U.S. AIRCRAFT CARRIERS

U.S. AIRCRAFT CARRIERS

AN ILLUSTRATED DESIGN HISTORY

By Norman Friedman

Ship Plans by A.D. Baker III

To Charles McCabe, Jr.
Norman Fr—
December, 1985

Naval Institute Press
Annapolis, Maryland

Library of Congress Cataloging in Publication Data

Friedman, Norman, 1946–
   U.S. aircraft carriers.
   Includes index.
   1. Aircraft carriers—United States. I. Title.
V874.3.F74 1983   623.8′255′0973   82-14357
ISBN 0-87021-739-9

This edition is authorized for sale only in the
United States, its territories and possessions,
and Canada.

Printed in the United States of America

Contents

Foreword

For the past twenty years, at least, no naval ship of the United States has been subjected to more analysis, rhetoric, and emotionalism by its supporters and critics alike than the aircraft carrier. Protagonists abound, both in and out of uniform. The carrier has often been swept up in roles-and-missions debates, leading to allegations, at times justifiable, of interservice rivalry, even intraservice dispute. Yet, it is of more than passing significance that throughout its operational life, the most consistent acclaim of the carrier has been sounded by the commander at sea, where the true test is inevitably made. Thus, when someone gives the aircraft carrier a rigorous, objective analysis, as Norman Friedman does here with distinction, one is left with a perplexing sense of the disparity that currently exists between the uncertainty of the carrier's future in the U.S. Navy and its vital accomplishments of the past.

No force had more lasting impact on the outcome of the Pacific War in World War II than the fast carrier task group, in combination with an effective submarine interdiction campaign. Air superiority at sea proved then, as now, that no naval force can remain tactically viable without adequate air cover. In the vast expanse of the world's oceans, now considered vital to U.S. interests, such air support will continue to be essential and will be provided predominantly from at-sea bases—in other words, from aircraft carriers.

As Dr. Friedman accurately points out, carrier-based air power was the only significant air threat the U.S. could muster to counter the southerly thrust of the North in the early months of the Korean War. Later, carrier air power dominated the air scene over the lengthy span of the eastern front and coastline to the Soviet Union and China.

Our Vietnam experience proved again the invaluable flexibility of sea-based air power. A fact often overlooked or underappreciated, especially by those who make a clear distinction between "power projection" and "sea control" missions, is that it was the omnipresence of U.S. aircraft carriers that estab-lished and maintained the uncontested "sea control" which permitted the successful prosecution of power projection tasks.

Given these historical perspectives of the carrier's wartime performance, one is hard pressed to find a more convincing empirical example of a truly cost-effective warship. The *Essex*-class aircraft carrier turned out to be a dominant factor in three wars, suffering virtually no losses while being totally responsive to the requirements of "maneuver warfare." In peacetime crisis response, the aircraft carrier demonstrated its value again and again by being the military option most consistently desired and employed by the national leadership.

Despite this record, the aircraft carrier is threatened with extinction at the very moment in history when it constitutes our principal dimension of superiority over the Soviet Navy. Paradoxically, as the debate rages on over the future utility of the carrier in U.S. naval strategy, the Kremlin indicates its awareness of the carrier's value by laying the keel of the first of a new class of full-fledged aircraft carriers.

How many crises and wars must there be in which the presence or absence of aircraft carriers proves critical before we have the vision to realize that this warship still has a long and useful life ahead? If only one lesson were to be drawn from the Falklands-Malvinas conflict, it is that the British government made a critical error in permitting the premature demise of the Royal Navy's aircraft carriers. Regrettably, it is a lesson that has probably been learned too late for Britain to rectify, given the prevalent pressures there to hold down naval investments.

For the serious student of naval warfare in search of a balanced exposition of the design evolution of the aircraft carrier, this book is invaluable. While the pages that follow primarily present a history of the engineering design considerations of the carrier throughout the past forty years, the reader is exposed to invaluable perspectives of the interplay between various interest groups—the fleet, OPNAV, the ubiquitous system analysts, the civilian leadership, and the ship designers themselves. Such insights are made all the more valuable when one appreciates that they come from the pen of one who has given far more study to the influence of the carrier on the course of naval history than most and whose research is untarnished by personal exposure to the political and bureaucratic infighting that has spotted the carrier's past.

Perhaps what one can best conclude from this masterful description of the myriad controversies that have surrounded the development of key features of the aircraft carrier is that, on balance, estimates of its intended functions have been elusive indeed. In action, at sea, the carrier has proved to be a much more flexible platform than its design engineers had conceived, able to adapt rapidly to the many variables in naval missions and tasks, from strategic nuclear strike to antisubmarine warfare, reconnaissance, sea control, power projection, and just plain overwhelming crisis presence. The carrier has likewise proved able to adjust readily to the astonishingly swift improvement in the performance of its main battery—the aircraft itself. Failure to perceive the carrier's inherent adaptability is not a recent phenomenon; as Dr. Friedman illuminates, even the *Lexington* and the *Saratoga* were initially criticized for being overdesigned.

Thus, let me suggest that a primary task confronting today's naval planners and design engineers is to predict with greater accuracy, after having reflected carefully on the lessons of the twentieth century, the utility of the aircraft carrier for a good portion of the twenty-first. After all, CVN 71, under construction today, has the potential to serve for fifty years. Let me suggest further that far more consideration be given to the challenge of determining how to design the carrier to eliminate, or substantially reduce, its dependence on catapult and arresting gear, features I believe will become increasingly vulnerable to debilitating combat damage as advances are made in the already formidable antiship missile. Proof of the carrier's wartime utility will lie in the ship's ability to fight vigorously and successfully in the heat of conflict while sustaining battle damage.

What is needed now, as is clearly evident in the pages that follow, is a willingness on the part of designers, operators, and civilian decision makers alike to be visionary and yet practical. They must recognize the unmatchable flexibility built into the carrier, so amply demonstrated in combat, as a strength that should be capitalized upon for decades to come. The demise of the aircraft carrier, which is still the backbone of the striking power of the navy, is not yet on the horizon. Air superiority at sea remains a fundamental tenet of those who advocate naval superiority itself, and will remain so for decades. At the same time, air superiority will be retained only insofar as we look aggressively for new concepts and technologies while being equally vigilant in proceeding now with the construction of the best carrier we know how to build.

ADMIRAL THOMAS B. HAYWARD, USN (RET)

Acknowledgments

Parts of this book originated with the Naval Ship Engineering Center's project for a technical history of U.S. aircraft carriers, sponsored by Dr. Reuven Leopold in 1977. I am grateful to Dr. Leopold and to his then assistant, Dr. Robert S. Johnson, for supporting and assisting me. For help at the Naval Ship Engineering Center, I am grateful to Herb Meier, a former carrier designer, and also to Kit Ryan and Philip Sims. Mildred Grissom and Charles Wiseman very kindly gave me access to many BuShips and NavSEC records still under navy control, and Mrs. Lorna Anderson of OPNAV located many of the files of the former Ship Characteristics Board. I am grateful to Dr. B. D. Bruins for his insights into the fiscal pressures of the fifties as revealed in these navy records and in his own study of the U.S. cruise-missile program. Dr. David Rosenberg contributed greatly to my understanding of the U.S. nuclear strategy of the early postwar period and, therefore, of the origins of the super-carriers.

I appreciate assistance with and access to the facilities of the Navy and Old Army Branch of the National Archives (particular thanks go to Elaine Everly); to the wartime BuShips files at Suitland under the National Archives' control; and to navy-controlled files at the Federal Record Center. In each case the staffs were extremely helpful. For assistance at the Naval Historical Center (General Board and wartime SecNav/OPNAV files), I am grateful to Dr. Dean Allard and to his staff, particularly Cal Cavalcante, Gerri Judkins, Kathy Lloyd, and Martha Crowley. Mrs. S. M. Edwards of NavSea, now retired, provided finished plans on microfilm of many of the carriers and carrier projects. Mrs. Susan Weidner of the NavSea public relations division provided invaluable assistance, and Anna Urban shepherded the nuclear carrier chapter through the clearance process.

I am also most appreciative of the assistance of the two naval air history offices: NavAir History, under Dr. William Armstrong, and Op-05 (DCNO [Air]) History, under Clarke Van Vleet. They provided much of importance on the development of naval aircraft, most of the catapult and arresting-gear story, and much of the policy story of the 1949 flush-deck carrier. The National Maritime Museum in San Francisco produced the rare magazine from which the sketch of the P4-P convertible liner was drawn.

Arthur D. Baker III acted both as illustrator and as critic of the text, catching many errors and making worthwhile suggestions. He also provided the majority of the photographs reproduced here; Christian Beilstein lent many of the others.

Other good friends also deserve thanks for generous assistance: Charles Haberlein, David Lyon, Norman Polmar, and Christopher C. Wright. They supplied me with significant material from their collections as well as invaluable comments and corrections. I thank them for many errors caught; those not caught are my own responsibility.

My wife Rhea deserves special thanks for her patience, encouragement, and very material assistance. This book could not have been written without her active help.

It would also have been entirely impossible to write without the extreme patience and care of my typists, Helen Iadanza, Anne Marsek, and Maureen Pritchard of Hudson Institute.

Key to Line Drawings

AAP	AA plot
AE	Aviation electronics workshop
AMR	Auxiliary machinery room
AS	Aviation stores
BM	Bomb magazine
BR	Boiler room
BU	Bunk room
CAT	Catapult machinery
CG	Crew's galley
CH	Chart house
CIC	Combat information center
CM	Crew's messing
CPO	Chief petty officer's berthing
CS	Crew's space
CT	Conning tower
DP	Dry provisions
EDG	Engineering diesel generator
EM	Elevator machinery
ER	Engine room
EVAP	Evaporator
FO	Fuel oil (ship)
FP	Flag plot
FW	Fresh water
GAS	Aviation gasoline
HR	Handling room
IC	Interior communications room
MAG	Magazine
MR	Machinery room
OM	Officer's mess
OS	Operating station
PH	Pilot house
PR	Plotting room
PR	Pump room
RM	Rocket magazine
RR	Ready room
SC	Secondary conn
SG	Steering gear
SSTG	Ship's service turbo-generator
ST	Stores
TORP	Torpedo storage
W	Windlass room
WR	Wardroom (and berthing)
WS	Wing stowage

U.S. AIRCRAFT CARRIERS

Introduction

Six decades have passed since the emergence of the aircraft carrier in the U.S. Navy, and four decades since the carrier became the dominant element of U.S. seapower. As this is written, no successor appears in sight, despite claims for missile-firing submarines and surface ships and the acknowledged vulnerability of carriers to some forms of attack. No other type of warship is nearly as flexible as a carrier, which can operate an infinite variety of weapon systems by changing her mix of aircraft. This potential is perhaps best illustrated by the development of the multi-role carrier, the CV, a descendent of the more specialized attack (CVA) and ASW support (CVS) types—the CV is essentially a CVA with minor internal changes to accommodate ASW aircraft.

This book traces the history of the design of the ships themselves, not their aircraft or operations, even though the latter two exerted powerful influences on carrier development. Research, executed originally for the Naval Ship Engineering Center to discover just how carriers had grown so large, was part of a general reevaluation of the large-deck carrier in the mid-seventies. Although security requirements make it impossible to provide an account of post-1950 carrier designs as detailed as that of earlier ones, it is clear in retrospect that the controversy over the size and cost of the carrier is by no means a new one, and that there have been many attempts to arrest what seems to have been an inevitable history of growth. Thus the reader may be somewhat surprised to learn about the *Forrestal*, the prototype of modern U.S. carriers, actually being an austere version of the earlier, abortive *United States*, or about the much larger carriers nearly laid down in the mid-fifties to accommodate new naval aircraft then in prospect.

Another issue relevant to current controversy is the role of mobilization. At present the U.S. carrier force is limited in numbers by the high cost of individual carrier battle groups. Although the plan to increase the force to sixteen ships may well be realized, that would still be far short of the number required. Similarly, the U.S. Navy suffered before World War II from a treaty limit on its total carrier strength, a limit below what the then-current war plan (ORANGE) required. The solution envisaged in the twenties and thirties was the conversion of suitable merchant hulls during mobilization. This was not a means of avoiding expensive naval construction in peacetime, but rather a way to overcome an unavoidable gap between requirements and peacetime realities. The escort and light fleet carriers that actually fought in World War II were designed on rather different lines, but nonetheless they illustrated the possibilities—and the very real limits—of such mobilization thinking. Current proposals for quick conversions of container ships may be the result of similar thinking, and they may benefit from the earlier lessons.

The design histories themselves illustrate the degree to which capabilities must be traded off within even relatively large ships. As in other warship types, apparently major reductions in military capability, accepted in the first place to secure major economies, often gave disappointing results. Yet at the same time apparently minor economies produced seemingly disproportionate losses of capability. Carrier capability is particularly difficult to assess because so much depends upon the details of carrier operation. For example, the aircraft capacity of a carrier is often equated with her hangar capacity. Yet U.S. Navy doctrine before World War II always envisaged the hangar as little more than storage for aircraft either not in use or under repair. Effective carrier capacity was, then, the size of the air group a carrier could launch in a single operation. At first that was a func-

The USS *Enterprise* epitomized the fast carrier task force of World War II. She fought in almost all of the great carrier battles, from the early raids on Wake and Marcus islands to the attack on Okinawa, where a kamikaze finally put her out of action on 14 May 1945. Her aircraft even fought at Pearl Harbor. She was the first carrier to win a Presidential Unit Citation (27 May 1943). Presented to the State of New York for preservation as a war memorial in 1946, she was reacquired by the navy in 1952 and, sadly, stricken and broken up when efforts to turn her into a memorial museum failed.

tion of the size of the flight deck; later aircraft were sometimes added in the hangar, and could be lifted onto the flight deck during the launching operation. Thus wartime carrier operations often exceeded pre-war estimates. By way of contrast, it was British practice to keep all aircraft in the hangar; they were struck below upon landing. The British view, then, was that carrier-air-group size was what the hangar could hold, at least until the middle of World War II. With the postwar advent of the angled deck and simultaneous launch and recovery operations, the full deck load of aircraft can no longer be parked, and U.S. carrier capacity is now a combination of that on the flight deck and that in the hangar.

Carriers were the first warships for which the weights of various components were not the prime determinants of ship size and configuration. Today all warships are volume critical or even length critical (as are destroyers and cruisers). In the case of carriers, volume became the dominant issue because the essential components of the ship (gasoline, magazines, hangar space, expanded crew quarters, maintenance ships, and even the aircraft themselves) were all relatively light for their volume. Moreover, almost from the beginning flight-deck configuration determined carrier configuration. Given that flight-deck length could usually not be traded off against width, the carrier hull generally approached a fixed length despite the choice of beam. By way of contrast, a battleship hull was generally sketched on the basis of a tentative balance trading off machinery weight (more power for a shorter ship) against hull weight (more weight for a longer, slimmer hull requiring less power).

Just what determined flight-deck length, the key issue in carrier design, changed abruptly in 1953 with the advent of the angled flight deck. Before that date, U.S. carrier flight decks were zoned, with a landing area aft and a parking and re-arming area forward. Typically the entire air group would be parked aft for mass takeoff, the size of the air group limited by the deck length required for aircraft to roll. Late in World War II catapult launches were frequently used and more aircraft could be carried because the catapults reduced the length an airplane needed for a conventional takeoff. Other factors considered in determining takeoff length included the wind the ship could generate over her flight deck by steaming at high speed. When the air group landed, it was parked forward. The aircraft had to fit forward of a crash barrier defining the fore end of the landing zone and be "respotted" aft for another group launch. Toward the end of the era of straight flight decks, when catapult launches were common (indeed, essential for jets), carriers often operated with a landing zone aft, a parking and re-arming zone amidships, and a launch zone forward, the full deck-load launch tac-

tics of World War II having been abandoned because of the limited endurance of jet aircraft. In theory aircraft could then be recovered and launched simultaneously, although that was difficult at best. In addition, the location of the parking area immediately forward of the crash barrier was quite dangerous, since from time to time aircraft did crash through or over it as they landed.

Increasing aircraft size complicated matters, since larger aircraft required longer arresting gear runouts as well as larger parking zones. In effect an angled (landing) deck is an attempt to get around this problem by separating the landing area from the parking and takeoff zones. One consequence is that the size of the parking zone no longer figures prominently in the overall determination of flight-deck size. Indeed, since it permits free use of elevators during flight operations, the angled deck makes a deck-load strike unnecessary. The net effect of adopting the angled deck was to shift the determinant of the lower bound on flight-deck size from the size of the air group as a whole to the characteristics of its highest-performance aircraft. This change deeply affects any attempt to achieve a minimum carrier. It may be significant that operations aboard a VSTOL carrier may so resemble those aboard the old straight-(axial-) deck carriers as to bring the earlier criteria back into prominence. VSTOL carriers as small as 10,000 tons are commonly discussed, whereas there is no real hope of building a full jet carrier of less than five or six times that size.

The design of a carrier cuts across bureaucratic lines more than that of any other type of warship, owing to the intimate involvement not only of the usual ship and ordnance design community, but also of the aviators and aircraft designers. Until 1945 U.S. carriers were designed on the basis of characteristics, or staff requirements, formulated by a council of senior naval officers, the General Board. The board was formed in 1900 to carry out long-range war planning, and throughout the interwar period it imposed on the navy what was in effect a long-range program. Until the late thirties it had considerably more power, for example, than did the newer Chief of Naval Operations (CNO). However, during World War II, Admiral King, combining the offices of the CNO and Commander-in-Chief U.S. Fleet (CominCh) in his own person, dominated characteristics decisions to the extent that a new characteristics organization was needed. In 1945 the Ship Characteristics Board (SCB) was created within the office of the CNO (OPNAV). The SCB attempted to impose greater operational influence on ship design decisions. However, it lacked the prestige of the General Board, which consisted largely of very senior officers in their final billet, and from the late forties onward the influence of long-range planning on ship design was intermittent at best. The General Board itself was dissolved early in 1951, its last carrier studies being those associated with the *Forrestal* class. The General Board era is graced by voluminous hearings before the board, since representatives of the operational forces and the technical bureaus were all questioned during the preparation of new characteristics. As a result, the board's influence and its decision-making powers, particularly during the period of its relative decline in favor of OPNAV from the late thirties onward, may appear to us to be greater than they actually were. However, it is apparent that until that time the General Board was the principal professional advisory body consulted by the Secretary of the Navy, and as such wielded very great power.

The technical bureaus, in charge of actual design and construction, were independent bodies responsible only to the civilian Secretary of the Navy; hence the importance of the General Board as a coordinating organization. Ship design was the province of the Bureau of Construction and Repair (C & R), although machinery and radios were designed by the Bureau of Engineering (BuEng). In 1940 these two were amalgamated into the Bureau of Ships (BuShips), a development often described as the ultimate victory of C & R over its old rival. Weapons, including bombs and torpedoes, were the responsibility of the Bureau of Ordnance (BuOrd). A separate Bureau of Aeronautics (BuAer) was established in 1921. Unlike its sister bureaus, it had authority over a lot of operational doctrine and personnel assignments, as well as the development of aircraft and, through its ship installations branch, such related ship systems as catapults and arresting gear. Thus, in carrier design discussions of the prewar period, BuAer had a more accurate understanding of operational realities than the other design bureaus. There were, however, wartime complaints that the aviators were unnecessarily excluded from OPNAV decision making, and in 1943 Admiral King established a separate Deputy Chief of Naval Operations for Air, Op-05. The new power of the DCNO (Air) was particularly evident in the fight over the flush-deck carrier from 1946 to 1949.

After the war naval aviators virtually dominated discussions of future U.S. naval development. As a result of their influence, the number of carriers was the starting point for much U.S. planning by the late fifties. The other major focus of U.S. postwar concerns was ASW, which required a coordinated leadership and major investments in specialized carriers and naval aircraft. Amphibious assault was a poor third, although it did gain in interest following the Korean War and led to a special breed of helicopter carrier. Here the marines were the lead organization—no DCNO was directly involved.

Effective long-range planning within the naval establishment ceased with the demise of the General Board and the navy's reaction to a series of budget crises. The outpouring of resources for the Korean War seemed to assure the end of budget constraints. Following the end of that war a new CNO, Robert B. Carney, saw the need for a long-range analysis of the fleet to take into account the great variety of competing technologies already in sight. The result was the Long Range Objectives group (LRO, Op-93), which he formed within OPNAV and which had considerable influence in the late fifties. It was disestablished in 1971, after making the first major U.S. proposals for a new ASW helicopter carrier, which became the sea control ship (SCS). After 1970 there was again a hiatus, marked by a series of disconnected ad hoc studies, and long-range planning was resumed only with the formation of Op-00X in 1981. Given the regular progression of CNOs and the inertia inherent in the construction of ships, which might take almost a decade from concept to commissioning, the late sixties and the seventies saw few attempts to reformulate U.S. naval doctrine or redesign a fleet built around the large-deck carrier. The chief exception was the effort of Admiral Elmo Zumwalt, Jr., who as CNO sought to introduce classes of less expensive carriers. He failed, although the Carter administration tried to adopt some of his positions following his retirement.

Again, given the lack of a firm navy-wide long-range plan in the seventies, organizations not linked to the normal chain of responsibility became quite powerful. The most important was probably Admiral H. G. Rickover's nuclear-power unit, which contributed to the end of the proposed conventionally powered "light" (60,000-ton) CVV and vetoed proposals for mixed nuclear and non-nuclear plants (these might have reduced the building cost of future large-deck carriers). Admiral Rickover has also been considered responsible for the demise of the SCS, although the fixed-wing aviation community undoubtedly can share credit.

The bureaus themselves experienced some changes after the war, most notably in the merger of BuOrd and BuAer into Bureau of Naval Weapons (BuWeps) in 1959. More important was the 1966 decision to change the bureaus from independent organizations to commands under the overall authority of OPNAV, BuShips and BuOrd forming parts of the Naval Sea Systems Command (NAVSEA), and BuAer (by then divorced from BuOrd) becoming the Naval Air Systems Command (NAVAIR).

From the late forties onward, moreover, the civilian Department of Defense (DOD) exercised considerable power, particularly veto power, over the carrier program. Carriers were now the most visible manifestation of seapower and by far the most expensive. They were also a major target of interservice rivalry, especially since the air force saw them as a threat to its claim to postwar primacy. James Forrestal, the first Secretary of Defense but also a previous Secretary of the Navy, was largely responsible for the approval of the large carrier *United States* despite fiscal stringency; his successor, Louis Johnson, cancelled the heavy carrier in favor of additional bomb-ers. Through the fifties the role of the Secretary of Defense was much more passive, even though decisions limiting the growth of the navy budget automatically translated into reductions in the attack-carrier program. Robert S. McNamara began a new era of DOD analysis and activism; his staff prepared

Since 1945, U.S. carriers have been the principal means of projecting American power in Third World crises. Here the *Oriskany* is shown at Yokosuka, Japan, about 1952 or 1953, with U.S.-built *Tacoma*-class frigates in the background. Alongside her a *Commencement Bay*–class escort carrier shows a deck load of Grumman AF (Guardian) ASW aircraft; the *Oriskany* is loaded with Skyraiders and Panthers. Note the emergency conn under the overhang of her flight deck, just abaft the Mk 63 director controlling her two twin 3-in/50s.

special position papers on all major defense programs including, naturally, the attack carriers and their aircraft. He is probably best remembered for his decision against nuclear power in CVA 67 (which became the *John F. Kennedy*), and perhaps less so for his later conversion in favor of carriers in general and nuclear carriers in particular. That it was McNamara who approved the most recent class of U.S. carriers, the *Nimitz* class, underlines the very long time lags that plague the carrier construction program. Actual approval of the third of the three ships McNamara proposed did not come until FY 74, and for the next five years the fate of future carriers was debated. Considerations included the threat of Soviet antiship missiles, the promise of VSTOL, even the feeling, under the Carter administration, that the carrier was far too much an instrument of U.S. intervention abroad, precisely the argument used by the navy to justify a strong carrier force. Only with the election of the Reagan administration, which brought the activist, carrier-minded John Lehman to the position of Secretary of the Navy, has this process apparently been reversed. Whether the Reagan carrier program will survive the stress of fiscal limits on defense is, at this writing, not entirely clear.

The account that follows emphasizes, if anything, the intricacies of the relationship between carrier concept, design, and operations. Much of the book is based on the records of Preliminary Design, a branch of C & R and BuShips and the organization responsible for the initial concept of the carrier. The reader should not ignore the significance of the later stages of design, the passage to a detailed contract design and then the development, often at the shipyard, of working drawings that had sometimes changed considerably from the original ship concept. However, most of these changes, which often had great impact on the actual operation of the carrier, represent a level of detail too fine for this account, which is concerned more with conflict and tradeoff among carrier characteristics.

Finally, it should be emphasized that the carrier is unlike any other warship in that she is part of an integrated weapon system, a major element of which is her aircraft. They are discussed here only where their characteristics directly influenced the ships. I have described carrier operations and aircraft at length elsewhere.*

Carrier Air Power (Greenwich, England: Conway Maritime Press, and New York: Rutledge Press, 1981).

1

The Role of the Carrier in the U.S. Navy

The history of carrier design and construction centers on the evolving role of the carrier and her air group, a role that has changed radically over the six decades of carrier operations in the U.S. Navy. The experience of World War I gave rise to the idea of a carrier, which was supplemented by theoretical war games at the Naval War College, followed by full-scale fleet exercises (fleet problems). The latter sometimes revealed previously unsuspected carrier capabilities. The first two U.S. fleet carriers, the huge *Lexington* and *Saratoga*, had their size (and inherent capability) fixed by the battle-cruiser origins of their hulls, and so were well adapted to rapidly evolving aircraft. Although at first they were criticized for being "over designed," they remained viable throughout the interwar period. Their sheer size made new kinds of carrier tactics possible, and experiments with them inspired some of the changes in the role of the U.S. Fleet itself between wars, when a strategy for dealing with the principal prospective enemy, Japan (ORANGE), was developed.

Experience during World War II further modified carrier-operation concepts, although not nearly as radically as is sometimes maintained. However, the combination of Allied naval triumph, the emergence of a largely land-oriented nation, the Soviet Union, as the principal prospective opponent, and above all the advent of nuclear and then of thermonuclear weapons had profound effects on the development of the carrier, as did the later appearance of long-range missiles such as Regulus and Polaris. An important background theme, after 1945, was the national debate on an appropriate strategy, carried out largely behind closed doors by navy and air force advocates of strategic nuclear bombardment. One of the outcomes of the debate was to focus attention on the carrier, particularly the very large one the navy hoped to lay down in 1949.

Throughout her history the carrier has exerted considerable influence on the structure and even on the missions of the U.S. Navy, far beyond the expectations of her proponents. Organizational considerations within the navy had a profound effect on carrier development and operation. The U.S. attitude was to integrate aviation into the larger goals of the navy, rather than to foster the development of an aviation branch that might consider itself opposed to other sections of the navy as a whole.

For their part, the aviators sought to gain allies within the navy. Perhaps the most significant such development was the determination that carriers (and for that matter, air stations ashore) were in future to be commanded only by naval aviators, as mandated by the President's Aircraft (or Morrow) Board of 1925. The prestige of aviation in the U.S. Navy shows in that decision: a variety of senior officers, including Admirals Halsey and King, opted for aviation training so that they could command such units. Organizationally, the aviators continued to feel that they had been slighted until the establishment of the DCNO (Air) in 1942. However, the important point is that aviators could command ships and, later, larger formations. For example, the lesson was soon learned in peacetime exercises that the carrier had to be flagship of the formation screening her, and prewar aviators (such as Admiral King) commanded

Steam catapults were an essential element of the jet carrier. The newly converted *Hancock* shows just how long the C 11 catapult was. Her original pair of H 4s terminated forward of the forward elevator, which could serve them.

The sheer size and speed of the *Lexington* and *Saratoga*, resulting from their battle-cruiser origin, endowed them with capabilities surpassing those required by early carrier aircraft; in the fleet problems these carriers demonstrated previously unsuspected potential, which was soon translated into operational plans. Here the *Lexington* is shown with the fleet at Lahaina Roads, Maui, 16 February 1932. U.S. aircraft carriers generally parked their aircraft on the flight deck, the hangar being used for maintenance and for storage of aircraft not in use. Consequently they could operate larger air groups than could foreign carriers of similar tonnage, and they could launch larger "deck-load strikes" more rapidly.

Air Forces, Battle Force, one of the major elements of the U.S. Fleet. (Admiral King himself rose to the position of CNO in 1942 but, somewhat surprisingly, his success has never been identified with that of U.S. naval aviation. Rather, King represented the integration of naval aviation into the larger entity of the navy, having had a wide variety of non-aviation commands and experience.)

The carrier began as an integral element of a balanced fleet whose primary offensive weapon was the heavy gun. During the interwar period, the U.S. Navy gradually developed the carrier aircraft as an offensive weapon in her own right, and added an important capability to strike land targets deep inland. The primary question throughout this period was the vulnerability of a carrier to counterattack, both by heavy-gun ships and by aircraft. The U.S. battleship designs of the late thirties showed major sacrifices in firepower and even in protection in order to achieve high speed to screen fast carriers. The action off Samar in the Philippines in October 1944, where a group of escort carriers was surprised by Japanese battleships, indicated how real the threat of the heavy-gun ship remained. Carriers were, however, fast enough to evade most battleships.

Almost from the beginning, then, the chief threat to their existence was the airplane. From the mid-twenties on, dive-bombing appeared to be an extremely potent threat to relatively lightly protected ships. At the same time, treaty restrictions on carrier displacement made it impossible for U.S. designers to provide what they considered adequate flight-deck armor to repel dive-bomb attacks. Moreover, repeated experiments seemed to demonstrate that the carrier's own fighters would be unable to protect her, given the very limited warning picket ships could provide. The only solution was to destroy the enemy carrier before she could find and strike the U.S. carrier. That conclusion had important tactical consequences.

Initially, carriers operated close to the battle fleet, providing the battleships with such vital air services as reconnaissance and spotting, and controlling the air over the gunnery engagement. However, in the late twenties and early thirties a succession of major fleet exercises showed that the battle fleet itself was relatively easy to spot from the air, so any nearby carrier would soon be destroyed. U.S. carrier doctrine, therefore, was to operate carriers independently, at least until all opposing carriers could be neutralized. Moreover, it was not considered wise to operate carriers in groups until their ability to protect themselves against surprise air attack was much better developed.

The critical development in carrier design was the combination, after 1942, of radar, the combat information center (CIC), and the effectively directed combat air patrol (CAP). From 1939 onward some improvement in carrier self-defense had been attempted in the form of doubled fighter complements and airborne scouts to direct larger standing CAPs. However, only with radar and the CIC did the carriers achieve a significant level of self-defense. The Battle of the Philippine Sea in June 1944 was probably the culmination of this development, in that it represented exactly the type of attack which, in the prewar period, would have been considered fatal: a mass surprise air raid against a concentration of carriers tied geographically to a relatively limited area, in this case the sea around Saipan. Radar and fighters protected the fast carrier task force, and the chief result of the battle was the destruction of the attacking Japanese aircraft. Indeed, from about 1943 on, fighter aircraft rather than ship antiaircraft guns were the major defense of the carrier task force, a situation that continued after the war, and that had important effects on the composition of carrier air groups.

Carriers were valued at first for the reconnaissance and artillery spotting their aircraft could provide the battle fleet, and for the denial of these advantages to an enemy; the strike power of the carrier was, at first, very much a secondary asset. The former roles were extremely important in the context of battle-line engagements as they were understood during and immediately after World War I; indeed, they continued to dominate Royal Navy thinking through the beginning of World War II. Operations in the North Sea showed that existing surface fleets were badly deficient in both strategic and tactical scouting. Strategic reconnaissance can be defined as providing intelligence about the approximate position, speed, course, and composition of enemy naval formations, information a distant fleet commander might use to seek or to avoid action. During World War I, German Zeppelins performed this function, and the British placed fighters aboard their battleships to deny the Germans such information, and thus to prevent the High Seas Fleet from either cutting off sub-units of the Grand Fleet or evading action with the entire Grand Fleet. The Zeppelins were effective. The British relied instead on a combination of code breaking and radio direction finding, partly because of their failure (despite considerable effort) to develop successful long-endurance strategic reconnaissance aircraft. However, with the experience of World War I in mind, they did attempt, on the eve of World War II, to develop special fleet-shadowing aircraft, relatively slow but of great endurance.

Tactical intelligence can be defined as the detailed picture of an ongoing battle a commander needs for effective tactical decision making. Before the advent of aircraft tactical intelligence was usually the province of scout cruisers, which were intended to make and then to maintain contact with the enemy forces. By compiling and sifting the cruisers' reports, a commander could form an integrated picture of a developing engagement, particularly in its opening phase. However, each cruiser had only a very limited radius of vision, hardly encompassing the entire battle area. Navigational errors, a major problem at Jutland, often created considerable confusion as

well. A single observer high over the battle area could probably form a much better idea of the relative positions, courses, speeds, and even identities of the approaching and engaging forces. Such tactical reconnaissance was the major initial motive for providing aircraft for the British Grand Fleet, and the unsuitability of floatplanes in North Sea conditions led directly to proposals for the earliest carriers.

During World War I the battleship gun was unquestionably the most effective naval offensive weapon, at least against heavily armored ships; advances in naval construction, such as blistering, had largely discounted its chief rival, the torpedo. Moreover, the battleship gun had a longer maximum range than the torpedo, although limitations in fire control did not always permit ships to make use of that potential. Here aircraft also played a vital role. They could observe the fall of shot, even well beyond the horizon, and radio down corrections. At very long ranges most ships could be penetrated through their deck armor, whereas at shorter conventional battle ranges recent battleships would enjoy the protection of their vertical (belt) armor. The fleet that could use extreme ranges effectively would, then, have a decisive advantage. This was clear to the U.S. Navy by the early twenties, when it agitated for increased elevation (range) for the guns of its older battleships and rapidly developed spotting aircraft. As a corollary, denial of the air over a battle to enemy spotters and protection of friendly spotters might be decisive factors in a naval engagement, quite apart from any direct offensive capabilities of the aircraft. Moreover, aircraft might well be able to derange the fire control of enemy battleships by strafing their relatively vulnerable fire-control positions aloft. Thus strategists envisaged vital roles for naval aircraft at sea well before such aircraft could directly damage ships in a battle line.

Two other naval-air missions emerged from World War I. One was antisubmarine patrol. Submerged submarines could not be detected efficiently from the air and presented little threat to a fast-moving force, but they had to move on the surface, out of sight of their targets, before submerging primarily to attack. Aircraft could enlarge the circle of visibility of the force, keeping nearby submarines down and thus neutralized. This situation persisted almost to the end of World War II, since diesel-electric submarines of the time could sustain maximum submerged speed (of no more than about 10 knots) for no more than half an hour; even that high submerged speed did not suffice to attack fast naval formations. Only with the appearance of the snorkel could submarines achieve any measure of immunity from airborne search, a change that shows in the late wartime and early postwar changes in ASW tactics and weapons. The sub-

From a tactical point of view, radar was probably the most revolutionary development for carriers in World War II. Two stages in its evolution are shown aboard the large carrier *Saratoga* (*above* and *facing*). In May 1942, with her prewar bridgework drastically reduced and twin 5-in/38 guns fitted, she had the "mattress" of a CXAM-1 air search radar at the forward end of her large funnel. A Mark 4 dual-purpose fire-control radar is visible above her bridge, with the new microwave SG (for surface search and navigation) partway up her foremast. The mast is topped by an early form of the standard U.S. aircraft homing beacon, the YE. The radio-direction-finding loop on the forward face of her bridge represented an earlier generation of electronics. The second photo, taken at Puget Sound in August 1944, shows a standard late-war outfit: two air search radars, an SK on the foremast and an SC-2 aft (for backup), an SM height finder for fighter direction (on the forward edge of the funnel), and a combination of a Mark 4 and the new orange-peel Mark 22 atop her two Mark 37 5-in directors. A stub mast near the after end of the huge funnel carried the YG secondary aircraft homing beacon. Note the large air intakes along her side below the flight-deck (and hangar-deck) level, which were characteristic of the *Lexington* and *Saratoga* throughout their lives.

marine threat during World War I was sufficient to leave a deep impact on postwar thinking, both in the United States and abroad.

Finally there is the role for which carriers are best known, the independent offensive attack. During World War I both sides developed torpedo bombers, but only relatively light torpedoes, far too small to sink a contemporary capital ship, could be lifted. Despite this limitation, aerial torpedo attack was attractive to the Royal Navy as a means of neutralizing a German battle fleet unwilling to leave home to fight a superior Grand Fleet. Although the war ended before it could be implemented, British interest in torpedo attack by carrier aircraft continued. American observers with the Grand Fleet were aware of such ideas, and continued to develop them after the war. From a postwar British point of view, the most important potential of the torpedo bomber was its ability to slow down a hostile battle line, forcing it to fight. For the U.S. Navy, the same airplane that was powerful enough to lift a torpedo was also powerful enough to lift heavy bombs; as early as 1923 the U.S. Navy incorporated a notional carrier air raid on the locks of the Panama Canal in a fleet problem. The

bombs used, however, were not effective against maneuvering ships at sea, a point often conveniently overlooked by interwar critics of heavy-gun capital ships. Dive-bombing, introduced in the mid-twenties, had revolutionary implications: for the first time aircraft could reliably hit rapidly maneuvering targets such as warships. The dive-bomber could not build up enough speed in diving for its bombs to penetrate thick deck armor, so that it could not be expected to destroy capital ships. It could, however, wreck a carrier's flight deck and so disable it.

During the twenties, U.S. doctrine increasingly detached the battle line from the carrier, so as to allow it to concentrate, at the outset, on destroying enemy carriers. For example, the standard U.S. carrier air group of the early thirties included in its four squadrons a scout squadron whose task it was to find the enemy carrier or carriers before its own ship was discovered. Cruiser and battleship floatplanes took over battle-line scouting and spotting functions, and aircraft used for these purposes vanished from the standard carrier air groups. In addition, the carriers ceased to function as depot ships for battleship and cruiser aircraft. The first U.S. carrier designs had incorporated facilities to service floatplanes that the battleships and cruisers might launch early in a battle, but that they would be unable to recover during it. It had been hoped that maintenance facilities aboard the carrier might also be used by those floatplanes. However, a carrier operating some considerable distance from the battleships could not have serviced such aircraft. The great U.S. interest in carrier catapults in the early twenties had largely been predicated on launching cruiser and battleship floatplanes; the abandonment of those early catapults reflects evolving carrier doctrine.

To achieve maximum offensive power against enemy carriers, U.S. tacticians developed the technique of the deck-load strike, which became the basis for U.S. carrier design: carriers were designed to launch the maximum number of aircraft for a strike in a single operation. Some inflexibility had to be accepted: with all the aircraft aboard, the takeoff

area forward was fully occupied. If only one airplane were launched, it could not land aboard when the landing area was filled with the rest of the aircraft waiting for takeoff. Catapults, particularly those on the hangar deck, could help, as could the secondary arresting gear provided at the bows of U.S. carriers of interwar design.

In both the case of the floatplanes and the case of flight-deck flexibility, U.S. interest in, and competence in the construction of, catapults can be traced back to a decision made before World War I to emphasize such devices as the standard navy approach to air power at sea. The approach was modified greatly by observing early British experiments with carriers.

Carrier air-group assignments reflected evolving tactics. For example, in 1929 the *Saratoga* carried four squadrons: one of fighters, one of dive-bombers (actually fighter-bombers, the same type the fighter

Photographed after a Mare Island refit in April 1944, the *Essex* shows how wartime electronic improvements crowded the small islands of the new fleet carriers. Improvements in command and control are also evident in the enlargement of the flag plot (the space under the number 18) at the expense of a quadruple Bofors gun. The primary radars visible are the SC-2 secondary air search set (27), the SM fighter direction set (23), and an SG surface search set sponsoned out from the funnel (37) atop a lattice mast. Note, too, the IFF antenna on the yardarm (38), the YE homing antenna (29), and one of two large loudspeakers ("reproducers") to control flight-deck operations (32). Increasing congestion in the island structure made it necessary to design more compact (if less efficient) radio antennas, the "whips" (35). The director forward of the forward quadruple Bofors gun is a Mark 49 (34), the unsuccessful predecessor of the ubiquitous wartime Mark 51.

squadron flew), one of scouts (Vought Corsairs, the type also flown from capital ships), and one of heavy-torpedo and level bombers (Martin T4M-1s). Within a short time the fighter-bomber squadron had been reclassified as a second fighter squadron and the scout squadron enlarged at the expense of the torpedo bombers. The lesson of Fleet Problem XI (1930) was that scouting was both essential and difficult, the two opposing carriers spending four days in futile searches for each other. By the early thirties a new generation of high-performance fighters had been developed as "scouts," but only the Grumman SF-1 (an adaptation of the FF-1) operated as such. The other aircraft of the same generation became "scout bombers" or light dive-bombers, and further advances in aircraft design produced a multi-purpose scout bomber which could lift the heaviest bomb then in service, the 1,000-pounder, and also serve as a fast scout. The outstanding example was the Douglas Dauntless, the SBD.

By 1938 the *Saratoga* had the standard prewar carrier air group, four squadrons of about eighteen aircraft each: one of dive-bombers, one of scouts (scout bombers, the earlier spotting types having been given up in 1937), one of torpedo bombers, and one of fighters. A fifth fighter squadron, for better CAP performance, was added in 1939 despite the operational problems it entailed. The scout squadrons were abolished during World War II, their aircraft amalgamated with those of the dive-bombing squadrons. One reason why was that improvements in CAP effectiveness had greatly reduced the importance of the preemptive strike on enemy carriers. Moreover, with radar, a reduced number of scouts could cover the same areas.

Within the battle fleet, the carrier increased offensive as well as reconnaissance range, and she added the entirely new capability of attacking and destroying targets deep inland. U.S. interest in such attacks was an important factor in the evolution of the ORANGE (Pacific) war plan, the joint army-navy document that formed the basis for much prewar naval planning and construction. As described in greater detail in chapter 6, ORANGE required the fleet not only to destroy Japanese naval and air forces, but also to seize a series of bases close to Japan, ultimately bringing her military installations and war industries under aerial bombardment. Prewar fleet problems included strikes on the Panama Canal, Pearl Harbor, and even the oil refineries of Los Angeles. At first, the element of surprise enjoyed by the carrier appeared to give her the advantage. However, improvements in land-based aircraft changed the balance by the late thirties. Now land-based reconnaissance aircraft could easily outrange the carrier strike planes, and it seemed likely that a

carrier would be detected and struck during her long run-in toward the target. It was argued that unless carriers were provided with longer range attack aircraft, they would be too vulnerable to land-based planes, which were not limited in performance by carrier flight decks. Thus it was a surprise, not least to the naval aviators themselves, that carriers were so successful in the island raids early in 1942. This expected vulnerability to land-based aircraft was little more than a corollary to the intense concern with attack by enemy carriers, but where air control at sea could be assured by the destruction of a few enemy carriers, no such security could be assured against land-based air forces, with their greater resources.

In the antiship role, the carrier was in an anomalous position by 1939. She could destroy any warship short of a battleship, and it was even unlikely that a battleship would be able to successfully attack a carrier with alert scouts and an effective surface screen. The key issues here were the relatively light weight of carrier torpedoes, limited by aircraft performance, and the limits on dive-bomb armor penetration. Moreover, no single carrier could mount an air strike intense enough to score many torpedo hits on a battleship, and carriers operating in company were supposedly only exposing themselves to attacks they could not fend off. Torpedo-attack tactics themselves were less than satisfactory, as the experience of the Battle of Midway proved. Indeed, for a time in the early thirties the U.S. Navy seriously considered abandoning aerial torpedoes completely, a step actually taken in the design of the *Ranger*.

World War II experience showed that these prewar expectations were false and that the carrier could indeed replace the battleship as the dominant type of warship. For example, even the relatively small torpedoes carried by British Swordfish sank Italian battleships at Taranto. Radar and the CIC/CAP made it possible for U.S. carriers to concentrate in large formations that could launch massive air strikes, such as the ones that sank the Japanese super-battleships *Yamato* and *Musashi* in 1944 and 1945. Even so, Japanese battleships could overwhelm smaller concentrations of weaker carriers, as they did off Samar at almost the same time.

The great success of fast-carrier attacks through the middle of 1944 can be traced to a combination of Japanese tactics and carrier tactics. The Japanese could mount only a small number of separate raids, given the need for many aircraft to attack each ship in order to damage her sufficiently. Thus the Japanese could not saturate the CIC organization, which plotted incoming raids in order to direct fighter interceptors to engage them. In a more general sense, thanks to the CIC/CAP organization, the fast carriers could be concentrated tactically, with up to five (three of the *Essex*-class and two of the *Independence*-class) from several task groups making up the fast carrier task force. As a result, surprise carrier air strikes could often overwhelm the defenders, particularly in the case of a small island with few resources.

This situation changed abruptly in the Philippines. For the first time, the Japanese could control massive land-based air forces. Carriers, particularly the escort carriers providing direct support to troops ashore, often could not leave restricted areas and thus could not enjoy tactical surprise of any kind. Moreover, the kamikazes introduced at Leyte usually attacked alone and from many different directions.

Individual aircraft were more difficult to detect on radar, particularly over land, and the sheer number of individual raids overloaded the manual CIC organization.

There were several possible solutions to this problem. One was the prewar idea of increasing the range of carrier bombers, which Admiral Marc Mitscher, Commander, Fast Carrier Task Force, proposed. The suggestion led to the design of the North American AJ Savage, which in turn became the first carrier nuclear bomber. Another was increased reliance on shipboard antiaircraft weapons for last-ditch defense, resulting, in the postwar period, in the 3-T

The light fleet carrier *Cowpens* (*above* and *facing*) shows late-war standard carrier electronic equipment in these 15 May 1945 Mare Island views. The white lines indicate alterations, which include a Mark 57 radar-equipped blind-fire director alongside the flight deck and forward of the island, relocated catapults (with a second catapult added), and the replacement of the usual secondary air search radar by an SP height-finder dish. The yardarm carries TBS antennas at its ends for ship-to-ship communication, as well as VHF dipoles for ship-to-air communication. Note, too, the diesel generator exhausts with their mufflers, abaft each of the two visible funnels. The view aft shows a radar-controlled twin 40-mm gun (with the dish on the gun mount but the circled Mark 63 director remote) and a twin 20-mm gun replacing the former single mount, a standard late-war weight-saving measure. The cruisers in the background are probably the *Louisville* and the *Pensacola*.

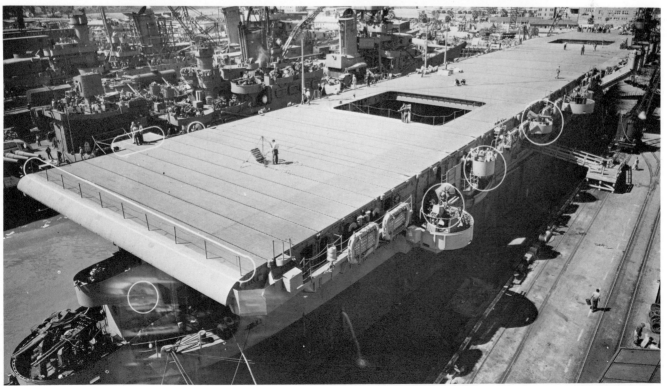

Belleau Wood received a refit similar to that of the *Cowpens*, although oriented more heavily toward radar countermeasures: she shows a TDY jammer at the after end of the small platform carrying her SP fighter-control radar, and her yardarm carries countermeasures receivers. The small box between the receivers is a "Nancy" infrared beacon.

family of antiaircraft missiles. Finally there was the notion of preemptive attack on enemy airfields, the functional equivalent of the prewar concept of preemptive destruction of the enemy carrier. To this end, carrier air groups were again reorganized, with large fighter-bomber squadrons that could neutralize airfields and supplement more conventional attack units. Typically, in the summer of 1945, fast carriers had double fighter units (thirty-six aircraft) and double fighter-bomber units (thirty-six aircraft) as well as somewhat reduced torpedo and dive-bomber complements (thirty aircraft). Fighter squadrons included special-purpose aircraft, typically four photo-reconnaissance fighters and four night fighters. Later there was a shift back to the specialized attack aircraft. New light carrier air groups organized at that time were made up exclusively of fighters as opposed to the previous mix of twenty-four fighters and nine torpedo bombers. In effect, the heavy carriers would be used for preemptive strikes, the light carriers for providing them with fighter cover.

Night attack was an important problem from 1943 onwards, since the Japanese showed great aptitude for conducting night raids with a small number of long-range torpedo bombers. There were two alternative approaches to this problem. Carriers could specialize in night operations, with specially trained crews and specialist aircraft, or detachments of night fighters could operate aboard fleet carriers. In 1945 the standard night carrier air group was set at thirty-seven fighters and eighteen torpedo bombers, the small numbers reflecting the relative difficulty of night operations. Specialized detachments were more common, but they imposed the load of twenty-four-hour-operations on their carrier. The problem was particularly worrisome from a postwar point of view, since land-based radar-equipped bombers would be able to attack a carrier force at night or in weather that carrier aircraft could not fly in. Probably, too, they would be able to use long-range guided weapons, such as the German Hs 293, which could appear from beyond shipboard gun range. Carrier fighters would be an effective counter, if they could be launched and vectored to their targets, and if they could engage using their own radars. By 1945 it was clear that the last two requirements could generally be met, but work was still proceeding on a means of recovering aircraft under all-weather conditions. The means emerged, after the war, as the carrier-controlled approach (CCA).

The kamikaze experience led as well to CADILLAC, the airborne early-warning (AEW) aircraft. As long as all radars in the task force were aboard ships, low-flying aircraft could approach quite close without being detected. AEW radars were lifted well above the task force, transmitting their radar pictures directly to carrier CICs for effective fighter control. In one version of CADILLAC, a converted B-17 bomber carried not only the radar but also a rudimentary CIC, for even better air control. In 1945 the largest carrier aircraft, the Avenger torpedo bomber, could carry only the radar. (The current Grumman E-2 combines radar and CIC in a carrier-suitable package.) From a carrier point of view, the CADILLAC increased the effectiveness of carrier fighters, but at the same time it took up valuable deck, hangar, and maintenance space aboard the carrier. After the war, it was found that the large CADILLAC radar (APS-20) was the best available airborne detector of submarine snorkels and periscopes, so that carrier commanders had to choose between allocating their AEW detachments to antisubmarine or antiaircraft patrols.

Enemy saturation of the CIC/CAP organization on which the safety of the fast task force depended was a particularly worrisome problem, and one which could not really be addressed with 1945 technology. However, from the end of World War II onward there was increasing interest in automating the CIC to

Carrier fighter-controllers could direct day fighters into visual contact with incoming attackers; at night, the actual interception required a smaller radar aboard the fighter itself to take over once the airplane had been vectored into position. Two early-model night-fighting Corsairs of VF(N)-101 are shown aboard the *Enterprise* in 1944.

overcome such saturation. That generally meant automating the "book-keeping" so the CIC could keep track of incoming raiders. After a series of abortive approaches, the naval tactical data system (NTDS) was finally developed, going to sea aboard the carrier *Oriskany* in 1962. Current practice includes an airborne equivalent aboard the E-2, the airborne tactical data system (ATDS).

The postwar navy viewed the 1945 experience as paving the way for future carrier operations. Carriers would generally be attacking land targets against land-based opposition, and that opposition would probably involve long-range bombers dropping guided missiles. The Soviets, the most probable future enemy, had captured the German missile technology in 1945, and within a few years U.S. carrier commanders considered the missile bomber the greatest threat they faced. This view persists almost four decades later, with the efforts the Soviets have made to deploy advanced air-to-surface missiles. Although the U.S. Navy developed its own surface-to-air missiles primarily to counter the missile threat, carrier fighters remained the primary means of fleet air defense at least through the mid-sixties, given the deficiencies of the 3-T program. The achievement of

all-weather operation (largely through the success of CCA) made fighter defense an effective counter to the bomber that had appeared at one stage vulnerable only to shipboard missiles.

The other major carrier role in World War II was ASW, generally involving escort carriers striking at German submarine concentrations revealed by a combination of code breaking and radio direction finding. By 1945 the submarine threat had changed: the new Type 21 and the forthcoming Type 26 (Walter) submarines would be far more difficult to detect, and they might be able to frustrate radio direction finding by the use of a new generation of "burst" transmitters. Nor could it be assumed that code breaking would be successful in any future war. As in the case of the guided missiles, the Soviets had captured much of the relevant technology, and it appeared that the Battle of the Atlantic might soon have to be refought. It was argued, soon after the end of World War II, that the submarines might best be defeated by an aggressive bombing campaign against their bases, combined with aerial mining of their exits to the open seas. Such a strategy would exploit the inherent geographical advantages of the Western Allies. The attack on Soviet naval bases has been a

Modern carriers such as the *Midway* (shown here after a Hunters Point refit on 17 December 1970) must operate at all times in virtually all weather; the electronic consequences are evident. The primary radars were the ubiquitous SPS-37A (97), with its IFF (109) for long-range air search and SPS-30 (96) with the associated IFF (108) for height finding; the *Midway* also had an SPS-10C (98) for surface search. All-weather air operations required CCA radars: an SPN-6 (81) to "marshall" approaching aircraft, the two dishes of an SPN-10 (82) for precision short-range control, and the dish of an SPN-12 for airspeed measurement (83). Other air-related electronics included the conical "Phasor-90" ship-to-air radio antennas (33 through 44, some of them not visible in these photographs), the SMQ-6 receiver for radiosonde (weather balloon) signals (115), and a TACAN navigational beacon at the masthead (80). Although ECM warning antennas such as the AS-616/SLR (88) are visible, the jammers, carried by this time aboard all U.S. carriers, are not. Finally, the *Midway* (in common with most U.S. warships) carried a commercial navigational radar, a Raytheon 1500B Pathfinder (99). One of the most important radar features of U.S. carriers, AEW is represented here only by a receiving whip, an AN/WRR-1 (100).

consistent theme of U.S. carrier doctrine since the late forties. Given the relatively small number of attack aircraft a carrier or even a carrier group could accommodate, it was essential that each aircraft have maximum effect; this alone might explain navy interest in very heavy attack aircraft, although it must be admitted that nuclear weapons (which they alone could carry) must have seemed synonymous with the military future.

In 1945 the great problem of the carrier navy was bureaucratic: there was no longer an enemy surface ship to counter, and some in the army air force suggested that, apart from ASW, the navy was largely obsolescent. In particular, they did not appreciate the considerable difference between carrier tactics and targets and those of land-based air forces during World War II, a difference crucial to the postwar strategic debate. That is, against land objectives, the carriers usually struck at key targets that could be neutralized in one or at most a few days of attacks.

That represented a balance between the strike capability of the carrier task force, the mobility of the force (which permitted it to hit a variety of widely dispersed targets over a brief period of time), and the vulnerability of a carrier formation operating for an extended period in one area, hence with predictable movements. By way of contrast, long-range bombers such as the B-29s could attack the same metropolitan target again and again, and they could bring in enough bomb tonnage to flatten an area target. Again, given the limited bomb loads of individual naval aircraft, strikes were generally made against particular point targets, such as Japanese warships in sheltered areas. In a broader sense, the strategic (heavy land-based) bomber force had been designed to achieve what might now be called a countervalue attack, the destruction of Japanese population and industry on a very broad, even indiscriminate, scale, as a means of forcing Japan out of the war. Carrier strikes were much closer to counterforce in current parlance, which emphasized the destruction of particular elements of the enemy's ability to fight. Postwar analyses of the relative value of carrier and land-based bomber strikes on Tokyo, for example, tended to highlight the difference in bomb tonnage dropped by the two forces. However, the numerous small carrier aircraft were attacking a variety of dispersed targets, and bomb tonnage was at best a poor measure of their effectiveness, even if it was not a poor measure of the effectiveness of heavy bombers.

In the postwar debate the navy argued that it could develop an improved capability to attack land targets through the construction of larger carrier bombers, great improvements in carrier and task-force air defense, and achievement of a seaborne capability to deliver atomic bombs. It also argued against the prevailing air-force concept of a future war. It was generally agreed that the size and power of Soviet ground and tactical air forces would permit the U.S.S.R. to overrun much of Europe and the Middle East early in any future war, and that a constricted U.S. budget and ruined Western Europe would be unable to maintain comparable forces. The air force view was that only nuclear bombing could stop a Soviet offensive, and that in view of the small size of the nuclear stockpile that attack would have to be concentrated on Soviet industrial and population centers. It postulated a period of mobilization prior to the outbreak of war, during which a viable air defense of North America would be erected and bomber bases abroad established. Upon the opening of hostilities, the air force would mount its strategic air offensive, in what it called the "decisive phase." Army and navy forces would be requred only to "mop up" afterwards; the air force suspected that navy agitation for a new carrier and for a new generation of naval attack aircraft was no more than an attempt to gain a major role in what had, until then, been an air-force monopoly. Emotions ran particularly high because the air force was just then being established as an independent service, and because, as the decisive element in any future war, it had hopes of gaining the major portion of the limited postwar military budget.

The navy argued that air force attacks on Soviet industrial centers were unlikely to be decisive in any sense, and that a future war would be much closer in format to World War II. It would probably begin with little or no strategic warning, and the first and most urgent task would be to slow down the Soviet offensive before, for example, it pushed allied forces out of the air bases from which any strategic air offensive would have to be mounted. Thus the initial crucial air operations would be tactical strikes on Soviet communications and on Soviet forces in motion, strikes that might best be mounted by naval aircraft already forward deployed aboard carriers. In a second phase, the United States would mobilize its own forces while attempting to draw down Soviet war potential; advanced bases would be seized overseas. Limited footholds would be secured in Europe and the Dardanelles during a third phase, which would also include a sustained bombing offensive. Finally, the last phase of the war would see the systematic destruction of Soviet industry, internal transportation, and war potential. Only in this last phase would the fast carrier task force not be essential, as by then land bases close enough to the Soviet Union to support sustained offensive operations would have been secured.

From 1945 onward, the navy argued that carrier strike forces were an ideal means of insuring peace in the midst of a variety of minor peripheral challenges. For example, a single carrier in the Mediterranean might be able to overwhelm any of the land-based air forces along the shores of that sea in the late forties, and even a decade later the air arm of the Sixth Fleet was the dominant Mediterranean air force. Navy plans crystallized in the call for the construction of four carrier task forces, each built around one of the new flush-deck carriers (which could accommodate heavy bombers): a *Midway* and two modernized *Essex*-class carriers.

What the navy probably had in mind was the now-familiar arithmetic of one forward-based carrier supported by two others, so that one carrier can always be working up and another refitting or returning from forward deployment. In principal, four was the minimum number of task forces that would allow for one carrier force always on station in the Mediterranean.

The new carriers would be too large to pass through the Panama Canal. Therefore at least one task force would have to be stationed permanently in the Pacific—reinforcements from the Atlantic would be slow, since the ships had to steam around the Cape. One task force was a minimum, providing forward deployment only about a third of the time in the Western Pacific. The Mediterranean was vital both for Western oil supplies and for launch areas from which Soviet oil fields in the Caucasus could be attacked, the navy arguing forcibly that by denying the Soviets oil early in a war a land advance could be countered. Typical carrier operating areas in the 1955 war envisaged in 1948 for planning purposes were the Norwegian and Barents seas, the Arabian Sea, the Mediterranean, and the Pacific. A January 1948 navy internal study argued that

there is no spot within the USSR which cannot be reached from four such carrier task forces, suitably deployed. . . . If 1955 targets were the same as 1947 targets and four such task forces were available to us, it would appear that the most effective and early assault would be from two forces in the Barents Sea, one in the Norwegian Sea, and one in the Mediterranean. The D-Day probable disposition for our carrier task forces would dictate a slightly different arrangement, such as one force in the Barents Sea, one in the North Sea, one in the Mediterranean, and one in the Arabian Sea. This deployment fails to cover targets in Eastern Siberia, but . . . the present USSR target system makes this an unproductive area for attack, only five targets of secondary importance being known to exist there . . . .

More generally, the navy stressed the mobility of the carrier strike forces and their ability to supply tactical air power, both offensive and defensive, early in a war with the Soviets, despite a lack of U.S. bases abroad. This argument in favor of the attack carrier is still one of the strongest.

Defensive air power could be important in a critical area such as the Mediterranean, close to Soviet air bases. For example, a 1948 study of carrier-task-group operations in the Mediterranean by the staff of the Commander-in-Chief, U.S. Naval Forces, Eastern Atlantic and Mediterranean (CinCNELM) emphasized protection of the Mediterranean line of communication against air attack. This task would require destruction of aircraft in the air (convoys serving almost as magnets for air attack) as well as on the ground; attacks would also be mounted on the enemy infrastructure supporting his air offensive. Carriers would also be essential to the defense of the Cairo-Suez area, with escort carriers furnishing convoy air defense outside that particularly hazardous area. CinCNELM wanted, at a minimum, a task group of three fast carriers in the Mediterranean at all times, with another in readiness in the Atlantic Fleet. The CinCNELM study was hotly debated within the carrier community; in retrospect it is interesting because of its emphasis on the air, rather than the submarine, threat. That shift became more pronounced after a reevaluation of the Soviet submarine program in the Low report of 1950 showed that the Soviets had not yet begun to mass-produce the feared German-type submarines. On the other hand, they already had a massive tactical air force, much of it subordinated to the navy.

Through the late forties, the navy tried to counter air force claims that strategic bombing could be decisive, one study noting that damage to Germany (which had been far from decisive) during World War II had been equivalent to that of 500 atomic bombs. Moreover, the navy argued, there were relatively few bases within B-29 range of Soviet targets, and even fewer of those would survive the early phases of a war. That would be particularly the case once the Soviets had nuclear weapons of their own.

The decisive issue, in the end, was money: the air force strategy was attractive because it was the least expensive, even though the navy argued that a realistic application of that strategy would involve the construction of extremely expensive foreign bases. The carrier *United States*, the prototype heavy-attack carrier, was therefore cancelled, and attack-carrier strength was scheduled to decline in FY 50 from the eleven large carriers of FY 47 and FY 48 to only eight, in two task groups. Fiscal pressure continued, and when the FY budget was debated in 1949, the army and air force proposed further deep cuts, even to the elimination of carriers in the active fleet. General Eisenhower initially proposed six fleet carriers and eight carrier air groups (down, respectively, two and six from FY 50). When his figures failed to fit budget guidelines, he cut them further, to four carriers and six carrier air groups, which the CNO, Admiral Denfeld, described as "below the level where [carriers] could be utilized for sustained operations in the face of significant air opposition." Even so, this low level was endorsed by Secretary of Defense Louis Johnson on 5 July 1949. Admiral Denfeld considered eight carriers and ten air groups a minimum, a level achieved by January 1950 with the decommissioning of four carrier air groups. As of January 1950, the Joint Chiefs of Staff authorized an operating level of only six carriers. However, the new CNO, Admiral Forrest Sherman, successfully argued for a seventh, to keep one carrier continuously active in Western Pacific waters, in view of the "deterioration of the political situation in the Western Pacific and Southeastern Asia." This level was reached in May 1950 with the decommissioning of the *Kearsage* for modernization. A month later, with the outbreak of the Korean War, the issue was moot, since carriers were the only tactical air power available.

Despite crippling financial problems, there was interest within the Truman administration in a rapid buildup of U.S. military forces, particularly after the Soviets exploded a nuclear bomb in 1949. It was soon estimated that by FY 54 the Soviets would have 200 bombs, a figure equated with the ability to destroy 100 U.S. targets. For planning purposes, then, FY 54 was set as the date the Soviets would be able to go to war with the United States. A National Security Council study, NSC-68, was ordered, partly to decide whether the United States should go on to develop the H-bomb. The study concluded that the United States should abandon the nuclear-only strategy, and that it should arm to fight a war in FY 54.

NSC-68 was not far from the navy's concept of a war against the Soviet Union. In a detailed presentation, for example, it demanded that at the outset of a war forces protect the mobilization base while offensive forces were being built up, conduct offensive operations to keep the enemy off balance, and maintain the vital lines of communication within the alliance. The authors also stressed the mobilization element of victory, which had proved so important in both world wars, and the potential for which was present even in a largely disarmed United States.

NSC-68 was still under discussion when the Korean War began in June 1950; at that time it was the closest thing the United States had to a mobilization plan, even though it was oriented to a world war rather than to the particular Korean problem. In any case, Korea was widely perceived as the opening move in such a war. The FY 54 maximum guidelines almost immediately became interim goals to be achieved (and, in some cases, considerably exceeded) by the end of FY 52. In its final form of November 1950, NSC-68 called for FY 51 carrier forces to consist of nine fleet and four (plus one in reduced commission, for training) light carriers, with twelve carrier air groups and six escort carriers. At the end of FY 52 there would be twelve fleet carriers (fourteen air groups), five light carriers, and ten escort carriers. In fact Korean mobilization outpaced these estimated: there were fourteen fleet carriers in service at the end of FY 51 and sixteen at the end of FY 52.

Carrier performance in the tactical role was surely a major reason for the resurgence of the type. When North Korea invaded the South in June 1950, the only tactical forces in place were two U.S. aircraft carriers. The North Koreans soon overran all land bases on the peninsula, and only the carriers could supply tactical attack aircraft for the surviving U.S. and Korean ground forces. Although they did not enter combat at once (largely, it would appear, because it took time for the U.S. government to decide upon an appropriate U.S. role in the war) carriers were decisive, and they supplied a large fraction of tactical sorties through the war. They did so against virtually no air opposition at sea, although the prospect of such opposition required them to mount elaborate air defenses that diluted their strike potential. At the end of the war, carriers were the only mobile tactical forces available to deal with the remaining potential sources of conflict in the Far East, Indochina (Vietnam), and the Formosa Straits. From 1951 onward, then, strong U.S. attack carrier forces were maintained in the Western Pacific to deter further conflict. When that conflict came, in the form of the Vietnam War, they were available to strike while land airfields were being built up. Moreover, the mobility of the carriers provided some element of tactical surprise, particularly when their attacks were coordinated with those of land-based aircraft in the theater.

Operationally, Korea differed considerably from World War II. The fast carriers exploited their mobility relatively seldom, remaining in a restricted launch area while flying a combination of close air support and interdiction strikes, a pattern they would repeat off Vietnam. By the end of the war, carrier and land-based aviation had been integrated, all strikes being ordered by a joint operations center ashore. Typically carriers flew strikes for three days out of four (two out of three for unmodernized carriers), retiring on the fourth day for underway replenishment.

Korea also marked the introduction of jet aircraft into combat, and carrier air group composition evolved to suit the larger unit size and much larger fuel appetite of these aircraft. A typical air group of 1950 consisted of two jet fighter squadrons (for interception as well as for strike escort), two piston fighter squadrons (fighter-bomber), and one attack squadron, each of fourteen or fifteen aircraft, plus an increased complement of special-purpose aircraft. The latter typically included three night (propeller-driven) fighters, two photo planes (modified fighters), two night-attack bombers, four ECM aircraft, and three AEW aircraft. There was a conflict in the use of the scarce AEW resource: should it be employed for carrier-group air defense or antisubmarine defense? The latter was important because as yet there were no ASW carriers fast enough to accompany fleet carriers, yet with carriers operating in relatively restricted waters the threat of the large Soviet submarine force in the Far East was quite real.

As the war continued, more jet fighters were added, particularly after it became clear that they could function as fighter-bombers. Typically the two piston squadrons were replaced by a third jet squadron. In 1953 this was still primarily a day-defense organization. However, the thrust of carrier development since 1945 had been toward use of carrier fighters as the primary defense against an all-weather, day or night threat, in the form of a fast missile-bearing bomber. Within a few years, therefore, the carrier air-group organization shifted once more, ships typically operating one day-fighter (interceptor) and one night-fighter squadron, plus a squadron of fighter-bombers (light attack) and one of medium-attack bombers (Skyraiders). Again the balance between offense and defense was shifting, particularly since the jet fighter-bombers required no strike escorts. By the mid-fifties typical squadrons numbered fourteen aircraft, and many carriers operated detachments of heavy carrier bombers (such as the North American AJ Savage) as well.

The new *Forrestal*-class showed a further shift toward offensive firepower, with a full heavy-attack squadron of twelve aircraft and a second light-attack squadron, for a total of forty-eight attack aircraft (twelve per squadron) and only twenty-eight fighters, plus perhaps ten special-purpose aircraft. The *Enter-*

prise, sized by factors other than her air group, was even larger, with a second medium-attack (Skyraider) squadron and a larger heavy-attack squadron. The flexible carriers could accommodate, virtually without modification, major changes in the offensive-defensive air balance, and so could the flexible aircraft, the same basic types of which operated between 1950 and 1956 as interceptors, all-weather fighters, and then as fighter-bombers. After 1956 there were further shifts. The day fighters were replaced by high-performance Crusaders, useful primarily to gain air superiority over a strike area. The all-weather or fleet air-defense fighter was the McDonnell Demon (F3H); it and the Crusader were later replaced by a single fighter, the McDonnell Phantom (F4H or F-4), which combined in one airframe (it was hoped) the air-superiority and fleet air-defense roles.

From 1950 on the navy developed a nuclear-delivery capability. The previous year the Air Warfare Division (Op-55) had proposed a deemphasis on nuclear attack. The carrier air group would be fighter-heavy for air superiority. Heavy-attack aircraft were important but limited in application, their nuclear role primarily tactical. They would also be used for long-range mining and reconnaissance; hence they operated as detachments rather than as integral elements of carrier air groups. From 1951 they were based ashore as composite squadrons, at Port Lyautey in the Mediterranean, coming aboard as required. In 1953 a Pacific counterpart deployed to Atsugi Naval Air Station in Japan for operation from modernized *Essex*-class carriers. Only in September 1950 was authority granted to carry some bomb components aboard ship, and nuclear components themselves were not routinely carried until at least 1953.

The first nuclear operations, assigned in October and November 1950, were the naval missions to destroy Soviet naval capability (presumed to be primarily submarine bases) within a 600-nm radius of the Mediterranean, Norwegian, and Bering seas. However, within a year carriers were also being tasked with a support mission for NATO ground forces. Their sea-control mission was then defined as including attacks on Soviet airfields "threatening command of the seas" as well as support for amphibious and mining campaigns. By 1952 the Sixth Fleet was considered an important means of outflanking a Soviet advance in Central Europe; that year nuclear weapons were allocated for tactical purposes for the first time. This is not to say that the navy had emerged entirely victorious in its inter-service fight. For example, the air force still maintained that the carriers would not survive in a general nuclear war. However, a January 1954 navy presentation on carrier-task-force objectives showed relatively few

purely naval targets: it listed 352 Soviet and Allied airfields, 54 shipyards, 44 naval bases, and 66 areas to be mined in wartime.

The strategic situation had once more been transformed, this time by the appearance of the hydrogen bomb, several orders of magnitude more powerful than the nuclear weapons of the forties. Now advocates of strategic air attack could once more argue the case for the total destruction of the enemy's ability to fight through a rapid air offensive, and this time the air force had the means to attack in its large force of jet medium bombers (B-47s) deployed around the Soviet periphery. The navy remained skeptical. It could also argue that, by striking the Soviets from the Pacific and the Mediterranean, it could enhance the bomber offensive by diluting Soviet air defenses. On 5 February 1954 the Joint Chiefs endorsed navy participation in U.S. strategic-attack planning, and from the mid-fifties on carriers often maintained one or more nuclear-armed attack planes on catapults on continuous alert, to be launched in the event of war. At the same time, however, the flexibility of the carrier and her ability to operate in less than general war continued to be emphasized within the navy. Also, the considerable shrinkage in the size of individual nuclear weapons tended to blur the distinction between nuclear (heavy) and conventional (medium or light) bombers within the carrier air group; by the mid-fifties any navy fighter-bomber could list a substantial nuclear weapon from a carrier deck. The nuclear role was so important by the mid-fifties that the successor to the fighter-bombers, the A-4 Skyhawk, was designed with a primary nuclear-delivery mission in mind. Early versions had only a very limited conventional bombing capability.

Having assured navy participation in joint strategic-attack planning, the CNO, Admiral Robert B. Carney, sought to develop coherent navy plans for the coming decade. On 20 April 1954 he established an ad hoc committee to study long-range shipbuilding plans and programs, under Vice Admiral Ralph A. Ofstie. Earlier shipbuilding plans, even those involving carriers, had not been coordinated with any larger navy strategic concept. Moreover, several technologies developed under intense pressure after World War II, including jet strategic bombers (which alone required large flight decks), defensive antiaircraft missiles (which might change the balance of offense and defense within the carrier task force), and nuclear power. Longer-range ASW sensors and weapons were all mature enough to enter service. All these technologies would surely affect the coming navy program. The committee sought a navy goal for the 1970 era and then developed a shipbuilding program to match. It stressed the importance of fleet air defense through long-range missiles and also called

Reactions to the advent of jets and heavy attack aircraft shaped the postwar U.S. carrier force. This is the reconstructed carrier *Lake Champlain*, off Norfolk on 1 November 1952, prominently displaying amidships the nylon crash barrier developed specifically for jet operation. Also, the three planes on her flight deck represent stages in aircraft development: the wartime Hellcat, the late-war and early postwar Corsair, and the postwar Banshee. At this time the U.S. Navy still favored a very strong shipboard AA battery of 5-in/38 and radar-controlled twin 3-in/50 guns. Note, too, the prominent housing for an escalator—characteristic of reconstructed *Essex*-class carriers—leading from a protected ready room under the armored hangar deck to the flight-deck level, alongside the island structure.

for attempts to apply nuclear power to cruisers, aircraft carriers, and submarines.

Much more important, the committee's final report formulated a navy view (subsequently endorsed by the CNO) quite at variance with the then-current concept of "massive retaliation." Since the Soviets were developing their own nuclear strike forces, the committee envisaged a strategic balance between the two superpowers, which meant the United States would be unable to deter Soviet or Soviet-proxy actions at lower levels of violence. It followed that the Soviets would be able to fight in many of the unstable areas around the Eurasian periphery, and that the carriers would perform an invaluable tactical role in such wars, not to mention their ability to show naval "presence" in such a way as to prevent the outbreak of such conflicts. In fact such carrier operations have been an important fixture in the postwar world. Examples are far too numerous to mention here, but they include the rapid buildup of forward-deployed forces during the 1961 Berlin crisis, when a third carrier was added to the Sixth Fleet and (along with one in the Seventh Fleet) loaded with air groups consisting almost entirely of attack aircraft. Recently, given the declining carrier-force level, the converse has been evident: when U.S. carriers had to be withdrawn from the Pacific to support operations in the Indian Ocean, the Japanese became nervous about Soviet naval forces in the Western Pacific, even though it could be argued that the remaining U.S. forces were more than a match for them. The carrier had, by that time, assumed such importance in local eyes that the presence of a Soviet semicarrier, the *Minsk*, was considered significant quite beyond its limited combat potential.

The ad hoc committee looked toward a transfer of deep-strike functions to long-range missiles (such as the Regulus) within the fleet, freeing carrier aircraft for just the tactical mission the committee's political analysis demanded. It also expected a decline in the need for high-performance fleet fighters. They would not be needed over the objective area (which by 1970 would probably be defended by missiles) because the attack aircraft of the future would penetrate by stealth rather than by brute force at high speed and high altitude. This was the origin of the Grumman A-6 Intruder. It would have STOL performance, and would be able to operate from ASW support carriers (CVS) as well as from conventional attack carriers. Moreover, it was confidently (if incorrectly) predicted that by 1962 there would be a vertical takeoff fighter capable of intercepting enemy aircraft with heat-seeking missiles, and that by 1965 it would be able to operate from "heavy-support ships" other than carriers. Given the STOL attack bomber and the VTOL fighter, there was a real hope of reducing car-

rier size and cost without a major loss in fleet (as opposed to single-ship) capability.

Each of five carrier strike groups in the 1970 fleet would comprise three attack carriers and one ASW support carrier, a combination described as "the minimum required for effective sustained strikes, using largely conventional weapons, in limited war." The carriers would be supported by a missile-armed converted battleship for long-range missile attack, for air control (with a missile cruiser as alternate), and for primary inner-zone air defense against high-altitude attack. Supporting ships would be four missile cruisers, three missile frigates, six destroyers, and two submarines for distant early warning and for rescue. The attack-carrier air group was envisaged as sixteen to thirty-two conventional and four to six VTOL fighters, six to twelve heavy-attack aircraft, twenty to thirty-two of the new low-altitude strike aircraft, four to six photo aircraft, and four AEW aircraft. Both the attack and the ASW carriers would be missile-armed for self defense, and the ASW carrier would accommodate four to six of the new VTOL fighters, four AEW aircraft or helicopters, twenty-four ASW helicopters, and sixteen of the new attack aircraft to contribute to task force striking power.

Air defense would be mounted in great depth, using the new long-range Talos missile and VTOL fighters aboard support ships to extend outward the surveillance and air-defense zones of the task force. The conventional fighters would form a CAP that might intercept attackers 150- to 250-nm from the task force, with VTOL fighters operating at shorter ranges, backed up by very heavy missile fire from the force. An important element of task-force operation would be air control by the missile ships, allowing the carriers to remain silent and so much less detectable. The great advantages of the VTOL fighter in this scheme were its quick reaction time and the fact that it probably would not interfere with normal carrier-deck operations.

As a minimum, one task group and one reduced task group (less two attack carriers and nine support ships) were to be maintained in each of the two fleets to permit an attack within two or three days after an alert. Elements sufficient to form another within a week were also to be available in each fleet. The figure of five task groups was deduced from the standard readiness factor of one in three, or two in three in an emergency; it represented a minimum force level. Carriers available in 1970 would include the six existing *Forrestal*s, the three *Midway*s, and six new nuclear-attack carriers; all of the *Essex*es would be out of the attack-carrier force, although five of the SCB-27Cs would be available for operations with the strike forces. Other forces envisaged at this time included a missile-submarine strike force and a seaplane (P6M) mobile strike force, as well as a surface defensive force. Support carriers would include one SCB 27C, all nine SCB 27A *Essex* conversions, and two new nuclear ASW carriers.

Great hopes were entertained for helicopter sonar, both towed and dunked. For example, the planners hoped for a 10,000-yd range within five years, and twice that range five years later, with all-weather operation by 1960. Helicopters would be operated from twenty-five escort carriers (CVHEs: nineteen *Commencement Bay*-class carriers, two *Saipan*s, and four new nuclear helicopter-carriers) as well as from twelve new barrier escorts, or CVHGs.

From the late forties onward direct attacks on Soviet submarine bases and mining of their exits had formed the basis of U.S. wartime ASW strategy. In addition, developments in submarine passive sonar made barrier operations off the exits viable, if enough ASW submarines could be built or converted. Convoy operations, as futile as they appeared to be (in view of advances in submarine technology) were a poor third, with hunter-killer operations least effective in the absence of effective code breaking or tactical radio direction finding. SOSUS was an effective substitute for code breaking, in that it permitted the location of submarines at a great distance, and with its introduction ASW carriers became an important means of prosecuting submarine contacts in mid-ocean. Ultimately they were replaced by land-based aircraft, as the longer-range P-3 Orion replaced the Neptune of the forties and fifties.

The ad hoc committee envisaged a series of barriers, which would be combined with the navy contribution to continental air defense. A distant barrier would consist of fifty ASW submarines (SSKs); an ocean barrier of thirty-five to forty Terrier-armed PBGs; an outer offshore barrier of twelve CVHGs in the Atlantic and twelve to fifteen PBGs in the Pacific; and an inner contiguous barrier of sixteen to twenty-six PBGs or YAGRs. The CVHGs would be useful both as barrier units and as convoy escorts. The barriers would be supplemented by mobile hunter-killer forces and also by convoy escorts, although the latter were not emphasized. In particular, it seemed unlikely that the large number of escorts remaining from the World War II programs would be retained much beyond 1965. Barriers "could reduce the . . . requirements for escorts through reducing the number of submarines able to reach and to operate effectively on . . . major shipping lanes." Improved sonars and shipboard helicopters would also cut the number of escorts required. Moreover, the barrier ships would double as escorts.

SOSUS would be used with shore-based aircraft as back up; the PBGs were to operate out of range of Soviet air attack, primarily for detection of sub-

marines and bombers, with limited kill capability against submarines. The CVHG and inner Pacific PBG barriers would have air control of shore-based interceptors as well, and the Atlantic ships would have low-altitude air surveillance and control with helicopters and ship-based fighters. The inner line of pickets (PBGs or YAGRs) would be able to control interceptors, and they would also have ASW search and kill capability. The ad hoc committee reported that the multiple barrier system would succeed because of its "diverse types of equipment and the use of mobile backup forces. A single barrier, or multiple barriers, utilizing but one basic type may be countered, but a system employing multiple threats in depth is more likely to succeed."

Although it was not mentioned explicitly, the long-range objectives report included a counter to a new threat, the fast Soviet nuclear submarine. Previously, carrier strike forces had been virtually immune to submarine attack by virtue of their high speed. However, they could not be sure of evading nuclear submarines, and therefore they required specialized ASW support, in the form of one support carrier for every three-carrier strike formation. By the sixties, such assignment was standard U.S. practice.

Like the strike-carrier policy, the ASW policy of the ad hoc committee was only partly realized. There was no major barrier construction program, and in 1965 the existing air-defense barrier forces were abolished. However, the basic strategic shift from convoy and base strike to barrier and attrition warfare was accepted, albeit in somewhat modified form. Advances in submarine sonar permitted the submarines to move back to the Greenland–Iceland–United Kingdom Gap, and their numbers fell below those advanced in the ad hoc report. In the North Atlantic itself, attrition became the province of long-range shore-based aircraft and of hunter-killer groups, the latter built around fixed-wing carriers (CVSs) rather than around the CVHEs envisaged by the ad hoc committee, partly because helicopter sonars did not develop nearly as quickly as expected. In addition, the ad hoc committee failed to realize one of the most important peacetime ASW functions, "cold-war trailing," in which U.S. ASW forces maintained active trail of selected Soviet submarines primarily to deter the Soviets from submarine operations in the North Atlantic.

A somewhat sanitized version of the long-range report was issued in 1958 under the title "The Navy of the 1970 Era," approved by the CNO, Admiral Arleigh Burke. It explicitly established the primary carrier mission as limited rather than general war, although carriers were only withdrawn from the general war plan (SIOP) after 1966.

By that time the carrier force had stabilized at the

fifteen-ship level, with a typical forward deployment of two carriers in the Eastern Mediterranean and three in the Western Pacific. The latter made up for a general lack of U.S. tactical strike bases within range of Soviet and Chinese targets. In addition, from 1952 on it was U.S. policy that, upon the outbreak of war, the Atlantic carriers in U.S. waters would form part of a NATO Strike Fleet that would proceed north to attack the Soviet bases on the Northern Flank, primarily the submarine bases around Murmansk. In recent years, the mission of reinforcing the Northern Flank appears to have replaced the nuclear strike as an initial navy concern. (The Sixth Fleet is responsible for the Southern Flank mission.)

From the late fifties onward, even before Vietnam, there was a gradual decline in carrier construction due to a combination of rising shipbuilding cost, new naval technology, and the shift toward a submarine-based strategic force, Polaris. Where the ad hoc report had seen a missile-based long-range strike force as an integral component of a strike fleet, Polaris was a separate (and very expensive) system, which had to be financed out of the same limited navy budget that supported the carriers. It was impossible, for example, to finance a new nuclear carrier each year from FY 58 through FY 63. Thus a 1960 navy planning document looked forward to the survival of only twelve attack carriers by FY 72. The Pacific force would have to be cut to two carriers, and it would be impossible to maintain a ready carrier in each of two essential Pacific sectors. Deployments to the South Atlantic and to the Indian Ocean would also have to be reduced. In a general war, there would have to be some reduction in attack-carrier nuclear assignments, some targets being transferred to submarines or even to NATO land-based aircraft. There was a bright side to this forecast for the carrier's future: some flexibility would be restored to carrier operations, which were rather tightly constrained by fixed general-war requirements in the Mediterranean and the Northwest Pacific.

A reduction in the total number of carriers added pressure to the existing tendency to increase the number of strike aircraft per carrier. One hope was for improvements in ship-based antiaircraft missiles, which might take over much of the responsibility for killing long-range missile-carrying bombers as well as low fliers. Carrier fighters would then operate largely against snoopers, small raids, and in the long-range attrition role against larger raids, since the fighters could fly well beyond a long surface-to-air missile range. An objective of at least forty-three attack aircraft per carrier was stated, at least one-third of which were to be all-weather, high-payload, long-range (heavy-attack) types. The remainder would operate in all weather, but would be largely limited to visual weapon delivery. All would be armed with long-range stand-off missiles to negate the growing Soviet surface-to-air missile armory.

As for the carrier task group itself, a reduction to twelve ships would imply a reduction from three to two carriers per force, the minimum acceptable level. In 1960, two carriers per task group was a far from ideal number; standard doctrine at the time called for three carriers to operate in company.

Concerning the ASW support carriers, in 1960 there were nine, five in the Atlantic and four in the Pacific. Generally two had to be forward deployed with the attack carriers, for a total requirement of at least six; indeed, in 1960 the fiscally unconstrained planning objective was five in each fleet, half of them forward deployed. Requirements included both cover for deployed strike forces and offensive operations against concentrations of hostile submarines. There was also the important cold-war requirement, which could be met only by long-endurance ships and sea-based aircraft, no matter what the improvement in long-range shore-based aircraft with their wartime prompt-kill capability was. The CVS force was, however, a victim of the war in Vietnam. Although ten CVSs were in commission in 1965, within five years that number had fallen to four. Moreover, the primary CVS airplane, the Grumman S2F Tracker, was no longer capable of dealing with Soviet nuclear submarines.

A new aircraft program was begun to buy enough S-3A Vikings for six carriers (for two forward deployments), but it was too late. As part of his program of economies to permit a major force modernization, Admiral Zumwalt, the new CNO, agreed to a plan to transfer the task group ASW function to the strike carriers themselves, redesignating the attack carriers multirole carriers, or CV rather than CVA. At the same time he proposed a special-purpose helicopter/VSTOL carrier, the sea-control ship, which under some circumstances would have resembled the World War II ASW escort carrier in function. It was never, however, built.

Although the 1960 projection was somewhat more pessimistic than it had to be, the carrier force did decline sharply in the sixties and seventies as the role and even the viability of the carrier came into question again and again. In 1963 Secretary of Defense Robert S. McNamara reviewed prospective carrier-force levels for the period through FY 72, the same period the 1960 report had considered. He had inherited a prospective program of one carrier every other year, down from the annual carrier of the fifties and of the ad hoc report, with ships scheduled for FY 63, FY 65, and FY 67. The CNO pressed for maintenance of the fifteen-carrier force, although the chairman of the Joint Chiefs proposed a reduction to fourteen in FY 70 and to thirteen in FY 72. The air force, the traditional foe of the carrier, went much further, calling for the retirement of one carrier every year after FY 65, to have a force of only eight by FY 71. In 1963 the navy was operating seven *Forrestal* and post-*Forrestal* carriers, with an eighth, CVA 66, under construction; there were also five *Essexes* and the three *Midways*, and there was agitation for an additional carrier (which became the *John F. Kennedy*, CVA 67). McNamara decided to recommend retention of fifteen carriers (with CVA 66 replacing one *Essex*) through FY 69, continuing the earlier plan to build one new carrier in FY 67 but cancelling the carrier previously approved for FY 65, and deferring one previously planned for FY 69 to FY 70.

Since the carriers were being withdrawn from the strategic role, the major issue in McNamara's mind was the comparison in capabilities between air force and navy tactical aircraft. The air force claimed that its new rapid-deployment capability would allow it to take over much of the rapid-reaction role of the carrier. The secretary's Draft Presidential Memorandum on CVA Forces (December 1963) pointed out that the forward-based forces were essential to prevent an enemy from denying the United States the ability to move home-based aircraft into an area. Forward-based carriers would be essential to maintain local air superiority to cover the arrival of the land-based composite strike air forces in the theater, particularly when land bases or their defenses had been damaged by surprise attack; forward-based carriers were also needed to provide tactical air power "in situations where bases are not immediately available.... Either the bases themselves or the overflight clearance to gain access to them may be denied (perhaps unexpectedly) by political considerations." McNamara could also envisage temporary augmentation of land-based aircraft during periods of "peak demand" in a land battle, as well as the classic missions of amphibious support and sea control.

He saw a decreasing need for carriers based on a combination of increasing capability per carrier in projecting tactical air power, "the introduction of large number of fast-reacting, long-range, survivable missiles into our strategic nuclear forces," and "the increasing worldwide mobility of land-based tactical air." The navy would later argue that, although carrier capabilities had indeed increased, that had only been in proportion to the general level of military technology, so that in some important sense a large nuclear carrier with about ninety aircraft operating in 1970 would have an effect analogous to that of a modernized *Essex* with an air group of a similar (numerical) size two decades earlier.

Secretary McNamara opposed inclusion of the carriers in the SIOP role because he considered all such "dual-capable" systems questionable. For example, levels of loss quite acceptable in a conventional war would, in a dual-capable system, be an unacceptable depletion of U.S. strategic strength, which was by definition a reserve for escalation control of a war. Thus he was determined to withdraw them from the SIOP beyond FY 66. Moreover, he was placing great emphasis on the nuclear survivability of U.S. strategic systems, and he considered a carrier far too "soft" against nuclear weapons to be acceptable. He does not appear to have taken very seriously arguments that a carrier might survive by deception and mobility, whereas the "hard" land-based missiles (Minuteman) would not. He did argue that only the forward-deployed carriers would be important in a nuclear war. Those carriers retained in American waters would, however, be extremely useful in a non-strategic war; McNamara cited, for example, the importance of Second Fleet carriers in major contingency plans against Cuba. Finally, he argued that the SIOP assignments in fact restricted the flexibility of the carriers in nonstrategic situations, and that the need to train pilots and have them stand nuclear alerts in itself reduced carrier capability in nonstrategic warfare. "Of course, this in no sense precludes the carrying of some nuclear weapons in the magazine of a carrier that is bought and operated for the conventional war mission to give it a tactical nuclear strike capability as well."

With the end of the SIOP mission, the navy was realigning the air groups of the carriers, reducing the fighter squadrons from fourteen to twelve aircraft, and increasing the size of the light-attack squadrons from twelve to fourteen as deck space became available. This change was scheduled for FY 65, and the McNamara paper also recommended approval for a new navy light-attack bomber, then called VAL (now A-7), to further increase carrier striking power in a tactical role. He also valued the manned fighter for its ability to counter low-flying attackers, which would generally escape the surface-to-air missile fire of the carrier task force; the existing F-4B, however, was not fully effective against such aircraft because of deficiencies in its radar, which would not be corrected until the emergence of the F-4G/J.

Within a year, the carriers were again in combat, in Vietnam, where they were proving their practical, as opposed to theoretical, value. Throughout the Vietnam War, the navy had to maintain force levels in the Western Pacific well above the peacetime ones on which the fifteen-carrier force level had been based. For example, by June 1965 there were five attack carriers in the South China Sea, operating from two launch areas, Yankee Station off North Vietnam and Dixie Station off the South, the latter used to work up newly arrived air wings. A converted

Secretary McNamara proposed in February 1966 the construction of three more nuclear carriers to maintain a force level of fifteen: eight *Forrestal*s and post-*Forrestal*s, three *Midway*s, and four nuclear carriers. Indeed, he was soon to propose the design and construction of a three-carrier nuclear class (which became the *Nimitz*) as a single-unit procurement to save money. Meanwhile the ASW carrier *Intrepid* was operated in the Gulf of Tonkin as a "limited" attack carrier, to make up the number for the heavy continuous deployment in the Far East. Crises elsewhere in the world made it impossible for McNamara to denude the Atlantic Fleet to match—in 1967 it was fortunate that two carriers were available in the Mediterranean for the June war.

Carrier operation in Vietnam placed heavy demands on individual ships and thus accelerated the demise of the older carriers, at just the time when new carriers became more difficult to buy. For example, the standard pattern of two attack carriers on Yankee Station and another (or an ASW carrier with a limited attack group) on Dixie Station was initially supported by only four deployed carriers, which thus had to spend over 80 percent of their time at sea. From June 1965 five carriers were deployed to the Western Pacific; even they averaged 75 percent of their time at sea. Moreover, this deployment did not allow for the Northern Pacific operations demanded for SIOP readiness until the carriers were withdrawn from that plan. To some extent the Vietnam War was sustained through deployments from the Atlantic, at least one of whose six carriers was generally off Vietnam. However, the remaining five still had to support at least two and sometimes three attack carriers in the Mediterranean, a very considerable strain.

Despite Secretary McNamara's enthusiasm, the carrier force declined in the early seventies. For example, he announced a program to build new nuclear-attack carriers under the FY 66, FY 68, and FY 70 budgets. In fact, however, these three ships were authorized under the FY 67, FY 70, and FY 74 budgets, a longer stretch that reflected uncertainty over the value of the attack carrier in the Nixon administration. Meanwhile, the surviving World War II carriers wore out; the last two modernized *Essex*-class attack carriers, limited in capability in any case, were laid up in 1975 and in 1976, and the *Franklin D. Roosevelt*, the least satisfactory of the *Midway*s, was decommissioned in 1977 upon completion of the nuclear carrier *Dwight D. Eisenhower*. That left a total of thirteen active attack carriers, with one more nuclear carrier under construction and two *Midway*s clearly approaching the end of their active lives. In 1975–77 the navy proposed construction of a fifth nuclear carrier to replace the remaining *Midway*, but once more controversy over the value of the carrier erupted. The Ford administration proposed this ship for FY 78, with additional nuclear carriers to replace the *Forrestal*s at a rate of one every two years. However, it also began design studies for a new non-nuclear carrier somewhat smaller than the large *Nimitz* class, ultimately designated the CVV.

There were attempts to make more efficient use of this reduced force. For example, when he took office

The outstanding feature of the modern carrier is her ability to remain at sea for substantial periods. That requires a considerable investment in fast underway replenishment ships such as the oiler and ammunition carrier *Sacramento*, shown simultaneously fueling the carrier *Kitty Hawk* and the frigate *Sample* in March 1978.

A variety of more or less futuristic schemes for unconventional carriers has been proposed. This 325-ft SWATH ship was proposed by the David W. Taylor Naval Ship Research and Development Center in 1980 to operate short takeoff, vertical landing (STOVL) fighters.

in 1971 as CNO Admiral Zumwalt made an extensive analysis of the problems of the fleet, which included a low retention (reenlistment) rate. He proposed reducing the separation of men from their families by assigning some ships, including carriers, home ports abroad; this move would also have the effect of increasing the fraction of time those ships would be available, lessening the impact of the inevitable reduction in the total carrier-force level. Although the proposal for providing home ports in Athens did not prove successful, it was possible to give a home port to a carrier in Japan.

Given delays in carrier construction, the force level appeared to be set at twelve large carriers and an aging *Midway*, allowing for forward deployment of four rather than five carriers (two instead of three in the Western Pacific); the Carter administration proposed that the remaining *Midway* be replaced, not by another *Nimitz*, but by a new carrier, the CVV, of limited capability more closely comparable to the ship she would replace. Once more events came to the rescue of the carrier force. Continuous carrier operations in the Indian Ocean in 1979–80 showed not only

the value of the nuclear carrier, but also how thin the total carrier force had been stretched. President Carter reluctantly approved the fourth *Nimitz*, CVN 71, and the limited-attack carrier was dropped. Moreover, the subsequent Reagan administration entered office with a commitment to a much more activist foreign policy, which in turn would require a stronger attack-carrier force. For example, it discussed a permanent U.S. carrier force in the Indian Ocean, which would entail a level of operations not obtainable at lower force levels. A total of sixteen attack carriers was proposed as a minimum acceptable level, to be achieved by a combination of new construction and the reconstruction (SLEP, Service Life Extension Program) of existing heavy carriers. In addition, the *Midway*s are to be retained at least through the 1980s; early in the Reagan administration there were plans as well to draw one or two *Essex*es from reserve for reconstruction. This last proposal, however, encountered considerable congressional opposition, not least because the costs involved are by no means well determined. In the end, the proposal was dropped.

2

Beginnings: The Langley, Lexington, and Saratoga

Like other major fleets, the U.S. Navy became interested in shipboard aircraft even before World War I; indeed, the United States was the first country to launch a plane from a ship. In 1910 a U.S. naval constructor, Captain Washington Irving Chambers, rigged a short flat platform on the foredeck of the scout cruiser *Birmingham*, from which Eugene Ely made the world's first shipboard takeoff on 14 November of that year. Ely landed aboard a similar deck on the armored cruiser *Pennsylvania* on 18 January 1911, while she rode at anchor. An hour later, with the primitive arresting gear removed, he flew off for shore. These developments did not, however, lead directly to the design of a U.S. carrier. The flat deck was cumbersome, and Ely had to land abruptly, just before his airplane crashed into the cruiser's superstructure.

When Glen Curtiss successfully tested a floatplane in January 1911, navy attention turned in that direction. The floatplane was simpler to operate, and landing it appeared less dangerous. The floatplane could also be launched from aboard ship with a catapult, a device Chambers invented at the Washington Navy Yard in 1912. The rapid development of the catapult in the U.S. Navy began when a rather cumbersome fixed-track type was fitted aboard the armored cruisers *North Carolina, Seattle, Huntington,* and *Montana* in 1916–17, even though the contraption interfered with the firing of the ships' after turrets. These catapults were removed when the ships were assigned to

convoy (antiraider) duty in 1917. Navy floatplanes had already seen limited service at Vera Cruz, Mexico three years earlier. Catapult-launched aircraft were, at that time, unique to the U.S. Navy, and they were considered essential aids to scouting—that is, to the cruiser mission. Thus, early versions of the General Board characteristics for the battle and scout cruisers of the *Omaha* class gave specifications for aircraft.

The earliest official U.S. interest in *carrier* design appears to have been inspired by British war experience. Relations between the two fleets were extremely close after America's entry into World War I in April 1917. Several U.S. officers later prominent in the development of shipboard aircraft served with the British Grand Fleet, where they were able to observe carrier experiments firsthand. Admiral William S. Sims, commander of U.S. naval forces in Europe and a revolutionary figure in the development of big-gun fire control, became an early advocate of such aircraft, in which he shared an interest with two other major gunnery figures, Percy Scott and John Fisher of the Royal Navy. He was responsible for fitting a launching platform onto the battleship *Texas*, over the protests of the then CNO, Admiral William S. Benson. Operational experience was particularly important because it showed the advantage of wheeled airplanes over catapult-launched floatplanes decisively. The latter could not be recovered under many common North Sea conditions; with the former, something closer to all-

The *Lexington* and the *Saratoga* were the first true U.S. aircraft carriers. Here the *Saratoga* steams through the Panama Canal in February 1928, with a pair of floatplanes on her flight deck near the flywheel catapult that would launch them. Note that the outer portions of platforms for her 5-in/25 AA guns have been folded up to clear her of the lock walls.

Two views of the conversion of the *Langley* emphasize how primitive she was: her coal-unloading cranes were removed and a series of thirteen steel truss towers was erected on each side to carry the flight deck. The bridge was unaltered, and the smoke pipes aft were carried out her sides. The interior view shows the rails for a gantry crane used to carry aircraft from the holds to an elevator, the latter visible in the lowered position.

weather operation was possible. Also, the weight and drag penalty of floats was considerable, although it was not always perceived. For example, both the French and the Italian navies were using floatplane fighters aboard their capital ships as late as 1940, while the U.S. Navy had flirted with the same concept in the twenties.

Carrier design was a matter of considerable complexity even in 1917. It was, therefore, fortunate that the British naval constructor S. V. Goodall (later British director of naval communications) was seconded to C & R. When he arrived late in 1917, Goodall carried plans of many of the newer British designs, including such carriers as HMS *Hermes*. He also brought accounts of British policy and of war experience, such as the analysis of battle damage at Jutland.

Goodall's ideas on carriers were significant because they formed a starting point for American doctrine and development. In June 1918 the U.S. director of naval aviation suggested characteristics for a carrier. That August, Goodall summarized British experience for the benefit of those determining such characteristics:

Air fighting has become a feature of naval operations, and the tactical movements of a fleet before an engagement opens will most probably be governed by information obtained from air scouts. . . . A series of fights between opposing aircraft will most likely be a preliminary to a fleet action. A fleet should therefore be attended by reconnaissance machines and fighting machines. . . .

. . . an armament of four 4-in AA guns is insufficient, and a larger number of heavier guns—preferably 6-in—should be carried, together with one or two AA guns. Although such a ship should not by any means be regarded as a fighting ship, it should be sufficiently powerfully armored to be able to brush aside light vessels of the enemy, so that its machines can be flown off in comparatively advanced positions.

A torpedo armament of about 12 upper deck torpedo tubes should be provided in order that if, at any time, through any fortuitous circumstances, she should find herself in the presence of large enemy vessels, she would have the opportunity of inflicting some damage and at the same time be a sufficient menace to make it undesirable for the enemy to approach very closely and inflict a knockout blow with one or two shots from heavy guns.

Torpedo protection is considered essential, as the ship would be a valuable unit operating most probably in the vicinity of enemy submarines.

Side protection should be as good as that of light cruisers. . . .

The speed proposed—namely, 30 knots—is considered a minimum. It should be equal to that of scouting forces with which the ship would work, and in view of the 35 knot speed of the U.S. battle cruisers

and scout cruisers, it is for consideration whether a higher speed than 30 knots should not be provided. . . .

At this time Goodall either did not know or could not reveal that the Royal Navy planned to use its carriers, with torpedo planes as their main weapon, for strikes on the German High Seas Fleet. In any case the proposed U.S. characteristics of 1919–20 followed Goodall's suggestions, with the single exception being the large number of torpedo planes included in a carrier's air group. At this time fighters were valued for their combined functions of fleet air defense, air control, and what would later be called antisnooper patrol (for denial of strategic reconnaissance, such as was accomplished in the wartime Grand Fleet). Even at this primitive stage, such carrier roles were well appreciated. The hard-headed General Board, which included the president of the Naval War College, who was charged with testing new tactical and technological concepts on the game board, wanted carriers in numbers—and wanted them soon. A July 1920 three-year building program called for four carriers (as well as three battleships and one battle cruiser); the following July the board asked for three carriers as its highest priority.

In the absence of experimental U.S. carriers, the General Board had to rely on the theoretical war games of the Naval War College, an organization instrumental in such earlier materiel developments as the introduction of the big-gun battleship into the U.S. Navy. At a 1922 General Board hearing, Captain Laning from the college summarized a year of table-top carrier engagements.

The games have not proven that aircraft will entirely dominate the situation, but they have brought out the fact that—as much as any other auxiliary [non-capital ship] type, and perhaps more than any other—aircraft can exert a decisive influence in all stages of a campaign and particularly in the battle stage. . . . For instance, unless you get control of the air sufficient so your spotting planes can spot or if you let the enemy use spotting planes and you don't have them, you suffer the equivalent of 4,000 yards loss in range. This is because if you are using top spot it is good for only 20,000 yards range while with airplanes you can increase your effective range to 24,000. Thus, having control of the air, if only for spotting gunfire, can become the decisive factor in battle. If you do not have your spotting planes up there and the other fellow has, you will lose out. . . . If the enemy has superior speed (and the British fleet has a fleet speed superior to ours) and has airplanes up while we have not, he will have such an advantage in range and accuracy that he would tie us up. All he needs to do is to keep the range over 20,000. . . . we also found other results were aircraft *directly* affect the trend [of a

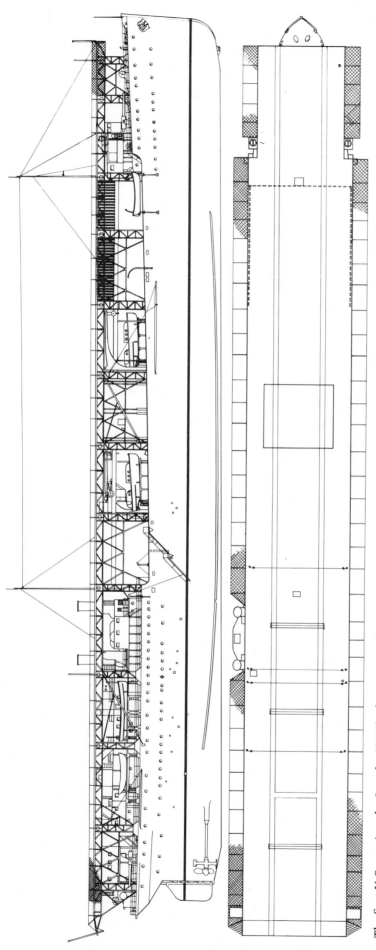

The first U.S. carrier, the *Langley* (CV 1), about 1930, after the removal of her catapult. Note that her bridge remained in its preconversion position. She was armed with four 5-in/51 guns.

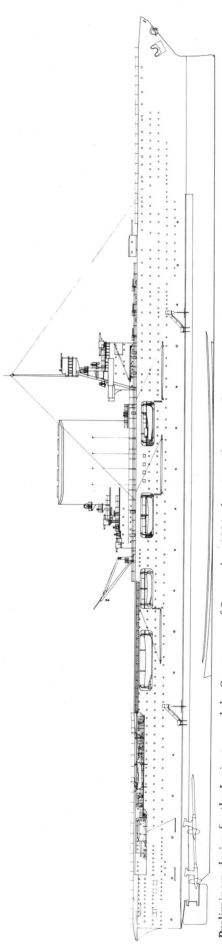

Preliminary design for the *Lexington* and the *Saratoga* as of September 1921, showing a battery of six 6-in/53s (three twin mounts, as in the *Omaha*-class cruisers), and twelve 5-in/25 AA guns. There were also to have been six single 21-in torpedo tubes, three on each side, grouped right aft above the protective deck. The only major features not evident here are two catapults: a long track extending from the forward elevator to the bow, and a turntable type to port abeam the 5-in guns on the flight deck.

battle]. If you can succeed in getting home a bombing or torpedo attack, you may injure one or more battleships and doing only that may give you the preponderance of gunfire that will ultimately win the battle. Of course there is difficulty in getting the attacks of those planes home for they are heavy planes easily destroyed by fighting planes and we have them on nothing except aircraft carriers.

The problem was the long time it was assumed would be required to launch carrier aircraft stowed below decks: nine minutes per bomber, six per fighter; the carrier would have only four bombers and eight fighters on deck for quick launch. BuAer could do nothing to get the bombers aloft more quickly, but it proposed that the fighters be carried aboard the battleship as catapult aircraft, so that more could be put in the air within a short period. Game experience suggested that the fleet with more fighters aboard its battleships could gain, and then exercise, command of the air, both for spotting and for strikes. In fact, carriers could accommodate much larger numbers of aircraft on their flight decks, and the performance penalties associated with catapult operation doomed the battleship-fighter concept.

Ultimately the concept of basing fighters on surface combatants was abandoned; floats imposed too great a performance penalty. However, the need to launch a large number of aircraft in quick succession from a limited deck was urgent. It was met in part by intensive training of the deck crews and in part by increasing the number of planes that could be packed together at one end of the flight deck prior to takeoff. The latter was achieved through the design of more compact aircraft (with such features as folding wings) and the provision for maximum flight-deck ("parking") area. But by 1930 a problem had arisen: heavier aircraft required longer deck rolls, and thus the farthest forward position in which an airplane could be parked was pushed back. The solution in World War II was use of the catapult, although for some time the device was opposed because it was cumbersome and because takeoffs from it were far slower than those from a more conventional deck roll. Catapults did not become popular until after it had been demonstrated in World War II that, aboard escort carriers, they were the sole means of launching certain aircraft.

The notion of the carrier as an essential component of the battle fleet motivated the U.S. Navy to press early for large and capable ships. In August 1918 Goodall thought that his rough recommendations would result in an 800-ft, 22,000-ton carrier—something a bit larger than HMS Furious. That October, C & R produced its first sketch design: 825 feet on the waterline, about 24,000 tons, to make 35 knots on about 140,000 SHP, with a battery of ten 6-in and four

AA guns. The sketch preserved is somewhat ambiguous as to the placement of funnels, but it appears that a pair of islands, one on either side of the flight deck, was contemplated.

This study was soon put aside, but work resumed in March 1919, since the General Board was interested in designing a carrier for its FY 20 program. This time the characteristics called for a ship with a speed of 35 knots and a capacity for twenty-four fighter/reconnaissance aircraft and six bombers. She would also act as depot ship for fifteen light reconnaissance aircraft to be based on the battle cruisers and scouts operating with her. The battery was to consist of four 8-in, six 6-in, and four 4-in AA guns, as well as a twin torpedo tube on each beam.

In 1918 perhaps the most characteristic emphasis of U.S. capital-ship design, and one reflected in most of the early carrier studies, was on underwater protection. New U.S. battleships and battle cruisers were to be provided not only with the usual layers of filled and void side protective compartments, but with turbo-electric machinery as well, which could be subdivided far more efficiently than the more conventional, compact, and lighter geared turbines. Typically, the turbo-generators proper were placed in large centerline compartments, the boilers occupying separate wing compartments. An incidental feature of such power plants was the ability—of some significance in U.S. carrier operational procedure between wars—to run astern at high power.

Preliminary Design reacted to the 1919 characteristics by modifying (on paper) the only high-speed large-ship design it had, the battle cruiser. The version used was the early 34,800-ton, 35-kt design, and not the 43,000-tonner actually laid down. As in the 1918 sketch, twin superstructures were contemplated, with a single 8-in gun fore and aft of each and the 6-in guns along the ship's side (two in a gunhouse aft, beneath the flight deck). Each superstructure would carry a cage mast. On this basis it appeared that the General Board characteristics could be met on a ship with about 29,180 tons (normal) displacement. At this stage Preliminary Design had in mind the modification of an existing design, primarily to simplify calculation. No one expected the battlecruiser hulls under construction (to a different design) to be converted.

In FY 20 and again in FY 21 Congress refused to authorize carrier construction; it was hard enough squeezing out funds to complete the large program of wartime capital-ship construction, which included six large battle cruisers. These ships were not even laid down until the period between August 1920 and January 1921, and it is not clear how badly the General Board wanted them anyway in view of the possibilities presented by airborne scouts. Certainly

This September 1922 photograph shows the *Langley*'s original single large funnel to port and the small house on the fantail for a carrier-pigeon coop.

Preliminary Design began to consider alternative uses for their material as early as July 1921.

Meanwhile all Congress would provide for in the way of carriers was the conversion of the slow collier USS *Jupiter* into the experimental carrier *Langley*; it is clear from General Board records that the *Langley* was never regarded as a combatant. That is not to imply that the *Langley* was converted from a worthless auxiliary; in 1919–20 the fleet was still largely fueled by coal and colliers were in short supply. As a collier the *Jupiter* was the prototype of the U.S. turbo-electric ship. Although slow, she could back down at full power and was thus, in a sense, double-ended. She was recommended for conversion by C & R, her advantages including large holds and hatches for stowing aircraft and hoisting gear already in place. Design work on the *Jupiter* was completed in July 1919.

She entered Norfolk for conversion in March 1920, emerging as the first U.S. aircraft carrier (the *Langley*, CV 1) on 22 March 1922. Of her six former cargo (coal) holds, the foremost was used to store aviation gasoline and the fourth was to used to hold elevator machinery and, below that, the magazine. The other four holds stowed disassembled aircraft, which could be lifted out by a 3-ton gantry crane traveling fore and aft under the flight deck. The *Langley* had no hangar deck in the modern sense, as aircraft were not stowed ready for flight. Rather, they were assembled on the former collier upper deck, loaded into an ele-

vator (which in its "down" position stood 8 feet above that deck), and then hoisted onto the flight deck. A former *Langley* pilot recalled that it took 12 minutes to get an airplane off the elevator and onto the former main deck for disassembly. The former collier bridge, well forward, was retained in its original position, the flight deck being built over it.

At this time the carriers were considered not only as platforms for wheeled aircraft but also as depot ships for floatplanes carried aboard cruisers and battleships. Thus the *Langley* had two cranes to lift aircraft from the water onto her "hangar" deck. She also had one, and later two, flight-deck catapults. Initially a unit similar to those that had been aboard the armored cruisers was installed, consisting of two parallel tracks, 94 feet long, sufficient to launch a 6,000-lb airplane at 55 knots. Within a few years, however, she had two compressed-air catapults (A Mk III), which BuAer records identify as turntable types, but which in fact were set into her flight deck fore and aft. They last operated in 1925, and on 25 July 1928 were authorized to be removed, just as catapults were being considered for hangar-deck installation in a new carrier, which would become the *Ranger*.

Possibly the chief problem in the *Langley* design was smoke disposal. She had a flush deck, with a short folding funnel to port and a smoke opening below flight-deck level to starboard. In theory, either opening could be used depending upon the wind. The

Anchored off Cristobal in the Canal Zone in 1930, the *Langley* shows her final configuration as a carrier, with two tiltable funnels to port. The flight-deck masts could be dismounted for flight operations. By this time her two flight-deck catapults had been removed.

The most striking thing about the *Langley* conversion was the almost total lack of structure under the flight deck. This photograph was probably taken about 1926 or 1927.

starboard opening had special water sprays for cooling, but even so it was not particularly successful, and within a short time the *Langley* had been refitted with a pair of hinged funnels to port, which could be lowered during flight-deck operations. Although the smoke-disposal issue for the *Langley* was regarded as settled, the problems encountered must have made C & R and BuEng reluctant to attempt a flush-deck design for the far more powerful *Lexington* that followed or, for that matter, for the *Ranger* a few years later.

The *Langley* was never more than an experimental carrier, unable to keep up even with battleships, let alone operate with fast scouting forces. About 1925 it was proposed that her sister ship *Neptune* be converted as an additional training carrier, outside the total tonnage limits for carriers imposed by the Washington Treaty (that is, the Five-Power Treaty), but the suggestion was rejected by the General Board. The *Langley* herself was retained as a carrier at least partly because, as an experimental ship already in existence in 1921, she did not figure in the

U.S. treaty tonnage allocation. However, after the passage of the Vinson-Trammell Act in 1934, she was included in the total carrier tonnage that the Untied States was permitted by law to operate. She had to be removed from the carrier category when the *Wasp*, permissible under the treaties, was built. The *Langley* was converted to a seaplane tender, with about half of her flight deck being removed, at Mare Island in 1936–37.

Besides large-carrier design, Preliminary Design investigated a proposed conversion of the *Omaha*-class light (scout) cruiser already under construction and severely criticized for her very limited battery. C & R saw such a conversion as a way of overcoming congressional reluctance to authorize new carrier construction. The *Langley*, already undergoing her first conversion in 1920, was far too slow to function effectively as a fleet carrier. Work based on the *Langley* conversion was begun in April 1920, and a flight deck supported by trusswork was incorporated into the cruiser design.

As in later flush-deck carrier studies, the disposal

of smoke generated by a high-powered plant (90,000 SHP in this case) was a problem from the beginning. Preliminary Design hoped initially to support all four funnels of the original cruiser design on sponsons entirely outboard of the flight deck "and to so arrange the uptakes that the entire waste-gas discharge from each group of 6 boilers could be diverted to one stack, so that all the gases and smoke could be discharged to leeward. In addition, each stack was to be so mounted that the top end could be revolved aft and downwards so that the stack would lie horizontally on the sponson while discharging. Difficulties were encountered in arranging this, on account of the excessive size of the stacks and uptake ducts." About 15 May an alternative, the "Yarrow antisubmarine smoke system," was proposed, consisting of "the application of a water-jet or spray introduced in ducts leading outboard from stack and connected with stack, so that when desired the smoke could be shut off from the stacks and diverted into the side ducts. The action of the water jet is claimed to induce a strong draft, in excess of the natural draft through the stack. The outboard discharge ducts are to be turned downwards after clearing the ship's side and the smoke after being cooled off and condensed by the water jet falls, rather than rises, from the discharge duct." This last system was actually tested, apparently unsuccessfully, in the Langley.

Unlike the Langley, the converted scout would have a true hangar deck. Indeed, there was concern that air flow under the flight deck, if unduly constricted, might spill over onto it. Commander Kenneth Whiting of the Aviation Section (the predecessor of BuAer), one of the men promoting the Langley conversion, asked specifically that the girders under the flight deck be made deeper for better air flow there, and that the hangar below them be fully enclosed on its sides with a 10-ft clear head room. At this point (24 May 1920), however, the preliminary designers, having started with a fixed hull rather than with a fixed air group, had no definite figure for the number of aircraft to be accommodated. The same situation would, of course, apply to the battle-cruiser conversion that resulted in the Lexington.

Small-scale sketches had been provided of four airplane types: the Martin torpedo plane (a large twin-engine bomber), the Loening amphibian (a seaplane), and the VE-7 wheeled fighter/trainer. On 25 May figures for an air group were finally obtained: there was to be one-third as many seaplanes as either the VE-7s or the Loenings, with one VE-7, one Loening, and one seaplane each to be carried fully assembled, and two each of the VE-7s and Loenings if possible. Commander Whiting asked for a three-gun battery, with one forward and two aft. There would be a single elevator.

As in other conversions of ships not originally de-

signed as carriers, it would be necessary to add considerable ballast to overcome the top weight of a flight deck and aircraft. Preliminary Design proposed 1,000 tons of concrete in the lower parts of some oil spaces, which would entail a small loss of cruising range and a considerable increase in displacement. It expected the hangar to be able to accommodate twenty-eight to forty aircraft, depending on how much area of the upper deck was retained for such requirements as passage and working space.

The General Board was unimpressed; on 16 December 1920 it advised the Secretary of the Navy to persevere in the attempt to obtain a large carrier rather than accept two unsatisfactory ones. Opinion was not unanimous, however. For example, Admiral Sims, president of the Naval War College, did not concur.

It is agreed by all concerned that the fleet needs to be provided with regular aircraft carriers as soon as practicable—and for power of offense these vessels should, of course, carry torpedo planes. . . . even assuming that such a vessel [a large carrier] should be appropriated for in the pending [Appropriation] Bill, it would probably be from three to four years before it could be placed in actual service, whereas two converted cruisers would be available in much less time.

The main characteristics of a regular aircraft carrier are well known and experimental work is not needed to determine them. A 30-knot platform is, however, needed in order to train the personnel and to develop the details of planes and their landing gear under the condition in which they will be used. This development cannot be safely carried out to the same degree in a 14-knot vessel of the Langley type. It is that the higher speed so facilitates landing on board that a more efficient type of plane can be developed and used if 30-knot platforms are available for training.

Aircraft carriers are in use on the gameboard at the War College, and problems in which they are used show their efficiency in scouting to be such as to refute the statement that "experimental work is in reality the main argument for the conversion of the scout cruisers," as assumed by the General Board.

The more urgent argument is that the fleet needs aircraft carriers, and that these converted cruisers will supply them in much less time than we can hope to get the larger vessels. But the principal argument in favor of the proposition is that converting two of the ten scouts to aircraft carriers will very materially increase

(i) The areas the ten vessels can cover in scouting
(ii) The efficiency of the group as a scouting line—as an information getter, and
(iii) The efficiency of the group as a fighting force, particularly if opposed by vessels of greater individual gunpower than the unconverted scouts.

Sims assumed that each scout would carry six torpedo bombers; Lieutenant Commander W. A. Edwards, who had been his aide for aviation during World War I, had assured him that one-third of the aircraft on board could be assembled on deck and ready for flight when the carrier reached the scouting line. These six aircraft could, he assumed, fly off at intervals of half a minute, and the remainder could be airborne within the next thirty minutes; that is, all could be off within thirty-three minutes of the signal to release aerial scouts. He derived his analysis from British experience.

Ten scout cruisers spaced 30 nautical miles apart (at the limit of visibility) would cover a front of 300 nautical miles. However, the front covered could be extended to 640 nautical miles if the carrier aircraft were credited with a range of 200 nautical miles each. As the General Board had specified an endurance of 4 hours at 100 miles per hour, Sims expected an increase to 1,040 nautical miles.

For its part, the General Board maintained that the fleet was sorely in need of scout cruisers, as it would have none at all until the ten under construction were completed. Moreover, the board believed that the conversions would have little operational value, because they would carry only twelve fighters and six torpedo bombers, all but one of the latter being disassembled; "instead of a good surface scout cruiser we would have an inferior aircraft carrier . . . [consequently] the General Board believes that every effort should be made to obtain from Congress immediate authorizations for properly designed airplane carriers." Perhaps the chief legacy of the scout-cruiser conversion plan was a series of studies for the conversion of the new heavy cruisers in the mid-twenties, followed by a series of "flight-deck cruiser" studies in the thirties.

Design work on a full fleet carrier, to be built from the keel up, proceeded. In October 1920 Preliminary Design worked out cost estimates for 10,000-, 20,000-, and 30,000-ton carriers of either 25 or 31 to 35 knots, ranging from a design based on the scout cruiser to one based on the 1919 carrier. The General Board wanted a battery of sixteen 6-in/53 and eight 5-in AA guns, but Preliminary Design suspected that "it would be very difficult to arrange for the number of guns specified on account of interference with the operations of flying on and flying off, stowage of boats, and general interference with work on the flying deck." No estimates of aircraft capacity were given, but a C & R sketch of a 20,000-tonner (660 × 69 × 35 feet) of 30 knots (90,000 SHP) was rejected as showing too little aircraft stowage.

By this time a distinction was being drawn between aircraft fully assembled for flight, aircraft partially assembled but ready for rapid assembly (that is, folded), and entirely disassembled aircraft held as a reserve. The General Board characteristics of November 1920 (for FY 22) called for an air group of twenty-four torpedo bombers (sixteen partly, eight fully assembled) and forty-eight fighters (sixteen fully, thirty-two partly assembled) plus "stowage in hold [for] 50 percent of above in disassembled condition." This requirement to stow reserve aircraft over and above hangar stowage would be an important consideration in U.S. carrier design through the *Midway* class, accounting for the characteristic deep girders and gallery deck of most U.S. fleet carriers. U.S. carrier designs of the early twenties show a T-shaped elevator at the forward end of the hangar for fully assembled airplanes and a smaller rectangular one aft for folded aircraft. The latter was limited in dimensions by the run of the propeller shafts around the elevator lifting machinery. At flight-deck level, the T-shaped elevator was abaft the flying-off area, and the smaller elevator was forward of the arresting gear. A takeoff run of 150 to 200 feet was considered sufficient for aircraft operating from a fast carrier.

Preliminary Design compiled all the data it could from wartime notes of British operations, as no new data had been obtained since the armistice. For example, it was known that the island arrangement planned for HMS *Eagle* had been tested in the flush-deck carrier *Argus* "to determine effects of air currents induced by this structure. This was not considered successful." Not essential to the British was a fully enclosed hangar or a "means for handling from hangars to launching position, of such nature as to permit getting off all planes, in succession, as quickly as possible." Smoke disposal was recognized as a problem.

> . . . in new designs for the English Navy smokestacks would not be led so far aft as on *Argus*. Exhaust from stacks would be led overboard on either side. On *Argus* when smoke exhausts astern with wind abaft the beam or astern, there is a tendency for gases to be drawn into vent system. On *Argus* exhaust is led beneath fly deck to stern, where they open to atmosphere. When draft cannot be supplied naturally, there are elbows which lead out to ship's side, and by adjusting dampers the gases are drawn out of uptakes by blowers and ejected overboard. Telegraphs operated from bridge with which men stationed at blower motors are notified when to close shutters, open dampers, start and stop motors, etc. . . . .

British experience suggested a speed of at least 30 and preferably 35 knots, both in order to work with cruisers and to generate a wind over the flight deck of 35 knots. Moreover, a carrier would have to turn into the wind to launch and recover aircraft, and she might rapidly lose position within the fleet if the latter were steaming with the wind.

Further, it appeared wise to place the arresting gear at both bow and stern, so that aircraft could land over either end of the ship. In a heavy wind, for example, an airplane could reduce the effective wind-over-deck to a safe figure by landing against the motion of the ship, that is, over her bow. Within a few years, however, the double-ended flight deck found on U.S. carriers would be considered more a feature of survivability than of usefulness in heavy weather.

The November 1920 characteristics called for sixteen 6-in/53s "arranged in two anti-torpedo groups on each side" and enough 5-in/25 AA guns to permit "four guns to bear in any direction," as well as one twin above-water torpedo tube on each side. In theory the carrier would be fast enough to outrun nearly all opposition, except destroyers and cruisers. Her own air group would be her primary air cover, the 5-in guns providing an antibomber barrage. Four torpedo tubes would provide a final defense against heavy units that might appear unexpectedly at night or in bad weather. Some question was even raised as to the value of the 6-in guns. At a February 1921 General Board hearing, Admiral W. L. Rodgers of the Naval War College argued that "the ship will have her aircraft along, and she herself, as against the attack of other aircraft, will have to depend very largely on her own aircraft and her own barrage fire. But the six-inch gun does not have elevation enough for barrage fire. For getting away she has her speed to rely on—there is nothing faster than she. Battle cruis-

ers she cannot stand up against. . . . [In any case] the question is whether an anti-aircraft battery is not of more importance than the anti-torpedo boat battery. . . ." Admiral Charles B. McVay of BuOrd replied that the antitorpedo battery was vital to surface attacks. This remained an important issue through World War II, and it was dramatized by the sinking of the British carrier *Glorious* by German battle cruisers in 1940. However, only the first two U.S. carriers had the excess tonnage, in the end, to be able to afford a single-purpose (antisurface) gun battery in addition to a heavy antiaircraft battery. Many of the designs leading up to the next carrier, the *Ranger*, showed cruiser (6-in/53) guns, but in the end she introduced the eight-gun heavy antiaircraft battery characteristic of later U.S. carriers.

By this time prospective carrier displacement was about 35,000 tons, with the battle cruiser (she had a massive 180,000 SHP turbo-electric power plant) again forming the basis of the studies. The disposal of her great volume of smoke presented a number of problems. C & R proposed to vent smoke through the sides (with an alternative hatch in the flight deck), as in HMS *Furious* (which had only half as much power and therefore only half the problem). Even on 35,000 tons the power plant—developed in the first place

The *Langley*'s unique internal structure is visible in this photograph. Forward, past the lowered elevator, crewmen are working on a Vought 02U "Corsair." Note that, in its lowered position, the elevator is by no means flush with the hangar deck. Overhead gantries are clearly visible, as is a heavy fore-and-aft girder for a traveling crane.

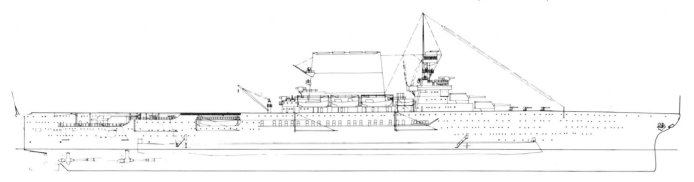

Contract design for the *Lexington* and the *Saratoga*, 1922. The oval opening right aft is for twin torpedo tubes.

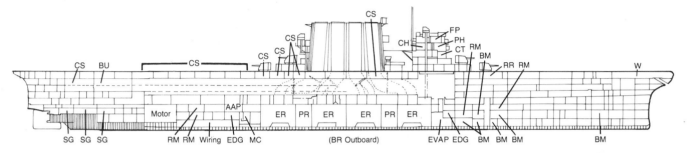

The *Saratoga*'s inboard profile, 1945.

with underwater protection in mind—consumed so much of the internal volume of the ship that no useful level of torpedo protection could be provided.

Some of the proposed features of the design were modern. It included a conventional island superstructure on the starboard side, as well as a flight-deck catapult. There were two roles for the latter. In her role as depot ship for battleship and cruiser floatplanes, the carrier might lift them from the water, but she could best catapult them off. It was also argued that catapulting would be the best method of launching wheeled aircraft in heavy weather, since the catapult track would keep the airplane directionally stable during takeoff, and it could be timed to take the pitching of the ship into account. However, the catapult contemplated was by no means powerful enough to launch aircraft too heavy to make conventional rolling takeoffs. That function would not be carried out until World War II.

In contrast with hangars on later U.S. fleet carriers, the hangar was entirely enclosed within the hull, with the flight deck forming the strength deck and the deck immediately below it being reserved for crews quarters and similar spaces. The hangar itself occupied only a portion of the hull volume, although the hull proper had to be broadened aft to accommodate its full 80-ft width. A hold below its after end held reserve (disassembled) aircraft. In no way did it resemble the lower hangar of British carriers, which held aircraft ready for flight.

The battery consisted of six 6-in/53s (in twin

mounts, one forward of the island, and one on each side aft), twelve 5-in/25 AA guns, and six above-water torpedo tubes, pointing aft, the latter presumably to discourage pursuit by heavy ships.

It appeared that the General Board characteristics could be met (and, in a few cases, such as flight-deck dimensions, actually exceeded) on a displacement of 39,000 tons (normal). Probably the chief defect of the carrier design was its limited magazine stowage, substantially less than that desired by BuOrd (for example, 91 rather than 200 1,500-lb bombs, 330 rather than 600 500-lb bombs).

The General Board adopted this sketch design in preference to several smaller ones and despite misgivings about the lack of torpedo protection. The design was, in fact, so close to battle-cruiser dimensions that some members of the General Board suggested the battle-cruiser hull plans be adapted for the new ship as an economy measure.

In July the General Board urged that three carriers of this large type be built as a matter of the highest priority. Nearly simultaneously the Secretary of State called for an international conference limiting naval armaments to meet in Washington on 12 November 1921. It cannot have escaped the General Board (or, for that matter, Preliminary Design) that the expensive battle cruisers would be prime targets for cancellation. Thus on 25 July Captain Robert Stocker, on his own authority as chief of Preliminary Design, ordered a study of the conversion of one of the battle cruisers to a carrier, with the ship completed

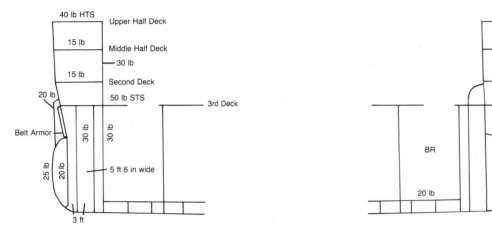

Cross sections of the *Saratoga* as built (*left*) and as blistered in 1942 (*right*).

"Drawing room" or preliminary design model of a study for a 32.75-kt carrier, November 1920. The large guns were twin 6-in/53s, as in the *Omaha*-class light cruisers; the single mounts were 5-in/25 AA weapons. There was no island; smoke exhaust was carried both port and starboard through the large square cutouts, with boats in the oblong openings further aft. The uptakes forward would have served a group of four boilers, with ten more further aft, and turbo-generator rooms abaft each group of boilers. There was to have been a single elevator, just abaft the after uptakes. A preliminary weight breakdown shows a tonnage, on trial, of 35,000 tons. There were also sketch designs of 29.5- and 34.75-kt flush-deck carriers. The Type A 1922 carrier (May 1921) showed a flush deck with telescoping uptakes. That design differed from the earlier ones in having all the uptakes concentrated on the starboard side; this was an intermediate stage leading toward the decision to provide a conventional island structure.

This official model shows scheme B for the aircraft carrier of 1922; scheme A was a flush-decker. There were two short catapults (port and starboard) just forward of the bridge, as well as three much longer ones extending from the forward elevator to the bow. The main battery of sixteen 6-in guns was mounted half in twin casemates forward and half in twin gun houses aft, with twelve 5-in AA guns alongside the flight deck aft. The design drawing, dated 5 May 1921, shows a stern quite different from that of the battle cruiser; presumably this was a design to utilize material accumulated for the *Ranger*. However, characteristics would have matched those of the battle cruiser; a length of 850 feet on the waterline (with a 900-ft flight deck), a beam of 94 feet, and a draft of 29 feet at 39,000 tons. The 7-in vertical belt would have been covered by a 2-in deck. The sketch shows no blister.

up to the top of her side belt. According to a design memorandum, "he stated at the time that no suggestion for such a change had been made, but he felt that he might be questioned in regard thereto. . . ." Such was the likelihood of cancellation that Preliminary Design also studied the conversion of a battle cruiser into an Atlantic liner at this time.

The battle cruiser would have good antitorpedo protection, as well as much larger magazines than the aircraft-carrier design provided for—sufficient to stow all of the required bombs. On the other hand, the cruiser had very different lines aft, much narrower than those of the carrier, and it was feared that air currents would not be so favorable to landings. If the two twin 6-in mounts were placed aft as in the carrier design, they would require sponsons. Hangar space would be about 16 percent less than that in the specially designed carrier, stowage space for spare aircraft would also be lost. "The ship spaces are in general smaller and less conveniently arranged, and the emergency fuel capacity is less. On the other hand, the wing spaces for crew, boat handling, etc., and the magazines and bomb stowage are larger. . . . The arrangement of uptakes is inferior on the converted battle cruisers as they cover the machinery space. The battle cruiser has a slightly longer landing space than the Carrier design as the after elevator is about 28 feet further forward." The latter was in turn a consequence of the finer lines aft and, therefore, of the narrower run of the propeller shafts. Due to her narrow lines aft, the converted battle cruiser was expected to trim 6 feet 11 inches by the stern in "normal" condition; due to a nominal 40,000-ton limit on her normal displacement, she was not allocated any ballast. In this condition, moreover, she would have a metacentric height of only 5 feet, compared to 7.2 feet for the specially designed carrier of about 1,000 tons less. The extra thousand tons, and the beamier hull form of the battle cruiser (104 feet 11.25 inches over the top of her sloped armor, 101 feet 1.5 inches on the waterline, compared to 97 feet for the carrier), would cost half a knot of speed, down to 33.5 knots from 34.

As an alternative, Preliminary Design considered using material already gathered for the least advanced battle cruiser, the *Ranger*, only 2.5 percent complete as of 10 September 1921. Such a conversion would have the advantage of permitting funds already appropriated for the battle cruiser to be used for the carrier, which the General Board preferred.

In December it appeared that the keel-up carrier would cost about $27.1 million, as against a conversion cost of $22.4 million plus the $6.7 million already spent on one of the least advanced ships; costs would be somewhat lower in the case of more advanced battle-cruiser hulls.

The Washington Conference greatly simplified matters by mandating the cancellation of all six battle cruisers. Proposals had already been made to complete two of them as carriers, and in view of the treaty that became an economic way of salvaging some of the vast sum already spent on the battle cruisers. However, an upper limit of 27,000 tons on new carrier construction had been set, far below the requirements of conversion. Assistant Secretary of the Navy Theodore Roosevelt, Jr., suggested an exception: carriers converted from existing capital-ship tonnage (which would otherwise be scrapped) might displace up to 33,000 tons on the new standard basis. The first two U.S. fleet carriers, the *Lexington* and *Saratoga*, were completed on this basis, as were the Japanese *Kaga* and *Akagi*.

The problem was that the converted-battle-cruiser design came to about 36,000 tons in standard form (that is, normal displacement less fuel oil and reserve feed water). Clearly there was no hope of shaving off the extra 3,000 tons. For example, in February 1922 Preliminary Design tried out schemes in which half the power plant was removed. That might have saved enough tonnage, but the General Board was quite unwilling to make the corresponding sacrifice in speed.

The project was saved by a clause in the Washington Treaty permitting the modernization of existing capital ships to protect them against air and underwater attack—in other words, to permit the addition of deck armor and blisters, up to 3,000 tons beyond their treaty displacements. Such a clause, it was argued, should apply to capital ships converted to carriers, that is, to the two ex–battle cruisers; for their entire lives the *Lexington* and *Saratoga* were carried in official lists at 33,000 tons with the footnote stating that this figure "does not include weight allowance under Ch. 11, pt. 3, Sec. 1, art. (d) of Washington Treaty for providing means against air and submarine attack"—3,000 tons of "means." Preliminary Design went so far as to estimate the actual weights involved: against air attack it credited all of the inclined armor over the steering gear, except the 12-lb plate required for structural purposes (266 tons), and the protective deck, again with the exception of the 12-lb structural plating (1,267 tons). Against submarine attack were credited the waterline blister (272 tons), the structure of the lower bulge outboard of the outer longitudinal bulkhead (270 tons), and the torpedo-protection bulkheads of the original battle-cruiser hull (1,100 tons, again excluding structural material)—a total of 3,175 tons. Had these weights not been counted, the ships would have come out well above the treaty limits: in 1928 C & R estimated that the *Lexington* would displace 35,689 tons, the *Saratoga*, 35,544. Indeed, in 1925 a more legalistic Secretary of the Navy actually went so far as to ask whether the two ships could be completed within the treaty limit of 33,000 tons, only to discover that rather radical changes (such as a 50 percent reduction in power) would be required. He demurred.

Even so, the design was very tight. For example, the armor protection originally provided for the battle cruisers was somewhat reduced. Thus the 17-ft-deep belt was cut to 9.3 feet in height (although the original thickness, 7 to 5 inches, was retained). However, the 2-in protective (third) deck was retained. The thicker deck (3 inches on the flat, 4.5 inches on the slopes) over the steering gear, provided for the original battle cruisers, was also retained.

There was very little margin on 36,000 tons, and even such minor weights as emergency diesel generators caused problems. BuEng complained in August 1922 that

> all provisions, stores, equipment, spare parts, etc., are included [in the standard displacement] and it is believed that [this] amount . . . should be reduced by the 151 tons (of the generators) so as to provide the necessary absorption of this weight. It is believed that this reduction should be made in any case, since it is a well-known fact that other navies do not provide stores in their ships covering any such period of time as is done in our Navy, and this constitutes a distinct handicap in laying down a new design. The additional stores not carried on the ship's trials could be regarded as on board temporarily, as undoubtedly they would be in time of war, since the amount of stores on board would be reduced to the very minimum, all excess stores being left at the Fleet base except when shifting from one base to another. It is understood that during the discussions of the question of stores during the (Washington) Conference the American representatives wished to provide a certain percentage of the total displacement to be allowed for stores and equipment, but this was objected to by the British representatives, and was, therefore, left out, but it is not believed that we should penalize ourselves as a result. . . .

Preliminary Design later estimated that a reduction in the stores allowance from ninety to sixty days would save 64 tons (128 tons for a reduction to thirty days). Moreover, the stores allowances in the converted design were based on those for the battle cruiser; they were considered generous, and could be halved, for a saving of 115 tons. The supply of potable water was already low for a capital ship (29.5 gallons per man instead of the usual 40), but it appeared that 30 tons could be cut without serious consequence to the vessel's efficiency.

The sketch design for the conversion, which was almost in its final form, was submitted by C & R on 22 April 1922. By this time the battery had been fixed as eight 8-in guns in twin gunhouses (instead of the 6-in battery of earlier studies), twelve 5-in/25 AA guns, and four 21-in torpedo tubes (ultimately there were none). A capacity of seventy-two aircraft was claimed, which corresponded to the FY 22 characteristics. The 8-in gun was adopted because, given the limitations of the Washington Treaty, many 8-in gun cruisers were expected to be built; the carrier would have to have some means of dealing with fast enemy surface ships at night or in bad weather. Early designs, both for 6- and 8-in gun carriers, had called for one twin gunhouse before the superstructure, and two more disposed to port and starboard below the flight deck aft. The two 8-in gunhouses aft limited flight deck width to 60 feet, and early experiments aboard the *Langley* convinced the aviators that the full 84 feet were needed. In October 1923 the General Board therefore authorized mounting of these two gunhouses on the flight deck proper, at a cost in the carrier's ability to fire at portside targets. Moreover, the weight of the island and battery was even less balanced than previously. Proposals to correct the consequent list included the removal of one boiler. In addition weight compensation for the new main-battery arrangement was achieved by mounting only one catapult (rather than three, as had been proposed) forward, and none (rather than one) aft. In fact the boiler was not removed, and through most of their operating lives the two ex–battle cruisers had to be ballasted (at the expense of usable fuel oil) to overcome their inherent list.

The final *Lexington* design was based on that adopted in 1919 for the battle cruisers, with inclined side armor and blisters for underwater protection, an arrangement inspired largely by HMS *Hood*, whose plans Goodall had brought to the United States in 1917. Unlike the hangars on all later U.S. carriers designed up until 1945, her hangar was a fully enclosed, integral part of the hull structure, the flight deck also functioning as the strength deck. In consequence, the hangar was quite small by standards set for later ships such as the *Ranger*, which had much less tonnage and much more hangar deck area (that is, a far larger proportion of a smaller deck was devoted to the hangar). Forward, the ship incorporated a flight-deck catapult, a unique flywheel-powered device invented by Carl Norden, better known for his work in fire control and bombsights. The value of the catapult was limited, particularly when the role of floatplane depot ship waned, as the large carriers became divorced from close cooperation with the battle line. The catapult issue would also be important in the *Ranger* design, completed just as the *Lexington* and *Saratoga* entered service.

At first there was some question as to whether the giant ex–battle cruisers represented the best possible

Here the *Saratoga*, with her distinctive funnel stripe and flight-deck lettering *S-A-R-A*, recovers her air group and parks it forward. One of the great problems of early U.S. carrier operations was the virtual impossibility of launching aircraft while recovery was taking place. Indeed, no aircraft could be launched until the entire air group had been manhandled ("respotted") aft. (Hence the variety of schemes at the time for multiple flight decks and flight-deck catapults.) Note the prominent crane, forward of the 8-in gunhouses, used for hoisting aircraft from the water onto the flight deck.

The *Lexington* is shown early in her career. The big carriers had complex island structures, which devoted much space to surface and AA fire control. At its sides the uppermost level carried 5-in rangefinders, with an AA director, shielded, between them. Below the director were 5-in and 8-in fire-control stations (a pair of similar stations were abaft the island). Below the fire-control stations was a fully enclosed flag plot. Next came the top of the pilot house, carrying a 20-ft rangefinder, and the pilot house proper, surrounded by the navigating bridge, with a chart house and an emergency cabin aft. Barely visible aft of no. 2 turret is an armored conning tower, abaft which is the main radio station. The meteorological platform (including the air intelligence office) is situated below that. The prominent platform on the upper level of the big stack carried an aviation control station (pri-fly), with a secondary conning station below that. The *Lexington* here carries Boeing F2B-1 fighters and Martin T3M-1 torpedo bombers. Both types of aircraft have axles designed to catch fore-and-aft arresting wires, which were soon abandoned.

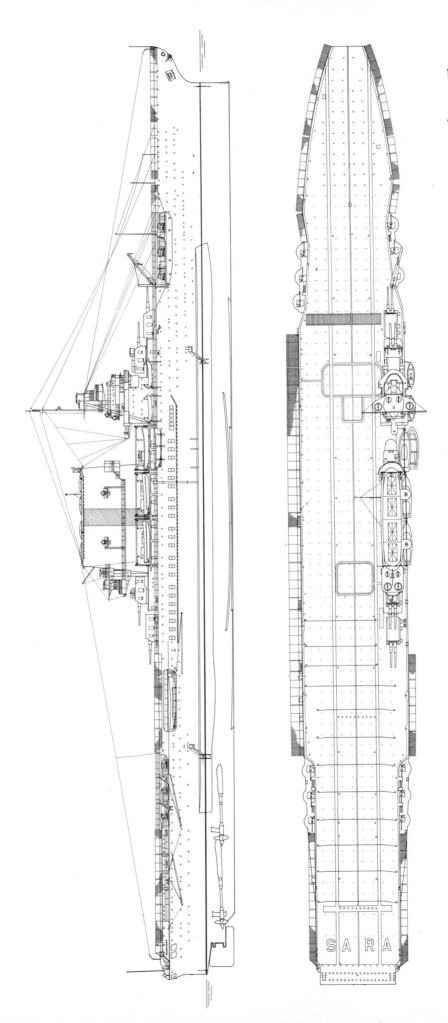

The *Saratoga* (CV 3), shown in 1936. Note the dark line down her funnel to distinguish her from the *Lexington*. Note also 0.50-cal machine guns atop 8-in gun houses. The windbreak (palisade) is folded down abeam no. 1 gun house, and there is no forward arresting gear.

investment of tonnage, given the amount the United States was allowed under the treaty limit. Part of the problem lay in the proper interpretation of the capacity or capability of a carrier. If, as was apparently assumed in the early twenties, capacity was equated with hangar capacity, then the smaller *Ranger* was certainly a better investment. However, operating experience soon showed that, for U.S. carrier tactics, the central issue was the size of a single deck-load strike the flight deck could accommodate. The two giants also demonstrated an ability to operate aircraft in weather conditions quite beyond what might have been imagined when they were designed. Doubts about the value of very large carriers, reflected in the choice of much less tonnage for the *Ranger*, vanished in the spectacular operations of the two big carriers in Fleet Problem IX of 1929.

Despite the General Board's insistence on quick construction, Congress was not eager to appropriate funds for the two big carriers, and work proceeded slowly as costs escalated.

Alterations in the first decade of service were comparatively minor, although a large modernization was planned in the late thirties. The catapult was removed in 1934 after relatively little use. In 1936 the *Lexington* had her bow widened. Most noticeably, both carriers received a considerable machine-gun battery as a defense against dive-bombers. In 1929 both ships were armed with experimental machine-gun batteries: two twin 0.50 caliber in the *Saratoga* and two sextuple 0.30 caliber in the *Lexington*. They were not successful and were removed. The *Ranger* was the first U.S. carrier designed for such weapons, with a total of forty 0.50-cal machine guns; by the summer of 1933 there were also the new *Yorktowns*, with quadruple 1.1-in machine cannon, in prospect.

A light battery for the big carriers had to be considered. The problem was the extent to which such a battery would interfere with flight operations. The *Ranger* had introduced galleries to accommodate her weapons, and the *Yorktowns* had theirs fore and aft of the island structure; the *Lexingtons* had 8-in guns. BuOrd proposed placing machine guns atop the forward superstructure, abaft the funnel, atop the superfiring 8-in turrets, and later, in new sponsons at the ends of the ship. Both the forward superstructure and funnel positions would interfere with 8-in fire control; however, galleries alongside the funnel were entirely practicable. Guns atop the 8-in mounts were rejected for the moment in view of interference with the heavier guns; moreover, it appeared that only one gun could be mounted in each position. A BuOrd proposal to mount the guns in the 5-in galleries was rejected because space there was already at a premium. BuAer considered most of these locations undesirable, and proposed the elimination of the two superfiring 8-in turrets in favor of light antiaircraft weapons; when the 1.1-in machine cannons became available they could be mounted in these positions. C & R agreed, to the extent that it alone of the bureaus considered the removal of the 8-in mounts the only solution short of an unsatisfactory compromise.

After considerable debate, the General Board in November 1934 approved a plan for mounting forty 0.50-cal machine guns: two atop no. 2 turret, six on a specially constructed platform above no. 3 rangefinder (atop the pilot house), six guns on either side aft on extensions of the 5-in galleries, and eight guns in a specially constructed platform at the stern. The two athwartship spaces fore and aft, then assigned to the catapult machinery room and to the arresting gear room, would be converted for temporary ammunition stowage and handling. Alternatively, two quadruple 1.1-in machine cannon could be installed on the forward platform and two more on the stern platform, at the cost of fourteen 0.50-cal machine guns. Estimated costs were, respectively, $386,000 and $880,000 per ship—quite substantial sums in the thirties. Thus the following February the CNO, acknowledging the urgency of protection against dive-bombers, felt that such expenditures were "not warranted until such a time as a satisfactory weapon for defense against diving attacks has been developed and thoroughly tested in service." The General Board recommended that the plans be completed but that installations be experimental only "to the end that the general problem of defense against dive bombing attacks and the peculiar problems obtaining with [sic] carriers may be investigated."

Thus only installations involving no structural work were to be carried out: two guns atop no. 2 turret and six guns on either side aft in 5-in gallery extensions. In fact C & R pointed out that, at most, only two guns could be accommodated in the gun galleries aft, and Puget Sound pointed out that the *Saratoga* could be fitted only with the two mounts on no. 2 turret. The gun-gallery installations would interfere with the control lever for the arresting gear and with the net, but the yard did suggest an alternative location that would permit installation of six guns on either side aft, 5 feet below the flight-deck level. By 1936 the *Lexington* had four such platforms at her ends, each with four machine guns, as well as a gallery enclosing her funnel with twelve more. About 1940 four more 0.50-cal guns replaced the 5-in rangefinders on platforms fore and aft, as these instruments were incorporated in modified 5-in directors (Mark 19). It appears, however, that the *Lexington* did not mount machine guns atop her 8-in turrets

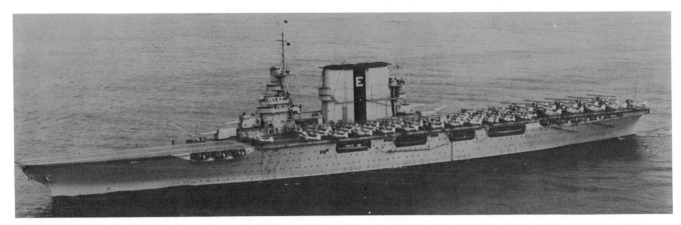

This late 1930s photograph shows the *Saratoga* after an attempt was made to provide her with light AA guns: machine guns are atop no. 2 turret, on her foremast, and abaft her big funnel. Unlike her sister, the *Saratoga* did not have her flight deck widened forward before World War II, and she began the war in essentially her prewar configuration.

In the last intact photograph taken of her, the *Lexington* is already down by the bows after being torpedoed. Her 8-in guns had been removed at Pearl Harbor to be added to local coastal defenses, and no 5-in/38s had as yet been added; note the omission of directors and rangefinders associated with the 8-in battery. This photograph is too indistinct to show details of the extemporized light AA battery, but its extent is evident: gun galleries run along the large stack at two levels, along the flight deck, and in the former boat stowage aft. Also visible is her radar, a CXAM-1 at the forward end of the stack.

before 1941. Her sister retained her experimental turret-top installation at least through 1937.

In 1940 the antiaircraft batteries of these ships were again strengthened. In common with other major U.S. warships, they were scheduled for 1.1-in quadruple machine-cannon installation, with 3-in/50s (locally controlled) as interim replacements. One such gun replaced two 0.50-cal machine guns of each of the four machine-gun sponsons, and another was mounted on a deckhouse between the funnel and the bridge structure. Two 0.50s were mounted atop each of the superfiring 8-in turrets, for a total of twenty-eight machine guns, including the four in the tops. By the outbreak of war, the 3-in/50s had all been replaced by quadruple 1.1-in machine cannon. Further weapons were fitted after the outbreak of war. The *Lexington* had her 8-in guns removed in April 1942, and when she was sunk in May at the Battle of the Coral Sea she mounted a total of twelve quadru-

ple 1.1-in machine cannon, as well as thirty-two 20-mm guns and her original twenty-eight 0.50s. It appears that the machine cannon replaced her 8-in guns (none in no. 1 position). As for the lighter weapons, 20-mm guns were added in a long gallery at 01 level abeam the funnel and in a gallery in the former boat recess, as well as in a new gallery below the pilot-house level. At this time the *Saratoga*, which still had her heavy turrets, was listed with nine quadruple 1.1-in and thirty-two 20-mm guns, having landed her 0.50s.

There is every indication that by the late 1930s the navy in general knew quite well that the General Board had been right to go for size in its first carriers. Although the *Lexington* and *Saratoga* both required large refits just before the war, neither needed any radical change to accommodate the combat aircraft of World War II. That in itself is remarkable, in view of the great changes in aircraft design over two decades. Undoubtedly flexibility in air group was a great incentive towards the General Board's adoption of big carriers from the start. As for the problem of flying off aircraft fast enough, it turned out that good deck crews rather than battleship and destroyer catapults were the answer.

Thus Captain Marc Mitscher, the aviator who would later command the fast carrier task force, testified before the General Board in 1940 as follows:

We have always felt, a good many of us, that the *Lexington* and *Saratoga* were the best ships we have ever built for all purpose ships, carrying the protection and armor of a cruiser. We will have twelve carriers that need cruiser protection and that cannot be sent out on independent missions unless they have cruiser protection. I feel that we have two carriers, the *Lexington* and *Saratoga*, that can be sent out on independent missions and if they lose their cruiser protection they can still protect themselves with their aircraft and armament. Therefore we feel we should look into that field for future carriers over and above the twelve that we have now that are more or less restricted in their activities.

By the late thirties it was generally agreed that both of the big carriers required modernization, but because they were the most powerful carriers in the U.S. Fleet, it was difficult to withdraw them from service for the time required. The same was true of HMS *Hood*, which as battle cruisers they had been designed to rival. The *Lexington* never was modernized, and the *Saratoga* received only piecemeal alterations, in view of the severe wartime carrier shortage.

As in the cases of many other warships, the two carriers gradually gained weight. Between 1928 and 1936 they gained 2,282 tons (1,290 tons of equipment and stores and 992 of additional structure) and 17 inches of draft; in 1935 the top of the armor belt was 8 inches below the waterline at full load. C & R proposed what it considered a minimum modernization in December 1936. A blister on the starboard side would correct the inherent list due to the weight of the island; it would also reduce draft by about 11.5 inches, if no other weights were added. Without the blister, about 890 tons of fuel oil were normally carried in portside fuel tanks beyond the amount on the starboard side, for a considerable reduction in useful fuel load. C & R also envisaged miscellaneous damage-control improvements, such as fuel-oil arrangements to facilitate shifting oil, the installation of two 850-kw and one 200-kw emergency diesel generators, and aviation improvements. The latter included completion of bomb and torpedo handling and stowage (in the *Saratoga*), additional gasoline outlets to the flight deck, modernization of the arresting gear

The *Lexington* was refitted in 1936. One of the more important improvements was the widening of her flight deck at its forward end, as shown. Here she passes through the Panama Canal, January 1939. Note that what appears to be gun tubs atop her bridge structure actually protects 5-in AA directors.

and barriers (and installation of forward arresting gear in the *Saratoga*), widening of the forward part of the flight deck and lengthening of the after part, enlargement of the after elevator (and speeding up of both), and installation of two flight-deck catapults.

BuAer agreed, but it wanted more: a better antiaircraft battery and additional fuel. As for the first, since the two ships had small hangars, they generally carried a larger proportion of their aircraft on the flight deck than did later carriers, and so often could not use either forward or after groups of 5-in guns. While aircraft were being respotted, at times none of the 5-in guns could be used.

The great size and speed of these vessels result in a limited cruising radius. At 25 knots, the minimum acceptable when flight operations are imminent, which would probably be a normal condition in wartime, the range is recorded as 4851 miles. . . . Range has frequently been a vitally limiting characteristic in Fleet Problems. During the relatively short Fleet Problem in the Hawaiian-Midway area in 1935 the *Lexington's* supply was reduced to a dangerous amount within the space of about five days. Furthermore, these ships must rely on evasion for their protection and this means the ability to run away at high speed. Under the foregoing conditions the fuel consumption is enormous. Elimination of the inherent starboard list by the addition of the blister will, it is understood, increase the effective fuel capacity by about 750 tons. At 25 knots this would add about 500 miles. . . . The range thus provided, approximately

5300 miles, is still considered to be definitely in-adequate. It is recommended that at least 750 tons of fuel be added. . . .

BuAer also recommended removal of the 8-in guns and their replacement by antiaircraft weapons and fuel oil (on a weight basis).

In evaluating the loss of military effectiveness through elimination of the 8-inch battery it is falla-cious to consider these ships as potential cruisers after the flight deck has been damaged. Unless this occurs in the final critical naval actions of a war, the carrier, in the opinion of the Chief of the Bureau of Aeronautics, should be sent immediately to a base for necessary repairs. The number of carriers available will warrant no other procedure. Actual main battery engagements with even one cruiser must be avoided as long as it is physically possible. Cruiser attack must be opposed by cruisers while the carrier uses its speed to escape. . . . Use of the 8-inch guns while air-craft are aboard would unquestionably seriously re-duce the operating equipment. Use of these guns dur-ing aerial missions would be limited to relatively short and very definitely fixed periods of time unless recovery of squadrons were discounted. . . .

The General Board felt that "considering the[ir] age and general condition . . . all repairs and renew-als necessary to maintain the ships in good condition for service should be undertaken and should have priority over any of the alterations which have been included in the proposed modernization program." It rejected removal of the 8-in battery for reasons that would be cited again in the 1940 hearing at which Captain Mitscher spoke.

The *Lexington* and *Saratoga* with their 8-inch bat-tery and armor protection are better suited for dis-tant service in war than other carriers carrying lighter batteries and with less protection. While it is considered essential to provide cruiser protection for carriers whenever possible during war operations, there is no assurance that such protection can always be afforded. Considering the number of carriers built and building, the missions to which they may be assigned, and number of cruisers that may be avail-able in war, the extent and effectiveness of cruiser protection that can be assured to the carriers without seriously depleting the cruiser strength needed else-where is problematical. The Board does not foresee the employment of the *Lexington* and *Saratoga* as cruisers per se, but believes that the power afforded by their armor and turret guns is of very considerable potential value for meeting situations under which they may have to operate with scant support from other ships. Moreover, during low visibility and at night when surprise attacks may be expected in spite of cruiser protection, or after suffering reduction in speed from any cause and evasion from gunfire is not possible, the 8-inch battery might be vitally useful. . . .

On the other hand, the interference between air-craft and antiaircraft guns might be eliminated if 5-in guns replaced the 8-in weapons atop the flight deck. The General Board preferred the alternative of reduc-ing the number of aircraft on the flight deck, perhaps even to the extent of retaining a squadron in the hangar until the deck had been cleared.

Another possible weight saver was elimination of all side armor; in the 1925 studies of weight reduction this had been evaluated at 1,280 tons. Removal of only the starboard armor would eliminate most of the inherent list and would also reduce draft by about 4.5 inches. However, since the sloping armor was internal, its removal would be difficult at best. Moreover, if the ship burned about half her fuel oil, the belt would be exposed and would become an important defensive element.

As for steaming radius, the board found that the *Lexington* and *Saratoga* actually compared favorably with other ships at high speed. Some mileage had been lost to increased displacement and to the con-version of some fuel tanks for gasoline stowage, and of course carriers steaming away from the fleet at 25 knots and then speeding up to rejoin could not make good the same distance as the fleet itself. Exercise data showed that steaming radius at 25 knots was 4,421 nautical miles when operating aircraft, 4,937 nautical miles when steaming steadily with no flight operations contemplated; at 10 knots these figures were 9,556 and 13,207 nautical miles.

In Fleet Problem 16, during the movement of the fleet from the West Coast to Midway Island and back, the daily fuel expenditure of the *Saratoga* varied from 2½ to 10 percent of her total fuel capacity. The planes were operated on alternate days from San Francisco to Lahaina, for about 70 percent of the days between Honolulu and Midway. . . . The Main Force with which the *Saratoga* operated steamed 5724 nm during this time, while the *Saratoga* steamed 10,247 nm.

The steaming radius of the carriers may be in-creased by approximately 14 percent by the installa-tion of the blister which will permit full use of the total tankage now installed . . . and might be further increased by approximately 3 percent by conversion of void spaces into fuel tanks. . . . This is the max-imum increase in steaming radius that can be obtained by enlarging their fuel capacity. A further increase in steaming radius can result from the in-stallation of arresting gear at the forward end of the ship as proposed since it should reduce the depar-tures from formation course and speed required for plane operations. *Operating methods themselves are an important factor in steaming radius and study of these methods offers a valuable field for improvement.*

In August the CNO generally approved the board's list of improvements, adding as first priority a gen-eral overhaul of the main engines and auxiliaries. The

5-in battery was to be modernized with remote-control gear, but there would be no replacement of the 8-in guns.

Even so, nothing could be done until 1939, when the international situation made any extended modernization difficult. Thus, in approving the program for the two carriers in December 1939, the CNO required that the work be done in two separate (relatively short) periods, the first of which would include the installation of the blister and of the new after elevator. By this time, too, there was some question as to whether the blistering could be accomplished within the usual limit of a beam of 108 feet, as set by the locks of the Panama Canal. In April 1940 C & R wrote the CNO to inform him that he could choose either a considerable loss of speed within the 108-ft limit, or a loss of buoyancy in the blister; in fact lines for a 1,685-ton blister (with a 5 percent gain in cruising radius) had been sent to Puget Sound for modernization. Alternatively, the beam limit could be discarded; after all, a project for a third (wider) set of locks for the Panama Canal would probably soon be approved by Congress, with construction scheduled for completion in 1946. This same project permitted the use of a beamier hull in the *Midway*-class carriers and in the *Montana*-class battleships; the United States would not explicitly abandon the Panama Canal standard until after World War II, in the design of the super-carrier *United States*. C & R considered the disadvantage of having two carriers (out of seven) unable to transit the canal balanced by the improvements it could promise on the basis of a gain in buoyancy of 2,200 to 2,300 tons, compared even with the 1,940 tons originally hoped for in the largest of the proposed blisters. Maximum beam would probably be 112 feet.

Even this proposal failed: by the spring of 1940 there was no hope of even a relatively short major refit. All that could be done was to install radar (the CXAM-1 air search set at the fore end of the big funnel and the YE aircraft beacon) and the new antiaircraft battery already described. Removal of the 8-in guns was ordered early in 1942; the *Lexington* surrendered hers in Hawaii for coastal defense. She was lost before any further work could be done, but the *Saratoga*, after being torpedoed by a Japanese submarine off Hawaii, 11 January 1942, underwent repairs at Bremerton extensive enough to permit much of the prewar planned refit to be carried out.

BuShips argued that a big blister would release the liquid load needed to counterbalance the island structure, regain buoyancy lost through the years of weight growth, and improve stability.

Each of these factors contributes a material improvement in resistance to war damage. At present two more substantially complete layers of liquid are required in torpedo protection on the port side than on the starboard side to counterbalance the island. . . . with one layer on the starboard side to meet minimum requirements for protection, three layers are required on the port side and no appreciable tankage remains available for counterflooding on that side. . . . Further, with the reduced depth of liquids on the starboard side the amount of flooding will be greater because (a) there are more empty tanks to flood and (b) the damage in the empty compartment will be more extensive. . . .

The blister would also increase metacentric height by about 3 feet, and it would cost only a quarter-knot—as well as passage through the existing Panama Canal locks. Meanwhile, it was also proposed that the 8-in guns be replaced with twin 5-in/38s, and the existing twelve 5-in/25s with twelve of the heavier 5-in/38 single mounts.

BuShips estimated that the *Saratoga* would be out of action for four to six weeks at the least for repairs to her torpedo damage, and that installation of the starboard blister would require only a month more. The twin 5-in/38 mounts, moreover, were immediately available from stocks that had been manufactured for the light cruiser *Amsterdam* (CL 59), already under conversion to a light carrier. The *Saratoga* emerged from Puget Sound on 22 May with a large blister, and with a battery of sixteen 5-in/38s, having replaced her sponson 5-in/25s on a two-for-three basis. Some weight was saved by removal of top-hamper. An open bridge (such as was being fitted to many U.S. warships at this time) was built atop the flag plot. The tripod foremast was replaced by a light pole. The stack was also lowered. At this time the *Saratoga* finally received the wider forward flight deck and the lengthened after flight deck first envisaged in 1936. She also received a pair of Mark 37 5-in directors (with Mark 4 radars), a secondary air-search radar (SC, at the after end of the funnel), and four quadruple 40-mm guns (each replacing one 5-in/25), retaining her original five quadruple 1.1s. At this time she had thirty 20-mm guns. The *Saratoga* was again torpedoed on 25 August 1942, and suffered from the vulnerability of her turbo-electric plant: she was short-circuited, dead in the water, after the flooding of a single boiler room. Repairs at Pearl Harbor in September and October included further increases in antiaircraft battery: the remaining 1.1s were replaced by quadruple Bofors guns, for a total of nine such weapons, and twenty-two 20-mm guns were added, for a total of fifty-two.

In July 1943 the *Saratoga*'s commanding officer proposed that the 40-mm battery be increased to twenty-four mounts, even at the expense of 5-in and 20-mm batteries, 5-in ammunition, some 5-in hoists, and miscellaneous items such as flight-deck wooden

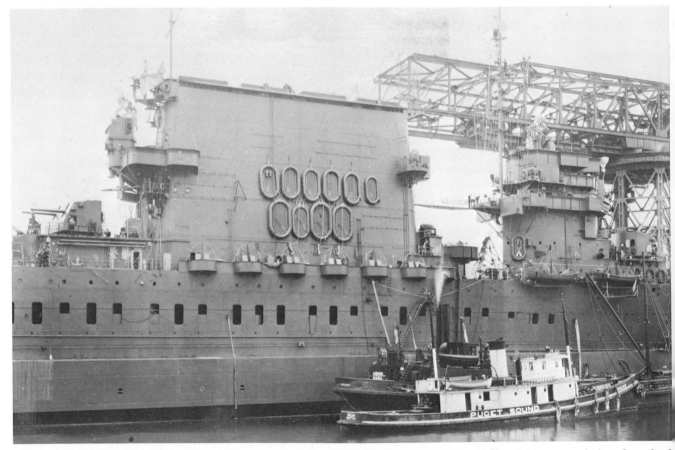

War accomplished what numerous prewar memos cound not: the *Saratoga* was stripped of her 8-in guns and also of much of her top hamper, as these two Puget Sound photographs of 14 May 1942 show. The new open bridge was a standard modification of the time, the U.S. Navy having taken to heart the British view that it was essential for effective operation during air attack. Below the bridge were the old flag plot and, one level further down, the pilot house and navigating bridge, the latter with a new windscreen. The old conning tower remained. The funnel was stripped of its pri-fly, and the secondary conning position plated in.

In 1943 the *Saratoga*'s commanding officer requested a major increase in his light AA battery. Although his ship was heavily loaded, her great length must have simplified arrangement, and this 2 January 1944 Hunters Point view suggests the density of the new battery. Although the twin-engine patrol bombers on deck do not seem too large for the ship they were, in fact, deck cargo.

covering. At this time the 20-mm gun was beginning to seem less effective than at the outbreak of war, but the 5-in had not yet benefitted from widespread use of proximity fuzes. BuShips proposed two schemes: in one, the 20-mm battery was to be reduced from fifty-two to twenty-four guns, and a total of twenty-three quadruple and two twin 40-mm guns were to be mounted; alternatively, four of the single 5-in/38s could also be removed, and two more quadruple 40-mm guns added. Other weight removals included the forward arresting gear and some 5-in ammunition. In fact, in the refit which followed, the 40-mm battery was increased at the cost of all but sixteen guns of the 20-mm battery. Weight was the problem.

By this time the *Saratoga* was badly overweight: in the light-service condition her displacement was estimated at 43,840 tons. Scheme A, in which all the 5-in guns would be retained, was estimated to give a light-service displacement of 44,147 tons, with a full-load figure of 48,552 and a calculated maximum load of 50,846 tons. At full load her belt would be almost 3.19 inches below water, despite the blister. These figures compare with an optimum battle displacement calculated by BuShips in February 1942 as 44,100 tons (full load was then 48,500 tons, including 8,542 tons of oil). These figures, moreover, did not include the 235 tons incident to installation of a new after elevator, which the *Saratoga* still awaited.

BuShips could only sadly comment that

. . . in common with most vessels that have been in commission for some time [she] is operating at drafts

far in excess of any that were considered possible at the time of her design. . . . Although the maximum load (calculated) is less than that reported by the ship of 52,000 tons, the difference may be accounted for by incidental load increases continually occurring during the life of a ship. The negative armored freeboard in the full and maximum load conditions exposes the ship to the danger of extensive flooding from all types of bomb hits. Bombs exploding near the shell on the third deck would be extremely dangerous because of the large area of third deck which would be exposed to flooding. . . . Deep running torpedoes will probably not cause much extensive third deck flooding because of the smaller chance of disturbing the transverse subdivision on this deck. Shallow running torpedoes will, however, present the same hazards as bomb explosions. The Commanding Officer should be made aware of the dangers incurred whenever the ship is operating at drafts which place the third deck below the waterline. . . . The changing battle conditions appear to offer justification for carrying no greater liquid load than that required for the underwater protection system of the ship. . . .

Refitted at Hunters Point from 9 December 1943 through 3 January 1944, the *Saratoga* received two portside sponsons for twin Bofors abeam the island structure; she also received seven quadruple mounts in the former boat recesses to port, two in the boat recess to starboard, three more outboard of the island at flight-deck level, and two more in the bow machine-gun galleries, supplementing two guns already there. By this time she had an SK air search radar; in a summer 1944 Puget Sound refit it was

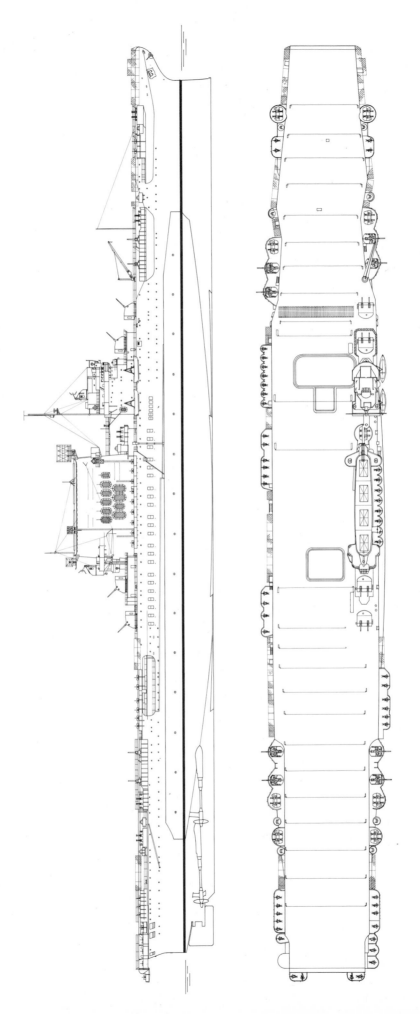

The *Saratoga* (CV 3) as refitted, shown in January 1943. Note the arresting wires, forward as well as aft, for over-the-bow landings.

The *Saratoga* emerged from another, relatively minor refit at Puget Sound later in 1944; this underway view is dated 8 September. At this time she was fitted with flight-deck catapults.

The *Saratoga* is shown running trials in Puget Sound after her last, post-kamikaze refit on 15 May 1945. The old aircraft crane forward of her island has been replaced by a new collapsible type. About half her hangar deck has been filled with berths; the after elevator has been eliminated.

moved to the pole foremast and replaced on the funnel by an SM fighter-director set, the *Saratoga* then having the full standard U.S. carrier radar outfit of one fighter-director and two air search sets. At this time, too, she was fitted with a pair of the standard H Mk II hydraulic catapults. They were considered essential for night operation because of the guidance they provided for an airplane taking off in total darkness. The *Saratoga* was designated a night carrier and with the carrier *Ranger* formed Car Div II at Pearl Harbor, training night pilots and developing night-fighter doctrine. In January 1945 she was sent to Ulithi to form a night-carrier detachment with the *Enterprise* for Iwo Jima.

On 21 February six Japanese aircraft scored five hits on the *Saratoga* in three minutes. Later she was bombed again. Once more she went back to Bremerton for repairs. Although her flight deck forward was wrecked, her starboard side penetrated twice, and large fires had been started in her hangar deck, she was able to recover her aircraft within three hours. By this time her operations were increasingly hampered by limited elevator capacity, particularly in the after elevator, which had been due for replacement as early as 1936. After Iwo Jima, the after elevator was deleted entirely, and a new forward elevator, about 44 feet square, was fitted. Much of the after end of the hangar deck was filled with two decks of berthing compartments, particularly for officers (by this time all of the prewar ships were severely cramped).

The *Saratoga* ended the war in this configuration, and, as surplus, she was expended in the atomic test at Bikini following "Magic Carpet" service for returning troops.

3

Carrier Spectrum Studies and the USS *Ranger*, 1922–29

By the early twenties the General Board regarded naval aviation at sea as a pressing need. Although there has been much rhetoric about the undue influence of the "gun club," and indeed although later the General Board chose to emphasize battleships over carriers, in the early twenties the board appears to have seen the carrier as very much the wave of the future. It was eager, not merely to build to the limit allowable by the Washington Treaty, but also to obtain the maximum number of effective aircraft at sea. In its studies, which led to the construction of the medium carrier *Ranger*, the board was at a considerable disadvantage, since the United States had virtually no operating experience with carriers; nor was there any great fund of foreign experience on which to draw. Moreover, the British had ended their cooperation with the United States in naval aviation soon after the end of World War I. Yet it was essential that characteristics for a new carrier be drawn up as rapidly as possible, well before the two ex–battle cruisers would be completed, if funds were to be appropriated and new ships authorized by Congress.

Although the *Langley* then in service was considered an experimental carrier, and although she participated in fleet problems designed to discover the possibilities of fleet aviation, it appears that the General Board relied far more heavily on the Naval War College for knowledge. At Newport new technological concepts could be modeled and studied at length through standardized games. Again and again this approach permitted the United States to achieve quick technological progress without waiting for experimental ships (and even squadrons) to become operational. War games largely decided the characteristics of the *Ranger* and later eliminated the proposed flight-deck cruiser. Such techniques live on in the endless computer-based analyses of proposed weapon systems now current, but Newport was in a unique position in the interwar period. It was the sole depository of such analytical expertise, and thus was in a decisive position: the president of the college was a major advisor to the General Board and, through it, to the Secretary of the Navy.

Thus the *Langley* functioned more as a testing ground for specific technologies such as arresting gear. She could also test the capability of a carrier deck to support particular types of aircraft. For example, experience in her operation effectively killed off U.S. interest in large twin-engine carrier aircraft until the eve of World War II. There were, to be sure, surprises. Perhaps the most spectacular was the success of dive-bombing, demonstrated against the fleet at San Diego in 1926. In the case of the *Ranger*, dive-bombing appeared to be so much more effective than

The *Ranger* was the first U.S. carrier built as such from the keel up. Limited in displacement, she spent much of the year in noncombat roles. Here she transports a deck load of army P40 fighters early in 1943. They were flown off to land at North African bases.

Newly completed, the *Ranger* shows her original and short-lived 5-in battery arrangement, with two 5-in guns on the forecastle and only two in the sponsons. There is no Mark 33 director for these weapons—the island superstructure carries only a small rangefinder. Finally, note how far aft the after elevator (in the down position) is located.

torpedo attack that torpedoes and torpedo planes were actually excluded from the ship in her final design—a result hardly to be expected from the Newport analysis. Moreover, because she was a flush-decker, the *Langley* could not test the peculiar virtues of an island superstructure as a means of controlling flight-deck operations, a point not apparent until the *Lexington* and *Saratoga* entered service. As a result, throughout the preliminary design series that led up to the *Ranger*, the aviators demanded, and obtained, a fully flush flight deck, with all of its attendant problems of funnel gas disposal. The island structure was added only well after the carrier's keel had been laid, bringing problems of weight compensation, overweight, and effects on other ships that had to be built within a fixed "global" (total) carrier tonnage.

Within C & R, studies of new specially built carriers began as early as 1922, largely on the basis of the *Lexington* design just executed. However, the General Board did not submit characteristics for a new carrier until 1927, after the completion of a long series of sketch designs that well illustrate the choices available at the time.

Perhaps primary among them was unit size. To an extent previously unimagined, the Washington Treaty limit of a total carrier tonnage as well as a maximum unit tonnage imposed strict choices on a designer. After completion of the *Lexington* and *Saratoga*, the United States was allowed just 69,000 tons more, which could be distributed in many ways. Only carriers smaller than 10,000 tons were unregulated, and there seems to have been a consensus that they

would be impractical, although the Japanese did build such a ship in their *Hosho*. The maximum was 27,000 tons; but the General Board thought in terms of a standard design, which meant either 23,000 tons (three ships), 17,250 tons (four), or 13,800 tons (five). The issue recurred in the design of the *Yorktown* (CV 5) class in 1931, although with different results, largely because by that time operational experience had been secured for both large (*Lexington*) and small (*Langley*) carriers. In the twenties no one was aware of the spectacular, nearly all-weather capability of a very large carrier, and size was much more an issue of total fleet, as opposed to individual airplane capacity. Somewhat remarkably, in view of the way the *Wasp* (CV 7) design developed, there seems to have been little feeling about the relationship between unit-size and survivability, an issue which later became quite emotional. To some extent, sheer speed was considered a means of protection from attack by surface ships.

Preliminary Design began work on new carrier designs as early as July 1922, well in advance of any General Board request. It tried a variety of schemes (see table 3-1): design 276 was set at 23,000 tons, the displacement on which three carriers could be built. The alternative 277 was the maximum: 27,000 tons. Either aviation (double-level hangar for increased aircraft capacity, design 281) or protection (design 282) could be emphasized, in each case at the cost of machinery volume and hence speed. Two other sketch designs, 286 and 293, were used to explore the possibilities of smaller hulls.

Table 3-1. 1922–23 Schemes

	276 Sep 1922	277 Oct 1922	281 Jan 1923	282 Jan 1923	286 Apr 1923	293 June 1923
LWL (ft-in)	710-0	766-0	890-0	680-0	625-0	660-0
Beam (ft-in)	87-0	90	86-3	101-0	68-6	80-0
Draft (ft-in)	27-0	27-1	25	29-0	20-6	24-6
Std (tons)	23,000	27,000	27,000	27,000	11,500	17,000
Normal (tons)	25,000	29,250	29,500	29,250	13,000	19,000
End at 10 Kts (nm)	10,000	10,000	10,000	10,000	10,000	10,000
SHP	118,000 (GT)	140,000 (TE)	59,000 (TE)	69,000 (TE)	46,800 (GT)	58,000
Speed (kts)	31.5	32.5	27	27	28	28
8-in Guns	8	8 (4×2)	9 (3×3)	9 (3×3)	6 (2×3)	9 (3×3)
5-in AA Guns	12	12	12	12	8	8
TT (21 in)	4	4	4	4	4	4
Belt Width (ft-in)	6-0	6-0	8-6	10-0	11-0	10-6
Thickness (in)	3	3	2	8, 5	3.5, 2.5	3.5, 2.5
Flying-off (ft-in)	—	—	459-0	245-0	316-0	273
Landing Run (ft-in)	—	278	385-0	240-0	304-0	332
Hangar Area (sq ft)						
Large Plane	8,890	10,500	17,500	10,600	11,500	7,450
Small Plane	7,190	7,700	4,500	11,400	—	15,300
Stowage	—	—	8,500	—	5,280	—
	probably 60 aircraft	probably 75 aircraft	double hangar; one elevator	short flight deck, no. 1 turret on centerline; "protected" carrier	one elevator	

The 23,000-ton project began early in July 1922; Preliminary Design generally followed the *Lexington* conversion. "It was assumed that a satisfactory ship should have the highest speed and greatest airplane carrying capacity compatible with full torpedo protection and the maximum armament allowed by the treaty, together with as much armor as possible without unduly reducing the other desirable qualities." The designers tried (unsuccessfully) for 35 knots, since aviation personnel wanted a speed as high as this.

Battle-cruiser (turbo-electric) machinery was preferred; however, a first cut with the full 180,000-SHP plant led to a 794- by 91- by 74-ft (deep) hull, which would probably come to 30,400 tons (normal)—far beyond the 25,000 tons (normal) expected to be consistent with 23,000 (standard). Geared turbines of considerably reduced power had to be accepted and hull length kept down to control weights. The first sketch design showed a main hangar for twenty torpedo planes as well as a smaller, shallower hangar over the boilers with a capacity of about forty "combat" (fighter) planes. No provision was made for stowage of aircraft in knocked-down condition.

The 27,000-ton design was developed as insurance against the failure of the smaller one, and even on that displacement there was the problem of internal arrangement. For example, because the hull was considerably shallower (65 instead of 74 feet) than that of the ex–battle cruisers, the hangar had to be dropped to the protective deck covering the armored belt, which in turn also covered the machinery. Thus the uptakes had to be carried across the hull through or under part of the hangar, and the designers broke the hangar up into three parts, of full 21-ft depth fore and aft of the uptakes, and of shallow 12-ft depth over them, the latter for fighters. The main aft and the shallow hangars would be served by one 60-ft elevator, the forward hangar by a 30-ft elevator that would also serve the forward end of the shallow hangar. At the flight-deck level, the after elevator was the fore end of the landing space, 278 feet long, since it would take aircraft below after they landed. A crane opposite the main elevator could also pick seaplanes from the water and deposit them onto it, and the bow accommodated two catapult tracks.

In effect 4,000 more tons bought about fifteen more aircraft, calculated on the basis of a larger hangar area, a knot more of speed (32.5 knots, still less than the 35 desired), and slightly more deck protection (80 versus 70 pounds on the flat, 4 versus 3 inches on the slopes). Both designs included 6-ft wide, 3-in belt armor; by way of comparison, the converted battle cruisers had 7-in belts and 80-lb (2-in) armored

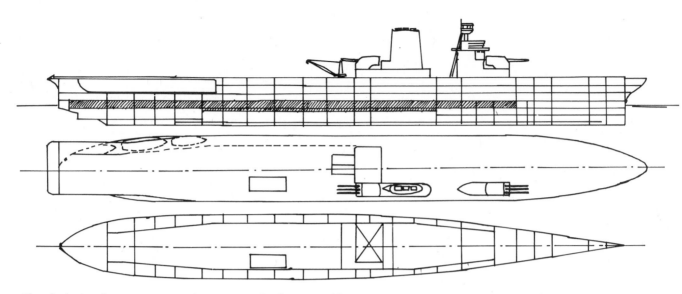

Sketch design for a 13,000-ton (11,500 standard) carrier (design 286), 1923. The guns are triple 8-inch.

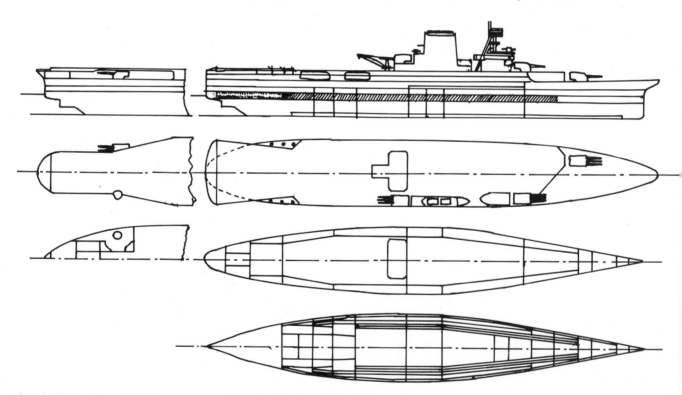

Sketch design for a 29,000-ton protected carrier (design 282), 1923.

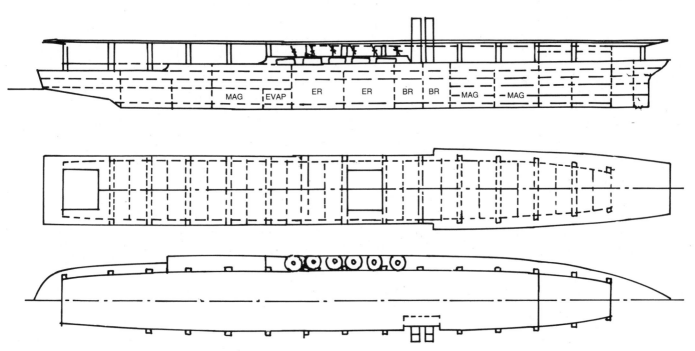

Sketch design for a 10,000-ton unprotected flush-deck carrier, 1926. The entire battery of 5-in AA guns is mounted amid-ships. This was scheme 2.

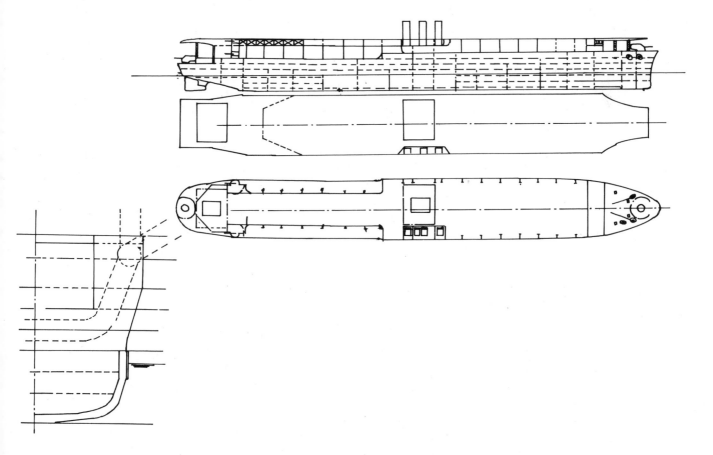

Scheme 30, sketch design for a protected 13,800-ton carrier, 1926. The gun houses and casemates carried 6-in/53 cruiser guns.

decks; it was believed, in 1922, that they could support one hundred aircraft, compared with seventy-five in the 27,000-ton design or sixty in the 23,000-ton. The turbo-electric machinery in the larger ship was an intangible advantage, since in previous U.S. capital ships such machinery had been associated with minute compartmentation for improved protection against underwater attack. It could be argued that such protection would be particularly important for a carrier, some of whose principal enemies (submarines, destroyers, and cruisers) were armed with torpedoes. Moreover, a carrier would normally be able to avoid such opponents during daylight hours, thanks to her own aircraft; at night the torpedo was often the weapon of choice. The 23,000-ton-carrier design showed that, as unit tonnage was drawn down, ship protection, particularly against underwater attack, would have to suffer.

Later, a 27,000-tonner design (282) more strongly oriented towards protection showed a flat 2.5-in protective deck covering an 8-in belt, with turbo-electric drive; however, power was reduced to about 70,000 SHP and speed, therefore, to 27 knots. Hangar-deck area approximated that of the original 27,000-tonner design, but the flight deck had to be cut back to provide space for a triple 8-in mount on the forecastle, another being mounted on the flight deck proper. The hull itself was shortened considerably to save weight.

In the end, the studies appeared to show that the minimum satisfactory carrier displacement was 27,000 tons, and that the choice on this figure was either high speed (32.5 knots) and heavy-gun armament with moderate protection, or much lower speed (27 knots) with either heavy protection or with very large aircraft capacity (the double hangar). Speed was expensive, since it had to be bought by lengthening the hull almost to *Lexington* length. As the hull weight grew, the gun battery would have to be reduced, and indeed the machinery might grow so rapidly in volume as to constrict the hangar deck. The flight deck would also be reduced, since the island would have to grow to accommodate the enlarged smoke pipes to dispose of the increased products of a larger machinery plant.

All of these schemes lay dormant until May 1924, when Representative Carl Vinson suggested to the CNO that, if rough characteristics were worked up quickly enough, he could get a carrier into the new naval bill. The General Board hearing was rushed, but it gives a fair picture of carrier thinking at the time. As before, the primary questions were speed, battery hangar space, and protection—experience was as yet too nebulous to permit any serious estimate of the size of the air group.

Speed was valued primarily as protection against

cruisers; the Washington Treaty had encouraged the large-scale construction of fast 10,000-ton heavy cruisers that could certainly threaten any carrier operating independently. Admiral Bloch of the General Board considered a 35-kt speed useful, particularly as "any sea will knock the 10,000 tonner more than it will this ship." The threat of numerous heavy cruisers would continue to be a factor in carrier design through the early part of World War II, particularly as carrier operators discovered that fast carriers normally operated well apart from the battle fleet, even when combining tactically with it.

The aviators were beginning to agitate for a flush deck, which would add many design problems. For example, Captain McBride, head of Preliminary Design, doubted that 8-in guns could be provided unless they were mounted on the flight deck proper. Looking at the only major carrier operator, the Royal Navy, he could see two alternatives: a flush-deck carrier dependent upon her consorts and her own air group for defense, or a heavily armored, heavily armed carrier. Heavy guns should go into a balanced—that is, heavily protected—design. McBride saw a swing toward the flush-deck "soft" carrier in British reconstructions of the three "large light cruisers" *Courageous*, *Glorious*, and *Furious*; in fact the first two were to be completed with large islands, but that was unknown in 1924.

The flush deck seemed best for aircraft, for maximizing the size of the air group and reducing the chance of an accident during landing. Wider beam would be no substitute. ". . . As they land and with a varying degree of wind, if they are given a slant towards the side that has the island, they must give up all idea of landing at that trial and start out and do it over again, whereas if they have a clear deck, even if the beam is less, they can go ahead with their landing because there is nothing to hit against." The aviator Lieutenant Commander Marc Mitscher (who would ultimately command the fast carrier task force) agreed, pointing to the air currents and eddies set up by the island.

The question was just what qualities to emphasize. Admiral Bloch noted that even with high speed, surprise attack in the night or the fog was always a threat. He wanted 35 or 36 knots, which McBride knew was impossible. Surely a larger ship rated at 32.5 knots could generally outrun a 32.5-kt cruiser. A carrier thwarted at the high-speed end, Bloch noted, might operate on the weather bow of the battle line; speed beyond the 21-kt fleet speed would be necessary only to allow the carrier to take up her position. Surely 6 knots would suffice, which brought matters back to the 27-kt designs. Admiral Hilary P. Jones disagreed on the grounds that tactics were not yet well enough understood. He thought of the carriers as scouts until action was imminent, when they would fall back on the main body for support. He therefore preferred high speed (33–34 knots) and long radius over gun battery. Mitscher favored a fast flush-decker with 6-in guns.

Later, in the fleet problems, the carrier commanders would discover that such mutual support could be suicidal for the carrier. Her main enemies were enemy aircraft, particularly dive-bombers, and her main hopes for survival were evasion and the offensive power of her own air group against the enemy carriers. It was discovered that the sheer size of the battle fleet made its discovery relatively easy for enemy airborne scouts: if the carrier were nearby, she too would be discovered—and neutralized, if not sunk. This tactical issue appears not to have been understood at Newport in the early twenties, although it became a fixture of fleet problems almost as soon as carriers appeared on both sides of them. Indeed, by the early thirties the absolute need to deal preemptively with enemy carriers led the United States to provide a specialized squadron of long-range scouts aboard each of its carriers. Identical aircraft were used for dive-bombing, whence the SB or scout-bomber designation of U.S. dive-bombers of World War II.

In the 1924 hearings there was some discussion of steaming radius, which of course did not directly enter into the standard displacement. McBride showed how it entered indirectly. For example, 10,000 nautical miles might require 2,500 tons of fuel, therefore a two-thirds-fueled 27,000-tonner (with 300 tons of RFW) would displace 29,000 on trial. If the radius requirement were 20,000 nautical miles, that might mean 3,300 tons of fuel, or a trial displacement of 31,000 tons—and more powerful machinery to maintain a fixed trial speed. The endurance speed on which such figures were based was not set at 15 knots, which paralleled other General Board characteristics policies.

The two sets of characteristics presented to Representative Vinson hardly resolved matters, as they merely reflected the two primary possibilities, the lightly protected fast carrier of 32.5 knots with eight 8-in guns and sixty aircraft, and the slow (27.5-kt) carrier with seventy-two aircraft and a 6-in (versus 2-in) belt. Each would also have deck armor, but the slow ship would have two decks. Also, each would have a catapult to fly off battleship and cruiser floatplanes, which would land alongside during a gunnery battle. Total construction cost was estimated at $26.5 million for each type, and the sixty aircraft of the fast carrier would cost another $2.5 million.

The bill failed, and carrier-design work was suspended until 1925–26, in preparation for the FY 29 program and the General Board's Five Year Plan.

That produced a series of flush-deck carrier-design sketches, culminating in the USS *Ranger* (CV 4).

With the failure of Vinson's bill, the General Board resolved to seek a much smaller carrier, and the aviators decided to demand a flush deck. That in turn ended the projects for carriers with 8-in batteries, and several of the subsequent sketch designs showed light cruiser (6-in/53) weapons instead, even though the latter might be considered unrealistic in view of the appearance of heavy (8-in) cruisers in the world's navies. Small unit size also precluded the type of protection that had been incorporated in all of the 1922–23 studies.

As yet, the U.S. had very little experience in carrier operation; only the slow experimental *Langley* had been built. The Royal Navy was, however, a major carrier operator, and it had actually tried the flush deck that the aviators craved. In October 1925 Commander J. C. Hunsacker, assistant naval attaché in London, described the problems with a flush deck to the General Board.

> They have great difficulty with . . . smoke disposal. When the [*Furious*] first came out she became so hot in the after part of the ship they had to interrupt the trials and send her back. She heated up like an oven—the whole after part of the ship. They took her back to the dockyard and had her there several months and worked extra insulation in her and ripped away the after part of the ship for about 300 feet to let the air get in and blow around these decks to keep them cool. I am told unofficially that they have . . . made great improvement so far as the heating up of the ship goes, but the poor commanding officer is still marooned in his cabin. He can't open his port or stick his head out without being asphyxiated. The smoke that comes out of these after ducts fills up the rear of this region of the ship and . . . rides there, and the captain's quarters are where they were in the original *Furious*—under the main deck aft. He has to go underneath through the passages in order to come up to the deck. . . .
> . . . the gossip is they [the *Courageous* and *Glorious*] will not be like the *Furious* but will have an island. In the meantime, the aviators on the *Hermes* and the *Eagle* have learned to be no longer afraid of the island. . . .

However, the message to C & R was clear: new designs must have the flush deck. Preliminary Design began work on a new cycle of such sketch designs, covering a wide range of displacements. Admiral J. D. Beuret, chief of C & R, described the problem.

> . . . We do not know . . . how many airplanes can be delivered to the air for offensive purposes from a deck of a given area; nor do we know what should be assumed as a rate of wastage . . . I mean what proportion the planes that are stowed in the hangar should bear to the planes that can be operated from the

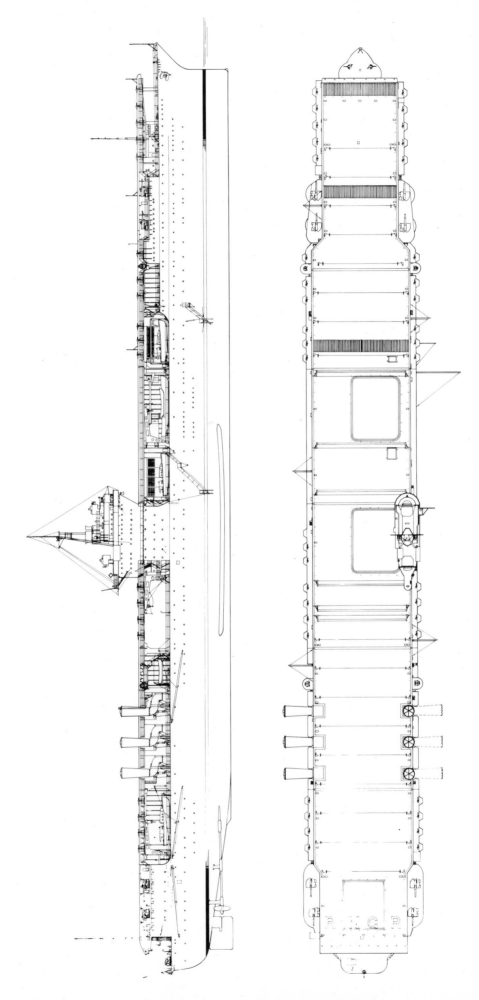

The *Ranger* (CV 4), in 1940, armed with eight 5-in/25 and forty 0.50-cal machine guns. Note her bow arresting wires, fitted after completion; unlike later carriers, she did not have a secondary LSO platform on her starboard side forward.

deck. . . . In its studies the Bureau has assumed . . . 250 feet necessary for the arresting gear . . . a minimum space of 250 feet forward of the arresting gear should be applied for taking-off space and in addition room for parking planes. At the present time they want, for a bomber, 250 feet minimum run and you would need a certain number parked. You could park on the arresting gear before the action but after that you couldn't park there. Now, our studies indicate that on an airplane carrier of a standard displacement as small as 10,000 tons it is impracticable to provide emplacements for even a limited number of 8-inch guns. . . . You either have to have a cruiser or an airplane carrier. . . . it looks as if for the airplane carrier of this size you would have to limit the battery to 6-inch. Even that is with restrictions in the arc of fire. . . . You might possibly follow out the *Lexington* and *Saratoga* arrangement if you had an island type and put one or two guns above the flying deck, but if you had any number of guns they would have to be below the flying deck. . . . So far as concerns the practicability or the possibility of developing a satisfactory design of airplane carrier on 10,000-tons, our preliminary studies indicate that if you go up to about 32-⅓ knots speed—that is, the speed of our present cruisers—you have to do away with the protection. . . . If you install protection, . . . like 2-½ inches on the side and an inch on the deck over the machinery spaces and the magazines, which the Board has more or less taken as the minimum protection—you would have to reduce the speed to about 30 knots. . . .

10,000 [tons] is the biggest carrier we are allowed to build that is not within the treaty limits, and 23,000 is one-third of our disposable tonnage inside treaty limits. . . . The smallest carriers would give you a greater deck area in the aggregate and would, I think, give you a greater aggregate hangar space if you wanted it. . . . a small carrier has the advantage, of permitting you to distribute your airplanes more widely, if that is a tactical advantage—but on the other hand, the larger vessels are more seaworthy, but again, we don't have information as to the conditions under which flying of airplanes will be limited by the weatherlines of the airplane itself or by the tossing about of the ship. . . .

[The relative ton-cost is in favor of the larger carrier] with the same speed. The speed makes quite a difference in the cost and for the same speed your machinery is relatively more expensive on the small vessel than on the large one.

In general, Beuret's analysis held through the prejet era, as long as U.S. carrier aircraft rolled to takeoff and as long as the principal tactic was the deck-load strike. He was, however, severely hampered: he could not know the lower limits on carrier size, owing to seakeeping and the minimum effective air-group size for an individual carrier, the latter a tactical issue that would not be resolved for some time. As for the issue of wastage, a 50 percent figure would obtain in U.S. carriers until World War II, and a common fixture of prewar planning was the assumption of a wastage of 25 percent per month in combat. Thus the standard figure of 50 percent amounted to two months' stores, and was in line with the supply of stores that large warships were designed to carry. The need for space to carry such aircraft led in turn to the characteristic U.S. hangar design, with deep girders above the hangar deck from which aircraft, some of them disassembled, could be suspended ("triced up"). This stowage was gradually usurped by the enclosed gallery deck, so that as functions were moved from, for example, the island structure into the gallery deck, it was enlarged, and spare-aircraft stowage suffered. The most striking example of such contraction was in the *Essex*, where, in the design stage, a major shrinkage of the island structure was associated with a decision to halve the spare-airplane complement.

Another question, familiar to those who followed the evolution of postwar carriers, was the relationship between carrier size and aircraft characteristics. For example, BuAer specified a maximum wing spread of 53 feet. A decision in favor of a 10,000-ton carrier would impose more severe limits on future carrier-bomber developments than would one in favor of 23,000 tons—but in 1926 no one could say how serious that limitation would be. There were, of course, catapults: the long catapults of the *Lexington* would be able to launch 10,000-lb airplanes; surely the 10,000-ton carrier would not do as well? Admiral Jones commented: "I think you could get the 10,000-pound plane off, but you would be limited as to the number you could carry because it would take all your disposable length forward of the arresting gear to get the one plane off. . . . We assumed the 250-foot run, but our actual length of deck forward [of the 250 feet for arresting gear] might be in the neighborhood of 300 to 350 feet."

Captain W. H. Standley, director of War Plans, compared the tactical and strategic values of large and small carriers, with three small carriers to one large one, and with the aggregate small-carrier air group at least equal to one large-carrier air group.

Such comparisons that I would be able to give would be more in the nature of opinions based on rather uncertain demonstrations, war games and what not, but from strategic considerations, in favor of the smaller type, you would have . . . greater flexibility in the plans because of the greater number. They would probably be of greater value in offensive screening because of the greater number. Now, as against that, you would have a dispersal of forces because for each carrier you are going to require certain other types for defense. For example, at the present time I think they are calling for a division of destroyers for each aircraft carrier. You are going to have to have a certain number of destroyers with each smaller type. Now, of course, an advantage with the larger type is the greater facility with which you can use planes under all conditions of weather.

Beuret found an 11,500-ton design particularly attractive, but he could not develop a carrier small enough to come under the 10,000-ton lower limit set by the treaty. By mid-February Preliminary Design had developed a series of sketch studies (table 3-2) and on 10 March the General Board held another hearing. Beuret found that the 10,000-lb bomber set an effective lower limit on carrier size, owing to the required hangar and flight-deck dimensions. He favored the smallest practicable design, 13,000 tons, one-fifth of the 69,000 available. Its key advantage was that a force of five 13,000-ton carriers would have a total deck area about 15 or 20 percent greater than the allowable force of three 23,000-ton carriers. The small carriers would cost about 20 percent more "due mainly to the higher proportion of machinery, which is expensive weight, for a given speed on the smaller than on the larger carrier."

The next question was vulnerability. Admiral Beuret considered any carrier highly vulnerable, in that a useful level of protection would entail excessive sacrifices in such major characteristics as speed or hangar capacity—as the 1923 studies had shown. In particular it would be nearly impossible to protect the flight deck and hangar. That is, although on 23,000 tons a useful level of underwater and hull protection was possible, there could be no protection for "the main characteristics of the ship—its airplane operating facilities." It seemed to follow that the force of smaller carriers would be better because the inevitable loss of some would not eliminate the entire force.

The hearing now turned to aviation facilities. BuAer wanted a clear deck width of 80 feet to accommodate bombers, "based on the wing spread of the plane and on the necessity for . . . some additional width to allow for inaccuracies of landing and also to make it unnecessary [to] get your plane too closely centered in going off." Commander K. Whiting of BuAer explained in addition that

there were two reasons for selecting 80 feet. In our retarding gear the athwartship wires, which are used to retard the plane after they engage the fore and aft wires, are designed for 80 feet and if we cut them down it subjects the plane to a larger strain . . . because the loads come on the plane much faster. Also,. when parking the planes on deck ready to take off, if you cut down the width of the ship five feet . . . you can [park] two [rather than] three rows of planes [abreast]. We selected 80 feet as the minimum width and also 80 feet appeared quite easy to obtain on a 10,000 ton ship.

[As for landing,] in the *Langley* type which is only 65 feet, the deck disappears entirely from view of the pilot about 100 feet before he reaches the deck of the ship. With 80 feet he will have a good view of the deck as he approaches.

A deck about 665 feet long would be necessary to operate the 10,000-lb bomber that was BuAer's primary offensive weapon. The bureau also favored a double-ended flight deck on the grounds developed in 1920 (see chapter 2), with arresting gear fore and aft. Bow as well as stern arresting gear remained a standard feature of U.S. carrier design as late as when the *Midway* class were being constructed, and carriers through the *Essex* were to be fitted for such double-ended operation. This requirement was not abolished until 1944, and later carriers inherited an associated

Table 3-2. Flush-Deck-Carrier Schemes, 1926–27

	Scheme 29 9 Feb 1926	Scheme 30 6 Feb 1926	Scheme 31 8 Feb 1926	Scheme 2 13 Sep 1927
LWL (ft-in)	790-0	680-0	600-0	620-0
Beam (ft-in)	84-0	71-6	65-0	71-0
Draft (ft-in)	25-0	22-6	20-6	18-0
Std (tons)	23,000	13,800	10,000	10,000
Normal (tons)	25,500	18,600	11,500	11,600
End at 15 Kts (nm)	10,000	10,000	10,000	10,000
SHP	105,000	92,000	83,000	53,500
Speed (kts)	32.5	32.5	32	29.5
6-in/53 Guns	8	8	—	—
5-in AA Guns	12 × 37 mm	12 × 37 mm	12 × 37 mm	12
TT	2	2	2	—
Belt Width (ft-in)	10-0	10-0	—	—
Thickness (in)	2.5	2.5	—	—
Hangar Area (sq ft)	49,000	31,000	23,800	—

Note: There are 2 elevators in each scheme, one right aft, one abaft amidships.

requirement: they had to be able to back down at high speed for a prolonged period.

It followed that catapults might best be placed at both ends of the ship, for true double-ended operation. "We have catapults at each end of the *Langley*, one at the bow and one at the stern. We asked for them on the *Lexington* and *Saratoga*. We asked for three at each end and we contemplated putting the three aft right at the retarding gear without interfering with it. But, owing to the weights it was decided to install one catapult at the forward end of the ship and reserve a space for another, so it is possible to put another in there later."

The carrier would have to be adaptable to future naval aircraft; the board wanted some estimates of future limits. Existing arresting gear was designed to deal with a 10,000-lb airplane landing at 60 mph. Admiral Moffet of BuAer expected a 10,000-lb carrier bomber to take off in 250 feet (15-kt wind) or 100 with a catapult; the British had taken off a 6,800-lb torpedo plane in 78 feet with a 22-kt wind. Moffett expected the big bomber (10,000 pounds, 60-ft space) to remain in the air for four hours at 90 knots. It was best approximated by the CS, designed to carry a torpedo or a 1,000-lb bomb. A fighter might take off in 80 feet (250 for a two-seat fighter). It would stall at 50–55 knots, the bomber at 60. Moffett saw the scout/torpedo bomber as the limit for future development.

In an October 1927 hearing on characteristics Lieutenant Commander B. C. Leighton of BuAer proposed as an ideal air group two fighters to cover every bomber; he expected to carry thirty-six bombers and seventy-two fighters on a 13,800-ton, 29.4-kt carrier (twenty-seven and fifty-four in a 32.5-kt ship); these figures included planes in the hangar and on deck. This type of analysis was very much at odds with later U.S. practice of expecting bombers to attack essentially without fighter cover, the fighters being withheld primarily for carrier air defense in view of the extreme vulnerability of the flight deck from which they operated. Thus the standard air group of the immediate pre–World War II period consisted of one fighter squadron, one scout (bomber) squadron, one dive-bomber squadron, and one torpedo/horizontal bomber squadron, each consisting of eighteen aircraft.

The aviators demanded a flush-deck (island-less) carrier design; Whiting testified that although there was no U.S. experience with the island type of carrier,

we do know that any obstruction on the flying deck extending above the flying deck sets up eddy currents in its lee. An island must necessarily be forward of the retarding gear and the ship must be headed into the wind when the planes are flying aboard . . . so that the lee of the island is that part of the deck occupied by the retarding gear and the part of the deck which the planes have to fly through or fly to in coming aboard.

They come in over the stern and the eddy currents set up by the island go well to the stern of the ship. We find the wind varies as much as 15 degrees very quickly. That would mean if you were carrying the wind dead ahead and you had the island on the starboard side, if the wind shifts to the starboard side the whole area [of] the retarding gear would be covered by disturbed air, which makes it difficult for the pilot coming aboard. He can't see that disturbed air and the first indication he has is when he feels the plane bouncing around. . . .

[However,] I talked with the British air attache here who was in command of the *Hermes* for two years and he seems to think it depends a good deal on the fore and aft location of that island, whether it is bad or not, . . . as well as the length of the island itself. He states there is considerable difference between the *Eagle* and the *Hermes*. I believe the *Hermes* has her island further forward than the *Eagle* and doesn't have so much disturbed air as they do in the *Eagle*, or at least the disturbed air is in such a position that the plane goes through it before they reach the stern of the ship in flying on. Then, of course, the island itself occupies space on deck.

. . . From what this British captain says, his pilots . . . rather like the island after they get used to it because it gave them something in view all the time while coming aboard—a point of reference—which you haven't in a flush deck. When they went to the *Argus*, which had no island, they invariably came to grief in attempting to land—broke the landing gear or the wheels of the plane.

Thus the island might even be useful as a point of reference.

. . . if a plane doesn't get into the retarding gear he is very likely to come in collision with the island. . . . it is very difficult to decide. Of course, a flush deck ship gives you greater area on deck to handle planes. It seems very desirable.

Admiral Phelps asked what percentage of landings on the *Langley* missed and had to go off again, because they made up the percentage apt to come in collision with the island.

A very, very small percentage. I should say it is not one in fifty, because, you see, after you fly the first plane aboard if it isn't removed from the deck the next plane must get into the retarding gear. In one or two cases the pilots were unsuccessful. In one case he missed it entirely and hit three planes parked on the deck and wrecked all four planes. That was due to the pitching of the ship and an inexperienced pilot. . . . Of course, when he misses he is apt to hit hard and start a fire. That is very serious on a carrier. There is so much gasoline lying around and a fire caused by a plane is very likely to be . . . serious.

Beuret compared the *Lexington*, a carrier of maximum displacement and "intensified military characteristics," to a 13,800-ton, 25-kt carrier with no military characteristics beyond heavy machine guns. The smaller carrier would actually show a greater useful enclosed volume. An alternative sketch design for a protected (2.5-in belt, with a 1-in deck, deep in the ship, covering it) 13,800-ton, 32.5-kt carrier showed that both armor and speed would cost in aviation features, giving protection more than speed.

Given a flush-decker (an aviation-oriented ship), the main design problem would be disposal of the uptake gases. In the *Langley*, which had relatively low power, the ship could steam sufficiently off the wind to keep the smoke off her deck. However, it was not clear that the rough air due to the smoke could be disposed of, nor was it clear that a similar measure would suffice for a much more powerful ship; there was, after all, the cautionary example of HMS *Furious*. For example,

> the moment the ship steams with the wind on the quarter at a speed below the speed of the wind, that smoke goes from the stern all the way forward and makes the ship almost uninhabitable. She almost gases herself. . . . Then the uptakes take up room in the hangar space that might be used for planes. . . . you always run into conditions where you steam with the wind at a speed less than the wind and you are going to have that gas all the way along the ship. We tried that on the *Langley*. We had one stack that pointed down to the water. It had a large water spray. We could eject all the gases from that stack. We tried it out and we found we could get all the gases out of it. But the gases, as they cooled, eventually formed eddy currents and eventually found their way to the boiler rooms and made the ship uninhabitable.

> [With the habitability of HMS *Furious* in general,] they had a lot of trouble. The uptakes were cased in and they had a large number of ventilators like wind scoops, half of them pointed forward and half aft. After a short trial they took her back to the Navy Yard and had to take all that plating off the side. . . . That was because they found hangar space got so hot it was dangerous to stow planes in it.

> They have spent a good deal [of money] and I don't think they have solved the problem. On the *Argus*, which is the same type of ship—I mean as far as smoke disposal goes—they have an arrangement in which they can run all the smoke into a very large room or compartment for a period of two minutes. That is all right for flying aboard, but I don't know how rapidly they can shift from one condition to another nor how much it affects steaming speed.

The engineers much preferred to circumvent the problem and stick to an island design; but for a carrier aviation characteristics were predominant, and BuAer was able to enforce its demand for a flush deck.

In contrast with accepted carrier doctrine, in which the ships were expected to operate with the (slow) battle line, Captain W. S. Pye of the War Plans Division wanted the new carriers to operate with the fast cruisers of the scouting force, which would mean a speed of about 32.5 knots. BuAer argued that high speed was too expensive, that 32.5 knots (rather than,

say, 29.4) would cost a quarter of a carrier's striking power, an unacceptable sacrifice. Moreover, in practice the 10,000-ton cruisers of the scouting force rarely exceeded 25 knots.

As Lieutenant Commander Leighton of BuAer argued before the General Board in October 1927, fast cruisers could combine tactically with a slower carrier, part of whose effective mobility was vested in her aircraft. "If you have the airplanes on the scouting line with the striking ranges that the airplanes have, it becomes possible, even with a considerable reduction in ship speed, by using the long range of the airplane, to concentrate your striking effort without concentrating the position of the ships as you must do with your cruisers."

Pye summarized the War Plans Division view. "We consider it desirable to have the largest number of the smallest carrier that can effectively operate at least one squadron of planes and have a speed not less than the speed of the 10,000 ton cruisers. . . . The newer carriers to be built will give a greater flexibility in operation and greater safety in operation due to numbers by building a large number of the smaller type."

Tactically, he expected to assign to each carrier a destroyer division to operate with it, a step already recommended to the CNO for the *Lexington* and *Saratoga* when commissioned; the destroyers would defend against submarine attack, and also against surface attack by heavy ships. Pye did not say that the effective sea speed of the destroyers, particularly in rough weather, would limit the speed and indeed the seakeeping ability of the carrier. In practice, the new large carriers were generally assigned cruisers rather than destroyers as escorts, the latter lacking either sea speed or endurance to match the carriers. By the late thirties the standard tactical unit was a large carrier and three heavy cruisers, acting as plane guards and as a means of countering heavy enemy surface ships met by surprise. By then actual fleet exercises had shown their value. If the carrier did indeed combine tactically with the heavy cruisers, she could share their maximum sea speed, which was much closer to 32.5 knots than might have been forecast in the late twenties, when the new heavy cruisers were as yet only paper projects. Moreover, by the late thirties it was understood that a carrier maneuvering into and out of the wind to launch and recover aircraft would need some excess of speed over her escorts merely to maintain a respectable speed of advance. This last issue does not seem to have been appreciated in 1927, when the only U.S. carrier, the *Langley*, operated only a relatively small air group which did not entail very long excursions into the wind.

From all points of view, then, a relatively slow 13,800-ton carrier seemed attractive, and it was this type that the General Board chose for the characteristics it submitted to the Secretary of the Navy on 1 November 1927. Although it envisaged the construction of five such ships in all, Congress actually approved only one as part of the FY 29–FY 33 five-year Program.

At this late date, C & R was still ready to pursue the other alternatives: 10,000, 17,250, and 23,000 tons. It also continued to press for an island-type carrier, given the problem of smoke disposal; C & R admitted, however, that even with an island and high funnels the problem might not be satisfactorily solved. The best it could hope for, and indeed the solution it adopted, was to place the boilers abaft the machinery and lead the uptakes through funnels that could be folded down for flight operations. Unfortunately, although moderate power could be accommodated in this way, very high power (for cruiser speed), upward of 100,000 SHP, would create severe problems of trim if the machinery were placed aft. "Subject to final expression of opinion by the Bureau of Engineering [which agreed], it appears probable that choice will have to be made between high speed and a clear [flush] flying deck.... Our only experience with smoke disposal is confined to the installation on the *Langley*, which is only 7,000 horse power...."

Four separate 13,800-ton studies were prepared. Three varied in power as well as in machinery, and the fourth incorporated a double flying deck. There were also two 10,000-ton carriers with alternative types of propelling machinery, and two 17,250-ton alternatives. Only the 13,800-ton schemes were seriously pursued, the board choosing between a fast carrier with a 700-ft flight deck and stowage for 81 aircraft, and a slow (29.4-kt) alternative with a 770-ft flight deck and stowage for 108 aircraft.

The board was willing to accept the shorter flight deck, but not the reduction in air-group size. It was also influenced by the smoke problem, which would clearly be much simplified at a lower power; 53,000 SHP (as adopted) would buy 29.4 knots in trial condition.

Lieutenant Commander Leighton (BuAer) testified that

> on [the] question of length of flying deck, as you increase the length of deck beyond a certain limit you don't get near the proportional gain. That is, we require about 250 feet clear aft for the arresting gear and we need about 350 feet forward for take-off. So, if your deck is only 600 feet long you can't have any airplanes on deck except the one taking off. The rest must be below. If you have a 700-foot deck there is 100 feet available for stowage of machines on deck ready for flight.... If you go from 700 to 800 feet you double the deck stowage capacity. If you go from 300 to 900 feet you increase the stowage space only 50%. So that somewhere around 600 feet is the critical length. One hundred feet in a 700-foot deck means a great deal more than 100 feet added to an 800-foot deck.

At this late stage the gun batteries envisaged were still closer to those of light cruisers than to those of carriers as they were later designed. For example, the 13,800-ton scheme 30 of 6 February 1926 showed eight 6-in/53 single-purpose guns (twin enclosed mounts at the ends, plus four guns in two double-level casemates on the stern quarters), two triple torpedo tubes (21-in), and only twelve 37-mm AA guns. At the same time the new heavy cruisers were being designed with the same antiaircraft weapon, a heavy machine gun being designed by John Browning. Delays in its development led to their equipment, instead, with the 5-in/25. Similarly, by the time characteristics were being prepared, the General Board had abandoned the single-purpose antisurface battery in favor of twelve 5-in/25 AA guns, supported by "the maximum number of machine guns [0.50 caliber] that can be installed clear of flying deck with effective arcs of fire." The latter were essential to countering the dive-bombers then becoming prominent.

These considerations were incorporated in the FY 29 carrier. The first ever built as such from the keel up for the U.S. Navy was the *Ranger* (CV 4). Her design reveals a number of ironies, the greatest being that, despite the numerous sacrifices involved in providing a full flush deck, she was completed with an island structure. She introduced several features common to other U.S. carriers designed before 1945: an open hangar, a gallery deck around the flight deck (in some cases, extending under it), and provision for cross-deck catapults. The latter provided the rationale for adopting the open hangar but were omitted as an economy measure before the *Ranger* could be completed. Note that the open hangar would only later be valued for the ability to warm up aircraft prior to lifting them to the flight deck. The requirement for an open hangar, and the separate requirement for a heavy machine-gun (0.50 caliber) battery in turn led to the institution of the gallery deck. With the dive-bomber being the most potent shipboard weapon, the General Board was willing to delete torpedo stowage from the characteristics for the *Ranger* during 1931, again as an economy measure.

C & R made the size and arrangement of the flight deck and hangar the focus of the design. For example, in order to obtain the widest possible flight deck, it accepted a hull with an unusual degree of flare, admitting that

> under some weather conditions this may cause more pounding than would be obtained with a vessel of the hull form of the light cruisers. The great length of these vessels, however, renders less probable the encounter of waves of sufficient length to cause a maximum amount of pitching. Pitching should be of small consequence in waves less than 600 ft long. As waves in excess of this length are comparatively rare, the adoption of this extreme flare is believed to be jus-

tified. It has, however, been considered desirable to provide the maximum possible freeboard....

Catapults would be installed only in the next (*Yorktown*) class; in February 1928, they represented

the [arrangement] desired by the recent conference [with *Lexington* and *Saratoga* officers] and the one recommended strongly by the Commander of Aircraft Squadrons of the Battle Fleet, in recent correspondence. It permits flying off the ship from two levels which under some conditions of operation appears highly desirable. This is provided for on certain foreign carriers by flying off forward under the bridge on the level of the main or hangar deck but this is accomplished only at the expense of considerable freeboard, which is of great importance in a long ship, and of reduced length of flight deck.

At the officers' conference, flight-deck catapults were rejected in view of their interference with normal flight-deck operations; catapults on the hangar deck

have the advantages of making it possible to launch planes of varying types at will without re-arrangement of parking on the flight deck, of providing stand-by launching points in case of damage to flight deck, and of getting the initial effort in the air in a minimum time. Any catapult has the further advantage of being able to launch seaplanes that cannot otherwise be launched from carrier decks. It was recognized that a very small time interval between launchings was necessary in order to realize any of the advantages of catapults to a very marked degree. These considerations argue that as many catapults as possible should be installed on the hangar deck.... Two was the maximum number that could be provided due to the necessary provisions for large bays to give sufficient wing tip clearance for large planes.

At this time the naval aircraft factory at Philadelphia had already demonstrated that airplanes up to 3,000 pounds could be launched cross-wind in wind velocities up to 26 mph; cross-wind launches of aircraft up to 3,000 pounds had often been made by catapult-equipped battleships and cruisers at sea. The two catapults would have to be near amidships because, in a flush-deck carrier, any location near the bow could interfere with the navigating bridge, not to mention part of the antiaircraft battery. At this time the available units were the P-type (powder fired) already developed for battleships and cruisers; one was to be between the elevators and one abaft the stacks, each with a 60-ft clear bay for wing-tip clearance. The athwartship catapults had to be arranged so as to clear the elevators; it proved impossible to locate the forward catapult between them. Thus the after elevator had to be moved forward to clear the forward of the two catapults, so that in the end the two elevators were only about 40 feet apart and nearly amidships, a

most unusual arrangement. Even then, no space could be found for the forward catapult. Both were offset to starboard to provide the maximum free path around them. There were originally to have been only two elevators, as in the earlier carriers; the *Ranger* was, however, completed with a third smaller elevator right aft.

The flight deck itself was wood, laid atop very thin steel plates (about 0.10 inch) which were to act as a fire break. A few years later the commander of the battle force, commenting about the characteristics of future carriers, wrote that local damage to such a deck could be repaired relatively easily by spiking steel plates over the holes in it, and that a repair-party station was being provided just under the flight deck accessible to the galleries on the *Ranger* and the new *Yorktown*.

The *Ranger* design introduced the flight-deck galleries that were later characteristic of U.S. practice. They replaced the booms and netting of the *Lexington* and *Saratoga*; the General Board commented that "they are expected to provide gun positions for the maximum number of machine guns that can be mounted.... The minimum (should) be 20. Although these galleries are not strong enough to withstand a heavy sea, the great freeboard of the ship is such that they would probably be rarely exposed to the full force of the sea if the ship is properly handled. They will afford desirable additional space for the crew in good weather in a very ... crowded ship."

Throughout the prewar period, defensive weapons competed with flight-deck area. The characteristics for the *Ranger* approved by the General Board called for twelve 5-in guns, but C & R could provide only eight, in four sponsons just under the flight deck. Even then it had to pare deck length by 25 feet and narrow the ends of the flight deck from 86 to 62 feet for a total of about a quarter of its length; the cost would be 4 to 6 percent of the maximum number of aircraft the carrier could fly off. Two more guns might have been mounted on the forecastle deck, but then they would interfere with the navigating bridge that was to be located there, under the forward edge of the flight deck. In the *Yorktown* design, which did not have to provide such unobstructed vision forward (because the later ship had a conventional island), the battery arrangement went through further contortions, including guns on the centerline forward, before reverting to exactly the same *Ranger* arrangement.

When the island was fitted and the navigating bridge brought out from under the deck overhang forward, the antiaircraft battery was temporarily rearranged: the *Ranger* was completed with two of her four forward guns on the forecastle beneath the forward end of the flight deck, and with two of the

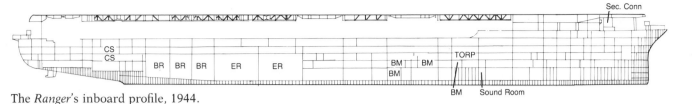

The *Ranger*'s inboard profile, 1944.

The *Ranger* is shown soon after completion, with her bow 5-in guns moved to the sides of her flight deck. The foremost of her palisades (windbreaks) is rigged.

after guns on the hangar deck right aft. Neither location was wholly satisfactory, and the guns were all relocated to the gallery-deck locations envisaged earlier.

Guns were not the only problem: they required directors, which C & R tentatively located on each side amidships to reduce further depredation of flight-deck area and avoid smoke interference from the funnels aft. The exact method of mounting was to be decided in the detail design. To reduce size and weight, BuOrd thought it might be practicable to incorporate director, rangefinder, and spotting glass into one instrument, as indeed proved to be the case in the Mark 33 directors that the *Ranger* and later prewar carriers received.

There was no hope of any reasonable degree of protection on the limited displacement. For example, C & R could not provide a conning tower in any useful location, since there was not enough height between

forecastle deck and flight deck to combine both a navigating bridge and a conning tower. Furthermore,

It has been the usual practice of the Bureau to locate magazines below the waterline and . . . one deck height from the inner bottom on all types of ships in which such an arrangement is practicable. This is standard practice on battleships, is largely complied with on light cruisers of large size, but cannot be met on small light cruisers and destroyers. It will not be possible to meet this desideratum completely on these vessels due to their comparatively light draft. So far as practicable, they will be kept below the waterline and away from the ship's side, but they will be immediately above the inner bottom.

Although the *Ranger* was much smaller than the converted battle cruisers, she had a much larger hangar, 552 feet by about 65, compared to 440 by 66 on the earlier ships (with their fully closed hangars) and 640 by 62 on the *Yorktown*s. She introduced stow-

Within a short time the *Ranger*'s guns had been rearranged. Also evident in this early photograph are the 50-cal AA machine guns along the edges of the flight deck and the unusual location of the two amidships elevators. By this time two 5-in directors (Mark 33) had been installed.

age for forty assembled fuselages between the flight-deck girders, with sufficient headroom that such stowage did not interfere with the movement of aircraft on the hangar deck proper. Compared to earlier practice, special effort was made to consolidate aviation shops, the resulting arrangement being much more compact than that in the ex–battle cruisers. During detail design the planned location of spare wing panels was changed from the platform deck, very deep in the ship, to a compartment on the main (hangar) deck just off the rear of the hangar proper, so that the long panels no longer had to be passed through a succession of hatches. Instead, for quick assembly, a spare fuselage could be lowered from the overhead, wings broken out of an adjacent compartment, and a propeller brought up from below.

A two-level ready-room structure was provided on the starboard side of the hangar, ultimately in the location just below the island structure. In addition, there was a single large space assigned to a combined aviation intelligence and air plot.

Finally, as the *Ranger* was being built, BuAer rather suddenly withdrew its demand for a flush deck (which had dominated the entire design process) and an island was added. Initially a rather small one was envisaged, but later it grew considerably. The 1931 sketch design, which would become the *Yorktown*, already showed a conventional island superstructure. However, since the *Ranger* had been designed and laid down as a flush-decker, the installation of an island added considerable difficulty. Even so, a 22 November 1932 letter signed by the four technical bureaus maintained that effective 5-in fire control would be impossible "unless provision is made for mounting the directors above the level of the flight deck. Furthermore, it appears essential to provide an elevated position in order to obtain efficient air and ship control." By this time, the value of a primary air-control position ("pri-fly") from which the entire air group could be seen had been demonstrated aboard the *Lexington* and *Saratoga*. The original letter visualized an island restricted to fire control, primary air control, and secondary ship control, so that the primary bridge would still be under the fore end of the flight deck. This was still not quite enough, although the change would add considerably to the cost of the ship. At an informal General Board hearing on 23 December, the chief constructor complained that some means would have to be found to add about $2 million to the $19 million originally approved; if no more money were found

> the ship will be completed as far as the hull and machinery are concerned. She will go to a Navy Yard and remain for overhaul three or four times as long as she normally would, and then would go to sea for a very brief period and return to the Navy Yard for a

Beginning with the *Ranger*, U.S. carriers were designed to stow reserve aircraft above their hangars, as this April 1937 photograph of the *Ranger* shows. Consequently hangar decks had to be quite deep, and deep girders had to be provided overhead. Spaces not used for stowage became part of the gallery deck. Note the rail used to move aircraft.

so-called annual overhaul which would be repeated for two or three years, never being at any time a satisfactory efficient operating unit. . . .

The small island approved [in November] by the General Board was satisfactory for fire control, half-way satisfactory for air control, and but partly satisfactory for ship control. It still left difficulties with the rail (folding) masts which if down are considered a menace on rolling and if up, are a menace to aviators. The [proposed larger] island, with a tripod mast, gives better radio facilities and also better ship communication, as regards flag hoists, signals, etc. We propose to take off the wing platforms and radio masts and not utilize the up and down platform. The pilot house [in the bows] would be left for secondary ship control. We have done about the best we could with a series of compromises. It is considered far better than the original. . . .

The small island was somewhat more satisfactory from a viewpoint of fire control than the present [larger one]. There is no secondary fire control in this scheme. Probably the greatest objection is the vulnerability of the island structure. . . .

The island is aft because of the flight deck structural strength on account of the expansion joint, and to keep clear of the flying-off area. Aeronautics did not

want it any more forward. The next joint would bring it too far forward. It is in the same relative position as on the *Lexington* and *Saratoga*. From an aviation point of view that is the ideal location. The flight deck on the *Lexington* and *Saratoga* is a strength deck but the *Ranger's* is fitted with expansion joints principally to get an open hangar deck. The necessary shifting of boat stowage will blank one catapult opening. As regards flight deck considerations and obstruction there is no change in this larger island from the smaller one except for the catwalk around the bridge.

The ship will probably be a better sea-going ship with the island except as regards damaged condition. It started out with a metacentric height of six feet and has been reduced from that to 5.8 and will probably go down to 5.4. . . .

He ended by pleading for a quick resolution, since every delay was costing money, and nothing would be saved by retaining the small island the General Board had just approved. Somewhat sheepishly the assistant chief of BuAer admitted that

at the time the original design for the *Ranger* was approved there had been no operating experience with the *Saratoga* and the *Lexington* and the concep-

Three photographs of the *Ranger* (*above* and *facing*) taken in Hampton Roads on 18 August 1942 summarize early war modifications, which are circled. Note the extensive application of splinter protection to all weapons, including those mounted before the war. She was little modified after this.

tion of a carrier was based on the experience with the *Langley*, which at that time operated only with a maximum of twenty planes. The air officer stationed on the forward platform could see far enough aft to see all planes land and to control the landing, with this small quota.... When, however, the complement was increased to 32 planes, it became difficult and almost impossible for the air officer from his forward position ... to see any plane landing after the 12th or the 15th. The same situation would occur on the *Ranger* after 15 to 20 planes had landed, and she has a complement of 72.

When the General Board considered new carriers and flying-deck cruisers more experience with the *Saratoga* and *Lexington* was available. Their island had been found satisfactory with no smoke interference and with no danger of being struck by planes. In fact, to date no plane has struck the island although one has run into a turret....

... There is [now] no opposition to the island idea in the Bureau of Aeronautics. The large island is better than the small island previously recommended since it affords facilities for the main ship control and for fire control and air control. The smaller island had no air plotting facilities, radio room, and other features installed in the larger....

In addition to landing control at the stern of the ship, air control on the bridge is necessary for emergencies, such as the landing of partially disabled planes and the like.

The General Board accepted the enlarged island with primary ship control that day.

Several features had already been eliminated in the interest of saving money, the two athwartship catapults being merely the most prominent. A more subtle measure was the elimination of torpedo stowage aboard the new carrier, adopted late in 1931 in view of the rising fortunes of the dive-bomber and the declining efficacy of the torpedo plane. Torpedo stowage was replaced by increased bomb stowage, a decision the General Board based in part on the expressed views of CinC Battle Force and also CinC U.S. Fleet, owing to the obvious vulnerability of the slow tor-

pedo bombers then in service. For example, as early as his FY 28 report the latter recommended the course of action that BuAer was then taking: development of a heavy dive-bomber that might replace the torpedo bomber as the primary carrier offensive weapon; "the bombing target offered by aircraft carrier decks, in particular, suggests the development of the type of bombing plane recommended.... The advantage of suppressing an air offensive before it is launched may have a far-reaching effect upon the engagements of main forces...." Thus as early as 1932 there was only one torpedo squadron left, VT-1S aboard the *Lexington* having exchanged its torpedo bombers for BM heavy dive-bombers. The *Ranger* and later the *Wasp* each had a second scout squadron in place of the usual torpedo squadron, so that they carried two squadrons of scouts, one of fighters, and one of dive-bombers. However, in the other fleet carriers the torpedo bomber regained part of its earlier prominence during the thirties, due in large part to the emergence of a new high-performance torpedo bomber, the Douglas TBD Devastator—which would be fatally deficient in World War II.

The *Ranger* epitomized the new importance of the dive-bomber: she was among the first U.S. warships armed with light automatic weapons (in her case the forty 0.50-cal machine guns) designed specifically to defeat the dive-bomber. She was also the first to prove the inadequacy of existing defenses, since in February 1938 she used the new drone aerial targets, which could fully simulate a dive-bombing attack. By that time the danger of a dive-bomber attack was well appreciated, and the supposed antidote, the 1.1-in machine cannon, was in full (some might say premature) production.

Her light antiaircraft battery was increased as part of the general improvement to U.S. Fleet air defenses in 1940–41, so that in September 1941, after a refit at Norfolk, the *Ranger* mounted six quadruple 1.1-in machine cannon and only twenty-four of her original forty 0.50-cal machine guns. Of the former,

The *Ranger* was refitted at Norfolk late in 1942, after her participation in the North African invasion. The major change was the addition of Bofors guns in place of the former 1.1s. Unlike later U.S. carriers, she was not refitted with gasoline pipelines outside her hull.

two were mounted on raised platforms at either end of the island structure, two at the after ends of each of the four 5-in galleries, port and starboard, and two on the fantail. By the middle of the next year her planned ultimate battery was set at six quadruple 40-mm guns and as many 20-mm guns as could be accommodated, and she was carrying a total of thirty of the latter weapons. By this time the *Ranger* was badly overloaded, and she never quite attained the sort of antiaircraft battery relatively easily applied to other carriers. Nor did she have the sort of topside space they enjoyed. For example, it appears that the after pair of quadruple 1.1-in machine cannon was cramped, and for a time it was intended that the pair be replaced by twin rather than by quadruple Bofors guns. Ultimately these positions were given up, and quadruple Bofors were installed on the centerline fore and aft, beyond the flight-deck overhangs. After a refit she emerged in January 1943 with six quadruple Bofors and a total of forty-six 20-mm cannon, as well as the original eight 5-in/25s. She had already operated in support of the North African invasion and during October 1943 formed part of the Home Fleet force raiding German shipping in Norway.

However, by that time she was both obsolescent and badly overweight. For example, in the fall of 1943 her 20-mm battery was reduced by six guns to save weight. In January and again in December 1943 Admiral King ordered materials collected for the *Ranger* to be modernized at Norfolk for a combination of improved underwater protection and the ability to operate modern aircraft. That would entail blistering, modernization of the elevators, the installation of catapults, and strengthening of the flight deck. Concurrent improvements, for greater operational efficiency and better damage control, would be made to the battery, the CIC, and the bulkheads. There would also be a complete machinery overhaul. The result would be a capacity of seventy aircraft and a maximum speed of 28 knots, the latter insufficient for fast carrier task force operations.

The work would be done at Norfolk, and it was expected to delay completion of the new *Essex*-class fleet carriers *Shangri-La* and *Lake Champlain*, each considerably more valuable than the refitted *Ranger*. Instead, the refit (May–July 1944) was limited to improvements required for training, with facilities to control night fighters, including a new SM height-finding radar. Her flight deck was strengthened and a flight-deck catapult (H 2-1) installed; as partial weight compensation, all of her 5-in guns were landed, leaving her with only light antiaircraft weapons.

Of the seven fleet carriers that the U.S. Navy began

World War II with, only the *Ranger* saw no combat service in the Pacific. She was the slowest of them all and, like the unfortunate *Wasp*, she had no underwater protection. As soon as new carrier completions began to increase the number of carriers, she was relegated to training duty. As the debate over the *Yorktown*s and then over the *Wasp* shows, her major defects were obvious even before the war: beside physical limits on air-group operations, low speed, and a total lack of protection, she could not operate in common Pacific swells nearly as comfortably as could the larger ships. Her design was predicated on an estimate of the minimum efficient carrier size, and in the absence of experience, the bureaus could not estimate that size properly. They thought the *Langley* quite efficient, not realizing until the advent of the two *Lexington*s just how much a carrier could accomplish in moderately heavy seas.

The *Ranger* ended her service as a night-fighter training ship, as shown here, with a new SP radar atop her mast and an SC-2 below it. By this time she was so badly overweight that all of her 5-in guns (as well as their two Mark 33 directors) had to be removed. The stern view was taken in June 1944; the other photograph is undated. Note how the funnels can be tilted, giving the *Ranger* the closest U.S. approximation to a flush-deck carrier prior to the appearance of the *United States* in 1949.

4

The *Yorktown* Class

The *Yorktown*s were in a sense the first modern U.S. carriers. They were the first to be designed on the basis of operational experience with the fleet, as opposed to the experimental *Langley* carriers; and theirs was essentially the design adopted for the *Essex* class, which for many years dominated the American carrier force, at least in a numerical sense. The *Yorktown*s story also illustrates the tension between advocates of a larger number of smaller carriers and a smaller number of larger and more capable ones; but unlike the debates over the *Lexington* and *Ranger* designs, this one derived from operational experience with both types: the *Lexington* and *Saratoga* were taken as representative large carriers, and the *Langley* as a representative small one. Operating experience included behavior in rough weather, an issue that would be raised again and again—it came up most recently in the debates over the size of the *Forrestal* and her successors.

The carrier-size discussions had to consider the total-tonnage limit set by naval-limitation treaties: 52,000 tons. At the time of the *Ranger* design her displacement, 13,800 tons, had been set by the preference for five carriers of moderate size rather than four or fewer larger ones; it seemed to the General Board that enough aviation facilities could be accommodated on 13,800 tons for that to be a satisfactory carrier. The remaining tonnage could be broken into four or more *Ranger*s, three 18,500-ton carriers, or two of 27,000 tons. Or a compromise solution could be accepted: one more *Ranger*, and two 20,700-ton carriers. This last option was particularly attractive, as the General Board considered groups of two carriers tactically useful. It actually adopted this compromise.

Another major factor was the demand for protection, which had been completely lacking in the *Ranger*. This concern paralleled the increased interest in protection for cruisers, which had produced a radical change in design policy in the *New Orleans* class. In fact, when C & R proposed slow-cruiser designs in 1930 that heavily emphasized protection from 8-in fire, this bias was described as characteristic of opinion throughout the Department of the Navy.

The design process began with a 22 May 1931 BuAer letter to the Secretary of the Navy, proposing a shift to an 18,400-ton carrier design in order to achieve

1. A speed of 32.5 knots.
2. Antitorpedo bulkheads for protection intermediate between battleship and cruiser standards (soon protection against cruiser shellfire was added).
3. A horizontal protective deck over the machinery, magazines, and aircraft fuel tanks (later it would be noted that a 2.5-in deck would keep out 1,000-lb bombs dropped from 5,000 feet, which indicates the kind of threat then visualized).
4. Increased internal operational facilities, to consist of
   a) a hangar deck (with 15 feet of clear headroom) devoted exclusively to aircraft stowage.
   b) a change in the arrangement and number of aircraft elevators.
   c) improved bomb handling.

The *Yorktown* (CV 5) at anchor at Hampton Roads, 30 October 1937. She was destined to win fame as a fighting carrier in the early days of World War II and to be lost during the Battle of Midway on 7 June 1942. Note the boat crane alongside the island and the heavy aircraft crane abaft it.

The new carrier *Yorktown*, still flying her builder's flag, is shown running trials off Rockland, Maine, on 12 July 1937. She lacks only her light AA weapons.

d) two flying-off decks. This idea was probably inspired by HMS *Furious*- and *Courageous*-class conversions, and by the Japanese *Kaga* and *Akagi* conversions, all completed before 1930 and all characterized by upper and lower flying-off decks (the lower was a forward extension of the hangar deck); the idea would recur in some of the nuclear-carrier studies of the fifties.

e) improved antiaircraft machine-gun defense using larger caliber guns and eight to twelve 5-in guns.

BuAer hoped to duplicate the flush deck of the *Ranger*, and wanted a single hangar with either a secondary flying-off deck forward or two hangar-deck catapults as an alternative means of rapidly launching the air group. There might also be a second lower hangar adjacent to shops and stores, which might alternatively be used to assemble spare aircraft. There would be four elevators, the two amidships serving both hangars, the two at the ends serving only the upper one; ammunition hoists would directly serve both the flight deck and the open lower flight deck or catapult area of the upper hangar.

This was a great deal to ask, even on 20,700 tons: the *Essex*, 27,100 tons, would be protected against 8-in fire alone and would have only intermediate torpedo protection, with a single open hangar. Thus the evolution of the *Yorktown* design illustrated the usual lesson of reality versus expectation.

At a 27 May General Board hearing on the FY 33 program, for which the new carrier was intended, Captain Lewis Coxe of War Plans stated "that the aircraft carrier should be reconsidered with a view to increasing size. The 13,800 tons is not quite enough for them. I am not prepared to say anything about their armament. I understand the general opinion now is that the 5-inch two purpose gun is considered sufficient.... However, it seems to me that this relegates them to the role of battle line carriers."

That is, without 8-in guns they could not hope to operate independently, since they might well fall victim to one of the numerous heavy cruisers that had been built by Japan as a result of the Washington Treaty. The *Lexington* and *Saratoga*, after all, had been armed with 8-in guns, and Coxe wanted the idea re-examined—as indeed it would be later in the design process. As for size, experience with the *Langley* in rough weather had already shown that 13,800 tons was probably too little. The two big carriers had demonstrated their ability to fly off and land on aircraft in almost any weather. Although BuAer wanted sketch designs of 13,800-ton ships as well as larger ones, the contest appears in retrospect to have been between three units of 18,400 tons and two of 20,700 almost from the outset.

To reduce displacement to 13,800 tons, BuAer was willing to dispense with its double hangar, and allow protection on the level of the 9,600-ton 6-in cruiser then in prospect rather than on a heavy-cruiser level. Eleven-foot hangar headroom would be acceptable, and the catapults might be eliminated as well.

By 1931 operational experience had been obtained; and doctrine for carrier employment made the relative value of high speed much clearer than it had been when the *Ranger* characteristics had been set in 1927. Carriers were to operate in raiding forces or in forces relieving U.S. bases, as strike forces, as scouting and screening forces, and with the battle fleet, in offensive screen or in fleet action. Naturally different carrier characteristics would be suitable to different employment; the unprotected *Ranger* was often described as useful only in the battle line.

Admiral Laning of the Naval War College considered heavy cruisers sufficient for scouting and screening; perhaps cruiser-carriers might be useful for such roles.

> ... The tonnage allowed for aircraft carriers should all be devoted to larger carriers suitable for offensive operations. ... They must have a speed at least equal to cruisers and destroyers. Carriers haven't sufficient air power to stop many cruisers, and if they can't stop them when the cruisers have superior speed, ultimately the cruisers are certain to catch and destroy them. ... at least one carrier ought to be provided to work with the battle line. There is no doubt about it that once the battle line sends up its planes, there is no chance of those planes getting back as long as the fight is going on. They must have somewhere to go and there should be carriers that planes, both from cruisers and from battleships, can go back to to refuel and be taken care of. They may get so many on the carriers that some of the planes will have to go overboard, but the fact remains that we can save the pilots. ...

Admiral Pratt, the CNO, also considered heavy cruiser speed—32.5 knots—essential, but primarily because he wanted his carriers and heavy cruisers to form scouting and offensive striking groups to operate ahead of the battleships. His fleet organization called for one carrier to operate with each of three 8-in cruiser divisions.

Only Commander R. K. Turner of BuAer disagreed; he was willing to accept a lower speed, "its exact determination [to] depend to a certain extent on certain of the other features ... such as the amount of protection and the number of airplanes ... that can be carried. ..." However, even he admitted that the speed of the *Saratoga* and *Lexington* helped prevent the ships from getting separated from the rest of the force, and helped them gain distance to leeward if it was necessary to turn against the wind and launch the planes.

High carrier speed resulted in operational penalties. Admiral Marvell recalled that

> if there are only two [cruisers] with the carrier, the commanding officer of the cruisers would like to have an excess speed of about ten knots over the carrier, on account of the fact that the carrier is so erratic in her movements. She will suddenly make a turn and you have got to get ahead again. ... Three [cruisers are] necessary on account of the fact that you can't regain your position. We caught it once off the coast of Cuba at the end of the last game where the carrier changed course. The *Northampton* was on the starboard bow and the *Memphis* on the port bow and the Island of Cuba was not over fifteen miles on the starboard

beam when the *Trenton* appeared and would have gotten the carrier because the only thing it could do was run away. It could not run away straight because the island was in the way but the *Northampton* was able to interpose. ...

The next issue was protection. Admiral Laning wanted deck protection, because he considered air rather than surface (cruiser or destroyer) attack the primary threat.

> Just the nature of their work draws the aircraft attack to them, because, if you can put the carriers out of business you also put out all the aircraft attached to them. Whenever we play a game at the [War] College, strategical or tactical, the thing each side tries to do first is to put the enemy's air forces out of action. It is essential that be done because the air forces, while they rarely deal a blow that is of itself decisive, nevertheless, the influence of the things aircraft do carries through or becomes cumulative, and has a decisive effect on the outcome. ...
>
> [The only way you can get control of the air is by destroying the carrier.] We formerly thought that by fighting in the air we could get control in the air like we can on the surface, but we find that no number of defensive airplanes can keep off all air attacks. ... Everybody, immediately there is a fight of any kind, seeks to put the enemy's aircraft out of business, and the only way to do that is to ruin the flying decks of his carriers. The only way to do that is with aircraft. If carriers have the speed, it is very difficult for any cruiser to get within gun range of the carrier. ...

In the Naval War College's gaming rules, used to evaluate alternative designs, "one bomb ruins one half the deck and two bombs would put it completely out of commission so that you can't handle the planes. You can't send them up or take them on. That is the rule we work on and it is very nearly correct."

Deck protection would keep the flight deck intact. However, it was not clear whether the fire hazard, about which nothing was as yet known, would not in itself be a major threat to carrier survivability, whatever the level of deck protection. The Naval War College was willing to avoid an evaluation of the fire hazard largely because the carrier would be put out of action more easily by 500-lb (that is, dive-bomber) weapons breaking up her flight deck.

As for active protection (guns) there were two distinct classes: machine guns to defeat dive-bombers and heavier weapons for use against high-altitude (horizontal) bombers. The latter guns were also considered helpful for destroyer attack. The dive-bomber was by far the greatest threat, so that automatic weapons were regarded as more important than 5-in guns. Agitation for the improvement of automatic weapons continued through the thirties, paralleling U.S. work to develop dive-bombers as the primary carrier offensive weapon.

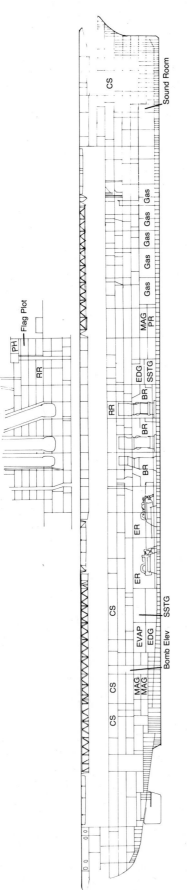

The *Yorktown*'s inboard profile, 1941.

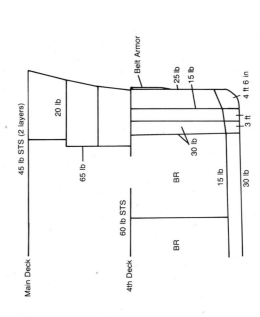

The *Yorktown*'s cross section. The upper deck shown is the hangar deck.

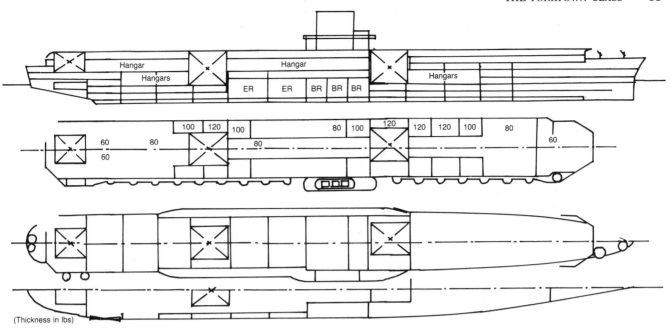

(Thickness in lbs)

Scheme E, a 20,700-ton protected carrier of 1931.

There was also increasing interest in protection against gunfire. In part this might be traced to a general movement away from unprotected ships such as "tin-clad" heavy cruisers; in the cruiser case, this shift resulted in the *New Orleans* class. Too, recent maneuvers showed that carriers often did find themselves within gun range. Commander Turner noted that "a carrier, which takes so long to build and is so important a combat unit of the fleet, ought not to be [designed] in such a way that ordinary gun fire would sink her. It might put her out of commission as a carrier but she could be saved and be back in commission as a carrier with a new outfit of planes after a comparatively small amount of work on her deck."

The other important issue was aviation features, in particular the speed with which the carrier could launch and recover her aircraft. Commander Turner continued: "Admiral Reeves, I understand, thinks that three flights can be taken off of the *Saratoga* and *Lexington* in one day provided the entire day is used, but it is seldom that the tactical situation would be such that more than two flights could be taken off in one day, since it is probable that attacks would not be made the first thing in the morning and the last thing at night. In most of the maneuvers not more than one attack flight has been taken off in one day."

Admiral Rock of C & R agreed that flight-deck protection would be useful, especially since bombs penetrating the flight deck would destroy the hangars. One participant in the hearing recalled that in the 1920 bombing tests a bomb penetrating the forecastle of the old battleship *Virginia* blew the whole forecastle deck off. Rock felt that if bomb damage could be limited to indentation—as the British armored flight deck was later claimed to do—the danger of bombs would be eliminated and the carrier

could get her planes on and off more easily. The problem, as in later attempts to secure flight-deck protection, was the weight required to defeat realistic attacks. For example, the German *Ostfriesland* had a 1.875-in upper armor deck (including 1 inch of steel equivalent to the U.S. STS) that was unable to stop bombs dropped on it in the 1920 bombing tests. It would take 2.2 inches of armor to stop a 2,000-lb bomb dropped from 4,000 feet, which in 1931 was considered a realistic threat. Such a deck was entirely beyond the top-weight capacity of a 20,000-ton carrier—as indeed it would be beyond that of a much larger ship a decade later, given standard U.S. aeronautical features.

The latter were clearly as important as armor protection. Indeed, throughout the thirties the U.S. Navy promoted a policy of achieving carrier security by striking against the enemy carriers first. It followed that success would come, not from an ability to absorb damage nearly so much as from an ability to launch the largest possible strike in the shortest possible time. There would be little belief in the efficacy of defensive fighters until about 1940, and that would be justified only by the advent of radar for early warning. Thus the *Yorktown*-design history shows early hopes for a combination of heavy protection and improved air facilities, the former being sacrificed to maintain the latter. Some of the air features BuAer wanted appear odd to modern eyes, but all are understandable in the context of operations as they were conceived in 1931.

The two-level flight deck was supported for several reasons. According to Admiral Taylor of War Plans, "as it is now you have to leave half your deck for planes coming back. It is very spectacular to see the *Saratoga* and *Lexington* going off with a whole deck full of planes and have them fly off . . . [but] not one of them could get back until all those are flown off." The carriers even had to fly the full deck load off before they could launch a single observation plane. Admiral Taylor expected to "use the planes on battleships for observation [but one time] the weather came on rough [and] the carrier was dependent on securing her own information. In order to get this information we had to fly off all these planes and they circled around until they could get these two observation planes off and then it was too late."

Commander Turner stated that "the biggest thing that interferes with rapid effective operations is the rearrangement of the planes required for getting the planes off that you want, and [the difficulty of] flying planes on at the same time that you have other planes parked to fly off. . . . The width that you have got on a flight deck is in that respect very important as are also the number of elevators and the size of the hangars."

One solution, as mentioned earlier, was a two-deck carrier, with aircraft flying off both the primary deck and a lower flight deck leading directly from the hangar. Aircraft could be launched from the lower deck even when the upper was being used for landing-on or for parking. There were several objections. The lower flight deck would be wet, and water entering it might destroy aircraft in the hangar. Aircraft warming up to take off from it would fill the enclosed hangar with exhaust gases. Neither flight deck would be satisfactory: the upper one would be too short. Aircraft rolling down the lower one would have to avoid the supports of the upper flight deck. BuAer did want studies, but it was skeptical, since Britain and Japan had had problems, even operating a considerably smaller number of planes.

Alternatively, a conventional one-flight-deck ship could operate with a clear deck, landing aircraft being struck below at once to maintain the ability to launch aircraft at all times. That was, in fact, standard British practice, and it was shunned by the U.S. Navy because of the limit it imposed on the tempo of air operation. The proposed solution was faster service (by four rather than the usual two or three elevators) between the flight and hangar decks. Even so, the need to bring heavy aircraft up to the flight deck would slow operations somewhat. In return, it would be far easier to launch small aircraft (which might be parked on the flight deck) rapidly, no matter how much of the air group was aboard. Experiences seemed to show that it was seldom necessary to launch heavy aircraft rapidly, but that during the flying day the small aircraft very frequently had to be launched and recovered, even with the heavy aircraft aboard. If (as in standard U.S. practice) all operational aircraft rode the flight deck, the "spot" of heavy aircraft ready for launch would fill the recovery area, and preparation for the recovery of light aircraft would preclude a quick launch of aircraft parked forward on deck to clear the arresting gear.

The final design incorporated, not the secondary flying-off deck, but its functional equivalent, a hangar-deck athwartships catapult. Similar catapults appeared in the *Wasp* and *Essex* classes and in the *Midway* design. Other navies, such as the Royal Navy, did not experience the same problem—they struck aircraft below as they landed, so that there was never the flight-deck congestion of an entire air group parked forward after landing. The standard U.S. air tactic, however, was the deck-load launch, in which the carrier generally had either the forward or the after end of her flight deck entirely covered by that deck load. Hence the interest in finding a means to fly off a single scout or observation airplane. As for elevators, in the end the design showed three.

Another concept was the double-ended flight deck, with arresting gear placed at both ends of the flight deck so that aircraft could land over the bow if the carrier steamed aft. It was fitted to all U.S. carriers during the thirties and was only eliminated in 1944. According to Admiral Laning, "we very frequently find in operation at the War College that you have to go before the wind and launch your planes over the stern. It all depends on the wind. A carrier should have a wind from ahead to launch its planes but sometimes you can't run a carrier into the wind because the enemy is there. . . ."

The antiaircraft battery would have to contend with both heavy (level) bombers and dive-bombers; the latter could be countered only by automatic weapons that would compete for space with the larger dual-purpose guns. Although ideally three 5-in guns were required to engage an attacking airplane, BuOrd suspected, correctly, that no more than eight 5-in guns could be accommodated, two on each bearing. Dive-bombing was the prime threat, and only machine guns could supply enough volume of fire to destroy a dive-bomber in the very short time available. Only with the advent of the VT (proximity) fuze in 1942 would heavier guns become a useful counter to such attackers. Meanwhile, the best BuOrd could do against the dive-bomber was to provide as many 0.50-cal machine guns as possible: the characteristics the General Board finally adopted called for forty. The threat was so severe that a heavier weapon, the 1.1-in machine cannon, was pressed ahead on a crash basis.

Overall, the hearing suggested that, whatever the benefits of a small-carrier design, it would probably be ineffective. Admiral Rock defended the *Ranger* design, but had to admit that boosting the speed of a 13,800-ton carrier to 32.5 knots would require a shorter, lighter hull (680 by 74 versus 730 by 80 feet) and the abandonment of underwater protection,

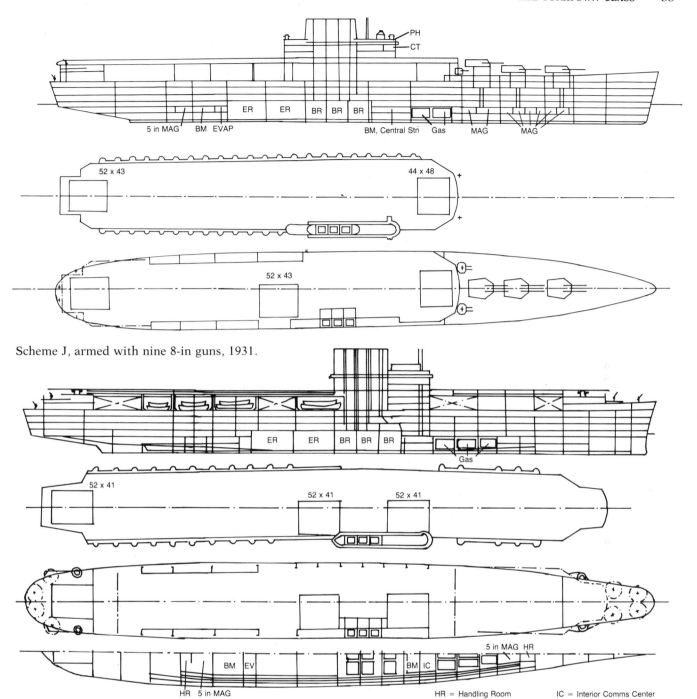

Scheme J, armed with nine 8-in guns, 1931.

Scheme I, the 20,000-ton carrier the became the *Yorktown*, 1931. Note the arrangement of the 5-in AA guns at the ends.

although perhaps not protection against 6-in fire. On 18,000 tons he could provide heavy-cruiser armor (but not flight-deck protection) and what he called 60 percent underwater protection (three bulkheads instead of the five of a battleship). Aircraft capacity would roughly match that of the *Ranger*. On 20,700 tons he could provide four rather than three elevators and heavy-cruiser armor—but still only incomplete underwater protection. All of these designs would have eight 5-in and eight heavy machine guns. Rock was not very hopeful of getting the second flight deck at any of these displacements because of its weight

and the space it required. He also could not guarantee a flush flight deck, which would have meant using folding funnels; no one knew how the *Ranger*'s horsepower would perform. A 13,800-ton, 32.5-kt ship would need roughly twice the *Ranger*'s horsepower (101,000 versus 53,000 SHP), resulting in twice the volume of hot gases to be dispersed.

The *Langley*'s hinged funnels had been acceptable (albeit with far less gas than the *Ranger* would produce), indeed much superior to those of the *Saratoga* and the *Lexington*, which "like to run a little off the wind in order to bring the gas away from the ship";

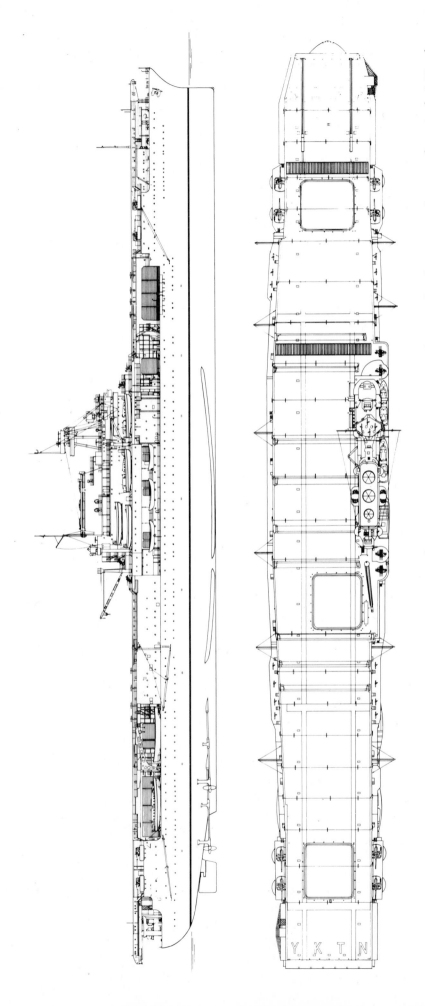

The *Yorktown* (CV 5), in 1940, only slightly modified since her completion. She was armed with eight 5-in/38, four quadruple 1.1-in, and twenty-four single 0.50-cal machine guns. The plan view shows aircraft outriggers extended; they are stowed in the elevation. Note the forward arresting wires and the platform for an LSO to control over-the-bow landings, as well as the two windbreaks.

and BuAer thought folding stacks without any island structure were essential. Very similar aviation demands would be made twenty years later in the *United States* (CVB 58) and *Forrestal* (CVA 59) designs, which again were expected to suffer from severe smoke-disposal problems.

Commander Turner of BuAer had to admit, however, that in fact the island structure produced little in the way of hazardous wind currents; the chief adverse effect of an island structure was exhaust gas. However, such would be a problem no matter how it was vented, and the U.S. constructors (unlike their contemporaries in Japan) never were fully satisfied with anything but a vertical funnel. Indeed, it was the smoke problem that restored the island structure in what became the *Yorktown* design.

Actual aircraft capacity carried little explicit weight. For example, the *Ranger* had been designed for a maximum complement of 108, although her normal complement was intended to be 75 plus 8 spares. In fact, Commander Turner of BuAer credited her with a maximum of 90. The *Lexington* and *Saratoga* had operating complements of 70, based on two small to one large plane; their maximum operating complement was estimated at 110. However, the effective air group depended on the size of the deck area available for spotting aircraft. For example, in the winter 1930 maneuvers, the big carriers flew off 82 aircraft spotted on the flight deck at daylight, although later in the day they operated an effective air group of 52. The reduction was due to a requirement to reserve both flying-on and flying-off areas; spotting was restricted to amidships. Turner noted that the 90 and 110 figures were based, instead, on a complete deck spot *and* a full hangar below. Thus the *Ranger* could spot 76 on deck. The *Ranger*, *Yorktown*, and *Wasp* all had folding outriggers to enlarge the effective deck space and, therefore, the striking power of the ship. It is not clear just when this innovation was conceived.

At this time the standard air group consisted of one squadron of eighteen heavy-attack bombers; one of twelve scouts (eighteen on the *Ranger*); and two of fighters, either single- or two-seat. At the time of the hearings, BuAer was planning a new air group of four eighteen-plane squadrons: one of dive-bombers with 1,000-lb bombs, one of large single-seat fighters with 500-pounders, one of scouts, and one of pure fighters. An alternative proposal was to have one squadron of heavy aircraft usable either as high-level bombers or torpedo planes, one of 1,000-lb dive-bombers, one of long-range two-seat fighters to be employed as scouts, and one of single-seat fighters capable of dive-bombing with 500-lb bombs. There was also a proposal to include in carrier air groups a limited number of very long-range aircraft (at least 1,000 nautical

miles) for "strategic scouting." In fact the two-seat scout and heavy dive-bomber categories were merged in the VSB, or scout-bomber, class, the outstanding example of which was the Douglas Dauntless, the SBD. The requirement that single-seat fighters be able to dive-bomb was abandoned, as was the "strategic-scout" concept.

Armed with these considerations, Preliminary Design retired to sketch 13,800-, 18,400-, and 20,700-ton carriers, all with substantial protection. Indeed, despite the *Langley* experience, BuAer thought for a time that a 31-kt, 13,800-ton scheme B would be selected. It combined substantial protection (better than CAs 37–8) with a wider flight deck and more aircraft than the two faster alternatives. Preliminary Design observed that the half-way point, 18,400 tons, was at best a poor compromise, and it was abandoned.

In contrast to the *Ranger* studies, all of these designs included large island structures incorporating uptakes. BuAer merely demanded that fixed stacks be of the greatest possible height, so that pilots could fly in below their gases. BuAer was forced, first, to accept that a fast (32.5-kt) flush-decker could not be built. At a 30 June 1931 meeting it capitulated, accepting the proposal that future studies include a bridge forward of the stack, with passage around it, a flying control station just forward of the stack, and as an alternative, a bridge under the forward end of the flight deck. By this time, moreover, operations of the *Lexington* and *Saratoga* had shown that the "island type" did not make plane landings hazardous.

One idea was to move the stack forward so as to leave the maximum length of landing-on deck. At the 30 June meeting, Turner insisted that the flight deck be 85 feet wide, 80 abeam the stack; he was told that (on a 13,800-tonner) this might be done in the 31- but not the 32.5-kt ship. Ultimately a scheme in which the flight deck bulged outwards to port abreast the stack was adopted.

Two 20,700-ton schemes, D and E, were to have the *Ranger* air group, protection as in heavy cruisers, and 32.5-kt speed. Underwater protection could not have the depth (that is, number of torpedo bulkheads or resistive power) usually provided in a battleship; but "protection against the explosion of bombs alongside is probably more important because [it is] much more likely to be needed. Inasmuch as the penetrative effect upon the hull to be anticipated from a bomb exploding at a distance is less than that of a torpedo exploding in immediate contact, whereas the side area [affected] may easily be greater, [we have provided] fewer bulkheads carried to a greater height above water than in battleship practice."

Three features could not simultaneously be realized on 20,700 tons: the double flight deck, the

Table 4-1. Evolution of Schemes for the *Yorktown* Design, 1931

	CV 4	A	B	C	D	E	F
Std Disp't (tons)	13,800	13,800	13,800	13,800	20,700	20,700	20,700
Trial Disp't (tons)	—	—	—	—	—	—	—
LWL (ft)	730	675	675	650	800	820	775
Beam (ft)	80	74	74	74	80	80	—
Draft (trial) (ft)	20.8	21.25	21.25	22.0	20.5	23	—
Depth (ft)	51.0	42.0	42.0	42.0	55.0	64.0	—
SHP	53,000	105,000	77,000	122,500	101,000	99,000	107,000
Speed (kts)	29	32.5	31	32.5	32.5	32.5	32.5
Radius (15 kts)	10,000	10,000	10,000	10,000	—	—	10,000
Battery: 8-in	—	—	—	—	—	—	—
5-in	8	8	8	8	8	8	8
Torp Bkds	—	—	—	—	—	—	4
Pro Against	—	6-in	*	†	CA 37/8	CA 37/8	6-in
FD (ft)	726 × 86	670 × 80	670 × 80	645 × 74	575 × 80 255 × 45	730 × 74	715 × 80 640 × 69
Hangar (ft)	560 × 64	500 × 57	500 × 57	475 × 56	430 × 66	426 × 66	—
Elevators (ft)	2 52 × 41 1 40 × 35	1 52 × 41 1 52 × 35 1 40 × 35	1 52 × 41 1 52 × 35 1 40 × 35	1 52 × 41 1 52 × 35 1 40 × 35	3 52 × 41 1 40 × 35	2 52 × 41 1 40 × 35	3 52 × 41 1 40 × 35
Aircraft	83	65	65	57	77	74	90

Note: Scheme I was the basis of the *Yorktown* design, scheme H, for the *Wasp*. There was also an I1 design with 6 6-in guns plus the 8 5-in of scheme I. Schemes A through H are dated July 1931; I through L (and variations) were dated August (when H and I were chosen), the others were presented that November.

*Somewhat better than CA 37–38.
†Somewhat worse than CA 37–38.
‡"Scant."
§5-in/40 (gun built as 5-in/38).

armored flight deck, and the protected hangar. Scheme D provided for a double flight deck, E a single armored one plus provision "for stowing a small number of planes with wings folded in auxiliary hangars placed low in the hull and partially protected against gun fire." Each was designed to mount thirty-two heavy (0.50-cal) machine guns as well as the usual eight 5-in AA guns. Air groups were estimated at seventy-seven for D, seventy-four for E, sixty-five for A and B, fifty-seven for the 650-ft C, and eighty-three for the *Ranger*.

Preliminary Design also produced scheme F, a single-deck carrier armored against 6-in fire, with a ninety-plane air group. It was the direct ancestor of the *Yorktown* design. Four elevators were provided, as in scheme D (three in the single-deck scheme E). An alternative scheme G showed how poor a compromise 18,400 tons was: eighty-three aircraft could be carried, and there would be three torpedo bulkheads, but protection against 6-in fire was scanty at best. It would have been pointless to pursue the scheme.

A General Board hearing concluded that 13,800 tons was too little; instead C & R was ordered to try alternative designs on 20,000 and 15,200 tons. That is, the board looked to the allowable carrier tonnage, and considered adding 1,400 tons (deducted from two ships of 20,700) to the third class of ships, which

would be unsatisfactory at best but which could be improved by growth from 13,800 to 15,200 tons. Thus Preliminary Design (and the General Board) always had to juggle two designs simultaneously. Two schemes, H of 15,200 tons and I of 20,000, were presented to the General Board on 2 September 1931. The board liked both, and proposed that the two of 20,000 tons be laid down in FY 33, followed by the 15,200-tonner in FY 34.

The Depression intervened. The two 20,000-ton carriers were ultimately built with industrial-recovery funds, and the smaller carrier, which became the *Wasp*, was not laid down until 1936. Carried out in parallel, both designs showed protection against 6-in shellfire, although only scheme I showed underwater protection, and each was to have eight 5-in DP guns. Aircraft capacities were, respectively, seventy and ninety. Characteristics for the large carrier proposed by the board on 7 October 1931 included a 708- by 80-ft flight deck, two double-ended hangar-deck catapults, three express elevators, forty 50-cal machine guns, and 6-in protection (10,000–20,000 yards at a 60° target angle), including bulk gasoline stowage (but no armored flight deck). The smaller carrier would have a 630 by 80-ft deck; otherwise she matched the 20,000-tonner. Her protection would cover magazines only. Indeed, an internal C &

G	H	I	J	K	L	M	N	O
18,400	15,200	20,000	25,000	25,000	20,000	15,200	27,000	27,000
—	17,400	22,700	28,000	28,000	22,700	17,400	30,250	30,250
745	690	770	800	840	740	665	900	830
—	77.5	80.3	88.0	86.0	81.0	78.5	87.0	89.0
—	21.7	24.6	25.5	25.0	25.0	22.3	25.0	26.5
—	50.0	51.5	52.0	53.5	52.0	50.5	53.5	55.0
107,000	120,000	120,000	138,000	132,500	105,000	108,000	131,000	140,000
32.5	32.5	32.5	32.5	32.5	31	31	32.5	32.5
10,000	10,000	10,000	10,000	10,000	10,000	10,000	10,000	10,000
—	—	—	9	—	6	4	—	10
8	8§	8§	8	16	8	8	16	8
3	—	1½	3	4½	2	—	4½	3
6-in‡	6-in	6-in	8-in	6-in	6-in	6-in*	6-in	8-in
685×80	630×80	708×80	540×86	732×86	500×80	445×80	780×86	555×86
610×67	570×66	645×68	520×74					
—	—	—	—	670×74	440×68	390×60	715×74	530×74
2 52×41	2 52×41	53×41	3	3	2	2	3	3
1 40×35	1 40×35							
83	70	90	65	100	60	45	108	68

R memorandum would later note that the 15,200-ton schemes were not satisfactory because of the attempt to embody in them characteristics that were too severe. Of the air groups, 40 percent in the 20,000-tonner and 33.5 percent in the 15,200-tonner would be of the largest carrier type. Endurance was set at 12,000 nautical miles at 16 knots, although C & R was to try for, respectively, 17,250 and 15,000 nautical miles.

There the story might be considered ended, but in fact the Secretary of the Navy was prompted to return the General Board's characteristics on 14 October.

He noted that the *Lexington*s, with their 8-in batteries, were now well liked, and asked for new studies of carriers armed with such weapons, the largest allowable under the Washington Treaty. The largest carriers that could be built on the tonnage remaining to the United States were two of 27,000 tons, and the General Board asked for studies of 20,000-, 15,200-, and 27,000-ton ships.

Contemporary interest in a "flying-deck cruiser," a 10,000-cruiser with a short flight deck, was strong. The secretary may also have been influenced by the concept of independent operations raised in the May hearing—which would, incidentally, arise again in the case of the *Midway*s.

The new set of studies was actually somewhat more extensive than what the secretary had asked for; it included 6-in guns and a 25,000-ton ship. On both the large displacements pure carrier and 8-in gun types were compared. They are listed in table 4-1, and are best described as unimpressive, with relatively small air groups on even the largest displacements. On smaller hulls, such as that of scheme M, not even the gun battery was numerous enough to be effective. The General Board reported on 10 December that mounting an 8-in battery on a carrier would involve shortening the flight deck unduly and reducing the number of planes materially.

The studies suggested 25,000 tons as the lower limit for an 8-in gun-armed carrier; even she would take only 65 planes, so that two such ships would provide only 130 planes and two flight decks. The board's program would add three decks and 250 planes—nearly twice as many aircraft. In addition the long stretch of forecastle (about 250 feet) on the 25,000-ton 8-inch carrier and the turrets thereon offer a serious hazard to planes. Large planes, heavily loaded, which at stalling speed are quite sluggish, may not have gained sufficient flying speed by the time they reach the end of the flight deck. This danger might be augmented by eddy currents set up by the turrets and bow. These hazards may be accepted in the flying-deck cruiser with its comparatively short deck, as it will carry only light planes; but they accentuate the need of a long deck for carriers which will send off all types of planes. The flight deck should be long enough to permit the safe launching of heavy bombers on short notice under normal operating conditions and with little or no wind. For efficient operation this envisages a deck long enough for the take-off, plus a considerable space for planes spotted forward of the barrier, and the area necessary for landing planes.... The flight deck of a carrier should be at least 630 feet long and if possible over 700 feet [versus 540 for 25,000 and 555 for 27,000 tons].... Even if we were to reduce the 8-inch battery to a minimum—one turret—on the 20,000 ton carrier or to two on either the 25,000 ton or 27,000 ton carrier, the gain in flight deck would not be sufficient to justify the 8-inch gun installation.

Schemes for 6-in guns on 20,000 tons were also tried. (I-1 had two 6-in turrets abeam, so that the flight deck could be carried forward at reduced width; I-2 through I-5 were of reduced speed; L-1 and L-2 had three or two triple 6-in turrets in place of the two triple 8-in of scheme L.) None of these schemes was particularly attractive: 6-in guns were not so valuable as to be worth a serious loss in air group or even in flight-deck width. Alternatively, three 6-inchers could be mounted in broadside positions in each waist in the space reserved for the forward a catapult.

The Secretary of the Navy, assuaged, approved the General Board characteristics on 15 December 1931, and C & R submitted a sketch plan on the twenty-eighth. At this point the sketch design showed 5-in guns arranged as in the *Ranger*, two on each quadrant in flight-deck cutouts. The flight deck length itself had been determined by the General Board characteristics rather than by the length of the hull, which in turn was a matter of optimum hull form for speed. Numerous questions, it turned out, remained as yet unresolved, including the matter of underwater protection, which had been emphasized so often in the evolution of characteristics.

A first general-arrangement plan was completed on 1 February 1932. However, the magazine and gasoline stowage proved too small, and BuAer asked that the forward end of the island be moved about 25 feet aft to facilitate operation of the forward arresting gear (for landing while the ship was steaming astern); the after end would be extended back 20 to 25 feet to make up for the space lost forward and also to allow the crane located immediately aft of the island structure to serve the midships elevator. The bureau also wanted 17 feet of hangar clearance, and it was suggested that the 5-in battery be relocated to lengthen the flight deck. In addition, the stowage of boats on the hangar deck conflicted with aircraft stowage.

In order to protect the enlarged magazines, the armor deck and side belt fore and aft over magazines and gasoline stowage had to be raised from the first platform (as in cruisers) to the fourth deck, a location that would be standard in the *Essex* class as well. An increased complement of officers required additional quarters, and it was proposed that the flight deck be raised 8 feet so that the admiral's, captain's, and staff offices could be placed amidships abreast the island structure on the gallery deck. In consequence the machinery had to be moved aft 20 feet, the island itself shortened 8 feet, and the flight deck lengthened by 4 feet, which gave a net increase of 32 feet forward of the island.

We agreed to give Aeronautics a clear head room of 17'-0 hangar deck and we had allowed 8'-0 above this for head room in quarters in flight deck structure. Investigating fuselage stowage under flight deck showed that they projected down into the hangar so far that it was impracticable to maneuver planes under them. The head room was therefore increased two feet to give about the same as *Ranger*.

It was found that the hangar area was about 1000 sq. ft. less than *Ranger* due to the 35-0 motor boats being stowed in the catapult bay aft and for'd. We tried to remove these boats and nest them in 50'-0 boats, but deck height under the gallery would not permit. So it was suggested [that the] flight deck [be extended] on starboard side abreast island structure for the location of these boats [as it was done in the] *Saratoga* arrangement.

The next problem was torpedo protection. "Due to the relatively shallow draft (24-0) and the limited protection space inside the vessel, it is evident that sufficient protection against torpedo explosions at normal running depth of 15-0 is not possible. Also the shape of the bilge is such as not to be efficient for bulkhead attachment, as compared with a battleship."

Just how inefficient the bilge's shape was C & R did not realize. It submitted preliminary plans to the underwater protection experts at the model basin, who observed that not only would there be less liquid and air in the system than in a battleship's, but that because a very round bilge had been accepted for better powering, a torpedo would strike at a point where there would be almost no air space. "A 400 lb torpedo charge exploding in contact would blow completely through the protection, fluid or no fluid [filling]; and the extent of the damage behind would depend largely on the chance as to the particular size and kind of projectiles which would be thrown through."

The only way out was to accept a much fuller midships section (coefficient 0.95 instead of 0.89) with the consequent increase in required power and machinery weight, which would be unpleasant in a ship limited so tightly by treaty. In this way the outer compartment of the protective system could be ex-

The *Yorktown* is shown in service, probably about 1939, fully equipped, with her palisade rigged to protect the utility floatplanes from wind-over-the-deck. Note the catapult sponson protruding from the catapult bay just abaft her forward 5-in guns; there was a similar sponson on the starboard side.

tended to within 4 feet of the bottom of the ship. An incidental problem was that, in order to get a fuller midships section, the designers had to take volume out of the ends of the ship, which resulted in the finest-ended ship in the navy. The fine ends in turn supplied relatively little buoyancy, so that the ship would have to withstand about 2 percent greater bending stresses in a seaway; but it was felt that this increase would be balanced by the deeper bilges. All of this difficulty was accepted on the ground that the ship was designed to resist air attack, meaning both torpedo attack and bomb attack. The torpedo protective system would also resist the effects of near misses, although the underwater protection experts noted that in tests on the hull of the uncompleted battleship *Washington* in 1924, a 1,000-lb charge exploded 40 to 50 feet from the ship, "drove in the shell over a very large area and flooded numerous compartments."

The other side of protection was the requirement to resist 6-in shellfire, and this conflicted with torpedo protection, since the designers tried to save weight by using heavy torpedo bulkheads (30-lb nickel steel), each of which counted as equivalent to 0.42 inches of armor. Unfortunately the design of the antitorpedo system was predicated on the elastic behavior of the bulkheads and their light weight. (If the bulkheads did shatter, the resulting pieces would cut into bulkheads deeper in the system). The characteristics equated to 4-in belt and bulkheads, but with three heavy torpedo bulkheads this could be reduced to 3.25 inches of belt over the magazines forward and 2.75 inches over the other vitals further aft (frames 35 to 64 versus 64 to 168). The belt was covered by a 60-lb STS protective deck, thinned to 40 pounds outside of no. 2 torpedo bulkhead. In addition, a 30-lb STS longitudinal bulkhead was run between frames 35 and 168 between the third and fourth decks to avoid flooding the fourth deck in the event of side damage above the belt (in battle condition it was estimated that the fourth deck would be only 3 feet 2

inches above the waterline). The new design also incorporated the new longitudinal (rather than the former transverse) structure for better strength at reduced weight.

From the point of view of protection, the greatest shortcoming of the design was that fire and engine rooms did not alternate, so that a torpedo penetrating the relatively poor underwater protection could immobilize the ship. Compartmentation was good enough to save one of these ships from destruction, but a BuShips war damage report would suggest that the *Hornet* was lost precisely because she was immobilized, and because U.S. forces were unable to tow her out of the battle area. Ironically, when she was ordered built to the *Yorktown* design, C & R was advocating alternating the engine and fire spaces (as they were installed in the much smaller *Wasp*), and BuEng hoped to install more compact high-pressure, high-temperature machinery, which would have been easier to subdivide. These proposals were rejected by the General Board in view of the urgent need for the new carrier.

On this basis contract plans were begun about 1 March 1932, but they were suspended so that work could begin on Heavy Cruiser 39 (the *Quincy*), for which Congress had appropriated funds; no money at all had been allotted any new carriers. There was, therefore, a considerable gap in time before the carrier design question arose again; money became available only under the National Industrial Recovery Act of 16 June 1933. At once C & R asked the General Board whether any changes in the 1932 plans were warranted.

C & R wanted to rearrange the 5-in battery to reduce the notches cut for them in the flight deck, placing three guns forward (one on the centerline in the bows) and five aft (one on the centerline in the extreme stern, four in the original sponsons). This new arrangement, by extending the deck forward, would increase flight-deck length to 729 feet, where the characteristics originally called for 708. Moreover, 5-in arcs for both high angles and for surface fire would be improved, and air flow forward might be smoothed if retractable plate wind breaks were built over no. 2 and 3 guns. In September 1932 BuOrd had proposed installation of the new quadruple 1.1-in machine cannon, a weapon intended specifically to counter dive-bombers; C & R wanted to provide four, replacing sixteen 0.50-cal machine guns on a one-for-one basis (albeit hardly on a weight-for-weight basis). Finally, the General Board had just approved deletion of torpedo stowage in the *Ranger*, and C & R wanted to know whether it could do the same in the new design.

The General Board approved both gunnery suggestions as advances in both defensive (antiaircraft) and offensive (air) characteristics; but it disapproved the elimination of torpedo stowage as a drastic cut in offensive antiship capabilities. They had been eliminated from the *Ranger* (December 1931) only as an economy measure. The CNO approved the General Board's action on 20 June, and the Secretary of the Navy concurred on 21 June.

In fact BuAer was not satisfied with the flight-deck extension it had won; due to the improved performance and heavier bomb loads of aircraft already in service or being contemplated, 1931 standards of flight-deck length were no longer adequate for an air group of about ninety aircraft. On 11 November 1933 the bureau called for further rearrangement of the 5-in battery to obtain the maximum possible flight deck; 794 feet (with a usable length of 778, as compared with 713 out of the then-contemplated 729). Costs would be minor: a delay of two to three months in the start of construction; an increase of about 400 tons (which would cut the remaining carrier from 15,200 to 14,400 tons); a setback of $500,000–$750,000; negligible loss in speed (0.1 to 0.2 knots) and GM (3 inches, an increase in the period of roll from 16.4 to 16.8 seconds); and reduction in the height of the belt above the waterline (3 feet 3 inches reduced to 2 feet 11 inches).

The C & R plan was predicated on retaining the two centerline mounts; the extended flight deck would limit their antiaircraft elevation to 20° when firing on the beam, and even this would require a substantial narrowing of the forward end of the flight deck (from 78 feet at 40 feet from the end to 56 feet 9 inches at the end). In addition, eight 0.50-cal machine guns would have to be relocated from the after galleries to the island, which would merely answer the fleet's criticism that the galleries were unsatisfactory because of overhanging wings.

BuAer and C & R had considerable support from the aviators, for an additional 6,000 tons should have bought more than 14 feet of flight deck. Flight-deck length, an aviation characteristic, seemed far more

important than any gunnery feature, and flight-deck length would be served best by going even further and mounting all the 5-in guns on sponsons, disregarding the loss in fore and aft fire. If, as some suggested, astern fire was by far the most important (since a carrier surprised by a surface ship would flee), then it would be worthwhile to extend the deck to the bow. A survey of carrier operating personnel established that if the flight deck were extended aft, it would pay to move the after elevator aft, running arresting wires over it. Similarly, the forward arresting gear would be moved forward. "The forward arresting gear will be very valuable, and its installation is favored. In this connection, the ship should have a backing speed of at least 20 knots and the astern control should be good, in order to facilitate use of the forward arresting gear. All portions of the forward arresting gear, and of the forward barriers, except the actual wires, should house flush with the deck."

The CO of the *Saratoga* wanted the 5-in guns moved so that the width of the flight deck at its ends would be at least 80 feet. He considered the galleries most useful for stations and for the escape of a flight-deck crew of several hundred in the event of accidents; as designed they were too narrow and too far below flight-deck level (rather than 3 to 4 feet below as desired). All machine guns should be removed from the galleries. Similarly, the CO of the *Ranger* would "accept . . . as a relatively cheap price to pay, the resultant reduction in firing arcs and in width of the forward and after portions of the flight deck. It may be noted in passing that the fire control problems would at the same time be simplified, at least as far as parallax is concerned" (if all the 5-inch guns were to go onto sponsons).

All of this seemed reasonable, and the General Board approved the C & R scheme (approved by the Secretary of the Navy on 20 November). However, BuAer, encouraged by suggestions that all the 5-in guns be mounted in sponsons, asked for even more the following June. Once more, it could be argued that little would be lost, and even that antiaircraft effectiveness would increase. This time the General Board refused. Further extension of the flight deck would cost $125,000–$250,000, and would require the use of light alloys of questionable effectiveness in order to remain within top-weight limits. As for a longer flight deck, the new controllable-pitch aircraft propellers could be relied on to cut takeoff roll by as much as 30 percent, and a third elevator had been supplied to so facilitate plane handling that a larger area would be available for takeoff than had originally been contemplated. Surely the 65 feet already added would be enough. On the other hand, the relocation of the 5-in guns was approved on the ground that they would improve antiaircraft efficiency and even reduce the number of personnel required for ammunition handling.

The Secretary of the Navy signed this suggestion on 13 July, but BuAer had not given up. In a letter of 12 August endorsed by the CinC U.S. Fleet, it argued that the board had misunderstood the consequence of controllable pitch, which was merely to balance the higher performance of the new aircraft. There were bound to be serious problems in spotting the ninety-four aircraft assigned, and the hangar would be congested. Moreover, a bomb elevator had been placed in the center of the hangar deck to serve the newly relocated after magazines (frame 149), which had been advocated strongly by the forces afloat as a useful addition to the forward bomb supply system. However, the bomb elevator would require an area of clear deck around it, which would have been balanced by a longer flight deck. Without the longer deck a good deal of the advantage gained would be lost.

Furthermore, "the wartime [possibility that] part of the flight deck [might be] shot away cannot be overlooked. In anticipation of this type of damage the Bureau of Aeronautics is planning to have two way arresting gear wires available at all parts of the flight deck. Under this damaged condition the length of the remaining intact deck is a measure of the carrier's residual fighting power...."

As for the third elevator, it could not substitute for a longer deck, as was clear from the experience of the CO of the *Ranger*, who would have liked more length despite his ship's after elevator. Even so, the secretary found the General Board's views persuasive in his endorsement of 6 September 1934.

BuAer remained unconvinced and reopened the question in November. A compromise solution might be to wait and see how the weights went (keeping in mind the problem of how much would be left for the next carrier), while building in enough strength for later extension of the flight deck. The bureau noted that since the main reasons for rejection had been cost, the fear of bow damage in a seaway, and the problem of aluminum used for structure, it might be wise to extend the flight deck by the stern only. Sixteen feet would cost only 35–40 tons, $50,000–$75,000. In the end a compromise solution, allowing for a later flight-deck extension, was adopted. It was approved on 17 November by the Secretary of the Navy.

The ships were completed with both hangar and flight-deck catapults, rather than with the pair of athwartship double-acting hangar types originally contemplated. The prototype H Mk I was tested in 1935; it could launch a 5,500-lb aircraft at 45 mph in a length of 34 feet. Its success led to the H Mk II of the *Yorktown* and *Wasp* classes, which could launch a 7,000-lb aircraft at 70 mph (in prototype form it could launch 5,500 pounds at 65 mph in 55 feet); it was later developed into the H 2-1 (11,000 pounds at 70 mph in 73 feet) for escort carriers and also for the *Enterprise* as refitted in wartime. The first dead load was fired from the *Yorktown* on 25 July 1939, and the catapults of both ships were later tested with 03U observation aircraft and with SBC-3 dive-bombers. The hangar deck H Mk II was seldom used. For example, during FY 40 the *Enterprise* fired a total of fifty-five catapult shots, nineteen from the starboard flight-deck unit, seventeen from the portside one, and only nineteen from the hangar deck. However, with the catapults fully tested, use fell off, so that during FY 41 she fired only twenty-one times, three of them from the hangar deck. Generally small observation aircraft, weighing less than 5,000 pounds, were launched, the catapults on the flight deck permitting such launches even when large numbers of aircraft were spotted near the bow. CinC U.S. Fleet authorized the removal of the hangar-deck units from these carriers on 17 February 1942, in view of their unnecessary weight and their inability to launch the heavy aircraft then in service (flight-deck units of equal capacity could launch much heavier aircraft because they benefitted from "wind-over-the-deck" generated by the carrier's forward motion); the catapults that became surplus would be valuable, however, for the escort-carrier (then called the AVG) program. Pearl Harbor Navy Yard reported the removal of catapults from the *Enterprise* and *Hornet* on 26 June 1942. The *Yorktown* had already been sunk with her catapult aboard. Early war experience suggested that catapults were not worth their weight, and indeed on 29 April 1943 the captain of the *Enterprise* went so far as to ask to have his remaining flight-deck units removed. However, by that time the CVEs had shown just how valuable such catapults could be, and when his ship was rebuilt at Puget Sound that summer, two redesigned H 2-1s were fitted.

They were armed with eight of the new 5-in/38 dual-purpose guns (and were among the first U.S. warships so armed) controlled by a pair of Mark 33 directors atop a massive island, most of which was devoted to uptakes. There were four quadruple 1.1-in machine cannon fore and aft of the island, and in addition a total of twenty-four 0.50-cal machine guns, including four atop a rather large air-defense platform on the tripod mast. As inclined in March 1938, the *Enterprise* had on board a five-squadron air group of over ninety aircraft: eighteen fighters, thirty-seven scout bombers (half of them functioning as scouts, half as light dive-bombers), eighteen torpedo bombers, eighteen heavy dive-bombers, and six utility aircraft (VJ). Three years later she was operating

eight-four aircraft and carrying thirty-seven as spares, most of them triced up over her hangars. Fully loaded, she then carried about 670 tons of ammunition, including both aviation and ship (gun) ordnance.

Although the *Yorktown* design was relatively old by 1938, the pressure of rearmament led to its duplication in the *Hornet* (CV 8) when additional carrier tonnage was authorized after the expiration of the Washington Treaty. In July 1938 C & R design priorities emphasized the new 45,000-ton battleship (which became the *Iowa* class); it was estimated that no new carrier design could be ready for as much as fifteen months, a year late. The alternatives were to duplicate the existing *Yorktown* with its known deficiencies or else to consign some of the designs to private firms, as had actually been done in 1933. The *Yorktown* design was repeated because it did not appear that much more could be achieved under 20,000 tons, and the *Hornet* (CV 8) was built to it under the FY 39 program. She differed from her sister ships in having Mark 37 rather than Mark 33 5-in directors, and she lacked the massive foretop characteristic of her near sisters. BuEng wanted a new propulsion system arrangement (which might have overcome the vulnerability to underwater attack that actually immobilized the *Hornet* in her last battle), but had to settle for improved superheaters. Turbo-

The *Yorktown*, at anchor at Hampton Roads, 30 October 1937, shows several features characteristic of later U.S. carriers: the sliding metal shutters enclosing an open hangar deck, the large crane (aft) used to lift aircraft onto the hangar deck, and the sponson for the athwartship catapult. The small rangefinder atop the bridge served the 5-in battery for surface fire, supplementing the stereo rangefinder in the Mark 33 director one level above.

THE YORKTOWN CLASS 95

The *Hornet* differed in minor ways from her two near-sisters, most noticeably in the substitution of Mark 37 for their Mark 33 directors. Note the prominent conning tower.

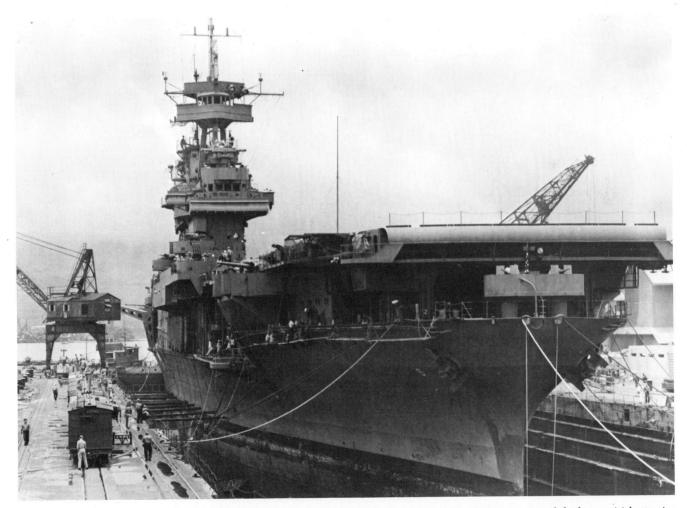

Early war modifications to the CV 5 class were not extensive, partly because they already incorporated the heavy AA batteries being installed in other ships and partly because they could not be spared for major refits. The *Yorktown* is shown undergoing hasty repairs at Pearl Harbor just prior to Midway, where she was lost. The only really visible change is the elimination of the pilot-house rangefinder; the CXAM-1 radar antenna is turned edgewise and can barely be made out.

This photograph, taken at Pearl Harbor in May 1942, shows detail changes in the *Enterprise*: the elimination of the boats and their crane; and the addition of degaussing cables and what appears to be an external fuel line. Note the early YE homing beacon above her air search radar.

The *Enterprise* is shown on 7 June 1943, having benefitted at this point from forward base work only: 20-mm guns and some radar have been added, but not many major power-operated light weapons.

electric populsion (for increased astern power) was also briefly considered.

Early modifications included radar and additional antiaircraft weapons. One of six prototype CXAM radars was fitted to the carrier *Yorktown*, atop her tripod mast, in 1940; the *Enterprise* received the improved CXAM-1, and the *Hornet* the more powerful SC, which had a smaller antenna. The performance of the latter was disappointing, and during the summer of 1942 the *Hornet* was fitted with the larger antenna of a CXAM salvaged from the battleship *California* at Pearl Harbor. If this was combined with the SC transmitter, it would have been roughly equivalent to the later SK of the *Essex*-class carriers. It appears that only the *Enterprise* survived long enough to be fitted with a secondary air-search set, an SC-2 sponsored out from her massive funnel, late in 1942. As refitted in 1943 she received a new SK for long-range air search, as well as an SM height finder, and this basic radar outfit remained to the end.

The original antiaircraft outfit of all three ships consisted of two quadruple 1.1-in machine cannon stepped forward of the island, with a third on the flight deck just abaft the massive airplane and boat crane, and a fourth further aft on the gallery-deck level to starboard. In August 1941 a general policy of substituting twin 40-mm mounts for quadruple 1.1-in and 20-mm mounts for 0.50-cal machine guns was announced. Neither weapon was available until the following year, and photographs of the *Enterprise* in February 1942 show the 0.50s still in action. By June, however, all three ships had their 20-mm batteries: twenty-four guns for the *Yorktown* and *Hornet* and thirty-two for the *Enterprise*. At this time the planned ultimate battery was six twin 40-mm and twenty-four 20-mm guns, the 40-mm positions including the bow, where the gap between the fore end of the flight deck and the bows proper provided useful space. It appears that the *Yorktown* was lost at Mid-

way with her original quartet of 1.1-in guns; shortly thereafter the two survivors each received a fifth quadruple 1.1-in mount in the bows. The very considerable overhang of the flight deck aft prohibited any similar mounting in the stern. In addition, 20-mm batteries were reinforced by August, so that there were, respectively, thirty-eight in the *Enterprise* and thirty-two in the *Hornet*. Meanwhile planned batteries were also reinforced: ships this large could replace their quadruple 1.1s with the much heavier quadruple Bofors gun instead of with the twin Bofors of similar weight. Thus late in August an antiaircraft battery of four quadruple and three twin Bofors guns, as well as thirty (thirty-two in the *Hornet*) 20-mm guns, was approved as the "ultimate" standard.

The *Hornet* was lost before she could be further modified, but during post-damage repairs in November 1942, the *Enterprise* had her four flight-deck quadruple 1.1s replaced by quadruple Bofors guns; her 20-mm battery was now increased to forty-six weapons. By this time she must have begun to show symptoms of overloading. Both of her sisters had been lost to underwater damage, and in January 1943 suggestions were made that she be blistered, at the least to restore the buoyancy she had already lost through overloading. At the same time she could be modernized; the changes made late in 1942 had been no more than incidental to damage repair in the forward base at Noumèa.

The *Enterprise* was, therefore, taken in hand at Puget Sound on 20 July 1943 for a refit from which she emerged in October. The most visible improvement was in her antiaircraft battery: she received a total of six quadruple 40-mm guns (four in the original 1.1-in positions, plus two at the hangar-deck level on the port side aft) and eight twin 40-mm guns (one in the bow, two on each side at the gallery-deck level forward of the forward pairs of 5-in guns, two port and starboard in the galleries abaft the after

Refitted at Puget Sound, the *Enterprise* (*above* and *facing*) shows her late-war appearance in these 2 August 1944 photographs. The overhead view shows the class's characteristic bulged flight deck, maintaining a constant width around the island. Note, too, how the blister, almost invisible, is faired into the hull.

Refitted at Puget Sound, the *Enterprise* shows her late-war appearance in these 2 August 1944 photographs. The overhead view shows the class's characteristic bulged flight deck, maintaining a constant width around the island. Note, too, how the blister, almost invisible, is faired into the hull.

groups of 5-in guns, and one more, at the after end of the island, abeam the airplane/boat crane). She received a total of forty-eight single 20-mm guns, plus two experimental mounts: one twin and one triple, both of which were soon replaced by single weapons. Perhaps almost as importantly, she received a pair of Mark 37 directors to replace her Mark 33s, and a new radar outfit: SK, the new SM height finder. She retained the SC-2 for secondary air search. She emerged from the yard fitted to support the first night fighters in the fast carrier task force, which entered combat in November 1943. The *Enterprise* was blistered to a beam of 95 feet 5 inches. Her old gasoline stowage was replaced by new built-in saddle tanks for increased survivability. Her island was rearranged, the two ready rooms formerly in its lowest level being moved into the gallery deck with those already present there; a CIC was built in the island proper. Her hull was permanently degaussed, and two 1,000 gallon/minute diesel and two 1,200 gallon/minute turbine fire pumps were installed. H 2-1 catapults were substituted for the former pair of H IIs on the flight deck. Fully loaded (condition VI), she now displaced 32,060 tons, compared to 25,484 tons as first inclined in 1938. She carried thirty-six fighters (F6F-3), thirty-seven scout bombers (SBD-5), and eighteen torpedo bombers (TBF-1).

Damaged by kamikazes in the spring of 1945, the *Enterprise* was again refitted, emerging at the very

end of the war with a battery of fifty-four 40-mm guns (eleven quadruple and five twin mounts): two new quadruple mounts were installed on a new sponson on the port side forward at hangar-deck level (in the former athwartship catapult bay), another new mount was put on the gallery deck level to port, and two twin 40-mm mounts forward (port and starboard) were replaced by quadruple mounts. By way of weight compensation, the bow twin Bofors gun was eliminated and the 20-mm battery reduced to sixteen twins. In addition, the Mark 37 directors were refitted with lightweight shields, and the fixed fog fire-fighting system was removed except in way of the gasoline stowage. However, an additional quadruple mount proposed to replace the twin Bofors gun abaft the island was not approved, as it would have required removal of the large boat and airplane crane abaft the island, which were considered too useful. In addition, proposals to clear the sides of the hangar deck by relocating the quadruple Bofors there to the galleries were rejected on structural grounds.

The substitution of 40-mm for 20-mm guns was quite general throughout the fleet in the summer of 1945, as the lighter weapon was considered useless against kamikazes. BuOrd "strongly recommended against the sacrifice of 36-20 mm to gain 8-40 mm barrels, because the arcs of fire of the quads were restricted to about 160 degrees whereas the 20-mm were scattered along the galleries with excellent arcs

Having served in virtually every Pacific battle, the *Enterprise*, a victim of kamikaze attack, was under refit at the end of the war. Here she runs post-refit trials in Puget Sound on 13 September 1945. She never operated aircraft again and served only as a troopship for returning servicemen before entering the reserve fleet. Perhaps the most interesting change visible in this photograph is the installation of radar-controlled Mark 57 directors fore and aft, near the 5-in guns, for local blind-fire control.

of fire. Evaluation of weapons studies favored the 20 mm.''

New blind-fire directors were also fitted: four Mark 57s for the paired 5-in/38s and adjacent Bofors guns in each quadrant, as well as four Mark 63s each controlling a group of two or three Bofors mounts. In addition there were four Mark 51 optical lead-computing directors for each pair of 5-in guns, and seven more for individual control of 40-mm mounts, giving a total of twenty-one directors, including the two long-range Mark 37s in the island structure.

According to the weekly SCB memorandum,

BuShips has authorized a number of alterations based on battle experience similar to changes being made in CV 9 class. These include additional fire hose, fire plugs in island structure, improved elevator pit drainage, and airline mask system in machinery spaces. Flight deck airplane outriggers, waterway covers, and shore power facilities are to be removed as compensation. A second surface search radar (SU) is to be installed on mainmast extension.

The *Enterprise* emerged from this refit just as the war ended, and instead of returning to battle she was employed to return U.S. troops from abroad. She was considered the symbol of American victory in the Pacific, having fought in almost every battle. BuShips compiled a war damage report listing all damage done to her between 1942 and 1945 as a tribute to the fast carrier task force, and in 1946 she was scheduled to be turned over to the state of New York as a permanent war memorial. Unfortunately, in 1949 this plan was suspended; subsequently she was reclassified as an ASW support carrier, although no modifications were ever made and she was already elderly. She was declared unfit for further service in October 1956 and stricken the following January, but scrapping was delayed while the *Enterprise* Association sought to convert her into a museum. They failed, and she was broken up the following year at Kearny, New Jersey.

The *Enterprise* is shown at the close of her combat career. On 14 May 1945 a kamikaze struck her flight deck just abaft the forward elevator. A bomb penetrated to the third deck, where it exploded in a rag storeroom. The elevator was blown into the air and a large fire started in the elevator pit and among aircraft on the hangar deck. Note that the flight deck just abaft the elevator has bulged upward and that paint on the island has blistered and peeled as a result of earlier damage. On 18 March off Kyushu she was struck on her forward elevator by a dud bomb, which ricocheted into her island. On 11 April she was narrowly missed by two kamikazes, fore and aft, and the bomb from the after one exploded near the turn of her bilge, causing severe shock damage in her after machinery space. The *Enterprise* was refitted, but the work was not completed in time for her to see further combat in the Western Pacific. She is shown offloading ammunition (note the crane aft) prior to her final refit at Mare Island.

5

The Return to Smaller Dimensions, 1934–39

Given the limited tonnage established by the Washington Treaty after the construction of the *Ranger*, the United States had to follow the two large *Yorktown*s with a second small carrier, which became the *Wasp*. She was derived from the 15,200-ton carrier developed in parallel with the preliminary designs for the larger ships, and incorporated many of their features. However, as is usually the case when a small ship succeeds a much larger one, most of those concerned in the *Wasp*-design decisions wanted to achieve large-ship features in the small hull imposed on them. Four decades later a similar drama would be played out in the case of the medium carrier (CVV) designed after the United States had built a series of *Forrestal*s and their nuclear cousins. In the case of the *Wasp*, the unfortunate designers had to demonstrate just how constricted the choices actually were at a General Board hearing on 20 August 1934.

The *Wasp* was authorized by an act of 27 March 1934 as a tonnage replacement for the *Langley*. Although the latter did not figure in the Washington Treaty totals, she was included in the total carrier tonnage allowed the U.S. Navy by the Vinson-Trammell Act. The *Wasp* was ordered from Bethlehem Quincy on 19 September 1935.

During the construction of the new carrier, her designers sought to use every ton remaining under the treaties; there was no longer, as there had been in the twenties, a desire to stay well below treaty limits so as to insure against accidental violation. By the end of that decade, U.S. cruiser designers were under pressure to use every one of their permitted 10,000 tons to obtain useful protection, and the usual design margins were no longer being tolerated. Similarly, because no large margins were ever allowed in the *Wasp* design, there was constant pressure as the actual (as opposed to designed) tonnages of the two large carriers under construction fluctuated. The *Ranger*, not commissioned until after the *Wasp* design had been begun, gained 700 tons during construction, largely through the addition of her island, a change ordered after she had been laid down. At an August 1934 General Board hearing Captain Chantry, responsible for the preliminary design, observed that carriers were particularly susceptible to such weight growth. After all, they represented rapidly developing technology. For example, the catapults to be installed in the *Wasp* as well as in the two larger carriers (and the *Hornet*) were only paper projects in 1934, and it was not even certain whether (or how many) catapults would be installed in those carriers—yet they would add substantial weight to all of these ships.

The *Wasp* was, moreover, designed before any operating experience had been gained with any of the specially designed carriers of her generation, and in-

Although she marked a return to smaller dimensions, the *Wasp* was based on the design for the *Yorktown*, not for the *Ranger*. She is shown emerging from Norfolk Navy Yard on 8 January 1942 after a refit, little changed except for her search radar forward.

The *Wasp* is shown on trial, 22 and 23 February 1940, complete except for her light armament. Note the folded catapult sponsons fore and aft, the catapult bays shuttered, and the absence of the hangar-deck crane of the previous class. A boat crane is visible alongside the island, stowed parallel to the superstructure.

deed before the designs of the two 20,000-ton carriers had been completed. Thus the open hangar deck, later so important because it allowed aircraft to be warmed up before they were brought up to the flight deck for launching, had not as yet been tried. Admiral King (then chief of BuAer) even opposed the warming-up of aircraft in the hangar, largely in view of his experience with the closed hangar deck of the *Lexington*. There was as yet no clear consensus on the value of a secondary flying-off deck or a hangar-deck catapult. Nor had there been any experience of the seagoing behavior of a relatively small carrier. Although some skepticism concerning her probable seagoing characteristics existed, the *Ranger* was commissioned on 4 June 1934, by which time much of the *Wasp* preliminary design already existed.

Preliminary Design began with the assumption that the new carrier should be designed for 14,150 tons. This allowed for a margin of 150 tons and a 175-ton excess on each of the two "20,000-ton" *Yorktown*s, whose design displacement included another 200 tons of margin; all of these figures seemed extremely small to Chantry. When the *Yorktown* design had been set at 20,000 tons, 15,200 tons had been left for a third ship. Of that figure, 700 had gone to overweight in the *Ranger* (for her island, an extension of her flight deck, and minor changes in features such as light armament and bomb stowage). Another 500 tons was going into margin; but if the margins were to be disregarded, and some minor violation of the total tonnage limit accepted, CV 7 could be designed for up to 14,500 tons.

Other initial assumptions included an armament equal to that of the *Yorktown*s (eight 5-in/38 guns, four quadruple 1.1-in machine cannon, twenty-four 0.50-cal machine guns), a period of roll of about 16 to 17 seconds, and a long cruising radius, at least the 10,000 nautical miles at 15 knots of the *Ranger*.

Beyond that, it was a question of which features to emphasize. The basic Preliminary Design study (scheme 1) emphasized aviation features: three elevators and seventy-two aircraft in a 695-ft hull covered by a 740-ft flight deck (see table 5-1). Sacrifices had to be made in speed (29.5 knots on 67,000 SHP) and in protection: scheme 1 was limited to a 50-lb underwater deck over the magazines and gasoline tanks forward; the magazines aft and the steering gear were to be protected by a 50-lb deck and by 4-in to 2-in transverse bulkheads. There would be no underwater protection, no side belt, nothing at all over machinery and boilers.

Alternative schemes emphasized other features. Scheme 2a stressed speed and power, for 32 knots on 120,000 SHP at the cost of a reduction in aviation features (fifty-four aircraft, two elevators, and a 680-ft flight deck on a 640-ft hull). It was far more efficient to buy speed with power than with a longer hull under the condition of limited displacement. Scheme 5a emphasized protection, and showed the cost of *Yorktown* standards: a 4-in to 2.5-in waterline belt two-thirds of the waterline length, covered by a 67-lb STS deck (fourth-deck level), would cost a reduction in speed up to 25 knots (35,000 SHP) and acceptance of scheme 2a aviation features. Scheme 5a did,

however, have the important virtue of including torpedo protection.

Neither scheme 2a nor scheme 5a was particularly attractive, so Preliminary Design tried one compromise, scheme 6. This had the aviation features of scheme 1 (except that the flight deck had to be held to 695 feet on a 650-ft hull); and it retained the side (underwater) protective system of scheme 5a while accepting the partial deck protection of schemes 1 and 2a. Speed was an unattractive 25.5 knots at the 35,000 SHP of scheme 5a—the power plant's dimensions had almost certainly been determined by the constricted internal volume left by underwater protection.

Preliminary Design also considered several schemes for flying off the hangar deck. In one, a centerline catapult was mounted on the forecastle below the flight deck; planes would be rolled onto a short lift leading to it. BuAer preferred an alternative in which planes would take off, under their own power, from a long forecastle deck extending to abaft the island. In such a design the flight deck would have to be raised and shortened so that planes could take off from under its forward end. The hangar deck would have, in effect, two levels: the forecastle and a deeper level aft. The forward elevator would have to be relocated to the after end of the forecastle to serve the deeper part of the hangar aft as well as the shallow section forward. In yet a third scheme, intermediate between these two, a shallow hangar forward would be large enough to park about one squadron; from this section planes could be rolled onto a catapult forward. In this case the flight deck would have to be raised about 2.8 feet (as compared to 6 feet for flying off the hangar deck).

At the hearing, Admiral King, who was then chief of BuAer, noted that interest in hangar-deck flying off was largely a consequence of Japanese and British experience in that direction. In an interesting contrast to the later U.S. practice, he observed that

> the Bureau . . . has as yet no definite views on this question as to two launching levels. In the first place it has been the practice in our carriers, and a very safe practice, that engines are not warmed up or any other similar risk taken within the hangars. The use of two launching levels would make it inevitable that planes would have to be warmed up between decks. The second main consideration . . . is that . . . the pilot would have to get under way and go down a tunnel until he emerged into the open and that is one reason for giving him at least a glimpse of the open deck forward. I think we are inclined to be somewhat skeptical. . . . Those considerations led to the studies here which are dependent on the success of the development of the flush deck catapults. . . .
>
> At present on all our carriers, built and building, it takes a good deal of management, foresight and good

Table 5-1. Schemes for the *Wasp* Design

	1	2a	5a	6
Std Disp't (tons)	14,150	14,150	14,150	14,150
LWL (ft)	695	640	590	650
Beam (main deck) (ft)	90	90	90	90
Draft (ft)	21.34	21.59	22.14	21.5
Hull Depth (ft)	52.5	52.5	52.5	52.5
FD (above keel) (ft)	80	80	80	80
Elevators	3	2	2	3
Length of FD (ft)	740	680	625	695
Aircraft	72	54	54	63–66
Speed (kts)	29.5	32	25	25.5
SHP	67,000	120,000	35,000	35,000
Belt (2/3 LWL) (in)	—	—	4 2.5	—
Deck	50 lb*	50 lb*	60 lb†	50 lb
Splinter Pro	no	no	yes	no
Torp Pro	no	no	yes	yes

Note: Scheme 1 was the basis of the *Wasp* design. All schemes incorporated a battery of 8 5-in/38s, 16 1.1-in guns, and 24 0.50-cal machine guns. These alternatives were presented in an 18 August 1934 C&R memo.

*At level of first platform, over magazines, avgas, steering gear.

†At fourth deck over all vitals.

luck to be able to launch planes at the same time you are landing them. Unless it can be shown that the second launching level can be worked in with the upper launching level to increase flexibility of operation, there is no object to be gained of sufficient magnitude to warrant the complications that are involved. The main purpose of introducing this feature was so that all hands might have a look at it. . . .

The new flush-deck catapult, which would become the H II, was as yet no more than a project that might or might not succeed. King feared that any carrier design dependent upon it might well be discarded in the event of its failure. For his part, Chantry was

a little surprised at [King's suggestion that the hangar in the *Yorktown*s was perhaps too deep] because the whole design was laid out to make . . . use of every inch of space under the overhead of the flight deck. It was necessary to use all of that space to accommodate the stowages required for spares, wings, fuselages, and also quarters. . . . Contract plans will show you that every bay overhead has been used for stowage . . . that must be provided for some place in the ship and it is almost impossible to provide below decks for stowage of the large fuselages and large wings. . . .

All of the dual-deck designs were based on scheme 1, which was clearly the best balanced. Admiral Woodward of the General Board asked to what extent it could be better protected, for example, at the cost of the amidships elevator (120 tons). In fact much more was required. For instance, the torpedo bulkheads in schemes 5a and 6 cost about 750 tons, with a total of about 1,450 tons for ballistic protection in scheme 5a (of which 600 to 700 tons were consumed by side armor). A partial protective deck in scheme 1 already cost 525 tons, and to extend that deck to full coverage would cost another 500.

Some weight out of the total allowable for the United States could be added if the two large carriers were completed within their designed weights (350 tons), and 100 to 150 tons would be released if the flagship feature of earlier carriers were omitted. Even more could be released by the removal of the 8-in turrets of the *Lexington* and *Saratoga*. Of these alternatives, the General Board chose the paper one: in September 1934 it recommended that "the unobligated 350 tons at present temporarily assigned to CVs 5 and 6 should be transferred to CV 7, thus permitting the "standard displacement" available for the latter vessel to be considered as 14,500 tons"—even though the two large carriers were then very far from completion. As for the two possible physical expedients, many within the fleet (and particularly among the aviators) considered the 8-in guns valuable, and the flagship feature was important, particularly for a

ship that might operate alone, with only cruiser escorts.

Perhaps some saving might be gained from the fact that, like the *Ranger*, CV 7 would not operate torpedo planes; consequently, her aircraft might be smaller than those of the last two heavy carriers. Admiral Greenslade of the General Board went further and asked King (as well as representatives of the CNO) whether perhaps CV 7 should be a specialized carrier. King was unenthusiastic.

I assume that the point raised is as to the question of a battle line carrier or a straight carrier. What we know about the exercises in the Fleet and on the game board at the War College, forecasting what is likely to happen when the real thing comes along, we feel that the battle line carrier is pretty much of a mistake because it would have to be in the vicinity of the main action and would probably be the first target hit by enemy planes. The practice to date seems not only to be to separate the carriers at some distance from the main body but likewise to separate them from each other. So that on these premises this ship should be what we call a straight carrier and not made up for a so-called battle line carrier. . . .

King strongly preferred scheme 1 to the far slower schemes 5a and 6.

You get into very serious difficulties with the 25 knot carrier, in the ability to launch planes [designed to take off with 25 knots of wind-over-deck]. . . . It takes some time to work up to full power and that limits the flexibility of her operations. . . . Those practical considerations of getting up to a condition with a necessary air speed over the deck inclined us very strongly to at least 29.5 knots.

We are not so much concerned about landing speeds. . . . whereas 25 knots wind over the deck is essential for launching planes especially from the forward spotting positions, a 20 or 21 or 22 knot speed is adequate for landing planes. With the adoption of flaps—which we were reluctant to undertake but which we felt would be inevitable—the control of landing planes is quite marked. However, the flaps or the variable pitch propeller or the combination of them have not nearly overcome the difficulty of the high performance planes and it is for that reason that we have gone into the matter of accelerating take-off even to the extent of catapults.

King did, however, prefer scheme 1 to the faster scheme 2a; his bureau liked the idea of the additional planes and the longer flight deck better than the prospect of the extra 2.5 knots.

Although foreign two-deck carriers had inspired the dual-deck ideas, U.S. intelligence was poor enough that King had to admit to having very little definite information about the success of the foreign ships, apart from the fact that "all the evidence goes to show that none of them have nearly approached

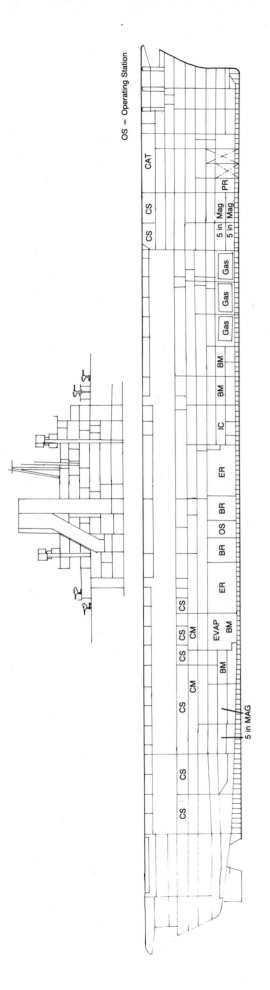

The Wasp's inboard profile.

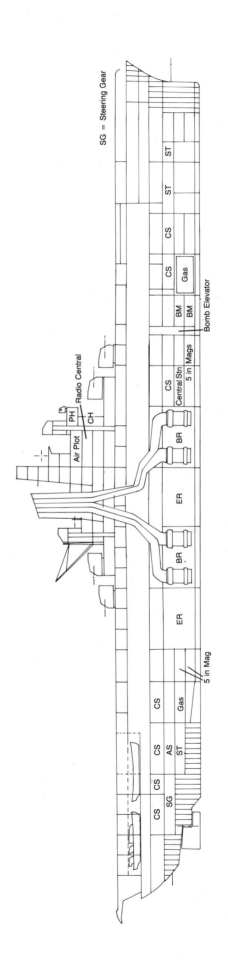

Light carrier design of 1938, the first U.S. design to show twin 5-in guns on the flight deck.

our speed in launching and handling planes. The second deck, in our minds, is a question of getting additional flexibility which is a matter of great importance. It is for that reason that the three elevators were introduced in the CV 5 and 6 and I . . . say by all means that the CV 7 should have three elevators."

Captain Van Keuren of C & R, however, pointed out that the HMS *Glorious* had operated on two levels and had suffered damage on the lower even in "some pretty fair seas." Captain Chantry answered that the sketch designs did indeed take this question into account, that in fact all of them allowed for about a 40-ft freeboard forward, or one-deck height over a cruiser; indeed,

> if you attempted to launch off the bow of the ship without such freeboard you would find in many instances this to be totally impossible and very dangerous. . . . The CV 5 and 6 are designed for a probable later installation of a tranverse catapult across the after end of the hangar deck and have big rolling curtains covering big openings in the side of the hangar in order that planes may be launched . . . out of the sides of the hangar. At that same location there is provided a crane starboard, and another port, for probable use in picking up damaged planes or seaplanes from the water and bringing them into the hangar through those large openings. . . .

C & R did not then expect to install the catapults and planned to use the cranes to handle boats, which were to be stowed on the hangar deck. Given the slow pace of catapult development, Chantry included none in the series of *Wasp* sketch designs, nor were there the large cranes or the boat stowage on the hangar deck.

> There is, of course, the large crane on the flight deck which picks planes up from over the side and lands them on the middle elevator on the flight deck. [The catapult] has a rather profound influence on the design [because] the boat stowage provided on the CV 5 and 6 and served by those [hangar deck] cranes is installed in pockets cut out of the hangar deck and the crane height with the boat on slings is such that only one large boat can be stowed in each pocket. . . . We cannot nest the boats. . . . We have to take more room both out of the hangar deck and along the island to accommodate the boat stowage than would be necessary if we don't have those cranes and use specially designed davits. . . . So the question is, does the design have to provide for probable later installation of transverse catapults, and does it have to provide cranes, in addition to the flight deck crane. . . . CV 5 and 6 when finished can't pick up planes from over the side with those cranes unless the boats stowed in the way of the opening are disposed of otherwise.

Note that, when completed, the large carriers instead had hangar-deck catapults athwart the forward ends of their hangars. The *Wasp* was unique in having athwartship catapults at both ends of her hangar deck.

Admiral King finally asked for scheme 1, but with modifications to reflect any possible addition of displacement. He preferred not to include transverse catapults on this restricted tonnage, but did want some improvement in protection to be provided by a complete armored deck and antitorpedo bulkheads. "No consideration whatever (should) be given to side belt armor," he concluded.

Captain Chantry wanted something more specific in the way of relative priorities of protection. Scheme 1 devoted 500 tons to armor, and in fact more tonnage was to be arranged later.

> We have felt that the RANGER, running around with huge quantities of bombs, gasoline, and 5-inch ammunition and with tops of magazines well above the waterline, is a . . . potential source of grave danger even though convoyed, and we have tried to improve that. We have kept, in this design, the ammunition just as low as it possibly can be and we have put a 50 pound deck above it and carried it to the side of the ship. At the sides of the ship the deck is something like two feet below the waterline. We were not able to install an underwater belt outside of that. . . . This deck covers the bombs and 5-inch ammunition and the gasoline, and aft it covers the bombs and 5-inch AA. Around the steering gear aft we have a protective box. It seems a matter of grave doubt as to whether you should provide a design that has no protection whatsoever to the huge quantity of explosives that must be carried.

This protection did not include any substantial cover for the potentially explosive aviation gasoline—400 tons of it for CV 7, 475 for CVs 5 and 6. Both gas and ordnance allowances were proportional to the size of the air group, and hence to deck area rather than to displacement: a smaller carrier, which could not be so well protected, would actually have to carry a larger proportional tonnage of gasoline and ammunition than would one of her larger sisters.

The General Board approved scheme 1, at 14,500 tons, modified so far as possible for better protection, with a superstructure similar to that of the 20,000-ton carriers, but otherwise generally similar to the *Ranger*. Transverse catapults were to be installed "if development gives promise of efficient use." Armament would match that of the larger carriers, with four 5-in/38s, four quadruple 1.1-in machine cannon, and twenty-four 0.50-cal water-cooled machine guns, with a pair of Mark 33 directors in the island for the 5-in guns.

The Secretary of the Navy approved the characteristics, including the transfer of 350 tons, on 22 October. At first it seemed to Preliminary Design that a great deal of protection could be provided. Torpedo

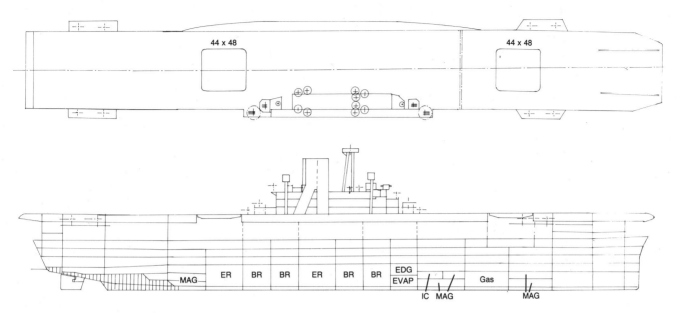

CVX of 1941.

bulkheads were out of the question on volumetric grounds, but late in 1934 it appeared that a 2- to 3-in belt could be provided over the machinery spaces (as in the larger carriers), covered by a 60-lb fourth deck; 50-lb decks could cover the magazines, gasoline, and ship- and fire-control spaces around the central station at the ends underwater. The main belt (as well as the ends of magazines and the sides of an after armored box over the after magazines and steering gear) would be closed by 4-in bulkheads. However, as the design progressed the usual weight squeeze made this generous scale of protection seem less and less attainable. In the end the side belt had to be given up and the decks equalized at 50-lb STS (1.25 inches); the transverse bulkheads remained, but they were trimmed to 3.5 inches.

The ship was fitted with 25-lb (0.625 inch) STS where a belt might otherwise have gone. This was backing for the provision of a true armor belt in the event of war, when treaty limits would no longer apply. However, it appears that the *Wasp* never was so fitted, nor the necessary belt armor ever procured and stored.

In proposing the original protective scheme, which gave immunity against shellfire (but not torpedoes) comparable to that afforded the large carriers, Preliminary Design had made provision for weight reduction in case the ship exceeded treaty limits: first the side belt could be eliminated, then the thickness of deck and internal protection reduced. The former step would still leave a protective deck over the machinery, and if treaty requirements were nullified, the belt protection could be added later.

To BuAer it seemed that this armor was a ludicrous waste of weight. In a 31 January 1935 memorandum to C & R it argued that "it is a mistake to handicap a carrier by giving it a shortened flight and hangar deck in order to provide protection against gun fire which at best is scanty. . . . Recommendation is being made to the Secretary of the Navy to make this ship as long as possible on the given displacement irrespective of the amount of protection obtained."

Preliminary Design felt that its position had been grossly misstated. Although the CV 7 hull was 40 feet shorter than that of the *Ranger*, the flight deck of the new ship was actually 12 feet longer, and its area 16 percent greater. Moreover, the *Ranger* design to which the BuAer comments clearly harked back was by no means acceptable: it allowed far too little metacentric height. Were that problem to be cured by an increase in beam, and the length held constant, the only way to avoid increased displacement would be by reducing draft. That might seem at first to represent a reduced hull weight, but in fact the reduced draft would mean a shallower ship girder and hence heavier scantlings to sustain the higher stresses implied.

Another way to appreciate the problem was to begin with the CV 7 design, then delete the armor (whose center of gravity was below that of the ship as a whole) and transfer that weight to a longer hull (whose center of gravity would be above the net center of gravity of the ship) and a heavier flight deck (whose center of gravity would surely lie high in the ship). The net effect would be a higher center of grav-

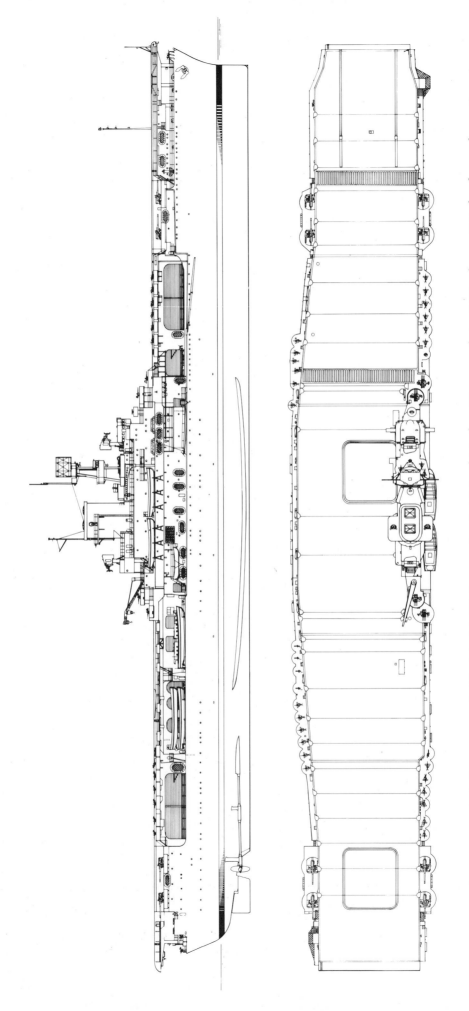

The *Wasp* (CV 7), in January 1942. She was armed with eight 5-in/38, four quadruple 1.1-in, thirty-four 20-mm, and nine 0.50-cal guns. Note her forward arresting wires and two windbreaks (folded down). Provision was made for an LSO to control over-the-bow landings (small starboard platform forward).

ity and hence a reduced metacentric height. The cure, as in the *Ranger* case, would lead to a heavier hull; and in order to remain within the displacement limit, the ship would have to be shortened substantially—to roughly where she had started from.

In fact any reduction in draft would be unfortunate for such diverse features as propulsion (which demanded a good beam-to-draft ratio), hull strength, seakeeping qualities, and the need for volume below the waterline to stow ammunition, gasoline, and other materials not to be exposed to shellfire.

What is interesting about this little controversy is how illogical the major design choices seemed to observers outside the design team. It appeared inconceivable that the hundreds of tons added for what BuAer considered a totally useless side belt could not go instead into better aviation features; in fact, there was both no belt and no lengthening—but BuAer did not know that in January.

When built, the *Wasp* had several unusual features. To conserve valuable weight, she was designed with an asymmetrical hull, so that no ballast would be required to balance the weight of her island structure. Her builders later explained part of her high per-ton cost on this basis. She also had an unusual machinery arrangement, midway between the *Yorktown*'s highly vulnerable scheme and the scheme of alternating engine and fire rooms on the *Essex*. The forward and after engine rooms were separated by two sets of three abreast boiler rooms, each containing a single boiler, and separated fore and aft by three abeam compartments for boiler-operating stations. The only other U.S. design with this arrangement was the contemporary *St. Louis*-class light cruiser, which also marked a transition from conventional to alternating machinery arrangements.

The *Wasp* had the first U.S. deck-edge elevator, a feature characteristic of later U.S. carrier designs. Originally a conventional three-elevator layout was planned, but BuAer decided instead, early in 1935, to adopt the new type. There was no hope of demonstrating its operation without actually installing it in a ship for a complete service test; the more conventional plunger-type elevator could be restored if it failed, and all structures for that purpose were provided and the manufacturer was required to build the necessary parts. The elevator was fitted on the port side of the forward catapult bay. It was T-shaped, the cross supporting the two main wheels of an airplane, the boom its tail. The entire elevator could fold up out of the way for storage. Its success inspired the use of a much larger deck-edge elevator in place of the initially planned midships unit in the *Essex* class. In the *Wasp*, it appears to have been as much a weight saver as a means of improving the flow of aircraft on the flight and hangar decks.

Despite attempts at weight saving, the *Wasp* came out heavy; in November 1939 C & R estimated that she was 692 tons overweight in light condition, even counting the usual 100-ton margin; she had a standard displacement, when built, of at least 15,400 tons (as against 14,700 in the final design). Moreover, the aircraft were much heavier individually than they were when the ship was planned. In July 1940 BuShips reported that their weight had doubled since the contract plans had been prepared in 1935, so that the original estimate of 157.2 tons for four squadrons and 50 percent reserves had grown to a more realistic figure of 300.7 tons, including 200.5 for the four active squadrons. This added weight, so high in the ship, could only have the most unfortunate consequences for her stability. The bureau asked that

The vertical girder in the *Wasp*'s forward catapult bay is actually the folding deck-edge elevator, the ancestor of the much larger unit installed in the *Essex*es.

Early modifications to the *Wasp* included bringing the gasoline line outside the hull, as in this pre–Pearl Harbor photograph, probably dated late 1940.

the reserve aircraft not be loaded. "In separate correspondence the Commanding Officer will be cautioned as to the total liquid load of fuel, fresh and reserve feed water, gasoline or compensating or ballast water which he should maintain on board. . . . Under present conditions without an armor belt the *Wasp* has the stability characteristics of a merchantman and must be handled accordingly."

The *Wasp* was also too slow, with a rated speed, at 70,000 SHP, of only 29.5 knots. Admiral King, then Commander of Aircraft, Battle Force, wrote to the CNO on 7 April 1939 that

> with the increasing speed of carrier based aircraft the safe wind velocity over the deck required for landing and take-off increases.
>
> At the present time a 30 knot wind is required for some types of planes with full bomb and fuel load. If there is no surface wind the ship must make this speed.
>
> The *Ranger*'s clean bottom full power speed at 16,000 tons displacement is 261.5 RPM, or 29.38 knots. Since her average operating displacement is over 18,000 her clean bottom speed is 255 RPM, or 28.65 knots. These speeds are reduced at the rate of 3 RPM per month for time out of dock. The *Ranger* has now been out of dock 202 days resulting in a full power engine speed of 26.5 knots and a reduction due to fouling of 2.3 knots giving a speed through the water of 24.2 knots.
>
> During the live bombing practice held 29 March it was necessary to use a long take-off run, because the surface wind was about 4 knots, and the maximum speed through the water attainable was 24.2 knots. With a long-run take-off it is not possible to spot the usual number of planes on deck which results in a considerable increase in time of take-off and consequent serious reduction in military effectiveness. . . . Another disadvantage . . . is the long time required to

> work up maximum speed. This is a serious handicap when expeditious take-off is required.
>
> At the present time the other carriers do not suffer from this condition because they have a clean bottom full power speed of at least 32.5 knots which is sufficient to permit a 30 knot wind over deck with the present 9 month period between docking. . . . A policy of docking the *Ranger* at least every 6 months and always just before a cruise such as the present one plus the use of the newly developed Mare Island underwater body paint should operate to promote her military effectiveness.
>
> It is strongly recommended that every consideration be given to increasing the speed of the *Wasp*, now building, to at least 32 knots and that future carriers be designed for speeds of 34 knots.

His superior, Admiral E. C. Kalbfus, tended to agree, particularly when the speeds of the new fast battleships were taken into account. The slower the carrier, the more the fleet would disperse as she launched and recovered her aircraft, steaming into the wind for extended periods. He wondered whether the *Ranger* and *Wasp* could be given increased power: "important sacrifices of other military characteristics and the expenditure of a considerable sum may well be justified by increases in available speeds. . . ."

BuEng concluded that little could actually be done for the *Ranger*. She would require 97,000 SHP to make 32 knots, but at best she might be fitted with the 75,000-SHP plant in production for the *Atlanta*-class light cruisers, for a speed of 30.7 knots. Although engine and fire rooms would be large enough, BuEng saw some problems in the replacement of the existing propeller shafts by larger ones. It estimated the cost of such a modification at $3.7 million.

As for the *Wasp*, she would need 130,000 SHP to reach 32 knots with a clean bottom. There were two possibilities for improvement over the existing plant. The existing boilers

> can be modified so as to give an increased output from 25 to 30 percent greater than now designed by the addition of suitable internal baffles in the steam drum and the addition of downcomers to improve circulation. As a result of this increased boiler output it would be possible to obtain approximately 25 percent more shaft horsepower by a new design of turbines and condensers. . . . Such a change would result in a clean bottom speed of about 30.7 knots and, furthermore, would insure that under foul bottom conditions a speed of about 29.7 knots would be realized.

The change would cost about $2 million and seven months' delay. Alternatively, a completely new 100,000-SHP plant, based on that being designed for the *Iowa* class (with two rather than four shafts), could be installed in the existing spaces for a clean-bottom speed of 31.5 knots, at a cost of about $4.1 million.

BuAer enthusiastically supported the attempt to gain speed.

> The design of carriers subsequent to the *Ranger* has consistently incorporated speeds in excess of 32 knots and considerably greater tonnage. . . . The recent operation of modern aircraft has served to accentuate the serious handicap which design speeds of less than 32 knots impose and indicates that the *Wasp* will be seriously deficient in this respect upon joining the fleet if the contract speed of 30.2 knots, only, is realized. . . . [She] can be very considerably improved in value to the fleet as a carrier unit by incorporating, prior to delivery, the maximum increase in speed indicated as being practicable. . . . this action would delay her commissioning until about December 1940.
>
> In regard to the *Ranger*, because of her shorter and narrower flight deck and other operating restrictions, in comparison to the *Wasp*, the Bureau is of the opinion that the increase in speed obtainable will not result in an effective carrier unit and believes that the expense of such a change is not justified at this time. . . . Other means of alleviating this limitation, namely reduction of interval between dockings, lightening of the ship, and the availability of full boiler power while operating, [should] be exhausted prior to a modernization program. Such a program, if undertaken, should include other features in addition to speed and should not place the *Ranger* out of commission during the absence of either the *Saratoga* or the *Lexington* from the fleet. . . .
>
> The political aspect of the change proposed for the *Wasp* should be considered in its possible adverse effect on future naval construction.

That is, Admiral Towers of BuAer feared that Congress would become uneasy at the virtual reconstruction of a carrier not even completed. The two materiel bureaus (C & R and BuEng) estimated that the *Wasp* would be delayed seven months and the *Ranger* would require a full year of work, for completion in, respectively, December 1940 and August 1941. The *Saratoga* was scheduled to begin modernization in January 1941 (for a period of seven months) with the *Lexington* following immediately after her.

The General Board shied away from any extensive reconstruction; at the end of August it recommended merely that the *Ranger* and the *Wasp* be docked often enough to avoid any undue loss of speed, particularly after the new plastic antifouling paint was applied. Every effort was to be made to increase the effectiveness of the two ships' machinery plants, but it was noted that "no further changes [should] be authorized on *Wasp*, that the contractor be notified to this effect, and that every effort be made to complete *Wasp* at earliest practicable date." However, the board did ask BuEng "to investigate thoroughly the practicability and advisability of certain modifications in the high pressure turbine installation of *Wasp* for increasing effectiveness of operation at high speeds with a view to possible accomplishment at some future Navy Yard period. . . ."

This was a period of rapid improvements in machinery, often at little or no increase in weight. For example, relatively small improvements in the battleship *North Carolina*, particularly the change to higher steam conditions, had brought an increase in power from 115,000 to 121,000 SHP. In September, BuEng reported that a 12.5 percent improvement in the *Wasp* could be obtained, for an increase of about 0.6 knots, merely with new nozzle rings for the high-pressure turbines and two rows of turbine blading; the original propellers would be used, at a somewhat higher speed. The change would be made at a navy yard after delivery. However, trials were actually more successful than expected: "the ahead speed of the ship, under clean bottom conditions, is in excess of one knot greater than designed, due to the greater power developed and a better propulsion coefficient than estimated." On three high-speed runs the *Wasp* averaged 73,906 SHP for 30.73 knots; power on the third run was limited by a defective receiver pipe, so the average of the first two was slightly over 75,000 SHP. Moreover, "during these runs No. 1 nozzle in the forward engine room was closed. This was because all bleeding was done in the after engine room to permit water rate measurements on the forward unit. The use of this nozzle in normal operation, bleeding from both units, would increase the maximum power about 4 percent, i.e., 78,000 SHP. There is therefore a margin of about 11 percent. . . ." Sea speed at a service displacement of 18,060 tons and with a 15 percent allowance for sea conditions and fouling was estimated at 29.8 knots, compared to 28.7

for the designed power. BuEng could now abandon the additional project to add another 12.5 percent of power with a clear conscience—"any further increase in ahead power would reduce engineering margins too great an amount."

Even so, the *Wasp* remained much slower than the other carriers. Low speed was not so much an impediment to operation in company with fast task forces as it was a severe limitation on actual air-group operation. Carriers before the era of catapults were unusual among major warships in that their maximum speed determined their operational capability; the combination of speed and flight-deck size was critical. The *Wasp* was deficient in both respects.

In common with the other carriers, she was scheduled for rearmament with 40-mm and 20-mm guns, the latter available long before the former. Thus in June 1942 she still had her quadruple 1.1-in machine cannon, but the original battery of twenty-four 0.50-cal machine guns had been replaced by thirty-two 20-mm guns, six of the 0.50s still being retained. At the time the planned ultimate battery was four quadruple 40-mm and thirty-two 20-mm guns. That was "the maximum battery that weight and stability conditions will permit . . . premised on the removal of about 20 tons of weight, a portion of which is now covered by projected weight removals"; the latter included elimination of the armored conning tower in favor of splinter plating around the pilot house. Even this battery was difficult to accommodate because the *Wasp* was so small. Although the two 1.1-in mounts forward of the island would be relatively easy to replace, two similar mounts abaft the island would present much greater difficulty, requiring relocation of some of the arresting gear, "and would result in an appreciable encroachment on the flight deck area." Instead, a platform for a 40-mm mount was installed on her port quarter at Norfolk. It held the only such weapon she received; the *Wasp* was lost on 15 September 1942, still carrying four quadruple 1.1-in mounts. At that time she had a CXAM-1 air-search radar, acquired during a refit at Norfolk in January 1942. The 40-mm mount was installed during a 1942 refit after service with the British Home Fleet.

She was lost to gasoline explosions following torpedo hits, the first of three torpedoes having struck while the flight-deck fueling system was in use. It appears that her loss, along with the earlier destruction of the *Lexington* through gasoline explosion, inspired the extensive changes made to gasoline stowage in the *Essex* class and the *Enterprise* when the latter was modernized.

Although the *Wasp* was acknowledged to be unsatisfactory from birth, interest in smaller carriers did not die off completely. In 1938 Congress approved another 40,000 tons of carrier construction, tonnage eventually expended in the *Hornet* and the *Essex*.

There were, however, some who suggested that some of it go into 10,000-ton light carriers. In November 1938 Admiral R. L. Ghormley of the War Plans Division wrote that a larger number of such smaller carriers might yet have its advantages, even though unquestionably the larger carriers would provide a greater economy of effort in tons of ship and number of ship personnel per plane carried. War Plans did recommend building two more 20,000-ton carriers (which became the *Hornet* and *Essex*) to make eight heavy units "for Fleet and other Striking Force purposes." The division argued that the large carriers were not well adapted to the type of sea-control warfare the United States might face in an Atlantic war, a case only then becoming important in U.S. planning. There was also the possibility of a Pacific war in which dispersed rather than concentrated operations would be the rule.

Virtually all earlier U.S. planning had been designed to increase the efficiency of a concentrated fleet, an organization most useful in a fleet-on-fleet battle. Such a fleet might be described as more capable of seizing command of the sea than of exercising it, i.e., of interrupting enemy trade routes and sea communications while protecting friendly ones.

Conventional naval theory maintained that effective sea control could best be achieved by the defeat of the enemy fleet, followed by a blockade. However, Ghormley found it sobering that Britain, "with her outstanding strategic postion, and her outstanding Navy, including units designed (for that time) to exercise command of the sea," had found it difficult to counter surface raiders such as the *Emden*. Submarines were an even more difficult problem. In both cases, command of the sea had been assured at the outbreak of war, but that had not eliminated very expensive naval problems. Moreover, the unique geographical position of Great Britain made it relatively easy for sea routes to Germany to be denied. Neither in the Atlantic nor in the Pacific did the United States enjoy a similar advantage.

The United States has a fleet strength sufficient to obtain essential command in the Atlantic against any opponent save England, to obtain command in the Eastern Pacific, or to dispute command in the Western Pacific. . . . Whatever the situation, the problem of *exercising* command of the sea will be a difficult one. Our superior strength may force, and probably will cause the other fellow to spread out. We must be ready to spread out to get him.

Opposed by Germany or Italy or both, our problem is to interrupt their trade routes while giving economical but effective protection to our own. The same holds for the Pacific. When we consider the problem of running down *Emdens*, we immediately recognize the advantage, or necessity of covering an extended area with a widespread mobile based air scouting force supported by gun power adequate to the need.

As in the case of the larger *Yorktown*s, early war modifications to the *Wasp* were restricted to splinter protection and radar; 20-mm guns replaced the earlier 0.50s.

The current [U.S.] conception of a carrier has centered largely on one capable of carrying 72 planes, with gun power, speed, protection modified to fit into a limiting global [total] tonnage. . . .

The tactics involved in the employment of our "large" carrier may be summarized as follows:
—Requires about 30 minutes to launch all planes.
—Requires about 60 minutes to take aboard all planes.
—Must head into the wind for a period of about 30 minutes to launch planes (carrier catapults may modify this somewhat).
—Must head into the wind for a period of about 60 minutes to take aboard all planes.

—Vulnerable to attack due to large number of planes dependent on one flight deck.
—Vulnerability causes carrier to be normally kept removed from probable enemy proximity. This causes "dead head" flying and adds to the difficulty of coordinating air operations with those of other forces.
—When separated from major surface units, large carriers normally require cruiser and destroyer protection.
—The "large" carrier carries mixed types of planes—fighters, bombers, torpedo bombers, and scout bombers.
—The "large" carrier subordinates gun power to air power. It concentrates on *air striking power*. . . .

Generally speaking the area that can be patrolled effectively or searched by a carrier with 72 planes exceeds very little that which can be searched by a carrier of 36 planes. If it were found necessary to patrol an area 500 miles by 1200 miles, it could be done better with three small carriers carrying a reduced number of planes than with two large carriers. If large carriers only were available, three would be used for the task just the same.

For scouting we need numbers of carriers in order to spread them out; we need to reduce their vulnerability (as regards the number of planes put out of action by a damaged flight deck or by underwater damage); we need some increased gun power in order to reduce their dependence on close and constant cruiser protection. We can reduce the number of planes per carrier and improve the efficiency of search operations for a given number of planes, by making the primary function of these planes scouting. They should be able to carry bombs and have sufficient maneuverability and gun equipment to act in the capacity of fighters, but the primary requisite is scouting. 18 to 24 of such planes will provide a very efficient unit for this purpose.

A carrier constructed for the general purpose of operating with cruisers in *exercising control of sea areas* will fill other functions or needs also. . . . For lack of a proper designation [it] is called a "scouting carrier". . . .

Ghormley's analysis is not entirely unfamiliar more than four decades later; we still have a relatively small number of heavy carriers, and for some important sea-control missions, most notably ASW, they are clearly far too large to do the job efficiently. There is also serious question still as to whether a more numerous fleet of smaller and more dispersed units would not be less vulnerable to attack, and studies of alternative carrier fleets continue to occupy many. Ghormley's comments reflect the shift of U.S. naval concern from the single-fleet engagement of an ORANGE war to the trade- and sea-control warfare that might characterize U.S. involvement in a European war or, indeed, in much of a realistic and protracted ORANGE war. A current observer might wonder whether somewhat analogous arguments could be applied to a fleet of heavy U.S. carriers that was best adapted to the most stressful general-war mission (direct attack against Soviet land bases) but inefficient at sea control, or even incapable of covering sufficient sea areas due to its limited numbers.

Displacing about 10,000 tons, the "scouting carrier" would be "sufficiently large that landing deck [would] be reasonably steady under most of the sea conditions to be expected," and it would be armed with eight 6-in/47 dual-purpose guns, so that two such carriers would at least equal a 10,000-ton light cruiser in fire power. It would have elevators fore and

aft and two deck catapults. Ghormley freely admitted that such craft would be expensive in terms of total tonnage and personnel and would suffer under fixed total carrier tonnages; he maintained that "the tonnage required for 'scouting cruisers' should not be related to any tonnage authorization now in existence, but should be the subject of additional authorization by numbers and approximate individual tonnage." Admiral Zumwalt might have said much the same thing when he advocated the "sea-control ship" almost forty years later.

Some of the functions Admiral Ghormley envisaged were later carried out by small escort carriers of roughly the size, if not the gun power or speed, he proposed. Included in these functions were ASW operations, both offensive ("locating and attacking submarines in the areas of shipping routes") and defensive (through continuous air patrols flown by carriers in company with the convoys). In fleet operations small carriers would form part of the advanced scouting groups, "where their reduced vulnerability in loss of plane strength, their increased gun power, and the shorter time required to get planes into the air and back on board will permit them to operate efficiently. . . . They [will] supply information to our striking units, including our large carriers, that will permit the latter to stroke enemy units with maximum power. . . ."

In fact it is not clear whether everything could be obtained on only 10,000 tons. At the verbal request of Admiral Horne of the General Board, C & R developed a sketch design for a 10,000-ton carrier, which it presented in December 1938. The proposed carrier was entirely unprotected, with a 648- by 70-ft flight deck, two elevators, and an air group of two squadrons of scout bombers, with no fighters or torpedo bombers at all; a third squadron could be accommodated on her hangar deck, and there would be two flight-deck catapults. By this time compact high-pressure, high-temperature machinery was well advanced: on 10,000 tons, 100,000 SHP (four shafts, as in the new light cruisers) could be provided for a speed of 32.5 knots and a respectable endurance, 12,000 nautical miles at 15 knots (compared with 10,400 for the *Ranger* and 20,000 for the *Yorktown*s). In order to accommodate the usual carrier gun battery of eight 5-in/38s, C & R had to mount them in pairs on the flight deck, an arrangement later adopted in the *Essex* class; it hoped also to accommodate three quadruple 1.1-in machine cannon as well as twenty-four 0.50-cal machine guns.

Gasoline and bombs were to be stowed fore and aft to facilitate service of aircraft landing at either end of the flight deck. The ship would carry spare parts but no spare aircraft. In contrast to earlier standard U.S. design practice, the flight deck would be part of the hull proper, and the double bottom would be carried up to the hangar deck, in accordance with cruiser design standards. The net effect was far more promising than had been expected, and the General Board had to carry the design the following June as an alternative to the heavy carrier eventually built as the *Essex*.

This proposal had several important consequences. It appears to have inspired Captain McCain of the *Ranger* to suggest in turn a small armored scout carrier the following March. Although McCain considered small size and a limited air group as important as flight-deck armor, the General Board was most impressed with the latter feature, and requested studies of large armored flight-deck carriers which evolved into the *Midway* (see chapter 9). However, the General Board was able to dismiss the small carrier on the basis of the seakeeping experience of the small *Ranger*, half again as large, which often failed to operate in Pacific swells. (Ironically, Ghormley had characterized the *Ranger* as a conventional, that is, "large," carrier).

Again, this sort of discussion surfaces today. It has often been generally agreed that smaller units would be better in a strategic sense, but actual design development has shown that necessary (as opposed to desirable) features cannot be accommodated on the desired tonnage. That was certainly the case with Ghormley's twin dual-purpose 6-in guns.

Another major consequence of the Ghormley paper was that it attuned both C & R and BuAer to the possibilities and limitations of the small carrier. Two years later, when the President became concerned that there were far too few carriers in prospect, he asked the bureaus to plan for the conversion of light-cruiser hulls, of roughly Ghormley's proposed size, to small carriers. Armed with studies of the limitations of such a ship, the bureaus were able to kill the project. The President demanded late in 1941 that it proceed along the austere lines already approved for the escort carriers. One result was a considerable delay in the appearance of the CVLs. Another may have been a belief on the President's part that the bureaus were far too willing to "gold plate" their designs, even at a time of national emergency, a feeling which appears to have carried over to his distrust of the *Midway* design when first proposed in mid-1942.

Advocates of the light carrier made one more attempt: on 15 July 1940 a member of the General Board asked BuShips for a study of a 15,000-ton 32-kt carrier with mine and torpedo protection—but without armor against bombing and shellfire—which the bureau designated CV-X (see table 5-2). As in the 1938 design, the tonnage limit was too tight: unless speed were reduced substantially below 32 knots, there could be no torpedo protection and no triple bottom. That was hardly a surprise: CV-X was about the size of the *Wasp* (which came out to 15,000 tons), but

Table 5-2. Light Carrier Designs

	1938	CV-X July 1940
Std Disp't (tons)	10,000	15,000
Trial Disp't (tons)	12,200*	18,000
LWL (ft)	600 (651 oa)	670
Beam (ft)	66 (93 ext)	82
Draft (ft)	21–11	22
SHP	100,000	120,000
Speed (kts)	32.5	32
Aircraft	78†	63‡
Avgas (tons)	271	400
Elevators	2	2
Catapults	2 H II	2 H II
Battery	8 5-in/38	8 5-in/38
	4 quad 1.1-in	4 quad 1.1-in
	24 0.50 cal	10 0.50 cal

*13,350 tons fully loaded.
†Operating complement given as 36 scout (dive-) bombers.
‡27 fighters, 36 dive-bombers.

considerably faster. Unlike the 1938 ship, CV-X had her 5-in guns in single mounts at the deck edge.

CV-X was hindered by the increasing weight of naval aircraft. Although her design incorporated two H 2s (as in earlier fleet carriers), they would be unable to launch the new aircraft. She would be able to accommodate only one of the H 4s then being designed. Moreover, her flight deck was so short at 707 feet that only about 45 percent of its length could be used for parking aircraft after recovery, although 57 percent might be used to spot aircraft before launching; some aircraft would have to be struck below upon recovery. That in turn would require maximum elevator capacity, yet in contrast with earlier carriers, CV-X would accommodate only two elevators. BuAer commented further that the forward elevator was set so far forward "that, once the small area of flight deck ahead of it is filled with parked airplanes in recovery, the landing intervals will be increased due to the necessity for striking all of a certain number of airplanes below, over this elevator, in order not to exceed the flight deck capacity forward of the barriers." Nor was BuAer confident that CV-X would be able to operate a large air group (representing great top weight), given the problems of the very similar *Wasp*, which would probably have her air group restricted for that reason.

The key argument, and the obituary of all such prewar studies, was that "practically all past and present advances in the military performance of carrier airplanes have been gained with an increase in size and weight of the individual airplane, and with higher landing speeds and greater take-off runs," that is, with larger minimum limits on flight-deck (and, therefore, carrier) size.

6

The ORANGE War Mobilization Carriers

Throughout the interwar period, U.S. naval thinking was dominated by the limitations imposed by the naval treaties, limitations that often made satisfactory war planning extremely difficult. Like other navies, therefore, the U.S. Navy sought legal means of circumventing the limitations in treaties, or at least of preparing for the abrogation that would surely follow any outbreak of hostilities. The first category included both the issue of the 3,000 tons of "protection" in the two *Lexington*s and Admiral Moffet's idea of the flight-deck cruiser, which was essentially a flight deck built as part of cruiser tonnage whose total would not be regulated by the Washington Treaty. (Discussion of the flight-deck cruiser is deferred until a subsequent cruiser volume, since it soon became a true combination of conventional cruiser and carrier characteristics.) More spectacular, and also more covert, was preparation for mobilization in the event of war, when a sudden expansion of the carrier force would be required. Since new hulls took, on average, about three years to build, mobilization planning always had to embrace the conversion of existing ships. Although there were some discussions of flight-deck conversions of existing and planned cruisers as early as 1925, those ships were vital elements of the battle fleet. Any new carriers, then, would have to be built on merchant hulls.

What distinguishes the prewar merchant conversions from the wartime CVE program is the resemblance of the former to full fleet carriers. There was no willingness before the war to accept the austere standards that made the CVE practicable; indeed, it does not appear that the prewar planning program had any substantial influence on wartime developments. Rather, the program was an exercise in the extent to which non-naval hulls could be adapted to make up for prewar treaty (and budget) limitations. The carrier conversion planning was only part of a very large interwar program of identifying suitable merchant hulls for naval use in wartime. C & R maintained a file of general arrangement plans of such ships and developed the necessary conversion plans. These ships were all required for the execution of the principal prewar national army-navy war plan, ORANGE, which envisaged a fleet advance across the Pacific against Japan. No peacetime navy budget could support the vast number of auxiliaries, including transports, that any realistic ORANGE Plan required.

ORANGE required very substantial naval air forces even in its early interwar versions—ultimately Japan was to be defeated from the air. In a typical version, the original ORANGE Plan of 1929, fleet units were to be dispatched to the Western Pacific,

The U.S. Navy planned an air war in the Western Pacific, but its resources were stringently limited by treaty; in 1933, for example, there were only three fleet carriers. They are shown here at Colon, in the Canal Zone.

XCV conversions became practicable with the advent of fast American liners in the thirties. The *President Hoover* is shown running her trials, June 1931.

where the Asiatic Fleet would be fighting a holding action against Japanese forces. If M were mobilization day, it was hoped that the main force of the U.S. Fleet could be concentrated in Hawaiian waters on M + 30. Subsequent concentrations in those waters were to be formed at thirty-day intervals for a variety of purposes. They would carry the expeditionary force and replacement personnel and aircraft, as well as the supplies necessary to support the fleet and associated troops. An advanced fleet base was to be seized in the Western Pacific. If possible Manila Bay would also be defended and developed as an advanced fleet base. In addition, it would be essential to provide sufficient protection against possible Japanese raids in the Canal Zone, before Japanese naval forces could be contained in the Western Pacific. Since the ORANGE Plan opened with an estimate that hostilities might well begin without warning, such containment early in the war would be impossible. Similarly, Hawaii would have to be defended as the principal outlaying naval base, and indeed as the base at which convoys would be concentrated at monthly intervals for passage to the Western Pacific. It was, incidentally, envisaged that portions of the Hawaiian Islands might be taken by the Japanese early in the war.

Operations would largely be mounted from the advanced bases, and much of the plan concerned their buildup for sufficient fleet and air support in the foward areas. Moreover, it would be essential to provide repair and support in the forward areas, as well as repair and dry-docking facilities in the Western Pacific. Once initial advanced bases had been secured, stocked, and defended, army forces in the theater would be built up to seize additional advanced bases closer to Japan's main islands, which in turn would be built up for continuous operations. Ulti-

mately bases close enough to Japan would be secured for an air offensive by both army and navy aircraft, leading to the destruction of ORANGE naval, military, and air bases, as well as "activities engaged in the production and transportation of war necessities, by intensive air attacks." This air offensive was essential, since ORANGE did not envisage anything approaching the logistical (or manpower) buildup necessary for an invasion of Japan.

Sea control around Japan would be secured by "the destruction or disorganization of the ORANGE fleet, the practical destruction of ORANGE aviation, the conduct of intensive Naval Operations in the SEA OF ORANGE against ORANGE Sea Communications, [and] the increasingly effective patrol of all approaches to ports in the ORANGE MAIN ISLANDS." Submarines would be used against Japanese commerce "under the same rules of international law as apply to surface vessels, unless and until the action of ORANGE in this respect forces us to do otherwise."

In its broad outline, the 1929 plan summarizes U.S. naval strategy in the Pacific in World War II. We were unable to hold the Philippines and, therefore, had to seize operating bases in the Western Pacific, perhaps most notably Ulithi, from which the fast carriers could indeed operate at length further West. The Philippines were seized in part as a major base area for the direct invasion of Japan, a step apparently not contemplated in 1929. Moreover, the ORANGE Plan does not, at least not explicitly, suggest the devastating effect that its blockade strategy would surely have on Japan, given the latter's dependence on overseas sources of raw material and even of fuel. It is remarkable in retrospect that the 1929 plan contemplated the use of aircraft for the major role of subduing Japan, as the B-29s were

Beside additional fleet carriers, the ORANGE Plan called for large shipments of replacement aircraft to the battle zone. During and after World War II the escort carriers fulfilled that role. For a time they were fully armed. This is the *Cape Esperance*, and the aircraft on deck date the photograph to about the Korean War period. Although the air force fighters and liaison aircraft are all cocooned to avoid sea corrosion, the four Hellcats forward appear to be ready for flight. Navy aircraft were rarely cocooned, since they were designed to be corrosion resistant. These Hellcats may well have been the F6F-5K drones tested against shore targets in Korea.

actually used in 1945. Amphibious operations were a major feature of the ORANGE Plan, as was the use of naval and land-based aircraft. Moreover, although the planners did not explicitly allow for the loss of any of the warships in U.S. hands at the outbreak of war, they did expect a loss of 25 percent of aircraft and pilots for every month of combat. Indeed, much of the logistical plan that accompanied the main ORANGE Plan was an attempt to provide sufficient replacements, in the form of men and aircraft, to continue to prosecute the war.

As its explicit concentration on aircraft suggests, the ORANGE Plan required considerable numbers of both aircraft and carriers, well beyond the two large and one small carrier available in 1929. The first concentration would depart Hawaii for the Western Pacific. It would include twelve battleships and all three carriers, the latter with ninety fighters, seventy-two observation planes (including those on battleships and cruisers), and fifty-four torpedo and bombing aircraft. With the fleet would sail a large

expeditionary force of about 20,000 marines, 18,000 army troops, and enough logistical support for the advanced fleet base.

The carriers would each have only a two-month supply of reserve aircraft (the usual 50 percent), so that the supply of spare crated aircraft would soon become critical. However, as of M + 30 there would be no further active carriers available to the United States. Moreover, the next convoy, with 55,000 army troops, would exhaust the remaining battleships, all ten light cruisers having been included in the first. They would add only twenty fighters, ten observation planes, and four torpedo and bombing aircraft to the total, including aircraft aboard the seaplane tender *Wright*, the only remaining specialized aviation ship in the fleet.

All further active manned aircraft would be aboard converted merchant ships, either carriers or seaplane tenders. The latter were considerably easier to convert than were full carriers, and in 1929 it appears that the limitations of floatplanes compared to landplanes were not nearly so evident as they were a few years later. Unfortunately the same advance in landplane performance also made the conversion of a merchant ship into a carrier a much more difficult project, and so reduced her value in the context of mobilization.

Thus the M + 90 concentration was to include sixteen fighters, eight observation planes, eighteen bombers, and transports for 40,000 army troops, 10,000 marines, and army aircraft (which would also be carried by earlier convoys). On M + 120 and afterward, monthly convoys would each carry up to 50,000 troops per month, as well as "maximum practicable additional aircraft for the Fleet."

The high expected rate of aircraft loss in the Western Pacific made the conversion of a large number of specialized transports for replacement aircraft and pilots (XAPV) essential. The 1929 ORANGE Plan shows, for example, a total of 103 manned and 12 unmanned "fleet augmentation aircraft" in the M + 60 convoy, of which all but 9 seaplane torpedo bombers (manned) would be aboard ships of the fleet train; those 9 would be aboard a converted seaplane tender. That concentration also included three converted aircraft repair ships. In the M + 120 convoy, the first of the converted carriers would transport, beside her manned "fleet augmentation" aircraft, a fleet replacement air group of 27 VF-VBs, 36 VO-VSs, and 18 land-based and 9 floatplane torpedo bombers. Presumably the large hold capacity of a converted merchant ship would make her particularly useful for such service. In later convoys, unmanned fleet

reserve aircraft were distinguished from "fleet augmentation" aircraft and "fleet replacement" aircraft, the latter transported aboard train vessels. That is, the XCVs were considered as augmenting the base strength of the fleet as it built up in the Western Pacific, whereas reserves and replacements were means of overcoming expected attrition. Since the ORANGE Plan made no explicit allowance for losses of warships, the XCVs did not represent replacements for the relatively fragile carriers. New construction did not enter any of these equations, since it would take so much time to build even the smallest specially designed carrier.

In the late thirties the entire concept of a major fleet movement westward at the outbreak of war came into question. General Board discussions of new battleship construction, for example, began to include mention of independent carrier raids early in a war, well before battle fleets could come into contact. The first of the post–Washington Treaty U.S. battleship designs, which resulted in the *North Carolina*s, were endowed with very high speed (by U.S. standards) so that they could operate with fast carriers; later the *Iowa* and *Alaska* classes were justified on a similar basis. It is not clear to what extent the gradual evolution of U.S. war planning for a conflict with Japan affected the concept of a steady buildup in Hawaiian waters once the fleet had steamed west to seize its advanced base. The expectation of stronger initial Japanese resistance should have somewhat relaxed the time scale for the buildup of carriers. On the other hand, the carrier strength necessary to

Later in the 1950s the aircraft transports were stripped of all but surface navigational radar, and all guns were removed. This is the *Cape Esperance*, carrying navy Banshees and Skyraiders. At this time she was designated a T-CVU (utility carrier) and was civilian manned by the Military Sea Transportation Command. Not long afterward she and her *Casablanca*-class sisters were replaced by *Bogue*-class C-3 conversions, which were more economical to operate.

achieve naval superiority in the disputed area of the Western Pacific would be greater at the outset (when no converted carriers could possibly be available), and the prospective loss of the Philippines relatively early in a war would also greatly complicate matters.

As early as 1923 plans were drawn for the wholesale conversion of existing merchant ships to types performing a variety of naval missions. Most were auxiliaries, and indeed prewar planning experience in this area may have proven useful when large numbers of conversions were carried out for World War II. The list of ships required to make up deficiencies included carriers.

The first version of the basic mobilization document, WPL-10 (May 1924), shows a requirement for nine second-line converted carriers, to be ships of 13,000 or more gross tons, 600 by 54 feet or more, with watertight subdivisions and a maximum sustained speed of 25 knots. The list of available ships was sadly inadequate: there were only seven in all, none of them approaching the speed requirement and most of them elderly. The *Leviathan* was the largest of the lot, but she was a coal-burner, and that limited her ability to fuel at sea. The only oil-burners were the Atlantic Transport Company's 15,442-tonners, the *Manchuria* and *Mongolia* (1904; 14 knots, with 12,000-nm endurance at that speed), and the U.S. Shipping Board's 18,372-ton *Mount Vernon* (1906; 20 knots, with 5,000-nm endurance at that speed). The U.S. Shipping Board could also supply four coal-burners: the *Leviathan* (1913; 54,282 tons; 21 knots; 4,905 nautical miles), the *Agamemnon* (1902; 19,361 tons; 20 knots; 4,600 nautical miles), the *America* (1905; 22,621 tons; 15 knots; 8,620 nautical miles), and the *George Washington* (1908; 25,570 tons; 15 knots; 8,900 nautical miles). All were ex-German liners seized in 1917, and few would survive for more than a few years. Moreover, all had alternate mobilization assignments as troop ships, a function of great importance in a trans-Pacific war.

Matters did not improve very quickly. A revision of WPL-10 (July 1925) showed eight liners (it added the Atlantic Transportation Company's *Minnekahda* [1917, a 17,281-ton coal-burner capable of 16.5 knots with a 10,000-nm cruising radius]). The *Leviathan* had been converted to oil fuel (for a cruising radius of 5,673 nautical miles at 24 knots), and somewhat more optimistic figures were provided for the other ships. However, of the eight, all but the *Agamemnon*, *Leviathan*, and *Mount Vernon*, the three fastest (21, 24, and 22 knots, respectively), had priority assignments as troop ships.

War planning did not reflect the shortage of appropriate liners, and there is no evidence that the government policy of the time favored special appropriations for ships suitable for conversion— that came only later. The ORANGE Plan of 1929 shows the first XCV joining the fleet concentration at Hawaii on M + 120, carrying eighteen fighters, eighteen fighter-bombers, and eighteen torpedo bombers. She was not an escort carrier: she was, in effect, a slow fleet carrier. XCV 1 would be converted at Boston Navy Yard, with a second ship (XCV 2) completed at New York on M + 120 and loaded with eighteen

Some of the aircraft-transport conversions were elaborate. This is the *Core* in Saigon Harbor in 1962, with two large cranes added on deck to handle cargo aircraft. Her deck load includes a training version of the Cougar fighter, which the marines used in gunfire support spotting during the Vietnam War, three Albatross amphibians, and a cocooned Crusader fighter.

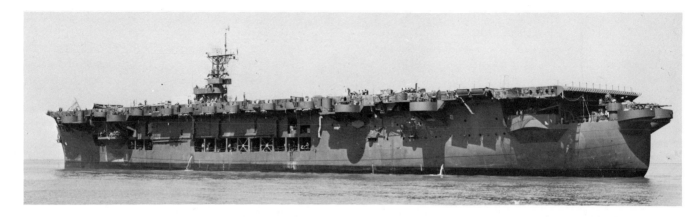

The *Chenango* is shown after a September 1943 Mare Island refit. The ex-tankers of the *Sangamon* class performed, in effect, as fleet carriers during the drastic shortage of the latter in 1942–43; they supported the North African landings as well as operations in the Pacific. Unlike some Atlantic escort carriers, they had no short HF/DF mast forward.

fighters and eighteen scouts at San Francisco fifteen days later, for arrival at Hawaii on M + 150. Thus two conversions were considered roughly equivalent, in plane-operating capacity, to a single fleet carrier. The other seven XCV then contemplated were to follow at the New York and Philadelphia yards at intervals of thirty days, the last joining the fleet in Hawaii a year after M-day.

The great flaw in this plan was the absence, in the U.S. merchant marine, of suitable fast merchant ships for conversion. In the twenties the only really large fast ship was the *Leviathan*, 950 feet long and capable of 23 knots. She was so important that detailed plans were debated before the General Board in 1926. One member commented that if the *Leviathan* were given a ramp rather than an elevator she would be able to accommodate two takeoff positions. A few years later U.S. Lines contemplated construction of a very large fast Atlantic liner, and C & R immediately drew up carrier conversion plans.

In June 1929, WPL-10 did not even list large liners for conversion, as these ships had all been assigned as troop transports. Moreover, it was admitted that conversion time might be too lengthy for any mobilization program. Requirements had, by then, been relaxed to 17,000 gross tons and 20 knots on oil fuel (radius 6,000 nautical miles), with at least a 500- by 50-ft flight deck. The air group would comprise up to seventy-two bombers; armament would be six 6-in guns, eight 3-in AA guns, and eight machine guns. An alternative converted carrier (small) might be 450 to 500 feet long (400- by 60-ft deck), 11 knots (oil fuel, with a radius of 6,000 nautical miles), and made to carry two squadrons (eighteen VFs, eighteen VBs). She would have four 6-in guns, four 3-in AA guns, and eight machine guns. Both classes were to be able to survive a single underwater hit and were to have periods of roll of not less than 14 seconds.

By this time there were three fleet carriers in service and a fourth (the *Ranger*) under construction;

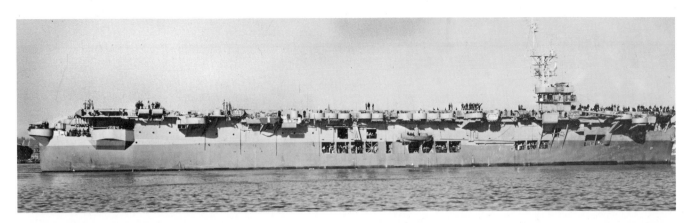

The *Suwanee* is shown at Puget Sound on 26 January 1945, after a refit. She appears to have a fighter-director radar on her mast; at this time many escort carriers were being fitted as fighter-director ships to support amphibious operations, and one escort-carrier commander maintained that his ships were actually facing more combat hazards than were the larger fleet carriers, since the former were tied to the beachhead and could not enjoy the advantage of tactical surprise.

ORANGE required only six small XCVs, and WPL-10 listed a total of nine candidates for conversion. Four were motorships: the *California* (445 by 59.8 feet, 11.5 knots), *East Indian* (445 by 58 feet, 14 knots), *Missourian* (445.1 by 59.8 feet, 11.5 knots), and *William Penn* (439.6 by 60.2 feet, 11 knots). The *James Otis*, *John Adams*, and *John Jay* were 439.6- by 60.2-ft, 11-kt steamers; the *Manukai* and *Manulani*, 480.6- by 62.2-ft, 12-kt steamers. Conversion plans have not been located, but these ships were freighters, and apparently they would have become, in effect, CVEs.

Matters did not improve until after 1929, when several fast liners were built in the United States. Panama-Pacific lines completed three turbo-electric liners in 1928–29: the *California*, *Pennsylvania*, and *Virginia* (600 feet, 18.5 knots). U.S. Lines completed the 705-ft *Manhattan* and *Washington*, each 21 knots, in 1932–33. Matson completed the 582-ft, 22-kt *Ma-*

lolo (later the *Matsonia*) in 1927 and the 632-ft, 20-kt *Mariposa Lurline* and *Monterey* in 1932. The Dollar Line (later American President Lines) built the 654-ft, 21-kt *President Hoover* and *President Coolidge* in 1931. These classes formed the basis for a new cycle of studies.

In 1933, for example, the two ships in the *President Coolidge* class, the three in the *Mariposa* class, and those in the *Manhattan* class were scheduled for carrier conversion. Although XCV plans were drawn for them, the *Californias* headed the list of projected wartime cruiser conversions, which included the *Malolo*. By this time naval aviation was considered so important that the war plan called for twelve XCVs, although conversion plans existed for only ten, including the *Californias*. Thus WPL-10 included the conversion of two old coal-burning liners, the *Monticello* (ex-*Agamemnon*) and her sister, the *Mount Ver-*

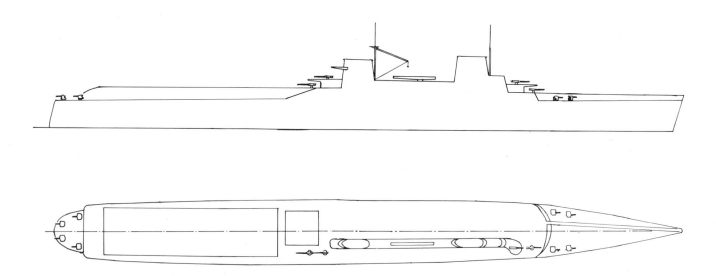

C & R plan for a carrier conversion of a proposed 980-ft high speedliner, 18 July 1928. The battery was four 6-in Mark 13s and eight 5-in/25 AA guns. This design was proposed for North Atlantic service by a specially formed Blue Ribbon Line in the Fall of 1927. The liners would have had flight decks even in commercial service (for mail planes), and it appears that the aircraft carrier features were intended partly to gain a large U.S. government loan. The project, which was rejected as economically unsound by the U.S. Shipping Board in April 1928, remained alive through that summer.

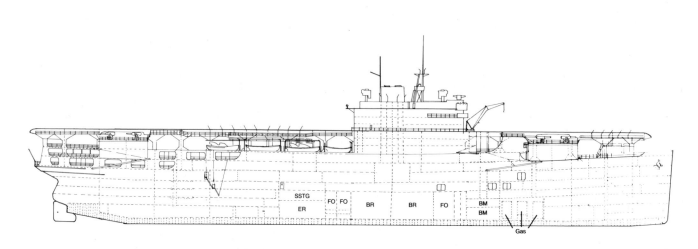

Plan for carrier conversion of the liner *President Hoover*, 1935.

non. Both were unsuitable, given their lack of stability (for example, they had a negative GM of 2.6 feet in the light condition); they would have to be blistered. In December 1934 the bureaus suggested their omission. The war plan as then written contemplated a total of fifteen carriers, three fleet and twelve converted. However, with the completion of the *Ranger* and the laying down of the *Yorktown* and *Enterprise,* the carrier total would come to sixteen without the two old coal-burners. BuAer concurred, and the next January both were assigned primary classification as troop transports. The Atlantic Transport Company's ex-Belgian liner *Columbia* (ex-*Belgenland,* 1917, 696 feet, oil fuel, 18 knots) was added to the XCV list. She was, however, broken up in 1936.

In April 1935 C & R noted that no XCV conversion could be completed in less than 180 days, and then only if some preparation were carried out before M-Day. The war plan in force at this time required completion of four XCVs within that period, at M + 90, M + 120, M + 150, and M + 180. The bureau considered elevators a controlling factor and was developing a cable-type one to facilitate conversion. It urged the design of an elevator that firms might bid on. War Plans feared that

> it will be necessary to give information to commercial concerns which might disclose the intention to convert merchant ships to carriers, and even to the extent of identifying the particular ships which have been selected.... Weighed against this chance of disclosure is the expediting of the conversion program. These converted carriers will be the first to augment the Fleet, thus will provide the first increase of operating planes of the carrier type in the Fleet. Anything which will assist in the early departure of these carriers is important....

Elevator plans were purchased under the FY 36 program and detailed conversion blueprints prepared. Their typical characteristics are shown in table 6–1.

The Maritime Commission replaced the former U.S. Shipping Board in 1936; one of its functions was to provide the fleet with ships suitable for wartime conversion. The Maritime Commission's hull no. 1, the *America* (723 feet, 23 knots), was a replacement for the *Leviathan.* In November 1937 Admiral William D. Leahy, acting Secretary of the Navy, asked the Maritime Commission to contract with the building yard, Newport News, for a set of carrier conversion plans. However, at about the same time the future of the XCV was bleak: a C & R sheet of 1939 shows 360 days for conversion—the other longest conversions took only one-third this time.

The April 1939 version of ORANGE showed 5 fleet carriers, 2 seaplane tenders (the *Langley* had by this time been converted), and 8 small seaplane tenders

Table 6-1.

	California	*Manhattan*	*President Hoover*
LOA	601-1¼	705	654
LWL	594	685	630
B	80	86	81
T (load)	32-3	30-0	32-0
Disp't	30,250	32,700	31,063
SHP		30,000	26,500
Speed	18.9	20	20.5
Cruise	17,350	11,000	15,000
Avgas	138,600	130,762	136,000
VF	27	27	27
VO	18	18	18
VB	15	15	15

Note: In each, eight 5-in/38 DP, forty 0.50-cal MG.

(AVPs) in the initial concentration, with a total of 113 scout bombers, 72 torpedo/level bombers, 90 heavy dive-bombers, and 90 fighters, among other aircraft. By this time the seaplane tenders were perceived largely as a means of moving the navy's heavy long-range patrol seaplanes, 186 of which were included in the original movement. No aircraft at all could be included in the M + 60 concentration, but M + 90 was to include the carrier *Wasp* (presumably to be completed on an accelerated basis), as well as two new large and small seaplane tenders. For M + 120 only converted seaplane tenders could be provided, two XAVs and two XAVPs; no converted carriers would yet be available. They were reserved for the M + 150 to M + 360 part of the logistical plan, which was not generally further elaborated.

In October 1939 an OPNAV summary included the *California*s, *Mariposa*s, *Manhattan*s, the *President Coolidge,* and the *America.* "Admittedly these vessels are not inherently entirely suitable, and are only selected as the best which can be obtained from those available.... All of the above ships have gun foundations built in, but these foundations will be of no use if converted to carriers, as they are on present deck, which will be blanked by flight deck...." Conversion would cost about $6 million per ship.

On the other hand, in 1939–40 the commission did plan a new 25-kt liner designed specially for ready conversion to a carrier, the P 4P. Speaking before the Society of Naval Architects and Marine Engineers in 1940, Admiral E. S. Land, a former chief constructor and then chairman of the Maritime Commission, described the origin of the P 4P. Three of the *Presidents* then serving on the West Coast–Orient route were aging, and another of them, the *President Hoover,* was lost in December 1937.

Some time after the preliminary consideration of this service had been undertaken it was learned that Japan contemplated building two 24-knot passenger

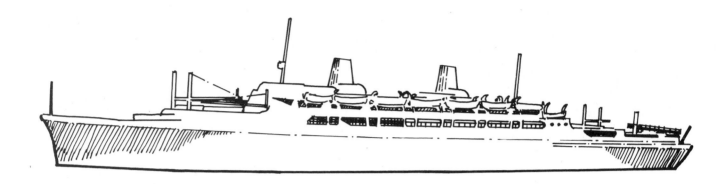

P-4P, the Maritime Commission design for a liner convertible to a carrier. This sketch was made from a photograph of a Maritime Commission model, published when bids were requested in 1940.

liners of very great size to operate in the trans-Pacific service. Continued study developed the fact that a 24-knot speed for our proposed replacements would make it possible to maintain a 42-hour schedule with two new P-4's as compared with the three originally contemplated.

It then became apparent that the great size of these ships (due both to their high speed and to the large deadweight resulting from the big cargo capacity and big amounts of fuel required) would make possible their satisfactory service as airplane carriers. Accordingly, it was determined to design these ships so that their conversion for airplane carrier service could be carried out with the greatest facility. While the structural features and the location of machinery necessary to bring this about, together with the effect on size of the large power plant necessary to give the maximum speed required, resulted in a very large vessel and one which is in some respects expensive, it is felt that nothing is involved which interferes appreciably with their satisfactory operation in the normal merchant service.

At this time Admiral Land listed the navy requirement of a total of sixty-five ships for conversion upon mobilization, including three carriers, one auxiliary cruiser, and nineteen tenders. The commission proposed to meet the need for hulls suitable for conversion to carriers with three "Ambassador"-class liners; these would be used for South American service, and the project would be separate from that providing for the Pacific service. A table of the ten-year Maritime Commission program showed a potential total of thirteen P 4-class (22-kt or more) passenger ships: three for the New York–Europe run, three for the South American run, three for the Pacific run to Australia and New Zealand, and four for the Pacific run to the major Asiatic ports. The Pacific ships were projected at 22,000 gross tons, the Europeans at up to 26,000, and the South Americans at 14,000.

Plans and specifications for two ships, to be operated by the American President Lines, were issued by the Maritime Commission on 13 February 1940. Cost was estimated at about $22 million, and the ships would carry 1,000 U.S. civilian passengers and a crew of 500. At the time, only three U.S. civilian yards were considered capable of building such ships—Bethlehem Fore River (Quincy), Newport News, and the New York Shipbuilding Corporation (Camden)—and all three had large navy commitments. However, on 10 September the Maritime Commission announced receipt of one bid, from the much smaller Seattle-Tacoma Shipbuilding Corporation (later Todd-Tacoma), a company then building only destroyers and smaller merchant ships. It offered two ships at $28,450,000 each (fixed price), the first to be completed in 1,080 days, the second in 1,445 days. It appears that no contract was ever let.

With the German successes in the spring of 1940, the navy began to claim a larger and larger fraction of total national shipbuilding capacity. "For a time there was more than a slight tendency on the part of the Navy Department to forget its need of merchant ship auxiliaries. . . . The Maritime Commission on its part held that most types of merchant ship would be of definite value in time of war, and that, should the present war prove long or short, both the normal cargo vessel of the C types and the passenger cargo vessels of the C-3 conversion types would be national assets. The same statement held for the large fast tankers." Ironically, indeed, both the C-3s and the tankers would form the basis for escort carrier conversions in 1942. However, in 1940 Land did find it difficult to justify the construction of large ships such as liners. He fell back on the carrier-conversion capacity of the P 4P, which "could be built and completed for airplane carrying and operating purposes so that, if necessary, she would be a valuable naval unit. On the other hand, after the emergency has passed such a ship having a great steaming radius, great cargo capacity and high speed, providing her draft be not excessive, can hardly fail to furnish satisfactory transport for freight and passengers on some of the great water routes of the world."

Not long afterwards, J. E. Schmeltzer, the associate director of the commission's Technical Division, wrote that "the main idea was to build the hull, power plant, etc., as a carrier and adapt it to merchant requirements with only necessary and acceptable changes. The Commission hopes to build five. . . . It is intended to write off about $8 million of the estimated $20 million cost as national defense features."

For example, in common with then-current warship-design practice, the new ship was to have had her machinery in two separate units, one for each shaft, each with a 29,000-SHP (maximum output 44,000 SHP) turbine. The two units would be separated by two smaller auxiliary rooms containing the main evaporating plant. Carrier conversion would be facilitated by a design in which, even in peacetime, both funnels were on one side of the ship. It appears that the Maritime Commission hoped to use national-defense funding to buy a radical new type of machinery, since the projected P 4 plant would have operated at 1,200 pounds per square inch (but at only 750°F) on a regenerative cycle: steam being exhausted from the high-pressure turbine would be returned to the reheater section of the main steam generator before entering the intermediate-pressure turbine.

A 15 percent reduction in fuel consumption, compared with that in a normal steam plant operating at the same pressure and temperature, was claimed, as well as a much flatter fuel-economy curve, giving about the same economy at half, normal, and full power. Another unusual machinery feature proposed for the P 4P was variable-pitch propellers. The combination of national-defense and liner features would produce a very large ship, with an estimated displacement of 41,000 tons and a length of 760 feet (unconverted).

By 1940 aircraft had so improved that the conversion of large liners no longer seemed nearly so attractive. Moreover, the treaty limits had been breached, and large numbers of *Essex*-class fleet carriers were on order, albeit for delivery only from 1944 onward. Even so, it appeared that satisfactory liner conversions would be lengthy at best. That November the CNO ordered BuShips to end the preparation of con-

version plans; the Secretary of the Navy had already quashed P 4P and other Maritime Commission hopes with his statement that "the characteristics of aircraft have changed, placing more exacting demands upon the carrier . . . such that a converted merchant vessel will no longer make as satisfactory an aircraft carrier as was the case when the plans for these vessels were being drawn."

The XCV program did survive, but only on paper. As of 1941, conversions were to provide space for seventy-two aircraft (four squadrons of fighters and bombers), although complements were sized for sixty. The last revision of WPL-10 (September 1941) noted that since conversion would require about a year, it was unlikely to be ordered. However, plans had been distributed for four classes: the two *Manhattan*s, the two *President*s, the three *Mariposa*s, and the three *Uruguay*s (ex-*California*s), which together would have provided a total of ten ships.

The other two major carrier operators also faced treaty and other restrictions on total aircraft-carrier tonnage, and both Britain and Japan considered merchant-ship conversions during the thirties, apparently without U.S. knowledge, at least before the outbreak of war. For Britain, the important issue was defense of trade against surface raiders and submarines, and inexpensive carriers were essential. There were some informal discussions in the Royal Navy in 1926 about using auxiliary carriers (considered analogous to armed merchant cruisers) in order to free fleet carriers for vital missions. Details have not survived, and no staff requirements (characteristics) were issued. In 1931 a study of convoy arrangements led to a suggestion that some merchant ships be fitted with a catapult and a landing-on deck, an arrangement that must have resembled the one first adopted for the U.S. prototype escort carrier, the *Long Island*, a decade later. However, ships so fitted were to have retained their centerline funnels. Outline plans for fitting a variety of existing ships, from 14,000 to 20,000 gross tons (15 to 20 knots), had been evolved by 1934; they generally envisaged a hangar, an elevator, and a landing deck 285 by 65 to 300 by 80 feet. Although these conversions were extremely austere by contemporary U.S. XCV standards, the British director of naval construction (DNC) estimated that they would require nine to twelve months each. Further study showed that the centerline superstructure would cause problems, and attention shifted to diesel ships, which would be easier to modify with a full-length flight deck. Again, this is precisely the line of reasoning the U.S. Navy followed in 1940–41.

Thus by 1935 the Admiralty had specific requirements for merchant ships suited to conversion to what it called trade protection carriers: gross ton-

The only changes the *Chenango* shows in this January 1945 view are improved electronics (indicated by the circled mast area) and a whaleboat amidships.

nage between 10,000 and 20,000 tons, diesel machinery for the highest possible speed, an endurance of at least 6,000 nautical miles at 14 knots, a flight deck at least 70 feet wide, stowage for twelve to eighteen aircraft, and a 4.7-in AA battery. Plans for two typical conversions, the *Winchester Castle* (diesel, 20,000 tons, 631 feet) and the *Waipawa* (diesel, 12,500 tons, 516 feet), each with twin screws, were prepared in 1936, and DNC suggested that specific merchant ships be earmarked for emergency conversion—which he estimated would require twelve months. The next year five ships were selected: four Union Castle liners (the sisters *Winchester Castle* and *Warwick Castle*, completed in 1930–31, the *Dunvegan Castle*, completed in 1938, and the *Dunottar Castle*, completed in 1936) and the Pacific Steam Navigation Company's *Reina del Pacifico*, completed in 1931. Staff was too limited, however, for details of the projected conversions to be worked out at the time, and of the five ships two became armed merchant cruisers and three, troop ships. Meanwhile, outline plans had been completed in December 1936 and a provisional staff requirement issued by the Naval Air Division in March 1937. Studies were resumed after the crisis that resulted in the signing of the Munich Pact but, as in the United States a few years later, full fleet carriers were given priority, particularly since it was expected that, with the completion of six armored carriers between 1940 and 1942, there would be a total of thirteen full fleet carriers, sufficient for all requirements.

From a U.S. point of view the significant consequence of all of this work was that, once war had broken out and the requirements for convoy protection had once again become evident, there was a base

upon which to build. The British director of air material proposed the conversion that became HMS *Audacity* on 5 December 1940, a staff requirement was stated on 12 December, and on 2 January 1941 a German prize then being refitted as an armed boarding vessel was allocated (initial information was provided to the shipyard on 17 January and the ship was completed on 26 June 1941). By that time the United States already had the *Long Island*, but plans for the *Winchester Castle* conversion were provided by the Admiralty in 1941, and they did influence the U.S. CVE designs, at least in detail.

As for Japan, trade protection and the treaty limits do not appear to have been such significant issues. However, the Japanese were uncomfortably aware of the industrial superiority of the United States and had to plan unusual measures for their own mobilization. The 1938 supplement to the Vinson-Trammell Act appears to have been particularly sobering, because it showed that the U.S. Congress could vote an unlimited increase to the statutory size of the navy, an increase the Japanese knew the United States could maintain. The 1938 bill itself included 40,000 tons of carriers, which became the *Hornet* and *Essex*. In order to maintain at least a 7:10 ratio, the Japanese now planned to convert merchant ships and certain auxiliaries (some of which incorporated features intended for conversion) to carriers. The most spectacular were the two 24-kt liners—ironically, exactly the ones Admiral Land referred to in connection with the P 4P project—laid down for the NYK Line in 1939. Planning for their construction began in 1936, as the Japanese were withdrawing from the system of treaty limitations, and both received naval subsidies. The two ships were designed specifically for conver-

Although no liners were ever converted to fleet carriers, some of the escort carriers approached fleet-carrier capability, at least in the types of aircraft they could operate. Of the conversions, the former tankers of the *Sangamon* class were clearly the best. Here one steams alongside a *New Orleans*–class cruiser of similar dimensions. The *Sangamons* could be distinguished by the openings in their sides above their former tanker main decks.

sion, naval design requirements including a greater height between decks, a stronger main deck, the more extensive wiring that a liner would require, better subdivision, and a longitudinal bulkhead in the engine spaces. The liner design also made provision for later construction of hangars, installation of elevators, and extra fuel and avgas tanks. In 1938 the Japanese Navy supplied 60 percent of their building cost. They were taken over for conversion under the 1940–41 budget in response to the U.S. "Two-Ocean Navy" Act of 19 July 1940, together with the *Kasuga*

Maru (which became a CVE); the submarine depot ships *Takasaki* and *Tsurugizaki* had already been converted as replies to the Vinson-Trammell Act of 1938. The two ex-liners were the only merchant ships in the world completed as XCVs. Other Japanese conversions produced rough equivalents of CVEs, but the *Hiyo* and *Junyo* came closest to the abortive U.S. concepts of the thirties. The complexity of their conversions suggests, moreover, that abandoning the XCV concept was not a bad idea.

7

The *Essex* Class

The *Essex* class best symbolizes the success of the U.S. carrier. Designed on the eve of World War II, these ships formed the basis of the fast carrier task force, which won the great victories of 1944–45, and served in both Korea and Vietnam. Now there are proposals to withdraw one or more from reserve for further duty. They comprised the most numerous class of U.S. fleet carriers and are certainly the most affectionately remembered. Yet as early as 1945 they were considered obsolescent, cramped, poorly protected. In common with virtually all other U.S. warships of prewar design and wartime construction, they were seriously overweight and indeed had lost some of their originally designed power of survival because of top weight.

Yet they must be adjudged extremely successful. In World War II they operated what turned out to be the largest air group adaptable to U.S. deck-load-strike tactics. The larger *Midway*s did have larger air groups, but it appears that their greater numbers could not be efficiently operated. The smaller *Independence* class had a higher accident rate and, indeed, could not operate as many aircraft per ton of displacement, that is, per unit cost. They may also have been the smallest size carriers that could be modernized advantageously after the war: they could be converted to operate jet aircraft and still accommodate a useful air group. Certainly the British found that the "overhead" of specialized aircraft (such as AEW and ASW) set a lower limit on the useful size of a jet carrier. The limited size of the *Essex* must have

facilitated rapid production, so that twenty-four units were completed, most of them in wartime. That figure alone made it inevitable that the *Essex*es would dominate the postwar fleet, barring congressional willingness to finance any substantial new construction program. However, it was the adaptability of the basic design that allowed the U.S. naval-air arm to modernize effectively and fight so well in Korea, which in turn contributed, perhaps decisively, to the continued construction of carriers for the U.S. Navy.

Like the contemporary *Baltimore*-class cruisers, the *Essex*es were a halfway design. They were developed after the end of the treaty regime and thus were considerably larger than comparable ships designed a few years earlier. However, the press of events dictated that their design would be developed from that of the earlier, treaty-bound class, so that they were somewhat smaller than ships later deemed ideal. For example, they had torpedo protection short of battleship standards and, indeed, only slightly improved over that of the earlier *Yorktown* class (CV 5). In common with contemporary cruisers and battleships, they did introduce alternating engine and boiler rooms, an important protection against underwater damage that might penetrate the limited side protection. Similarly, they did have some deck protection intended specifically to counter bombing, where earlier carriers had been armored primarily against shellfire. However, they were not large enough to accommodate the armored flight deck of the later *Midway*s, and proposals for flight-deck

One of the first "long-hull" *Essex*es, the *Ticonderoga* displays her pair of bow 40-mm gun mounts in this August 1944 photograph. She also shows a cutout in her flight deck to provide an overhead arc for a third Mark 37 director, which was to have been mounted on her port catapult sponson to control the four portside 5-in guns. Note the deck slots for her two H 4B catapults forward and the cross-trees on her radio masts, from which wire antennas were slung. The later whips, by way of contrast, were active elements and required no wires between them.

Although earlier U.S. carriers had "double-ended" flight decks, the *Essex*es were the first in which speed astern was a design consideration. Here a TBF Avenger lands over the *Yorktown*'s bow while the carrier steams astern in 1943. Note that the plane could be recovered without disturbing the full load of aircraft parked in the usual takeoff position aft.

armor were rejected in the course of their design. Finally, the increased weight margins which became possible with the end of the treaty did contribute materially to their adaptability in wartime and even to their capacity for later reconstruction or, in the case of ASW and helicopter carriers, conversion.

It does not appear, in retrospect, that the *Essex* design owed anything to considerations of production, but the yards did succeed in greatly accelerating their construction. For example, the lead ship, the USS *Essex* (CV 9), was ordered in 1940 for completion in March 1944; she was commissioned instead on the last day of 1942, fifteen months early. Similarly, the *Yorktown* was more than seventeen months early, the *Intrepid* seventeen months early, and the *Hornet* six months early. Both the *Intrepid* and the *Hornet* had been laid down behind schedule. Throughout the war fleet carriers enjoyed a very high priority, and aside from the gear-cutting problem that afflicted the entire wartime ship program, did not suffer from any major bottlenecks; in 1944 Rear Admiral E. L. Cochrane, chief of the BuShips, reported that "the carrier program encountered fewer cases of delays resulting from material shortages than other programs owing to the high priority which [it] enjoyed." Carriers had first priority until May 1942, when landing craft for North Africa moved to top priority, and even then they continued above most surface ships, so that the *Essex* was completed in only seventeen months. By the time the destroyer escorts had moved to top priority late in 1942, most of the material for the fleet carriers was already in the pipeline.

Even so, the expected delays in carrier completions had by then led to the crash program in cruiser-hull conversions (the *Independence* class) to provide carrier hulls in commission in 1943. Meanwhile, during 1942 the U.S. Navy lost four out of its seven prewar fleet carriers.

The *Essex* class began with a single hull, planned in 1939 for construction under the FY 41 program, to absorb tonnage still available under the Vinson-Trammell Act. That law authorized sufficient tonnage to bring the United States up to the totals allowable under the Washington Naval Treaty, and so constituted a tonnage limit even after the expiration of that treaty. A 20 percent expansion program of 17 May 1938 added 40,000 tons to the originally permitted 175,000, providing for the *Hornet* and also for 20,000 tons of new carrier, which became CV 9. Beside the statutory total tonnage limit, there was also a 23,000-ton limit on individual carriers imposed by the London Naval Treaty of 1936. The new carrier design was funded under the FY 40 program for construction in FY 41.

By that time, however, it was clear that the U.S. Navy needed much more rapid expansion. The "Two-Ocean Navy" Act of 14 June 1940 provided for three more carriers (CVs 10–12)—which had already been ordered under a CNO directive of 20 May. Upon the fall of France, Congress voted an additional 70 percent expansion, with another seven fleet carriers (CVs 13–19) being ordered under a 16 August 1940 directive. Two more of the initial series, CVs 20–21, were ordered under a further expansion program, just after the outbreak of war on 15 December 1941. Hull nos. 22 through 30 were absorbed by the *Independence*-class conversions of light-cruiser hulls, and the first eleven ships absorbed the available slips for the first two years of the war. Six were awarded to Newport News, the lead yard, four to Bethlehem Quincy, and one to Norfolk Navy Yard. An additional ten were ordered from three navy yards on 7 August 1942 under the second war program (1943–44 for FY 43): CVs 31–35 from New York, CVs 36–37 from Philadelphia, and CVs 38–40 from Norfolk. Of these, CV 32 was later reordered from Newport News, to reduce

The new carrier *Yorktown* is shown off Norfolk Navy Yard on 27 April 1943. She was typical of the earliest *Essex*-class carriers. The large folding sponsons evident on either side of the forward hangar opening were extensions of the hangar-deck catapult. Note, too, the five radio towers, characteristic of these ships, which folded down for flight operations; the antennas proper were strung lengthwise between them. "Short-hull" *Essex*es were armed only with one quadruple 40-mm mount fore and aft, the after one off the centerline. The deck-edge elevator has been folded up. The tripod mast carries an SK air search antenna, with a smaller SC-2 at the after end of the funnel. The *Yorktown*, in very much modernized form, is preserved as a memorial at Patriot's Point, South Carolina.

congestion at New York Naval Shipyard. Three more were ordered on 14 June 1943 under an FY 44 program intended to exhaust available authorized combat tonnage: CVs 45–47, one each from Philadelphia, Newport News, and Bethlehem Quincy. Finally, in 1945 a program of six was proposed: CV 50 from Bethlehem Quincy, CVs 51–52 from New York, CV 53 from Philadelphia, and CVs 54–55 from Norfolk. However, this program was disapproved by the President on 22 March 1945, a month after the contracts had been provisionally awarded. Of the twenty-six others, all but two were completed, one of them, the *Oriskany*, to a modified design (see chapter 13).

Admiral Cochrane maintained that the number of available slipways was quite sufficient and, indeed, had not been a limit on the program. The major yards

were, fortunately, in the process of expansion as the *Essex* program began. Thus Newport News began with two slipways; the *Essex* was laid down on the ways on which the *Hornet* (CV 8) had been built, and the new *Yorktown* (CV 10) on ways vacated by the new 35,000-ton battleship *Indiana*. However, in 1940 the navy had awarded contracts for two new building docks, so that Newport News could accommodate four *Essex* hulls simultaneously. Bethlehem Quincy (formerly Fore River) had only one large slipway when it received an award for four carriers. However, two new ways were under construction, and two carriers were laid down on them as soon as they had progressed far enough. The fourth ship succeeded the first on the original slip. Ultimately eight were laid down at Newport News and five at Quincy. The three major East Coast naval shipyards built four each (three at Philadelphia). The 1940 expansion program had provided two new building docks at both New York and Philadelphia, and one new dock at Norfolk; all were completed in record time, well ahead of the needs of the carrier program.

The available tonnage, 20,400, was to be concentrated in a single ship of maximum size in view of the success of the *Yorktown*s and, as Rear Admiral F. J. Horne of the General Board indicated in July 1939, because

> experience with the *Ranger* shows that a sea-way tends to reduce her operating ability considerably. Also this carrier, and the *Wasp* of comparable tonnage, have a speed not in excess of 29 knots, so that neither of these two carriers will be entirely satisfactory for all of the varied missions an effective carrier should be capable of undertaking. Nor is there incorporated in either of them many of the basic characteristics considered desirable, or even essential, for an effective aircraft carrier. . . .

> Study of various displacement possibilities . . . indicates that a standard tonnage in the neighborhood of 20,000 tons gives the most advantageous arrangement of most essential features and at the same time gives the greatest percentage of aircraft carrying and operating capacity with relation to individual tonnage. . . . Experience has shown that with a tonnage below 20,000 standard, the larger and heavier types of aircraft, such as torpedo-bombers, cannot be operated effectively.

> A well worked out plan for a carrier of 10,000 tons standard displacement with a speed of 32 knots clearly indicates that a maximum of 36 aircraft of medium size could be operated from such a carrier. Such a displacement indicates a vessel, however, that could not operate effectively in even a moderate swell such as is habitually encountered in the Pacific.

The single strongest driving force in the *Essex* design appears to have been a desire to operate a larger air group of individually larger aircraft. Flight-deck area equated to operable air-group size. The *Yorktown*s had been designed to operate ninety aircraft, but by 1939 they were down to eighty-one larger ones, and there was no question but that the new generation of naval aircraft would be much larger and would need longer deck runs to takeoff (that is, that parking area in existing flight decks would be reduced). Given a clear area on the *Yorktown* deck of about 64,962 square feet for eighty-one aircraft, it could be estimated that 72,180 square feet would be required for ninety aircraft (891 by 81 average width compared with 802 by 81 feet). The greater length could not be achieved on anything like the 20,000 tons available; the only alternative was to rearrange the flight deck. Preliminary Design sought to reduce

the areas lost to cutouts for antiaircraft guns and to the island structure itself. It had already experimented with deck-mounted 5-in guns in its abortive design for a 10,000-ton carrier in 1938, and the following year proposed elimination of the starboard deck-level 5-in guns in favor of enclosed mounts superimposed on the island. However, the portside weapons were retained, since the deck guns would be unable to fire across the flight deck when aircraft were on deck. This consideration contrasts with contemporary British doctrine, which envisaged striking all aircraft below decks in the face of air attack. The island was further constricted when ready rooms were moved from it to the gallery deck immediately below the flight deck—where they became vulnerable to attacks on the flight deck itself, as the U.S. Navy learned during kamikaze attacks in 1944–45. Indeed, the *Essex* design consumed much more of the potential gallery-deck area than had earlier U.S. carriers; the usual overhead stowage for spare (disassembled) aircraft was, then, much reduced. As in the *Yorktown*s, the hangar was essentially open, so that aircraft could be started up before rising to the flight deck; it could be closed off by light-tight roller shutters.

The new generation of naval aircraft required more gas (200,000 gallons even for the original seventy-four-airplane group). In July 1939 the General Board estimated the gasoline requirement on the basis of an average consumption per airplane of 37 gallons per hour, a maximum operating day of eight hours, and a total of seventy-four aircraft, or 21,900 gallons per day. At 25 knots the carrier would steam about 10,000 nautical miles, or sixteen days, and it seemed reasonable to allow for air operations for two-thirds of that time, or ten days, or 219,000 gallons. The figure was about 230,000 gallons by the time of contract design (August 1940). Tanks, surrounded by voids, had to be provided within the limited armored box in the hull, a box shared with magazines and also with the machinery. The latter in turn required more length, as alternating engine and boiler rooms were desired for survivability; the fleet wanted greater power as well (to maintain or increase speed).

Ready rooms were a more subtle air-group consideration. Admiral Horne wrote that "there can be material improvement . . . as to size, location, and equipment. The facilities provided should . . . permit maintenance of a high state of efficiency of pilots . . . waiting for flight operations. There should be a separate ready room for each squadron . . . and each compartment should have ample ventilation, even to the extent of providing air conditioning if necessary." The commanders of both the *Yorktown* and *Enterprise* considered their existing ready rooms unsatisfactory,

Steaming through Puget Sound following a refit, the *Yorktown* displays mid-war modifications. They include the replacement of three of her original five radio masts, which were considered a hazard, with three slender vertical whips, added aft. The 40-mm battery has been increased to seventeen quadruple mounts; one in the island has been eliminated and ten added: five on the starboard side at hangar-deck level, one aft, two in the gallery deck to port, and two on the former port catapult sponson. Note, too, the change in radar arrangement attendant on installation of a height finder. The ship is shown at anchor on 6 October and under way on 30 September 1944.

partly because of confusion created when two or more squadrons occupied the same ready room. Moreover, some of the existing ready rooms were not well enough ventilated, particularly for pilots in flight clothing ready to man their planes.

The new flight-deck arrangement increased the 5-in battery to twelve guns, four in twin mounts, at a cost of 400 to 500 tons. It allowed for up to eight weapons firing on either beam, since it was believed that the two superfiring twin mounts could generally fire across the flight deck. Proposals for even larger guns, such as the 6-in/47 DP then being developed, were rejected, since the guns would interfere with aviation facilities; the 5-in/38 gun seemed to be the best heavy-carrier weapon. BuOrd commented that the new base-ring mounts already in production would afford a simpler ammunition supply and would permit adequate protection: it proposed eight twin mounts (which could not be accommodated).

Fleet and carrier commanders all wanted a high volume of fire as well as gun mounts protected against splinters, blast, strafing, and weather.

The 5-in gun was useful primarily against level and torpedo bombers. Dive-bombing was best countered by automatic weapons; Admiral Horne claimed that "such aircraft attacks constitute the greatest, as well as the most probable, hazard to carrier operations, in that one well-placed bomb on the flight deck may well cause complete cessation of aircraft operations and at the same time cause the loss of all aircraft from that carrier that remain in the air." The four quadruple 1.1-in machine cannon of the *Yorktown*s were to be retained, one near each pair of twin 5-in/38s, one near each pair of single 5-in/38s to port. However, there was considerable divergence of opinion concerning the 0.50-cal machine gun, with officers endorsing anywhere from ten to forty weapons.

These basic features characterized all the variants of the basic CV 9 design that were considered, although the design itself grew in 1939–40 from the original 20,400 tons to 27,100 as ordered. There were several forces at work. First, improvements the fleet wanted in a new carrier (increased speed, a larger air group, greater protection, a heavier battery) were difficult to meet on an increase in displacement of only 600 tons. Changes in design standards, such as the shift to alternating engine and boiler rooms or the provision of a separate boiler operating station, in themselves required more displacement, yet nowhere in the design papers is there a suggestion that these advances be abandoned in the interest of limiting growth. Moreover, any growth in the weight of one component of the carrier would be multiplied several times. For example, the fleet wanted the ability to steam astern for a sustained period, and one means to that end was turbo-electric drive—which, on the original 120,000 SHP, would have added 400 to 500 tons to machinery weights alone and increased the length of the machinery spaces. In order to retain sufficient volume for magazines and aviation fuel within the protected volume of the carrier, the designers would have had to enlarge the hull, more than consuming the 600 tons allowed them under the original rules. Fortunately, as this narrow margin was consumed, the designers were able to accept greater and greater design displacements, the treaty and other links having been abrogated by the outbreak of World War II.

The enlarged air group was to include another squadron of fighters to make a fifth squadron. For many years it had been apparent that the single-fighter squadron with which carriers were equipped represented an insufficient margin for self-protection, to the extent that standard carrier tactics called for the achievement of air superiority at sea by the elimination of enemy carriers at the outset. However, it appears that in 1939 the idea of much stronger combat air patrols supported by aerial pickets gained currency; in May 1940 the outgoing Commander of Aircraft, Battle Force, Admiral Blakely, was reporting favorably on the operation of five squadrons, including two fighter squadrons, aboard the Yorktown. Radar still lay in the future, and the best early warning available was that provided by scout aircraft attached to the fighter groups. Thus when the General Board circularized the fleet concerning a new carrier in May 1939, its first question was the need to operate a fifth squadron. That in turn implied a larger flight deck, given standard U.S. carrier operating procedure. Note that it did not necessarily mean a larger hangar, although the virtues of a double-deck hangar, as in the British Ark Royal, were briefly considered.

Tentative characteristics of 19 July 1939 called for "the effective operation of four squadrons of aircraft in one launching, a total of seventy-four aircraft," including seven utility aircraft; the hangar was to be able to accommodate a full eighteen-airplane squadron set up and ready for flight, but with wings folded. In addition, the standard carrier characteristics of the time called for 50 percent spare aircraft, stowed partly disassembled, to make up for battle damage. The extra squadron added eighteen fighters plus a scout bomber for liaison with each fighter squadron, or a total of thirty-eight scout bombers (one scout and one bomber squadron). By June 1940 the extra squadron was being considered a spare, and the carrier would operate only the original seventy-four aircraft in a single launch. Moreover, the spare aircraft requirement was halved, as fuselage stowage was clearly a problem. Note that the gasoline stowage requested did not increase as the air group did. By late 1940 the requirement to operate a fifth squadron had been discarded in view of the increased unit size of modern aircraft; it would be employed only in emergencies. The General Board did, however, add nine fighters to the originally planned squadron of eighteen, for a total of eighty-two aircraft (including thirty-seven scout bombers, eighteen torpedo bombers, three observation and two utility aircraft). Trial displacement calculations of November 1940, for example, were based on Grumman F5F-1 fighters, Brewster SB2A-1 bombers, and Vought TBU-1 torpedo bombers—all types that never entered service—and twenty-one spares.

The Yorktown and Enterprise, the first really satisfactory fleet carriers, had been in service for only about a year; the next large carrier, the Hornet, had been laid down to their design not because they were the best possible (they were not), but because her completion was considered urgent. In May 1939, then, the fleet had just enough experience to criticize the 1931 concepts embodied in the two earlier ships, and Preliminary Design had just enough time to make effective use of that criticism. It considered the Yorktown hangar-deck arrangement flawed, and wanted to move the forward elevator far enough aft to leave a space free for storing utility planes or damaged aircraft, clear of fore-and-aft traffic on the hangar deck. Conversely, it was argued that efficient operation on the flight deck was more important than the efficiency of the hangar deck, and that the elevators should be kept as far apart as possible. The amidships elevator was perceived as a means of striking aircraft below after they had been recovered in either the forward or after arresting gear. At this time two hangar-deck catapults (as in the Wasp) appear to have been contemplated. C & R had just provided an experimental deck-edge elevator for the Wasp; alternatively, Preliminary Design argued, the amidships elevator could be moved "somewhat further forward to permit its use regularly during landing operations in the after arresting gear; and second, to move the forward elevator, if fitted, somewhat farther aft as has been mentioned previously to clear the hangar-deck catapult and give more run for small planes taking off forward. This will facilitate its use likewise during landing operations over the stern while some planes are spotted on deck forward and the relocated No. 2 elevator [amidships] cannot be used." Up to four catapults, as in the *Wasp*, could be provided.

The fleet wanted both high speed and high sustained astern speed, the latter "to permit landing in the forward arresting gear without true wind (22 knots has been given as the desirable relative wind for safe carrier deck landings). . . . Alterations have recently been completed permitting the *Lexington* to operate astern at 20 knots, which has apparently been accepted by the ship without serious objection." Such operation, which may seem bizarre to a modern reader, was valuable both tactically and from the point of view of damage-limitation. Although earlier carriers had been fitted with arresting gear forward, it appears that the *Essex* class was the first in which such astern operation was a major design consideration. Perhaps the greatest virtue of recovery over the bow was its contribution to the survivability of the carrier's air capability, despite the vulnerability of an unarmored flight deck. That is, a single bomb hit at either end would still leave one elevator, one takeoff deck, and one set of arresting gear intact. Forward arresting gear was not removed from U.S. carriers until 1944. High astern speed placed a considerable strain on any conventional geared-turbine plant; for a time, Preliminary Design considered substituting turbo-electric drive, intrinsically capable of generating full power astern and also superior from the point of view of damage control. That was why it had been adopted in U.S. battleships during World War I and also in the battle cruisers that ultimately became the *Lexington* and *Saratoga*.

At a General Board meeting in July 1939 Captain Smith of BuEng maintained that high-speed backing for over ten or fifteen minutes would damage the ahead turbine blading of a conventional geared plant. Turbo-electric drive would cost 400 to 500 tons at the 120,000-SHP level accepted in the earlier *Yorktowns*, although it might buy 25 to 30 percent better fuel economy at 15 knots. However, given limits on the standard (unfueled) displacement, such economy was relatively unimportant at the time. BuEng did observe that a similar weight increase applied to conventional geared turbines might buy up to 145,000 SHP, for 34 knots in a 20,000-ton carrier.

Otherwise the original design generally followed that of the earlier *Yorktown*. The armored conning tower of earlier carriers was abandoned in the interest of shrinking the island structure; an armored pilot house was to be substituted, which appeared "advantageous from the point of view of continued readiness for action and for defense of the ship-control party against surprise attacks either by aircraft or light surface craft."

The restriction of protection against light-cruiser fire, which survived into the final *Essex* design, was itself an indication of the limitations under which the ship had been designed. That is, like the U.S. Navy, the Japanese Navy operated a large force of heavy cruisers that might reasonably be expected to engage carriers operating independently in the early stages of a Pacific war. By way of contrast, Japanese light cruisers generally operated with destroyer flotillas supporting the Japanese battle fleet; the *Mogamis* (which were converted to heavy cruisers, albeit unknown to the United States before the war) were the sole exceptions. Protection against 6-in fire at the specified ranges required 4-in side armor and 1.7-in deck armor (for a 60° target angle). At similar ranges, protection against 8-in fire would have required much more; even at 17,000 yards the 8-in fire could penetrate 5 inches of side armor, and at 21,000 yards a 2-in deck would be needed. Moreover, 8-in fire would be accurate at longer ranges than 6-in, so that 24,000 yards (2.5 inches, 100 pounds) was suggested as most appropriate at a General Board hearing; in fact that is the thickness adopted in the first major CV 9 design, CV 9E. As for underwater protection, the level adopted for the *Yorktowns*, and limited by treaty-set hull dimensions, was only slightly increased. It was, to be sure, improved later by a change in liquid loading (the two outer layers rather than the two middle layers were flooded), but that did not make up for its basic defects.

There was considerable interest in deck armor; BuOrd wanted protection against a 1,000-lb demolition bomb dropped from 10,000 feet, which could penetrate both the ship's structure and the existing 1.5-in armored deck without breaking up. A 2.5-in deck would stop it, but every inch added to deck thickness would cost 650 tons. However, BuOrd argued, without those 2.5 inches the ship would be endangered if 1,000-lb bombs hit.

There was also the flight deck to consider; here the proposed standard was the 500-pounder, and the chief advocate was Captain John S. McCain of the *Ranger*. He actually preferred a relatively small carrier, as long as it could be protected against bombing. Again and again he told the General Board that any U.S. carrier, if her flight and hangar decks were crowded with fueled and bombed aircraft, was a potential inferno, and that friendly fighters could not guarantee the security of any flight deck. His views were rejected largely because of the physical cost of effective flight-deck armor, a cost confirmed by the sheer size to which the succeeding *Midway* class was driven. For example, 60-lb (1.5-in) STS steel would be required to defeat even 500-lb bombs, and those weapons were rapidly being displaced by much larger ones. A *Yorktown*-size deck that thick would itself weigh 1,460 tons, and the increase in ship displacement would be several times as large, taking into account the much heavier structure needed to support the flight deck and the greater beam needed to restore stability because of top weight. Moreover, the flight deck would not substitute for the anti-gunfire-armored deck deep in the ship, since the side armor would not rise to its level; shells would still be able to penetrate between flight and protective decks. According to Preliminary Design, "the deck over the vitals of the ship would have to be, therefore, protected by a lower armored deck unless protection against gun fire can be omitted entirely, which appears off hand to be a step which present knowledge of probabilities could hardly justify." Finally, it was argued that armoring the flight deck would be extremely difficult in view of the number of openings (as for arresting gear, barriers, lighting equipment, catapults, elevators) in it. Estimates of the cost of an armored flight deck ran as high as two-thirds of the air group, a figure that seems plausible in view of the decline in British air groups attendant on the Royal Navy's adoption of armored flight decks after 1936.

In July 1939 Preliminary Design offered the General Board a choice between a reworked *Hornet* with turbo-electric drive and more gasoline (258,000 gallons compared with 178,000 for the *Yorktown* or *Hornet*) and an armored flight-deck carrier without torpedo protection. The increased gasoline stowage would be obtained by eliminating the usual voids surrounding such tanks, covering only their tops and ends with cofferdams, but letting them extend out to the inner bulkhead of the side (antitorpedo) protection. Neither was acceptable. The General Board was unwilling to give up torpedo protection entirely, and the proposed hull tanks for gasoline were unpopular at best. For example, Admiral Towers, chief of BuAer and former commander of the *Lexington*, noted that the *Langley* had actually suffered a gasoline-tank explosion at sea. Instead, the General Board issued tentative characteristics for a reworked *Hornet*, with an 800- by 80-ft flight deck, an 18-ft clear hangar height, and a midships elevator "located as far as practicable towards the island side of the flight deck" to minimize interference with flight-deck operation. Admiral Towers had personally rejected the proposed deck-edge elevator. There would be two catapults on the flight deck, as well as a double-acting one

on the hangar deck, firing athwartships. The speed requirement was reduced to 33 knots (20 astern for up to an hour) and the carrier would accommodate 200,000 gallons of gasoline in tanks surrounded by voids. The C & R proposal for twelve 5-in/38 guns was accepted, and the new ship would have the four quadruple 1.1-in machine cannon of earlier U.S. carriers.

This was so close to the existing *Hornet* design that Captain Chantry of Preliminary Design thought at first that his organization would hardly be involved, that the CV 9 design would be entirely the responsibility of Final Design, with Preliminary Design merely redrawing the hull lines. Machinery design appeared to be the only issue. The chief alternatives, given a realistic standard displacement of 23,000 tons or more by October, were based on a sketch design for a new 60,000-SHP turbo-electric unit, two of which could provide 120,000 SHP, and three of which could provide 170,000. Each would contain two boilers and a turbo-generator. Alternatively, a geared-turbine installation of 60,000 SHP (two shafts and four boilers, as in a destroyer) or 85,000 SHP (two shafts, four boilers) was envisaged. None was entirely satisfactory from the perspective of protection or internal space. For example, any single, very large compartment would present a serious flooding hazard if the torpedo protection of the ship were breached. The 170,000-SHP turbo-electric plant required two 72-ft rooms and a total length of 348 feet, far beyond that of any other scheme. Both it and the 120,000-SHP electric-drive scheme required 2 feet more of headroom than the *Yorktown* plant, which in turn required a higher armored deck, added top weight, and then more beam to restore stability; the carrier grew to 26,200 tons (see table 7-1).

As for the geared-turbine schemes, the engine and boiler rooms of the 170,000-SHP version were considered too long at 52 feet. In the 60,000-SHP version, it appeared that the boiler rooms would be rather cramped, and that this would have to be lengthened 6 feet to an even less acceptable 58 feet. Fortunately there was an alternative already in production: the 75,000-SHP plant of the new *Atlanta* class, which could be paired for 150,000. It could fit within a length of 224 feet for engines and boilers (202 for the 120,000-SHP geared version, or 214 if longer boiler rooms were accepted), plus 28 feet forward for evaporators and 28 aft for auxiliary generators. This showed the best subdivision of all, with two 44-ft engine rooms (48 feet for the 120,000-SHP plant), and two 40-ft and two 28-ft boiler rooms (two 52- or 58-ft ones in the 120,000-SHP scheme). It was adopted as scheme CV 9E, with torpedo protection considered adequate to defeat 500 pounds of TNT, a 100-lb (2.5-in) protective deck rather than the 60-lb deck of the *Yorktown*s, and a speed of 34 knots ahead, 20

Table 7-1. Evolution of Schemes for the *Essex* Design, 1939–40

	CV 9A	CV 9B	CV 9C	CV 9D	CV 9E	CV 9F	CV 9G
Std Disp't (tons)	26,200	25,300	23,900	23,300	24,250	26,000	27,200
Trial Disp't (tons)	31,270	30,860	29,100	28,700	30,900	32,200	33,400
LWL (ft)	856	836	820	820	820	820	830
Beam (ft)	88	87.5	88	86	88	91	96.3
Draft (trial) (ft)	26	26.4	25.2	25.5	25.9	26.5	26.0
Machinery Type	TE	GT	TE	GT	GT	GT	GT
SHP	170,000	170,000	120,000	120,000	150,000	150,000	150,000
Speed Ahead (kts)	35	35	33	33	34	33	33
Astern (kts)	25	20	25	20	20	20	20
Depth (main deck) (ft)	54.5	53.5	54.5	52.5	53.5	54.0	53.5
Width (mach spaces) (ft)	60	60	58	58	57.5	57.5	57.5
Depth (torp pro) (ft)	14	13.75	15	14	15	16.8	19.4
FD (in)	—	—	—	—	—	—	2.5
HD (in)	—	—	—	—	—	2.5	—
AD (in)	1.5	1.5	1.5	2.5	2.5	1.5	1.5

Note: CV 9F formed the basis of the *Essex* design. A depth of 15 feet was considered sufficient to resist 500 lbs of TNT.

astern, at 24,250 tons. (Note that the *Hornet*'s 120,000-SHP plant was considered obsolete; it did not operate at high steam conditions, nor did it incorporate alternating engine and boiler rooms for survivability.)

There matters might have ended but for continued interest in deck protection. In the same joint memorandum (December 1939) for the General Board that described the five sketch designs, the bureaus added that "after the speed characteristics have been determined the Bureaus proposed to investigate the effect of protecting the main [hangar] deck with about 2½ inches of Special Treatment Steel. This will require some additional displacement, some added beam [which would improve torpedo protection] and some loss in speed. However, there would be a decided advantage in keeping bombs from detonating within the strength hull of the ship and rupturing the main structural members."

Advocates of the armored flight deck were still active, and on 25 October the General Board went so far as to issue tentative characteristics for a ship with a 2.5-in armored flight deck (as well as a 1.5-in lower armored deck) but only eight 5-in guns, two elevators, and two catapults. It appears that this project was inspired by spotty reports of the new British armored flight-deck carriers.

Admiral Towers did not like the idea; he considered an armored flight deck sensible only in the context of British operating practice. The Royal Navy struck its planes below as they landed (and consequently was far less efficient in intensity and rate of strike operations), whereas a U.S. carrier would always have many of her aircraft on deck. Even were the flight deck to resist penetration, a bomb exploding on it would be extremely destructive. It was essential to keep the bomb out of the vitals; an explosion in the hangar deck might not damage the ship proper beyond what could be repaired relatively quickly. This was the origin of the armored hangar deck incorporated in the *Essex* design.

Moreover, there would be no point in reducing the air group below four squadrons. Admiral Towers felt that if cost were no limit, the *Lexington* and *Saratoga* would be the best carriers, since they could resist shellfire attack better than the *Yorktown*s.

Many of the same points would be repeated in the 1940 hearings on more powerful carriers; both times Towers and others from BuAer came out in favor of an 8-in main battery, looking toward independent carrier operations in the face of enemy cruisers, and not fewer than twelve 5-in AA guns. Admiral Horne of the General Board favored a big ship that could resist 8-in shellfire and three torpedo hits; Towers considered this sort of ship equivalent to the *Lexington*s.

The rest of a 31 October 1939 General Board hearing was concerned with determining the appropriate thickness of deck armor. It was necessary to distinguish between the heavy-case demolition bombs then in service, which might break up on impact, and the new armor-piercing (AP) types. Admiral Furlong of BuOrd noted that

—A 500-lb bomb dropped from 10,000 feet will be rejected by 1.9-in STS.

—A 1,000-lb heavy-case bomb dropped from 10,500 feet breaks up on a 2.5-in STS; the same bomb dropped from 10,000 feet will just be rejected by 2.4-in STS. However, a 1,000-lb AP bomb (18 percent rather than 50 percent explosive) will penetrate 2.88 inches of STS.

—A 2,000-lb bomb dropped from 10,000 feet breaks on 3-in STS; from 9,000 feet, it pierces 2.9 inches.

These ideas were shelved temporarily when the General Board adopted the 25,000-ton CV 9E proposed (with a 100-lb protective deck) in December. As an alternative, a new scheme, CV 9F, replaced the original fourth (protective) deck with the combination of a 100-lb hangar deck and a 60-lb armored fourth deck; the latter would keep out 6-in shells at ranges below 18,700 yards. The hangar deck could not be counted as protection against shellfire because shells could enter the vitals by way of the soft sides beneath it. C & R considered the main advantage of the armored hangar deck was "that bombs up to 1000 lb size would be kept from detonating inside the hull proper, and the danger of serious damage to the main strength members of the hull minimized." The cost would be increases in displacement (25,950 rather than 24,800 tons) and beam (91 versus 88 feet), and a loss of speed.

The other alternative to CV 9E was an armored flight-deck carrier, signated scheme CV 9G: on comparable weights, the 100-lb deck could be placed at the flight-deck level. This scheme was not complete until January 1940 (it is discussed in chapter 9). It was less than satisfactory, and the basic choice was between CV 9E, protected only against shellfire, and CV 9F, protected against some bomb effects at the expense of some protection against shells, some increase in size, and some decrease in speed.

At an 18 January General Board hearing, the chief of BuAer preferred CV 9F because it offered greater protection at relatively minor cost in other characteristics. However, he was unsure that the new and far heavier aircraft in prospect could be accommodated in the numbers specified; the requirement for an extra squadron was reworded to "provide as practicable, during development, for the operation of at least nine additional VF-type aircraft."

As for specific features of the CV 9F design,

the greatest improvement to the flight deck capacity can be made by reducing the length of the island structure.... the spotting pattern is reduced from five to about three planes abreast in the region of the island and gun mounts.

Carrying the sides of the flight deck in a straight fore and aft line to the ramps at bow and stern is important in parking after landing, and spotting prior to take off, when area at the extreme ends of the flight deck is at a premium.... [However, this would blank off the overhead arcs of the port 5-inch guns.]

The after elevator has been moved forward from Scheme CV 9E. This is vital to launching so that planes can be brought up from the hangar, after warming up there, and can enter the take off taxi line with planes from the area abaft the elevator. By this arrangement launching intervals can be maintained with a 45 second elevator operating cycle.... The capacity of the elevators should be increased in proportion to the increase in airplane weights, i.e., from

9000 to about 14,000 lbs. The speed as at present specified for CV 8 elevators is satisfactory, i.e., 45 second round trip. (10 sec. load, 12.5 sec. moving, 10 sec. unload, 12.5 sec. moving). The size, 44 × 48 feet, is satisfactory.

Preliminary spotting studies show that only three squadrons of the projected largest type can be spotted on the flight deck for launching unless all wings are folded except the leading six planes. This means that one squadron must be warmed up in the hangar and brought up over the elevators to launch—as is now done on Ranger, and will have to be done on Wasp. (Yorktown and Enterprise frequently bring up a few planes, less than a squadron, in launching now—and will have to employ this method more and more as the take-off runs of planes increase.) A study of take-off runs shows an annual increase. This is a result of the increasing performance of planes (higher wing loading). Inevitably unassisted take-off runs will continue to increase [in length, which] emphasizes the necessity for obtaining the optimum arrangement and operating efficiencies of the elevators so that the hangar may be employed as a warm up area prior to launching.

On 31 January the General Board submitted characteristics, which the Secretary of the Navy approved on 21 February, reflecting the main features of CV 9F. The flight deck (at least 850 by 80 feet) was to be equipped with two flush-deck catapults, with a third (double-action type) athwartship on the hangar deck. The latter had to be built on the hangar deck, with ramps to move planes over it, because that strength deck could not be cut. The hangar, with an 18-ft clear height, was to be served by three inboard elevators, the amidships one of which BuAer wanted offset as far as possible toward the island in order to facilitate movement of aircraft on the hangar deck.

An increase of 6,500 tons over the 20,000 of the Yorktowns bought

—An increase in flight-deck length, which would allow effective operation of four squadrons in one launching operation
—Greatly increased subdivision, including rearrangement of the power plant to allow it to survive the effects of one hit; a triple bottom against magnetic mines; and an effective side protective system
—A 25 percent increase in avgas
—Four more 5-in guns
—Better protection, for the armored hangar deck included
—An increase in propulsive power

The third bottom was a last-minute addition, proposed at the 18 January hearing; on 25 January C & R reported that it would cost 300 to 500 tons (0.2 to 0.25 knot)—hence the rise to 26,500 tons.

The 31 January characteristics included specific standards for ballistic protection: resistance to 6-in (105-lb AP, 2,800 ft/sec) shellfire between 11,250 and

18,700 yards (with a 4-in belt over 30-lb STS, and 1.5-in fourth deck);* and protection against bombing, defined by a 2.5-in hangar deck, which was enough to stop a 1,000-lb GP bomb. The latter could not be counted as antishellfire protection, since shells could pass through the large unarmored portion of the side of the ship above the fourth deck. On the other hand, the 2.5-in hangar deck could initiate fuse action in large AP bombs, the fragments of which would be stopped by the fourth deck. In the *Essex* class as built, the main belt, 10 feet deep, tapered from 4 to 2.5 inches at its lower edge. It extended between frames 39 and 166 (508 feet, or almost 62 percent of the waterline length).

The designers sought to minimize openings in the armored hangar deck; they reported that "a large portion of the ventilation air will be taken into the ship at the ends beyond the 2½ in deck in order to limit the number of openings." This choice seems to have been one of the few basic flaws in the *Essex* design. In action, the single long ventilating trunk too often served as a conduit for asphyxiating smoke and burning gas. It had disastrous effects on the *Franklin* and was eliminated from later ships, as well as from earlier ones during their postwar reconstruction. As for the basic protective concept, it seems unfortunate in retrospect that the prospective destruction of the flight deck was regarded relatively lightly at the same time the gallery deck immediately beneath it was being much more fully utilized, first for ready rooms and then for a CIC as well.

One problem in protection was the many openings required in both the protective fourth deck and in the hangar deck. The former had to be closed against shellfire, the latter against bombing. Thus the main openings in the hangar deck, the elevator pits, required 2.5-in plating on their bottoms and 50 pounds of STS splinter armor around their sides; and the bomb elevator trunks had to be given protection comparable to that of the side belt (4-in plating tapering to 1-in, up to 5 feet above the protective deck). However, there were no armor gratings (for example, in the steam pipes). To some extent the latter omission was later rectified by the provision of armored hatch covers and 80-lb plating over the uptake slopes. Provision of the elevator trunk armor, additional splinter plating for exposed personnel, and an increase in armor over the steering gear from 1.5 to 2.5 inches were all recommended well after the contract design was under way; they contributed to a final rise in displacement to 27,100 tons. Only the splinter protection was compensated for (in part, by a reduction of the 5-in gunhouses to 30-lb plating). All of the

protection changes were approved by the Secretary of the Navy on 28 November 1940.

By the spring of 1940 the navy was expanding very rapidly, and the design workload was such that some of the work of Contract Design had to be entrusted to a design agent, Bethlehem Quincy. The new carrier design was so urgent that Contract Design began as the preliminary design was only 40 percent complete, the contract with Bethlehem being awarded on 2 April 1940. As an indication of the complexity of the design, in 1944 Rear Admiral Cochrane, then chief of BuShips, claimed that an *Essex*-class carrier required 9,160 separate plans (45 for preliminary design, 115 for contract design, and 9,000 shipyard working plans), compared to 8,150 for an *Iowa*-class battleship or 6,200 for a light cruiser. The bureau found it difficult to coordinate with Bethlehem, and on 6 September that organization left the program. To some extent its place was taken by Newport News, which on 3 July became the lead yard in the *Essex* program.

General-arrangement plans, completed in August, show an increase in the fighter complement to twenty-seven (plus nine extra fighters and one bomber under crowded conditions). The flight deck was enlarged: a study of the Panama Canal locks showed that an overall width of 113 feet 2 inches could be passed over the lock walls, which permitted a maximum flight-deck width of 109 feet (94 abeam the 5-in gunhouses). The specified flight-deck length was also exceeded: 862 feet plus 4-ft 9-in curved ramps fore and aft. The flight deck was served by three elevators, and bomb hoists provided ordnance at both flight- and hangar-deck levels (lower hoists to the third deck, upper to flight and hangar decks).

The new heavier aircraft required a more powerful catapult: the hangar-deck unit had to be extended over the side of the ship onto a portside sponson and then onto a hinged sponson beyond. The cost was 100 tons beyond the 127 required for the catapult proper. As compensation the portside flight-deck catapult was eliminated, and the net flight-deck catapulting rate was maintained by doubling the pumping capacity of the hydraulic system.

Four air-conditioned ready rooms, as specified, were to be provided, two just aft of the midships elevators and two forward of the after elevator, all of them inboard on the gallery deck with good access to the flight deck. Ready room no. 1 had extra space, to accommodate all twenty-seven fighter pilots.

The bomb elevators were somewhat smaller than those of the *Yorktown*s, with three hangar and three (rather than two) flight-deck delivery points. Elevator size was reduced because it seemed impossible to provide protective hatch covers for the openings in the armored hangar deck: here survivability was considered more important than the ease with which

*These figures differ from those used in the *Yorktown* design because a 90° rather than a 60° target angle was specified, in common with U.S. cruiser designs of the time. At 60° the 4-in belt would keep out a 6-in shell at 8,700 yards.

aircraft could be armed. Preliminary Design commented that

> the smaller elevators provided for CV 9 are designed to carry about half as many bombs per trip. . . . It will probably be possible to increase the speed at which these elevators operate and to reduce the loading and unloading intervals. It appears that the bottleneck in bomb deliveries is in the time required to tail and fuze bombs at the transfer points or to stack bomb crates on skids in the magazines. The capacity of elevators on previous carriers appears considerably greater than required, as they were based on specification requirements for a round trip in two minutes whereas they are able to make a round trip in well under one minute in service. The bomb-handling installation as a whole is designed to maintain the basic requirement for rearming the entire carrier based group of planes in 30 minutes. Considerable savings in weight and space have resulted. The elevator platforms are large enough to handle a contemplated 2000 lb demolition bomb.

The midships elevator caused difficulties in structural design, as its pit cut the main deck (which was the upper flange of the ship girder). At first it was proposed to set the elevator on the centerline (despite BuAer requests that it be set as far inboard as possible), increasing the weight of plating outboard of the opening. However, favorable reports of the performance of the prototype deck-edge elevator aboard the light carrier *Wasp* made such an installation acceptable to BuAer, and the coordinator of shipbuilding approved this change on 20 December 1940.

Other aviation changes included an increase in air group to eighty-eight and a requirement that the ship carry depth charges; these too added weight. Finally, the originally specified battery of four quadruple 1.1-in machine cannon was increased to six, four of them in the island structure. By way of compensation, the 0.50-cal battery shrank to only eight weapons, all of them on the island structure. At the end of Contract Design, accommodations were planned for 230 officers, sea cabins for the flag officer, chief of staff, commanding officer, and navigator, and pipe berths for 156 CPOs and about 2,100 enlisted men, for a total of 2,486 men. Thus the contract design came out to 27,100 tons (standard), a 600-ton increase over the weights forecast in the preliminary design and in fact beyond the unit displacement allowed for new-construction carriers under the old Washington Treaty of 1922.

The *Essex*es were part of the last generation of U.S. warships to be designed without major provision for radar. That meant cramped antennas topside, with all their problems of mutual interference and smoke damage, radar rooms (and radar personnel) in a ship whose design was already relatively tight, and a CIC. On the other hand, radar was the solution to the problem of a carrier fighter defense: only it could provide sufficient warning and information to bring airborne or deck-launched fighters into position to intercept an incoming raid. Radar operation in turn required the integration of information from all available sources in a CIC, generally adjacent to (but not included in) a fighter direction office. Those sources would include both the ship's own radars and her lookouts, sometimes her ECM warning receivers, and information from other ships of the fleet. The CIC concept predated the *Essex* class, and ships were completed with relatively cramped CICs in their island structures. Ultimately, however, these functions were moved to larger spaces in the gallery deck, which offered considerable space but, unfortunately, no protection from bomb or kamikaze attack.

The *Essex*-class radar arrangements were both complex and individualistic, the latter so much so that ships can often be identified in photographs by their radars. At first the single massive tripod carried an SK for long-range air search, an SG for surface search, and the usual aircraft homing antennas. However, the failure of the *Yorktown*'s air-search radar during the Battle of the Coral Sea led to a demand for a second air-search set as insurance against a similar failure in the future. In an *Essex*-class carrier, that meant the provision of a second (often lattice) mast sponsored outboard from the single compact funnel, carrying a smaller air-search set, generally an SC-2. Often a second SG was provided abaft the funnel, to make up for the blind spots represented by the major radars. There were, in addition, the usual 5-in fire-control sets. This was hardly enough, as it was soon discovered that efficient fighter controls needed accurate height information. Requirements for a height finder were formulated in the spring of 1942, and the prototype SM (CXBL) was installed aboard the carrier *Lexington* in March 1943; production sets were installed aboard the *Bunker Hill* in September and aboard the *Enterprise* in October 1943. In *Essex*-class carriers the height finder generally occupied the prime position formerly held by the big matress of the air-search set, atop the tripod mast. In the *Lexington*, for example, the SK was sponsoned out from one side of the funnel, the SC-2 from the other (atop a lattice mast). In some cases, the platform atop the tripod was extended aft to accommodate both an air-search set (often a dish-shaped SK-2) and the height finder; in others, the platform accommodated the smaller SC-2 on a short topmast, and the major air-search radar was sponsoned out from the funnel. Only at the end of the war did a combined air-search and height-finding radar, SX, appear, displacing the secondary air-search set and thus simplifying topside arrangement somewhat.

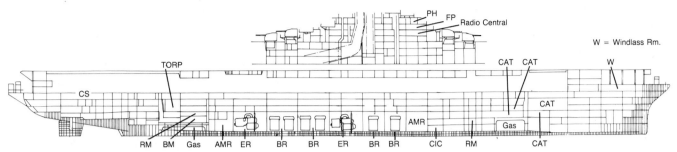

Essex-class inboard profile, to hangar-deck level.

All of these sets could search only up to about 75° above the horizon, and that only intermittently (SM). Thus aircraft undetected at long range, where they might be at a relatively low elevation, could attack from directly overhead undetected. By 1944 there was an urgent need for a radar to search this volume, since the fast carriers were beginning to operate near Japanese land bases, and aircraft were difficult to detect overland at almost any altitude. The *Lexington* was fitted with an unsuccessful prototype (SO-11), and by 1945 a zenith-search antenna had been developed to combine with the existing surface-search radar (SG-6 and the postwar SPS-4 were of this dual type). As an interim measure, night-fighter radars were installed, pointing directly upward, aboard several carriers: the *Ticonderoga* led, with an AN/APS-6A in her starboard catwalk. She was followed by the *Hancock, Bon Homme Richard*, and (probably) *Boxer* with army-type SCR-720s; a similar set replaced her APS-6A, and similar sets were installed in the battleship *North Carolina*, the command ship *Appalachian*, and the destroyer *Bristol*. A contemporary navy radar magazine, the classified journal *CIC*, noted that "a dive looks like a dive on the B-scope (display)—the target echo moves rapidly downward while the C-scope indicates nearly constant angle."

That these zenith-search sets could not be positioned in the island structure testifies to the extent to which carrier islands had already become congested. In addition to the radars they had to accommodate ECM antennas, both for search and for jamming, which were both numerous and sophisticated by the end of World War II, as well as directors for the 40-mm and 5-in guns around the island—not to mention ship and air-control positions and a variety of radio antennas in the island proper.

By 1945 there was also an airborne radar fed into the carrier's CIC, Project CADILLAC, carried aloft by a modified torpedo bomber. From a carrier point of view, CADILLAC required expanded radar main-

tenance spaces, a special beacon onto which the CADILLAC data link transmitter could lock, and also a special receiver linked to a display in CIC. In addition, the special group of radar airplanes was typical of a whole series of specialized types that had to be accommodated as an "overhead" beside the combatant element of the carrier air group, and which added to its congestion. Other examples, already present aboard many carriers in 1945, were specialist night fighters and photo-reconnaissance aircraft. Before World War II there had been "utility" planes and even spotters to support surface action, but they were long gone by the end of the war. Although CADILLAC was not a very visible element of carrier structure, it began an important trend in the U.S. carrier force; CADILLAC is represented almost four decades later by the Grumman E-2C Hawkeye, which combines an airborne radar with an independent CIC and can control its own section of CAP fighters. Such "overhead" aircraft increase the net size of the carrier air group and thus generate pressure for the growth of the carrier, given combatant elements more or less fixed in number by operational requirements. Internally, the specialist aircraft often have disproportionate maintenance requirements. For example, the size of the Hawkeye was a major consideration in the choice of hangar-clear height in the abortive CVV designs of the mid-seventies.

The other major external change to the *Essex* class during World War II was the explosive growth of their antiaircraft battery, sometimes at the expense of aviation assets. Throughout the fleet, the quadruple 1.1-in machine cannon and the 0.50-cal machine gun were ordered replaced by, respectively, the 40-mm Bofors and the 20-mm Oerlikon in August 1941. These weapons were not yet available, but production would begin the following year; a twin Bofors weighed about as much as the quadruple 1.1s. However, such large ships as the carriers could accommodate quadruple Bofors in place of the 1.1s. As of August 1941, an additional pair of twin Bofors

In New York Harbor on 9 January 1945, the *Bon Homme Richard* (*above* and *facing*) is prepared for a yard period. Her bombs are unloaded on her deck-edge elevator. Note that although she had been fitted with the two portside catapult sponson 40-mm gun mounts, she had not yet received the starboard sponsons. Nor does she have the extreme outboard-gallery-deck 40-mm sponsons later mounted on her port side. All five outboard 40-mm mounts could be removed for passage through the Panama Canal. The *Bon Homme Richard*, the last of the short-hull *Essex*es, was completed with the enlarged flag plot of the later ships, indicated by the absence of a second 40-mm mount on the fore end of her island.

was planned, one in the bows and one offset to port aft under the overhang of the flight deck. At this time a total of forty-four 20-mm guns were planned, including six located outboard of the island at the first level above the flight deck. The rest were to be on walkways 4.5 feet below flight-deck level, on platforms that could be removed for passage through the Panama Canal. The very large number of 20-mm guns, compared to the light 0.50-cal battery originally contemplated, reflects the prestige this weapon had already developed in British service, a prestige it would not lose until its failure against kamikaze attack in 1944–45.

By the time the first ships had been completed, the bow and stern mounts had been made quadruples, so that there were eight in all; they also carried a total of forty-six single 20-mm Oerlikons. Even this battery did not satisfy all concerned. In July 1942 Commander of Carriers, Atlantic, proposed a radical rede-

sign of the *Essex* class in which the island would cease to encroach upon the flight deck: almost all functions would be removed from it, including the four quadruple 40-mm mounts. The 5-in battery would be relocated to provide a four-cornered defense, each corner having its own director. Other proposed improvements included a stronger flight deck, armor protection for the CIC, which was then located in the island structure, and better avgas protection. When the more radical proposals were weeded out, improvements in antiaircraft firepower and control remained.

In January 1943 BuShips proposed a much more modest improvement program. At the cost of 11 feet of flight deck forward and 7 feet aft, plus a considerable reshaping of the bow lines above water and the construction of a large stern sponson, the Bofors battery at each end of the ship could be doubled. As for 5-in directors, if the hangar-deck athwartships cata-

pult were removed, its portside sponson could support a third Mark 37 director, at the cost of some flight-deck area, which would have to be cut away to provide it with useful overhead lines of sight. The hangar-deck catapult would be replaced by a second unit on the flight deck, as in the design then being developed for the *Midway* class. In fact only six ships (CVs 10, 12, 13, 14, 17, 18) ever received the hangar-deck catapult; the *Essex* herself had no catapults as completed, and the *Lexington* only the flight-deck unit, due to delays in delivery.

A very radical plan, somewhat similar to that ultimately accepted for the *Midway*s, was rejected by a January 1943 conference between representatives of the bureaus and of Admiral King's office. It would have required an increase in beam so great that the carrier could not pass through the Panama Canal, an actual decrease in flight-deck area, and a decrease in the total cones of fire available to the twelve 5-in guns. This last decrease was due to the side-mounted weapons being unable under any circumstances to fire across the flight deck.

The result was a compromise: the third Mark 37 director would be mounted on the catapult sponson, and the flight deck above cut away just enough to provide it with an unobstructed view from 60° before to 60° abaft the port beam. As for 40-mm guns, the conference considered portside coverage insufficient, even though it could be argued that the four mounts on the island could fire to port. The additional bow and stern weapons could have 180° arcs of fire, and another would be mounted just abaft the third Mark 37 director on the former catapult sponson. The conference also favored CIC under the fourth (protective)

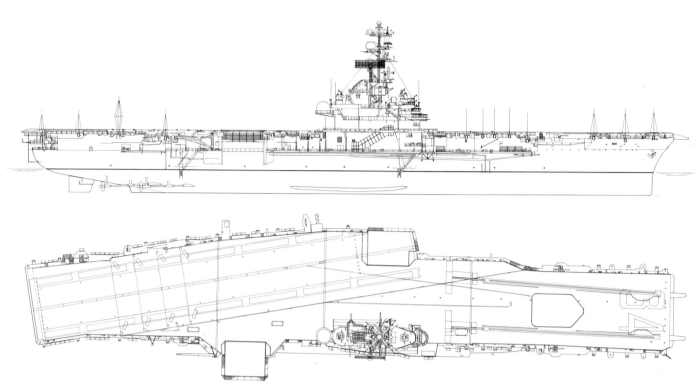

The *Oriskany* (CVA 34) near the end of her career, 1974. She still had four 5-in/38 guns, controlled by two Mark 37 (Mark 25 radar) and two Mark 56 (Mark 35 radar) directors; two of the guns and the two Mark 56 controlling them were later removed. Radars were the SPS-10, SPS-30, SPS-37A, Raytheon 1500B Pathfinder, SPS-12, SPN-35, SPN-41, and SPN-43. She also had TACAN (URN-20), satellite communications (SSC-3), and meteorological equipment (SMQ-1A, SMQ-6). The lattice outrigger visible on the port side in the deck view carried ECM antennas, as did a lattice outrigger from the island.

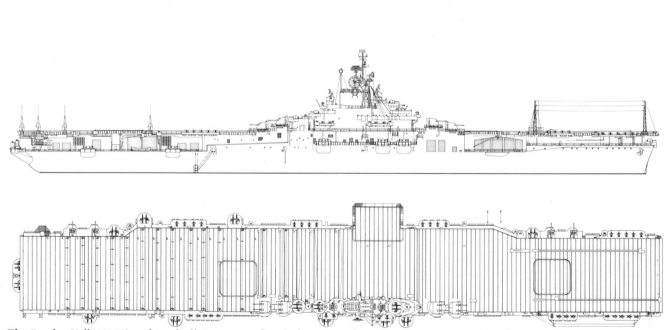

The *Bunker Hill* (CV 17), a short-hull *Essex*, as refitted after severe battle damage, September 1946. At this time she was armed with twelve 5-in/38, seventeen quadruple 40-mm, and thirty-five twin 20-mm guns. In the plan view, note the outboard platform for the SK-2 air search radar and the inboard one for the TDY jammer; other radars included an SC-3 and an SM-2 (height finder). Fire controls were two Mark 37s (Mark 12/22 radar), four Mark 57s (Mark 29 radar), and seventeen Mark 51 mod.

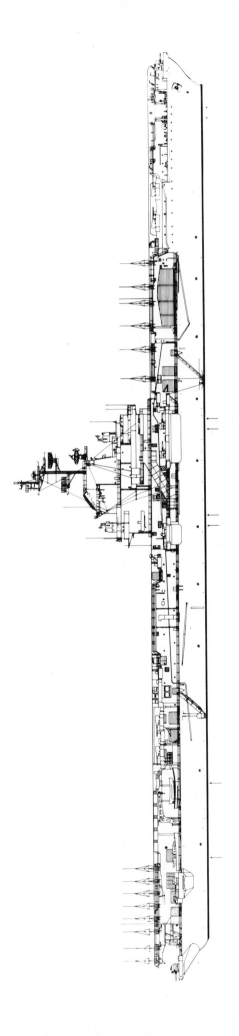

The *Wasp* (CV 18) newly converted to SCB-27A configuration, November 1951. She was armed with eight 5-in/38 and twelve twin 3-in/50 guns, although the conversion design showed fourteen of the latter. Arrows indicate planned positions for twin 20-mm guns, which were not installed. Radars were the SG-6 (surface/zenith search), SR, SX, and SPS-6B. The platform at the after end of the island was reserved for an SPN-8, and an SPN-6 was to have gone atop the island, abaft the mast; instead it was later installed on the SPN-8 platform. The empty platform projecting forward from the mast was intended for an SPS-10.

In these April 1945 post-refit photographs the *Ticonderoga* displays standard late-war modifications: a reduction in radio masts and a great increase in 40-mm battery, including two portside mounts on the former catapult sponson. Also clearly visible is the small platform for the landing signal officer on the port side of the flight deck aft; a vertical screen protects him from the stiff wind-over-the-deck. The hangar deck has been closed off with roller curtains on its sides and aft. The starboard-side 40-mm sponsons could be removed to allow the carrier to pass through the Panama Canal. The sponsons did not long survive the end of World War II in active *Essex*-class carriers, although ships drawn from reserve for Korean duty retained them, and they were a feature of the SCB 27A reconstruction program.

deck, but noted that since space would be scarce there it would be impractical to relocate the air plot similarly.

Now there was resistance. The Commander of Air Forces, Atlantic, did not want any reduction in flight-deck length. Moreover, he was unimpressed with the proposed CIC location. "Experience with carriers lost in the present war seems to indicate the opposite. Personnel loss in the island structure has been comparatively light, while many of the so-called protected stations, such as central station, have been among the first that had to be abandoned. It is recommended that these stations remain in the island or else on the deck immediately below the flight deck and abreast of the island."

However, the proposed changes were pressed ahead, and on 4 March 1943 the Secretary of the Navy formally approved new characteristics for the *Essex* class, providing for the shorter flight deck, the third director, all eleven quadruple 40-mm mounts, the second flight-deck catapult, and relocation of the CIC and fighter-director station to positions under armor.

Now the issue was the extent to which ships under construction (and, indeed, with high priorities for completion) could be altered without unacceptable delay. For example, on 19 March Newport News (which was building CVs 10–15 at the time) reported that it could install the improved ventilating system in CVs 15 and 21 (not yet laid down); the new relocated and redesigned gasoline tanks in CVs 15 and 21 only; a strengthened flight deck in CV 11 and later ships; the new flight-deck catapult and the shorter flight deck in CVs 14, 15, and 21; the additional director in CVs 15 and 21 (with structural work only in CV 14); the extra bow and stern 40-mm mounts in CVs 14, 15, and 21; and the relocated CIC and fighter-director station in CVs 15 and 21 only. Ships with the new bow mounts and the associated clipper bows were known as the "long-hull" group; CVs 9–13 at Newport News, CVs 16–18 at Quincy, and CVs 21 and 31 at the New York Navy Yard were completed to the earlier "short-hull" design. They all received the enlarged stern sponson and the portside quadruple mount on the former catapult sponson, but not the clipper bow. The latter proved a mixed blessing, as it caused excessive slamming in service. After the *Ticonderoga* buckled her hangar (strength) deck amidships in a postwar passage around Cape Horn, the entire class had to be strengthened.

The portside Mark 37 was not really satisfactory, given its limited sight arcs, despite some sacrifice of flight deck above it. BuAer wanted the cut eliminated. It presented "a serious hazard to aircraft taking off since in effect it reduces the width of the flight deck by 6 ft 3 in at a point 216 ft from the bow. The handicap to flight operations resulting from this cut far outweighs the potential availability of a third

Mark 37 director." Only the *Ticonderoga* and the *Hancock* actually had the cut, and they were modified to eliminate it, a second quadruple 40-mm mount replacing the Mark 37 director. The characteristics now changed to allow for a local 5-in director, initially a Mark 51, for each of the two groups of 5-in guns on the port side. At the end of World War II many ships had the new Mark 57 radar director controlling these weapons. Moreover, in July 1944 the VCNO authorized restoration of the original flight-deck length in view of arguments that very slight movement of the guns and their directors fore and aft would give "a useful although not as effective gun arrangement as that with the deck removed." Puget Sound Navy Yard developed a proposed two-mount bow arrangement not requiring a new clipper bow, but it was rejected as not worth the weight and personnel involved, if the flight deck were kept at its original length.

That made a total of up to twelve quadruple 40-mm mounts, and by the summer of 1943 up to fifty-five 20-mm guns were also specified. In June two quadruple 40-mm and two 20-mm guns were ordered mounted on the starboard (after) boat sponsons of the short-hull units for increased firepower to starboard; this improvement was later extended to all the *Essex*es. Two more were later mounted at gallery-deck level forward of the after group of 5-in and 40-mm guns; and finally three could be mounted in detachable sponsons outboard of the island, to be removed for passage through the Panama Canal. That made a potential total of eighteen quadruple 40-mm mounts. In most ships one of the two forward in the island structure was later removed to permit expansion of the flag plot on the level below; in early *Essex*-class carriers part of this modification was relocation of the CIC to the gallery deck, although in at least some cases the CIC was relocated to the hold (below the lower armored deck) during construction.

Fire-control arrangements were complex, not least because space, in the island at the ends and at the gallery-deck level, was very limited. Thus the bow 40-mm guns in "long-hull" *Essex*es with the full flight deck had to be controlled by Mark 51 directors at the forward ends of the flight deck, since the restored deck would have blanked off a director mounted behind and above them. The island accommodated two Mark 37 (5-in) directors, as well as up to four 40-mm (or auxiliary 5-in) directors, two of them in the island proper and two in elevated positions between the island and the twin 5-in mounts. Early ships had a mixture of the unsuccessful semi-enclosed Mark 49 and the much simpler Mark 51. Later some ships had the radar-equipped Mark 57 (incorporating a dish on the director) or the Mark 63 (with a dish on the 40-mm mount). Plans in 1945 called for elimination of the Mark 57 mounted forward of the pilot house, and

At Hunters Point on 15 January 1945, the *Randolph* displays her characteristic "long" or clipper bow, with its paired 40-mm quadruple mounts, as well as five new starboard gun sponsons. The 20-mm gun galleries on her island have also been extended, and she has the enlarged flag plot adopted in mid-war.

the installation of Mark 63s in two other island positions. There would be a total of two (portside) Mark 57s, six Mark 63s (three at the ends of the ship), and nine Mark 51 directors, controlling seventeen quadruple 40-mm guns. In some cases Mark 57s and Mark 51s could control 5-in as well as 40-mm fire, multiplying the number of targets the ship could engage. There was no significant shortage of 5-in directors: the two Mark 57s in the portside galleries could control the open 5-in mounts there.

By 1945 the single 20-mm gun had largely been discredited, and carriers were being re-armed with twin mounts, which weighed little more than the earlier single type; the specified ultimate battery was thirty-five such weapons (the interim was sixty-one single mounts). However, there was still considerable interest in a lightweight weapon that could rapidly and independently engage incoming targets (such as kamikazes) with very high firepower, and BuOrd tested a variety of such devices. One was the army quadruple 0.50-cal mount, fitted instead with four 20-mm aircraft-type guns (Hispano T31 or M3). Designated Mark 22, it was "a radical compromise of strength and reliability in order to attain maximum fire power." Mark 22 was driven by a gasoline-engine-powered charger and battery, with an on-mount supply of 200 rounds per barrel; its outstanding features were a cyclic rate of 2,800 rounds/minute and a working circle of only 14 feet, 4 feet more than that of the single or twin 20-mm guns (and comparable to that of the twin Bofors). As an alternative, installation of army Mark 31 0.50-cal quadruple mounts was planned, with experimental mounts actually aboard

the carriers *Wasp* (six), *Lexington* (six), and *Cape Gloucester* (four). It was expected that six could replace ten twin or fourteen single 20-mm guns, or that four could replace six twin or nine single 20-mm guns; in the experimental ships replacement was one for one.

With the end of the war the disadvantages of these very heavy batteries, in terms of personnel, top weight, and maintenance, came to outweigh their value, and the ships completed postwar had fewer mounts. They lacked the three detachable sponsons abeam the island, the two extra quadruple mounts on the port gallery deck aft, and the two on the starboard hangar deck aft; in a few cases it appears that sponsons that were fitted (such as those replacing the former catapult sponson) were not used. In the case of the after starboard guns, removal was necessary to provide the carrier with sufficient boats for normal peacetime operation, and the removable sponsons would have interfered with free passage through the Panama Canal.

Internally, there were major attempts to improve survivability. The first of these was the modification of the underwater protection, from the prewar standard of inboard and outboard voids with liquids sandwiched between, to a new system with two outboard liquid layers and two inboard voids. This system was also introduced in the *South Dakota*–class battleships.

The gasoline stowage was redesigned after the loss of the *Lexington* to gasoline fires and explosions. The forward tanks were moved slightly aft to a point where the torpedo protection system was deeper and

The newly completed *Ticonderoga* shows both her long bow and her flight-deck indentation (for a third Mark 37 director) in this 30 May 1944 photograph. Note also her enlarged flag bridge (one rather than two quadruple 40-mm guns forward on her island).

contained an additional bulkhead. The tanks themselves were redesigned and fitted with a saddle tank 30 inches thick; it would be filled with seawater after the gasoline in it was used, so that after about 25 percent of the gasoline had been consumed the main supply would be covered entirely in water.

As in the armament changes, early ships were not completed with the revised gasoline system, which required some internal rearrangement and reduced avgas capacity to about 209,000 gallons.

There were major changes in subdivision for better survivability. The ships were designed for berthing on the second deck and messing on the third, which meant that bulkheads would be pierced above the third deck. However, early U.S. experiences with underwater damage suggested that maximum compartmentation would be best; the ships were redesigned to make the second rather than the third deck the damage-control deck, (that is, the deck below which bulkheads were unpierced). This improvement was effective only for CVs 21, 32–40, and 45–47; it was authorized for earlier ships, but whether it was made in wartime is unclear. The improvement was associated with revision of the ventilation system. Quite early the vent running along the second deck had been criticized; it was a

tunnel present[ing] an unbroken avenue along two-thirds of the length of the second deck from which ventilation ducts led to most of the volume of the ship below, including machinery spaces. Since this trunk is always under negative pressure, the introduction of flame, smoke, or toxic gas into any part of it would result in the instantaneous spread of flame, smoke, or gas through a large part of the ship. That this apprehension was well-founded was later demonstrated by the *Lexington* (CV 16) when smoke tanks aft near the entrance to the tunnel were ruptured and toxic smoke was immediately spread through the ship. Since this tunnel was immediately under the hangar deck, a gasoline-handling area, it offered the

additional hazard of the spread of liquid gasoline along its length, in case of damage, with the consequent fire and explosion danger.

The BuShips solution was elimination of the trunk in favor of a series of vertical ventilation systems, from CV 21 onward (and as an alteration in earlier ships). The effects of this change included some encroachment on hangar space, and the aviators complained; the bureau's reply was that the duct presented a very grave danger. It might even cause flooding, since it penetrated bulkheads toward the ends of the ship which would otherwise have been solid up to the main (hangar) deck.

Counterbalancing improvements were the effects of greater loads than had originally been contemplated. Aircraft became both individually heavier and more numerous. In response to the former problem, flight decks were strengthened, a longitudinal beam being added in each panel. The increase in individual weight is suggested by a comparison of projected weights used to develop the Preliminary Design in 1940 and actual weights of operational aircraft in 1945; note that the weights of 1940 referred, in some cases, to projected rather than to operational aircraft. Thus, the 1940 fighter was the twin-engine Grumman F5F-1 of 6,784 pounds empty or 9,395 loaded, with the Vought Corsair (XF4U-1) of 6,896/9,476 pounds taken as an alternative. In 1945 the standard fleet fighters were the Grumman F6F-5 Hellcat (9,238/13,797 pounds) and the Vought F4U-4 Corsair (9,167/13,597 pounds). Similarly, the attack aircraft foreseen in 1940 were the Brewster SB2A-1 (6,881/10,928 pounds), the Curtiss SB2C-1 (7,028/11,155 pounds), the Grumman TBF-1 (8,367/13,540 pounds), and the Vought TBU-1 (8482/13,769 pounds). Again, there was considerable weight growth in the two types actually in service in 1945: a typical Avenger (TBF or TBM-3) had a loaded weight of 16,761 pounds in standard condition; and the Curtiss Helldiver (SB2C-5) came to 16,287 pounds. In each case that represented about 1.5 tons per bomber, loaded, and rather more per fighter, distributed among fifty or even one hundred aircraft at flight-deck level, about 55 feet above the waterline.

These heavier aircraft had to be accommodated in larger numbers than had originally been expected. The *Essex* was commissioned with a "double" fighter squadron of 36 aircraft, plus single scout (dive-bomber), bomber (dive-bomber), and torpedo-bomber squadrons, each of 18 aircraft; she also had an extra dive-bomber for liaison, making a total of 91 operational aircraft, plus 9 more (3 of each type) in reserve. As radar developed the need for specialized scouts was reduced, so that by 1944 the "scout-bomber" and dive-bomber squadrons had typically been amalgamated, for a total of 24 such aircraft. The slack was taken up by the fighters, which included specialized night interceptors and photo-reconnaissance aircraft. For example, in October 1944 the new carrier *Shangri-La* accommodated a total of 49 day fighters (F4U-2s), four night-fighting Hellcats, and two photo-reconnaissance Hellcats. By that time, however, fighter-bombers were beginning to displace the pure dive-bombers. By the summer of 1945 the typical *Essex* air group included one large fighter squadron of 36 or 37 aircraft, a fighter-bomber squadron of similar size, and reduced dive- and torpedo bombers of 15 aircraft each, for a total of 103 aircraft; the fighter squadron included specialist aircraft.

The heavier aircraft landed faster and required new arresting gear Mk V, a late-war modification that alone was credited with adding about 125 tons, all of it high in the ship.

Bomb loads also increased, and by the spring of 1945, in common with most other U.S. warships of wartime construction, the *Essex*es were weight-critical; in January, BuShips warned that "the margins of stability possessed by the earlier vessels of the CV 9 class have completely disappeared on CV 21, CV 31–40, 45–47 and that the Bureau will require complete weight and moment compensation for any changes or alterations requested or directed on these vessels in the future." The *Franklin* (CV 13) was inclined as typical of CVs 9–20. "Preliminary inclining data . . . indicate that this ship has suffered an even larger increase in weight and reduction in stability. . . . It is believed that the ships which have been in service some time compare unfavorably with new ships because of a general accumulation of weight of all kinds. While this remark applies particularly to permanent weight, the tendency is well illustrated by one specific item of load on the *Franklin*. . . ." The yard's inventory revealed that there was on board in topside locations an average of 800 rounds of 40-mm ammunition per gun barrel,

and 4,076 rounds of 20-mm ammunition per gun. The total weight was 247 tons, about 50 percent of the weight of the ship's complement of aircraft (empty weight). "The *Franklin* has adequate stability in the intact condition [but] the ability of the ship to survive damage has been seriously impaired because of loss of freeboard and stability. . . . The ship with one torpedo hit would take about the same list as the *Essex*, as originally built, with two torpedo hits. . . ." In July, after the *Franklin* and the *Bunker Hill* had very nearly been lost in action, the bureau went into greater detail.

The first ships of this class to be completed, the *Essex* and *Lexington*, were considerably lighter and had greater stability than estimated during the design stage. These margins provided considerable leeway for the numerous alterations later undertaken as the result of improved design standards and war experience. . . . Although the Bureau had provided in the original design a GM in Battle Condition of approximately 7.5 feet in order to assure excellent damage resistance for ships of this size and importance, it was decided on [a] recent review, taking into account reports of satisfactory service experience, that some reduction from this design figure was acceptable in [order to allow for modification]. . . . the GM should not be reduced below 6.5 feet in this condition. The primary consideration in reaching this decision was the list resulting from underwater damage along the sides of the ship. Secondary considerations were the tenderness of the ships when turning at high speed and the ability of the ships to carry an accumulation of water resulting from large-scale fire-fighting. . . . changes authorized in the most recent ships built would add about 1500 tons of weight in the Light Condition. . . . [But] the actual increase has been about 1750 tons. The GM had fallen to 5.5 feet and the Light Condition displacement was 2150 tons greater than the earliest ships, as built, and 400 tons greater than the latest ships, as built. . . . Inasmuch as the early ships have not received (and will not receive) all the alterations undertaken on the later ships (probably only about 1150 tons, instead of 1750 tons), it appears that the ships in service have gained on the order of 1000 tons which cannot be accounted for on the basis of authorized alterations.

Two ships of this class [the *Franklin* and the *Bunker Hill*] have returned after extremely heavy damage topside and two ships [the *Lexington* and the *Intrepid*] have been torpedoed near their sterns but . . . in none of these cases was the damage of such nature that the ship depended upon stability for survival. It should be noted in passing, however, that the *Franklin* developed symptoms of critical stability conditions due to fire-fighting water. The type of damage, i.e., two or more heavy explosions against the side underwater, which makes heavy demands on stability, has not yet occurred. In addition to the direct adverse effects of loss of stability, the probability of loss of the ship after

As an ASW carrier in March 1956, the *Valley Forge* illustrates the configuration of *Essex*-class carriers that remained operational after 1945. The massive radar on her tripod mast was an SX, a single unit that combined long-range air search and height-finding functions and greatly simplified antenna arrangement. Above it is an SG-6, a combination surface search and zenith (overhead) search set. Note also the enclosure of the two forward bridge levels. By this time most of the light AA guns had been landed, as evidenced by the empty gun tubs on the former catapult sponson at hangar-deck level forward. Also notable is the extent to which the hangar deck could be enclosed by roller doors, although structurally it was not part of the hull; even the deck-edge elevator opening could be covered. The aircraft on deck are Grumman S-2 (then designated S2F) Trackers, with an HUP helicopter (plane guard) amidships.

severe underwater damage is greatly increased if a severe list develops so as to impede damage control action, hamper access, derange mechanical installations, etc. Moreover, a large angle of heel in itself causes reduction of stability.... Prediction of the number of torpedo hits which a ship will withstand can not be made with definite assurance because of the number of variables involved, the most important one being the location of the hits. It is estimated however that in the case of these ships with 5.5 feet GM there would be a high probability of loss from three torpedo hits on one side; whereas with the GM increased to 6.5 feet for the same probability of loss would be reached with four torpedo hits on one side.

The problem was so severe that BuShips recommended a limitation of ready-service light ammunition to 500 rounds per 40-mm barrel and 1,440 per 20-mm barrel.

Finally, also in common with most U.S. warships at the end of the war, the *Essex*es suffered from overcrowding. Factors included the advent of radar, of greatly increased light batteries, and of larger air groups, which in turn required more maintenance personnel, more ships, and more spares. The spares themselves consumed space that might otherwise have gone to living quarters. The *Essex* preliminary design was based on a complement of 215 officers (98 ship, 22 flag, and 95 aviation) and 2,171 enlisted men (1,528 ship, 106 flag, and 537 aviation). In fact the *Essex* carried 226 officers and 2,880 enlisted men on her trials. The captain of the new *Intrepid* complained in 1943 about berthing. The carrier had 2,493 enlisted men's bunks, 301 bunks for officers, and provision for 268 hammocks in the mess halls, but the latter could not be used because there were as yet no provision for bags and hammocks. Messing began as early as 0500, ending at 2230, so that mess spaces really could not be used for berths. On trials, there were a total of 2,765 enlisted men and passengers in the crew spaces, as well as 332 officers; bunks had been placed in the admiral's cabin, the chief of staff's cabin, and the flag office. Messing aboard the *Intrepid* was also unsatisfactory, one reason being the location of accommodation hatches from the hangar deck: the forward steam tables could not be used without having the enlisted mess lines jam the wardroom hatches. The forward mess had to be used for the air department because of its odd hours (it often took up to four hours to feed the

Around 1959, the *Valley Forge* showed dual funnel caps, a feature she shared with the *Leyte, Antietam, Princeton,* and *Philippine Sea*. In each ship a new pole mast, similar to that installed in modernized SCB 27s, was fitted with a new base at the forward end of the funnel. Here the mast is topped by an SRN-6 TACAN, the navigational aid that succeeded the wartime and postwar YE. An SPS-6B is carried on the mast for air search; an SPS-8 height finder is mounted at funnel-cap level. When this photograph was taken, not all tactical aircraft had as yet been fitted for TACAN; some still relied on the earlier YE system, and the ship retained a YE beacon on a stub mast visible above the after funnel cap. On the side of the funnel is the small squat radome of a CCA (bad-weather-landing) radar, an SPN-8. Note that, to control her port 5-in open mounts, the *Valley Forge* had a pair of Mark 56 directors, the aftermost of which is visible just forward of the two guns it controlled. The boxlike structures, visible beneath her flight deck abaft the whaleboat, are ventilating ducts, which were meant to replace the centerline duct that had caused serious wartime problems. Like the Mark 56 directors, they were a standard postwar modification to this class.

department, compared with about one hour and forty minutes for the other messes).

In 1945 typical figures for the *Intrepid* were even worse: 382 officers (40 flag, 175 aviation, and 167 ship) and 3,003 enlisted men (100 flag, 135 air group, and 2,768 ship) were used for the BuShips overweight calculations. After the war the ship's complement figures were somewhat reduced as some of the light armament was eliminated, but even so the 1945 numbers represent about a 50 percent increase over the original design.

In 1945 the *Essex* was considered the ideal combination of ship and air-group size, but even so she had severe deficiencies, as in her capacity for avgas and its protection, which had been designed against shellfire rather than against bombs and bomb fragments. The fleet carrier design of 1945–46 (see chapter 10) was an attempt to remedy these shortcomings. A more direct attempt, the redesign of the incomplete *Iwo Jima*, failed with the cancellation of that carrier, although the *Oriskany* was suspended incomplete to become the prototype for the *Essex*-class reconstructions (see chapter 13). Meanwhile, many of the wartime ships were laid up in 1946–47. The severely

damaged *Franklin* and *Bunker Hill* were never recommissioned, although at least the latter appears to have been used for Project CADILLAC experiments after repairs. Of the others, the *Boxer* (CV 21), *Leyte* (CV 32), *Kearsage* (CV 33), *Antietam* (CV 36), *Princeton* (CM 37), *Tarawa* (CV 40), *Valley Forge* (CV 45), and *Philippine Sea* (CV 47) remained in service, having been completed at the end of the war or afterward. Of this group only the *Kearsage* was ever reconstructed, being withdrawn from service in 1950. The others were rerated as ASW support carriers as the rebuilt *Essex*es entered service during the fifties, beginning with the *Leyte* and the *Antietam* in August 1953. By that time unconverted *Essex*es were clearly inadequate as jet carriers; the *Philippine Sea* was the first laid up, in December 1958. Three unconverted ships became amphibious assault helicopter carriers in 1959 and 1961: the *Boxer, Princeton,* and *Valley Forge*. The *Antietam* became a training carrier at Pensacola and was fitted with the first U.S. angled flight deck for tests. The other two unconverted ASW carriers, the *Leyte* and the *Tarawa*, were both withdrawn from service in 1959–60, as converted carriers became available for ASW service.

The *Bon Homme Richard* was recommissioned for service off Korea (in much her original configuration) and then modernized. She is shown on 28 February 1952 with a pair of Grumman Guardian ASW aircraft on deck. Although these aircraft could be operated from escort carriers, experiments aboard *Essex*-class ships showed that the latter were far better adapted to postwar ASW operations; the result was the decision to reclassify several unmodernized ships as ASW support carriers, or CVSs, beginning in 1953. Note how little the ship had changed since 1945. Her 20-mm battery had been removed, as had several 40-mm mounts, the sponsons for which remained. Other 40-mm mounts were provided with on-mount Mark 28 radars coupled to modified Mark 51 directors, as in the aftermost starboard mount; three other mounts were added (two on the island and one on the after 5-in-gun platform to port). She retained her wartime SK-2 long-range air search radar, but a postwar SPS-6B replaced the earlier SC-2 as part of a policy of frequency diversification.

The last of the original *Essex* class, the *Bunker Hill* ended her days as an electronics test platform, with experimental long-range radio antennas aboard. She is shown at North Island Naval Air Station, San Diego.

8

Austere Carriers for War Production

During World War II the United States built three series of carriers: a fleet carrier descended from prewar designs, the *Essex* class; a second, an emergency light fleet carrier that reinforced the heavy carriers but traded off efficiency of operation for quick production; and finally, the very austere escort carrier. Both of the latter two classes owed much to the active support of President Roosevelt, who became a strong advocate of naval aviation as Assistant Secretary of the Navy under Josephus Daniels in World War I. In both cases, the President ordered prewar "gold-plated" standards, discarded in the interest of quick production for an ongoing emergency. In both cases, too, he appears to have been correct, at least at the beginning of the war. However, by the middle of 1942 the acceleration of heavy-carrier construction was beginning to tell, and the President's willingness to build large numbers of slow escort carriers rather than the *Midway*s seems in retrospect somewhat naive.

The converted merchant hull (escort carrier or CVE) was the first project under way, and the austere concept of a carrier it embodied was later applied to the conversion of nine light-cruiser hulls during 1942–43 to light fleet carriers or CVLs. In turn the CVE might be regarded as the much more austere equivalent of the XCV developed before the war, except that the CVE design papers do not show any reference to the XCV projects. The reason the CVE was built and the XCV abandoned was that the latter was intended as a second-line fleet carrier, whereas the CVE had the most austere platform that could still support those aircraft essential for the second-line mission of convoy air and submarine defense. These missions implied a lower level of risk than a fleet carrier might encounter and, coincidentally, a lower level of individual aircraft performance. In this sense the CVEs formed the lower (and the *Essex*es the upper) end of an implicit "high-low" mix, the descendants (CVS and CVA) of which shaped U.S. carrier policy into the seventies. The CVE story also illustrates the conflict between optimum design for operation and optimum design for quick production.

A subtheme is the way the CVE mission shifted over time to include aircraft transportation (a role envisaged before CVEs were ever considered combatants) and a close-support role which ultimately required aircraft approximating those aboard a full fleet carrier. Indeed, the sophisticated CVEs produced at the end of the war were virtually slow versions of the CVL, and British CVEs operated as fleet carriers in Southeast Asia. Aside from speed, the similarity between CVE and CVL was so great that when a new island specially adapted to ASW was designed after World War II, it was applied to both types of small carrier. Moreover, the entire CVL conversion was based on concepts embodied in the early CVEs.

The changing role of the converted carrier (CVE) is evidenced by her changing designation. The original

The *Commencement Bay* class comprised the ultimate U.S. escort carriers. Here the new *Siboney* steams through Puget Sound on 24 May 1945. She has a new type of island supporting both air search and fighter-control radars, and her massive hangar-deck sponsons carry four twin Bofors on each side. Note as well the two flight-deck catapults: a short H 2-1 and a long H 4C.

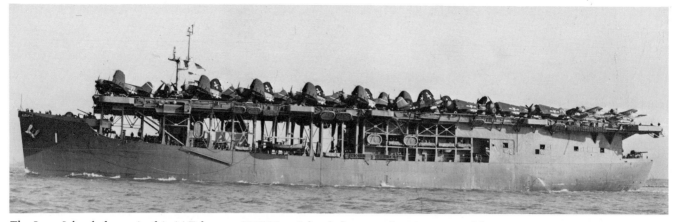

The *Long Island*, shown in this 14 February 1945 Mare Island photograph, spent most of the war as an aircraft transport. The outline of her original superstructure is visible abaft amidships. The plated-in area aft was a short hangar served by a single elevator; after her first conversion, she had only a landing-on deck with a catapult forward for launching. Later the flight deck was extended, as shown here, and the catapult relocated. As a transport, she was fitted with a more powerful catapult for delivering aircraft.

type symbol, actually applied to the U.S. prototype *Long Island*, was AVG, a modification of the AV symbol that denoted a seaplane tender and a clear indication of the secondary status of the type. On 20 August 1942 it was replaced by ACV (auxiliary aircraft carrier), still hardly the mark of a combatant. Only on 15 July 1943 were the ACVs redesignated aircraft carriers (escort) or CVEs, and they were always numbered in a separate sequence distinct from that of the fleet carriers (CV/CVLs). CVEs built in the United States but destined for the Royal Navy were numbered in their own BAVG series.

In many ways the CVL story embodies the contrast between standard peacetime production and design and the practices appropriate to mobilization, when far lower standards must be accepted. Like the CVE, the CVL was an attempt to achieve a rapid increase in the level of sea-based air power, using resources already in the production pipeline, in this case light-cruiser hulls. The decision to convert the light cruisers involved a judgement of the relative merits of rather austere flight decks and rather scarce light cruisers, the latter themselves required to support fast-carrier operations. In addition, carrier characteristics had to be balanced against building time. A major difference was the far smaller number of hulls suitable for CVL, as compared with CVE, conversion. Even fifty C-3s made little dent in the large U.S. wartime merchant-ship program, whereas the CVL program eliminated about a fifth of all potential U.S. light-cruiser hulls; the specially built *Saipan*-class light carriers of the 1943 program occupied cruiser building slips and required cruiser machinery that might otherwise have powered new heavy cruisers.

The U.S. escort-carrier program was deeply influenced by the close cooperation of the Royal and U.S. navies, even before the outbreak of hostilities.

The Royal Navy converted the first CVE (which was soon lost in action); ultimately most CVEs used by both navies were built in the United States. However, the two navies' requirements were not quite parallel. The Royal Navy was most concerned with trade-route protection; the U.S. Navy included among its most basic needs the movement of "expeditionary forces," especially across the Pacific. Thus from very early on, the U.S. concept of an auxiliary carrier included the support of landing operations.

As it was understood in 1941, aircraft had two quite distinct roles in convoy warfare. They could be used to beat off enemy aircraft, both the long-range snoopers that might home in other aircraft or submarines and the bombers directly attacking a convoy, as was often the case on the Murmansk run. They could also force enemy submarines to remain submerged, so that they could not close the convoy; and under favorable circumstances they could sink those submarines caught on the surface. Most of the submarines of World War II could not sustain high submerged speeds (which in any case often did not exceed convoy speeds) for more than a half hour; they had to surface to close or even to shadow a target convoy, unless they had the good fortune to be directly in the path of the convoy.

Thus air patrol, merely by extending greatly the secure area of sea surface around a convoy, could often protect it from U-boat attack. However, air ASW really became effective after Allied successes in code breaking permitted offensive attacks on U-boats whose approximate positions were known in advance—only aircraft could usually search fast enough to profit from such information. In addition, aircraft could often run down an HF/DF bearing to its U-boat source before the datum became "stale." In the Atlantic, U.S. escort carriers were generally em-

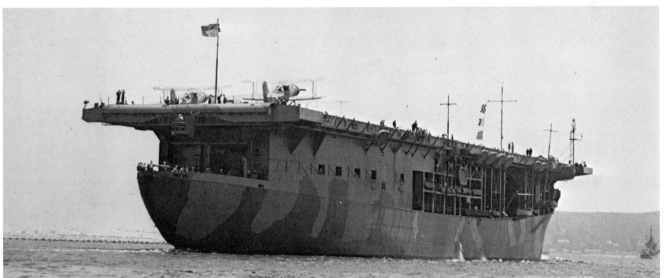

The *Long Island* was the first U.S. escort carrier. She was completed without an island superstructure, retaining her original merchant-ship bridge superstructure under her flight deck; bridge wings were fitted under the deck's forward end. Masts carried her radar and radio antennas. She was designated CVE 1. The significance of the number 751 in these early photographs is unknown. The aircraft are SOC cruiser floatplanes, seen here on their alternate wheeled undercarriages.

ployed in offensive hunter-killer (HUK) groups, in combination with destroyer escorts or ASW-modified destroyers, prosecuting HF/DF or code-breaking data. The Royal Navy more frequently used the mobility inherent in its escort carrier aircraft to allow the carrier to intervene defensively in an ongoing convoy battle. Also, it was responsible for the north Russia convoys, where air attack was as much a threat as the submarine.

The balance between alternative aircraft roles varied both with location and with the course of the war; the fighter function was so important at first

that the Royal Navy placed fighters on catapults aboard merchant ships (CAM ships) for one-time missions. In effect the small flight deck of an escort carrier made recovery possible and enabled the operation of ASW aircraft.

It appears that the CVE idea as implemented in World War II originated in the U.S. Navy. In mid-October 1940 President Roosevelt proposed a merchant-ship conversion for convoy (ASW) protection, entailing 6,000 to 8,000 tons, not less than 15 knots, and a flight deck for eight to twelve helicopters or STOLS. At about the same time, Rear Admiral

Halsey, Commander of Carriers, Battle Force, proposed a new class of auxiliary carriers both for pilot training (for force expansion in the event of hostilities) and for the transport of aircraft to overseas bases. He considered a 600- by 85-ft flight deck and a speed of 19 knots sufficient. Halsey's superior, Admiral Richardson, forwarded his suggestions to the CNO with a recommendation for conversion prior to the outbreak of war.

Admiral Stark, the CNO, held a series of conferences on merchant-ship conversions between 31 December 1940 and 23 January 1941.

> A requirement [was] the availability of a sister or similar ship which [could] be purchased by the British and altered in a manner similar to that being converted by the Navy. The conversion of both ships was to be by a private shipyard under contract in order that the Naval plans would be accessible for either ship. . . . these carriers [were to carry] small planes which could hover ahead of convoys, detect submarines and drop smoke bombs to indicate their locations to an attacking surface escort craft. It was also thought possible that these planes might carry a limited number of small or medium depth charges.

Tests with a Pitcairn autogyro proved unsuccessful, since the autogyro could carry only the smoke bombs and had no offensive characteristics. The autogyro seemed operable from a short flight deck, which would entail a relatively simple conversion. However,

> a partial landing deck was deemed impracticable, even for the autogyro, due to the turbulence of air caused by the afterhousing. Also the autogyro cannot come down vertically, as the pilot would be blind to the landing platform. The "take-off" and "take-on" from the bow of the ship by backing into the wind for recovery was also considered impracticable for the same reason (turbulence). A full length landing deck with arresting gear and a small plane [is] apparently the only prospect. All small planes will require arresting gear. This full length landing deck with arresting gear takes the ship out of the conversion class, about one and one-half years being estimated as the time required. . . .

This estimate was even worse than those for the much more elaborate XCV, and it appears less than realistic. It also represented a retreat to the flush-deck carrier "with [bridge] wings placed under the landing deck." The conference favored diesel power, which would reduce the volume of gas to be disposed of. By early January two diesel C-3s had been selected: the *Mormacmail* and the *Mormacland*, both building at Sun Shipbuilding and Dry Dock Company.

"The President, who considered U.S. entry into the war imminent, [threw] out any plan which would take more than three months; the President believed a job could be thrown together quickly by some fireman who was not worried about stability." The real issue was the level of sophistication either acceptable or necessary. Just as in the later case of the CVLs, the naval leadership wanted something close to a full carrier. Roosevelt knew he had to settle for less. He got a partial flush deck 305 feet long for landing on and a catapult forward for launching, the latter available as a result of deferring the modernization of the *Lexington* and the *Saratoga*. Newport News thought it could convert a C-3 in about three months on this basis. The *Mormacmail* was initially redesignated APV 1, a "special escort ship" or perhaps a transport (AP) with heavier-than-air aircraft function (V). She was taken over on 6 March and emerged on 2 June 1941 as the carrier *Long Island*, now designated AVG 1 (aircraft tender, general purpose).

The carrier had priority equal to that of the new fleet carrier *Hornet*. As completed, the *Long Island* had a partial deck extending 362 feet aft from the roof of the pilot house, which was still in the original merchant-ship position; BuAer required 350 feet for an SOC observation plane to land. The hangar deck below was flush, without camber, built flat above the original main deck abaft the engine-room bulkhead, with a single elevator at its forward end. The single H Mk II catapult was mounted at an angle of 30° to the centerline, launching aircraft at the forward port corner of the ship. The *Long Island* was ballasted with 1,650 tons to maintain a sufficient metacentric height, to keep the propeller immersed despite the light load and to hold the forward draft to a minimum of 16 feet 6 inches. Very considerable weights of fixed ballast were characteristic of the merchant-ship conversions, which might generally be described as inefficient uses of the available hull tonnage and volume; the same might be said, incidentally, of the XCVs planned before the war. Another stability feature was relatively thick deck plating, 30 pounds (0.75 inch), adopted not so much to increase strength but rather to reduce the stiffness evident in a builder's inclining experiment. Finally, she was fitted with a water-displacement system for her 100,000 gallons of avgas and 7,000 gallons of aviation lubricating oil. The gun battery was heavier than that common in later CVEs: one 5-in/51 gun aft, two 3-in/50 AA guns at the bows on the forecastle, and four 0.50-cal machine guns. The *Long Island* had an unusually great freeboard because, in effect, her flight deck was built atop a complete merchant-ship superstructure.

Captain D. B. Duncan, the *Long Island*'s first commander, described her as

> very dry in heavy weather. . . . She did not roll very much. . . . Pitching was normal for a ship of her size. She was better than I thought she would be and I

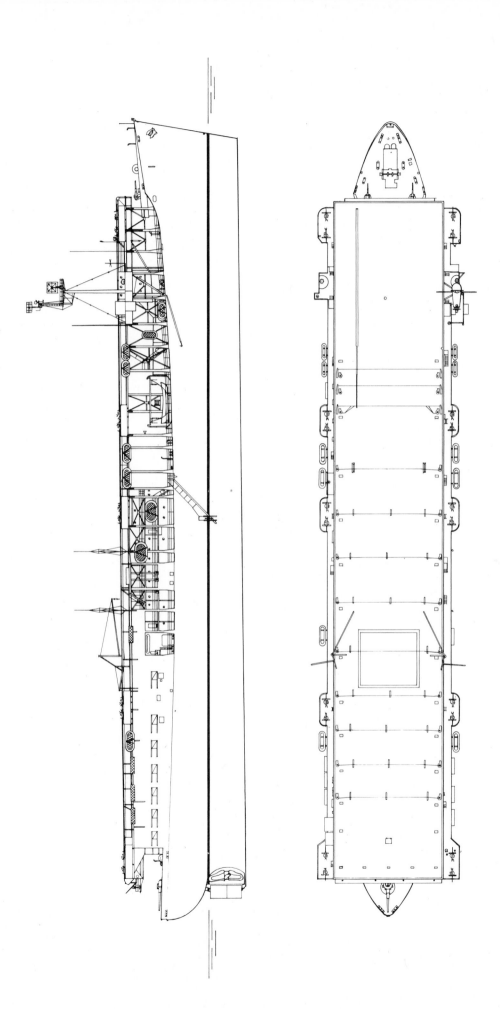

The *Long Island* (CVE 1), the prototype escort carrier, as an aircraft transport, June 1944. Note that she still retained her arresting gear at this time. The original freighter superstructure is visible amidships, forward of her short hangar.

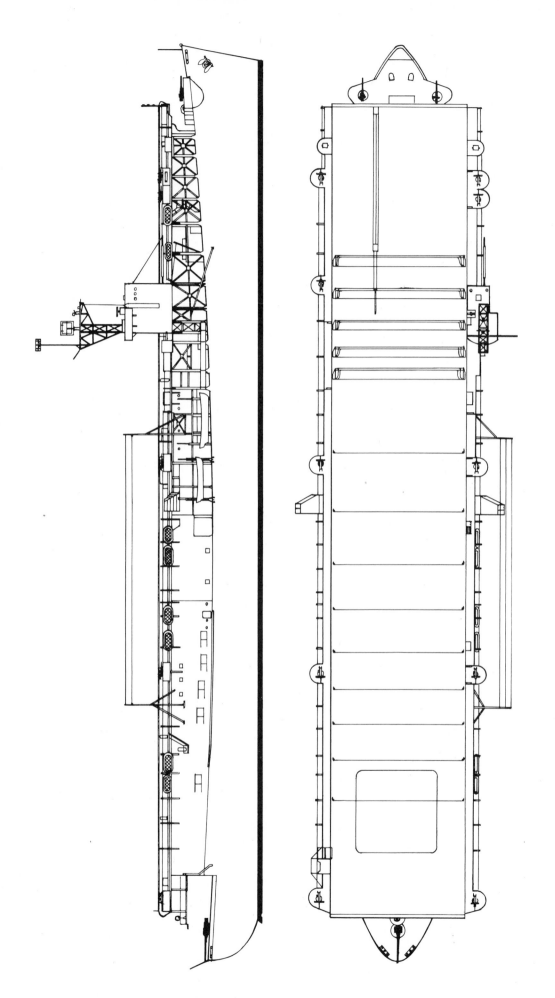

The escort carrier *Charger* (CVE 30), in April 1942, armed with one 5-in/51, two 3-in/50s, and ten single 20-mm AA guns.

think the new ones will be an improvement because they are one deck less in height. . . . I would not compare it with a large carrier as far as pitching is concerned but I have rolled worse on the *Saratoga* than I ever have on the *Long Island*. They are very dry. They ride the seas and don't plunge into them badly. I have seen the *Wasp* taking water over the flight deck when we were not getting a drop on the *Long Island*.

The short flight deck was unsuccessful, and on 15 September 1941 BuShips authorized Norfolk Navy Yard to extend it 77 feet forward over the pilot house; at the same time she was further subdivided to improve her damaged stability and floodable length. The 0.50-cal machine guns were replaced by 20-mm cannon the following year, and that November the 20-mm battery was increased to twenty guns at Mare Island; at the same time the catapult was relocated and set parallel to the centerline on the port side of the flight deck. These relatively minor additions added enough top weight that the fixed ballast had to be increased to 2,640 tons.

Although the escort carriers were essentially completely unprotected, some degree of protection for the bomb stowage was accepted. In common with many other U.S. escort carriers, the *Long Island* was fitted in March 1943 with 1-in (40-lb) longitudinal bulkheads of medium (rather than protective special-treatment) steel outboard of her bomb stowage, with water ballast between the bulkheads and the outer skin of the ship as torpedo protection. Finally, in February 1944 she was designated an aircraft transport, carrying and flying off aircraft but not recovering them. Her arresting gear and barriers were removed, and her flight-deck plating reduced to 5 pounds. She was then authorized to carry 250 tons of aircraft on deck and another 100 in her hangar, figures comparable with, for example, those of the aircraft complement of the fleet carrier *Wasp* in 1940.

The 14 January conference in the office of the director of fleet maintenance, which developed the *Long Island* scheme, considered the following variety of carrier-conversion roles:

—XCV
—Training carrier
—Escort
—Carrier supporting expeditionary forces
—Airplane transport with takeoff deck for the transfer of assembled aircraft to distances where they can fly to destinations
—Airplane transport without takeoff deck

Not surprisingly, the XCV was rejected, as was the training carrier, which was perceived for the moment as a gunless XCV. The escort expeditionary types were merged; so were the CVEs in service during World War II. However, they were considered unsuit-

able for transport of aircraft overseas "because of the limited deck space which would be available and the fact that no take-off deck is proposed"; the *Long Island* was then conceived as launching her aircraft by catapult, which would be a relatively cumbersome procedure.

Large liners were a much more attractive prospect, as they could carry about fifty aircraft to fly off, or up to one hundred if no takeoff deck space were reserved. It was already known that flying off would be far more efficient from a combat point of view than the delivery of crated aircraft. On 1 February 1941 the CNO made planning for the aircraft transport a matter of the highest priority, the large liner *Manhattan*, capable of 20 knots, being BuShips' first choice. Plans for conversion of the even larger *America* were ordered on 18 July, and a few days later the CNO was contemplating a total of six such AVGs, although only two more were ever identified: the *Manhattan*'s sister ship *Washington* and the Swedish liner *Kungsholm*, recommended by the Auxiliary Vessels Board on 20 December. Characteristics of August 1941 envisaged a 586- by 86-ft flight deck, with the pilot house built on flush at its forward ends and the uptakes diverted into hinged smoke stacks offset from the deck. Although the *Long Island* had succeeded in launching aircraft without a catapult, one was specified. There were to be two elevators, serving a hangar with a capacity of fifty-two aircraft. Aircraft themselves could weigh up to 17,000 pounds, compared with a 10,000-lb limit on the *Long Island*, and stowage for 190,000 gallons of avgas (and 7 percent lubricating oil) would be provided. A radius of action of 12,000 nautical miles at 15 knots was expected, and the battery would consist of four 5-in/51 guns, four quadruple 40-mm guns, and ten 20-mm guns. Although the XCV plans of 1935 had been abandoned, these conversions, which would take nine months each, were still impressive. They also interfered with the use of rather valuable merchant hulls at a time when the United States needed every berth it could find to ship soldiers overseas. The proposed conversions of the *Wakefield* (ex-*Manhattan*), *Mt. Vernon* (ex-*Washington*), *West Point* (ex-*America*), and *Kungsholm* as AVGs 2–5 were, however, cancelled by the CNO on 31 December 1941. All but one of these ships had been included in the earlier XCV program. The undecked aircraft transport concept did survive in several Seatrain train car ferry conversions (AKV).

The decked transport did not die completely; for example, in 1943 there were plans to convert the transport *Lafayette* (ex-*Normandie*) to "AP with flight deck." She had already lost most of her superstructure in the course of salvage operations after a disastrous 1942 fire. A 26 March 1943 memo lists aircraft capacities on deck.

	P-38	*P-39*	*P-40*	*P-47*
On whole deck	65	132	133	93
Clear of catapults	54	112	113	82

Meanwhile, the Royal Navy followed the rather different logic of trade protection, described in chapter 6. As German air attacks mounted from captured bases in France began to threaten convoys in the Atlantic, the idea of the fighter carrier emerged in the form of the *Audacity*, decked over and fitted with two arresting wires and a barrier. In distinct contrast to the *Long Island*, she was intended from the first to operate high-performance aircraft. There was no hangar and no elevator, although on her second operation she carried three spare wings in her well deck and three spare fuselages on deck.

In May 1941 the British Battle of the Atlantic Committee observed that "a great advance will have been made if our convoys can carry their own cooperation aircraft," and under the merchant-ship name *Empire Audacity*, the ex-freighter sailed with her first convoy in September. She was a fighter carrier; her air group consisted of four Grumman Wildcats (Martlets in British service), which managed to shoot down two long-range FW-200 bombers. The *Audacity* was torpedoed during a long convoy battle (Gibraltar to UK) in December, but her success inspired the Battle of the Atlantic Committee to suggest five more conversions plus six to be ordered in the United States under the Lend-Lease Act.

As early as January 1941, well before the *Audacity* had been completed, the Royal Navy requested more ships of her type, and in particular the four *Castle*-class conversions planned before the war. However, as in the case of the AVGs, this request was rejected because they were too valuable as fast merchant ships. (One of the four, the *Pretoria Castle*, was converted later in the war.) Instead, on 20 January 1941 the U.S. Navy was requested to act as agent for the acquisition of six *Audacity*-type auxiliary carriers from U.S. yards. On the twenty-eighth U.S. officers in London informed the Admiralty that they had their own conversion plans, which they considered superior; however, they did not disclose details. Thus on 1 April the Admiralty asked for six ships to be built to the plans of the *Winchester Castle*, which (on a hull far larger than that of the C-3) was to have had only a small hangar for six Swordfish torpedo bombers. The elevator proposed was too narrow for a fighter, so the ship would have to carry her six fighters on deck. Nor was there a catapult. The U.S. position was that the C-3 conversion was far superior, and in April and May three hulls, one of which had already been completed, were requisitioned by the U.S. Navy for conversion into what were then known as BAVGs; work began on the first, HMS *Archer*, even before the lend-

lease appropriation for her had been passed, and she was commissioned in November 1941. She incorporated the longer flight deck that had already been fitted to the *Long Island*, her half-sister.

Of the other five ships ordered for the Royal Navy, the *Charger* (BAVG 4) was retained by the U.S. Navy for training. The *Avenger* (BAVG 2) was lost to a torpedo hit and thus demonstrated the need for the side protection applied in 1943 to many American and British escort carriers. The *Tracker* (BAVG 6) was completed to a modified steam-turbine-powered design.

The U.S. Navy was well aware of British operational practice. In October 1941 the U.S. naval attaché to Britain reported on fighter protection for Atlantic convoys, which included both full carriers and catapult ships, the latter capable of launching but not recovering their aircraft.

> Escort vessels are better known as fighter catapult ships. The Royal Navy had four at one time but two have been sunk, one by submarine and one by an aircraft torpedo. Of the remaining two, one carries one Hurricane and one carries two. Three pilots are carried who stand watch in turn at the plane and the ships have the best RDF [radar] available. Owing to the service required, these ships do not carry cargo and accompany outbound convoys only to the range of the Focke-Wulf [200] when they return with an inbound convoy. By remaining always in the danger area the planes must be constantly on the alert, hence the necessity for three pilots. . . .
>
> To date these ships have had eleven encounters, resulting in 3 enemy shot down and the remaining evading destruction by escaping in clouds. It is felt that the presence of these ships in a convoy is causing the Focke-Wulfs considerable annoyance and their activity, at least in the Western Approaches, would appear to be slackening. . . .
>
> Future construction of these vessels depends to some extent on delivery of American converted carriers. However, it is contemplated installing two catapults and 4 fighters on future catapult fighter ships.
>
> Catapult merchant ships or CAM ships differ in that [they] are primarily cargo ships, fly the Red Ensign, carry one Hurricane and one pilot and only a semblance of RAF. Their results to date have been nil.
>
> There are 32 of these ships now reported in commission and no more are contemplated as it is felt that having so many planes and pilots out of the fighting area cannot be afforded. The RAF [not the navy] furnishes plane and crew. The reason for carrying only one pilot is that once the convoy leaves the danger area the pilot is immobilized for the remainder of the trip. . . . Usually two of these ships are in a convoy. When first placed on board the CAM ships the presence of the plane was such a secret that only the ship carrying the plane knew of its presence. . . . As a

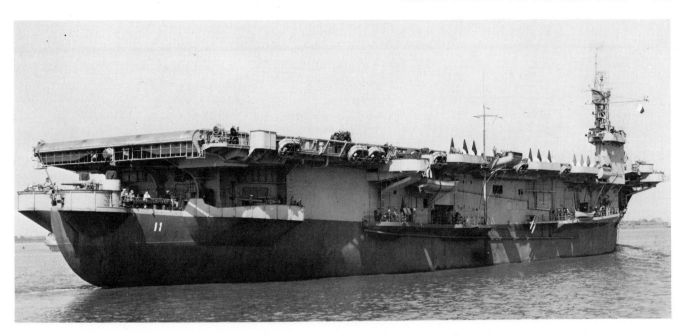

The escort carrier *Card* was typical of U.S. C-3 conversions. She is shown newly completed off Norfolk Navy Yard on 26 March 1943. Although the *Card* served as an ASW carrier in the Atlantic, at the time of these photographs she had not yet been fitted with an HF/DF, the essential sensor. Unlike the *Long Island*, she had a hangar deck running most of her length. The deck's sheer, which presented a problem to aircraft handling, is indicated by the galleries built out on both sides. Note the fuel lines brought outside the hull to reduce fire hazard. The air search radar is an SC.

result, when it was catapulted for the first time, the rockets made so much smoke and flame that the other ships in the convoy thought it was an enemy plane dropping bombs and promptly opened fire. No harm was done, however, and future convoys were advised of the presence of a friendly plane.

. . . To date convoys including CAM ships have passed through the danger area a total of 58 times without interference with a single enemy aircraft. Primary purpose of CAM ships is cargo carrying, so that aircraft carrying is subsidiary. Given the ship and all necessary gear, it requires about 14 days to fit catapult.

The *Empire Audacity* carries 6 Martlet I's. At first it was desired to carry 4 fighters and 2 Swordfish [bombers], in order to have protection against both

The *Croatan* shows the typical portside appearance of a C-3 conversion in this photo taken off Restoration Point, Washington, on 20 May 1943. In contrast with fleet carriers, CVEs and CVLs had fully enclosed hangars. Early C-3 conversions had eight twin 40-mm guns when completed: six alongside the flight deck, four forward and two aft, and two in the extreme stern, with a pair of 5-in guns sponsoned out just abaft the hangar.

The *Copahee* shows what appears to be a unique level of protection for an external avgas line in this 14 July 1943 Mare Island photograph: the "zipper" consisted of a line of structural supports. The position of the small portside uptake is disclosed here by its smoke plume.

air attack and submarines. Owing to the shortage of ships with good AA defense, it was seen that undue strain on the outbound trip would leave the ship defenseless on her return, so she was given maximum fighter allowance. Whether this system will hold in the future is open to argument. To date one enemy plane has been destroyed with no losses to themselves.

These diesel-powered carriers were not entirely satisfactory. For example, in September 1941 the commander of the *Long Island* complained that he could achieve a maximum speed of only 16.5 knots—he wanted a speed of 21. BuShips was skeptical, since C-3s were designed to make 17.5 knots at 18,700 tons, and the *Long Island* displaced only 13,000 for an estimated speed of 18 knots. A much larger plant, 25,000 SHP, would be required for 21 knots. The British later commented that diesel machinery had given them trouble in their escort carriers, and that the *Long Island* had also been plagued with breakdowns.

More to the point, by the middle of 1941 a large escort-carrier program was in prospect, and there were not enough diesel-powered C-3s under construction. That is, after the *Archer* four were available at Sun Shipbuilding, along with the *Hawaiian Shipper* being built at Federal. On 22 July BuShips advised the Maritime Commission to abandon the latter, as the conversion design would instead be applied to ships then under construction at Seattle-Tacoma and at Ingalls, all of which were steam-turbine driven—but, more importantly, all of which represented a type being built in quantity. HMS *Tracker* (BAVG 6), a converted steam C-3 hull, was capable of a sustained speed of 18.5 knots.

The first four production BAVGs differed from the *Long Island* in having hangars that followed the sheer and camber of the original merchant-ship deck, which proved to be a particularly troublesome feature of all the latter C-3 conversions. The pilot house remained amidships, under the flight deck, with

In this 17 October 1943 view, the *Croatan* displays the most prominent mark of a North Atlantic escort carrier, the HF/DF mast forward of the bridge. Note, too, the supports for her island structure. The island was built out over the side of the ship to clear the flight deck entirely, and so was not structurally supported by the hull or the hangar side.

bridge wings extended to the sides. Planning for BAVG 6 incorporated British suggestions: the flight deck was wider and the navigating bridge set forward rather than amidships. Moreover, because the hull was incomplete when it was delivered by the building yard, there was no merchant-type deckhouse amidships. The hangar deck could run the full length of the hull between two large elevators, restricted only in way of the uptakes. The flight deck, of 10-lb plating, could accept a 14,000-lb airplane, compared with the 10,000-lb plane for the *Long Island*, and the ship could carry 90,000 gallons of avgas and 7,000 of lubricating oil. A British account emphasizes much improved underwater protection with more transverse bulkheads.

Early experience brought home to the British the problems of a fully flush deck. "The British have found that it is unsatisfactory for an aircraft carrier of whatever type to be without a ship control station above the flight deck from which all-around vision is possible. With no single point from which the conning officer can survey the situation continuously, the ship is dangerously handicapped in her position in a merchant ship convoy and is continuously liable to collision and to surprise attack."

In February 1942 the United States had under construction three classes of flush-deck converted carriers: the C-3 conversions, the *Sangamon*-class tanker conversions, and the light-cruiser conversions (CVLs). All were ordered fitted with essentially the same very small island, "actually no more than a small open bridge," 6 feet wide, 4 feet from the starboard edge of the flight deck. It included captain's and navigator's sea cabins, a chart room, an open bridge with high bulwarks for ship and flight control, and sky lookout platforms extending 4 feet to either side. BAVG 3 and BAVG 5 were similarly fitted. That left the *Long Island* as the only flush-decker.

The *Tracker* thus became the prototype for a total of forty-four more C-3 conversion carriers built under the FY 42 and FY 43 war programs. That is, on 11 December 1941 the Auxiliary Vessels Board called for a total of twenty-four more AVGs for British and American requirements. The war program adopted the following year called for another twenty-four conversions in FY 43. However, even C-3s were not available in infinite numbers, and only twenty could be spared for the FY 42 series. They became CVEs 6–25 (initially AVGs 6–25). Half of them were assigned to the Royal Navy; all could handle both fighters and

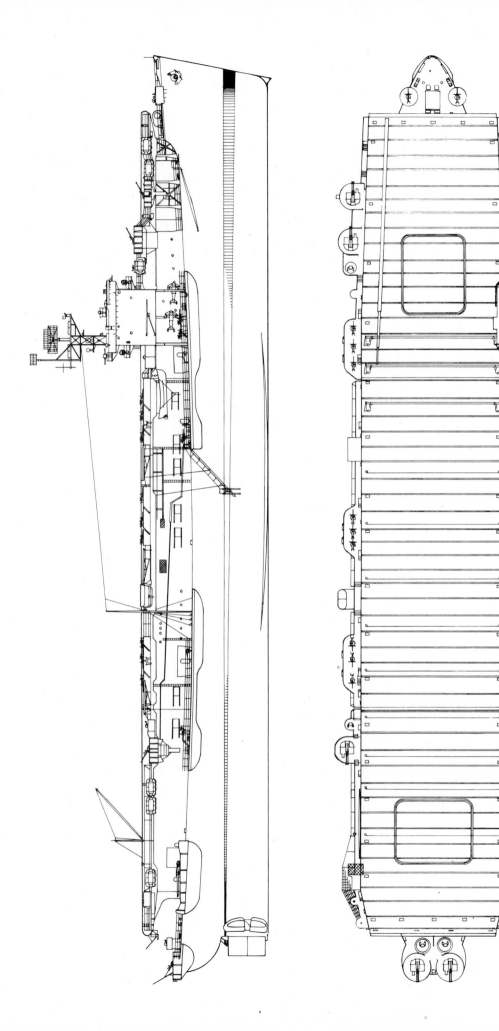

The *Bogue*-class escort carrier *Croatan* (CVE 25), May 1943, armed with two 5-in/51, eight twin 40-mm, and twenty-seven single 20-mm guns. The three booms projecting to starboard were aircraft outriggers. Radars were the SG and SC-3.

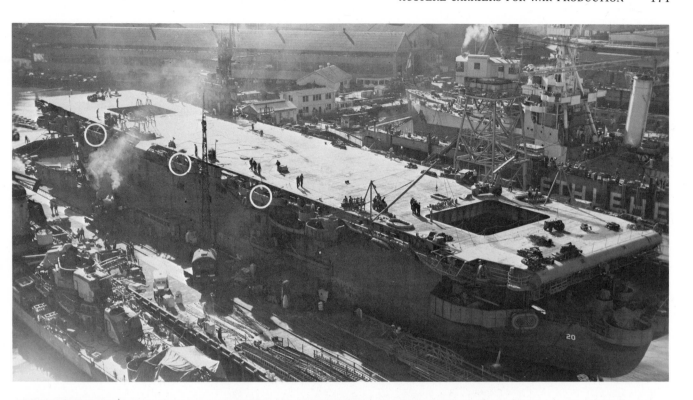

The carrier *Barnes* is shown under refit in San Francisco, 25 December 1944, along with the light cruiser *Detroit* and the destroyer *Beale*. Circles indicate changes, which at this time were relatively minor.

The C-3 conversion *Altamaha* was unusual in having a raised uptake on the starboard side aft, as shown in these February 1945 refit photographs taken in San Francisco. The circles indicate changes, which appear to have been minor. Note that, to save weight, all of her 20-mm guns were unshielded; the ultimate 20-mm weight saver, the replacement of single mounts by twin mounts, had not yet been carried out.

torpedo bombers. For the twenty-four ships of FY 43 a modified C-3 conversion was considered. The *Sangamon* was clearly better, but there were hardly enough tanker hulls for normal tanker duties. BuShips sought higher speed and better damage resistance through additional longitudinal bulkheads. The CVE 6 hull was extended by 35 feet amidships, with flight-deck length increased to 477 feet; it was estimated that this lengthening alone would gain 0.6 knots. Work continued through the summer and fall of 1942, but it gradually became apparent that any changeover would require several months' delay at the Tacoma yard in an urgent program.

In any event, no more than two or three of the FY 43 ships could be modified, and the new design would not appear in numbers until the FY 44 program. Since a modified *Sangamon* was already being considered for the latter, the VCNO decided to drop the lengthened C-3; on 24 October 1942 he stated that the next batch of twenty-four escort carriers would be similar in design to the *Sangamon*s; all of the FY 43 ships, CVEs 31–54, were completed to the original design. The only other available suitable hulls were four *Cimarron*-class fleet oilers, which became AVGs 26–29, the *Sangamon* class. (AVG 30 was the redesignated *Charger*, originally the British BAVG 4.) They were larger than the C-3s and could carry fuel for escorts. Moreover, they had national-defense features that had been included in their original designs. However, oilers were relatively scarce, and the decision to convert four of the twelve built was a delicate one, not to be repeated for the FY 43 program. Thus the FY 43 program consisted of twenty-four more C-3 hulls, AVGs 31–54. Of the FY 43 ships, only one, the *Prince William* (AVG 31) was ultimately retained for U.S. service. The *Sangamon*s were so clearly superior that they, rather than an improved C-3 design, formed the basis for the last series of U.S. escort carriers built under the FY 44 program, the *Commencement Bay* class.

Probably the greatest defect of the former C-3s was the camber and sheer of the original merchant hull in their hangar decks, making aircraft handling difficult at best and virtually impossible in rough weather; winches and cables had to be installed to move aircraft about. In addition, the hasty design of the conversion showed in the installation of the after elevator with its long dimension athwartships, making large aircraft nearly impossible to handle. On the other hand, according to an official comparison with the next CVE design made in August 1943,

the C-3 class has had approximately one year's operation as a CVE. It has proven to be an all around excellent CVE providing its speed and size limitations are taken into consideration. The ship handles very well at all speeds, and despite the fact that it has

one screw only, it is readily maneuverable under all conditions. Living conditions for both officers and enlisted men are above average. Built without air ports adequate ventilation was built in making it reasonably comfortable even in the tropics.

The fleet tankers were slightly slower than the C-3s, with a rated speed of 16.5 knots, and they were also much larger, with 484 rather than 442 feet of flight deck. However, the hangar deck between elevators was 20 feet shorter at 220 feet. It was built up from the main deck and therefore had no sheer, a distinct advantage. Given their considerable size, it is somewhat surprising that avgas stowage was only 100,000 gallons. However, the tankers did retain gear for fueling other ships at sea, and they could carry 5,880 tons of oil, compared with 3,290 for the former C-3s.

The fleet tankers were considered the most successful of the early generation of escort carriers, and by 1945 had been considerably modified; moreover, the final class, *Commencement Bay*, was a modified version of the *Sangamon*. The ships of the latter class were the first to have the twin-screw propulsion originally desired, although their engines were concentrated in a single compartment and thus vulnerable to a single hit. They did benefit from the protection of large wing tanks ballasted with seawater, as well as from a large fuel capacity and the ability to fuel escorts. Moreover, given their displacement and inherent stability, they could tolerate increases of flight-deck weight better than could the other classes.

The BuShips escort carriers were all designed to be armed with a pair of 5-in/51 single-purpose guns aft; British ships received 4-in guns instead. This choice reflected the realities of wartime production rather than any theory that such ships would not encounter air attack; in mid-1942 the designed or ultimate battery was changed to two 5-in/38 dual-purpose weapons, to be fitted as production permitted. Early conversions had, in addition, four quadruple 1.1-in machine cannon, scheduled for replacement on a one-for-one basis by twin 40-mm guns. The ultimate 20-mm battery numbered twenty in all of these ships. Late in 1942, however, the 40-mm batteries envisaged for the C-3s were doubled, and those of the *Sangamon*s increased to nine twin 40-mm guns. About a year later the *Sangamon* battery was set at two quadruple and seven twin 40-mm guns, the quadruple mounts being on the fantail. In June 1945, as part of the general improvement in fleet antiaircraft defenses, the two 5-in/38s pocketed on the main deck under the flight-deck overhang were to have been removed in favor of two twin 40-mm guns in the galleries, increasing the 40-mm battery to thirty-two for a total of twelve twin 40-mm guns aboard. The twelve 20-mm guns were to be replaced by thirteen

The *Charger* was intermediate between the *Long Island* and the standard C-3 conversions, and in fact had been earmarked for transfer to the Royal Navy. Like the *Long Island*, she was diesel powered and had only a partial hangar (note the absence of plating along her side). She had one 5-in/51 aft and two 3-in/50s forward. A light battery of six 0.50-cal machine guns was originally planned, but 20-mm machine cannon were mounted instead, as shown. By January 1944, when these photographs were taken, the *Charger* had been fitted with more modern electronics, including an SC-2 air search radar and a YE aircraft beacon. Apart from two airplane-delivery runs (to Bermuda and Guantanamo Bay), the *Charger* spent the entire war in Chesapeake Bay, being used to train pilots.

twin mounts. A Mark 57 radar director would provide blind-fire control for 40-mm guns in each quadrant (two forward, three aft) and another would control the two fantail mounts; there would also be seven individual Mark 51 directors (six twin mounts and one of the quadruple mounts).

The early CVE program might have ended with CVE 54, but for the President's belief that even more escort carriers were required to cope with the ongoing ASW disaster. Like the contemporary DE

program, this one peaked well after the decisive engagements of the spring of 1943. Both illustrate the problem of adjusting even austere mobilization programs to rapidly changing circumstances. In this case the result was an order suggested by the President for fifty small escort carriers.

Admiral Land, Admiral Robinson and I [Rear Admiral H. S. Howard, BuShips] were called to the White House [8 June 1942].... [The President] announced that more aircraft escort vessels should be

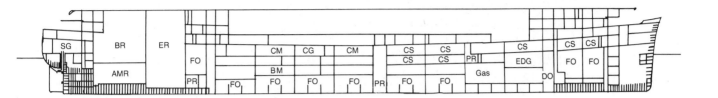

Sangamon-class inboard profile.

started immediately. Mr. H. J. Kaiser had impressed [the President] with the merits of a design prepared by Gibbs and Cox for an aircraft escort vessel suitable for quantity production and fitted with engines capable of giving the vessel a speed of around 20 knots. Mr. Kaiser had further informed the President that some of the ways at the Vancouver yard and at the Richmond No. 1 and Richmond No. 2 yards would soon be vacated and would thus become available for aircraft escort vessel construction. . . .

The paramount need of the new additional program is speed and to this end, after some discussion, it was decided that these vessels would be constructed by the Maritime Commission and inspected by them. In other words, it is to be a thoroughly Maritime Commission program, including the furnishing of all material such as arresting gear, catapults, etc., if such a procedure is at all possible. . . . the Gibbs and Cox design would have to be reviewed by the Navy Department as to its suitability for present aeronautical needs, inasmuch as it is believed to be based on the earlier conception of aircraft escort vessels such as the *Long Island*, which concept has been considerably modified during the development of the BAVG's. . . .

At a meeting later in June Admiral Land of the Maritime Commission explained that

the basic characteristic of the ships which were to be built was the delivery of airplanes abroad. The second characteristic . . . was the ability to use these planes from a flight deck when proceeding in convoy. . . . the ships were merchant vessels and not naval aircraft carriers or even aircraft escort vessels.

With regard to numbers, Mr. Kaiser apparently was extremely anxious to put two of his West Coast yards on this job to make use of his usual procedure of inter-organization competition. This would mean that a large number of vessels must be built as a minimum. . . . Mr. Kaiser wished to build not less than 100, although he would consider from 50 to 100, and Admiral Land stated that the figure of 50 should be looked on as a minimum. . . . plans called for the

delivery of the first ship in February 1943, deliveries to follow thereafter at the rate of 8 ships per month.

Fifty ships (CVEs 55–104) of this *Casablanca* class were ordered. Their design was carried out by the Maritime Commission under the title "small airplane transport with flight deck," although for all practical purposes they paralleled the other CVE designs and in some ways surpassed them. For example, unlike the C-3 conversions, they had flat hangar decks which, at 257 feet, were actually longer than those of either the C-3 or the *Sangamon*. On a smaller hull, displacing 10,200 tons fully loaded, compared with 13,900 tons for the C-3 or 23,900 for the former tanker, they had virtually the same aviation capability as and a much longer flight deck (477 feet) than the C-3. Moreover, the *Casablanca* class incorporated both twin screws and a dispersed machinery arrangement, each of two engines occupying a space with two boilers. This unit arrangement shows in the positions of the small uptakes, well separated along sides of the ship. By way of contrast, the former C-3s also show a pair of uptakes, but they are located at the same point along the length of the ship to either side of the flight deck. The *Sangamon*s showed four uptakes, all closely grouped at both sides at the extreme stern, as might have been expected in the case of tanker machinery arrangements.

Like the DEs, the *Casablanca*s showed the effects of the immense national shipbuilding program in their machinery: not merely were turbines in short supply, but even diesels were difficult to come by. Instead, the Maritime Commission selected old-fashioned reciprocating steam engines (five-cylinder Uniflow), a type already in production. Hull lines were based on those of the P 1-type fast transport (*Doyen* class): a longer mid-body, for a higher speed of 20 knots, was inserted, along with an acceptably long flight deck. Aft, the stern was fined, the shafts set further inboard,

The only unit of her class used for North Atlantic ASW, the *Santee* shows her characteristic HF/DF mast in this 12 October 1943 photograph. The openings in her side separated the original tanker main deck from the flat hangar deck built above it, the hangar proper, as in a C-3, being totally plated in.

and the skeg lengthened; there was a transom stern above water. Compared to the C-3s, they were both faster and considerably more maneuverable. Higher speed was valuable.

> Low speed [is a] serious, and at times, critical, handicap, especially when operating in the South Pacific or in the area of Doldrums. It requires 30 knots relative wind over the deck to launch a TBF with a torpedo, either by fly off or by catapulting with the original type catapult installed. On many occasions this relative wind was not obtainable and as a consequence torpedo planes could not be operated. Landing modern high speed airplanes with only 22 or 23 knots of wind over the deck is a serious operational hazard and results in a high loss of planes in operations.
>
> . . . the 2 to 2½ knots difference in speed of the two classes of CVE's is of vital importance in aircraft operations. Given 20 knots, even when operating in light winds often encountered in the South Pacific, it is almost always possible to get a relative wind of 25 or 26 knots over the deck. This increase in relative wind and the longer flight deck of the Kaiser type CVE will permit the operation of aircraft under all but rare conditions of light winds. This is not possible with the C-3 type.

Protection was limited to splinter plating around the island, gun stations, ready-service and clipping rooms, air-control stations, and torpedo stowage in the hangar; there was no underwater protection for the magazines. Moreover, the concentration of personnel in itself made for the possibility of very heavy casualties from a single catastrophic hit, as actually occurred in the case of the *Liscombe Bay*. The *Casablanca* hull was too small to accommodate the splinter bulkheads (outboard of bomb stowage) fitted to the C-3 conversions after the loss of HMS *Avenger* to a

torpedo. Moreover, it could be argued that the C-3 conversions were more survivable since their design was generally more conservative. Certainly nothing could be done while the class was in production, although Vice Admiral J.W.S. Dorling of the British Admiralty Delegation wrote to Admiral H. L. Vickery of the Maritime Commission in January 1943 that he was concerned with their vulnerability to torpedoes.

> I know it is late to start talking about modifications in design. . . .
> But the thought of sending these ships to sea as at present designed quite frankly fills me with dismay, particularly after the recent experience we . . . had when an auxiliary carrier sank practically with all hands after one torpedo hit near the bomb-room.
> These auxiliary carriers are such valuable ships, have such valuable equipment and above all, invaluable trained personnel, that if it is humanly possible I think we would be amply justified in any reasonable improvements which will help them to keep afloat when damaged.

As early as 5 February BuShips was asking the Maritime Commission to improve the protection of the bomb magazines from splinters accompanying torpedo attack, a modification then being made in the other CVEs by adding water-filled wing compartments outboard of the magazines. In the end it proved necessary to restrict bomb stowage to a centerline compartment, converting outboard compartments to oil-fuel tanks as protection for it. The remaining magazine compartment was to be provided with universal stowage of maximum capacity, but even so two out of the three compartments initially provided for bomb stowage had to be abandoned. There were, therefore, some considerable reductions. There were additions as well. The heavier bombs

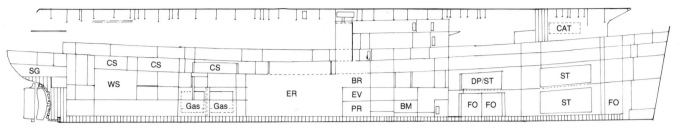

The inboard profile of the *Charger* (C-3 conversion).

FW = Fresh Water

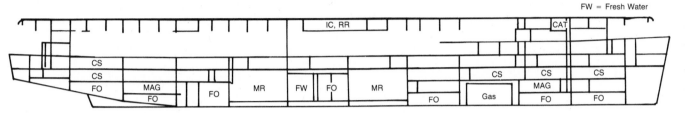

The *Casablanca*'s inboard profile.

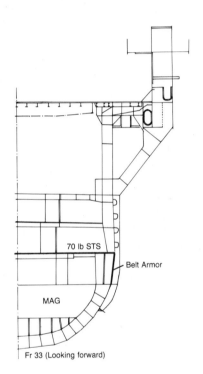

Cross section of the *Cowpens*. Note the blister.

were more compact per unit weight and so could replace larger numbers of smaller weapons. The transverse bulkheads, but not the longitudinals, of the new smaller magazine were protected with additional 40-lb STS plating.

British views of the vulnerability of escort carriers were more extreme than those of the U.S. Navy, perhaps due in part to the shock of losing the new carrier *Avenger* in the space of only a few minutes to a single torpedo; the Admiralty therefore adopted its own modification program. About 1,000 to 1,300 tons of ballast were added to new carriers to increase their stability, and buoyancy drums were fitted over the ballast in the wing deep tanks to reduce the list after a torpedo hit; the Admiralty also originated the system of bomb-magazine wing bulkheads, keeping weapons more than 10 to 15 feet from the ship's side. Avgas stowage was reduced to about a quarter of that originally provided, again to reduce vulnerability; in the C-3 steam conversions it was confined to one tank, the others being filled with seawater. Later the standard British fleet-carrier system of separate cylindrical gasoline tanks was fitted. HMS *Nabob* (CVE 31 class) was torpedoed in the Arctic on 22 August 1944 and survived a tow back to Scapa Flow. British constructors claimed that an unmodified (that is, U.S.) escort carrier would not have survived the hit, which left her badly down by the stern.

The final group of CVEs, the FY 44's *Commencement Bay* class, is best addressed together with the final *Saipan* class of CVLs, both representing compromises between the austerity of the early war emergency and the apparent utility of carriers below the level of fleet units. The original light fleet carriers (CVLs), by way of contrast, were essentially analo-

gous to the first waves of CVEs, except that they addressed a somewhat different problem.

In his CVL program, the President looked to conversions of cruiser hulls already under construction to make up for expected delays in the completion of the large fleet carriers (*Essex* class) already authorized. For example, the first of them, the first new carrier after the *Hornet* of 1941, was not scheduled for completion until 1944. The President began to propose conversion of some of the many cruiser hulls already on order in August 1941, but the idea was rejected at first in view of the time it would take to build such a carrier to peacetime standards. Conver-

The *Casablanca*s or "Kaiser" carriers formed the bulk of the wartime CVE force; here they are represented by the *Tripoli* (CVE 64, *top*) and the *Wake Island* (CVE 65, *above* and *facing*), as photographed on, respectively, 24 May 1944 and 9 November 1944. Note the HF/DF mast for North Atlantic ASW and the flat hangar deck, indicated by the straight line of the outboard sponsons. The prominent hangar-deck sponsons were used primarily for fueling at sea, the CVEs carrying substantial loads of cargo oil for destroyers and destroyer escorts.

sions were not actually ordered until January 1942, and then on a much more austere basis. Thus the first three CVLs entered service between the commissioning of the much-accelerated *Essex* in December 1942 and that of the next on 15 April 1943; the remaining six conversions all entered service during 1943. If it were argued that a CVL provided something less than half the air group of a fleet carrier, albeit at a much higher accident rate, the nine CVLs might be equated to more than four more fleet carriers in 1943, a considerable achievement.

In 1941 Preliminary Design could look back at what had become a history of cruiser-size carrier designs, beginning with a 1930 flight-deck cruiser with a 300-ft flight deck and nine 6-in guns. In 1934 there had been a twelve-gun flight-deck cruiser, its 200- by 65-ft deck amidships. The General Board had actually revived the idea in October 1939, again calling for a central, rather than an end, flight deck, and that November C & R and BuEng had returned a proposed 10,000- to 12,000-ton light carrier based on the 1930 design. In place of the General Board's proposed battery of three triple 6-in and four twin 5.4-in DP guns or three twin 6-in and three twin 5.4-in, the bureaus proposed a battery of eight twin 5-in/54s, this weapon having replaced the abortive 5.4-in gun in U.S. advanced antiaircraft planning. There were also projects for much larger flight-deck cruisers; a sketch design of December 1939 would have provided two deck catapults (one abeam the island, one astern), one elevator on a standard displacement of 12,000 tons, a battery of three 8-in/55 guns (one turret), and three twin and two single 5-in/38 guns, with a 420- by 71.5-ft flight deck. An alternative proposed the following January called for a somewhat smaller

deck (390 by 65 feet) and only one catapult, with the battery altered to two triple 6-in/47 guns and two twin 5-in/38 guns, as well as four quadruple 1.1-in machine cannon, all on 12,200 tons with somewhat thinner side armor. There were also the 10,000-ton carrier of 1938 and the 15,000-tonner (CVX) shown to the General Board in July 1940, the latter with two catapults forward, a 719- by 84-ft flight deck, a waterline length of 670 feet, a speed of 32 knots (120,000 SHP), and eight single 5-in/38 guns, four quadruple 1.1-in machine cannon, and ten 0.50-cal machine guns. It was to have had two elevators (44 by 48 feet, compared with 41 by 43 feet in the CVLs as built).

At first, then, the bureaus continued to think along such conventional lines despite the President's determination that they emphasize austerity. Preliminary Design based its studies on the 1938 10,000-ton carrier design, which had been adjudged efficient if limited in its ability to operate in a heavy swell. Admiral Howard of BuShips was willing to omit armor to save weight. Captain Cochrane of Preliminary Design felt that a conventional 5-in dual-purpose battery would encroach too deeply on the flight deck, so that the ship might (as, indeed, proved to be the case) have to depend on her own planes or an escort ship for protection against high-altitude bombers; in this sense even the initial, rather sophisticated design represented a departure from prewar standards. However, he did want single-purpose 5-in guns to protect the ship against surface attack.

Compared with the design actually adopted, the flight deck was similar in size (550 by 70 feet compared to the 552 by 73 feet actually achieved), the hangar was to have been longer (380 feet rather than 258 between elevators), and the elevators would have

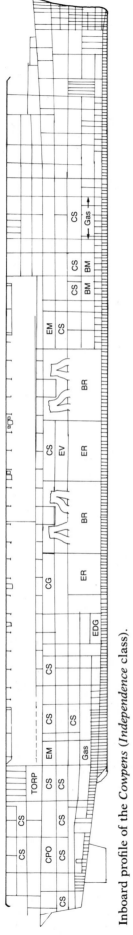

Inboard profile of the *Cowpens* (*Independence* class).

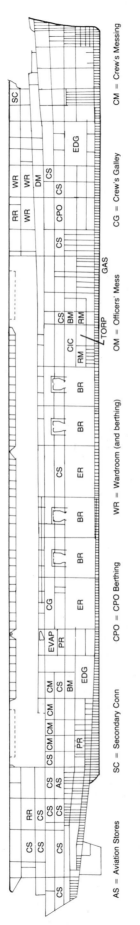

AS = Aviation Stores

SC = Secondary Conn

CPO = CPO Berthing

WR = Wardroom (and berthing)

OM = Officers' Mess

GAS

CG = Crew's Galley

CM = Crew's Messing

The *Saipan*'s inboard profile.

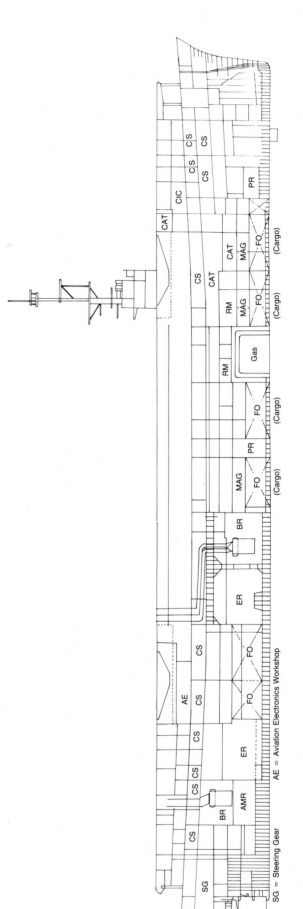

SG = Steering Gear

AE = Aviation Electronics Workshop

Inboard profile of the *Palau* (*Commencement Bay* class), 1955, in ASW configuration. Note the sonar, a QGA in a 100-in dome. Note also the unusual after boiler room.

been rather smaller (26 by 34 feet forward, 42 by 34 feet aft). There would have been 50 percent more avgas. At this stage an air group consisting of twenty-seven fighters and nine scout bombers was envisaged—that is, an *Essex*-class fighter group with a very limited strike component. The *Independence*-class characteristics would specify twelve fighters and eighteen attack aircraft (scout and torpedo bombers). As for the flight-deck structure, it would follow the escort carriers, with closely spaced bents that would preclude the sort of open hangar employed by the larger carriers. The island would contain the uptakes; it would be smaller than that of the *Essex* but would still reduce flight-deck area considerably.

Preliminary Design opposed the project because "it would upset the orderly construction of this series of cruisers, and would produce small, costly aircraft carriers of limited effectiveness [not much, if at all] earlier than the large aircraft carriers of the *Essex* class now building."

BuAer felt that the design "has a number of undesirable aeronautical features which combine to jeopardize seriously the probable usefulness of these vessels. . . . flight operations would be both hazardous and difficult." For example, the island seriously encroached on both landing and takeoff areas. "Take-off runs have constantly increased due to the addition of armor, leak-proof tanks and other military essentials. . . . Runs in excess of 350 feet may be frequently experienced. Such runs would have to start well aft of the island on a deck which is already limited in width."

The small forward elevator would accommodate only folded fighters (F4F-4s, F4U-1s) and observation planes. Everything else would have to remain packed on the flight deck during flight operations, which would limit the operating group to about eighteen

F4F-3s and six SBD-2s. This limit could, however, be overcome to some extent if folding-wing fighters were used. The sheer of the former main deck, which now became the hangar deck, would present serious problems in moving aircraft fore and aft, just as in a C-3 conversion (CVE). In addition, the already narrow hangar would be severely constricted amidships by the uptakes. The same narrow beam applied to the flight deck would probably create excessive turbulence in the approach and landing area abaft the ship.

It was no great surprise that on 13 October the General Board rejected the President's idea. To all of the disadvantages the bureaus had cited, it added that "the ship would be too small to be an effective carrier as it would be too lively in a seaway to preclude satisfactory operation of its planes except under most favorable sea conditions. The space available in the hull structure is so limited that a satisfactory arrangement of necessary carrier features such as plane and bomb elevators, gasoline tanks and piping, bomb storage and similar items cannot be secured. . . ." Even with many sacrifices made in the name of top weight, the ship would still require about 400 tons of fixed ballast.

The President was not to be put off. In a 25 October memorandum he asked the CNO to request a new cruiser conversion study since he did "not agree with the statement that the conversion of such a ship could be made little, if any, earlier than the completion of the big carriers of the *Essex* class now building. All you have to do is look at the dates of prospective commissioning of the latter."

Probably he was thinking in terms of his recent experience with the CVE program. The General Board still thought in terms of the rather sophisticated carrier sketched by Preliminary Design, and argued that lead times both for design and for the

The new "Kaiser" carrier *Hollandia* shows a typical layout in this September 1944 completion photograph. All eight twin Bofors were arranged around the flight deck, since there was too little space on the hangar deck aft to accommodate any; the Kaisers were unique among U.S. operational escort carriers in having only a single 5-in gun aft.

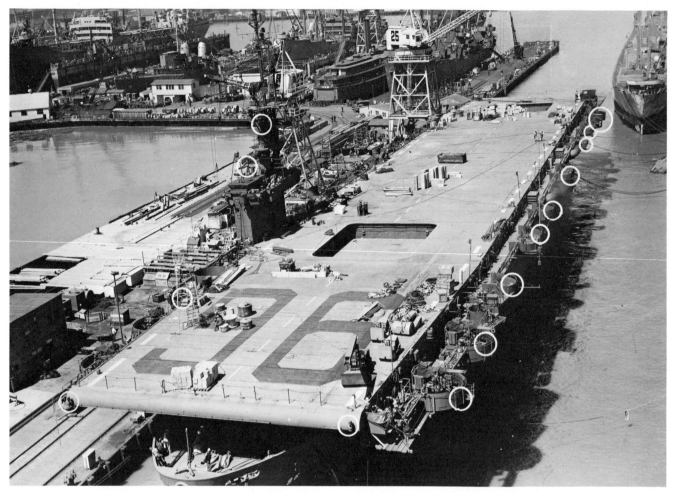

The *Salamaua* shows the standard improvements made to *Casablanca*-class escort carriers in this 1 November 1945 photograph. She had just returned to the United States carrying troops from overseas and would not again see carrier service, but even so she was fitted with an SP height-finding radar for fighter control. Note the single flight-deck catapult.

delivery of new material for a partially completed cruiser would mean that "even under the most favorable possibilities of such conversion, an assignment to the whole project of high priority would result in the delivery of the finished ship only about three months prior to the completion of the first carrier of the *Essex* class."

There was, however, an escape clause. According to BuShips,

the question of time for conversion is also affected by the conversion design. The Bureau prepared [its] preliminary study with the object of obtaining the maximum airplane capacity and the closest approach to present aircraft carrier standards for aviation features. . . . [It] did not consider that smaller capacity or lower standards would be justifiable in view of the expense and military value of the ships to be converted in their original role as cruisers. If, however, it were decided to accept a smaller flight deck, smaller plane capacity, and less effectiveness in air operations in other respects—somewhat along the lines of the converted AVGs [CVEs]—the conversion could, of course, be completed more quickly.

That was exactly the President's point; what was remarkable was that in the end rather better features were achieved as the cruiser hulls were blistered to gain stability against the added top weight. On 2 January 1942 the CNO, Admiral Stark, wrote Admiral Robinson of BuShips to confirm his directive to convert one of the light cruisers, expressing the President's delight; he foresaw a series of such conversions and hoped to "make a record on it."

Although BuShips began work on 3 January using the earlier plans, it soon shifted to a carrier design based on the contemporary *Sangamon* class (CVE), with the same flight deck. The cruiser main deck, with its camber and sheer, was the strength deck, and to avoid cutting elevator openings in it, the designers added a new flat hangar deck 4 feet above it, extending only between the elevators. They were able to achieve a clear hangar height of 17 feet 4 inches, comparable to that in a fleet carrier, in part because the flight-deck girders were quite shallow at 3 feet. That in turn was possible because there was no requirement for the new light carriers to stow spare aircraft triced up above the hangar, as in a fleet carrier. The flight deck was to be narrowed to only 60 feet at the forward end, to avoid changing hull lines to increase the flare of the relatively narrow cruiser hull. Weight and space were expected to confine the new carriers to the earlier H 2 rather than the H 4 catapult of the large fleet carriers, although two rather than the one of the escort carriers were accommodated.

A 315-ton blister solved the stability problems that had existed in the original cruiser conversion design, costing that ship 400 tons of ballast. Fuel stowage was actually increased compared with that of an unconverted cruiser, since the blister, when it was filled to the waterline, added 635 tons, as against a sacrifice of 225 to avgas stowage.

The designers began in hopes of avoiding any island superstructure at all. As in the flush-deck carrier studies of the twenties, they found gas disposal difficult, adopting at first a long horizontal uptake which was to have led aft under the flight-deck overhang from boiler room to the after end of the flight deck. However, even though the bridge was originally to have been under the forward end of the flight deck (as in original plans for the *Ranger*), there were difficulties: the new ship would require a radar mast, as well as a crane (of at least 14,000-lb capacity) to lift planes from the water or a dock to the flight deck. The designers initially thought they could combine it with the radar mast, the latter acting as a kingpost and located just off the flight deck proper. In fact, as completed, all the CVLs had prominent aircraft-handling cranes forward of their CVE-size islands. In the *Essex* class, a comparable crane had also been fitted, but it was installed at the hangar-deck level, to hoist aircraft into the large opening alongside the hangar. However, in the new design the hangar was essentially enclosed, as indeed it was in the CVEs. According to the characteristics, the hangar was "closed for darkened ship; curtained openings near the ends, port and starboard, . . . [permitted] warming up airplane engines. . . ." On the larger ships, after all, the fully open hangar had originally been adopted primarily to accommodate the athwartships catapult installation and then, in the *Essex*, the deck-edge elevator; the light fleet carrier needed neither.

Just as in the CVEs, there was a small island structure, authorized in February 1942, and the uptake arrangement changed to four simple smoke pipes led out of the starboard side of the hull abaft the island. The success, then, of a carrier of 100,000 SHP with an almost completely flush deck does bring into question much of the hostility C & R showed the flush-decker concept so loved by the aviators before the war. The same might, however, be said of several contemporary Japanese designs which, remarkably,

The *Independence*-class conversions of light cruisers paralleled the escort carriers in concept, although they were intended for fleet operations. This is the newly completed *Independence* off Philadelphia Navy Yard, 12 March 1943, still showing her original battery, which included a single 5-in/38 gun forward and aft. Both forward and after 5-in/38s were soon replaced by quadruple Bofors, and the light fleet carriers were unique in having all-automatic AA batteries. Note, too, the flight-deck extension to port to allow aircraft to be wheeled around a lowered forward elevator. The large flight-deck crane was necessary because there was no way to transfer aircraft from a pier or a barge into the closed hangar deck.

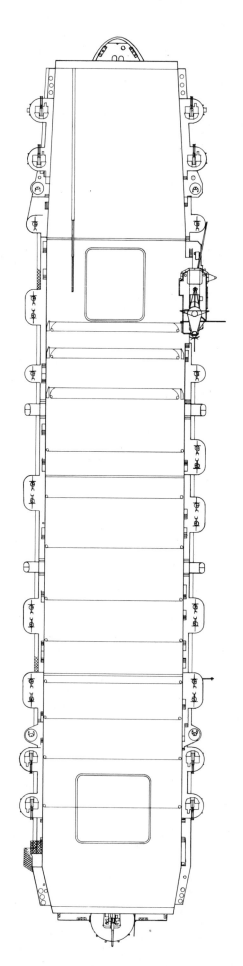
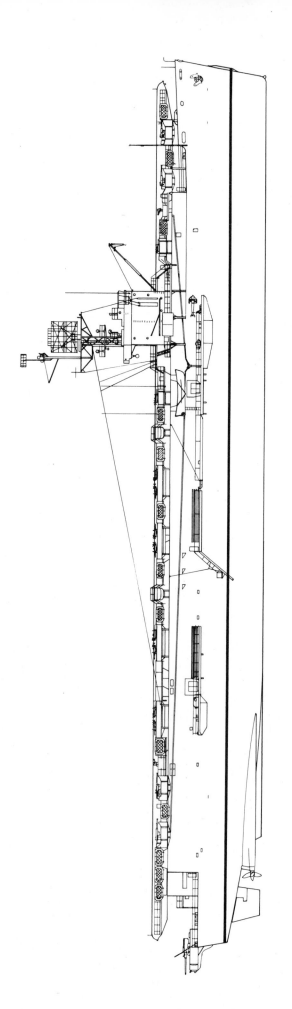

The *Casablanca*-class escort carrier *Nehenta Bay* (CVE 74), January 1944. She was armed with one 5-in/38, eight twin 40-mm, and twenty single 20-mm guns.

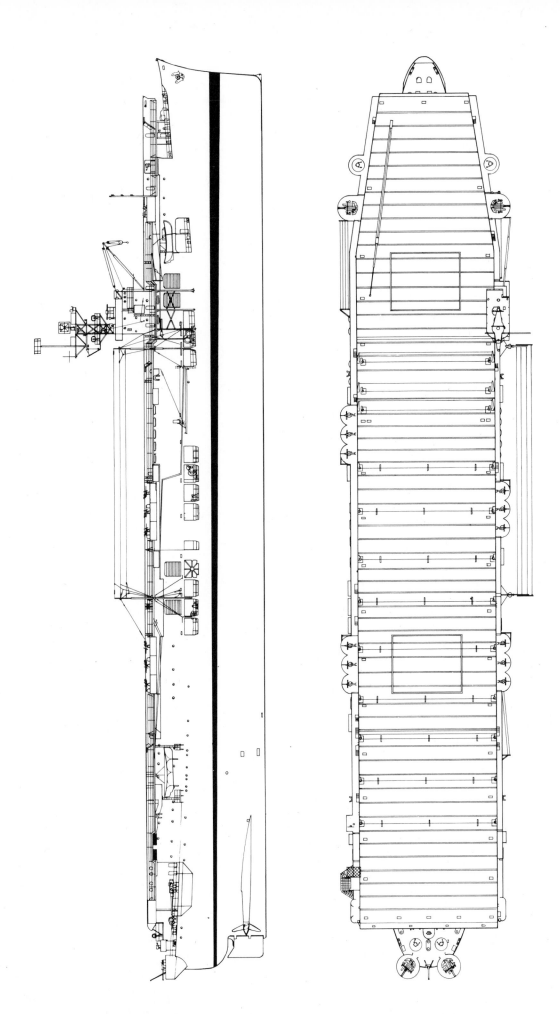

The *Sangamon* (CVE 26), a converted tanker, September 1942. At this time she was armed with two 5-in/51, eight twin 40-mm, and twelve single 20-mm guns. Note the characteristic openings in her side above the original tanker deck, designed to facilitate fueling at sea.

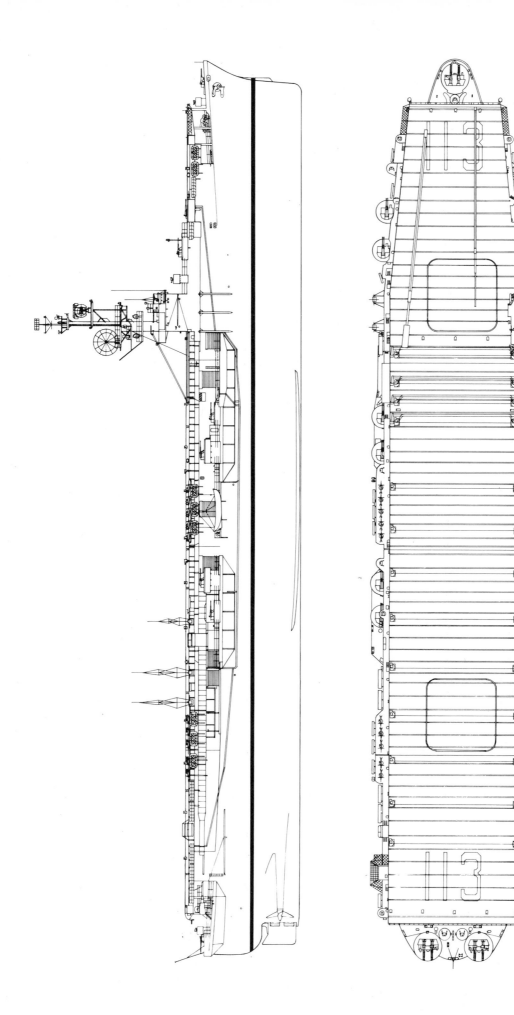

The *Commencement Bay*–class escort carrier *Puget Sound* (CVE 113), newly completed, in January 1946. She was armed with two 5-in/38, three quadruple and twelve twin 40-mm, and twenty single 20-mm guns. Radars were the SK-2, SP, and SG.

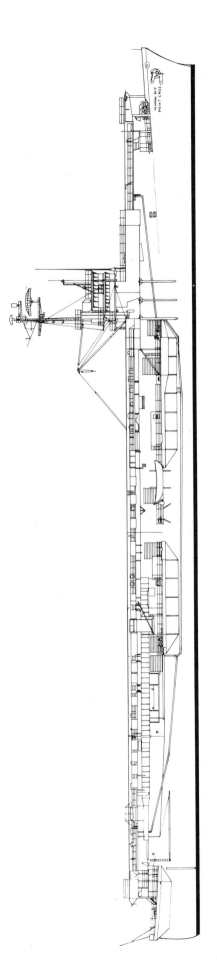

The escort carrier *Point Cruz* (CVE 119) as an unarmed aircraft transport (T-AKV 19), September 1965.

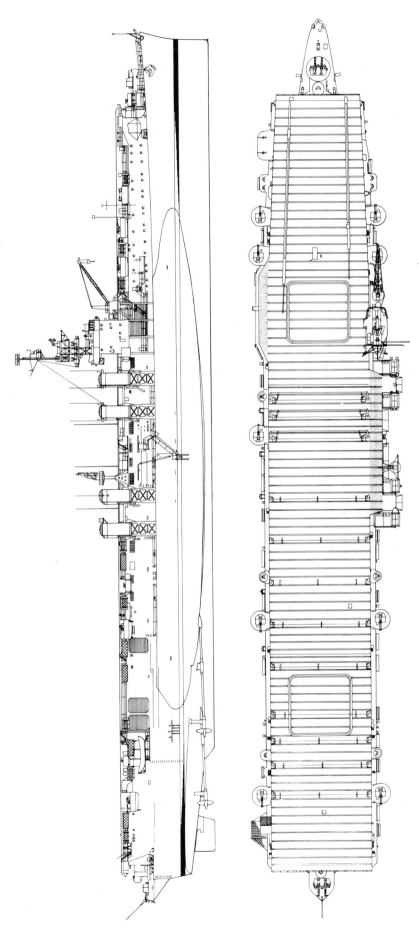

The *Independence*-class light carrier *Monterey* (CVL 26), July 1952. Note the longer port catapult.

did not figure in prewar discussions of U.S. carrier design either within C & R or in the General Board. Indeed, it appears that the Japanese adopted conventional uptakes in the island structures of their later carriers, primarily in order to concentrate those uptakes for protection; otherwise, they seem to have been quite satisfied by fixed uptakes turning downward alongside the flight deck. One important difference between this and CVE standards was the provision of a second air-search radar, on a stub mast just forward of the after pair of uptakes: all fleet carriers were required to have two such sets as insurance against the failure of one of them in combat. The wide separation between the two primary radars of the CVL appears often to have made for better radar performance than was enjoyed by the heavy fleet carriers. When fighter control radar was specified for fleet carriers, the CVLs had to surrender their secondary (SC-2) air-search sets, located on the island, in favor of an SP height finder there. The *Independence* received this modification during her 1944 post-damage refit, followed by the rest of the class, although the *Princeton* was lost unmodified.

The small island accommodated only a pilot house and chart house, with an open bridge above for gunnery control, sky lookouts, and fly control. The CIC and radar control rooms were located on the gallery deck forward of the hangar bulkhead, with air plot forward of the CIC at the same level. Even the small island had to be counterbalanced, and four portside blister compartments below the second platform level were filled with a total of 82 tons of concrete. Later saltwater ballast piping was approved for eight fuel oil tanks in the forward hold, to reduce trim by the stern and also to protect the forward magazines from under water attack, as in the CVEs.

Compared with a CVE, the aviation facilities were similar but better. For example, the elevators had a much faster cycle. While the first ship, the *Independence*, was fitting out, the VCNO authorized extensions in way of and between the stacks to park airplane "duds" that might otherwise have congested the flight deck proper. There was also an extension of the flight deck to port in way of the forward elevator, to bypass the elevator well and also to serve as a jettisoning ramp for damaged aircraft. (The *Independence* was completed without these improvements.) In addition, in March 1944 OPNAV authorized a second catapult (starboard side forward) at the cost of eighteen 20-mm guns and eighteen torpedoes, the first ship so fitted being the *Independence* herself. Some commanding officers did not consider this modification worthwhile, but it was authorized for the entire class in October 1944. Even with two catapults an *Independence*-class CVL was not the equal of an *Essex*. For example, the H 2-1 of the light

carrier would have required a wind-over-deck of 22.5 knots to launch the Grumman F7F-4N twin-engine night fighter, whereas the comparable speed for the H 4 of the larger carrier was 4 knots. Aviation fuel was on a CVE scale, 100,000 gallons of gasoline and 7,000 of lubricating oil being required.

The original cruiser main-battery magazines fore and aft were retained as bomb magazines, although (as in escort carriers) torpedoes were carried at main-deck level, in this case abaft the hangar. They rode the after airplane elevator to the flight deck, and there was a single bomb elevator to the flight deck on the port side forward. The capacity was not enormous, including, for example, 24 torpedoes, 72 1,000-lb bombs (divided between SAPs and APs), 72 500-lb bombs, and 162 of the small 100-lb general-purpose (GP) bombs. For example, that would permit an air group of eighteen scout bombers (and nine fighters), as originally proposed, to fly only four full long-range sorties with 1,000-lb bombs.

As for a gun battery, early proposals included two 5-in/38s, in this case fore and aft (after the relocation of the bridge), plus eight twin 40-mm and sixteen 20-mm guns, the latter all at gallery-deck level. The *Independence* was actually completed in this form, but the two 5-in guns were soon replaced, at the request of her commanding officer, by quadruple Bofors guns, which had greater power against air attack; the CVL would have to rely on her speed and her own aircraft to counter surface attack, something that prewar and even early wartime opinion did not foresee. On 8 February 1943 the VCNO authorized the addition of a ninth twin 40-mm gun, on the forward port side of the flight deck. On 6 August, as CVL 27 was completing, the VCNO authorized six more 20-mm guns, all in the galleries at the fore end of the flight deck, for a total of twenty-two such weapons. However, the 20-mm guns soon began to lose popularity to the more powerful 40-mm guns, and in January 1944 proposals were made for eighteen of the lighter weapons to be removed in favor of seven twin 40-mm guns. This was impossible from the point of view of top weight: a twin Bofors was much heavier than two 20-mm guns, and the guns were mounted high in the ship. However, it was possible to fit a fifth twin 40-mm gun on the starboard gallery forward. In the *Independence*, this change was made when the second catapult was fitted, although at least some ships ended the war with nine twin Bofors and with five twin 20-mm guns.

Armor was minimal for a light cruiser, except that splinter protection (15-lb STS, about 0.38 inch thick) was applied to the hangar side in way of the torpedo stowage and to exposed control spaces; bomb elevators and ammunition hoists were protected with 25- and 30-lb STS. That is, these ships might be consid-

The new light carrier *Monterey* is shown in June 1943. Note the stub mast for her primary SK air search radar between the two groups of uptakes, and the structures supporting the uptakes and the island itself. As in a CVE, the island was built entirely outside the flight deck and the hull.

The *San Jacinto*, the last of the *Independence* class, leaves the Philadelphia Navy Yard on 17 January 1944. The four prominent portside masts supported radio antennas and were folded outboard during flight operations, as were the lattice radio masts of an *Essex*. Note how the blistered hull was carried outboard of the straight-sided hangar, a narrow flat deck area showing amidships. The line of baskets for floater nets followed the flat hangar deck, which was built up above the original sheer of the cruiser hull.

ered protected against shellfire to about the extent enjoyed by the *Yorktown*s. They had no special bomb protection (as the *Princeton* proved by her loss) nor were they protected against underwater attack, their blisters serving rather to regain a measure of stability that would otherwise have been lost to top weight. However, after the severe losses of 1943 no fast American carrier was hit amidships (that is, in spaces protected in the larger ships) by a Japanese torpedo, so that this last gap was, operationally, of little moment. The prototype, the *Independence*, was torpedoed aft in November 1943, but survived and was restored to active service after a refit at San Francisco, completed in June 1944. While being refitted she received her second catapult.

During construction there was some fear of delay due to late delivery of the main belt armor. In particular, cruiser armor was class A, which could not easily be welded to blister framing outboard of the original hull. Class B was required, but in March 1942 BuOrd could only hope to provide it (in unhardened

form for the first ship, hardened for the others) from CVL 24 onward; the first two ships received no side armor at all. As compared with these unarmored hulls, the addition of about 360 tons of armor steel reduced speed by about a quarter knot, in addition to the 1 or 1.5 knots already lost by blistering; this additional loss was quite acceptable.

The conversion design was carried out on a crash basis, with much of the work done by the New York Shipbuilding Corporation at Camden, New Jersey; a representative of the builder even attended the initial 3 January meeting. On 10 January the chief of BuShips authorized the conversion of the USS *Amsterdam* (CL 59) to a carrier (CV 22). Admiral King examined the conversion plans and on 3 February wrote the Secretary of the Navy that

this ship will be a most useful unit, and [her plans] are sufficiently promising to warrant immediate steps towards the conversion of two additional ships of this class.

Off Hunters Point in June 1944, the *Independence* shows the unusual tumble-home hull form of her class. In the original cruiser design, the increased waterplane area compensated for added top weight, such as light AA weapons, and of course was used in the light carriers built on cruiser hulls. The deck cargo consists of twin-engine patrol bombers en route to the combat area.

Off Mare Island in July 1943, the *Independence* shows the forward end of her blister as well as the forward end of her hangar deck. The original CVL design called for a bridge and pilot house in that area, which later housed only a secondary steering station.

Examination of the prospective dates of completion of the 10,000 ton cruisers . . . indicates that it would be practicable to select two for conversion now which could be completed at approximately the same time as the *Amsterdam*. It is further considered that there are sufficient cruisers of this type under construction to warrant conversion of two more ships to aircraft carriers. If the decision is made now the very desirable result will be the completion of three small aircraft carriers at about the end of the year 1942, instead of one as now planned.

CL 61 became CV 23; CL 76 became CV 24. Later CL 77 and CL 78 became CV 25 and CV 26; and four ships not yet laid down as cruisers (CLs 85, 79, 99, and 100) became instead CVs 27–30.

Light cruisers were not the only hulls considered for carrier conversion during the President's carrier panic. A BuShips reference sheet shows a preliminary study of *Alaska*-class conversions (six hulls under construction or on order) of 3 January 1942 and even a preliminary study (June 1942) of an *Iowa*-class conversion, although a 12 June note stated that the conversion would not take place. At about the same time the conversion of a *Baltimore*-class heavy-cruiser hull was also considered. The original *Saipan* design would have been similar, although it would have been built from the keel up as a carrier. The *Alaska*-class conversion was particularly attractive, given the close affinity between that design and the one of the *Essex*. Compared with an *Essex*-class conversion, the *Alaska*-class conversion would show about 10 percent less aircraft capacity due to a shorter flight deck. That is, the heavily armored *Alaska* was both shorter and lower in the water, with three full decks rather than four, a difference of 11 feet in freeboard to the main deck. Cruising radius was 12,000 rather than 20,000 nautical miles at 15 knots. Moreover, the large cruiser had inferior underwater protection (a triple skin rather than the carrier's layers of protective compartments) because so much of her displacement had gone into protection against shellfire. BuShips expected to reduce that belt armor from 9 to about 4.5 inches, but even so could provide only two elevators and no hangar-deck catapult; about a thousand tons of ballast would be required. The lengthy delays inherent in such a project made it impractical, and work stopped on 7 January 1942.

Unquestionably the design to which the nine cruisers were ultimately converted was inferior to the one proposed by BuShips in September 1941, and even that was far inferior to the design of an *Essex*. But what mattered in January 1942 was speed of production—and that is what the CVL design ensured.

There were complaints even before the CVLs had really entered service. For example, in connection with the subsequent *Saipan* design, BuAer commented that

> perhaps the most general adverse comment regarding aircraft operation in the CVL 22s is the narrow hangar . . . due to the multitude of vent ducts and uptakes which pierce the hangar deck inboard of its outer boundary and to the fact that the flight deck supporting bents were not landed outboard of the hangar deck proper, i.e. on the blister. It is strongly recommended, therefore, that the maximum possible hangar width be achieved on this new class. . . .

More generally, the 1945 Pacific Fleet Board, going over lessons learned in ships' characteristics, recommended against any repetition of CVL construction in view of

> the CVL 22 type's lack of air group strength and lack of flight deck and hangar deck flexibility of operation (due, primarily, to lack of beam). . . . Their presence in a force containing large carriers provides CAP and other air details without compromising the readiness, launching or landing of complete strikes from the larger ships, but this advantage is not sufficient to warrant diversion of such tonnage as may be available in peacetime to this purpose. Ton for ton, CVLs can launch and land airplanes more rapidly than can CVs because airplanes must be launched or landed in succession regardless of ship size, but the overhead in screen vessels and ship's organizations, and complications of communications, maneuvering and aircraft rendezvous modify this advantage.

It appears, now, that conversion of the nine cruiser hulls to CVLs was expedient in that these vessels, completed as carriers, inflicted more damage on the enemy than they would have inflicted, probably, had they been completed as cruisers, but their lack of air strength, vulnerability, uncomfortable living conditions, lack of capacity for reserve airplanes, inadequate ship control and signal accommodations, catapult limitations, and unsuitability for night flying operations . . . are believed inherent in high speed carriers of this tonnage.

> Motion in a seaway, which it had been feared might prevent operations, is sufficient, at times, to make such operations much more hazardous than in the larger vessels, but this hazard is almost always accepted and the pilots and crew, by superior skill developed through necessity, make the operations successful. By judicious choice of speed, course, and acceleration, action can be reduced but the cost in landing casualties due to motion is, inevitably, higher than in the CVs, although still within acceptable limits.

Of the eight ships that survived the war, one, the *Independence*, was expended in the Bikini nuclear test of 1946. The other seven were all laid up in 1947. The *Langley* and the *Belleau Wood* were transferred to France in, respectively, 1951 and 1953 for service in Vietnam. The *Cabot* and the *Bataan* were refitted for ASW service (see chapter 16), the former being loaned to Spain in 1967. Finally, the *Monterey* served as a training carrier at Pensacola from 1951 to 1954, and was replaced by the larger light carrier *Saipan*.

Within a few months conditions had eased sufficiently for more sophisticated follow-ons to both the emergency types to be developed: the results were the *Saipan*-class CVLs and the *Commencement Bay*-class CVEs. Only the latter could be completed in time for the war, and even in their case only a very few ships entered combat. The prototype was retained in home waters to train new air groups for her sister ships, as the prototype C-3 conversion, the *Long Island*, had been. Remarkably, although the ultimate CVE design drew on CVE operating experience, the final CVL design was based entirely on expectations and on the experience of the initial design work, since most characteristics were set before CVLs had entered combat.

That was the *Saipan* class, which began as a CVL based on the *Baltimore*-class rather than on the *Cleveland*-class hull. Admiral King envisaged the CVL supplying local air cover for a pair of larger carriers in a task group, freeing their aircraft for offensive strikes. In July 1943 he instructed his VCNO in charge of ship construction to plan for more CVLs, since "in December 1945 . . . the Navy should have about eighteen CV type carriers in commission. The CVL building program will be completed in January, 1944, at which time it is estimated that seven of the original nine CVLs will be in commission, allowing two for normal attrition. [We want] to bring the number of CVLs up to the original nine as soon as practicable . . . to brigade one each with two CVs in a carrier division. . . ."

Two new CVLs were, therefore, included in the FY 44 program. King wanted somewhat larger flight and hangar decks, and BuShips had already begun to

The *Mindoro* is shown newly completed on 29 November 1945 (abeam) and, little changed, on 20 September 1947. Note the very heavy 40-mm battery, including three quadruple mounts (two aft). The postwar photograph shows many 20-mm positions empty, the result as much of low manning levels as of a loss of confidence in the weapon. In the summer of 1945 several ships of this type were fitted with army quadruple 0.50-cal machine guns in an attempt to increase their firepower.

The new escort carrier *Bairoko* steams on trials off San Pedro in a dark wartime paint scheme in this 10 October 1945 photograph. Note the very small uptakes, duplicated port and starboard and separated lengthwise because of alternating engine and boiler rooms. The crate-shaped objects on the radar mast were "reproducers." Note, too, the baskets for floater nets outboard of the flight-deck galleries.

develop such a ship on the basis of the *Baltimore*'s dimensions and machinery. Both ships occupied slips at the principal cruiser plant, the New York Shipbuilding Corporation at Camden, delaying completion of the large antiaircraft cruiser CL 147 (later cancelled) and shifting the heavy cruiser *Des Moines* to another yard. BuAer obtained a heavier flight deck, for 20,000-lb (ultimately 30,000-lb) aircraft, but BuOrd could not have the 5-in battery it wanted, and which it had lost in the original CVL design. Deck and side armor was somewhat improved, but there was no hope of providing torpedo protection in so small a hull. However, boiler rooms were further subdivided (there were four rather than the two of the original CVL) for better resistance to flooding, and the thicker protective deck was not stepped down over the magazines, as in a cruiser (and in the original CVL); the belt armor was also carried forward at the third-deck level. The result was increased volume for magazines as well as increased protected buoyancy. However,

the price was a decrease from the *Baltimore* scale of side armor (protection against 8-in shellfire) to the *Essex* scale (protection against 6-in shellfire).

By November 1943 BuShips had devised an improved hull form which required no blistering, but which reduced its similarity to the heavy cruisers under construction. The improved island resembled that being developed for the new class of escort carriers. The new carriers were also designed from the beginning with a second catapult, although both were still the H 2-1 type of the earlier CVLs. Only after the war would one be replaced by an *Essex*-type H 4B. There were also subtler improvements. For example, the *Princeton* had been lost owing to the explosion of her essentially unprotected torpedoes stowed in the hangar deck. In the *Saipans*, torpedoes were stowed in the best protected part of the ship, on the second platform deck. There were special port and starboard torpedo elevators, terminating, respectively, on the hangar and flight decks. Bombs

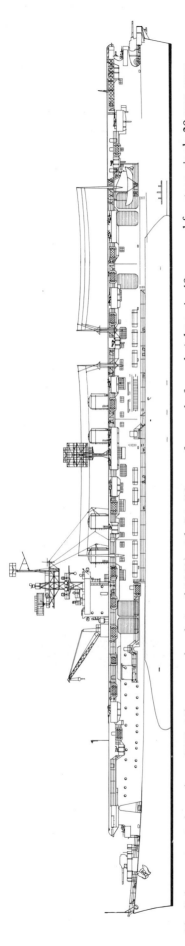

The light carrier *Independence* (CVL 22) as completed, April 1943, with 5-in/38 guns fore and aft, and eight twin 40-mm and fourteen single 20-mm guns.

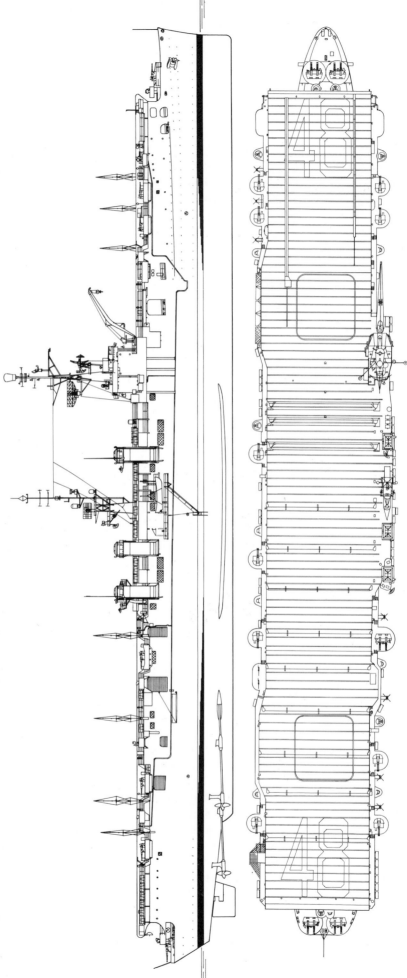

The light carrier *Saipan* (CVL 48), October 1956, at the end of her active carrier career. She was armed with three quadruple and ten twin 40-mm guns, controlled by six Mark 57 radar fire control systems (with Mark 28 radar) and eight Mark 51 mod 2s. Other major electronic equipment included an SPS-4 (surface/zenith search), SPS-6B, SPS-8, SR (after radar mast), SPN-2, SPN-12, TACAN (URN-3), YG (beacon), and HF/DF (after radar mast).

The *Saipan*-class light carriers, like the carriers of the *Commencement Bay* class, evolved from the designs of emergency conversions. The newly completed *Wright* is shown in this 15 March 1947 photograph. She carried, fore to aft, an SP fighter-control radar, a surface search radar, an SR-2 for long-range air search, and on the stub mainmast, an SR air search radar plus the radomes of the DBM radar direction-finding (countermeasures) system. In theory the combination of an SR-2 and an SR improved overall radar performance by employing two sets operating at different wavelengths; a few years later the *Essex* conversions combined an SPS-6 and an SR or an SC for similar reasons. The empty platform on the stub mast appears to have been intended for a TDY jammer.

from the forward magazine were brought up to the second deck by a centerline elevator and thence by torpedo elevators. As in late-war *Essex*es, fighter direction, air plot, and CIC were all under the protective deck, sharing in the extra volume brought by keeping that deck at third-deck level forward.

The island was larger than that previously employed, with captain's and navigator's sea cabins at flight-deck level, pilot and chart houses above, and flag plot, captain's bridge, gunnery control, fly control, and lookouts on the second level. It carried both search and fighter-control radars, with a secondary radar on the usual stub mast aft.

The resulting *Saipan* and *Wright* served continuously after the end of the war, both being decommissioned in 1956–57. At that time limited interest was expressed in an angled-deck conversion, presumably to keep the *Saipan* as a training ship at Pensacola. No design work appears to have been done, although an SCB project number was assigned. The two carrier hulls were, however, quite modern, and in 1962 the *Wright* began conversion to a national command post afloat, CC 2. Her sister began a similar conversion the following year, but instead became a major communications relay ship (AGMR 2, the *Arlington*). She alternated off Vietnam with the ex-CVE *Annapolis* until satellite communications made both obsolete. The NECPA role itself was abandoned about 1969: both former CVLs were decommissioned in 1970.

As for escort carriers, the FY 44 program finally permitted the navy to choose the type it liked best, the large *Sangamon*. Given sufficient time, new hulls could be built from the keel up, with work on what amounted to an improved *Sangamon* class beginning in the fall of 1942.

The Royal Navy received none of these escort carriers. In May 1943 it had stated a requirement for a total of fifty-two auxiliary carriers, to be reached by the end of 1944. The following August a joint U.S.-British ASW survey board criticized the Royal Navy for its delays in bringing U.S.-built CVEs into service, and recommended that the next seven be allocated to the U.S. Navy in order to have all available for ASW before the end of January 1944. Within three weeks of the survey board report, the U.S. Navy had informed the Admiralty that, given the combination of steel and electrical equipment shortages and U.S. requirements (presumably largely for the Pacific), no further British orders would be accepted. Thus the new CVEs would be wholly American in conception and in use.

The Royal Navy did complain that U.S. escort carriers needed extensive modifications to make them combat worthy, and moreover that the U.S. record in manning had not been so very much better than its own, with only nine of sixteen U.S. CVEs in combat by August 1943, compared to five British ones (with five more in September). On the other hand, the Royal Navy by this time was so short of personnel that it was employing merchant navy officers and men in the engine room and supply departments of most of its CVEs; airmen and aircraft were in short supply as well. Thus, of fifteen C-3 class (*Ruler*-type) carriers transferred after the U.S. Navy decision, nine were employed up to the end of the war only for training or transport. Britain obtained three ships nearing completion in the fall of 1943, but otherwise her attempts to get CVEs from merchant ships being built at home ceased.

BuShips reviewed prospects for future CVE production in a 24 August 1942 memo to the VCNO, who had announced an annual program of twenty-four

Both the *Wright* (*above*) and the *Saipan* (*facing*) were modified late in the forties for ASW operations, albeit not as elaborately as the *Bataan* and the *Cabot* a few years later. These photographs, undated, were probably taken in the early 1950s, when both ships had been fitted with tall HF/DF mainmasts and with the zenith-search derivative of the SG surface-search radar. Note, too, the SPS-6B, which did not enter service until about 1950, on the foremast. Plans to extend the life of one of these ships, which would continue to serve as a training carrier at Pensacola, were abandoned because of a shortage of funding for the FY 57 shipbuilding and conversion program. There had been some hope of fitting them with angled flight decks.

new escort carriers, under the Maximum War Effort program.

No directive covering the construction of aircraft escort vessels following the 1943 program has been received, but it is understood that it will provide for a larger number than 24 AVG's for 1944 since the first five hulls at the Seattle-Tacoma Yard, which follow the vessels of the 1943 program, will be converted to submarine and destroyer tenders instead of to aircraft escort vessels.

. . . The Bureau [of Ships] has taken steps looking toward the substitution of a revised design for the present design of the COPAHEE (AVG 12) class. This revision offers the advantages of an increase in length of 35-ft. and increased resistance to underwater and splinter damage because of the inclusion of new longitudinal wing bulkhead. Other characteristics remain the same as for the COPAHEE class. It was originally hoped that some of the later vessels of the 1943 program could be built to this revised design, but a review of the delivery schedule for these vessels and the plan progress for the revised design indicates that this will not be feasible. Aircraft escort vessels of the proposed program for 1944 could be built to the revised design with a probable rate of production 20% slower than if the present design were retained.

Two new factors deserve consideration in connection with the review of the aircraft escort vessel program:

—The Maritime Commission will presumably deliver 50 vessels of this type during 1943, an addition which was not contemplated when [the modified COPAHEE was proposed].

Recent emphasis on the probable use of the AVG type as combatant, or semi-combatant, ship leads to the question as to whether an improved type should not be considered. This would involve either a completely new design, or a design similar to the AVG 26-29 Class (ex-oilers). The revised design referred to [above], even though a marked improvement over the present design, would still suffer from the handicaps inherent in a conversion. Vessels of a new design could not, of course, at least initially, be produced at the rate at which either the existing or the revised design could be produced.

The VCNO concurred; on 24 October he asked that Seattle-Tacoma, the yard responsible in the past for the C-3s, produce twenty-four (or as near that num-

Since both the *Wright* and the *Saipan* were laid up after less than a decade of service, several plans for use of their hulls were framed. The *Wright* became a command ship, her flight deck forming an antenna "farm."

ber as possible) *Cimarron*s with improved damage resistance and, if possible, speed, so far as possible without interference in other programs or delay in completion. In this *Commencement Bay* design the principal improvement was separation of the engine rooms to protect against damage from a single hit. In addition, there were higher speed elevators, and the deck was designed for 17,000- rather than 14,000-lb aircraft. In May 1943 a second catapult, partially overlapping the forward elevator, was added to the design, providing these ships with both the usual CVE H 2-1 and the fleet carrier H 4C. There was a new, larger island, similar to that in the *Saipan* class CVL. Finally the battery was improved, with two 5-in/38s aft, and the bows flared to take a quadruple 40-mm mount forward; two more were mounted right aft. In addition, there were eight twin 40-mm guns as the ships were completed, for a total of twenty-eight barrels, plus twenty 20-mm guns.

The wing tanks were permanently converted to saltwater ballast, the heavy-duty cargo pumps and piping of the converted tankers being eliminated in favor of additional crew space. In contrast to the converted tankers, the new ships were limited to fueling escorts.

Speed was increased through more horsepower; structural strength was improved by making both the hangar deck and the main deck strength decks. Finally, the new design, although closely based on that of the *Sangamon* class, was more finely subdivided, with refinements such as saddle tanks for avgas. The FY 44 program finally ordered on 23 January 1943 consisted of only fifteen ships, CVEs 105–19; the FY 45 program added CVEs 120–27. The FY 46 program, the only part of the large proposed program that President Roosevelt approved in March 1945, was to have included CVEs 128–39, all of which were cancelled on 13 August 1945. After the war, the *Commencement Bay* class was the only surviving CVE type considered to be worth retaining in service, since only these ships could operate modern ASW and ground-attack aircraft.

9

The *Midway* Class

Although unlimited by treaty and similar restrictions in theory, the *Essex* class still retained many of the features of its limited forebears: given the very short time between conception and the beginning of construction, only so many changes could be made. Several other designs were likewise limited, such as the *Cleveland-* and *Baltimore*-class cruisers. Almost contemporary with this work, new and entirely unlimited designs were begun. Usually the motive was superior protection, often against the new weapons already in prospect, such as the "super-heavy" shells BuOrd was then developing. In the case of the *Midway*, the weapon in question was the bomb, and the new departure was to provide direct protection for the flight deck: the end of the treaties finally made possible the massive growth in displacement that earlier studies had shown would always be associated with such armor. The outbreak of war led to the cancellation of almost all of the new designs in favor of continued production of the interim types; the *Midway-* and *Alaska*-class 12-in gun cruisers were the sole survivors, although for a time it appeared that the *Montana*-class battleships would also be built. The large *Fletcher*-class destroyers can also be considered part of this post-treaty design generation, their relative simplicity (and also their great superiority over earlier types) saving them from cancellation.

As had been foreseen, useful deck protection for an American-style carrier implied great size and cost. President Roosevelt appears to have suspected that the navy tended to "gold-plate"; by early 1942 he had learned, for example, that the navy's rejection of a light-cruiser conversion for carrier use was based, not on the issue of how rapidly flight decks could be

procured, but rather on secondary issues of relative merit in far too elaborate a conversion. When he was presented with a proposal for four 45,000-ton armored flight-deck carriers as part of the "maximum war effort" building proposal for FY 43, he demurred; those four ships alone were not approved at once. Instead, in August 1942 Admiral King was instructed to ask responsible commanders for their views on the value of such large carriers compared to the value of a similar tonnage invested in ships of 11,000 tons. The President appears to have had escort carriers in mind. Admiral Nimitz had little enthusiasm for either tonnage extreme, reporting that the forces afloat found the 45,000-tonner "unnecessarily large and unwieldy, and concentrat[ing] too great a percentage of strength in a single hull. . . . The view is generally held that the 11,000 ton vessel is too small to meet the requirements of a first line carrier." Marc Mitscher, then commanding Patrol Wing Two of the Pacific Fleet and later Commander, Fast Carrier Task Force, found "apparent unanimity of opinion that the best aircraft carrier is in the 20 to 30 thousand ton class. There is no question but that speed of delivery of carriers is the all-important factor at the present time."

There was also some skepticism in the fleet as to whether even a 45,000-ton carrier could be adequately protected. For example, the new 1,750-lb bomb was advertised as capable of penetrating 7 inches of armor, far beyond what could be placed on a flight deck high in a ship. As one writer commented,

the fact that the powers at Washington are still in the discussion stage seems to conclusively prove that

At anchor in the Bay of Gibraltar in May 1954, the *Midway* shows her secondary conning station forward, just under the edge of her flight deck, and a new reversed-tripod radar mast, the pole topmast of which is topped by the new SRN-6 TACAN antenna.

such a vessel would not be ready to fight in less than three years. That is just about one year too late to be of any use in this war. . . . The controlling factor therefore seems to be time. We need carriers, plenty of carriers, and then more carriers. Conversions are not satisfactory chiefly because they do not have the speed and secondarily because of the limited flight deck. . . . We are going to lose some, probably many, but we are also going to lose the big ones if we build them. The smaller vessel will lend itself readily to quantity production and should come off the ways in about one-third of the time that it will take to build the larger. . . .

Another opposed an armored flight-deck carrier on the theory that the heavy flight deck would reduce stability, and that "the best defense against both bombs and torpedoes is speed and maneuverability."

The officers queried thought that the 11,000-ton carrier in question was the *Independence*, a converted light cruiser capable of 33 knots. In fact, King told them at the end of August, it was the *Santee*-class escort carrier, unprotected, of about 20 knots, a wholly unsatisfactory alternative. Comments from the fleet strongly favored continued production of the *Essex* class. That was not the issue: the proposed maximum war-effort program already contained many new fleet carriers. Rather, it was whether a portion of the program would be spent on a new, larger carrier. That the fleet tacitly accepted.

Four large carriers were, therefore, included in a Maximum War Effort shipbuilding program. President Roosevelt approved the program, with the exception of the four carriers, on 12 August 1942. On 8 October, after pressure from Admiral King and the General Board, he agreed to the large carriers, but only if the General Board could certify "that the program for the immediate construction of smaller carriers is adequate for the next two years" and "that greater speed can be made in the construction of these 45,000 ton carriers than is indicated in the report of the General Board of September 11th." The board replied that no more light carriers could be obtained except at the expense of cruiser tonnage, the need for which was now critical. The CVE program was considered adequate. But *Essex*-class construction was not addressed, nor could the General Board promise greater speed in heavy-carrier construction. It had previously pointed out, however, that the existing program allowed for a total of twenty-three *Essex*es, nine CVLs, thirty-six C-3 conversions (CVEs), four oiler conversions (CVEs), and fifty Kaiser carriers (CVEs), plus fifteen C-3 conversions for Great Britain. As for the President's proposed program of sixteen slow-type 11,000-ton carriers, there was not a sufficient number of slips or supplies of material or manufactured goods (such as propelling machinery). "If the suggested program is considered

of sufficient importance to justify the disruption of other programs now in progress and to warrant granting the highest priority, it can be taken in hand; even so, it is improbable that the first eight vessels could be completed in the Autumn of 1945 due to the difficulty of starting a new line of construction quickly."

The General Board estimated that if the four proposed 45,000-ton carriers were not laid down, it would be possible to obtain four *Essex*es (the first to be completed in the summer of 1945), or four carriers similar to the *Independence*-class CVLs (1945), or ten CVEs similar to the converted tankers (two late in 1944 and the rest by the end of 1945), all at Newport News. Other resources were the New York Shipbuilding Company, which was specializing in cruisers and had nine light cruisers already under conversion to carriers. If nine more conversions were ordered, three could be obtained in the summer of 1944 and six more during 1945. Bethlehem was building *Cimarron*-class tankers for the Maritime Commission at its Sparrows Point yard. Fourteen were under construction; if they were to be converted to carriers, three would be completed late in 1943 and the remainder during 1944.

The board considered the slow escort carriers of "problematical" usefulness, depending upon characteristics such as the number of aircraft they could operate "which in no single instance equal those of an acceptable all round aircraft carrier." Nor could the CVLs be considered anything but deficient, for all the reasons outlined in chapter 8.

President Roosevelt now made a contingent approval of the project, although his Secretary of the Navy, Frank Knox, considered the General Board's estimate of the time to complete the large carriers (two in the third quarter of 1945, one in the fourth quarter, one in the first quarter of 1946, with a possible delay of six months in each case before the carrier could enter combat) unfortunate. The President thought the war might well end in less than three years from the fall of 1942, and saw in his proposal for sixteen small carriers the possibility of having eight within a year and eight more by the fall of 1944 (and perhaps another eight by the fall of 1945, when the first 45,000-ton carrier would appear). Knox felt that the General Board was being unduly conservative to protect itself from criticism in the event that a faster (and more realistic) schedule failed.

The President trusted Captain Cochrane, probably in view of the personal interest that he took in the naval construction program; on 21 November he asked, confidentially, for the captain's own estimate of how well the 45,000-ton carrier program could be accelerated; he was inclined to approve the program, but felt the reply of the General Board was not satisfactory.

Off Hampton Roads on 20 October 1945, the *Midway* displays her original configuration, with a 5-in director mounted on the flight deck forward of the bridge and all nine 5-in/54 mounts on her starboard side. Note, too, the early-war-type radio masts along her flight-deck side. The large antennas atop her island belong to SK-2 and SX air search sets, the former scheduled for replacement by an SR-3, the direct predecessor of the standard postwar SPS-6 series. An additional air search radar, an SR-2 operating on a different wavelength, is barely visible abaft the island. Note, too, the ship's name prominently displayed on her hull. It appears that this practice was adopted only for the 1945 Navy Day fleet review in the Hudson, shortly after this photograph was taken.

Cochrane soon replied that the schedule for carrier construction could be accelerated if two ships were allocated, not to Newport News, but to the New York Navy Yard, whose drafting room had excess capacity due to the cancellation of the *Montana*-class battleships. Rather than lay down one ship every two months, the bureau could begin the first pair simultaneously in the summer of 1943, for completion about twenty-four months later; this interval was the best Cochrane could promise for such large ships. One advantage of this plan was that the ships could be built in building docks rather than on conventional slipways, which would "eliminate launching expense and hazard."

The General Board's estimate of limitations on slips and materials remained valid; Cochrane estimated delays in the completion of CV 15 (to keep a building dock clear at Newport News), CV 21 (shifted to clear ways for CV 15), and CV 32 (shifted from New York to Philadelphia or Norfolk to clear a building dock). The building dock at Philadelphia had to be rejected: it would displace two heavy cruisers and require the preparation of additional plans and materials. On the whole, Cochrane considered design work the critical element, and the one he had solved by using the New York Navy Yard drafting office.

The President remained skeptical, and on 8 December he asked his naval aide, Captain J.L. McCrea, if, in Cochrane's opinion, they were justified in building two of these large aircraft carriers. Were there any other types that could be more economically built?

Cochrane, now a rear admiral in charge of BuShips, replied later in the month that

we should go ahead with the big carriers. The initial undertaking of two of the four recommended by the Department would accomplish the most important part of the program, namely, starting the only two ships which we could lay down during 1943 and getting the detail drafting and design work in hand.

Should subsequent circumstances dictate the need for additional ships of the type they can be ordered later with very small loss in time of delivery and small increase in cost. . . .

As to other types of ships which we could more profitably build using the steel which would go into the big carriers, the present building programs are, in my opinion, very well balanced as they stand. . . .

Actually today, and the situation will apparently continue, hull steel, particularly plates, is very much less critical than is manufacture of main and auxiliary machinery for ships, especially large reduction gears.

The special treatment [ballistic] steel is still tight but even that will be far less troublesome than it has been during the past year when enormous demands came in for alterations to ships in the fleet as well as for the building program.

Actually, the two big carriers will help to balance the materials situation because they will require only eight sets of main machinery [four shafts per ship] against a large weight of hull steel and armor.

The President approved two ships on 29 December 1942 and a third on 26 May 1943. Newport News became the lead yard, and New York Navy Yard built only one ship—which, ironically, bore the President's name as completed. The new carriers were so large that they merited a new designation, CVB, a step approved by the Secretary of the Navy on 10 June 1943. Two further ships, which would have become CVBs 56 and 57, were proposed as part of the large 1945 program disapproved (except for escort carriers) by the President on 22 March 1943; they would have been built by Newport News.

In wartime, then, the *Midway* concept was hardly universally popular. Until 1945 the U.S. Navy suffered no severe flight-deck damage due to bombing; it lost carriers to underwater attack, and the improvements in the *Essex* class (alternating engine and fire rooms and better side protection) were a sufficient answer to that problem. The *Midway*s appeared just as the danger that had prompted their design was first becoming apparent in the Pacific. But even then it was argued that their very large air groups could not, in fact, be operated efficiently. In connection with the design of a postwar fleet carrier, Captain W. T. Raisseur of Op-05-3 described the relationship between carrier design, the size of air group, and the time required for a "complete carrier evolution, i.e., launching and landing of a stated number of aircraft." He estimated that the launching interval might be reduced to 20 seconds; experiences showed a 40-sec landing interval, which might conceivably be cut to 30. Since aircraft could not be launched and recovered simultaneously, the carrier would usually fly about half at any one time, recovering one strike and launching another while steaming into the wind

for about 40 minutes in all (for about forty aircraft in a "deck load"). CAP and ASW patrols would add about 8 minutes to the launching schedule.

Present schedules call for a maximum of 6 deck load strikes per day, 4 hours into wind. If the direction of the wind is unfavorable for flight operations and additional turns into the wind are required, a force employing such a schedule has difficulty in maintaining a striking position. With the maintenance of a striking position a governing factor, we may say that one-third of a normal daylight period must be accepted as the maximum time available for carrier evolutions.

A CVB with 144 aircraft would require six hours for the analogous operation, which would be unacceptable. In effect, then, the CVB would be unable to make full use of her much more numerous air group, an argument Raisseur used in favor of a smaller postwar carrier. He also advocated a flight deck designed to allow simultaneous launch and recovery, which would reduce CVB time for six deck-load strikes into the wind to four hours, the permissible figure. Otherwise, the CVB was hardly the way to increase the number of aircraft at the target: better to increase the number of smaller carriers. The keys to simultaneous launch and recovery were a radically redesigned flight deck and a new mode of operations, as in postwar designs (chapters 10–12).

Against this rather gloomy prospect, sheer size in the *Midway* class did have some major advantages at a time of very rapid growth in aircraft size. First, the length of the flight deck permitted installation of a longer version of the standard H 4 catapult (H 4-1), which therefore could accelerate a heavier airplane to a greater speed; the *Midway*s were the only U.S. carriers, for example, which in their unmodified form could operate the postwar AJ-1 Savage nuclear-attack bomber. Similarly, sheer size made for greater aviation-fuel capacity just as jet aircraft, with their vastly greater fuel consumption, appeared. The increase represented by the larger carrier was not, however, nearly enough, and indeed no carrier would have sufficient aviation-fuel capacity before reconstruction.

On the other hand, a very heavy flight deck could not be carried at a high enough freeboard; the *Midway*s did not have the freeboard-to-length ratio of the *Essex* class, and throughout their careers they have been considered rather wet. Moreover, built with war-damage lessons in mind, they were more minutely subdivided than either the earlier *Essex*es or the later *Forrestal*s, and so gained a reputation for relative discomfort. Reportedly, for example, the *Franklin D. Roosevelt* was broken up because she was so subdivided that she would have been too expensive to reconstruct. Her two sisters were, however, mod-

The *Franklin D. Roosevelt* was completed to the original design. She is shown at anchor in the Piraeus, Greece, in September 1946, part of a continuing U.S. naval presence in the Mediterranean. The three *Midways* spent most of their early careers in the Mediterranean, where they provided the initial U.S. Navy capability for nuclear attack.

The *Coral Sea* is shown at anchor on 3 December 1947. She was completed to a modified design, which included a revised island. Elimination of the original armored pilot house allowed movement of the forward 5-in director onto the island structure, clearing some flight-deck area. Note the absence of two of the after 5-in/54 mounts on each side. By this time all three ships had been scheduled for re-armament with the new twin 3-in/50s; since the new guns were not yet ready, the *Coral Sea* was completed without an AA battery. The bar-shaped radar just abaft her forward 5-in director was an SR-3, the shorter bar the associated IFF interrogator antenna; the radar abaft the island was an SR-2. Not visible is the new structure at the bow, under the flight deck, designed to seal the hangar deck against waves (the *Midways* were relatively wet due to their great length and moderate freeboard, the latter no greater than that of the much shorter *Essex*es). This bulkhead, a direct forebear of the "hurricane bow" of later carriers, housed a secondary conning position at its forward end.

Steaming off Norfolk after a refit on 15 June 1948, the *Franklin D. Roosevelt* (*above* and *facing*) shows the reduced main battery and revised island originally built into her sister ship. Note the prominent flight-deck crane, which replaced hangar-deck cranes in *Essex*-class carriers. Although the hangar of a *Midway* was nominally open, in fact there were no bays fore and aft through which aircraft could be hoisted. They had, therefore, to come aboard via the flight deck. Two of the Mark 56 directors used to control the portside battery can be distinguished in the port oblique view; one of them is between the two aftermost 40-mm mounts on the port side. The portside elevator is stowed in vertical position.

ernized, and they are the last war-built combatants to remain in first-line U.S. service.

From the first, the *Midway* design was predicated on improved protection, against both heavier (8-in) surface fire and against bombs striking the flight deck. In 1940 the aviators had a lively interest in protection against surface attack, particularly by the large fleet of Japanese heavy cruisers; previous carriers were "compromised" in the sense that they had been protected only against 6-in fire, which was all that could be afforded on a limited displacement. They even favored a more powerful antiship weapon, for use by a carrier accidentally encountering enemy ships.

From an aviation point of view, the *Midway* class marks the divide between the prejet, treaty-limited carriers and the very large postwar types predicated on heavy jet-attack aircraft. The *Midway* was the last U.S. carrier in which the flight deck was no more than a superstructure, and indeed in which "ship" characteristics could predominate over those specifically tailored to aircraft. When she was designed in 1941–42, any flight deck much more than 400 feet long would suffice for the small naval aircraft. The size of carriers has since been driven up by air-group requirements, to the point where minimum flight-deck dimensions can now be estimated from the lengths required for glide path, aircraft handling, and catapults. When the *Midway* was designed, the main requirement on flight-deck dimensions was that the deck be long enough to allow spotting of the air group en masse before launch, leaving enough runway for takeoff (allowing for wind-over-deck). Similarly, there had to be sufficient length to park the entire air

group forward, leaving space for aircraft to land on. Both requirements reflect U.S. air-group operating practices of the war and prewar periods: elevators were slow enough and aircraft endurance low enough that the key tactic became the deck-load strike (the quick launch of nearly the entire air group). Similarly, group landings required parking forward, as the centerline elevators could not operate while aircraft landed. Nor could the deck-edge elevator. U.S. carriers were still designed as surface-ship hulls with flight decks slapped down on them. As complex and carefully thought out as internal aircraft arrangements were, they did not yet dictate carrier designs, and it was still relatively easy to convert surface ships designed for other purposes to carriers.

In 1940, when the *Midway* design began, U.S. carrier doctrine for the expected Pacific War called for independent operations against Japanese lines of communication and surface raiders. The carriers would be escorted by strong cruiser-destroyer forces; in fact a major argument in favor of fast battleships (the *Iowa*s) and "large cruisers" (the 12-in gun *Alaska*s) was that they could screen fast carriers against surface attack by Japanese heavy and battle cruisers. However, the U.S. cruiser force, limited in numbers by treaty, might well be hard pressed to provide sufficient screening ships: in the face of eighteen large Japanese cruisers the navy would have to provide convoy escorts, fleet scouts, carrier screens, all out of a force of eighteen large heavy cruisers and nine large

light cruisers. Here neither tally includes smaller cruisers usually assigned to operate with fleet destroyer flotillas (the U.S. *Omaha*s and the new *Atlanta*s).

Thus it must have seemed significant to U.S. naval aviators when the British carrier *Glorious*, escorted only by two destroyers, was sunk off Norway by the German battle cruisers *Scharnhorst* and *Gneisenau* in June 1940. At this time there was no reason to believe that surface search radar would soon make chance short-range encounters more than unlikely; but even then it seemed foolish to assume that carriers would always be able to show their heels to fast gun ships. In July BuAer proposed to the General Board that the next carriers (those following CVs 9–12 just authorized) be armed with 8-in guns and protected against 8-in fire. The guns would force any heavy cruiser to keep her distance, and so indirectly preserve the carrier's aviation characteristics: it was improbable that a few 8-in hits would sink a 35,000-ton carrier, although they might well destroy her flight deck. Proponents of the heavy-gun carrier probably had the *Lexington* and *Saratoga* in mind as prototypes; at hearings they would refer to the unique characteristics of those ships, fitting them for truly independent high-speed runs. Indeed, at General Board hearings in November 1940 BuAer resisted a proposal to remove the 8-in guns of the two older carriers, despite the fact that it was intended to cure a critical overweight problem—which, incidentally, submerged most of their belt armor and so reduced their survivability in the face of cruiser fire.

The controversy over whether or not to compromise aviation features in favor of secondary antiship weapons has a contemporary flavor, although we might not expect to see the aviators in favor of the guns. The problem was that, in bad weather, a carrier was helpless without her consorts; but weather bad enough to prevent flying would hardly make the operation of cruiser gunnery impossible. The same would apply more strongly to night operations. A good part of postwar carrier evolution has been directed towards the sharp reduction of that portion of the time the air group cannot operate.

The other element driving displacement up, and the one for which the *Midways* are best known, was deck protection against bombing. That her flight deck was an invitation to bomb attack was well known. As early as 1931 the question of what appeared to be the extreme vulnerability of the carrier's main battery to air attack had been raised in connection with the *Yorktown* (CV 5) design. Although an armored flight-deck design was rejected at that time, this did not amount to dismissal of the problem. Rather, the U.S. Navy position was that bomb damage to a wooden deck would be relatively localized, and that almost certainly a length great enough to permit air operations would be left undamaged. In fact bow arresting gear was introduced in the *Yorktown* design precisely in order to permit air operations in the event of damage to the after part of the flight deck. The idea of flight-deck armor was raised again several times in connection with the *Essex* design; in scheme CV 9G (January 1940) flight-deck armor was considered as an alternative to the armored hangar deck actually adopted.

However, the strongest impetus towards heavier (and higher) armor was probably the striking success of German dive-bombers in Norway. The General Board asked for designs with enhanced deck protection in August 1940; while these were being prepared HMS *Illustrious* presented a rather impressive example of the value of an armored flight deck in the Mediterranean.

Until this time, U.S. doctrine had favored the expenditure of the limited weight allowed it by treaty on the offensive air group. It appeared, at first, that no practicable armored deck could resist any bomb; it would be better to face the fact that bombs would get through and either prepare to accept the consequences or try to stop the bomb deeper in the ship, where protective weight was easier to accommodate.

To what extent the prewar U.S. Navy was aware of British interest in armored flight decks is unclear. Apparently there were (accurate) rumors of British construction of such ships about the time the *Hornet* (CV 8) was being ordered (March 1939), but since U.S.

attempts to design an armored flight-deck carrier had failed, many within C & R suspected that these rumors were unfounded. Prewar General Board hearings suggest the scarcity of technical intelligence. Particularly good attaché reports were frequently referred to explicitly, since there were no classified fleet handbooks or standardized ONI publications on foreign programs. By 1940 there had been a marked change: the British were very free in their exchanges, and attaché reports preserved in U.S. design documents are often transcribed Admiralty documents. By mid-1941, when what would become the *Midway* design was under active discussion, details of British armored flight-deck designs were available to interested U.S. naval officers, and Americans were observing British carrier operations firsthand.

One key event in the story was a visit to England by then Captain Cochrane and Rear Admiral Mills of BuShips in the fall of 1940. The British allowed both officers to visit their new armored flight-deck carriers. After suffering a bomb hit that penetrated her flight deck, HMS *Illustrious* was repaired at Norfolk Navy Yard in 1941, increasing U.S. interest in the type. According to Cochrane, writing in 1945, U.S. sentiment at this time was that

> while the armored flight deck was still desirable, the British arrangement of armored sides to the hangar was not desirable in view of the hazards to planes exposed in the hangar in the event the flight deck was penetrated.... The *Midway* has an armored flight deck, a heavy hangar deck, and, in addition, heavy transverse bulkheads subdividing the hangar against such casualties as the *Franklin* later experienced, and with relatively open sides for the hangar so as to prevent the serious damage which the *Illustrious* suffered of a bomb burst in the hangar....

The carrier faced two quite different bomb threats: high explosive (demolition, or GP) bombs and armor-piercing (AP) bombs with fuses of varying delays. The GP bombs were designed to explode on contact; they would have little effect even on light armor and might break up if dropped from a high altitude against thick armor. GP bombs derived most of their effect directly from blast. By way of contrast, an AP bomb, whose weight consisted mostly of its case, was designed to remain in one piece while passing through one or more armor decks. It would then produce a shower of high-speed fragments.

Although an AP bomb would leave a relatively small hole in the flight deck, the consequences of penetration might prove severe. For example, an explosion in a magazine might easily destroy the ship. The best way to prevent such a hit depended upon the delay designed into the AP bomb. If the first armor the bomb encountered was the flight deck, the length of delay would determine whether the burst was in the hangar deck or further below. A long delay might

Off Norfolk on 10 January 1951, the *Franklin D. Roosevelt* shows her new 3-in/50 AA battery, and her two air search radars have been replaced by new SPS-6Bs. She also has the new SG-6 zenith search radar and Mark 25 for her 5-in fire controls. There were eighteen twin 3-in guns, and ten twin 20-mm guns were retained, despite some considerable skepticism as to their effectiveness. By this time all three *Midway*s could and did operate North American Savage (AJ) nuclear bombers, but only on a temporary (detachment) basis. Note the unusual base metal color scheme of several of the F9F Panther fighters parked forward on the flight deck. This was a short-lived Korean War experiment.

permit penetration of several decks. Once the bomb exploded, however, even a relatively thin deck might protect the spaces below the burst. In effect, there were two ways to protect against AP bombs: a single very heavy deck could be used to exclude the bomb entirely, or a sequence of relatively thin decks could be used. In the latter scheme, the uppermost armor deck would initiate fuze action, and one of the lower decks would neutralize the fragments. However, a bomb with a long enough delay might well pass through any series of thin armored decks prior to

bursting. The decks would probably not stop it: a series of thin decks could not equal the ballistic effect of a single deck of their total thickness, which might be able to stop a long-delay bomb from penetrating at all.

The choice of a single heavy deck would be a gamble, since any bomb heavy enough to penetrate it would meet no further opposition. Unfortunately, it was clear in 1940 that enemy aircraft could be modified to take heavier bombs far more easily than ships could be rebuilt with heavier deck armor. The single

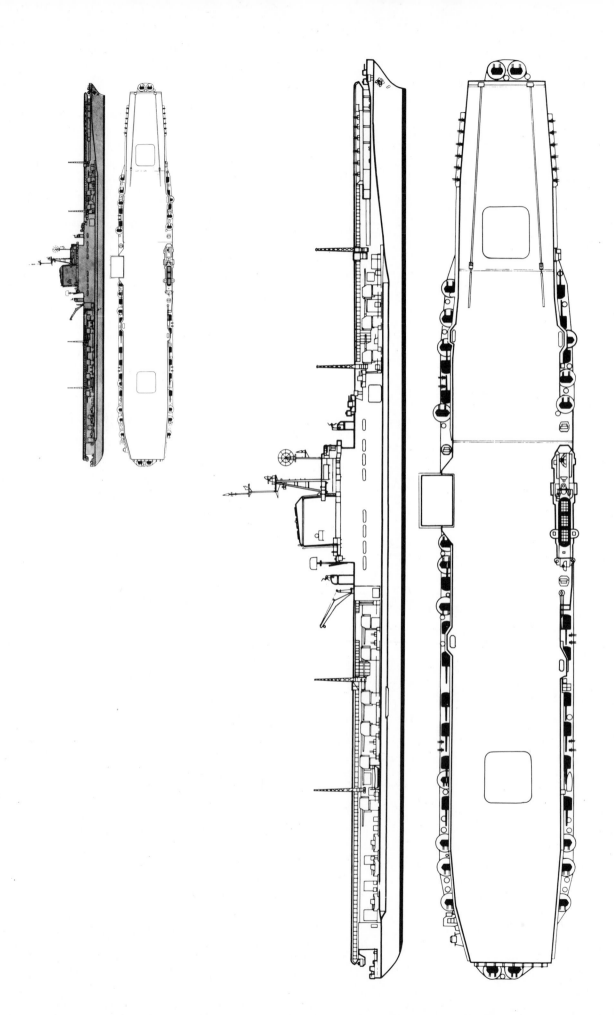

The *Midway* (CVB 41), 1945, as designed. This navy drawing shows an SP radar atop the tripod mast rather than the SX actually fitted.

heavy-deck scheme of protection had to be predicated on a particular bomb weight, and it appeared that AP bombs of quite feasible weight could penetrate any attainable single armor deck (which would have to be the flight deck).

This problem was nearly the undoing of HMS *Illustrious*. She did not have enough top weight available to allow for very much protection at the hangar-deck level, although she did have armored hangar deck sides to reject bombs falling far from the vertical. The 1936 staff requirement for the *Illustrious* and her class called for a 3-in nickel-cemented (NC) flight deck, which was expected to resist 500-lb bombs dropped by dive-bombers, or 500-lb semi-armor-piercing bombs dropped from 7,000 feet. The hangar floor had only splinter protection (1-in "D" steel) intended primarily to resist the effects of shells striking the side of the ship below the hangar. In fact the hangar deck was heavy only at the ends, over the magazines.

Even given an impenetrable flight deck, there remained the soft spots of the elevators. Before the war U.S. carriers had elevator tops made of aluminum for higher speed—an important offensive feature. However, a bomb penetrating an unarmored elevator would not merely put the elevator out of action—it might well pass into a magazine or a machinery space.

Any analysis of flight-deck protection had to take into account the fact that armor weight—and, more importantly, top weight—expended at the flight-deck level would exact a cost in protection to the vitals of the ship. Nor could it be assumed that bombs would have to pass first through an armored flight deck; they could pass instead through the sides of the hangar. The U.S. Navy required a nearly open-sided hangar deck so that aircraft could be warmed up below. As elsewhere, this was an offensive feature aimed at mounting a deck-load strike in minimum time; it impacted indirectly on the defensive considerations shaping the *Midway* design. On the other hand, it was argued that the open sides of the hangar would allow the blast of a hangar-deck explosive to vent. In several British and Japanese ships with closed hangars, hangar-deck explosions buckled the flight deck and even blew out elevators.

On 1 March 1939, even before discussion of what would become of the *Essex* began, Captain John S. McCain of the *Ranger* proposed a light carrier whose flight deck would be protected against at least a 500-lb bomb dropped from 10,000 feet. The entire air group would be spotted within the protected hangar, which would be served by two hangar-deck catapults. Admiral King, Commander of Aircraft, Battle Force, considered McCain's views on carrier size

essentially irrelevant, but suggested investigation of the armored flight-deck concept for future carriers.

However, he suspected that the penetrations of an armored flight deck with arresting gear would sharply reduce its viability. As an alternative, the entire hangar might be moved down in the ship, and an armored deck inserted below the unarmored flight deck. In his view, the primary virtue of the armored flight deck was protection of the hangar, not of the flight deck itself. King admitted that his proposal would require a closed hangar, as in the *Lexington* (CV 2), but felt that adequate ventilation could be provided.

Admiral E. C. Kalbfus, Commander, Battle Force, suggested that efforts should be made to develop both McCain's protected small carrier and a large protected carrier "capable of withstanding repeated bombing attacks, underwater attacks, and gunfire of at least 8-inch caliber." He suspected, correctly, that such a ship would be at least of *Iowa*-class size, and his 15 June 1939 letter is probably the earliest move toward the *Midway*s. General interest in carrier protection at this time led to increases in *Essex*-class tonnage; late in 1939 the General Board asked C & R to study the design of a protected carrier. A January 1940 design was evolved from the CV 9E *Essex* scheme (2.5-in armor deck at fourth-deck level, 25,000 tons) essentially in parallel with CV 9F (which became the *Essex*: 1.5-in armor deck, 2.5 inches on hangar deck, 26,000 tons). Another 1,200 tons brought the hangar-deck armor up to the flight deck, where it could resist non-AP bombs of up to about 1,000 pounds. However, this protection would be broken by expansion points, elevator openings, and even openings for arresting gear, elevators, barriers, and catapults. BuAer required an open hangar; it was impossible to guarantee that bombs falling through the hangar sides would not destroy the hangar deck or even penetrate deeper into the ship.

So long as the flight deck was not made a strength deck—that is, so long as BuAer continued to require an open hangar—a heavy flight deck would impose considerable structural problems in the form of "racking" or transverse stresses due to rolling or even beam winds. In addition, great weights high in the ship, even if compensated with increased beam, would probably cause large angles of heel on high-speed turns.

For all of these reasons, the General Board rejected the armored flight deck on 7 February 1940. Matters did not end there, however. On 1 August Admiral Halsey, now Commander of Aircraft, Battle Force, called the CNO's attention to reports that

—The British Director of Naval Construction (DNC) . . . stated that he considered it essential that the flight deck be protected over the hangars.

—The flight deck of British carriers is a strength member of the hull and therefore of heavier plating than the bridge or platform construction of U.S. carriers.

—A portion of the flight decks of new British carriers are apparently armored since the British DNC has stated that the armored section of the flight deck of their new carriers was sufficient to provide for landing planes.

Halsey's letter was inspired by one of McCain's, which cited experience in the Norwegian campaign. His commander, Admiral J. O. Richardson, CinC U.S. Fleet, disagreed since an armored flight deck would be very difficult to repair if damaged and the risk of bomb hits seemed small (no carriers were hit in Norway, and the overall percentage of bomb hits on all vessels was about 0.7 percent).

Meanwhile BuAer raised another issue. On 7 July it suggested that any new carrier (after the CVs 9–12 group already on order) be armed with 8-in guns; it seemed worthwhile to accept a larger carrier even at the expense of numbers (a 200,000-ton limit on new construction was in force). This proposal drew mixed reviews within OPNAV. The new 6-in/47 dual-purpose gun was suggested as an alternative, particularly as surface combat would probably occur only at very short ranges. On 2 August the General Board announced a hearing on carrier design "looking to the development of a new and improved type.... Among such matters is that of increased protection against bomb attack, as by making the flight deck of such thickness, say minimum 1.5 inch STS, as will exclude splinters, fragments, and small bombs." The hearing would also consider as alternatives an 8-in battery, a 6-in single- or dual-purpose battery, and a combined 5- and 6-in dual-purpose battery. Captain Marc Mitscher of BuAer, who would command the fast carrier task force four years later, pushed hard for the 8-in gun; he was backed by Captain Crenshaw of War Plans, who had to admit that he could not guarantee the presence of cruiser escorts in a global war.

Captain Cochrane of C & R emphasized the increased size that a new battery would require. This was more than the usual direct increase due to added weight, since power plants were available only in modest sizes. If the smallest was not powerful enough, then the ship would have to grow to accommodate a larger one. The situation is reminiscent of that of current nuclear and gas-turbine power plants, except that in 1940 the barrier against some intermediate plants was U.S. industrial capacity in the face of a mobilization emergency, rather than the sheer effort required for a wholly new reactor or gas turbine. In 1940 the choices were 150,000 SHP for the *Essex* and *Alaska* classes, 172,000 SHP, which would soon be adopted for the *Montana*-class battleships

(BBs 67–71), and 212,000 SHP for the *Iowa*-class battleships.

The alternative to adding power would be to accept a loss of speed; but high carrier speed was considered essential. In U.S. practice the carrier had to steam into the wind for 30 minutes to launch her air group and for 60 to recover it; she needed her speed to rejoin her formation. In effect high speed was associated with the size of the air group (that is, with the time required to launch and retrieve aircraft—wind-over-deck to launch was only about 25 knots). Thus it was considered unacceptable to reduce design speed much below 33 knots, which in turn meant that a design capable of, say, 32 knots on 150,000 SHP would have to be recast with the larger 172,000-SHP plant.

Mitscher was more interested in antiship than in antiaircraft guns. "Our aviators feel that they carry the most effective AA protection on the carrier itself in the fighting planes of the carrier and I believe that probably we could do away with some of the AA that has been recommended that we carry aboard carriers now." He considered radar the key to active defense of the carrier, citing British reports that their "detective system" allowed "plenty of time to get their airplanes in the air to meet any attack coming in." Shipborne antiaircraft protection was, then, a last-ditch defense against those few attackers who might leak past the carrier fighters. He could not get the preferred 8-in battery, however, because of the reduction in antiaircraft weapons it would imply. The 6-in/47 dual-purpose gun, often advertised by BuOrd, was still unacceptable in view of its very immature state of development: it would not actually become operational until 1949, in the *Worcester*-class light cruisers. That left the new 5-in/54s, under development as the secondary battery of the new *Montana*-class battleships. Higher velocity would give it significantly better antiship characteristics than the existing 5-in/38s, at a cost in rate of fire (due to a heavier shell and powder charge), that is, at a price in antiaircraft capability. It was accepted.

Aircraft were already a major contribution to top weight, a problem that an armored flight deck would exacerbate. At this time BuShips was imposing a 13,000-lb limit, and the new single-engine fighters were already approaching it (torpedo bombers of 15,000 pounds were envisaged); the *Wasp* (CV 7) had been ordered not to take aboard her spare aircraft for fear of top heaviness. It seemed to Mitscher that a strength deck/flight deck could take the weight of heavier aircraft, and that the added stability required to carry armor could also carry a heavier air group.

Commander Spellman of BuOrd reported on the deck thicknesses required to keep out bombs dropped from 10,000 feet. Proving-ground tests suggested that a 500-lb case bomb dropped from a high-enough altitude would completely penetrate a 3-in plate; from 4,000 feet it would penetrate an inch. He doubted that any deck without a considerable amount of thickness would protect against bombs heavier than the smallest (100-lb) type.

Views varied as to whether even this minimal protection was worthwhile. On 6 August the General Board asked for three studies to test the cost of various improvements to the *Essex* design (see table 9-1). In each, the fourth (protective) deck was to be increased from 1.5- to 2-in STS; the hangar deck from 2.5- to 3.5-in STS; and 1-in STS was to be replaced on or near the flight deck. The 1-in flight deck was intended to reduce damage in the event of an explosion just above or below the flight deck; it would also initiate fuse action and so allow a bomb to explode before reaching the vitals. Later BuShips would comment that, for rejecting small bombs, it was wiser to choose between very thin 20-lb plating (which would reduce distortion of the deck in the event of a hit) and a minimum of 2 inches.

—CV-A, with nine 8-in/55s, protected against 8-in heavy (335-lb) projectiles (see table 9-1). It was never worked out in detail, but BuShips estimated a displacement of 44,500 tons.

—CV-B, with sixteen 6-in/47 DPs (eight in twin mounts on the flight deck, eight in single mounts on galleries stepped down from the flight deck), protected against 6-in heavy (141-lb) projectiles. It came out to 38,500 tons and 900 feet in length. Even

with this lengthening, speed fell to 32.5 knots. Moreover, the flight-deck 6-in guns could not be dual-purpose because their gallery positions could not be brought clear of the flight deck as long as both a wide flight deck and transit through the Panama Canal were required. CV-B was presented on 16 December 1940.

—CV-C, with twelve 5-in/54 guns, came to 33,400 tons and length was increased to 880 feet in order to maintain speed. Although the hangar deck would be 40 feet longer than that of an *Essex*, any attempt to add more airplanes would add yet more displacement. CV-C was presented on 11 October 1940.

The order of priority was C, A, B, presumably on the theory that B was unlikely to materialize in the face of delays in the 6-in/47 gun program.

Meanwhile Captain McCain raised the armored flight deck issue once more.

I repeatedly endeavored while in command of the *Ranger* to visualize the effect of a bomb hit. . . . when planes were ready for takeoff the after half of the flight deck was covered with massed planes. The entire hangar deck was filled with planes gassed and ready. A bomb striking the *Ranger* would have had a fifty percent chance to strike the flight deck clear of massed planes. Because the hangar deck was completely filled with planes, this percentage would be further reduced by twenty-five percent for the ship as a whole, leaving only that forward part of the *Ranger* which included officers' and crews' quarters as a rel-

Table 9-1. Evolution of Schemes for the *Midway* Design, 1940–41

	CV-A	CV-B	CV-C	CV-D	CV-E	CV-F	CV-G	CV-H	CV-I
Std Disp't (tons)	44,500	38,500	33,400	28,000	45,000	35,900	39,500	37,400	40,000
Trial Disp't (tons)	51,200	45,600	40,600	34,600	52,600	43,100	46,700	44,600	47,300
LWL (ft)	900	900	880	788	900	880	880	880	880
Beam (ft)	111	103.5	100	95	111	101	106	102	106
Draft (trial) (ft-in)	32–4	32–0	28–2	29–6	32–6	31.6–0	32.6–0	32.3–0	33.1–0
SHP	172,000	150,000	150,000	150,000	172,000	150,000	150,000	150,000	150,000
Speed (kts)	33	33	33	31.5	33	32.5	32.0	32.5	32.0
Aircraft	112	91	83	64	120	110	110	110	60
5-in Guns	8	6	12	12	12	12	12	12	12
40-mm Quad	6	6	6	6	6	6	6	6	6
Belt (in)	7.6	5	4	4	7.6	4	4	4	—
FD (in)	1*	1*	1	1.5	2	1	3.5	3.5†	5
HD (in)	3.5*	3.5*	3.5	2.5	3.5	3.5	2	2	2
AD (in)	2*	2*	2	1.5	1.75–3.5	1.75	1.75	1.75‡	—
IZ (light) (thousands of yds)	11.25–18.7	14.6–28.4	9–28.4	11.25–18.7	14.6–28.4	11.25–28.4	11.25–22	11.25–22	—
IZ (heavy) (thousands of yds)	14.4–16.6	15–25.7	11.25–25.7	14.4–25.7	15–25.7	12–26	12–20	12.20	—
vs	6-in/47	8-in/55	6-in/47	6-in/47	8-in/55	6-in/47	6-in/47	6-in/47	—

Note: CV-E was the basis for the *Midway* design. IZ is immune zone, vs light/heavy projectiles of given caliber (105/130-lb 6-in, 260/335-lb 8-in) at a 90° target angle. Belts are all laid on 30-lb (0.75-in) STS. Light guns in CV-A, -B, -C are all quadruple 1.1-in (with eight 0.50-cal machine guns). Main battery in CV-A is 9.8-in/55; in CV-B, the guns are 6-in/47 (half DP, half SP). 5-in guns are 38 cal in CV-A and CV-D; otherwise they are 54 cal.

*FD armor over 696 feet, HD and AD over 500 feet.

†Middle bay only.

‡5.25 inches over magazines. IZ extends beyond 28,400 yards for magazines.

The *Franklin D. Roosevelt* is shown emerging from Puget Sound on 10 March 1954 after her last major premodernization refit. It appears that she received the semi-enclosed bow at this time.

atively safe place for a bomb to strike: namely, twenty-five percent of the ship's length.

When handling planes: that is, taking off or landing, which occupies twenty-five percent of a carrier's operating time, a bomb striking could hardly fail to crash a plane or cut an exposed gas line. With all planes in the air, the risk of vital damage was considerably reduced, but . . . the records will show that under conditions of mimic warfare the air group is aboard the carrier, in whole or in large fraction, seven-eighths of the time. . . . the damage of a bomb hit does not consist mainly or even necessarily of a hole in the flight deck. The danger lies in setting off highly inflammable or explosive material exposed or carried in planes. No carrier of any imaginable design can possibly survive the setting off of armed and massed planes.

The flight deck is essential to the performance of the ship's mission as a mobile base for planes. A large hole in that deck would put the ship out of action for some months. Thus protection of the flight deck itself is of fundamental importance.

The carrier whose planes are not protected while on board is in precisely [the same] situation [as] a main battery gun mounted on the open deck with unprotected ammunition around it.

In any probable war . . . the enemy fleet cannot keep the sea against our own fleet. He will be forced to withdraw to his home or frontier bases. Then, in order to make an impression on him, it will be necessary to combat land based planes and bases with carrier based planes. This would not be true in the initial stages of the conflict with respect to home bases, since an attack on them or even a venture within range of these bases would likely be too hazardous. However, it is undeniably the fact with respect to frontier bases. In an Orange war it will be necessary to clear out such bases in order to close the enemy sufficiently to hurt him. Such a combat would be a continuous performance and not an intermittent hit-and-run affair, and with the carrier as at present designed it is certain to result in great losses, for I do not conceive that once an advance is begun and attack underway that our fleet would turn back until an actual trial of strength had been made.

The director of War Plans wanted designs of British armored flight-deck carriers procured for study. Although on 18 November the General Board reiterated its view that the *Essex* class, which did not incorporate an armored flight deck, were the best carriers that could be had without going to excessive displacement, it continued the series of new studies.

Work also continued on CV-A, which came to 44,500 tons and introduced the 172,000-SHP *Montana* power plant. CV-A was the first in the series of studies to allow explicitly for a larger air group (112:

36 VFs, 38 VSBs, 38 VTBs). Its hull was probably the basis for the later CV-E that led directly to the *Midway.*

Meanwhile the Admiralty provided full details of the new British armored carriers, including their small gasoline (90,000 U.S. gallons) and aircraft (twelve VF fighters, twenty-four VTD bombers) capacities. Soon there was evidence of the value of the British armored flight deck: on 10 January 1941 HMS *Illustrious* survived six 1,000-lb and one 500-lb bomb hits, and a 1,000-lb very-near miss.

Within six months, U.S.-British cooperation was close enough for a U.S. officer, Lieutenant Commander Steadman Teller, to sail with the British Mediterranean Fleet. His report of 12 June 1941 indicated some of the defects associated with a heavy flight deck in a carrier considerably smaller than an *Essex.*

The armored flight deck of the *Formidable* (sister ship of *Illustrious*) was not struck by any bomb or shell while I was in the Mediterranean. Its effect upon the design and operation of the ship as a carrier was evident in the following ways:

—Reduces drastically the capacity for aircraft. Although *Ark Royal* and *Formidable* are about the same tonnage (22,000), the former, an old carrier, operates 54 aircraft but the *Formidable* is limited to 36.

—The reduced height of the flight deck above waterline in *Formidable* prevents aircraft being parked on deck in fairly rough weather. This does not concern the British but would require radical changes in our carrier system. Heavy spray was taken over the flight deck in Mediterranean and on one occasion I saw a small amount of green water. In an Atlantic storm the flight deck was swept frequently by green water; the forward end sustained damage from seas and ground tackle on the forecastle was torn loose.

—Aircraft elevator speed is reduced by the added weight. Although the *Formidable*'s elevators were not fully armored, they were heavier than *Ark Royal*'s. *Ark Royal* speed, 7–9 seconds for one way trip; *Formidable*, 13–14 seconds.

—The armored "box" formed by the flight deck, sides and armored doors must be vented in any case—witness *Illustrious* damage from hangar explosion. Standard orders on *Formidable* are (when day bombing attack is likely):
(1) Forward elevator down, after one up.
(2) Forward armored doors wide open, after ones shut.
(3) Lobby doors closed.
(4) Wire curtains up.
(5) Wire parties outside of hangar (in lobbies).

—The British Navy is not so sure that they can armor their carriers effectively. They insist that armor is necessary, but are not sure how they will obtain a satisfactory thickness.

My conclusions are that the British gave up almost 50 percent of their aircraft capacity to obtain partial protection of the carrier. The additional aircraft, particularly if they are fighters, will provide protection to the carrier. Furthermore, armoring a carrier at the expense of your main striking power is a defensive attitude. If carriers are to be used in an enclosed sea *without* the support of the shore based fighters, an armored deck is necessary, but it should be thicker than 3". If carriers are to be used for normal purposes, the additional aircraft capacity is more important than armor.

As a result of an informal request by the General Board (30 June 1941), BuShips decided to sketch a carrier of roughly *Essex*-class size, trading off length, speed, and air group for flight-deck plating and protective bulkheads. The bulkheads would divide the hangar deck in three to localize bomb damage (and thus, incidentally, answer the argument that no realistic level of flight-deck armor would exclude all bombs).

As for British experience, BuShips argued that the flight deck of the *Illustrious* was penetrated by a large (1,000-lb or heavier) AP bomb.

The fact that the existence of an armored flight deck forces the use of such heavy bombs is an important argument in favor of such a deck. On the other hand, this bomb did penetrate the flight deck and did gut the hangar by blast effect, fragments and fire. Moreover, if this bomb had struck a few feet further forward, and had had a somewhat longer delay in its fuze action, it would undoubtedly have entered a magazine and caused a disastrous explosion, since in the *Illustrious* the protective plating on the hangar deck is not extended over the central portion of the ship, including the magazines, protection for these spaces presumably being furnished by the lower side belt. . . . The question is often asked as to what the results would have been if a ship of the CV 9 class had been subjected to the same attack as the *Illustrious*. . . . Assuming the hits to have occurred in approximately the same locations in CV 9, as in the *Illustrious*, there seems no reason to believe that the CV 9 would not also have survived. The bomb striking the middle portion of the flight deck would almost certainly have had its fuze action initiated at the flight deck and therefore might have detonated before reaching the hangar deck, or it might have penetrated the hangar deck and detonated after penetration with severe, but probably not fatal, structural damage. . . . In case the bomb had detonated in the hangar of the CV 9 which has sides of light construction, there is some question as to whether the blast effect would have been as serious as in the hangar of the *Illustrious*. . . . Subject to confirmation by [small-scale] tests, it is believed that the provision of one-inch S.T.S. transverse bulkheads in the hangar will restrict the damage from blast effect in a relatively open-sided hangar to the section between two of these

Table 9-2. Estimated Altitudes (Feet) Above Which Decks Could Be Penetrated by Intact Bombs in 1941

	CV-D	CV-D	CV-D	CV-E	CV-E
	1.5-in FD	1.5-in FD 2.5-in HD	1.5-in FD 2.5-in HD 1.5-in PD	2-in FD	2-in FD 3.5-in HD
Horizontal Bombing					
500-lb HC	4,000	—	—	7,000	—
1,000-lb HC	3,000	10,000	—	4,500	—
2,000-lb HC	2,500	6,500	10,000	3,500	—
1,000-lb AP	1,000	5,000	7,000	2,000	8,500
1,600-lb AP	700	4,000	5,500	1,500	6,000
2,125-lb AP	500	3,000	4,500	1,000	5,000
Dive-Bombing (300 kts—60° dive)					
500-lb HC	1,000	—	—	3,500	—
1,000-lb HC	any alt	—	—	2,000	—
2,000-lb HC	any alt	3,500	—	any alt	—
1,000-lb AP	any alt	2,000	4,000	—	5,000
1,600-lb AP	any alt	500	2,500	any alt	3,500
2,125-lb AP	any alt	any alt	1,000	any alt	2,000

Note: In 1941, when these data were compiled, the 2,125-lb AP bomb was only contemplated and had not yet entered service.

bulkheads, and will protect the adjacent bays from a large part of the fragment attack.

Protection for the hangar of the *Illustrious* was achieved by material sacrifices in other characteristics of the carrier as compared with the *Essex* (CV 9 class). The direct comparison is obscured by the fact that the *Illustrious* is of smaller displacement than the CV 9 class and that the British practice of carrier operation differs materially from ours in the number of planes operated. Even allowing for these, however, there is a material difference in number of planes carried, speed, endurance, gasoline capacity, and bomb storage between the *Illustrious* and the CV 9 class. . . .

CV-D, like CV 9G the previous year, demonstrated that the *Essex* hull was too small to accommodate substantial flight-deck or hangar protection. Even a 1.5-in flight deck (and other armor on the *Essex* scale) would cost 900 tons of displacement, a reduction in ship length from 820 to 788 feet (which in turn would cost 1.5 knots in trial speed), and a loss of 19 aircraft, making a new air group of only 64. In submitting CV-D, Preliminary Design suggested an alternative design of about 45,000 tons, with 110 to 130 aircraft, and a 2-in STS flight deck, 3.5-in STS hangar deck, 2 inches over the vitals, and protection against 8-in shellfire. In effect this was CV-A with her 8-in battery traded in for an extra inch of flight-deck armor. Preliminary Design later offered to interchange flight deck and 3.5-in hangar-deck armor at the cost of another 1,000 tons in a new CV-E sketch design. This was very close to the compromise ultimately accepted in the *Midway* class.

BuShips saw the flight deck as a means of forcing an enemy to use heavy bombs to attack the hangar, that is, to reduce the number of bombs carried by the enemy and so reduce his number of hits. For example, a 500-lb heavy case bomb, in order to penetrate the flight deck of CV-E, would have to be dropped from more than twice the height necessary to penetrate the flight deck of CV-D (see table 9-2). Even so, it would take 6 inches to exclude the largest current AP bombs. In any case, of the 3.5 inches on the hangar deck, 2 were needed for strength, so that no more than 1.5 could be moved up to the flight deck; extra weight would be required to cover the greater projected area of the flight deck and to maintain stability. Thus a 3.5-in flight deck probably represented a practical limit, as long as the basic U.S. design practice of an open hangar was retained, that is, as long as the hangar rather than the flight deck was the strength deck.

BuAer found the CV-D design attractive. "The reduction in complement of aircraft . . . is not great enough to condemn the design. . . . It is proposed . . . [that] a certain portion of CV-9 tonnage [be diverted] to the CV-D design. . . . Except for reduction in the number of carriers, an even better solution appears to be to construct an equivalent tonnage in carriers of 45,000 tons displacement. . . ." A tonnage of 135,000 would buy three 45,000-ton carriers with a total of 390 aircraft, or five CV 9s with 415 aircraft.

BuOrd was less impressed with CV-Ds: the lower speed would make gun battles with cruisers more likely, and the 1.5-in deck would not stop a 500-lb

CV-E	CV-F	CV-G	CV-H	CV-I	HMS *Illustrious*
2-in FD 3.5-in HD 1.75-in PD	1-in FD 3.5-in HD	3.5-in FD 2-in HD	2-in HD 5.25-in over magazines	5-in FD	3-in FD
—	—	—	—	—	—
—	—	—	—	—	9,000
—	—	—	—	—	6,000
11,000	7,500	9,500	16,000	10,000	4,000
8,000	5,500	7,000	12,000	7,500	3,500
6,000	4,500	6,000	9,000	6,000	2,500
—	—	—	—	—	—
—	—	—	—	—	—
—	8,500	—	—	—	3,000
7,000	4,500	6,500	—	6,500	1,500
5,000	2,500	4,500	—	4,500	any alt
3,000	1,000	2,500	6,000	3,000	any alt

demolition bomb dropped from 6,000 feet. "Combined with the 1.5 inch flight deck [the 2.5-in main deck] gives inadequate protection to the ship [considering] the weight and stability expended." After all, a 3-in flight deck did not save the *Illustrious* from becoming disabled. If no deck thick enough could be provided, the bureau wanted the thinnest deck that would limit flight-deck damage due to a hangar-deck explosion—in other words, one that would not curl too much and would be certain to initiate fuze action. Probably 0.5-in STS would suffice.

At a General Board hearing on 24 September, there was interest in CV 9 and in CV-E, but almost complete agreement that in scheme CV-D the sacrifices in plane capacity and other characteristics were too great. War Plans considered CV-E too large from a handling standpoint and felt that the 120-plane air group might be difficult to operate. All participants did find some flight-deck protection attractive. The General Board turned back to CV-C as a prototype of reasonable dimensions and asked for the two following developments:

—An updating, to include the 1-in STS bulkheads, 40-mm guns, etc. This became CV-F, with a 3.5-in hangar deck and a 1.75-in armored deck. Displacement would be 35,900 tons and speed 32.5 knots.

—A study with a 3.5-in STS flight deck and whatever is required for strength at the main-deck level. BuShips noted that as a compromise heavy plate might cover only one bay of the hangar deck. CV-G (39,500 tons, 32 knots) would have 2 inches on her hangar deck and 1.75 inches on her protective deck.

As an alternative, CV-H (37,400 tons, 32.5 knots) had the 3.5-in flight-deck plating restricted to the midships bay.

BuShips presented CVs-F, -G, and -H on 24 November. In CV-H the heavy deck at the flight-deck level was lowered to the armored deck to give a total of 5.25 inches over the magazines under the two end hangar bays. Finally, there was its own CV-I, in which side and armored deck (antigun) protection was rejected completely in favor of a 5-in flight deck and a 2-in strength hangar deck. Even so, displacement rose to 40,000 tons, and the air group fell to sixty in view of the smaller hangar that had to be accepted. BuShips concluded that the 43,000 to 45,000 tons of CV-E was well warranted by comparison with the alternative schemes not so very much smaller.

These November sketch designs ended the series; on 27 December 1941, with a war emergency program in view, the chief of BuShips asked that "in view of the urgency of other design work now in hand . . . no further design studies of aircraft carriers be undertaken until such time as the General Board has determined approximately the size and general type of aircraft carriers which will be desired for future construction." BuAer had by this time been converted to CV-E, recommending it on 18 February 1942. The CV-E design provided a 3.5-in flight deck stressed to take 26,000-lb aircraft for takeoff, 22,000-lb aircraft for landing, embodying many of the lessons being learned at the time. The General Board agreed and sent CV-E characteristics to the Secretary of the Navy on 14 March.

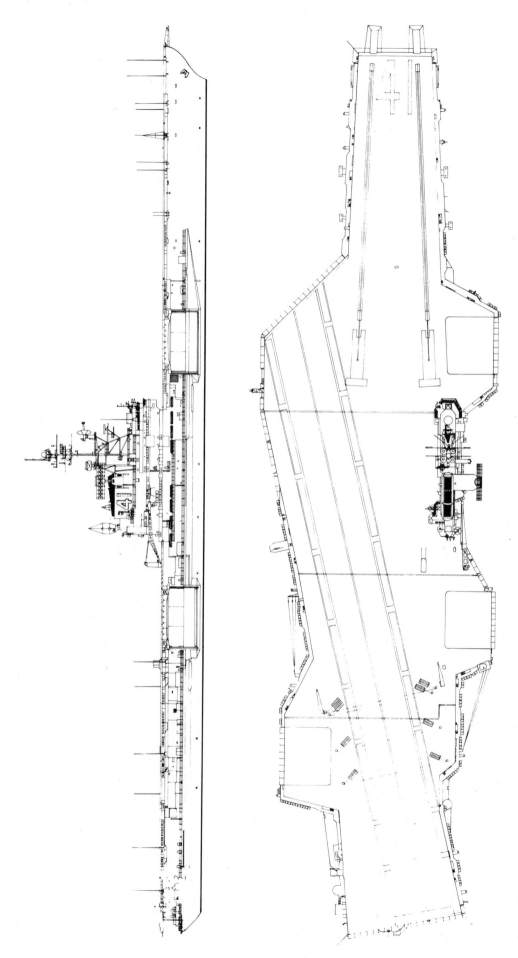

The *Midway* (CVA 41) as modernized (SCB 101.66), 1974.

. . . The General Board has taken notice of damage to carriers in this war, has considered the characteristics of our own carriers built and building, and has studied the characteristics desirable in aircraft carriers of unrestricted tonnage. . . . it is essential to have some tougher carriers which embody improved power of survival and which can engage in offensive operations without being easily placed out of action by a few light bombs, one or two torpedoes, or medium sized projectiles. The Board is of the opinion that the advantages to be gained by the considerable increase in standard displacement of this class of carrier outweigh the additional cost involved. . . .

The basic *Midway* design, then, reflected early British war experience as well as U.S. war losses. As the design evolved from CV-E, however, it changed to reflect a combination of war experience and developing aircraft technology. As approved by the Secretary of the Navy on 21 March 1942, the characteristics called for sixteen 5-in guns, either 38- or 54-caliber; and by June the air group was set at 120 aircraft (thirty-six VFs, forty-eight VSBs, thirty-six VTBs), or equivalently, a group of eighty-three aircraft of larger types already under development. Detailed analysis showed that the fuel required for endurance radius (20,000 nautical miles at 15 knots) would increase displacement by 2,500 tons, so that 172,000 SHP would not suffice; instead the *Iowa* plant (212,000 SHP) was adopted. However, the highly compartmented *Montana* arrangement was retained. An increase in waterline beam to 113 feet (to accommodate the new machinery, for example) could be tolerated, because the United States then planned to build a new set of Panama Canal locks (which were not, in fact, ever begun).

The machinery arrangement resembled, if anything, that which had been adopted during World War I (to improve damage resistance for capital ships, although now the turbines were geared). Geared-turbine units for the two outboard shafts were in after engine rooms abreast, separated by generator and auxiliary machinery rooms on the centerline. Three boiler rooms for each unit were located forward of the engine rooms. The inboard shafts were driven by geared turbines in forward centerline engine rooms separated fore and aft by pump and generator rooms; there were three boiler rooms for each unit outboard, two on one side and one on the other, with two groups in an alternating arrangement. Thus there were twelve separate boiler rooms, four separate engine rooms, and ten more separate machinery spaces (for pumps, generator, auxiliary machinery rooms, and evaporators), for a total of twenty-six separate spaces within the torpedo protection, as compared with eight main machinery spaces in an *Essex*-class carrier. Each of the four units could operate independently, and the inboard and outboard plants were cross-connected.

The 1 July letter from Commander of Carriers, Atlantic, had a considerable influence on the design. He asked particularly that the island be minimized; he noted that torpedo damage to the *Saratoga* was aggravated by the unbalanced weight of her island. It appeared that the location of 5-in guns fore and aft of the island was a major contribution to its height; for example, the two tiers of guns required high locations for pilot house and flag bridge merely to ensure sufficient forward vision. Hence he recommended that the 5-in battery be mainly distributed on both sides, with individual directors if possible.

Every effort was made to reduce the extent of the island during contract-plan development. The forces afloat wanted more island space, especially for the inclusion of a CIC, air pilot, and fighter direction station; BuAer cited the small islands of the CVE and CVL. The VCNO ordered that the CIC and air pilot be located on the gallery deck below the armored flight deck. The 5-in directors for the starboard quadrants were mounted on the flight deck fore and aft of the island, together with one of the two quadruple Bofors originally to have been located on the island; the other went on the gallery-deck level forward. Island width was reduced. As first issued, the contract plans showed a width of 16 feet, overlapping the starboard edge of the flight deck by 5 feet; this was later reduced to 11.5 feet, giving no overlap, with no projections below the second level.

All of this austerity brought reactions. For example, as completed, the *Midway* had a visual fighter director station included with the after air-defense station at the second level of the island abaft the stack. The prospective commander of the ship criticized her rather cramped bridge arrangements, and the CNO ordered a restudy. On 12 December 1945 the third ship, the *Coral Sea* (CVB 43), was ordered modified with an extended island structure, incorporating the forward 5-in director above the pilot house; armor protection for the pilot house was reduced from 6.5 to 2 inches as weight compensation. Similar changes were later made to the other two ships.

BuShips circulated revised, though still incomplete, contract plans in mid-September 1942. These showed eighteen 5-in guns (38- or 54-caliber), including two twin mounts forward of the island, as well as two quadruple and twelve twin Bofors. The initial design studies had shown an *Essex* arrangement of twelve guns, either 5-in 38s or 5-in 54s. As the value of antiaircraft weapons came to be appreciated more fully, four more guns were added in the starboard galleries, at a cost in flight-deck area; the flight-deck weapons were retained because of their overhead cones of fire. On the other hand, the aviators were beginning to notice these reductions in flight-deck area. By June 1942 BuShips was thinking in terms of guns mounted in relatively large numbers in the gal-

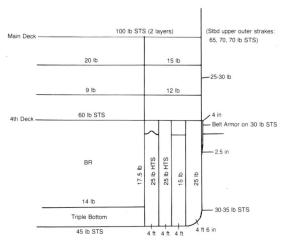

The inboard profile of the *Randolph* (long-hull *Essex* class), 1945.

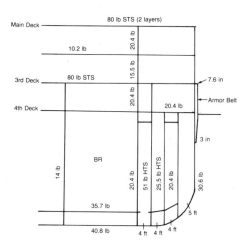

Midway-class cross section, to hangar-deck level.

leries—again, at a cost in weight—so that cross-deck fire would be less important. Thus a sketch design showed eight guns on either side. In September BuShips looked toward an eighteen-gun arrangement, with guns in four quadrants, and two twin mounts covering the forward starboard quadrant. Finally, by January 1943 the ultimate armament arrangement had been achieved: eighteen single 5-in/ 54s, all on pedestals built up from the main (hangar) deck, and none of them interfering with the flight deck. In March 1945 these positions were described as useful side protection for the open hangar. A major incentive for use of the single mount may have been the delay in installation of the twin 5-in/54s due to cancellation of the *Montana* class; even so, BuOrd would propose twin mounts for the projected CVBs 56–57 in 1945.

This battery required four 5-in directors: two on the island structure for the starboard quadrant and two in the portside galleries (one amidships, one aft). To some extent the latter development paralleled the short-lived portside Mk 37 for *Essex*-class carriers.

The light antiaircraft battery grew explosively. The 20 January plans (approved by the VCNO on 20 February) showed fifteen quadruple Bofors. Two would be on the forecastle, two on the stern, one on the flight deck forward of the island, and the rest in the galleries: one below the flight-deck mount at forecastle level and, on the hangar deck, three aft on the starboard side, six along the port side. A revision in the summer of 1944 added six more: one to starboard, five to port. Meanwhile the midships portside 5-in director was eliminated, although the after one, which cut off a corner of the flight deck, remained. When the prospective commander of the first ship complained that the remaining width (82 feet) was insufficient, the CNO directed that a study be undertaken, the consequence of which was the replacement

of the big director by a much smaller Mk 56 in the last ship (CVB 43).

There was one other problem. In the early stages of the design, the weight of the island had been counterbalanced by a heavy portside flight-deck overhang—which would have to be cut away to allow for the portside battery. In May 1943 BuShips proposed the reduction of the starboard belt from 7.6 to 7 inches to regain balance. The arrangement approved on 16 June 1943 contemplated 7-in (tapering to 3-in) armor on 30-lb STS backing on the starboard side; the port belt was to be 7.6 inches untapered and extended forward 3 feet.

The other major design change while the ships were being built was in their bows. The June 1945 typhoon showed that carriers were very much subject to weather damage forward, and it was already understood that the *Midway*s, very long in proportion to their freeboard, would be wet. Only the third ship, CVB 43, was still sufficiently incomplete to be affected: her side plating was extended upward to the flight deck at its forward end, with a transverse inclined bulkhead positioned at the fore perpendicular so as not to interfere with anchor handling. The bulkhead enclosed the secondary steering position, forward. This modification was later extended to the two earlier ships, the *Franklin D. Roosevelt* not receiving her enclosed bow until 1954. The next step, the fully enclosed "hurricane bow," appeared in reconstructed carriers a year later.

Finally, on 22 July 1943 the VCNO, at the suggestion of BuAer, finally eliminated the usual requirement for arresting gear at the fore end of the flight deck. This also meant that the demand for high astern speed could be overcome; the *Midway*s were required to make 17.5 rather than 20 knots astern.

Externally, the new carriers showed a much narrower island than the *Essex*, and one better adapted

As weight was added to the *Midway*s after 1945, the only available compensation was to remove guns, which in any case were considered less and less effective against fast modern aircraft. In this 8 August 1955 photograph, the *Midway* has emerged from a Puget Sound refit entirely without guns on her starboard quarter, her total battery reduced to ten 5-in/54s (seven to port). The hangar, enclosed only by roller curtains, was entirely unprotected. A 1945 review of *Midway*-class characteristics for two proposed new ships (CVBs 56 and 57) suggested that the hangar's primary protection from kamikazes was the row of 5-in gunhouses—which were all gone a decade later.

to the installation of radars. Initially two air-search (SK), two surface-search (SG), and one height-finding radar (SM) were authorized. The ships were completed with a short-pole foremast, a massive tripod, and a short-pole mast abaft the island, for large clear arcs. The *Midway* herself had SK-2 and SR-2 air-search radars, plus the massive SX combined height finder and air-search set atop the tripod (she was one of the first ships to receive the latter). Her two sisters were similarly equipped, except that the *Franklin D. Roosevelt* appears to have been completed with an SR-3—predecessor of the postwar SPS-6—forward. During refits in the early fifties both the *Midway* and the *Coral Sea* had their two forward masts combined in a single, more massive structure; its canted legs faced aft, and it carried a platform for an air-search radar (SPS-6B) halfway up and an SX on a platform at its peak, with a tall pole topmast for the TACAN navigational beacon.

As new as they were in 1945, the *Midway*s were all badly overweight. Most of the alterations in the design from 1942 onward had added weight, and most of that had been high in the ships; the principal saving grace was that the requirement for 25 percent spare aircraft had to be abandoned, due to a lack of space. The *Coral Sea* was completed with only fourteen rather than the original eighteen 5-in/54 guns (nos. 6, 7, 13, and 16 being eliminated). This was weight compensation for CVB (aeronautical) improvement program no. 1, approved in May 1947 and extended to the other two ships. Similarly, only the *Midway* and the *Franklin D. Roosevelt* were completed with the full outfit of eighty-four 40-mm guns; the *Coral Sea* was completed instead with empty gun tubs pending the installation of the new twin 3-in/50s in May 1949, the total being eighteen twin mounts.

The *Midway* differed in having twenty such mounts after she was refitted with them. By 1957, on the eve of a reconstruction, the *Coral Sea* was down to sixteen twin 3-in/50s. As early as 1947, there were proposals for a new battery of rapid-fire (Mk 42) 5-in/54 guns in place of the slow-firing weapons originally mounted, with BuShips promising eight or ten to replace the previous total of fourteen; at this time it could still count on the ballistic protection of the side belt for the 5-in magazines.

The major postwar alteration was CVB improvement program no. 1, designed to afford the *Midway*s interim capabilities to operate jet and heavy-attack aircraft. A McDonnell Phantom (FD-1) made the first U.S. carrier jet landing on the *Franklin D. Roosevelt* on 21 July 1946. The principal improvements were those required to operate the AJ-1 strategic bomber and provide for heavy- (particularly nuclear-) bomb handling, including spaces for the assembly of early-type nuclear weapons, which might take as much as twenty-four hours.

There was the usual crowding. In September 1947 members of the General Board embarked on the *Midway* to observe Operation SANDY, the test-firing of a V-2 rocket. They were then drawing up characteristics for the first postwar carrier, SCB 6A, and they saw the ship as a good object lesson in what to avoid.

The living accommodations provided for officer and enlisted personnel . . . are of such an unsatisfactory standard that they could cause a serious reduction in the effectiveness of the ship's company and air group in wartime conditions. . . . they undoubtedly have an adverse effect on general morale and, therefore, constitute a deterrent factor in the matter of reenlistments and transfers to the regular Navy.

. . . With the ship operating in latitude 28°30′, the

The *Coral Sea* was the last *Midway* to be modernized. She is shown on 15 April 1957 off Tacoma, about to enter Puget Sound Navy Yard. At this time she had been reduced to ten 5-in/54s and sixteen twin 3-in/50s (ten to port). One unusual feature of her radar rig was the World War II SK-2 carried abaft her island. This radar represented a return to long wavelengths, the shorter-wave SPS-6 series having shown marked deficiences in service. Ultimately a new series of UHF radars, such as the current SPS-43A, was developed to replace such wartime types without losing the benefits of the frequencies at which they operated. Note, too, the small radome just below the numeral 3 on the funnel: this was an SPN-8, the CCA radar, relatively common aboard U.S. carriers in the late fifties. Patches aft on the flight deck appear to indicate the removal of arresting gear pendants before the ship entered the yard for reconstruction.

temperature of the officer and enlisted berthing spaces immediately under the flight deck was such as to preclude the possibility of any refreshing rest during the daytime or during the first half of the night, a feature which would assume considerable importance during a period of continuous combat operations. The noise level of the blowers is a constant harassment. An insufficient degree of privacy is afforded the officers because of the lack of doors on staterooms, partial bulkheads separating the rooms, lack of doors on washrooms and heads, and the general interspersing of officers' and crew's quarters. Wash basins are generally not provided in the staterooms, necessitating in some cases a considerable walk to the nearest washroom.

The crew's living quarters are in general overcrowded. The commanding officer of the *Franklin D. Roosevelt* stated that, incident to Improvement Program No. 1 now being applied to that ship, 4-tier bunks have been substituted for 3-tier bunks in many of the crew's living compartments. He . . . had personally tried out the top bunks in the 4-tier installation and found that a man in a top bunk cannot roll over without striking his shoulder on the overhead.

The degree to which the living spaces for officers and the various enlisted ratings are dispersed and interspersed throughout the ship is apparently the result of battle damage reports stemming from our earlier carrier actions. It appeared to the observer, however, that this feature has been carried to such an extreme that the potential military effectiveness of the ship's company and air group has been impaired. In other words, inordinate stress has been placed upon the defensive qualities of the ship at the expense of her offensive potential.

The ships were also wet, both on the hangar and the flight decks. For example, they tended to plunge into heavy seas rather than ride over them, so that green water broke over the forward end of the flight deck. The latter was leaky, making the hangar deck wet in the rain as well as in a heavy sea. Flight-deck wetness was particularly significant because U.S. operating practice required aircraft to be parked for extended amounts of time at the forward end of the flight deck.

The *Midway* had been designed for a total comple-

The *Coral Sea* shows her final island configuration, just prior to modernization, in this 8 June 1955 photograph. Serving with the Sixth Fleet at the time, the *Coral Sea* had radar that was a mixture of wartime and postwar sets, with an old SK-2 abaft the island. The small oval antenna in the big dish, at its lower edge, was intended to improve high-altitude performance. The big lattice mast forward shows, from bottom to top, SPN-6 for "marshall control" of approaching carrier aircraft, SPS-6B for air search, SPS-8 for height finding (and a YE aircraft homing beacon on the right), ECM radomes, a surface/zenith search radar, ship-to-air radio antennas, and a UHF direction finder. The conical radome on the side of the big funnel was an SPN-8, for CCA.

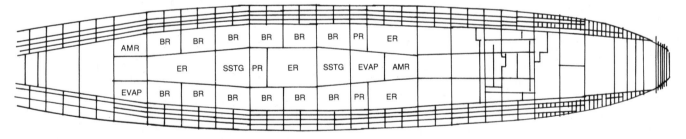

Midway-class machinery arrangement, showing subdivision and torpedo protection.

ment (ship and air) of 3,583, but by 1947 had aboard about 4,100, with more in prospect, given new jet aircraft and a new generation of airborne weapons. The General Board proposed that all new ships be designed with an allowance for complement growth, and that, as in the prewar *Saratoga* and CV-5 classes, living spaces not be located directly under the flight deck; the gallery deck was better utilized for ships and storerooms or air-conditioned ready rooms. Failing that, all living spaces in the gallery deck would have to be air-conditioned: the *Midway* arrangement was unacceptable.

For all of these faults, the *Midway*s were the only U.S. carriers available in 1947 that, without major modification, could usefully operate postwar weapons and aircraft. As such, they were among the last of the war-built carriers to be modernized: the *Franklin D. Roosevelt*, the first, began modernization at Puget Sound on 1 May 1954; the *Midway* followed on 1 September 1955, and the *Coral Sea* on 16 April 1957. These modifications are described in chapter 13.

10

The New Fleet Carrier of 1945

U.S. carrier design shifted dramatically after 1945, in the direction of the very large carrier intended primarily for strategic attack. However, before the course was set, attempts were made to realize the lessons of war experience in a new production carrier, a lineal successor to the *Essex*-class ships that had formed the basis of the fast carrier task force. Given the large number of such ships already either completed or nearly complete, there was no real hope that Congress would authorize any massive program of carrier (or destroyer or submarine) construction. However, Secretary of the Navy Forrestal was well aware of the danger of dismantling the design teams formed during the war, particularly since there was little hope that the postwar world would be a very peaceful one. On 10 May 1945 he proposed a program of new-design ships embodying wartime lessons: one was to be a new fleet carrier with aviation facilities "equivalent" to those of a *Midway*. BuShips "understood from informal discussions with the various agencies concerned that it is desired to develop an aircraft carrier, intermediate in size between the CV 9 class and the CVB 41 class in order to permit production of the new carrier with somewhat less expenditure of labor and material than is required for the CVB 41 class.... A standard displacement of 35,000 tons is desired."

Forrestal's program reflected wartime concerns; his proposed ship was also an interesting alternative to the much larger strategic carrier, the *United States*, which actually did form the basis for modern carriers. An evaluation of aircraft-carrier design was conducted in the fall of 1945 for CinCPAC.

Operations of the fast carrier task groups during the war have demonstrated that the CV 9 class carrier has admirably served the purpose for which it was designed. Its basic characteristics are fundamentally sound and correct. Through the services of a constant seagoing logistic group, a fast mobile force of air power was available and used to strike the enemy at will. Duration of these operations far exceeded what was thought possible when this class carrier was originally designed. The engineering plant is the most remarkable feature in that no major changes or alterations were necessary, and that it out-performed expectations with comparatively short periods of availability for maintenance. In the latter stages of the present war, these periods of sustained operations exceeded eighty days, although this was not recommended as a standard.

The element of surprise was always available to us, although it is not understood why the Japanese made no attempt to destroy our logistic group when it was within range of their bases. This same situation may never be enjoyed in future naval warfare.

There were, to be sure, weaknesses: lack of adequate protection (as seen in kamikaze attacks), reduced levels of stability (as BuShips had already stressed), limited arcs of fire for the antiaircraft battery, and vulnerability while aircraft were re-armed and de-gassed, a problem most dramatically demonstrated by the loss of the Japanese carriers at Midway.

Every naval officer was well aware of the success of the British armored flight-deck carriers in resisting kamikaze attack off Okinawa, while the U.S. "soft" carriers had suffered grievously. Even the 2.5-in han-

By 1945 the prewar *Essex* design was considered crowded and unsuited to the new generation of naval aircraft. With her air group on deck, the *Boxer* shows limited deck space, and access to two of her three elevators is cut off. The 1945 fleet carrier was to have solved such problems in a hull suited to mass production.

gar deck was not considered proof against bombs weighing 500 pounds or more, although the 1945 report did admit that it "has been of inestimable value in resisting bomb explosions in the hangar space and protecting the spaces below the hangar deck."

Passive protection had been the subject of a study by the carriers and aircraft tenders committee of the new Ship Characteristics Board (SCB). In a 28 July synopsis the CNO noted that

> armor protection should be provided for the most likely type of attack.... it seems sound to assume that the type of attack to which a carrier will be most generally exposed would be from aircraft bomb, suicide plane or from some type of guided missile. Underwater attack from either torpedo or mine or diving missile must also be provided for. Since it is possible to build or to construct both bomb and missiles of such size that they would penetrate almost any armor that could be carried, the committee is of the opinion that the best distribution would be to provide a reasonable degree of protection and at least to force the enemy to carry more than a simple airplane and engine combination in inflicting serious damage to the ship....

> Within the weight and stability limitations of a design, horizontal armor should be provided in the flight deck, hangar deck, and at a lower level over the ship's vitals. On the flight deck it is recommended that armor, minimum thickness of 2 inches (80 lbs), should be provided to extend over all hangar spaces. 40-lb STS should be provided at the ends of the flight deck. Hangar deck level should be armored with a minimum thickness of 2½ inches (100 lbs) to extend throughout the length of the hangar covering magazine spaces, engine rooms and gasoline storages; steering gear, although outside these spaces, should also be protected. A lower deck of at least 60 lbs STS should be provided over machinery spaces, magazines, steering engines and similar vital machinery.

> Fore and aft vertical armor should not be concentrated in an armor belt but should be distributed uniformly over the ship's side adjacent to the hangar and in way of machinery spaces and ship's vitals from a point at least 8 feet below the waterline to the hangar deck level. The minimum thickness of this material should be 1½ inches (60 lbs).... division of the hangar into protective subdivisions open at the sides but protected one from the other by athwartship vertical armored bulkheads as in CVB-41 is sound and should continue. Provision of at least 4 armored bulkheads is recommended, one at each end of the hangar space and 2 which serve to divide the hangar into 3 subdivisions.

> ... all elevators [should] be of the deck-edge type in order to preserve the maximum integrity of the protective features of the flight deck and hangar deck.... in the fore and aft locations [they] would also eliminate the necessity of piercing forward and aft transverse armored bulkheads. It is recommended that current methods of providing adequate underwater protection be retained....

The STS was intended to protect against near bomb misses, preserving the waterline against the effects of splinters. The CNO wanted the new carrier *Iwo Jima* (CV 46—scheduled for launch 1 June and completing 1 November 1946, about six months later than any other *Essex*) modified with 60-lb STS in lieu of belt armor, but she was canceled.

Protection also embraced the touchy subjects of the ready rooms and CIC. The fall 1945 report continued:

> It was demonstrated with large loss of life through Kamikaze hits that the gallery deck is not the location for pilots' ready rooms. As many as possible of the ready rooms should be located inboard beneath horizontal armor and protected access to the flight deck should be furnished [as indeed it was in the SCB 27 conversions five years later]. BuShips is now preparing final plans for relocation of ready rooms 2, 3, and 4 to the second deck on the CV 9 class carriers, utilizing the wardroom as number 2. Number 1 should remain in the gallery deck for scrambling purposes. This move will force some berthing of enlisted personnel into the gallery deck and it is considered to be an advantage to have gun and director crews berth in this location.

> Opinion varies radically as to the proper location of CIC but it is generally agreed that the gallery deck is unsafe.... Several commanding officers have expressed a preference for the 01 deck or the second deck. However, most flag officers have agreed that the island location is essential. An excerpt from an action report is quoted as an example:

> It has always been the opinion of the Commander First Carrier Task Force that CIC should be located in the island structure in close proximity to Flag Plot. Recent experience indicates more than ever the absolute need of close personal liaison between CI and Flag Plot in the efficient running of an operation. If at all possible, the Operations Officer should have his battle station in CIC as he is thus able to readily assimilate, evaluate and take action on the offensive phase of operations. Since CIC was moved from the island this has not been possible; also, it has been the experience of this Command that in seventh deck (i.e., protected) CICs some of the equipment does not function at maximum efficiency, due to distances involved, and the air conditioning is not adequate to take care of the heat from five radars.

> The island and 01 deck locations can be considered to be a little safer than the gallery deck location. The second deck [below the hangar] and hold spaces are better protected. Further technical advances in radar circuits and in co-axial cable may make it possible to get maximum value out of radar transmissions at these remote locations. CIC should be given the greatest protection possible compatible with the

operating requirements. The close personal liaison between the tactical control stations and CIC is an important consideration. The spaces now devoted to Radio One might easily be acceptable for an island location of CIC.

CinCPac commented that

> there is a certain inconsistency in our placing the CIC below decks within the armored box on battleships and cruisers, yet putting it in the crowded island structure of carriers. CinCPac definitely concurs in the below decks location for battleships and cruisers; in view of general preference of carrier officers for the island location, he is ready to concur in this, despite the apparent inconsistency. However, it is recommended that studies be continued with a view to locating CIC below decks but providing for visual presentation in Flag Plot and elsewhere of such information as is required but is not readily handled by voice communication.

Finally, only inadequate protection was provided against the great enemy of the carrier, fire.

> Fire fighting equipment has been improved remarkably but has not yet reached its optimum development. Hangar sprinkling systems and water curtains have been very effective. Foam has not been used extensively because it was more awkward to employ and not as relible. However, it is expected that a new fog foam equipment which will soon be installed will prove a very effective fire fighting medium. Sprinkling systems in ready service ammunition rooms in the gallery deck are subject to rupture in almost any crash which occurs in the vicinity. As a consequence, their value is doubted. It is quite possible to achieve the same effect by flooding with a hose or cooling the bulkheads with a hose.

CinCPac added that "more attention must be given towards the provision of smaller self-sufficient fire fighting parties in larger numbers at strategic locations throughout the ship." The greatest problem of all, the hangar fire, would prompt designers of the new carrier, and indeed of the SCB 27 reconstructions, to subdivide the hangar and later to provide separate fire stations throughout its length.

The ventilation system, particularly in a carrier with battle damage, was faulty, as was seen after problems with the "wind tunnel" in the *Essex* class.

> Ventilation throughout the CV 9 class is definitely not satisfactory, particularly when extensive operations are conducted in tropical climates. Some rearrangement of ducts will be necessary. Analogous to this subject is [*sic*] living conditions. In the design of future carriers, it must be borne in mind that these ships will spend a large proportion of their service life in warm climates. Health and efficiency of personnel deteriorate rapidly unless living conditions offset to some degree the enervating effects of these climates. Specific attention should be given to proper insula-

tion and ventilation of living spaces and to the expansion of air conditioning to working spaces in which personnel are required to spend long periods of constant mental effort.

> The most persistent problem in the CV 9 class carrier has been smoke, as result of battle damage, throughout the ship and particularly in the engineering spaces. Alterations have been approved which will provide for supply of air from either side, and this should be incorporated in all carriers.

The deck-edge elevator was popular among the aviators; it could move aircraft off the centerline of the flight deck as they landed, simplifying operation. Indeed, in the spring of 1945 proposals were made for the final *Essex*es to be completed with their forward elevators moved to the deck-edge. On 5 May Commander, Air Force, Pacific wrote to the CNO that

> discussions with fleet personnel have indicated that the deck-edge elevator is definitely more useful than the centerline type in operations on CV-9 class aircraft carriers. The outstanding advantage of the deck-edge type is that its operation still leaves nearly all the athwartships space available for fore-and-aft movement of aircraft. Thus it greatly facilitates the handling of aircraft during launching and landing operations. This is much more true of the forward (No. 1) elevators than of the [aft] in the landing area.
>
> The deck-edge elevator also possesses the following structural and safety advantages:
> —Permits smaller and lighter construction
> —Much less susceptible to the blast effect of hangar deck explosions
> —Does not reduce [armor] coverage over the hangar deck
> —Does not require an elevator well and its accompanying drainage system
> —Mechanical features are less susceptible to misalignment and other derangement.
>
> Current new construction CVs and CVBs commissioning in 1946 and later, and USS *Franklin* [as repaired should] retain the present after centerline and amidships deck-edge elevators, but replace the forward centerline elevator with a deck-edge type installed in the forward bay opening. The starboard location is preferable because it utilizes space not available for takeoff and because it minimizes the possibility of both forward elevators being damaged by a single bomb hit or near miss. Provision must be made, however, for the undiminished use of this as a nearby station for handling stores, fueling, and rearming at sea. . . .
>
> [In] future new construction, replace all centerline elevators. . . . Vessels having only two elevators should have the forward one to starboard, the after one on either side was found best for weight balance, adequacy of landing areas, etc. On ships having three, the forward two should be as described above, while the other one would be equally effective on either side.

The fleet-carrier designs of 1945 and 1946 were, above all, reactions to wartime experience, particularly the dramatic attacks of the kamikazes. Here the carrier *Essex* suffers a hit on her forward elevator on 25 November 1944. Fully armed aircraft on the flight deck were touched off, and a series of explosions killed fifteen men and wounded another forty-four. However, the ship was operational thirty minutes later. In part this vindicated prewar expectations that a thin wooden deck would be far easier to repair than a thin armored one, which might curl back after an explosion. A layer of steel under the wood was intended to confine fires to the flight deck proper, protecting the hangar to some extent. The large deck loads of aircraft used to achieve maximum striking power in U.S. operating practice made carriers vulnerable to fire damage; throughout the war considerable attention was paid to those means of fire fighting that are not given attention in a general design history, such as water curtains for the hangars, special fire-fighting stations, and various types of fire and fog hoses.

Real Admiral H. B. Sallada, chief of BuAer, generally approved the deck-edge idea for the *Essex* class, although in a letter of 21 July he wrote that "in view of the stage of construction of the three CVBs and the design work involved in such a change, it is recommended that no action be taken at this time. It is considered highly desirable to gain combat experience with these vessels at the earliest opportunity."

However, BuShips vetoed the idea on 18 August in view of the problems it raised in an *Essex*-class carrier: the proposed elevator between frame 40 and the island would add 125 tons at a high location to an already badly overweight ship; it would make transit of the Panama Canal impossible; underway replenishment would become more difficult. Probably most importantly, there would be "structural difficulties in the installation of elevator guides because of the flare of the ship at this point. The flare would require supports 15 feet outboard from the hull at about 10 feet above the waterline. This structure, even though heavy, would be subject to damage and misalignment from a relatively moderate sea."

War experience also showed that catapults were not merely useful but essential, and early proposals for a new carrier were designed to permit simultaneous launch and recovery of aircraft. Captain W. T. Raisseur of Op-05-3 analyzed the appropriate air group for a new carrier in a 30 June 1945 memorandum to an informal advisory board set up to consider its design. As noted in chapter 9, he considered the *Essex* air group about the most numerous any new

carrier could accommodate, although the aircraft might well be larger individually; he wanted to base plane dimensions on the largest existing fighter, the twin-engine Grumman F7F, and on a proposed new attack airplane, the Douglas BT3D, which would ultimately fly as the twin-turboprop A2D Skyshark.

Captain Raisseur proposed a flight deck with one port (aft) and two starboard (amidships and forward) elevators. In addition to the usual pair of catapults (forward), another was angled out on the port side, sufficiently for an airplane with a 50-ft span launched from it to clear one with a similar span sitting on the port forward catapult. This catapult would be served by the port elevator; the two forward, by the forward starboard elevator. Finally, Raisseur provided a fourth catapult from above; it would be served by the after (two-story) starboard elevator. Note that the fourth catapult might have been brought down to flight-deck level (and made symmetrical with the canted catapult on the port side) had the island been dispensed with and a flush deck adopted. The island could not have been moved abaft it in view of the requirement for a clear landing area. This flush-deck arrangement would later be adopted for the abortive *United States* (CVB 58) and for early *Forrestal*-class designs. Raisseur required that each catapult be able to launch a 15,000-lb airplane at 120 mph. Actual design schemes of 1945 incorporated a new H 8 catapult (H 4 in CV 9, CVB 41). Although this scheme resembles an angled-deck carrier, arresting gear was to be of the conventional axial-deck type.

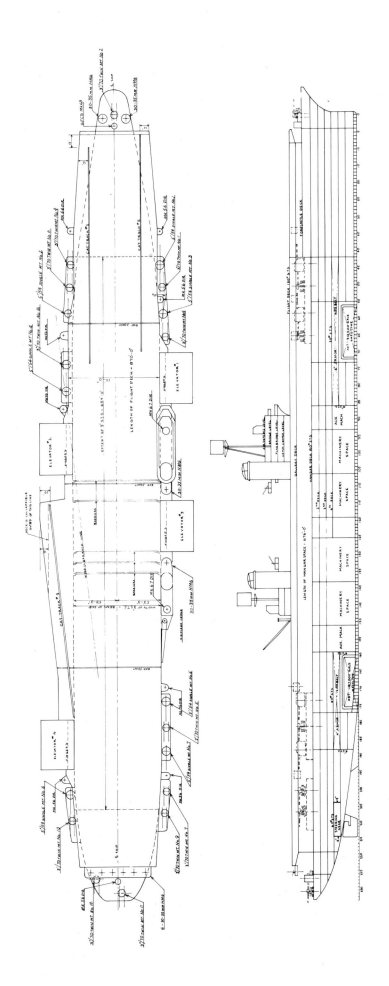

Fleet carrier scheme C-2, 8 May 1946.

This characteristic multiple-catapult/deck-edge elevator design would appear in the 1945–46 studies, the *United States* design (SCB-6A), and then in the original *Forrestal* design.

The other side of Raisseur's operational analysis led him to an air group of fifty-four F7Fs and thirty-six BT3Ds; on 9 July the board approved both Raisseur's air group and his flight-deck configuration. In view of the great gasoline consumption expected of future jet aircraft, "unless the necessary steps are taken to insure an adequate fuel supply for these planes, the endurance of our future carriers will be drastically reduced and certainly governed by this one factor. . . . the aviation gasoline capacity of our future carriers should be 500,000 gallons." This is compared with 365,000 gallons for the *Midway*, 250,000 for the *Essex*.

As for re-arming aircraft, according to the fall 1945 report,

> speed and flexibility are of paramount importance. Since frequent last minute changes in designated aircraft ammunition components are made, the larger 4,000 pound elevators now being installed are essential. The speed of these elevators should be the highest compatible with safety. Bomb elevators must be so located as to service directly the greatest number of magazines possible. The early CV 9 class carriers incorporated a very satisfactory arrangement of magazines and bomb elevators. Later ships, such as the *Shangri-La*, have a relatively poor arrangement and future design should not make the same mistake. The supply train of aviation ammunition components must have the speed and capacity needed for rearming as the strike planes come aboard and obviate the necessity of accepting the hazards of maintaining large stockpiles of these components on the flight deck prior to the return of strikes. Jettisoning ramps now authorized are believed to be adequate.

The other major influence on the configuration of any new carrier was defensive battery. Given the value of guns as a last-ditch defense against kamikazes in 1945, and the probability that in the future guided missiles would duplicate that experience, there was no question of sacrificing gun batteries. For example, according to the chief of BuOrd (2 July 1945), "the future field of anti-aircraft may well lie in the field of guided missiles. . . . launchers for such missiles may be a requirement in the near future. . . . the possibility of shifting to this new type of weapon should be considered in the construction of new vessels where practicable." For the immediate future, BuOrd could offer a new 3-in/70 twin heavy-automatic weapon, and perhaps a new 37-mm (later 30–35-mm) free-swinging one to replace the twin 20-mm gun. The bureau proposed that a single automatic mount (which became the present Mk 42) be in-

stalled fore and aft of the island, as in an *Essex*; these would be backed by three twin 3-in/70s in each portside and two twin 3-in/70s in each starboard side quadrant, in place of the earlier single open 5-in/38. This heavy antiaircraft battery would be backed by "as many 40mm quad mounts as may be practicable, but not less than 12," and "as many free-swinging automatic weapons of the 37mm or twin 20mm type as may be practicable after the above installations are considered. It is recommended that a minimum of 30 such mounts be provided. The arrangement of armament should provide for the maximum number of guns practicable which will bear ahead and astern and will be capable of tracking and firing across bow or stern, respectively."

Kamikazes were still diving on the fast carriers at this time; BuOrd wanted an individual director for each heavy weapon down to 40-mm guns, as a counter to saturation attacks. "A sufficient number of free-swinging heavy or light automatic weapons is considered necessary also to augment fire power and for use in the event of power failure. The Bureau of Ordnance recommends further, that consideration be given to improvement in protection against bombs and torpedoes. . . . the provision of side belt armor to defeat projectiles is of lesser importance. . . ." BuOrd's enthusiasm for the flight-deck 5-in mounts, which had been dropped in the *Midway*s but whose overhead arcs must have seemed most useful against kamikazes, would be carried over to the initial design studies for the new carrier.

The single greatest driving force behind the new carrier program was a demand for much heavier carrier aircraft. Thus the story of the postwar carriers began late in 1944, when, off the Philippines, Vice Admiral Marc Mitscher, commanding the fast carrier task force, conceived the need for a new generation of more powerful attack aircraft and a new class of fleet carriers to support them. One historian has suggested that Mitscher became interested in bomb loads as great as 12,000 pounds, and that by early 1945 he was already thinking along the lines that led to the carrier *United States*. In any case, Mitscher called for the formation of a special informal board to advise DCNO (Air) on the characteristics of a new carrier. The board was appointed to restudy U.S. Navy carrier requirements; an 11 May 1949 interval OPNAV history of the SCB-6A project (CVB 58) ascribes it to "pressure from Carrier Task Force Commanders who needed longer-ranged aircraft to accomplish war missions," which would certainly apply to Mitscher both in the Battle of the Philippine Sea and at Leyte Gulf nearly four months later.

The 12,000-lb bomb is significant because it became the basis for a new generation of U.S. naval-attack aircraft and hence for the *United States*,

CVCB 58, the ancestor of all U.S. super-carriers. Possibly this figure was adopted simply in order to provide naval aircraft with a nuclear capability; however, when first raised in the summer of 1945, it was discussed in the context of European experience. The navy was obsessed with ASW at this time, and it is seems likely that a capability against reinforced concrete U-boat pens looked very attractive, especially since the most probable adversary had very little in the way of an active surface fleet. The Soviets had captured a lot of advanced German technology; had the new U-boats deployed in any numbers, the last phase of the Battle of the Atlantic might have been a close-run affair indeed. It followed that conventional ASW might well require the assistance of deep strikes on enemy submarine bases; those submarines might resist any move to stop them once at sea. Such a mission might justify the operation of fast carrier task forces, even against an enemy with virtually no surface fleet and no sea lines of communication.

Only later did the navy begin to see strategic strikes on the enemy homeland as a vital carrier-task-force mission. This is not to belittle the raids that paved the way for such a strategy. The most famous was obviously the 1942 Dolittle raid on Tokyo; in February 1945 the fast carriers (led by Vice Admiral Mitscher, who would later champion the heavy-carrier bomber) also struck Tokyo. The raid proved relatively unsuccessful, probably because of the comparatively light bombs the carrier-attack aircraft carried. The fast carriers returned to Japanese waters in July 1945 and found greater success in attacks on the remaining Japanese shipping than they had had against industrial plants. Standard HE bombs may have been at fault in February: the B-29s began to succeed only when they switched over to large-scale fire raids. On the other hand, the carrier air groups were very well armed against ships and airfields, which they struck in July.

In both cases rather heavy ordnance was required, either a very heavy supersonic concrete-penetrating bomb or else a nuclear weapon, which in 1945 was just as heavy but rather more compact.

In any case, immediately after VE-Day BuAer began studies of new carrier-based horizontal bombers with greatly increased bomb loads. These were later described as necessary in view of the tentative conclusions of studies on the consequences of bombing in Europe, which presumably showed how relatively ineffectual bombs in use at the time were. Such studies would also have shown how effective German submarine pens had been in resisting conventional bomb attack. Undoubtedly, too, BuAer was encouraged by wartime experience with carrier operation of heavy aircraft, culminating in the catapult launch and recovery of a medium bomber (PBJ-1H) by the

carrier *Shangri-La* in November 1944. It does not, incidentally, appear that the 1944 tests were part of a carrier heavy-bomber program.

On 11 December 1945, Rear Admiral Sallada, the chief of BuAer, wrote the following to the CNO:

1. The largest bomb regularly carried by carrier-based aircraft in World War II was the 2,000 lb G.P. bomb, and the maximum striking radius of carrier-based aviation was about 400 nautical miles. Analysis of bombing results in Germany has revealed that lethal damage to many targets required 12,000 lb bombs. The handicap of inadequate strike radium in carrier-based aircraft in World War II is well-known, particularly in the earlier phases of the war.

2. A series of preliminary studies [has] been made in BuAer with the objective of determining what extension of range and of bomb size in carrier-based aircraft can be attained through technological advances in the foreseeable future. These studies reveal that development of propeller-turbines will permit considerably geater advances in bomb-load, range, and speed than can be attained in the immediate future with reciprocating engines or combinations of reciprocating engines and turbo jets. Insofar as weight and size are concerned, the results of the studies may be divided into three classes of aircraft, as follows:
   A. Those which will operate from present CVB class carriers, and remain within maximum capacities of CVB arresting gear, catapults, elevators, flight deck, and hangar deck.
   B. Those which will operate from present CVB class carriers in a restricted manner; i.e., incapable of being struck below, but capable of landing in light loading condition and of taking off without assistance in fully loaded condition.
   C. Those which will require a new class of carriers, with arresting gear, catapults, elevators, flight deck, and hangar deck of increased capacities, dimensions, and/or strength.

3. Results of studies to date indicate that aircraft employing propeller-turbines can be developed in each of the above categories with approximately the following major characteristics:

	A	B	C
Gross weight, fully loaded (lbs)	30,000	45,000	100,000
Gross weight, landing (lbs)	20,000	30,000	65,000
Bomb size (lbs)	8,000	8,000	8,000
Vmax/alt. (mph/ft)	362/S.L.	500/35,000	500/35,000
Combat radius (nautical mile)	300	1,000	2,000

In each case above, the 12,000 lb bomb can be carried with sacrifice of fuel and range. Also, an aircraft can be developed in each category above, around the

The carrier *Franklin* burns on 19 March 1945 off Kyushu, in what BuShips described as "the most severe [fire] survived by any U.S. warship during the course of World War II." She had just been returned to service in January following a fire on 30 October off Samar, which was the most severe experienced up to that time, and her survival in both cases was considered proof of the survivability of the *Essex* class. In this incident she was struck by two bombs, which exploded in her hangar among gassed and armed aircraft. Much of the subsequent damage was done by her own aircraft and their weapons; the explosions and fires were so severe that only two men survived from her hangar deck. At the time of the attack she had thirty-one aircraft on the deck, warming up, and twenty-two on the hangar deck (six of them not gassed and only five armed). Although the forward gasoline system had been secured, the after one was still operating. The hangar-deck explosions burst gas tanks on the airplanes in the hangar, and within a few seconds there was a tremendous gasoline-vapor explosion; blast and flames filled the hangar, and aircraft on the flight deck were thrown together. Then their bombs began to explode, most of them on the flight deck, some of them after falling through holes in the deck, adding to the damage below. All twelve Tiny Tim rockets on the flight deck were touched off, and although a few were propelled over the side, most exploded aboard. The vitals of the ship were protected by the armored hangar deck, which was penetrated in only a few places by an enemy bomb and several Tiny Tim rockets. In addition, 0.75-in armor plating on the floors of the CIC and air plot, located in the gallery deck, protected those spaces from explosions on the hangar deck. This armor had been added during shipyard repairs after the kamikaze attack of 30 October, which had inflicted the worst type of damage to be expected on a carrier loaded with gassed but unarmed aircraft. One might note that the damage done on 19 March corresponded roughly to that which sank three Japanese carriers at Midway. The *Franklin* survived the attack, largely because of the crew's courage and skill, demonstrated when they managed to spoil a Japanese bombing run on the ship with a locally controlled 40-mm mount in the island. At this time the fires were as yet not fully under control. The list to starboard evident in the photograph was characteristic of *Essex*-class carriers with large amounts of fire-fighting water below decks—most of the drainage from the flight deck was via starboard side spaces, including damaged vent and air intake ducts, uptakes, and bomb-elevator trunks. The *Franklin* was able to steam home under her own power for repairs at the New York Naval Shipyard, but she was never reactivated.

same bomb-load, employing reciprocating engines and turbo jets, but at a very great reduction in speed and range from the above figures.

4. BuAer recommends that a definite program be initiated to extend greatly the limiting ranges and bomb sizes of carrier-based aviation. Such a program would involve not only the development of the necessary aircraft, but also development in the fields of carriers, bombs, ground handling equipment for the aircraft, and bomb handling equipment. If such a program is initiated, BuAer recommends that it include the following:

      I. As soon as possible, in order to accelerate complete definition and solution of design and operating problems involved, an aircraft in Category B, employing reciprocating engines and turbo jets, with the object of attaining approximately the following characteristics:

Gross weight, fully loaded	
(lbs.)	41,000
Gross weight, landing (lbs.)	28,000
Bomb size (lb.)	8,000
Vmax/alt (mph/ft)	500/35,000 (jets on)
Combat radius (nautical miles)	300

      II. When stage of development of propeller turbines permits, a turbine-propelled aircraft in Category B.

      III. Fully coordinated design and development of carrier, aircraft, and all accessories and components in Category C.

      IV. Coordinated design and development of escort fighters to parallel that of long-range heavy bombers.

This was the formal origin of the heavy-attack program. Admiral Sallada's letter may well have been inspired by an 11 October proposal by the navy Air Development Research (ADR) organization at

Johnsville, Pennsylvania, to the director of RD&E for BuAer, on the possibility of tactical bombing by turboprop aircraft from specialized carriers. The alternative airplane characteristics of the admiral's letter are typical ADR products: they were intended as baselines against which aircraft-industry proposals could be evaluated. On 28 December the CNO authorized development of the 41,000-lb aircraft (which became the AJ Savage, the first U.S. naval heavy-attack bomber), subsequent development of a category B turboprop (which became the abortive A2J) and coordinated design and development of escort fighters to parallel the long-range heavy bombers. The fighters never materialized. Action on the category C bomber and its new carrier was deferred.

The bomber program "as outlined and approved is considered to be a logical step in the development of carrier aviation and is immediately applicable to the needs of the Navy Aeronautical Organization. It is desired that this program form the basis of postwar effort in the carrier aviation field, and as such should be assigned an appropriately high priority." The assistant secretary of the navy (Air) approved the program in January 1946.

The June 1946 characteristics for the 1945–46 fleet carrier reflect these ideas: the flight deck was to be stressed for landing a 30,000-lb airplane, and the elevators and catapults for operating one of 45,000 pounds (however, elevator dimensions were set by the much smaller BT3D). These figures describe the heavy bomber BuAer was developing, which it categorized as class VG (bomber, not torpedo or the later attack VA).

BuAer Data for VG Bomber (AJ-1)

	April 1946	*(As Built)*
Without bombs or gasoline (lbs)	28,000	30,776
Max. full load (lbs)	45,000	54,000
Max. landing (lbs)	30,000	
Length OA (ft-in)	56	64-1
Span (ft-in)	75	71-5
Span folded (ft-in)	45	
Max. height (tail) (ft-in)	24	21-5

Even the 45,000-lb bomber was clearly a tight squeeze for a CVB; any approval of such a development had to lead to a new generation of carriers with radically different characteristics. Indeed, they would have to reflect a new kind of operational environment. As the VG design evolved, it became apparent that the big bomber could not be stowed very easily in the hangar deck. The AJ was designed to spend most of its time permanently spotted on the flight deck. Its wings could fold, but one of the necessary measures of weight saving in the design had been the elimination of powered folding: it took fifteen to twenty minutes to prepare, fold, and strike

below. Tip tanks, necessary for range performance, had to be removed to reduce the total height of the folded airplane and meet hangar clearance limits: the AJ would be sent to the hangar deck only for maintenance. It would require catapult launch, as otherwise there would be insufficient space for a deck run plus a spot of ten or more aft. It could land on only after dropping its bombs and using up most of its fuel.

These factors suggest that a carrier with an air group of AJ and an axial flight deck might have found operations cumbersome. For example, the fighters could be stowed below and fired off the catapults forward; when the fighters were to be landed, the AJs normally sitting aft would have to be moved all the way forward. If no AJ flights were required, fighters would pass down into the hangar deck by deck-edge elevators and then up to the catapults by the forward centerline elevators, with the flock of AJs amidships, waiting for a landing airplane to miss the wires and the barrier and crash into them. Probably a specialized air group, comprising bombers and perhaps escort fighters, was intended. The latter would follow them off and would not have to worry about a deck park of AJs upon landing.

The informal advisory board began by analyzing variants of the existing *Midway* and *Essex* designs, seeking to accommodate "CVB aviation features" in something short of a CVB hull. Given the Op-05 analysis that the CVB-size air group was too numerous for efficient operation, it would seem (in retrospect) that the "CVB" features most significant were the long (H 4-1) catapult and the heavier-lift elevator. At first, however, the board emphasized a CVB-size flight deck on a smaller hull. One way to shave displacement (and, therefore, cost and some complexity) was to reduce armor. Thus a 12 April 1945 calculation sheet showed that with her side belt and third-deck STS (4,232 tons) removed, CVB 41 would displace 38,220 tons light (versus the 42,450 tons estimated in May 1943) and 52,610 on trial (vice 56,840; GM would fall from 10 to 9.1 feet). In those calculations, 450 tons of STS had to be left on the port side to balance the island, even if no side armor at all was required for protection. If the loss of weight deep in the ship was balanced by a reduction of 1 inch in flight-deck armor (1,040 tons), GM actually rose to 10.1 feet at the new trial displacement of 51,570 tons.

Exactly how these drastic reductions in protection, which characterized the whole series of schemes done in May and June, were justified is not clear. There must have been strong feeling that armor against shellfire (that is, side belt and third deck) was no longer relevant; but other kinds of protection, perhaps involving large weights, certainly would be needed still. A series of schemes dated 2 May was intended to operate a CVB air group of ninety-six VFs and forty-eight of the new torpedo/dive-bombers. Various reductions from *Midway* characteristics were tried: in scheme 1 the 5-in/54 battery was cut from eighteen to sixteen guns and the number of quadruple Bofors from twenty-one to twenty; armor was reduced to a 3.5-in flight deck and a 40-lb (vice 80-lb) hangar deck. Standard displacement fell from 46,050 to 37,560 tons, only 180,000 SHP was required, and GM actually rose from 10.4 to 12.7 feet. Waterline length was 860 rather than the 900 feet of a *Midway*. This began to approach *Essex* dimensions (820 feet).

In scheme 3 waterline length was further reduced to 840 feet (36,800 tons at the cost of another four 5-in/54 guns). Scheme 3 was so close to an *Essex* that another sketch design, 4, was drafted on the basis of *Essex* rather than *Midway* weights and data; however, even with a reduced air group (seventy-three VFs, fifteen VSBs, fifteen VTBs), it showed an insufficient GM (8.8 versus 9.7 feet in 3), perhaps due to the weight of the 3.5-in flight deck. A compromise scheme 5—840 feet, 34,980 tons, 3.5-in flight deck, 40-lb hangar deck, and twelve single 5-in/54 guns—seemed best. It would have a flight deck wider but not longer than that of an *Essex* (870 by 105 feet; the *Midway*'s was 932 by 115, with widths clear of the island). An increase of 10,000 SHP over the *Essex*'s 150,000 was required for 32.7 knots (the *Essex* was capable of 33.1 knots).

Scheme 5 was presented to the informal advisory board on 31 May. However, studies continued. Scheme 6 was a *Midway* stripped of protection (except for 110-lb plate—2.75 inches—on the hangar deck and the usual four 50-lb hangar-deck bulkheads): displacement fell to 38,210 tons and GM rose to 13.7 feet. Speed rose to 34.2 knots: it might well have been possible to achieve the required ship characteristics (about 33 knots) on a shorter hull with less power. Scheme 8 was now designed to embody the smallest ship that could incorporate the following characteristics:

—(a) *Flight Deck* of same length and breadth as CVB
—(b) *Protection*—none
—(c) *Speed*—33 knots (calculated 33.5 hts. by Standard Series, etc.)
—(d) *Power* based on (c) = 165,000 SHP
—(e) *Armament* 12-5″/54 sgl, 20–40/m Quad, 28–20m/m twins
—(f) *Aircraft*—same as CVB

The resultant dimensions are:
L = 875′—This was chosen not so much from speed considerations as from consideration of the shortest ship which structurally could support a 930 foot flight deck.
B = 105′—200 tons were put into the weights to take care of supporting the overhang of the flight deck both longitudinally and transversely.

D = 57.5′—This was not reduced from the CVB since it was felt that a ship having a 930 foot flight deck should have as much or more freeboard to that deck as the CVB. The effect of pitching in the shorter ship will probably be worse as far as wetness is concerned.

On this basis, scheme 8a of 7 June 1945 showed a standard displacement of 35,200 tons (GM about 9.7 feet at a trial displacement of 45,620 tons). Perhaps scheme 8a is the best measure of how far the *Midway* strayed beyond what was required to operate her air group, or more realistically, of how far her design was driven by protective considerations. Now Captain Raisseur presented the Op-05 view of a more appropriate combination of flight-deck configuration and air-group size, which the board adopted as the basis for further studies. Again, it seems remarkable in retrospect that, although the new carrier was in theory to be driven by aviation considerations, the designers had no real contact with the air community until late June, the advisory board having requested Op-05 views only at its 31 May session.

Scheme 8, presented to the board at its fourth meeting, 17 July 1945, was a demonstration that an entirely unprotected carrier would displace the 35,000 tons envisaged. Now the board requested two detailed design studies from which the effects of particular characteristics might be estimated.

Scheme A, extrapolated from CVB 41 with equal aviation facilities (in this case meaning hangar and flight-deck dimensions), had moderate armor and equal or higher speed. Raisseur's letter had been taken to heart. There were to be three heavy catapults "for launching projected types of planes. . . . a fourth may possibly be added during later stages of the design." All three elevators were preferably to be deck-edge. The air group was to comprise fifty-four F7Fs and twenty-eight to thirty-six BT3Ds (twenty-eight were accepted). Of avgas 500,000 gallons were required. Although the advisory board did not discuss the BuOrd armament recommendations, BuShips adopted them since they "appear to meet the requirements expressed by the Board in a general way." However, protection did not follow the ideas then being investigated. Instead, it was to comprise a 2.5- or 3-in flight deck, a heavy hangar deck (thickness as needed for strength), 80-lb 3- and 5-in magazines only, and a 4-in belt over main magazines and gasoline stowage. Hangar-deck bulkheads were not even mentioned. The island was expected to be greatly enlarged for CIC, among other features. "Some more encroachment on flight deck [is] acceptable." Underwater protection would match that of CVB 41.

Scheme B was to be held to 35,000 tons and otherwise reduced as necessary. BuShips worked from CV 9 flight-deck and hangar-deck dimensions, with 2-in STS on the flight deck and a 60-lb third deck. Vertical armor was to be reduced or even omitted if necessary, yet torpedo protection to CVB 41 standards was specified, which would have meant greatly increased beam as compared with the *Essex*. The battery would generally follow that of scheme A, perhaps with 5-in/38 in place of 5-in/54 guns. As for machinery, the carrier would have "two 80,000 SHP DD engines [the type later used in the *Mitschers*]— take whatever speed we get." BuAer estimated the air group at thirty-six F7Fs and eighteen BT3Ds. Gasoline stowage was reduced proportionately to 330,000 gallons.

The outcome of the A-series cannot have been heartening. As in many other design series, its originators, who were not naval architects, thought that omission of some (armor) weights would lead to major economies. Instead schemes A-1 (900 feet on the waterline) and A-2 (950 feet) were heavier than the *Midway* (scheme A-1 at 46,550 and scheme A-2 at 47,850 tons) as well as less stable in trial condition (their GMs were 8.6 and 8.83 instead of 10.2 feet). They had 3-in flight decks, 80-lb STS on the hangar and third decks (as in the *Midway*), the 4-in belt, three catapults, and three deck-edge elevators. The complete BuOrd battery was mounted and the *Midway* power plant retained.

The B-series was more encouraging. An 820-ft design marked "2nd shot B" displaced 33,799 tons (28,640 for an *Essex*), and yet incorporated 2-in flight-deck armor, 60-lb hangar and third decks, a 4-in belt, and three hangar bulkheads, as well as three catapults and three deck-edge elevators, all with better stability than those of an *Essex* (with a GM of 8.30 instead of 7.61 feet). The flight deck was actually wider than that of an *Essex* (102 rather than 96.5 feet). Light-weight destroyer machinery (3,430 tons dry versus 3,212 for an *Essex*, 5,415 for A and 5,165 for a *Midway*, according to a comparison of 17 September) was probably partly responsible for the success of the B design. Unfortunately, the hull was too short for high speed: even with the addition of 10,000 SHP, trial speed fell from 32.7 to 31.6 knots. An alternative B-2 design gained 0.3 knots by increasing length to 850 feet (34,432 tons). By September, an 860-ft hull (35,030 tons, 31.8 knots) had been adopted, and the flight deck enlarged accordingly (888 by 103 feet). Armament came close to BuOrd requirements (including 5-in/54 guns) but there would be only eight quadruple 40-mm and twenty twin 20-mm guns.

In presenting both series of studies to the General Board in a letter of 12 October, BuShips proposed that the low speed of scheme B might be increased at a relatively small cost in displacement by adoption of a new power plant. Outside of the flight and main-deck armor,

other armor protection, of moderate thickness, is concentrated around magazines, gasoline stowages, and steering gear, primarily for protection against rockets and other medium caliber missiles. . . . the side plating between the hangar deck and the waterline will be of heavy STS—probably varying from 1 inch near the waterline to 2 inches at the upper deck—to help small missiles and fragments from penetrating the ship's side and to reduce the danger from suicide plane crashes. The torpedo protection system in both studies has been tentatively assumed to be the same as the CVB-41 class but further developments in the underwater explosion testing program may indicate the desirability of making some improvements. [In fact a 13 September note on the sheet of characteristics suggests an increase in the depth of torpedo protection from 18 to 22 feet "in order to make necessary advance in the art."]

Bomb penetration data, tests of bomb explosions in contact with STS, and war experience with suicide plane attacks indicate that increasing the flight deck armor thickness of Study B from 2 to 3 inches would be very desirable, probably increasing its effectiveness more than the 50 percent indicated by the direct thickness ratio. . . . It appears desirable, therefore, to consider a third study, based on B, with flight deck armor increased to 3 inches, speed increased to 33 knots, and standard displacement probably somewhere in the neighborhood of 37,000 tons. The Bureau has already started this study. . . .

It became scheme C-1, which used the 212,000-SHP plant of the *Midways*. In its first version (9 November 1945) the plant and the 3-in flight deck (of *Essex* size, 870 by 96.5 feet) cost a rise to 38,000 tons; but speed rose to an acceptable 33.2 knots. However, the advisory board asked for an increase to 500,000 gallons of avgas at its 13 November meeting. The fuel itself would weigh only about 465 tons, but BuShips estimated that tanks, piping, armor, and the greater size of ship required would cost 1,600 tons more. Gasoline stowage alone required 20 feet more length; at the same time a preliminary estimate showed that the 212,000-SHP plant would be 8 feet longer than that of an *Essex*, so that the total length had to rise to 888 feet. Power was soon boosted even further, to 220,000 SHP, for a speed of 33.2 knots (39,610 tons standard, 50,210 full load—not so far short of CVB dimensions).

The flight deck, as in the *Essex* class, was 111 feet wide except at the island, which reduced it to 96.5 feet. The aviators wanted to offset the island so as to avoid this reduction. There would, of course, be costs: more structure to support the overhanging island, some problems with stability, even the increased weight due to a larger flight-deck area requiring 3-in protection. In April BuShips estimated 200 tons to move the island, but a net-weight growth of 775 tons (and a 1-ft beam) to increase flight-deck protection to 111 feet as well.

There was considerable discussion about fueling. "Admiral Mitscher stated that it was important for

Carriers remain so prone to fire damage that most advances in fire-fighting technology have originated with the carrier community. The *Forrestal* fire, the results of which are shown here, illustrated both the severity of the problem and the strengths of a modern carrier—not to mention the determination and skill of her crew. On 29 July 1967, while the ship was operating off Vietnam, an A-4 Skyhawk on the flight deck "started hot," its engine shooting out a long tongue of flame toward other aircraft parked nearby. The flame ignited a Sidewinder missile under the wing of an F-4 Phantom, which hit a 400-gallon drop tank under another A-4. Fuel spilled and ignited, and other aircraft on deck began to burn. Their bombs blew seven holes in the armored flight deck, and flames ate through six of the ten decks below the flight deck. The ship became so hot that, even a day later, water in passageways below decks was flashing into steam. Two-thirds of the crew helped fight this enormous fire, which burned for thirteen hours and left 134 dead and 64 others seriously injured; twenty-one aircraft were lost. Repairs took seven months to complete. In a somewhat similar accident, the *Enterprise* burned off Hawaii on 14 January 1969. A rocket under an airplane on no. 4 elevator ignited, hitting another airplane and setting off a chain reaction of explosions and fires. In places the flight deck itself sagged from the heat, and bombs blew five holes in it. Even so, the ship was capable of conducting flight operations within four hours. In each case, despite the size of the fire, the ship withstood what amounted to multiple flight-deck hits by major-caliber bombs, perhaps equivalent to cruise-missile damage. Many lessons of the *Forrestal* fire have been applied to U.S. carriers. For example, naval bombs now have heat-resistant jackets that delay "cooking-off" long enough to allow them to be dumped overboard in the event of fire.

the Bureau of Ships to reduce the time of taking gasoline to that required for taking fuel oil at sea. At present it requires about ¾ of the time to take fuel as is required to take gasoline."

The board also wanted to specify seaworthiness criteria in detail, especially the permissible angle of heel in high-speed turns.

Admiral Mitscher is understood to have stated that the heeling characteristics of the CV-9 class carriers are satisfactory. Harder to be able to state in the characteristics of the new design in specific terms what are the equivalent requirements for the C-1 study; the following specification is desired:

The tactical diameter under trial load condition at 25 knots, using standard rudder (about 18 degrees) shall be a maximum of 1,000 [1,200 was later accepted] yards with a maximum heel of 10 degrees resulting from turning.... The latter figure was 7 degrees in the CV-9 class which resulted in a heel of 17-½ degrees with standard rudder at 30 knots under combat load conditions, which was considered satisfactory.

Of course, nothing nearly this specific could be stated at the preliminary design stage.

Finally there was the 12,000-lb bomb. The characteristics submitted to the SCB specified bomb elevators sufficient to accommodate it.

These requirements were part of recommendations submitted by the informal advisory board on 23 January 1946. The following April they became the basis for a new C-2 study, which incorporated the offset island and a catapult sponsored out to port. Unfortunately, the combination of island and sponson came to about 150 feet, which "exceeds by 10 feet the assumed maximum width of future aircraft carriers on which were based the recommendations for a clear breadth of 154 feet for the projected third set of locks for the Panama Canal. The maximum width of the ship in way of the gun sponsons is 134 feet, some 4 feet less than the CVB-41 class. Further studies will be made to ensure that the catapult structure will fall within the finally selected clear breadth of the new

locks by providing a collapsible outboard end for the amidships catapult."

The island was reduced in overall bulk and split in two units, each with its own funnel, to reduce both air-flow disturbance and the risk of losing both uptakes to one hit. The starboard elevators were moved closer to amidships, the after one forward to "where it can be more advantageously used for striking planes below immediately after landing or for bringing planes up to flight deck during launching operations." The forward starboard elevator was moved aft to where the flare of the ship's side was less, reducing structural complexity and also the potential for sea damage. A fourth deck-edge elevator was added on the starboard side between the two islands.

All of these improvements in aviation facilities had to be paid for by the elimination of the 5-in/54 flight-deck guns. The island could be cut down two levels, and blast effects on the flight deck would be avoided. Note, however, how late in the design evolution (April 1946) this change occurred. As compensation, three twin 3-in/70 guns were added; but only four rather than the original eight quadruple 40-mm guns could be accommodated. By June sixteen twin 3-in/70 guns (no fewer weapons) would be specified.

The C-2 design was reflected in preliminary characteristics set before the SCB on 12 June 1946. Changes included the elimination of the 4-in belt in favor of the 60-lb STS recommended in July 1945; standard displacement was up to 40,400 tons.

This was really the swan song of the design. By mid-1946 BuAer had shifted its focus to the heavy-attack carrier that became the *United States* (CVB 58). For a short time the two carrier projects were carried on the SCB's books, but it was inevitable that they would merge, especially in view of the naval air community's feeling that the big carrier was the future of naval aviation. Thus SCB 6, the strategic carrier, became SCB 6A, nominally a general-purpose type. In this light the great significance of the postwar carrier project was the number of essential features it fed into the *United States* and then into the *Forrestal*, the prototype for the postwar carriers.

11

The Super-Carrier *United States*

The design of the *United States* was the direct ancestor of all American designs for subsequent carriers. It also represented a distinct break in both operational concept and design practice from the *Essex, Midway,* and 1945 fleet carrier. In contrast with the plans of these earlier ships, the *United States* design was determined above all by the characteristics of the heaviest aircraft the carrier was intended to operate: the new bombers BuAer began to develop at the end of 1945. In effect, they decided the size and shape of her flight deck and hull, in the latter case to an extent beyond anything imagined earlier. For example, in her design the flush-deck concepts of the twenties and early thirties were reverted to, the aviators believing that the island structure itself was a major impediment to aircraft growth and thus to the overall development of carrier aviation. Unlike their predecessors, moreover, they were able to press this view despite the usual protests that boiler gases would be almost impossible to dispose of without conventional uptakes.

Throughout the evolution of the design, tension existed between advocates of the pure heavy-attack carrier and those seeking a multi-purpose ship whose upper range of capabilities would include heavy attack. Differences arose over features such as the hangar. The pure heavy-attack carrier needed no hangar, since the bombers would (it appeared) be far too large to fit within one; at most she might need a small hangar for fighter escorts. Advocates of a more flexible carrier, of course, demanded a large hangar for the alternative non-heavy-bomber air group. Similarly, the heavy- (nuclear-) attack carrier would

need relatively little magazine space, since, although each bomb would be quite heavy, there would be relatively few of them, perhaps only enough for one hundred missions.

From another point of view, the *United States* symbolized the navy's postwar attempt to compete with the air force for a share of the U.S. nuclear stockpile. The air force viewed this competition as a struggle for the decisive strategic nuclear-strike mission. Navy attitudes appear to have been mixed; the navy often referred to nuclear weapons in tactical rather than strategic terms. Moreover, even as the air force succeeded in having the big carrier cancelled, navy plans for developing a nuclear strike force based on the existing *Midway* class and on the AJ-1 Savage bomber proceeded, so that the battle for the nuclear role was ultimately decided quite outside the issue of the existence of the *United States.*

From the point of view of subsequent developments, the choice to develop the *United States* design rather than that of the more flexible 1945 fleet carrier meant that the next carrier actually built, the *Forrestal,* would be closer to the former than to the latter; indeed, in design terms the *Forrestal* was a scaled-down *United States.* That had major implications for the size and character of subsequent U.S. naval aircraft, particularly fighters, and so for the effectiveness of subsequent carrier air groups when faced with land-based opposition. This sequel was filled with ironies. For example, the *United States* and *Forrestal* designs were predicated on attack-aircraft characteristics, a major element in the design of the latter being the choice to scale down the maximum attack

The *Forrestal*, shown here in November 1956, was smaller than the ship that was originally designed, the *United States*. It was the sheer size of aircraft that drove up the dimensions of the "100,000-pound carrier" and eventually led to her cancellation. Here the four big Douglas Skywarriors on the *Forrestal*'s deck are limited to 70,000 pounds.

The desire to operate a new generation of heavy attack aircraft was the driving force behind the *United States* design. The Douglas A3D or A-3 Skyraider, shown here landing aboard the USS *Independence* on 20 October 1962, was a prime example of the new aircraft, although it fell somewhat below the 100,000-lb weight set for the super-carrier, having been redesigned to operate from *Midway*-class heavy carriers after the cancellation of the *United States*. A parked Skyraider in the background, just abaft the tail of the landing airplane, gives some indication of scale: the two F3H Demon fleet air defense fighters alongside were among the largest of their day, designed at the upper limit of what was thought possible for conventional carriers in 1948. The object in the foreground is part of the system that made jet operations practical aboard modern carriers: a mirror landing aid, with its two arms of lights. The carrier's island shows other aids, most of them impractical aboard a full flush-decker such as was planned. The pole mast was topped by a TACAN navigational beacon, essential for long-range air defense by missile-armed fighters, with ESM intercept antennas and direction finders just below it. Below them is an SPN-6, an element of the carrier blind-landing system, with an SPS-10 (surface search) and SPS-12 (air search) below that. The big dish atop the pilot house is an SPS-8B, for long-range height finding and therefore for fighter control. The big "mattress" is an SPS-37A, and the small radome below it, an SPN-10, is also part of the blind-landing system. The Skyraider shown was from VAH-11, a heavy attack squadron.

bomber from 100,000 to 70,000 pounds. However, by the seventies the controlling airplane size would be that of the long-range fleet-defense fighter, the Grumman F-14, attack aircraft having ceased to grow. In addition, where the key issue in the *United States* design was a relatively short, sharp attack requiring a limited weight of ordnance per strike, the large hull volume associated with a large flight deck in the *Forrestal* and later carriers made possible the high-volume "trucking" air attacks of the Vietnam War.

From the beginning, Admiral Mitscher was the great and prestigious supporter of both the big-carrier bomber and also of the flush-decked carrier to support it. The formal origin of the program was the BuAer decision to develop a 100,000-lb bomber, too large for the proposed 39,600-ton fleet carrier to operate, and possessing a 2,000-nm combat radius at 500 knots. Given the bomber, a new carrier followed logically: referring specifically to "a future of atomic warfare and radically different aircraft propelling units," Rear Admiral H.B. Sallada, chief of BuAer, proposed to the CNO on 28 December 1945 that

> serious consideration . . . immediately be given to the development of an additional type [of carrier] . . . that will accommodate aircraft of about 100,000 lbs with a 2000 mile radius. The ship may be rather radical in design with, for example, no island and no hangar. A flight deck equivalent to the CVB 41 [*Midway*] class would accommodate about 14 planes. . . . 500,000 gallons of gasoline (as in the new Fleet carrier design) would permit each plane about eight full-range flights. Such a carrier would be capable of long-range bombing as opportunity afforded; at other times it would be available for more conventional operations.

Sallada already envisaged strategic bombing missions mounted from the 39,600-tonner and observed that she would be able to accommodate twenty-seven of his 45,000-lb, 1,000-nm attack bombers (which would probably be restricted to the flight deck).

Admiral Mitscher, who had originated the BuAer bomber/carrier program and was now DCNO (Air), seconded Admiral Sallada on 8 January 1946.

> Air operational considerations dictate that a new carrier design for a large bomber in the class indicated should be based upon the following considerations:
> —The number of aircraft to be operated should be 16 to 24.
> —The minimum number of sorties possible without refuelling or rearming should be approximately 100.

Such a carrier would require no hangar, because her aircraft would be so large that they would not fit in any conceivable one. The acceptance of a very small number of sorties, only slightly more than four per airplane, probably reflects an expectation that the aircraft would be nuclear armed. Several naval officers had worked on the Manhattan Project, and as DCNO Mitscher met two of them, Captain William Parsons and Commander John T. Hayward. The VCNO, Vice Admiral D. C. Ramsey, ordered the requisite studies of 7 February 1946.

BuShips began its sketch designs (tentatively designated CVB X) on the basis of the largest carrier it had developed to date, the *Midway*; an internal memo of 19 February, the first entry in the design history file for the "100,000 pound plane CV X," reported that the new carrier would have two catapults each twice the weight of the H 4-1 of the *Midway*s (600,000 pounds each, about 225 feet long) and that arresting gear would consist of three sets of four wires each, as compared to four sets in the *Midway*. Although the bombers would not fit below decks, a hangar would nonetheless "be desirable to enable use of carrier with smaller type planes." In theory, the new bomber would take off at 100,000 pounds and land at up to

90,000, that is, without their bomb load. Since no characteristics for the new bomber existed, Preliminary Design based its estimates on the largest navy bomber, the land-based P2V Neptune patrol bomber (60,000 pounds, with a 100-ft wing span, and 25 feet from the forward to the after wheels).

Informal characteristics for the study were clearly based on those of the fleet carrier already well under way (500,000 gallons of avgas, 12,000 nautical miles at 20 knots, 33 knots). It was to have a flush deck (although Preliminary Design protested that smoke would be a major problem, echoing its predecessors of the twenties). Aircraft characteristics were also reflected in a note that "plane armament consist[s] primarily of an 8000 or 12,000 pound bomb [which] will be of sufficient number for a total of 100 sorties. Special handling facilities for rearming the planes with these heavy bombs will be required." Protection would generally follow that of the new fleet carrier, with an armored flight deck, splinter protection along the sides from the hangar deck down to 8 feet below the waterline, and additional protection (1.5-in STS, like the sides) on the fifth deck, one and one-half decks above the designed waterline. However, in contrast to wartime carrier designs, there would be no armored hangar deck as such. As for armament, the wartime lessons of very heavy batteries clearly applied: the draft characteristics called for eight single 5-in/54 guns, two per quadrant, as well as at least twelve of the new 3-in/70 twin mounts. Single rather than twin 5-in/54s were, however, adopted in the interest of keeping sponson overhangs as small as possible.

At this time it was estimated that the BuAer ADR-42 heavy bomber would require 500 feet to land (using arresting gear) and that, including catapult, it would need 400 feet to take off. It would be about 90 feet long, with a wing span of about 116 feet (44 folded). These dimensions determined the minimum flight-deck size, and therefore the minimum size of the big carrier. That is, there would have to be enough space to land the entire air group to permit stowage of twenty-three aircraft while the twenty-fourth landed. It was assumed that at least 75 feet would be required to stow three aircraft abreast, so that twenty-four ADR-42s would require a flight deck 1,125 feet long, with a width of 132 feet. Fifteen bombers would reduce the flight-deck length requirement to 900 feet. In each case the overall hull length was estimated as 70 feet greater than the flight-deck length, and the beam to support the 132-ft flight deck would be 130 feet. In the shorter ships (fewer than twenty-four aircraft), that would require increased horsepower (with some consequent difficulty in internal arrangement) to make the design speed of 33 knots. The bureau did not note, as yet, that the flight-deck

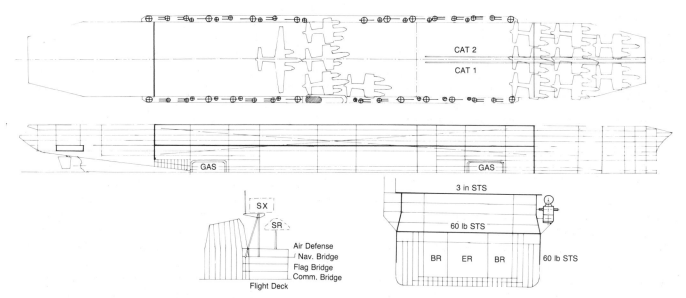

CVB-X design, 1946, with the flight deck showing the arrangement of aircraft amidships for launch and at the bow spotted after recovery. Heavy lines indicate the extent of deck and bulkhead armor. Note the use of splinter armor, as represented by the dashed lines, over the entire side. The director is a Mark 67. The single guns are 5-in/54s, the twins, 3-in/70s; small crosses are Mark 35s. Note the bulkheads, reminiscent of those of the *Midway*.

dimensions implied by the choice of the heavy bomber would mean the abandonment of the usual American requirement that warships be able to transit the Panama Canal.

BuShips did try to retain an island superstructure, protesting that stack gases and ship control would present enormous problems. The bureau therefore included a small island in CVB X, arguing that it could be located just forward of the barriers so as not to interfere with landing operations. The island would, of course, interfere with any takeoff not assisted (and controlled) by a catapult, and the aviators rejected it for just that reason.

A set of tentative characteristics corresponding to the CVB X study shows two catapults, "installed close together near the center line with one overlapping the other only slightly. The second is installed as a standby only." There were, then, to be no elaborate arrangements of sponsons for simultaneous launch of several aircraft, as in the contemporary fleet-carrier study. That made sense if aircraft with a 116- or even 125-ft span (the latter figure included a proposed BuAer wing-tip turret) were to be launched from a flight deck no more than 132 feet wide. This Preliminary Design draft of 24 April 1946 showed no hangar at all, although at a BuAer conference on the nineteenth "it was suggested that a study should be made wherein a small hangar with facilities for some

fighter airplanes be provided." By this time BuAer was beginning to fear that a 500-kt bomber would stand little chance against modern fighter opposition if unescorted, and it was making studies of very long-range escort fighters, such as the McDonnell Banshee. However, the hangar idea was too late for CVB X.

Given the size of its heavy-bomber air group, CVB X was estimated to displace 69,200 tons standard, or 82,000 tons on trial, with an overall length of 1,190 feet and a beam of 130 feet (154 over sponsons, 132 over flight deck). She would then be too large for existing dry-dock facilities, which would limit her to 1,050 by 113 feet on the flight deck. The only solution was hangar stowage: on 5 April BuAer announced that the tail assembly of the 100,000-lb bomber might be collapsed to within a 20-ft height. Given a hangar, the new limit of 1,050 by 113 feet might permit stowage of fifteen ADR-42s on deck, two abreast (to fit within the limited width). Ultimately the new carrier would incorporate a 28-ft clear hangar height.

At this point CVB X was a rather grotesque single-purpose carrier design, much more a complement to the fleet carrier than an alternative. Thus an Op-03 memo issued on 24 May 1946, the day the study was delivered to SCB, included among FY 48 projects both the fleet carrier and a hangarless 100,000-lb bomber carrier.

That same day Admiral Mitscher, then com-

This October 1948 drawing was the only officially released representation of the *United States*. It was described at the time as approximate only, and no design model appears to have been made. Note the open bow, abandoned in the "all-weather" *Forrestal* design, and the mixture of twin 3-in/70 and single (rapid-fire) 5-in/54 guns. Each of four catapults, spaced widely enough to be used simultaneously, is served by its own elevator. The drawing does not appear to be quite to scale, with jet fighters (probably F2Hs) about as large as land-based patrol bombers (Neptunes). The small jet fighter is probably intended to be an FH Phantom. Radar arrangements are not evident; in the subsequent *Forrestal* class there would have been three air search radars spaced around the flush deck, their scans synchronized and their "blips" portrayed on a single display to overcome the absence of a single large radar mast raised well above the flight deck.

mander of the Eighth Fleet, who had originated the big flush-deck carrier project, explained its rationale.

Basic aircraft carrier design has progressed steadily from the days of the converted collier *Langley* to the present in which the CVB class represents the latest in carrier thought. Perhaps the most effective of all U.S. Navy carriers was the *Essex* class, which operated so superbly in the Pacific during the past war and was the primary expression of our military-naval superiority there. Our new CVB class [the 1945 fleet-carrier study] represents but relatively slight improvement over the *Essex* class, with the armored deck as the outstanding difference. Increased size of these carriers is somewhat modified by decreased mobility because of inability to transit the present Panama Canal locks.

It is the opinion of Commander Eighth Fleet that present carriers are extremely vulnerable to bombing attack. Explosion of instantaneously fuzed bombs on the armored flight deck would probably render all island structure radio-radar outlets and primary ship control inoperative. Further it is believed that these existing carriers approach the ultimate in basic design under existing limitations. Foremost among these limitations is the island structure. This structure places a definite restriction on the size of aircraft which may be operated. The foreseeable future may well find that this limitation is unacceptable. Therefore it is considered that our thoughts as to carrier

design for the future should include design and construction of a flush-deck type. . . . Now, when we have an excess in carrier hulls over peacetime requirements, is the appropriate time to implement the above. . . .

In light of the above it is recommended:
(a) That design study of a flush-deck type aircraft carrier be started immediately.
(b) That upon completion of this study, immediate modification of an inactivated *Essex* type carrier to a flush-deck type be undertaken.
(c) That development of correlated radio and radar apparatus, including airborne AEW, be pressed.

BuAer's ships installations division was perhaps most aware of the problems a flush deck would bring, especially in smoke disposal; surely the small island acceptable in the fleet-carrier studies would not be too great a disadvantage. But on 13 June Admiral Stevens of BuAer wrote in a memorandum that he thought the island would place the single greatest restriction on future airplane design. Admiral Sallada concurred. So did Admiral G. F. Bogan, now Commander, Air Force, Atlantic.

This command concurs in the comments and recommendations. . . . While great difficulties and obstacles with existing radar and radio equipment will be experienced as well as ship handling and flight deck problems, the most direct method of overcoming such matters is to assign a CV 9 class carrier as a "dog" ship for the development of ship control, radar and radio facilities suitable for the proposed flush deck carrier.

It is recommended that the proposed carrier have armament designed solely to repel airborne attacks; accompanying ships would be relied upon to furnish protection from attacks by surface vessels. The armored flight deck has proven its worth and should be provided.

To eliminate large protruding antennae on the flush deck carrier, it is felt that the command ship of the force, a type other than the carrier, could handle all radar and communication functions rebroadcasting on low power to the carrier within the force or boosting the carrier's output transmissions as necessary. Electronic progress makes it obvious that any plot data required on the carrier is well within the realm of television broadcast from the command vessel or AEW planes.

In conclusion, this command recommends that consideration be given the idea of starting design of a flush deck carrier from scratch rather than converting a CV 9 class and that it be a ship whose design is not compromised by gun and group command considerations.

By this time the design of a specialized command ship, the converted cruiser *Northampton* (CLC 1), was well under way. Her configuration emphasized the large radar (ultimately the gigantic SPS 2) that a flush-deck carrier could not carry.

Serious planning for the new carrier began with a conference convened by DCNO (Logistics), who was in charge of SCB, on 19 June 1946. The carrier design would be based on the airplanes that could be carried; and as it was unlikely that the ship would be completed before 1952, DCNO (Air) was asked to estimate aircraft dimensions and weights for the 1952–60 period.

Meanwhile, active measures were taken to assure that the navy would have authority to deliver nuclear weapons; after all, nuclear delivery was the basis of the big-carrier design. On 24 July 1946 the Acting Secretary of the Navy, John L. Sullivan, wrote the President that

the atomic bombing of Hiroshima and Nagasaki and the first Bikini tests have amply demonstrated that the atomic bomb is the most effective single instrument of mass destruction ever deployed.

The high mobility of the Naval Carrier Task Force combined with its capacity for making successive and continuous strikes in almost any part of the world make this force a most suitable means of waging atomic bomb warfare. Carrier Forces are particularly effective during the early phases of a war when fixed shore installations may be temporarily immobilized by planned surprise attacks in force. Increased range of carrier aircraft, which will shortly be provided by new engines under development, will further increase the areas accessible to attack by carrier based aircraft. Also, the Carrier Task Force can provide a fleet of fighters to escort its bombers throughout their tactical range and thus insure maximum probability of successful accomplishment of the bombing mission.

In order to enable Carrier Task Forces to deliver atomic bombs, it will be essential to modify carrier aircraft and alter aircraft carriers to provide servicing facilities. This will require advance peacetime preparations. The aircraft carrier is well adapted for modification to provide the bomb assembly and technical facilities essential to the preparation of the atomic bomb for combat use. Excellent security can be maintained by assembling the bomb within the ship as opposed to assembly in elaborate and obvious installations ashore.

A memorandum of August 15, 1945, issued by you, requires specific Presidential approval for the Navy to receive such information as would be necessary to permit the Navy to prepare for use of the atomic bomb in warfare.

I strongly urge that you authorize the Navy to make preparations for possible delivery of atomic bombs in an emergency in order that the capabilities of the Carrier Task Forces may be utilized to the maximum advantage for national defense.

The President tacitly approved and on 19 November the CNO directed the DCNO (Logistics) to modify the three CVBs to permit the operation of AJ Savages carrying atomic bombs; these modifications (CVB improvement program no. 1) included stronger flight decks, larger bomb elevators, and larger stowage and handling facilities. At this time the AJ had just been ordered in prototype form; according to BuAer (letter of 7 November 1947), it "is the smallest plane which can carry the atomic bomb and it taxes the ability of the CVBs to the utmost. In other words the AJ design was forced to suffer considerably due to the size of the elevator, hangar deck height, catapults, etc." Hence the need for a new bomber (of over a 700-mile combat radius) and a new ship to carry it. In a sense the navy could consider the presidential authorization for carriers to project nuclear strikes an authorization for the big strike carrier. CVB improvement program no. 1 was completed on the *Coral Sea* by late 1947, on the *Franklin D. Roosevelt* by early 1948, and on the *Midway* by November 1948.

It is no longer clear whether the Savage was conceived from the beginning as a nuclear bomber. It certainly corresponded to the low end of the scale envisaged by Admiral Sallada in December 1945. However, the navy did consider a variety of large twin-engine aircraft for carrier use during World War II; in November 1944 it test-flew a PBJ-1H, a marine corps variant of the land-based Mitchell (B-25J) medium bomber, from the carrier *Shangri-La*, mak-

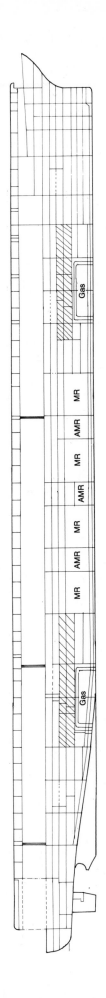

The *United States'* inboard profile. Magazines are shaded.

This seakeeping model (*above* and *facing*), under test in a wave-making tank at the David Taylor Model Basin, shows an early version of the *United States* design, without the big sponsons ultimately adopted. The aircraft are F7U Cutlass interceptors and a heavy jet attack bomber. Note that the funnels and masts were tested both in raised and in lowered (flight-operations) positions. The single mounts were 5-in/54 rapid-fire guns; the twins (bow, starboard bow, and right aft) were 3-in/70s, the most powerful available AA weapon. Presumably the amount of water taken over the bow was part of the inspiration for the enclosed-bow ("all-weather") *Forrestal* hull form.

ing catapult takeoffs and arrested landings. The Mitchell was certainly comparable in size to the Savage, and it was a developed version of the plane Dolittle had flown from the *Hornet* to bomb Tokyo in 1942. As for the Savage, only in the summer of 1946 did two naval officers of the then nuclear-weapons division of the Office of the Chief of Naval Operations, Captain Joseph N. Murphy and Commander F. L. Ashworth, travel to the North American plant to check its detailed compatibility with nuclear weapons, as then represented by the 60-in diameter, 10,000-lb "Fat Man." At this time such compatibility might more properly refer to arrangements for arming the bomb in flight, requiring special openings into the bomb bay (Ashworth himself had armed "Fat Man" en route to Nagasaki). No specific approval for the Savage modification was sought, since Secretary Forrestal considered it unnecessary, presumably in view of the President's blanket approval.

With the Savage program in motion, and BuAer's heavy-bomber program and heavy carrier under way on paper, proponents of a navy nuclear capability also sought an interim system that would end the de facto nuclear monopoly enjoyed by the air force. In mid-1947 Vice Admiral Forrest Sherman, DCNO (Op-

erations), was approached by Commander Hayward, who wanted him to lobby Congress for endorsement of the navy objective of developing a nuclear capability. Sherman preferred first to develop such a capability, which Congress might then endorse and support. The only existing navy airplane that could lift the massive bomb was the Neptune, ironically the same airplane BuShips had used as a stand-in for ADR-42. The largest existing carrier was the *Midway*, far smaller than the CVB X designed around the Neptune. Given the lack of any catapult powerful enough to launch a Neptune, Hayward had to resort to rockets, at the same time stripping his twelve aircraft of as much weight as possible. They became P2V-3Cs, and although the C represented a very marginal carrier capability, the planes were fitted with tail hooks. They were of limited value, being intended to ditch upon completion of their missions. They were also rather large relative to the *Midway* flight deck; one pilot remarked after the cancellation of the flush-decker *United States* that an accident with one Neptune would wipe out the island superstructure, giving the country a flush-decker after all.

The most important thing about the Neptune program was that it provided the navy with some semblance of a long-range nuclear capability even before the *United States* could be laid down. The first feasibility test was carried out by two Neptunes launched by rocket booster (JATO) from the *Coral Sea* on 28 April 1948. Hayward's aircraft (the twelve P2V-3Cs, pending availability of the Savage) were organized as VC-5 on 9 September 1948. On 7 March 1949 Hayward, now a captain, flew a Neptune from the *Coral Sea* carrying a simulated atomic bomb, followed by two other planes. He flew across the United States to drop the "bomb" on California, then returned to the East Coast twenty-three hours after takeoff. In September VC-5 received its first Savage, and the same month all three *Midways* launched Neptunes simultaneously, Hayward flying with the Secretary of Defense, Louis Johnson, who had that April cancelled the *United States*. Finally in 1950 the Savage was carrier qualified (after a carrier takeoff from the *Coral Sea* on 21 April) and the unwieldy Neptunes could be discarded in favor of fully carrier-capable aircraft. Meanwhile, non-nuclear components for atomic weapons were placed aboard the *Coral Sea* pending her Mediterranean deployment in September 1950. In theory the nuclear components would be flown to Port Lyautey, Morocco, aboard navy transports, and thence to the carriers by Savages, which would await their assembly. The *Franklin D. Roosevelt* was the next to deploy to the Mediterranean, and she, too, received non-nuclear components (February 1951); the *Midway* followed on her next Mediterranean cruise. From 1953 onward nuclear as well as non-nuclear components were deployed at sea, the navy having, in effect, won the battle symbolized by the *United States*.

The SCB produced draft characteristics for what it designated SCB 6A on 13 February 1947. They called, now, for a big carrier with a hangar of sufficient clearance to accept the largest aircraft in its air group. For planning purposes that group would consist of either (1) twelve to eighteen VAs (ADR-45A, 45,700 pounds, four turboprops, 750-nm combat radius, span 94 feet) and fifty-four VFs (XF2H Banshees), or (2) twelve VAs (ADR-42, now listed at 89,000 pounds, 2,000-nm radius, four augmented turboprops, span 110 feet) and fifty-four VFs (Banshees).

Note the substantial number of fighters, both for air superiority (self-defense) and for strike escort. Although the small number of heavy-attack bombers required only a small number of very heavy bombs, the flush-deck carrier was to have a substantial aviation ordnance load, described in a 1948 memorandum as 2,000 tons. Remarkably, the allowance for total aviation ordnance was not arrived at by any study of the air-group composition, but rather by scaling up from the *Midway* design, so that only in March 1949 was there a study of how to allocate that 2,040 tons. One reason was that magazine volume

was relatively plentiful in a hull large enough to support the immense flight deck required by the air group. At that time a typical air group was taken as fifty fighters and eighteen ADR-64A bombers, only the latter carrying bombs heavier than 250 pounds. Each fighter was assumed capable of carrying two 250-lb low-drag bombs. Bomber loads were based on patrol-plane practice, since land-based patrol bombers were the only aircraft of that size in current naval service. In addition, fighters might be armed with 20-mm cannon and also with the new 2.75-in high-velocity folding-fin rockets, and magazines fore and aft could be adapted to either.

Since each fighter would have either 4 20-mm cannon or 24 rockets, and each attack bomber 2 cannon, the air group as a whole would have either 236 20-mm cannon or 36 cannon and 1,200 rockets; with rockets in the main magazine, the ship could accommodate 12,000 rockets, or ten launchings. As many 250-lb low-drag bombs as possible (1,700 bombs, or 190 tons) were accommodated, as well as a 5-in and 11.75-in rocket load (based on that of a *Midway*) and the remaining weight, 1,200 tons (devoted to conventional bombs, universal stowage arrangements making for considerable flexibility). The entire discussion was relatively casual, perhaps reflecting a more intense interest in much smaller numbers of nuclear weapons. After all, the one hundred sorties frequently raised in earlier discussions would amount to no more than 536 tons, even if each bomb weighed 12,000 pounds, which in 1947 was already considered an excessive estimate.

According to the characteristics,

> special attention shall be given to rearming facilities which shall include ship facilities (similar to CVB improvement program no. 1) servicing the two forward bomb elevators, with lessened shop facilities servicing the two after bomb elevators and mechanized loading of large bombs at all bomb elevators. In general, facilities shall be provided for rearming the group within the time required to "land and respot" starting the operation with bombs below. A landing interval of 75 seconds may be used for planning purposes.

In the end elevators with a capacity of 16,000 pounds each were provided.

Flight-deck and launch arrangements were far more crucial. As with the fleet carrier, the SCB sought the ability simultaneously to launch four aircraft, two bombers, and two fighters, without interference, which in turn meant the adoption of the wide sponsons proposed for the earlier design. The tentative characteristics called for two bow catapults for bombers, with two others capable of launching a 60,000-lb airplane, even though fighters in existence at the time weighed less than a third as much. Ultimately, however, all four catapults were set at a 100,000-lb capacity. Elevators were to be positioned to permit rapid and simultaneous launch from all four catapults, "without mutual interference and without disturbing landing arrangements." The latter provision made the new flush-deck carrier the first in U.S. Navy practice to be capable of simultaneously launching and landing aircraft by design, although it might be argued that a conventional straight-deck carrier could achieve the same effect by catapulting off aircraft protected by her crash barrier.

As in the earlier flush-deck carrier studies, this one retained the 500,000-gallon avgas capacity of the fleet carrier, not quite twice that of a *Midway*; moreover, to balance the increased fuel capacity of the new aircraft, it would be piped to the flight deck at three times the previous rate, 150 gallons per minute, per outlet, for a total of 3,000 gallons per minute available at the flight and hangar decks. As yet jets were not expected to use a nonexplosive fuel, so the half million gallons of avgas required armored stowage below the waterline, where they competed for ship volume with the magazines and the massive engine rooms required for 33 knots.

BuAer simplified matters somewhat by deciding, in December 1947, that only half the air group would have to be catapulted on any one launch. Due to their lesser endurance, the fighters would launch last and land first. As for the strike aircraft, they would generally be spotted on deck prior to launch, not least because current elevator technology could lift only 60,000 pounds, so that heavy aircraft would either have to be handled on ramps or else armed and fueled on the flight deck only. Even though carrier dimensions were permitted to grow rather beyond the limits established for CVB X, it appeared that twelve of an air group of eighteen ADR-42s would have to ride the flight deck permanently, as would eighteen out of twenty-seven ADR-45s. Such aircraft would be rotated to the hangar for maintenance, much as was the case for Savages aboard the *Midway*s.

Several alternative flight-deck arrangements were tried, the designers finally choosing one in which the two fighter catapults were arranged on sponsons in the waist and the two bomber catapults occupied bow positions. There were four elevators: one right aft (with special arrangements to protect its well from a following sea), one on the port side just forward of the catapult sponson, and two on the starboard side, fore and aft of the catapult sponson there. In this arrangement the two forward elevators served the two bomber catapults, permitting removal of a dud from either catapult without respotting aft. The fore-and-aft division of elevators also corresponded to the division of the hangar into three sections by fire and blast bulkheads, a protective feature.

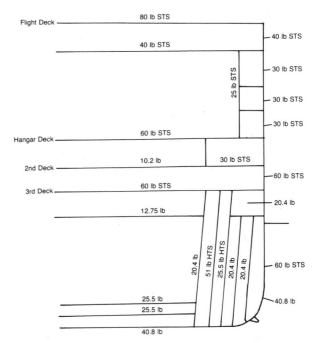

The *United States'* cross section.

Later the designers would comment that

the interrelation of the four catapults, four bomb elevators, and two special (nuclear) bomb magazines governed the arrangement to a considerable extent. The location of the catapults fixed the position of the bomb elevators which, assuming direct hoisting from below, located the special (nuclear) bomb magazines. With the after special bomb magazine pushed far into the stern, it became necessary to fit an underwater defense system relatively farther aft in the ship than has been done in recent carriers. The result was that the outboard shafting penetrated the system, necessitating the working of shaft alleys through and between the underwater defense system bulkheads. . . .

The heavily armored magazines had to be restricted to aircraft ammunition, since the ship's guns were located so far forward and aft that they could not be extended to match those locations. Thus all 3-in and 5-in ammunition, except for forward 5-in, was unprotected. "It was felt that the character of the ship ammunition was such that we could risk a hit in that type of magazine."

The catapults themselves were a problem, as they were to be far more powerful than any previously used. BuAer still believed that hydraulic-type catapults would suffice, their pumps driven by steam turbines rather than by the usual electric motors. However, the great moving mass of such a catapult, with its numerous sheaves and wires, made for enormous weight growth with each increase in capacity. In 1947 development began of the alternative direct-acting "slotted-cylinder" catapult powered by an explosive charge. Although such a device was not incorporated in the *United States* design, it did figure in the subsequent *Forrestal*, ultimately giving way to the current steam catapult.

Pilot ready rooms were another important aviation feature, their protection a sore point after the kamikaze damage of 1944–45. In the new carrier, as in the *Essex* reconstructions, they were placed deep in the hull, under the hangar-deck armor (on the fourth deck). That in turn meant a long climb from ready room to flight deck, which BuShips hoped to reduce by fitting escalators port and starboard from the hangar to the gallery deck, reducing a 47-ft climb to 29 feet.

Although it hardly seems likely that protection was a major consideration in Admiral Mitscher's demand for a flush-deck carrier, it was very much in the mind of any aviator who had survived the kamikazes. That meant deck armor above all, and any heavy weight high in a very large ship had to be difficult to accommodate. At the same time the great length of the new carrier effectively mandated that the flight rather than the hangar deck be the strength deck, a distinct departure from previous U.S. practice. BuShips argued that, if the flight deck were indeed the strength deck, any bomb penetrating it would seriously weaken the ship. It therefore split the required 3-in deck into a 2-in flight deck and a 1-in gallery deck, on the theory that this latter structure might take enough of the load to permit a low-speed run out of the battle area. A loss in direct bomb penetration had to be accepted: 2 inches plus a 1-in gallery deck were equivalent to only 2.5 inches in a single deck, but there was not weight enough for more. BuShips argued that the gallery deck would have the virtue of protecting valuable gallery-deck spaces from explosions on the hangar deck.

Under the flight deck were 1.5-in hangar (third) and sixth decks, the latter over the machinery only; outboard of the hangar proper the hangar deck was 2 inches thick. Over the special magazines the hangar deck was 4 inches thick, with additional 3-in armor decks at fifth- (forward) and sixth- (aft) deck level. These latter covered internal armor boxes within the overall protected envelope of the carrier, a new feature that was continued in later U.S. carrier designs. Thus the 1.5-in STS over the side of the ship, a recommendation since the spring of 1945, was supplemented by additional 3-in side and bulkhead armor surrounding the three armored boxes for magazines, aviation fuel, and the steering gear aft (4 inches in the latter case). This scheme of protection capitalized on the relatively dispersed character of the machinery, which could be expected to survive any single-point damage of the type airborne weapons might be expected to impose. Its main vulnerability was to underwater attack, against which the carrier had generous defensive spaces extending over most of her length, with a depth of about 22 feet.

As great as the weight expanded in protection was, the new carrier was not as well protected against bombing as was the earlier *Midway*: thick armor would have cost too much in top weight. Thus a 28 August 1947 BuOrd study evaluated various combinations of a 3-in flight deck, a 1.5-in hangar deck, and various protective decks over gasoline and magazines. It would take a 3-in lower deck to provide the same protection against dive-bombing as the *Midway* enjoyed, that is, protection against a 1,600-lb AP bomb dropped at only 1,500 to 2,000 feet. The reduction in flight-deck armor had to make matters worse, and in the *Forrestal* design BuOrd would strongly favor a return to a single thickness of armor there.

The structural choice of the flight deck as strength deck brought further complications, since both it and the hangar side joining it to the hull proper had to be cut. The hangar sides were enclosed with a double wall, the outside of 0.75-in STS, the inner of 0.62-in STS, designed more for strength than for protection—although the wall would tend to exclude fragments from the hangar. Special studies of stress concentrations around the large openings for deck-edge elevators were nonetheless required. On the flight deck, the slots for catapults were a major problem, as were bomb elevators, arresting gear, barrier sheaves, and even airplane hold-downs. Catapult slots were expected to be particularly troublesome. For example, the angle between the catapult and the centerline of the ship had to be limited to avoid weakening the flight deck. As a plus, it was argued that expansion joints, with all their attendant problems, would be eliminated, and that about 500 tons would be saved by making the heavy protection on the flight deck contribute to the ship's strength.

Protective considerations even extended to the carrier's unusual underwater form, a twin-skeg type resembling that of the battleship *South Dakota* and selected for much the same reason, to permit sufficient underwater protection over an internal magazine pushed aft by the need for internal volume. That is, the two aviation magazines, serving the two sets of catapults, were separated by machinery spaces massive enough to drive the ship at 33 knots and lengthened for protection against underwater hits powerful enough to break through even the generous side and bottom protection provided. The tunnel between the skegs reduced cross-sectional area aft without requiring any commensurate reduction in beam, that is, in the volume or depth of the antitorpedo system there. This was particularly important, given the great volume of the vitals containing both magazines and avgas.

In 1949 BuShips claimed that the *United States* would be able to withstand a 1,200- to 1,500-lb underwater charge (compared with the *Midway*'s ability to withstand an 800-lb charge), a weight nearly twice the average one of torpedo warheads used in World War II. Further, the bureau claimed that the ship could resist five 1,200-lb hits distributed in the worst possible way; more realistically, she would probably survive six or seven on one side, or even three or four penetrating hits on one side. An important feature was the side protective system, designed to provide the same degree of protection throughout its length. As for the skegs, they protected the inboard propeller shafts against torpedo damage. An elaborate system for counterflooding and pumping, developed on the basis of World War II experience, was to be installed as well.

The new carrier required more power than any previous U.S. warship, estimates ranging from 260,000 SHP at first up to 280,000 in the end. As in other features, her designers were able to consider a variety of radical alternatives, ultimately choosing a conventional four-shaft plant over five- and six-plant types. The scheme selected had the advantages of reduced length (in a ship badly in need of internal volume) and a small saving in weight, with problems of higher power per propeller (an unprecedented 70,000 SHP) and lower propulsive efficiency. Postwar machinery developments made available the choice of the new high-steam conditions (1,200 pounds per square inch, 950°); wartime practice was reflected in the unit arrangement, each of four compartments accommodating two boilers and one turbine, with ship service generators divided between the main machinery rooms and auxiliary machinery rooms.

Given these standard features, the principal issue in machinery arrangement was smoke disposal, and BuShips was never enthusiastic about the solution it had adopted. As in the very earliest U.S. carrier designs, smoke was to be discharged to either side depending upon the wind; even as the ship was being laid down wind-tunnel tests of her arrangement were in progress. In general, it appeared that the further aft the smoke pipes, the less the nuisance they presented; but such an arrangement carried its own difficulties, since the boilers were more nearly amidships. Initially the uptakes were run fore and aft between the hangar and fourth decks, and then up through the hangar walls to a crossover flue between the flight and gallery decks. However, this flue would not have been very well protected, and ultimately the crossover valving was moved under the hangar deck. Notes in the *United States* files suggest that because these arrangements were unsatisfactory, the designers looked forward to the advent of nuclear power (perhaps for a later ship in the series) to make the flush-deck carrier really effective.

Defense armament for the ship was almost, but not quite, an afterthought. As in the case of armor, it was a subject of emotional significance, given wartime experience. At first the characteristics called for a battery limited to the new twin 3-in/70 automatic cannon and to free-swinging automatic machine guns (that is, a 20-mm gun, although BuOrd consistently mentioned a new 35-mm gun in its postwar planning). However, in the end a mixed 5-in and 3-in battery, divided to give quadrant fire, was chosen. A new feature was the provision of four-sector fire controls. At first it appeared that eight 5-in/54 and eight twin 3-in/70 guns would be mounted, but in the end only six of the latter could be accommodated. Complications arose concerning seaworthiness and the necessity of keeping barrels (except for two bow mounts) below flight-deck level when elevated, the bottoms of sponsons being at least 20 feet above the waterline.

The end result was rather larger than CVB X, with an overall length of 1,090 feet and a molded beam of 130 feet; flight-deck beam was 190 feet. Although the design papers do not touch on docking limitations, a summary presentation given by BuShips in April 1949, just after the carrier's cancellation, mentions that the characteristics demanded she be capable of entering large graving docks and the largest floating dry docks (AFDBs). Thus it was hoped that waterline beam could be held to 125 feet, although in the end an increase to 130, "which we regarded as the practical limit for existing docking facilities," was necessary. "Actually the length of the CVA, also, is about the maximum for the large graving dock. As designed, the CVA 58 can be docked in ten graving drydocks and in a 13 section AFDB."

In the end, then, the super-carrier, for all the emphasis on aviation features, showed in her design process remarkably little attention to two of the issues greatly affecting the details of that design: the volumes to be devoted to aviation fuel and to aviation ordnance, both of which had to be protected as explosives. It appears that the figure of 500,000 gallons, almost casually arrived at in the fleet-carrier study (on a very different tactical basis), continued to govern the SCB-6A study in the absence of any kind of review. Similarly, magazine volume was based on that of a very different carrier, the *Midway*, again without any kind of tactical analysis. The precise origin of Admiral Mitscher's one hundred sorties is not clear, although one might guess that he thought in terms of two to four strike days between replenishment; a 500-kt airplane would cover the 2,000 nautical miles each way to and from its target in eight hours, for one strike per strike day, or four strike days for a twenty-four- or twenty-five-airplane air group.

The *United States* was, for three years, the focus of naval aviation attention and pride, as her name suggests. She was also honored with a new type designator, CVA, for "attack"—or, perhaps, "atomic." Her cancellation was a grave blow, and the continuation of detailed design work through the summer of 1949

The operational concept of aircraft on the *United States* survived in a series of heavy carrier bombers such as the Vigilante, shown aboard the *Enterprise* in April 1962.

reflects the extent to which the navy hoped that she would be revived. What must have been particularly galling was that Congress and the President had approved her construction despite strict limits on military spending; indeed the navy appears to have looked forward to the construction of four such super-carriers as the basis for four strike groups. Then, only nine days after her keel had been laid, the new Secretary of Defense, Louis Johnson, a man identified strongly with the development of heavy land-based bombers, cancelled her on 23 April 1949, virtually

without consulting the CNO. It is true that he did so at the suggestion of the army and air force representatives on the Joint Chiefs of Staff, but many at the time believed that the two other services were in collusion to strip the navy of both its independent air arm and its independent amphibious component, the marine corps; moreover, it might be argued that army and air force were still, in 1949, closer in outlook to each other than to the navy.

    The end of the super-carrier did not quite end the navy's hopes, however. There was still CVB improvement project no. 1 and the AJ-1 Savage, as well as the *Essex*-class modernization program. The carrier heavy bomber also survived, although its takeoff weight had to be trimmed from 100,000 to 70,000 pounds; it became the Douglas Skywarrior (A3D, later A-3). Moreover, much of the thinking that had gone into the *United States* survived in the subsequent *Forrestal* design, which is why the super-carrier is worth discussing in this much detail.

The cancellation of the carrier (in favor of more heavy bombers) was extremely controversial, but none of the navy arguments raised at the time proved effective. Indeed, the decision was only reversed thanks to the vast increase in defense funding generated by the Korean War. One of the ironies of the *United States* dispute is that the total navy pre-Korea super-carrier program was far less ambitious than the program actually executed a few years later. Thus it appears that the navy expected to build no more than four SCB 6As for four task forces, each comprising one super-carrier and two smaller ones, either *Midway*s or SCB 27As. The operation of such forces is described in OPNAV memos of the late forties.

At the time cancellation of the super-carrier seemed to be symptomatic of a total rejection of the navy and its values by an army- and air force–oriented defense and political establishment. Secretary of the Navy Sullivan resigned in protest, and many naval officers had to resign as the navy's case was made public during 1949. At one point a naval aviator even offered to shoot down an air force heavy bomber to disprove that branch's claims of invulnerability to interceptions.

The controversy was surely the most explicit example of the explosive political feeling surrounding the carrier, which controlled a large force of aircraft not under the auspices of the air force and yet capable of executing many of the same missions. Although the air force had to accept the construction of carriers in the early fifties, by the latter part of the decade it was again attacking carrier construction as inefficient on the ground that the carrier task force required massive fighter forces merely for self-defense. Only in the sixties did the air force begin to see carriers and land-based tactical aircraft as truly complementary, and even now arguments are still raised. For example, over the past four years, advocates of aerial refueling have claimed that this technique would permit aircraft based on U.S. soil to operate worldwide. And the struggle over the CVN 71 suggests that even now the carrier is not universally accepted. The *United States* controversy never quite ended.

12

The *Forrestal* Class and Its Successors

Navy hopes for a new flush-deck carrier did not die with the *United States*. First, the aviators still expected to develop a new generation of long-range carrier attack bombers, and they still believed that such aircraft would be hazardous to operate from any carrier with a fixed island structure, given the wing span they would require. It was true, however, that the 100,000-lb figure characteristic of planes on the earlier super-carrier could be reduced: BuAer had selected the 70,000-lb Douglas A3D Skywarrior (later designated A-3) as its phase 3 heavy bomber in March 1949. It could, therefore, accept a formal reduction in the carrier-bomber limit from 100,000 to 70,000 pounds after the cancellation of the large carrier. However, a new carrier of some type was still badly needed. Although the *Midway* could, in theory, operate the new bomber, that was only a very inefficient type of operation. Thus in August 1949, Op-55, the studies arm of DCNO (Air), proposed a *Midway*-size flush-decker or, failing that, a conversion of an *Essex*-class carrier to flush-deck configuration.

There was, moreover, reason to believe that a new carrier would eventually be authorized. Congressional willingness to buy the *United States*, even during a period of fiscal drought, along with the strong resistance to Secretary Johnson's attempt to emasculate the marine corps at about the same time, could be read as proof of considerable political support for the navy. Carl Vinson, the navy's strongest advocate in Congress, informally indicated that he expected Congress to back a new carrier significantly smaller than the *United States*. His suggested limit of 60,000 tons influenced the design of what became the *Forrestal*, much as treaty limits had figured in pre–World War II carrier designs.

There were no new carrier characteristics drawn up after the cancellation of the super-carrier. However, BuShips, confident enough that a new carrier would be authorized, continued studies without characteristics, seeking those sacrifices that would make for significant reductions in the overall size of a new carrier. When approval for the new heavy carrier arrived, BuShips, pressed for time, used these studies for the basis of the new design; they carried with them many of the decisions originally made for the *United States* and even for the 1945 fleet carrier, and relatively few of the ideas associated with what was, by 1950, a ship intended for very different service. That is, between 1946 and 1950 the navy concept of future carrier operations shifted from strategic strikes by a relatively small number of carrier-based heavy bombers to tactical air strikes by a much larger air group of smaller aircraft. Moreover, by 1950 it was clear that light atomic bombs, suitable for delivery by fighter-size aircraft, would soon be available; that year BuAer issued the requirements that later became the Douglas A4D (now A-4) Skyhawk. However, the new circumstances were reflected in the new

The new *Saratoga* shows her flight-deck layout in this 4 June 1956 photograph. Note how the forward portside elevator interrupted the runway of the angled deck. The elevator, a carry-over from the original axial-deck design, was intended to serve the port forward catapult. The proximity of the two waist catapults was also a consequence of the redesign. In the original flush-deck design, the outer waist catapult would have been on the starboard side, a position occupied in the final design by the island. The angle between the two waist catapults was limited because the flight deck was the strength deck—cuts too close to transverse could not be made.

carrier design primarily in the increased stowage space for aviation fuel, and not at all in increased magazine volume. Indeed, the latter appears to have been scaled directly from the volume provided in the *United States*, which in turn had been set almost casually by scaling up from the wartime *Midway*. Magazine volume was of little moment in the *United States* design, because nuclear weapons for one hundred sorties could occupy only a small fraction of her 2,000 tons of aviation magazine space. Matters were very different for a carrier such as the *Forrestal*, which might have to make sustained non-nuclear strikes in support of ground forces, as in Korea and Vietnam. Even so, magazine space appears not to have figured significantly in her design.

Thus the design of the *Forrestal* was very much the direct descendant of that of the *United States*. Once carrier construction had been renewed there was, then, pressure to test alternatives: carriers better adapted to aircraft-operating procedures, particularly after the adoption of the angled flight deck and the steam catapult, carriers of slightly smaller size, carriers with higher speed. For a few years the *Forrestal* design, appropriately modified, continued to be built simply because there was no other large carrier design available in a condition even approaching suitability for construction. In 1952–54, however, a variety of alternatives were examined, the *Forrestal* actually being evaluated as the minimum carrier suitable for modern naval aircraft. After that, attempts to design a new carrier were abandoned in view of the advent of nuclear power: there was little point in spending a large amount for an improved conventional carrier, when only one or at most two ships might be built to that design. Thus four *Forrestal*s and four improved *Forrestal*s (CVAs 63, 64, 66, and 67) were built, all testimony to the robustness of the original design.

The revival of carrier construction was very much a consequence of the Korean War. The North Koreans attacked on 25 June 1950, vindicating Forrest Sherman's plea that one carrier be maintained in the Far East at all times. On 11 July the Joint Chiefs agreed to postpone further consideration of reductions in the carrier force level, and the following day Secretary of Defense Johnson, the man who had killed the *United States*, offered Admiral Sherman a new carrier. Even then it was not immediately included in the new shipbuilding budget, that for FY 52. For example, a draft version of the new budget, prepared on 31 August, showed two *Essex* conversions (SCB 27), two guided-missile-cruiser conversions, a nuclear submarine, and a variety of other new types, but the only new carrier was an ASW escort carrier (SCB 43), which was listed as the twenty-third item in priority, the new destroyer escort being the first. The *Essex*

conversions were fourth priority, after the missile cruisers and a mine-hunter conversion program. By 28 October, however, a revised FY 52 program showed a new carrier (SCB 80) as eighth priority, the conversions having moved to sixth. The other high-priority projects were the destroyer escorts, the missile cruiser, a new minesweeper, the mine hunters, the nuclear submarine *Nautilus*, and a new landing ship (tank). Several of these projects reflected the realities of limited war in Korea, such as Soviet-inspired mine warfare and the continuing viability of amphibious assault. The ASW escort carrier had by this time been dropped entirely from the list of thirty items. Secretary of the Navy Francis P. Matthews approved the entire list on 30 October 1950, and the *Forrestal* design was born.

The name itself was something of a slap at Secretary Johnson and the air force. As Secretary of the Navy, James Forrestal had encouraged, first, the 1945 fleet-carrier design, and then the entire navy nuclear program, all the way from CVB improvement program no. 1 to the *United States*. As Secretary of Defense, he had continued to support the super-carrier, sometimes at the expense of the air force, and the tensions of the interservice dispute led to his breakdown and then to his replacement by Louis Johnson.

From FY 52 onward, then, the construction of a carrier every year was a major navy goal. No final force level was set, because the navy was so far from replacing all of its active wartime carriers that none could really be envisaged. In 1950 the Joint Chiefs had adopted as an FY 52 goal the twelve-carrier force defined by NSC-68. In December 1951, moreover, the Commander-in-Chief, Far East, asked that his air forces be augmented, and the following February the Joint Chiefs approved the deployment of a fourth carrier to the Western Pacific as a temporary measure. In order to avoid withdrawals from the Mediterranean, the CNO recommended that the attack-carrier force be enlarged from twelve to fourteen, and this was approved by the President on 28 February 1952, despite objections from the air force.

Although this deployment was to have ended with the Korean War, it continued for the twelve months following August 1953. Ultimately a peacetime level of fifteen carriers (for five forward deployments) was stabilized, and continued heavy-carrier construction was generally measured against a goal of twelve new carriers and three modernized *Midway*s by the end of the sixties. The pace of carrier building remained steady through the construction of the *Enterprise* of FY 58, and then faltered in view of the high cost of new nuclear and oil-fired carriers and the importance and cost of the new Polaris submarine-launched ballistic missile system. Although the navy leadership argued that the latter was a national system, and so had to use strategic funds such as those paying for air force heavy bombers and land-based missiles, in the end it was the navy general-purpose forces, and particularly the new carriers, that suffered. Thus the *Forrestal* class bridged the period of the greatest prestige of the attack carrier, when she formed part of the national strategic force and her bombers were very much on a par with the best the air force was flying. Although the carriers continue to be an essential element of the national power, they are no longer part of the ultimate strategic arm, nor are they ever likely to regain that position.

The BuShips designers did not operate entirely in the dark between April 1949 and late 1950.

> While it has not been feasible for OpNav to prepare characteristics, the Bureau has been furnished information as to what is wanted, by copies of OpNav correspondence and in conferences. At hearings of the General Board in consideration of this project, the Bureau presented rough studies based on extrapolation . . . to indicate the effect of the various characteristics under consideration. These studies showed that a ship meeting the proposed characteristics would be larger than the *United States*. In a conference on 8 November 1950 with the Chief of Naval Operations, the Bureau was given an idea as to the features which could be reduced in order to meet the limiting standard displacement. . . . Based on this information, a design study has been going forth in the Bureau on the highest priority and on a six-day week basis. . . .

BuShips wanted three studies available by 15 February 1951; one would be chosen and characteristics embodying it prepared by 1 March, with the preliminary design completed on 1 September and contract plans ready by 1 July 1952. The first contract would be let on 1 January 1952, and contract negotiations would begin on 1 December 1951 on the basis of the preliminary design. With construction scheduled on a normal forty-hour work week, the first ship would be completed 1 January 1956; with an all-out effort, this date might be advanced to 1 July 1955.

This was a very tight schedule, but BuShips actually did even better, contracting with Newport News for the new carrier on 12 July 1951; the new *Forrestal* was commissioned on 1 October 1955, despite having been redesigned (with an angled flight deck and steam catapults) during the course of construction.

In a 22 December 1950 memorandum to the CNO, the designers argued that even their proposed schedule was rather optimistic, requiring "a sandwiching of events not heretofore accomplished in a ship of this size. . . . decisions [must] be made and conflicting requirements resolved promptly. Further changes in characteristics during the design stages will have to be avoided." By way of comparison, thirteen months

had been required for the preliminary design studies (which were now called feasibility studies) of the *Midway*, and another nine for preliminary design proper, plus ten months for contract plans and specifications—a total of thirty-two months, compared with about a year altogether for what became the *Forrestal*.

DCNO (Air) described the new carrier as an all-weather attack aircraft carrier, arguing in September 1950 that

> first and foremost, . . . any replacement carriers should be suitable for conducting aircraft operations in all conditions of visibility and temperature so far as the carrier is concerned. Intensive efforts are being made to enhance the all weather characteristics of our carrier planes. One of the greatest hazards to all weather flying, so far as the carrier is concerned, is the presence of the superstructure. This means that all replacement carriers should be flush deckers which can operate with no obstructions above the level of the flight deck *when in a condition for recovering aircraft.*

All-weather operation also demanded an enclosed bow for a drier hangar and flight deck, a feature perhaps adopted in view of the severity of storm damage to carriers and particularly to their flight decks in 1945. It was retained in the face of General Board criticism that it unnecessarily restricted design of the vessel. One consequence of the adoption of the enclosed bow was a longer flight deck on a hull constrained in length by the Vinson tonnage limitation.

The aviators also called for an enlarged aviation fuel capacity, 750,000 gallons. This figure was based on wartime experience. At a General Board hearing Commander Counihan of Op-05 observed that

> we have never had enough aviation fuel in the ships. . . . It wasn't unusual in the last war to burn 40,000 gallons in a day's operation of repeated strikes and these jets are something in the nature of five times as expensive fuel-wise, so we figure that 750,000 gallons—and you have to leave some in your tanks—would give us three days' operation. . . . We expect to be using JP-3 (rather than gasoline) and we will design for it. BuShips says they feel there is no change in the fuel stowage and it is just as dangerous.

In fact even 750,000 gallons was low by later standards. What saved the big carriers was that fuel ceased to be an explosive and hence ceased to need protected stowage. In the fall of 1950 there was some hope that the lighter, more volatile, and more explosive fraction of aviation fuel could be split off and stowed under armor; this would be recombined later with heavy-end aircraft fuel (HEAF), which was not too different from bunker oil and could be stowed in conventional fuel tanks within the side protective

Shown here newly completed by Newport News on 29 September 1955, the *Forrestal*, with her massive angled flight deck and her four steam catapults, began a new era for U.S. carriers. Her flight deck was an integral part of the hull; the large openings in her hangar side, for four deck-edge elevators, posed major structural problems. She was designed for "all-weather" operations, symbolized by her high enclosed bow. Even so, the spray thrown up by the two forward gun sponsons limited her rough-weather speed. Prominent antennas included the four ship-to-air units at her bow and stern (TED/AN/URR-13), the TACAN, at her masthead, and an SPS-10, SPS-12, and SPN-6 below it. The pilot-house roof carried an SPS-8A height finder; the mainmast carried ECM antennas and, at its peak, a UHF/DF antenna. A small radome at the after end of the island carried an SPN-8 for bad-weather landing, and an antenna outboard of the funnel was used to receive weather-balloon data. The two tall masts could hinge to permit the carrier to pass under the Brooklyn Bridge to the New York Naval Shipyard (all large U.S. warships had this capability until the sixties). Only the *Forrestal* had the after mast.

(antitorpedo) tanks, outside the armor box. At first it was assumed that the heavier fuel would have to be blended with the lighter, so that a ship could carry (in effect) twice as much aviation fuel as in her protected tanks (the *Forrestal* would carry 1.5 million gallons). Later, all naval aircraft were fueled with JP-5, which was heavy enough for stowage in bunker tanks and required no lighter additive; protected tankage was needed only for the shrinking complement of propeller-driven aircraft, such as the Skyraiders. Still later, many carriers had their boilers modified to burn JP-5 instead of bunker oil, so that they could trade off operating (steaming) radius against airgroup endurance.

Operationally, carrier commanders did not as yet realize the thirst of the relatively new jet fighter in the fall of 1950. For example, in October 1951 Rear Admiral S. B. Spangler, Commander, Air Force, Atlantic, wrote to Rear Admiral T. S. Combs of BuAer that

> by March 1953 carrier air group 7 would have three squadrons of F9F-6, one of F9F-5, one of A2D [Skyshark, an abortive turboprop successor to the Skyraider or AD]. Assuming 80 fighters and 27 attack aircraft on a CVB, it needs about 65,000 gallons per group hour. This is about the rate at which the carrier can be refuelled with aviation fuel. At this rate there is something under 6 group hours on the CVB. Assume then that we use ship fuel in the aircraft, and cut steaming time to 9.5 days, then we get 23 group hours—and these are not terribly reasonable assumptions. For our own calculations we are using current fuel consumptions actually being expended under strike operations and these vary from 1.3 to 2.0 times the combat radius figures in the standard aircraft charts. Using equivalent figures, the current *Coral Sea* group has 18 group hours of fuel aboard, and they are fuelling after two simulated strike days. Carrier Air Group 7 then has 0.7 to 1 strike days of fuel. . . .
>
> One operation . . . scheduled 340 sorties for two jet fighter squadrons; of 355,000 gallons available, only 48,000 (41,000 usable) were left after 187 sorties. 340 sorties in four days for 36 aircraft is 4.6 hours per day (2.3 hours per flight)—in World War Two we averaged 9 hours per aircraft per day on strike days.

For example, on average the F2H-2 Banshee consumed 6,000 pounds of fuel (1,000 gallons) per flight, so that 340 sorties would require 340,000 gallons, leaving only 15,000 (of which 7,000 would be usable) for the piston-engine aircraft.

The aviators were willing to reduce the catapults to 70,000 pounds each in view of the reduction in the weight of the new attack bomber, and they wanted at least two, forward. "If other features of the ship design will permit, one or more additional catapults capable of launching 40,000 lb aircraft [is] desired." The lighter catapults would launch fighters. Another, subtler change was made. The *United States* had been designed for four hydraulic catapults (H 9 type),

which were extremely heavy and below which was required a lot of internal hull structure. However, since 1945 BuAer had been developing a much lighter high-powered catapult, the slotted tube. Where a hydraulic catapult achieved its power by means of a ram connected to the catapult shuttle by a series of wires passing over sheaves, a slotted tube directly connected the source of power to the airplane. In the BuAer design as then conceived, the catapult shuttle would be fired directly by a powder charge, and the *Forrestal* design originally allowed for 400 tons of such charges in a special magazine. Ultimately the explosive catapult failed its development, and fortunately an alternative slotted-tube system, the British-developed steam catapult, was available. However, both the steam and the explosive systems represented very considerable weight saving compared to the massive hydraulic catapult. Moreover, there was some question in 1950 as to whether wire-and-sheave construction could take the loads associated with the new generation of naval aircraft.

The aviators were also prepared to accept the loss of one of the four elevators of the *United States* design as well as a reduction in hangar-clear height to 19 feet. However, in contrast with the earlier design, they wanted escalators running the full distance from ready rooms to flight deck. They presented no specific requirement for aviation ordnance capacity for the new carrier, but DCNO (Air)'s proposed characteristics called for a load of 1,200 tons of aircraft. The earlier figure of 12,000 nautical miles at 20 knots was retained from the 1945 fleet carrier, although a sustained speed of 30 knots (war loaded) was acceptable. It was considered equivalent to 32 knots on trial.

Although the aviators dominated the design, BuOrd lobbied hard for a level of protection better than what had been accepted in the *United States*. It was particularly dissatisfied with the decision to split the flight-deck armor into separate 2-in and 1-in (gallery-deck) thicknesses, arguing that the minimum acceptable should be the 3.5 inches of the *Midway*, 60 pounds over that of the earlier carrier (and representing a weight gain of about 5,000 tons very high in the ship). The bureau argued that 3.5 inches would keep out all GP bombs up to 2,000 pounds, and that it would also keep out semi-armor-piercing (SAP) bombs up to 1,000 pounds.

> It is impracticable to carry enough armor to keep AP bombs from penetrating the flight deck, provided they are dropped from sufficient altitude to acquire the necessary velocity. . . .
>
> You have heard the view expressed that the shaped charge and the guided missile render armor of such doubtful value that we might as well do without armor. I do not underestimate the capabilities of these weapons, but I can not concur with this view.

Space and weight for the warhead of a guided missile are at a premium. If our armor forces the enemy to provide an AP warhead in order to penetrate, it will have seriously reduced the destructiveness of his missile.

As for shaped charge bombs, most of the energy of the detonation is expended in front of the triggering plate. It is true that the jet will penetrate into the ship and will be a serious fire hazard. This is better, however, than permitting the entire bomb to penetrate into the ship. The situation is different in tank warfare, where a shaped charge hit is almost certain to disable a tank, regardless of any thickness of armor it can carry, because of the density of vulnerable components inside a tank.

Even so, every inch of armor high in the ship represented considerable top weight. Indeed, it could be argued that the greater the clear hangar height, the greater the effect on stability of each inch. In particular, greater top weight would have to be balanced by a beamier hull, which in turn would add weight to the ship. For example, in February 1950 Preliminary Design estimated that 1,000 tons added at the flight deck would require, in addition, 10 feet of length (at 50 tons per foot) to maintain speed without increasing power, and 2 feet of beam (at 300 tons per foot) to maintain stability, for a total increase of 2,100 tons. Thus a 10-lb layer of armor added to the flight deck (400 tons) would require a net addition of 840 tons to the ship. Increased speed, on a hull substantially shorter than that of the *United States*, would entail increased power and therefore increased weight, so that a simple shrinkage of hull length might not suffice to save net displacement.

As early as 25 April 1949, two days after the cancellation of the *United States*, Preliminary Design was investigating the effects of various sacrifices. For example, elimination of one deck-edge elevator, half the catapults and arresting gear, 4 feet of hangar-clear height, all of the 5-in battery, and 20 pounds of flight deck and 10 pounds of hangar-deck armor (leaving, respectively, 60 and 60/40 pounds outboard/inboard), along with the adoption of lighter elevators attendant on a reduction in airplane weight to 80,000 pounds, reduced standard displacement only from the original 66,850 tons to 62,675. Alternatively, Preliminary Design tried to scale up from the *Midway*, a shorter ship, rather than down from the *United States*. In this case the hangar deck rather than the flight deck would be the strength deck. Estimates showing that a 960- or 970-ft carrier could be built on as little

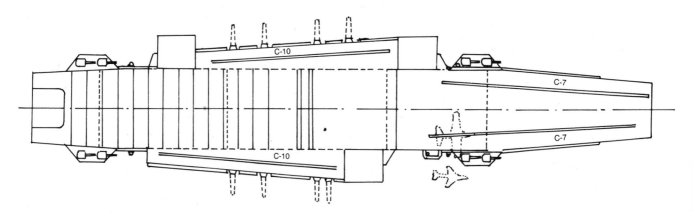

The *Forrestal*'s design, with a small fixed island.

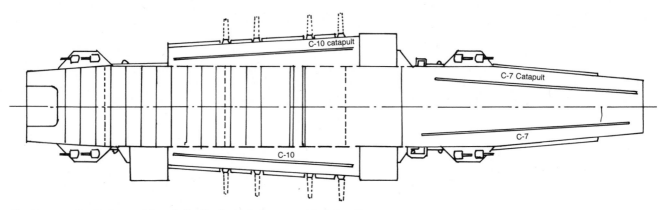

The *Forrestal*'s design, with a fully flush deck (retractable island).

as 52,000 tons may have been a factor in Representative Vinson's choice of a 60,000-ton limit. Ultimately, however, the *United States* was used as the basis of the new design, and the project that led to the *Forrestal* began as "CV junior" or the "AW (all-weather) carrier" late in February 1950.

The combination of additional flight-deck armor, additional protected aviation-fuel capacity, and the full *United States* requirements for guns (eight 5-in/54s and eight twin 3-in/70s) and hangar height added 7,000 tons to that ship, even if the lighter catapults were counted as weight-savers. Drastic sacrifices were in order. Two undated BuShips schemes, probably prepared early in 1951, illustrate the trade-offs involved. In each case a total of 5 inches of deck armor over the machinery was to be provided, much of it placed low enough in the ship to avoid stability problems. Each 59,900-ton hull was 980 feet long on the waterline, compared with the 1,090 feet of the *United States*; this choice in itself drove down the displacement. Side protection was reduced from the 60 pounds of the original ship to 45 pounds (1.125 inches), but there were to be four catapults and four elevators. On this basis the designers could choose a 25-ft hangar and 70 pounds (1.75 inches) on the flight deck, or a 19-ft hangar and 80 pounds (2 inches) on the flight deck, in each case supplemented by gallery-deck armor. Both schemes displaced 59,900 tons, just short of the Vinson limit, and both represented reduced batteries of, respectively, eight 5-in/54 guns (70-lb flight deck) and ten 3-in/70 twin mounts (80-lb flight deck). The first formed the basis for the *Forrestal* design.

That is, when they reported in November 1950 the BuShips designers proposed a 980- by 125- by 34-ft hull displacing about 57,500 tons; they sought a figure well below Vinson's to allow a maximum margin. On this displacement they believed they could provide only three catapults and three deck-edge elevators, as well as 1,000 tons of aircraft and only 1,000 tons of aviation ordnance. Three deck-edge elevators represented an absolute minimum, since for damage-control reasons the hangar deck would be divided into thirds by blast and fire bulkheads, each third forming a fire-fighting zone. A similar system was then being installed aboard the modernized *Essex*-class carriers. As for protection, although the 2-in flight deck of the earlier *United States* was to be retained, gallery-deck armor would have to be reduced to 0.75 inch. The 60-lb hangar deck and side armor of the earlier design would be retained. Finally, a 1,020- by 125-ft flight deck was envisaged, and there was some question as to whether even eight gun mounts would be available. Hangar height was set, in this design, at 19 feet.

On reflection, BuAer found the 19-ft hangar less than attractive. For example, the new A3D attack bomber turned out to require at least 22 feet of clear headroom. Since the aircraft were already driving the design, the minimum hangar height was soon set at 25 feet. That in turn doomed any attempt to achieve substantial flight-deck protection and created the need for a beamier hull. By late February 1951 Preliminary Design was reporting the 59,900-ton nominal displacement of the final version of the design, with a beam of 127.5 feet on the waterline and a 25-ft hangar. At this stage it appeared that all four catapults could be provided, as well as four elevators, the fourth being right aft. There would be eight guns, and all would be the automatic 5-in/54 type, somewhat lighter than the more sophisticated (and, as it turned out, less reliable) twin 3-in/70 guns. Again, all other considerations were subordinated to aircraft operation. By this time, too, a magazine capacity of

The *Forrestal*'s design, with a retractable island, after a BuShips design model. The large aircraft are A3D Skywarriors; the smaller one on the port waist catapult is an F3H Demon heavy interceptor.

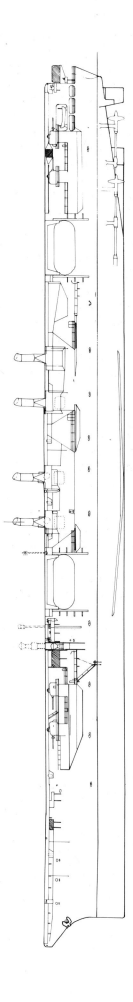

The *Forrestal*'s contract design, with a retractable island (as laid down). The shaded objects are radomes. Fore-to-aft details at the flight-deck edge are as follows: an SPS-10 for surface search, a Mark 35 director, 5-in guns, an SPS-6C for air search, a retractable TACAN (URN-3), secondary fly control (with retractable auxiliary fly control), an elevator, a hinged URD-3A direction finder, the after elevator, after guns, another Mark 35, an SPS-6C right aft, and below it an SPN-12 (small dish) for CCA. All three SPS-6Cs were to have been coordinated, feeding a common display.

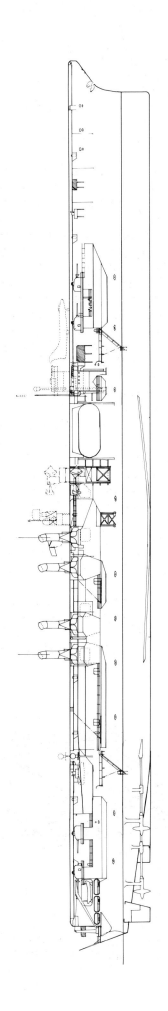

The *Forrestal*'s contract design, starboard side. Details, from left to right, are as follows: an SPS-10 (surface search) radome, 5-in/54 guns, a director, a retractable SMD-1 meteorological antenna, uptakes, a retractable platform carrying SPN-8 and SPN-6 (above) CCA radars, a retractable SPS-8 height finder (the position of the fixed island was considered as an alternative), an elevator, a retractable island with auxiliary ship control on its own hoist, an SPS-6C, guns, and a Mark 35 director.

1,800 to 2,000 tons of aviation ordnance was being reported. Given the shortage of time, the late February characteristics marked the design itself.

Late in the process the hull was redesigned, a conventional underbody and transom stern replacing the twin skegs of the CVA 58 design. Waterline length was increased from 980 to 990 feet. It was claimed that torpedo resistance would be improved, since the inner and outer shafts would be further separated in length. Another unusual survivability feature was a third rudder.

As for the structure above the flight deck, there was some sentiment favoring a very small fixed bridge over to a fully retractable structure, and designs for both alternatives were prepared. Characteristics of June 1951, which actually reflected the design developed by that time, called for "provisions . . . in the design so that a permanent island bridge structure may be installed between the after starboard catapult and the starboard elevator if after completion and evaluation the decision is made to do so. To this end, *as far as practicable,* space allocation, piping, wiring, and ventilation arrangements in the internal structure shall be such that the installation of a permanent island would be facilitated." This still meant a very small fixed island, perhaps 40 by 12 feet; the smoke pipes were still to discharge from below the flight deck, with all the attendant problems of internal arrangement.

> The desire to locate the smoke pipes well aft to minimize the smoke interference, coupled with the requirement that no uptakes penetrate a transverse watertight bulkhead below the hangar deck, led to an arrangement of the main machinery further aft than is customary. . . .
>
> With machinery further aft, the forward armor box was made somewhat longer than the after box. As a result, about two-thirds of gasoline and ammunition is stowed forward; one-third is stowed aft. . . . The shops required for special weapons are located in the forward armored box. . . . Four bomb elevators lead up from the magazines. One forward and one aft terminate on the hangar deck; one forward and one aft terminate on the flight deck.

Pilot accommodations differed from those proposed for the *United States.* In the earlier design, one ready room, sufficient for the largest squadron aboard, was to have been located in the gallery deck adjacent to CIC and air plot, with the others in more protected locations below the hangar deck. By way of contrast, the new design had a pair of twenty-five-man ready rooms in the gallery to scramble to the forward and after catapults, with an additional sixty-man room in the gallery deck amidships near CIC. The four large ready rooms (two each for forty-five men, and two each for sixty) were provided below the hangar deck, with escalator access to the gallery deck. The special scramble rooms could be described as features for tactical (World War II) operation, as compared with the more deliberate pace implied by ready rooms deeper in the ship, or located with respect to CIC and air plot rather than to the catapults.

As the design was developed, detailed improvements were made as well, such as weight saving in the underwater protection, which was absent in the *United States.* Just as in the earlier ship, problems arose with smoke disposal and the arrangement of radar antennas around the edge of the vast, flat deck.

The greatest change was the shift from that flush deck to the modern angled deck, which at a stroke solved most of the problems of the design. Indeed, it can be argued that the combination of angled flight deck, steam catapult, and mirror landing air, all British inventions, transformed carrier design and made practical the wholesale use of high-performance jet aircraft. Ironically, it was the United States rather than the Royal Navy that benefitted most from them.

The theory of the angled flight deck was simple. In a conventional or axial deck, a landing airplane headed down the centerline of the carrier, its path into the parked airplanes forward blocked only by a combination of arresting wires and a safety barrier. An airplane penetrating the wires and barrier would crash into the aircraft forward and start the sort of fire that would inevitably halt flight operations. Moreover, although in theory aircraft could be catapulted off during landing operations, such dual operation was difficult since the zone available for parking between landing and takeoff areas was extremely small. In the *Forrestal* and *United States* designs, massive sponsons and a vast flight deck made simultaneous landings and catapult launchings possible, but only barely so. In an angled deck carrier, the landing zone was angled out to port, away from the carrier island—and away from the parking and catapulting areas on the centerline of the carrier, forward. Thus an airplane that skipped over the barriers would simply fly off the end of a sponson, away from other aircraft. It would, indeed, be so far from the starboard edge of the flight deck that the presence of an island structure would not affect landing safety, and the smoke-disposal problem could be solved without prejudice to aviation features. In the case of the *Forrestal* the only substantial sacrifice was moving the starboard sponson catapult to the (now greatly enlarged) port sponson, where it somewhat interfered with the catapult already there. That is, it was now possible to load both catapults simultaneously, but not to fire both at once, as would have been the case previously.

The angled flight deck progressed rapidly from concept to construction. It was first proposed at a meeting at the Royal Aircraft Establishment in Bed-

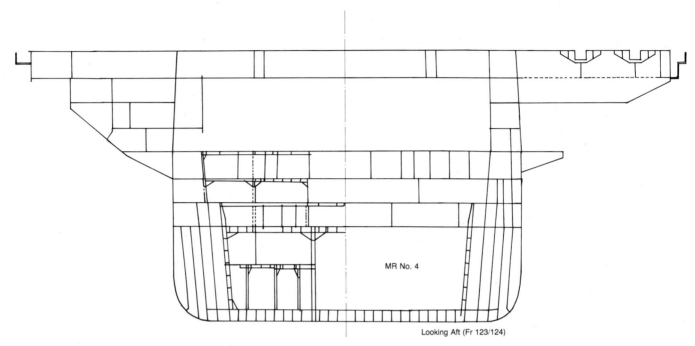

MR No. 4

Looking Aft (Fr 123/124)

The *Forrestal*'s cross section, looking aft.

ford, England, on 9 August 1951. Participants discussed the operation of heavy (30,000-lb) jet aircraft from the flight decks of the new carriers *Eagle* and *Ark Royal*, and the problems of operating undercarriage-less aircraft on the rubber-mat flight decks the Royal Navy had been developing since World War II. In each case, the angled landing zone offered a number of advantages, a U.S. commentator noting that the U.S. Navy had had no interest in the rubber-mat flight deck until the advent of the angled (or canted) configuration. The first tests were performed aboard the British light fleet carrier *Triumph*, which had a 10° angled landing path painted on for touch-and-go landings. Similar tests followed aboard the USS *Midway*, but in both cases the arresting gear and barriers remained oriented to the original axial deck. However, between September and December 1952 the unmodernized fleet carrier *Antietam* had a rudimentary sponson installed for true angled-deck tests, which soon proved superior.

By that time BuShips was already aware both of the opportunity and of the costs it might incur. In January 1953 the bureau proposed to the CNO a carrier for FY 55 with a canted deck and fixed island. Since new carriers were then being authorized on an annual basis, that would have meant the construction of three carriers of an obsolescent design, and on 4 May 1953 the CNO directed the entire *Forrestal* class to be fitted with the new angled deck. Although the Commander, Air Force, Atlantic Fleet immediately proposed a full island with uptakes, BuShips worked out both flush-deck and conventional island

designs. The problem was urgent, because Newport News was then at a stage of construction permitting rearrangement (such as relocation of elevators) with little or no delay, and at a cost of only $2 million—which, it was later estimated, was recovered by elimination of the complex retractable island. Modified characteristics incorporating the angled flight deck were issued on 7 October 1953, by which time a new arrangement (scheme 34) had been selected.

The rearrangement was considerable. For example, the formation of a parking space on the starboard side increased the importance of the starboard elevators, and the after port elevator was moved to that side, leaving only a single elevator to port, at the forward end of the big port sponson. The after centerline elevator, of little value in the first place during simultaneous landing and takeoff operations, was omitted in favor of a third starboard elevator. The original flush-deck design showed in some of the flight-deck arrangements, since it was impossible to dispense entirely with internal structures associated with elevators, bomb elevators, and control spaces. Thus the island structure was located approximately amidships, with one elevator forward and two abaft it, although most of the triangular parking space was forward.

The forward port heavy steam catapult (C 7) was moved forward 20 feet to allow for the relocation of the port elevator forward (to clear the landing zone), and the starboard fighter catapult (C 11) was relocated to port on the sponson, where it could no longer fire at the same time as the other catapult there. It

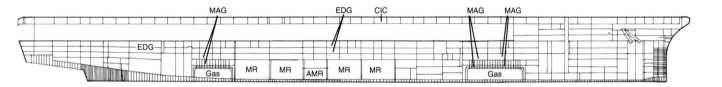

The *Forrestal*'s inboard profile as built.

was impossible to overcome this limitation, given the use of the flight deck as strength deck. That is, the catapults could not be installed with very great angles to the centerline of the carrier without considerably weakening the strength deck.

Although the ship retained massive sponsons on both sides, their shapes were considerably different than in the original flush-deck design. For example, the starboard sponson was changed from a simple sponson-type structure to a cantilever including the flight and gallery decks, except in way of the island, where it was carried down to the deck below the hangar deck.

At the same time the originally planned powder-driven catapults (C 7 and the lighter C 10) were replaced by British-designed steam catapults, a new version of the heavy C 7 and a new C 11, the latter actually the British BXS-1 which had first been tested aboard a repair carrier, HMS *Perseus*, in August 1950. It was tested in U.S. waters, powered by higher-pressure steam from the destroyer *Greene*, between December 1951 and February 1952. The success of the steam catapult was particularly fortunate for the U.S. carrier program, since the explosive slotted-cylinder types were encountering considerable development problems. One consequence of the change was the elimination of 400 tons of catapult charges. On the other hand, since the catapults bled steam from the boilers, protracted launch operations were sure to reduce maximum speed, and there was "a large increase in the requirement for make up feed [water] because of the contamination and subsequent loss of steam used in the catapults."

Internally, the number of hangar bays was reduced from four to three more nearly equal ones, each served by at least one deck-edge elevator, so that elevator service on the starboard side would suffice to support the normal recovery rate during landing op-

erations. The new arrangement also allowed additional hangar-deck parking space. There were subtler improvements as well. For example, the angled deck required fewer arresting-gear pendants, hence fewer arresting-gear engines and less internal space. The simplification of uptakes and the removal of some electronic spaces from gallery deck to island structure also saved space, so that more berthing space became available; a January 1954 design review claimed that a 28 percent increase in complement could be accommodated without dropping below the minimum standards then accepted.

There were also detail changes. The 5-in gun sponsons were lowered one deck to provide adequate space for ammunition hoists; the guns themselves remained at the same level. Consequently, the forward pair of sponsons thew up so much spray in heavy weather that they contributed considerably to reduced speed under such circumstances. Aviation ordnance requirements were set at 1,660 tons plus 165 tons of nuclear weapons, the original design allowing for about 2,000 tons of ordnance including the catapult charges. Between 1951 and 1954 requirements for bombs were little changed, but an expectation of increasing reliance on missiles for carrier and fleet air defense showed in a quadrupling of the Sparrow missile allowance, while 20-mm ammunition was halved and unguided rocket loads (FFAR and HPAG) were reduced by about 30 percent.

The *Forrestal* was built on an urgent basis, and her machinery design was limited in steam conditions (to the wartime figures of 600 psi and 850° of superheat) in order to conserve critical materials. In consequence, she was limited to 260,000 SHP. When the expected shortages did not materialize, later ships in the class were designed for the standard postwar conditions of 1,200 pounds and 950°, for 280,000 SHP, at a slight increase in machinery weight and a con-

Still in her original configuration, the *Saratoga* rides at anchor off Yorktown during the International Naval Review, 12 June 1957. The booms sloping down from the fore end of her flight deck are "bridle catchers," used to recover the wire bridles that hold an airplane to the catapult during launching. The portholes between them indicate the emergency or secondary conn forward, a feature common to all U.S. carriers of this period. Note, too, the small sponson for a Mark 56 director forward of the two visible 5-in/54 guns. The radar dish on the forward gun house was part of a Gunar, a director placed entirely on the mount.

siderable improvement in the rate of fuel expenditure. The steam catapults were, however, designed for the *Forrestal*'s conditions, and BuAer was unwilling to redesign them. Later carriers benefitted from a provision for 1,200 psi.

An important incidental benefit of the new design was improvement of electronic performance, due simply to the relocation of radar and radio antennas to much better positions higher in the ship. The large island accommodated a large height finder (SPS-8) atop a pedestal, plus a massive pole radar mast carrying an SPS-12 for air search, an SPN-6 for air-traffic control, and a TACAN aircraft beacon at its top. A second large pole mast carried ECM antennas. Both could fold down for passage under the Brooklyn Bridge, at the time a major requirement for U.S. warships. An SPN-8 for precision aircraft control (CCA) occupied a position at the after end of the island.

Four ships were built to the basic *Forrestal* design, although as early as 1952 alternative designs were being considered. The last two, the *Ranger* and *Independence*, had heavy C 7 catapults in place of their waist C 11s. This improvement was proposed by BuAer as part of a new carrier design program in 1954, and then applied to the FY 54 and FY 55 *Forrestal*s. All but the *Ranger* had their forward 5-in sponsons removed in the late sixties: high speed in rough weather was far more important than carrier guns for self-defense, particularly since the guns were already of limited value against fast aircraft. Ultimately the remaining quartet of guns were all replaced by Sea Sparrow point defense missiles. The *Enterprise* was the first ship fitted, but the *Forrestal* had her guns removed after they were burned out in a major fire in 1967, one basic point defense missile system launcher being fitted forward on the starboard side. Two launchers were fitted to the *Independence* in 1973, the *Saratoga* in 1974, and the *Forrestal* in 1976. The *Ranger* was initially fitted with the improved point defense missile system, retaining her last two 5-in/54 guns until 1977. By 1981 the *Independence* also had the improved system, and the other pair was scheduled to receive it.

By the late seventies even the *Forrestal*s were badly overcrowded. They were, moreover, beginning to show the effects of continuous hard service, and it was clear that replacements were not in sight. Just as in the case of the World War II–built units still in active service in the late fifties, the navy began to

Steaming off the Virginia Capes on 23 April 1965, the *Forrestal* shows several standard modifications. Her forward gun sponson has been removed, although her hull is by no means entirely free of spray-producing projections. Like the wartime carriers, she has begun to sprout extra antennas, most prominently a big lattice mast for a long-range air search radar, an SPS-43A. Note the heavy pole mast, well abaft the island, downward on its hinges for flight operations. Multicolored hoses amidships are used to fuel escorts; from the early fifties onward, a proportion of the fuel load of U.S. carriers was reserved for the escort ships, to permit the force as a whole to make high-speed transits. Jet-blast deflectors have been raised behind the two Crusader fighters on the forward catapults. Another Crusader waits on the forward starboard unit, and three Skywarriors are parked aft.

consider a reconstruction program, this time called SLEP (Service Life Extension Program). Much of the work is simple rehabilitation; for example, half the fire mains are to be replaced, 30 percent of the plumbing, and all of the oil-fuel transfer piping. Main and auxiliary machinery is to be reconditioned, and much of the plating will be replaced. Modernization will include the installation of three improved point defense missile systems (NATO Sea Sparrow) and three Vulcan-Phalanx close-in weapon systems, as well as new search radars (SPS-48C and SPS-49), an improved ASW tactical support center (TSC), and lesser improvements such as an additional weapons elevator. Catapults and arresting gear will also be modernized. For example, reportedly only four rather than the previous six boilers will be required for air operations, since the steam will be used more efficiently. After a bitter fight over which yard would carry out the refits, Philadelphia Naval Shipyard was selected by Vice President Mondale in 1976. The *Saratoga* is the first ship to undergo modernization, having entered the yard on 1 October 1980, for completion scheduled on 1 February 1983, at a reported cost of about $500 million—far more than her original price, but in grossly inflated dollars. She will be suc-

ceeded by the *Forrestal, Independence,* and *Ranger.* In 1982 the navy claims that SLEP will add fifteen years to a nominal thirty-year carrier lifetime. (Note that forty-five years exceeds the lifetime of the longest serving battleship of the first half of this century, the USS *Arkansas,* 1912–46.)

Given the almost ad hoc nature of the *Forrestal* design, it was natural that more deliberate alternatives would be explored. Late in 1952 BuShips reported to the Secretary of the Navy that "the appropriate place for CVA redesign appears to be the CVA included in the 1955 building program [i.e., CVA 62], since the need for the prompt construction of the 1954 CVA outweighs the delays inherent in a redesign." Looming over any such project was the prospect of nuclear power, the advent of which would require a new carrier design. In 1953 it was expected that nuclear power would become practical for either a late-design FY 57 or an FY 58 carrier. The latter date proved to be the correct one.

Most of the preliminary design of 1953 and 1954 was concerned with carrier size and improvements in aviation features. Size has been the most persistent theme in postwar U.S. carrier development: as carrier size increases, pressures to halt and reverse the trend grow. For example, the 1945 fleet carrier was partly an attempt to overcome the growth represented by the *Midway*; the *Forrestal* itself was a (congressionally mandated) reaction to the size and cost of the *United States*; the nuclear carrier designs of the late fifties (see chapter 16) were reactions to the size of the *Enterprise*; and the abortive CVV of the late seventies was a reaction to the cost of the *Nimitz*. Growth has actually been relentless, and constant pressure has been exerted to determine its sources and justification. Once continued carrier construction had been assured, BuShips could reasonably examine a range of carrier designs. In so doing it made clear the fundamental trade-offs under which it had to work.

By 1953 the design of the *Forrestal* appeared to lie within the range of possible attack carriers, the minimum being represented by the *Midway* modernization design (SCB 110) and the maximum by a ship providing *Forrestal*-like aviation facilities for a future 100,000-lb attack bomber (rather than the 70,000-lb airplane for which the *Forrestal* had been designed). The surviving documents suggest that BuShips initiated its own study of the range of carrier-size alternatives, ranging from a new ASW carrier through CVA 3/53, a minimum-size carrier for the 100,000-lb airplane (CVA 10/53), and a large carrier for large aircraft. Thus on 12 December 1952 Captain P.W. Snyder (Code 410) instructed the preliminary designers to "include in your present CVA studies a study to see how *small* you can make this ship—not bigger than 45,000 tons standard and probably smaller without serious loss in aviation capabilities. The projected CVA-41 (*Midway*) class conversion . . . will give you some guidance as to what can be done."

The *Midway*-size attack carrier, CVA 3/53, appears to have been inspired directly by the success of the modernization project. However, the carrier designers were operating under a new set of assumptions. Since their carrier would be scaled down from a *Forrestal*, she would have the enclosed hangar and deep hull of the newer carrier, with much greater freeboard than the earlier carrier (for dryness and also for greater clear hangar height). Greater freeboard in turn would add top weight, which would have to be compensated by greater beam. On a fixed displacement (chosen as a means of keeping down size), greater beam would imply lesser length. Aircraft capacity on both hangar and flight decks was much more a function of length than of deck area, so the CVA 3/53 design had to suffer by comparison with SCB 110. Moreover, the new angled flight deck with its massive sponsons in itself was a source of great top weight, and any carrier designed from the first to incorporate that weight would have greater beam than the *Midway*, designed under no such conditions.

Although first preliminary characteristics of 1 April 1953 called for a ship "to take the place of the *Midway* class while incorporating protection and design features comparable to those of the *Forrestal* class," the design study showed that no such result could be achieved on the displacement for which the *Midway* had originally been designed, 45,000 tons; in any case, by 1952 the *Midway*s were rated at 49,000 tons. Speed and endurance were to match those of the larger ship, as was the defensive battery (although 3-in/70 guns were considered an acceptable alternative to the 5-in/54s). The great consumers of internal carrier volume, and hence the features driving up carrier size so much, were underwater protection, protected aviation-fuel stowage, aviation magazines, and clear hangar height; some reductions in all were to be permitted. For example, the hangar would be only one foot higher than that of the *Midway* (18 feet 6 inches versus 25 feet for the *Forrestal*; ultimately, however, 23 feet had to be accepted). Gasoline stowage was set at the 500,000 gallons of the 1945 fleet carrier, about midway between the 355,600 gallons of the *Midway* and the 750,000 of the *Forrestal*.

Deck configuration presented problems, since a large deck angle would make for too large an overhang. One solution was to bend the deck twice, to use a greater angle for the landing area than for the area of the waist catapult. All three elevators, one per hangar bay, would have to be on the starboard side, but that would make the carrier relatively vulnerable to damage on that side. Aircraft capacity was measured by the number of heavy A3D bombers: thirty-two of them for the *Forrestal*, twenty-nine for the *Midway*, and only twenty-four for CVA 3/53.

As in some of the earlier carrier designs, propulsion was a problem, since there were only two plants available in the power range required: the 212,000 SHP of the *Iowa* and *Midway* (which could be boosted to 225,000 SHP using higher steam conditions) and the 280,000 SHP of the later *Forrestal*s. Anything intermediate would call for a new design, with all of its costs and risks. The CVA 3/53 studies incorporated the lower-powered plant in a hull intermediate in length between that of the *Essex* and *Midway*. For example, a first cut of 31 March 1953 showed a 900- by 124-ft, 49,195-ton ship with a 19-ft 2-in hangar, a 7.25° deck, and a sustained sea speed of 30.8 knots. On a smaller hull (850 by 119 feet), with protection reduced even below that of the *Forrestal* (which was already well below that of the *Midway*), a 23-ft hangar could be fit. However, the shorter hull could not accommodate as many aircraft.

These designs did not quite meet operational demands. For example, BuAer considered a 10° deck essential, although ultimately the best that could be done was a 9° one, in view of the overhang problem.

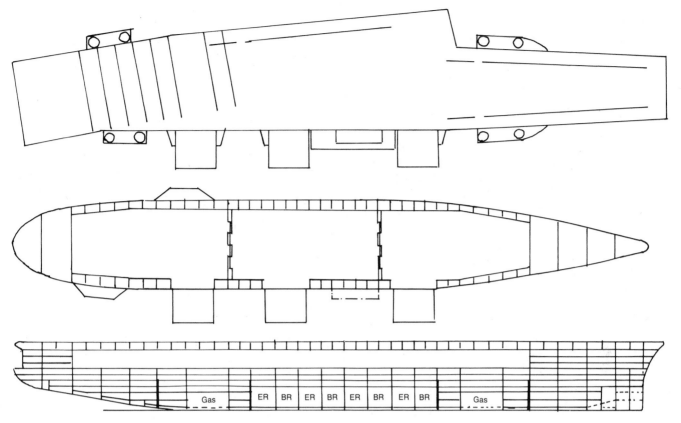

CVA 3/53 design.

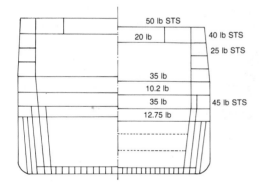

Comparison of the *Forrestal*'s (left) and CVA 3/53's midship sections.

On the other hand, there was more than enough volume for aviation ordnance; BuShips considered 1,400 tons (the *Midway* 1,376 tons) sufficient, but CVA 3/53 would accommodate 1,565, compared with 2,087 for the *Forrestal* as designed in 1953. Actual ordnance weights critically depended on bomb shapes, so that World War II–type bombs could be carried in far greater numbers than could the postwar low-drag types. Finally, BuShips analysis showed that flight-deck arrangements required a waterline length of at least 900 feet, which meant more problems.

By the end of June 1953, BuShips was describing CVA 3/53 as a 44,500-ton ship with a battery of ten 3-in/70 guns (twin mounts), costing $170 million,

compared with $215 million for a repeat *Forrestal*. It had to admit that the new carrier would hardly be a *Midway* equivalent.

These two designs have different degrees of protection. Another difference between these two designs is reflected in the number of aircraft which can be parked on their flight decks. Being longer, the CVA-41 Class conversion has more total flight deck area. It also has less area set aside for landing. If the canted landing strip of the CVA-41 were increased to a width of 112 feet, it would only have room to park 25 A3D's instead of 29 as shown in the tabulation.

The bomb protection and torpedo defense system scantlings on the CVA 3/53 have been reduced to about seventy percent of what was used on the

The *Ranger* steams through Hampton Roads shortly after her completion, on 22 July 1957. She differed in detail from the two earlier CVAs. Note, for example, that there was no notch at her stern, the flight deck and after bulkhead continuing directly into her transom. The two radio masts of the earlier ships were eliminated, as was the ECM mainmast. There were also differences in the form of the forward gun sponsons. However, the most important operational change, the substitution of a C 7 for the two C 11 catapults, is not visible here.

The *Ranger* is shown after a refit at San Francisco, on 10 February 1964. Her 5-in sponsons differed in shape from those of the *Forrestal* and the *Saratoga* and were retained after the guns were removed. The lowered deck-edge elevator shows just how close to the waterline the hangar deck was, partly because of the requirement for a great clear hangar height. The big dish antenna on the island is an SPS-30, successor to the SPS-8 series of height finders.

CVA-59. To maintain the protection standards of the CVA-59 would increase the Standard Displacement by about 2,000 tons. Thus the CVA-3/53 has about three-fourths of the aviation capabilities of the CVA-59 and about three-fourths of the Standard Displacement of the CVA-59.

The next step was a minimum carrier adapted for better aviation features. Work began in the fall of 1953 on a modified variant of CVA 3/53, designated CVA 10/53,

> the smallest successful carrier [which] would be able to launch the same air attack as the CVA 59 class. We also assumed it would have to endure the same landing loads and catapult the same weight aircraft. . . . on about the same displacement [62,300 tons full load] as the *Midway* [it] can mount the same attack as the *Forrestal* but with 15 fewer spare planes available for replacement usage [this presumably reflects re-

duced hangar volume]. . . . This ship has the same protection as the *Forrestal* [as opposed to two-thirds the protection in CVA 3/53]. It carries 67% of the aircraft ammunition of the *Forrestal*. Its gasoline capacity is a little less than half that of the *Forrestal*. HEAF capacities are more nearly equal—i.e., about 80% that of the *Forrestal*.

The underlying reason for pressure for increased aircraft carrier size is well illustrated by [the] history of growth of aircraft weight and size. Note the weight of the AJ and the A3D aircraft—the large atomic bomb carriers. It seems natural to expect, with the development of smaller atomic bombs, a concomitant reduction in the sizes and weights of the carrying planes. According to our colleagues in BuAer, however, the end of plane growth is not yet in sight. Actually, under the impetus of continued expansion in the use of jet aircraft, further weight increases in new aircraft designs seem inevitable in order to satisfy the needs for higher performance, adequate range, and greater useful military loads.

The transition from propeller to jet propulsion which naval aircraft are undergoing has likewise thrown the design of aircraft carriers into a transition stage. Some of the results of this transition, canted decks and steam catapults, are, of course, already with us. Another change less apparent, but still fundamental, is the shift in the aeronautical factor that exerts the predominant influence on the size of aircraft carriers. Up to and including *Midway* Class, it was possible to make the generalization that the number of aircraft to be carried and operated from an aircraft carrier was the most important aeronautical feature affecting the size of the ship. This was still true to a certain extent on *Forrestal* but, for any new designs taken in hand now, we can foresee a definite change. Individual airplane performance, specifically maximum airborne speed, has begun to control flight deck lengths and, through this dimension, the size of the aircraft carrier.

This follows because, in current and probably future designs of jet aircraft, there is a direct relationship between maximum airborne speed and landing and launching speeds. Since there are reasonably definite limits to the acceleration and deceleration that pilots and planes can assimilate, high take-off speeds demand longer and more powerful catapults while high landing speeds demand greater run-out lengths even with arresting gear of higher energy absorption capabilities.

The influence of landing and launching aircraft speeds is so pronounced that it is possible to evolve a rough formula for minimum required flight deck length. . . .

When we fix flight deck length, we also fix, within relatively minor limits, the length of the hull of the aircraft carrier required to support this flight deck. With these two dimensions and the related factor of flight deck strength determined, the size of the actual ship begins to take shape. We still have some freedom of action in determining such variables as ship speed, cruising radius, ship protection (including deck and above water side protection against bombs, underwater side protection against torpedoes and offensive armament) and capacity for useful load, such as aircraft fuel, aircraft ammunition and airborne guided missiles.

It is interesting to note that the variables of ship speed and cruising radius have remained practically constant for the last 20 years. Variations in aircraft carrier size stemming from other than aeronautical features have been primarily based on the desire to get tougher and better protected carriers.

In order to see what can be done in the way of getting a smaller attack carrier it is, of course, necessary to decide on the largest aircraft for which to design this carrier. After consultation with BuAer, it was agreed to use the same plane, A3D, the controlled *Forrestal*'s design since the use of foreseeable smaller planes would severely restrict the combat radius of the carrier's attack group.

To get a smaller ship, we have taken full advantage of the canted deck principle and cut flight deck length to the bone. Then, to push the ship as close as possible to a feasible minimum size, we have reduced certain other attributes of *Forrestal*, finally reaching a carrier [CVA 10/53] of about *Midway*'s size. . . .

Other possible combinations of ship characteristics could have been chosen and, within certain limits, would be equally feasible. For example, ship speed could have been reduced further to get more useful load like avgas or more guns. Horizontal protection could be skimmed in favor of other loads or a slight increase in speed. Because of the dangers of listing from unsymmetrical flooding, stability considerations make further reduction in side torpedo protection unprofitable short of its complete elimination.

Minimum flight deck length requirements for the A3D preclude further appreciable ship size reduction unless we are willing to accept the operational restriction of only operating this plane with a certain minimum wind speed over the flight deck. This is equivalent to an equal reduction in landing and launching speeds. . . . such a reduction in turn, permits a shorter flight deck length, reduced ship length and consequently displacement (although the resulting volume reduction may curtail other aeronautical capabilities unacceptably—a good example of the circularity of ship designs).

Part of the BuShips analysis of the CVA 3/53 exercise was a demand for at least 60-lb flight-deck protection rather than the 55-lb actually provided. CVA 10/53 restored the 60-lb flight deck, but that added top weight; beam had to be increased to 124 feet. On a fixed displacement, this in turn meant a shorter hull (844 feet) and lower speed at fixed power. Now 212,000 SHP achieved a trial speed of 30.7 knots and a sustained speed of 28.6, both short of the 32/30-kt requirements originally imposed on CVA 3/53.

The other end of the spectrum was the carrier of the future, designated CVA 100,000 pounds, to operate aircraft that BuAer expected would weigh about 100,000 pounds and take off at about 175 knots.

The Ships Installation Division of BuAer did their best to predict what sort of a carrier they would require in the mid-1960's. BuAer is afflicted with the same problem of weight growth as Ships, only to a much greater degree. A few examples to indicate this growth are:

	Originally Built	*Today*
AD	about 14,000 lbs	25,000
F9F	12,000	21,000
A3D	68,000 (as conceived)	78,000 (and the first not yet complete)

The [A3D] will probably grow to 100,000 lbs. You will also note the tendency towards larger planes, the end of which is not in sight. . . .

The combination of heavier planes and higher launching speeds poses a tough problem to the catapult designer. We have progressed over the years to

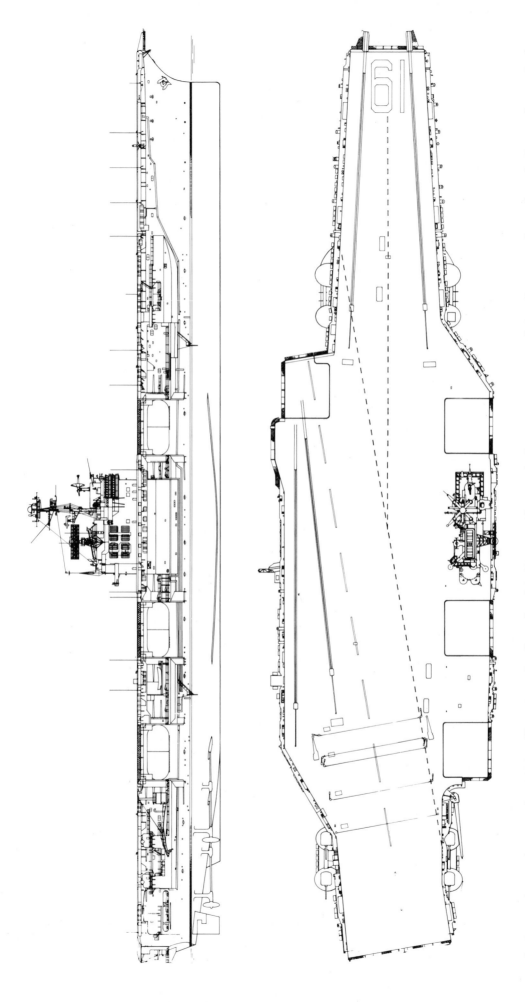

The *Ranger* (CVA 61), November 1973, still retaining her four after 5-in/54 guns. She was the last active carrier with 5-in/54 guns and was the only *Forrestal* to retain the forward sponsons. Radars were the SPS-10B, SPS-30, SPS-37A, SPN-42, SPN-43. TACAN was URN-20. She had two Mark 56 mod 16 fire control systems atop the island, port and starboard. As completed she had, in addition, two Mark 69 and four GUNAR (on-mount) systems. The Mark 56s on the sponsons were removed, and two Mark 56s replaced the unsatisfactory Mark 69 on the island. Plans to replace them in turn with the more capable (and heavier) Mark 68 were abandoned.

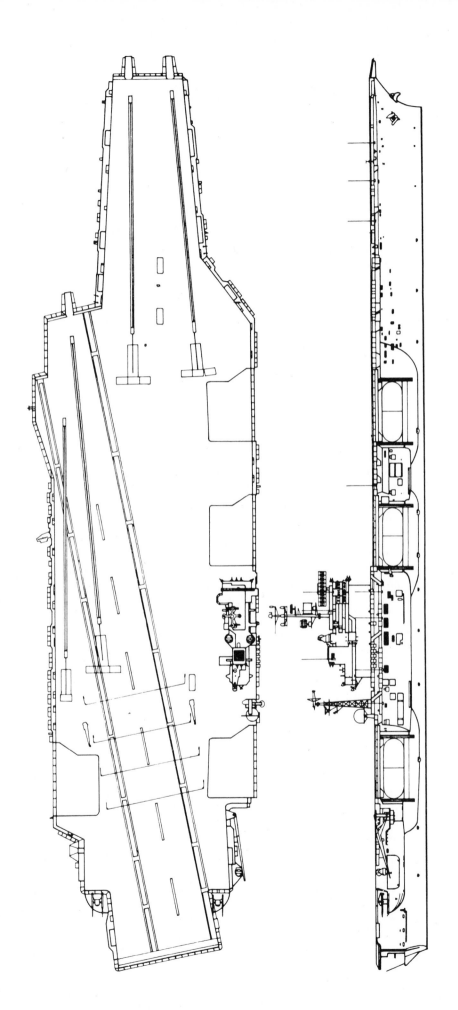

The *America* (CV 66), 1973, showing Terrier launchers on her quarters.

the C-7 catapult designed to launch about a 70,000 lb plane at a speed of about 125 knots. This catapult weighs about 346 tons. To launch the plane of the future, 100,000 lbs and 175 kts, will require a catapult estimated to weigh about 650 tons.

Along with the evolution of the catapult we have had a commensurate need for growth in arresting gear. At present we do not know how many G's a human being can stand. Recently 5 G's has been used as a criterion. [With fixed deceleration, higher landing speeds require] arresting gear of higher and higher energy absorbing powers. . . . we do not have estimates on sizes of arresting gear that would be needed for the plane of the future. However, they would be in the same order of increase shown in the catapult comparison.

. . . the minimum size ship [to carry the plane of the future] would carry the same number of planes as the *Forrestal*. Its tonnage and protection would also be the same. It would have two catapults vs. four on the *Forrestal*. Its speed would be somewhat less. Thus we have an object lesson in what penalties we have to pay when we go to larger aircraft. To obtain the same plane handling speeds as *Forrestal* we'd probably have to go to a ship about 1400 feet in length. . . .

A later sketch for a minimum carrier CVA 196 (?) with 150–65-kt (70,000-lb) planes of the sixties shows a ship of a full-load displacement of 80,000 tons (CVA 59 of 76,000 tons), with three 300-ft catapults (two forward, only one on the port sponson). The length of the single-waist catapult would preclude installation of a *Forrestal*-type portside elevator. A carrier for 100,000-lb aircraft required similar catapults—and 86,000 tons. In each case the air-group size was given in numbers of A3D heavy-attack planes: twenty-five for the *Forrestal*, twenty-three for CVA 10/53, twenty-five for the CVA 196(?) ship with 70,000-lb aircraft, and twenty-five also for the carrier to operate 100,000-lb aircraft. Both of the big-carrier projects incorporated avgas and aviation munitions capacities equal to those of the *Forrestal*, but their deck-edge elevators were larger (53 by 70 versus 52 by 63 feet). CVA 196(?) benefitted from a slight increase in length (995 feet versus 990) to achieve 33.6 knots; CVA 100,000 pounds required 295,000 SHP to make her 33.3 knots even on a length of 1,000 feet.

The net effect on the studies was to show that, although a smaller carrier might be built to operate 1953–60 aircraft, that would be to economize for little reason, since inevitable growth processes would soon make it obsolescent. Better to keep the *Forrestal* or some equivalent design and refit carriers to take the heavier aircraft that would surely appear.

The 100,000-lb aircraft carrier was an immediate rather than a long-term program, as weight growth in the principal attack airplane, the A3D, had already eaten away the margins built into CVA 59 for launching and arresting such aircraft under low-wind con-

dition. In connection with the design of the then-planned CVAs 62 and 63, Code 440 asked (20 January 1954) for a 100,000-lb, 150–75-kt carrier, which became CVA 1/54. Attention now shifted from overall design to ship features specifically intended for aircraft operation, not least to minimize the design effort involved. After all, CVA 62 was the FY 55 carrier. The proposed improvements were to
—Substitute new and more powerful arresting gear.
—Crowd no. 3 and 4 catapults into the port sponson, a poor arrangement but the best that could be made on a ship with a fixed island whose flight deck was also a strength deck. "The situation can be improved in the new design by fitting a new strength deck 4 ft. below the present flight deck which would then become a superstructure deck. The deck heights of hangar and gallery would each be reduced by about 2 ft. thus maintaining about the same ship depth. This type of construction would permit slotting the flight deck transversely to ensure a better arrangement for waist catapults [that is, a greater separation at the loading ends so that both could be loaded simultaneously. One would have to fire at an angle across the other, otherwise it would interfere with the two forward catapults]. . . . the inability to transversely slot the flight deck on CVA 59 class is its most serious shortcoming." As weight compensation one of the elevators might be eliminated.
—Balance the armored box again to move 60 percent of avgas and munitions forward (except SPARROW air-to-air missiles, which would be 60 percent aft). This jibed with a concept of flight operations in which the heavy-attack aircraft would fly predominantly off the forward catapults, the SPARROW-armed fighters off the waist catapults. An additional upper-stage bomb elevator aft was recommended.
—Eliminate the tumble-home and the centerline rudder of CVA 59.

Given the short time available, not all of the proposed improvements were practicable. The flight-deck structure required a wholly new design, which Code 440 admitted could not be prepared in time for the customary early contract award (CVA 62, FY 55); however, overriding priority in the bureaus and in OPNAV would make it possible to award a contract late in FY 55. As a fallback, the armored box could be balanced again and aluminum substituted for steel in the elevators for greater capacity. CVA 62 plans modified to this extent could also apply to the FY 54 carrier, CVA 61.

In fact, that is what happened, except that both FY 54 and 55 carriers received more powerful waist catapults. Some of the features of the CVA 1/54 design were applied to the FY 56 and 57 carriers (SCB 127, the *Kitty Hawk* class) and to the FY 58 *Enterprise*.

However, the proposed flight-deck structure proved a design disaster and never materialized. Among other defects, it would have reduced clear hangar height to 23 feet (which BuAer rejected), eliminated protection of the important spaces housed in the gallery deck, and been extremely difficult to maintain. The flight deck would also have added displacement to ships already at the upper limit of acceptability.

The new design was started on 25 January 1954. She would match the *Forrestal* in armament, protection (except as modified by flight-deck construction), speed (33 rather than 32 knots because CVA 60 was expected to make the former), and endurance. Aviation fuel capacity was set at 750,000 gallons of gasoline, of which 50,000 were reserved for helicopters and vehicles. The other 700,000 were to be blended with HEAF, raising the ratio to 3:1, so that the ship would carry 2.1 million gallons of the latter. A modified version of the existing C 7 catapult was needed to launch the 100,000-lb airplane at 150 knots (which with 25 knots wind-over-deck generated by the ship herself would give the required 175 knots). Unlike the *Forrestal*, CVA 1/54 would have four of the 250–75-ft C 7s, a feature later applied to the last two *Forrestal*s.

Off New York City on 3 July 1976, the *Forrestal* displays many of the modifications made to her class. Sponsons extending from her port flight-deck sponson carry the antennas of a deceptive ECM system as well as her mirror landing aid. A box launcher on her port quarter carries Sea Sparrow (BPDMS) short-range defensive missiles, and the small launching tubes visible on her quarterdeck are for chaff rockets. In combination, the deception system and the rockets were intended to drive Soviet-type cruise missiles off course; now their successors are being supplemented by the Phalanx close-in weapon system, a Gatling gun. The small cylinders ranged along the edges of the flight deck replace the earlier life raft; when these capsules hit the water, they break open and a raft inflates. The island shows an ECM array sponsored outboard and, well below it, a chaff launcher. Most of the antennas facing aft are part of the CCA system: an SPN-43 (replacing an SPN-6) near the top of the mast, then the big radome of an SPN-35, flanked by the two dishes of an SPN-42. The smaller dish is an airspeed indicator, an SPN-12. Above the SPN-35 is a "pri-fly," and the small square antenna above that is a satellite communication link, a WSC-1.

The elevators would be larger (80 by 52 feet) and two rather than one would be located forward of the island structure "to provide high rate of plane handling during recovery operations. . . . [Increasing] the length of the platform to 80 or 90 feet [would] provide for the trend in aircraft design to higher slenderness ratios." In February BuAer and Op-55 proposed a new elevator arrangement.

Two elevators forward of the island, which are not in the landing area, are considered necessary to accommodate an increased tempo in landing operations anticipated with all jet operations. Relocation of the port deck edge elevator to a position aft of the waist catapults will make this elevator usable during all launching operations. In addition, the port elevator, in its present location on CVA 59, is opposite the forward starboard elevator which will produce interferences in aircraft handling and spotting in the forward bay of the hangar deck.

The studies suggested that CVA 1/54 would be a very large ship, and limits on her dimensions were worked out. Length was limited by dry dock no. 4 at Pearl Harbor for a maximum waterline length of 1,080 feet. Beam was limited to about 134 feet by the size of building docks in the United States. Draft was set at 36 feet, the draft of a fully loaded *Iowa*-class battleship. An important issue was the depth of water a carrier, badly damaged but still afloat, would draw relative to the repair yards on both coasts.

The final studies for the new carrier, designated CVA 3/54, showed how expensive the new flight deck and a proposed increase in machinery subdivision could be: displacement rose to 62,690 tons light (79,940 fully loaded), compared with 55,510 (72,450) for CVA 61, the *Ranger*; waterline length would be 1,030 (rather than 990) feet, and 300,000 SHP would be required to maintain the 33.6 knots of the earlier carrier. Cost would be $224 million, compared with $200 million for the repeat *Forrestal*. More importantly, eighteen months would be required for the completion of the contract plans. The SCB was not enthusiastic about further carrier growth.

Indeed, the board soon reacted by sponsoring yet another attempt to prune back carrier size. As of August 1954 it was, in fact, willing to accept the elimination of one of the usual four catapults. The remaining three would, however, all be the heavy C 7 type. Elevators were to be enlarged from the former 63 by 52 feet to 70 by 52 feet, still far short of what had been hoped for earlier in the year, and capacity would rise only to 80,000 rather than to 100,000 pounds. Once more, in hopes of reducing carrier size, one elevator would be eliminated; it was argued that a single elevator could lift two fighters at once.

The basic issue was flight-deck size, determined by the characteristics of the A3D; in addition, the new

ship was to accommodate about 75 percent of the *Forrestal* allowances of aircraft, aviation fuel, and ammunition. A net landing length of 525 feet, 50 feet less than a *Forrestal*'s, was set by three distances: ramp to first wire (that is, glide angle) 150 feet, first to last wire 275 feet, and maximum wire run-out 250 feet. Allowances for the length of the airplane and for towing off the landing strip added 150 more feet. The strip would be 120 feet wide (between sheaves of the arresting gear). Similarly, the launching area was defined by the power stroke of the catapult (250 feet), the distance from catapult end to deck edge (20 feet), and the holdback structure, for an overall length of 352 feet plus another 50 for positioning gear and blast deflectors.

It did not matter how many aircraft were to be accommodated: the flight deck had to be at least 877 feet long, counting the angle of the deck and keeping the fore end of the landing strip clear of the catapult area, so that aircraft could be removed from the strip after they had been stopped. More realistically, another 150 feet had to be allowed for taxiing, for a total of 1,027 feet, which might be shaved to 1,000 by careful tapering of the inboard side of the landing strip. That length in turn determined a hull length of 940 feet, since an overhang of more than about 60 feet was unacceptable; indeed, 40 feet was a preferred figure. Again, this was a minimum: a 940-ft hull might well have insufficient internal volume.

Even hull depth was determined by aircraft operating considerations, in this case by the need for dryness in rough weather.

Freeboard to the flight deck should be about 6% of waterline length or 56.4 feet, and draft should be about 35 feet. Thus, the depth to flight deck would become about 91.4 feet. This, however, must be tempered by actual deck heights, of which the hangar deck is most important. If the clear hangar height can be reduced some 4 feet from the presently required 25 (and there are some indications that it can), the depth of flight deck can be reduced from 97 to 93 feet. This figure will be used.

In a further effort to decrease size, one layer of the underwater side protection will be eliminated with a consequent reduction in beam.

Weight savings would be substantial: 50 tons for every foot of length, 250 for every foot of beam, 230 for every foot of hull depth, as well as the weight of the torpedo bulkhead itself, and one elevator and one catapult. However, each elevator and each catapult would weigh more. Savings added up to about 7,000 tons, for a full-load displacement of about 64,000 tons.

The proposed new flight-deck structure presented so many problems that even the aviators ultimately had to give up on it, although it persisted through 1954.

CVA 5/54 became SCB 127, an umbrella designation for the FY 56 carrier design which became CVA 63, the *Kitty Hawk*. Characteristics drawn in October 1954 showed both the new flight deck and reduced loads, although aviation ordnance was set at 1,800 tons, little short of the full *Forrestal* figure. A 960-ft hull (130-ft beam, 97-ft depth) was to be driven by 220,000-SHP engines, for a trial speed of 32 knots (rather than 33.6 in a *Forrestal* with 60,000 more SHP), and avgas stowage was limited to 675,000 gallons, up from the 500,000 originally contemplated. There would be only three catapults and three elevators, and aircraft weight would be about 10 percent less than in a *Forrestal*.

These reductions were significant, but they were soon abandoned. Thus the tentative SCB 127 characteristics were soon revised upward, to include a fourth elevator (port side aft) and a fourth C 7 catapult. Emphasis was to be placed on improved flexibility in air operations for simultaneous launch and recovery. The catapults were to permit a launch on one while an adjacent one was occupied, both aircraft having a 75-ft wing span (compared with 72.5 feet for the A3D). A reduction in air group was acceptable to buy an improved layout as well as a substantial reduction in carrier cost and size. However, four elevators and four big catapults required something quite close to a *Forrestal*; a sketch design showed a length of 975 feet and a displacement of 57,000 tons (72,250 fully loaded), even taking into account reduced power and reduced loads, such as 1,700 tons of aviation ordnance. Op-05 sought the aviation features already attained in the *Forrestal*s, and was willing only to sacrifice self-defense weapons to cut cost and size.

Preliminary Design observed that, although the new design would be substantially less expensive to build than CVA 62, the need for new plans would increase net cost to roughly that of the earlier and larger ship. Similarly, building time would be comparable—but the new carrier would be delayed by the need for new plans and new types of components. Consequently, if the nuclear carrier were really so close to actualization that no more than one or two more conventional carriers would be built, it appeared "uneconomical in money, time, and manpower to build a ship with reduced overall performance characteristics merely to obtain phantom benefits of unrestricted land-launch capabilities."

By the end of 1954 it had been decided that CVA 63 would essentially be a repeat of CVA 62. Meanwhile, however, dissatisfaction with the *Forrestal*s remained, and the alternative carrier studies merely turned to another designation, SCB 153. In turn SCB 153 also failed, but some of its features were incorporated retroactively into CVA 63.

The new carrier study began as CVA 4/55, utilizing some of the material originally assembled for the SCB 127 project. The separate strength-deck concept was abandoned, but more effort went into rearranging the flight deck. For example, scheme N was devised to permit simultaneous landing and recovery without cutting the flight deck at a large angle to the centerline: the waist catapult was set to starboard between two deck-edge elevators, the island moved inboard to clear it. A third elevator was set to port. This apparently grotesque configuration actually made good sense, as aircraft were no longer to use the long axis of the flight deck in any case. Two alternative configurations were clearance for an A3D heavy-attack plane or for an F7U interceptor. A requirement for larger elevator dimensions was met by adopting an irregularly shaped elevator, 85 feet long on its outboard edge, 70 inboard. This was to accommodate the long nose of the prospective supersonic attack plane, the A3J (later redesignated A-5) Vigilante.

The flight deck ultimately adopted, however, was the one BuAer and Op-55B had proposed in February 1954, showing little catapult rearrangement (because the flight deck remained the strength deck) but a considerable realignment of the elevators, with the carrier's island moved well abaft amidships.

Another new aviation feature was a requirement for exotic fuel, which, like gasoline, had to be kept in special protected tanks within the armored box. This was a throwback to the problems of gasoline stowage aboard carriers operating piston-engine aircraft—and in the mid-fifties attack carriers were still operating some propeller aircraft, notably variants of the AD Skyraider and the AJ Savage. The new fuels were at the other end of the aircraft spectrum: high-energy fuel (HEF) or "zip" ("chemical") fuel, generally boron-based, extremely toxic and difficult to handle; and hydrogen peroxide (H_2O_2). Hydrogen peroxide was a combat boost fuel for aircraft already in service. Zip fuel was as yet a proposition, but it was thought essential to a new generation of super- and hypersonic-aircraft. All that could be said with any certainty was that the FY 57 carrier would probably commission well before zip was service approved. BuShips wanted, then, to rewrite the characteristics to reflect differing fuel loads depending upon the progress of the zip program, but the idea was rejected. In fact, one of the surprises of the fifties was that, although zip was initially specified for both the B-70 and the A3J Vigilante, in fact it was not needed. What was needed was a great deal more jet fuel, for larger, faster, and much hungrier aircraft.

Specified aviation fuel loads for the new SCB 153 carrier are listed below in thousand-gallon units,

The *Constellation* (*above* and *facing*), shown in the South China Sea on 2 October 1974, was a redesign of the original *Forrestal*, with much the same hull and propulsion. Designed for a conventional gun battery, the *Constellation* was completed instead with a pair of Terrier launchers, one on each quarter, served by SPG-55 missile directors on her quarters and her island. The SPS-39 three-dimensional radar on her island, above her main air search set, was also part of this system, recently removed in favor of the NATO Sea Sparrow close-in defensive one. In this and later classes congestion of the island was so acute that a lattice radar mast had to be erected abaft it, in this case carrying an SPS-30 for long-range fighter control. Conical antennas paired alongside the bridge are Phasor-90s, for ship-to-air communication, which replaced the arrays originally mounted in the *Forrestal*s at the edges of the flight deck.

according to characteristics of 8 August 1955. Note the quick demise of zip by the following February, and the move from avgas to pure jet fuel, which was easier to stow.

	CVA 63	SCB 153	SCB 127A (2/56)
HEAF (JP-5)	792	1,300	1,300
HEF (ZIP)	——	200	——
H₂O₂	——	200	200
Avgas	750	100	100

Here CVA 63 is the proposed repeat *Forrestal* design, which was not quite how the ship turned out.

Design studies began with the minimum hull that could carry the BuAer/Op-55 flight deck. This CVA 64A design came to 970 feet LBP—and $214 million (vice $196 million for a repeat *Forrestal*). Moreover, sacrifices had to be made: for example, it proved necessary to move the aircraft crane from the port quarter (sponson) up to the flight deck abaft the island, where it created an obstruction. Scheme CVA 64B was a larger ship, about *Forrestal* size, showing the new enlarged elevators. Scheme CVA 64C placed the improved flight-deck arrangement on the *Forrestal* hull. These schemes approached the goals of the

new carrier design—except that they showed no reduction in size. In scheme CVA 64D, all of the SCB 153 criteria were met, and the hull could accommodate almost a standard torpedo defense. There was also an improved machinery arrangement: the package came to $215.5 million, only slightly more than the rather less capable CVA 64A design. In fact somewhat more ship endurance was wanted, and in CVA 64E an entirely new hull was designed with greater ship fuel capacity. It would cost $230.5 million, which was too much. The other design studies were variations on the CVA 63 design: CVA 64F, with the new aviation fuels ($210 million), CVA 64G, with the new elevators ($210 million), and CVA 64H, with the new flight deck ($212.5 million).

None of them progressed very far. On 14 September the SCB 153 project was stopped in view of the progress of the nuclear-carrier studies: there was little point in a new carrier design if only one ship was to be built to it. Preliminary Design carrier personnel were reassigned to the nuclear project (CVA 9/55, which became SCB 160 and then the USS *Enterprise*), and CVA 63, the *Kitty Hawk*, not yet much advanced, was modified to incorporate the new flight-deck fea-

tures. In addition, as a matter of urgency, its elevators were enlarged by the addition of pie-shaped segments on their outboard edges. This solved the elevator size problem, and the solution was applied to CVA 64, the USS *Constellation*, as well. As completed, both ships were designated SCB 127A.

Despite the extent of carrier-design evolution since 1951, none of the new carriers had as yet been completed. Moreover, CVAs 63 and 64 were as yet designated for conventional gun batteries. They were completed instead with Terrier missiles, as in the CVAN 65 (*Enterprise*) design. They lacked the former forward sponsons, which allowed them to sustain high speed in rough weather, a increasingly important capability in the face of fast Soviet submarines. The carrier missile self-defense program was part of a larger task force missile defense effort; Secretary of Defense McNamara remarked in 1963 that it was a far more economical way of adding to task force air defense than was the construction of new missile-armed escorts.

Plans for missile batteries for CVA 63 through CVAN 65 initially called for four Terriers, one twin launcher replacing each pair of 5-in/54 guns. However, the forward sponsons were eliminated for seakeeping, an arrangement that left firing arcs very badly constricted forward. Only in the SCB 211 nuclear-carrier design for the never-built CVAN 66 (November 1959) were the Terrier launchers specifically arranged to allow for a "smooth" hull forward. The conventionally powered CVA 66 showed a similar above-water form for the same reason, and the reduction in battery was retroactively applied to the two earlier ships, which were still in an early stage of construction.

From a carrier-design point of view, the Terriers required their own three-dimensional radar (the electronically scanned SPS-39), which was mounted on the heavy pole foremast; the fighter-control (or long-range pencil-beam) radar, an SPS-8B or -30, was displaced to a new lattice mast abaft the island. By this time, too, the carriers were being fitted with a very large air search radar, SPS-37A, which had to be mounted directly above their bridges, where the *Forrestal*s mounted their smaller height finders.

It appeared that no further non-nuclear carriers would be built, but that was not to be the case. The cost of the first nuclear carrier was frighteningly high. Efforts were, therefore, directed toward some less expensive (but still nuclear) alternative. The building program, which had carried one attack carrier per year for FYs 52–58, carried none in FY 59 and 60. Unfortunately, the proposed austere nuclear carrier, SCB 203, was not acceptable.

For example, a 16 September 1958 memorandum from the DCNO (Air), Vice Admiral R. B. Pirie, to the DCNO (Fleet Operations and Readiness) reported a comparison between a proposed CVAN 66 (SCB 203), CVA 64, and the *Enterprise*, CVAN 65.

A smaller and cheaper CVA(N) for 1960 appears to be unattainable in view of the high cost of any nuclear power plant and of the aviation operating requirements. The decrease in the landing deck angle to 7 degrees, the reduction to three catapults and three elevators, and reduction of sustained speed [below 30 knots] are the primary unacceptable characteristics. The following conclusions have been made after complete evaluation:
—That CVA(N) 65 represents the optimum aircraft carrier of the foreseeable future.
—That in respect to specific items of deck space and aircraft loading capacity the CVA(N) 65 is a somewhat larger ship than requirement demands. This *bonus* results from the increased hull size dictated by installation of the nuclear power plant.
—That the *Forrestal* type attack carrier is a *completely adequate ship* for present and planned aircraft operations.
—That the single overpowering disadvantage of the nuclear powered aircraft carrier is *cost*. Initial procurement and the expense of periodic core replacement does not indicate economic advantage to nuclear power.
—That justification for nuclear power must stem from tactical military factors.
—That the FY 60 carrier, as a choice between a smaller version of the CVAN 66 (SCB 203) and a conventionally powered CVA 64, should be the CVA 64. The demands for an efficient carrier with respect to aviation requirements is not sufficiently fulfilled by the CVAN 66 (203) proposal. The gain realized in nuclear power is not worth the loss of the *Forrestal* or CVAN 65 deck and facilities arrangement.

Admiral Pirie recommended that the FY 60 CVA be a repeat CVA 64 modified to incorporate more modern electronics, such as fixed array radars and NTDS. "Guided missile provisions may be limited to space and weight only, dependent on a future decision as to exact requirements for air defense armament on this attack carrier." In fact two Terrier batteries were provided for the FY 61 carrier (CVA 66, the USS *America*), and similar batteries were mounted in the two earlier SCB 127s, CVAs 63 and 64. Otherwise, she was built as a slightly modified CVA 64, her design designated SCB 127B.

One major change was the provision of a big low-frequency sonar (SQS 23) in the forefoot. Similar installations were being made in ASW support carriers, but the intent in an attack carrier was different. It was a consequence of the development of nuclear-attack submarines by the Soviets. Such boats would, for the first time, be able to keep up with, and thus attack, fast-carrier formations. At the same time the threat of nuclear attack forced those formations to open up, so that the escorts could no longer be sure of maintaining an effective overlapping sonar screen. Hence the self-defense sonar for an attack carrier.

Although CVA 66 emerged as no more than a slightly modified CVA 64, several alternative designs were considered. The choice among them illuminates some of the compromises made in modern carrier design.

By 1959 aircraft growth no longer took place with the headlong force of five years earlier. Although the new heavy attack bomber, the A3J Vigilante (later redesignated A-5), represented a considerable advance in speed over its predecessor, the A3D, it was clearly the last of its line. The decision had already been made to adopt missiles such as Regulus and Polaris for heavy attack. Carriers would be relegated to a tactical role, and their primary attack airplane would be the relatively slow Grumman A2F (later A-6), designed initially with STOL characteristics. The fleet air-defense fighter of the future, the F6D Missileer, traded aircraft performance for missile performance and so made much-reduced demands on catapults, arresting gear, and flight-deck dimensions. In January 1960 the SCB circulated a request for comments on a new carrier to replace SCB 127B (the modified CVA 64 actually built as CVA 66) and SCB 211 (the rejected CVAN 66 design).

DCNO (Air) was unwilling to reduce carrier size; although the trend in increased aircraft size might appear to be levelling out, a carrier might last twenty years, and no one could guarantee against renewed growth. For example, larger aircraft might be required to accommodate the long-range air-to-surface missiles of the future. Nor could speed be sacrificed, if the carrier were to be able to operate in company with other attack carriers. The only saving available was armor: "a couple of inches of armor plating is hardly more than splinter protection against modern weapons, yet it imposes a tremendous penalty in topside weight plus the necessity for massive support structure. If not eliminated, this armor could at least be dropped to hangar deck level."

The Plans, Programs, and Budget Division (Op-722) saw no great reduction in the size, weight, or approach speed of future aircraft compared with that of the A3J and the F4H (F-4) Phantom: the usual 720–50-ft landing runway with Mk 7 arresting gear would be needed for the foreseeable future, and with

Table 12-1. CVA 66 Alternatives, January 1960

	CVA 64	CVAN 65	Scheme 60A	Scheme 60B	Scheme 60C
LWL (ft)	990	1,040	1,040	1,040	1,080
Beam (ft)	129	133	133	133	133
Draft (ft)	34	36	36	36	38
Light Ship Disp't	57,000	67,700	59,000	60,000	60,500
Full Load Disp't	77,137	85,000	85,000	85,000	85,500
SHP	280,000	—	280,000	360,000	360,000
Speed (sust) (kts)	31	—	31	33.5	35.0
Speed (trial) (kts)	33	—	33	36.0	37.5
JP-5 (tons)	4,007	6,426	7,200	5,050	4,550
Av Ord (tons)	1,800	1,800	2,000	2,000	2,000
Aircraft	89	98	98	98	98

it the *Forrestal*-size hull. However, hangar height might be drastically reduced, from the 25 feet of the earlier carrier to perhaps 21 feet, with an enormous saving in top weight. After all, only the A3D required more than 21 feet (and the A3D-2 could be folded to 15 feet 2 inches), and by 1966 only fifty-nine would remain in service. The LRO (Op-93) group concurred.

Fleet Operations and Readiness (Op-342) agreed with Op-05 but also stressed the need to avoid the "rough" sides of the *Forrestal*s, which limited carrier speed in bad weather by raising spray. Where such limitations might have been acceptable in the past, with speed limited to that of the screen, carriers now operated independently, without close ASW protection; submarine speeds had more than doubled; and it was more and more important for the carrier to be able to operate in heavy weather. Op-342 therefore wanted a dry hangar deck, an improved bow design for heavy weather, and smooth sides. It also suggested a self-protection sonar similar to the SQS-20 then being proposed for the fast replenishment ship (AOE).

BuWeps, which included the former BuAer and BuOrd, adamantly opposed any reduction in carrier aircraft characteristics or protection. Although currently projected aircraft were all operable from the smaller *Midway*-class carrier, the bureau expected an increase in aircraft cruise speeds to Mach 3, with increased length and height. For example, it postulated a 70,000-lb airplane with a length of 95 feet, a span of 40 feet, and a height of 25 feet, compared with figures of 73 feet 3 inches, 73 feet 3 inches, and 19 feet 4 inches for the subsonic-cruise Vigilante. These projected aircraft would easily match a fully loaded A3D or A3J in catapult requirements. BuWeps believed that this change was essentially inevitable, given the state of the art of aircraft design. The strongest argument in favor of the 25-ft hangar was that seven carriers had it. To adopt anything less in a new carrier would be to constrict aircraft design needlessly.

The bureau took the new A3J as the standard for future aircraft, with an upper limit on launch of 65,000 pounds at 150 knots, exceeding the capability of the existing C 7 catapult by 25 knots. Nor would the existing Mk 7 Mod 1 arresting gear suffice. However, the new C 13 and C 14 catapults would be able to launch the loaded A3J at zero ship speed, although the Mk 7 Mod 2 would still require 17 kts of wind-over-deck for recovery at 42,000 pounds. Flight-deck size was thus fixed by an approach speed of 150 kts at a 3° glide slope (230-ft approach), 60 feet from target touchdown point to forward wire, 350 feet of run-out, and 100 feet to turn off—a total of 740 feet, as in a *Forrestal*. The C 13 catapult had a 250-ft stroke, which fixed the length of the ship forward of the angled deck at about 350 feet—the same as on a *Forrestal*.

Most of those polled were unenthusiastic about any reduction in armor, and one wanted a considerable increase in underwater protection. BuWeps even argued that flight-deck armor weight contributed to the stiffness of the ship and thus to the carrier's "ability to operate the heavier and faster aircraft now being introduced."

So much for the smaller carrier. The alternative, a conventionally powered carrier on an *Enterprise* hull, was investigated by BuShips at the same time. All carriers, even those as large as the *Forrestal*, had been plagued by limited internal hull volume. In the new studies the narrower side protective system (designed for SCB 211 and actually incorporated in the *John F. Kennedy*) was employed, and the inner bottom deepened to add tankage. The results are shown in table 12-1. Although the *Forrestal*s had been designed for an endurance of 12,000 nautical miles, the replacement of some fuel oil by JP-5 had considerably reduced that figure. The larger hulls of schemes 60A through 60C could accommodate enough bunker oil for the full endurance figure, as well as more JP-5. Scheme 60B would be the first major U.S. warship rated at over 35 knots.

No costs were computed and the large-hull CVA was shelved early in 1960. There was one footnote. In 1963, after the failure of yet another attempt to obtain a nuclear carrier, BuShips developed sketch

To a considerable extent the *America* was a repeat *Constellation*. The new flight-deck arrangement employed in both classes is evident in these 18 November 1964 photographs of the newly completed ship. The port elevator has been moved back out of the path of landing aircraft so that it can serve the two waist catapults, and two starboard elevators now serve the clear parking error delineated by the angled landing runway and the forward catapults. Missiles are carried on both Terrier launchers, and the size of the SPS-43A air search antenna directly above the bridge is evident. The portside view shows the angled-deck sponson faired into the hull to reduce spray in rough weather. Note, too, the bow position of the anchor, which allows the SQS-23 sonar to be set into the forefoot.

designs for oversize conventional carriers, CVAL, CVAXL, and CVAXXL. The CVAXL was the largest ship that could be built and maintained in existing facilities: 1,080 feet long, 66,500 tons light and 97,360 tons fully loaded. It could carry 11,221 tons of JP-5 aboard (compared with 5,835 on CVA 67) and 3,150 tons of aviation ordinance, as in the CVAN 67 design (compared with 2,140 for CVA 67). CVAN 67 would have carried 8,071 tons of JP-5. An alternative *Enterprise*-size CVAL, 1,040 feet long, could accommodate 6,433 tons of JP-5 and 3,150 of aviation ordnance, in each case at the same steaming endurance as that of CVA 67. Displacements were 64,052 (light) and 88,150 (fully loaded) tons. CVAXXL was an attempt to combine the aviation loads (JP-5 and ordnance) of CVAXL with sufficient bunker fuel to achieve a much greater ship endurance, equivalent to the air group endurance represented by the increased JP-5 and aviation ordnance of CVAXL. The result was beyond U.S. graving dock capacity, 1,300 feet long, displacing 82,917 tons light and 110,719 tons fully loaded. Yet, it would not be very much more effective than a

CVAL-size nuclear carrier, with much greater steaming endurance, just as much aviation ordnance, and about two-thirds as much JP-5. In CVA 67 and CVAN 67 all avgas was to be replaced by 190 tons of aviation ordnance for comparison purposes. These data, all compiled for a CNA study of nuclear- and conventional-carrier battle groups, are interesting primarily as expressions of the outer limits of carrier design as they were understood in 1963–64.

With the change of administration in January 1961 the carrier program came under review once more. By this time there was another improved nuclear design (SCB 211A), which enjoyed considerable support from within the navy. One vital element was a new and far more compact side protective system. Although the new system saved weight, its volume saving was potentially far more important.

However, both Secretary of Defense McNamara and his CNO, Arleigh Burke, at first requested a conventionally powered carrier for FY 63. Even the relatively austere SCB 211A would be very expensive (one-third to one-half again as much as a CVA).

A design model of the *John F. Kennedy* shows the two major features abandoned before her completion, the bow sonar and the Tartar missile battery. The latter is indicated here by the twin Mark 11 launcher and by a representation of the SPG-51 missile director on the island. Note the extent to which the elevator sponsons are faired to achieve a "smooth" hull.

Moreover, no nuclear surface ship had yet been evaluated in service. The more general problems of the attack-carrier force show in the transition from the mid-fifties tempo of one per year to an implicit construction rate of one every other year; even that would be impossible to maintain through the sixties. By 1961, then, carriers were planned only for every other year after FY 63, a tempo Secretary McNamara reviewed in 1963 and which moved him to cancel the FY 65 ship.

Operational experience with the *Enterprise* and the *Long Beach* was so encouraging that the navy position shifted strongly in favor of a FY 63 CVAN. In view of the ambiguity of the situation, alternative nuclear and conventional designs were developed in parallel. However, Secretary McNamara rejected the navy position, and construction of CVA 67 (the USS *John F. Kennedy*) as a "fossil-fuel" carrier was ordered on 9 October 1963, about a year behind the FY 63 schedule.

At this time it appeared that a new major surface-to-air missile system, Typhon, would soon replace Terrier, Talos, and Tartar. Although it required a much greater investment in shipboard radars, Typhon could achieve better performance with a smaller weapon. As in the case of Terrier, a Typhon installation aboard a carrier would be more a contribution to overall task force missile firepower than to carrier self-defense as such. Given the great size and cost of the carrier, it could be argued that the additional cost of Typhon would provide a considerable capability at a cost well below that of a new Typhon ship. Early versions of the CVA 67 design therefore showed the Typhon radar controlling "medium-range" missiles (of Tartar size but Terrier capability). As an alternative, the new carrier could be armed with the much less capable Tartar, representing a similar investment in missile size and weight but a much smaller one in fire control.

Another new item of naval technology available for CVA 67 was the pressure-fired boiler, much more compact than earlier types. Moreover, it burned jet fuel, so that a carrier would no longer have to divide her tanks between JP-5 and bunker oil, but could freely trade off steaming radius against air-group endurance. Pressure firing was, in the early sixties, the great hope of the oil-fueled fleet, and it was a key element of the new surface escort designs (the *Brooke*, *Garcia*, and *Knox* classes). However, it would be discredited and then abandoned after the intervention of William F. Gibbs in the *Knox* design in 1963–64. In any case, no really large pressure-fired boiler was ever built, the maximum being the 17,500-SHP unit of escorts.

Use of JP 5 would fight corrosion by reducing contaminants; improve aircraft-landing approach visibility by lessening smoke density; reduce boiler maintenance; and above all increase operating flexibility by permitting trade-offs between ship and air-group endurance. Although pressure firing was not adopted, it turned out that conversion of conventional boilers to burn JP 5 would be relatively easy.

The SCB working-level meetings culminated in the preparation of "single-sheet characteristics" (29 November 1961), which called for
—A CVA 66 hull.
—Speed, endurance, and bunker-oil capacity as in CVA 66.
—Rearranged machinery: five 52-ft spaces (one auxiliary space sandwiched between two pairs of main machinery spaces). This cut off 20 feet (two 36-ft auxiliary spaces were consolidated into a single 52-ft space).
—Electronics as in CVA 66 except for Typhon (two medium-range launchers, forty missiles each, directed by a 7,000-element radar).
—A flight deck as in CVA 66 (but consideration of a 310-ft catapult).
—Ballistic protection as in CVA 66—but use of a new low-volume side protective system (developed for the nuclear carriers).
—Accommodations to increase by 58 officers and 318 enlisted men (the CVA 66 accommodated 411 officers, 4,171 enlisted).
—10 percent more aviation ordnance.

These somewhat schizophrenic requirements reflect a desire to cut costs by repeating the CVA 66 design while somehow making a few useful improvements. By no means did they represent the end of the process. For example, the Typhon system was large and expensive, requiring a separate sub-island to house its big phased-array SPG 59 radar. One idea was to substitute four Sea Maulers (the ancestor of the present Sea Sparrow PDMS). This would mean abandonment of the carrier contribution to integrated task force air defense, but it also would have saved much money—and weight. After all, the escorts accompanying the carrier would have the higher-powered systems. Design would be simplified since Sea Mauler carried its own radar on the mount.

Preliminary Design submitted its first studies of the SCB on 2 February 1962. They reflected a 22 January visit by the chairman of the SCB to BuShips. He suggested two studies.
1. One was a CVA limited in cost to $310 million, to be based on a repeat CVA 66 except that
  a) total aviation fuel would be increased from 1,850,000 to 1,950,000 gallons and aviation ordnance from 1,650 to 1,800 tons. The increased volume required could be gained only by the adoption of a new side protective system.
  b) the complement would grow from 411/4,171 to 481/4,724, requiring adoption of lower standards of habitability (that is, those specified

for destroyers and cruisers, 301 to 600 feet in length).
  c) Terrier was now to be replaced by two Mk 13 (single-arm) Tartars rather than by Typhon.
  d) the existing SPSs 39A and 30 height-finding radars were both to be replaced by the new SPS 48.
2. The other was a CVAN based on SCB 211 (it was known that the anti-CVAN decision might well be reversible). Changes generally paralleled those specified for the other study, except that JP 5 capacity was to be increased by a reduction in bunker oil to 500,000 gallons, and the complement was to rise from 413/4,242 to 487/4,485. Both were to have four C 13 catapults (with a 250-ft stroke).

These studies were circulated within the fleet. A severe North Atlantic storm inspired Commander, Naval Air Force, Atlantic, to revive the idea of the centerline elevator: the storm had not prevented flight-deck operations per se, but it had prevented the operation of the deck-edge elevators. Replacement of no. 1 elevator by a centerline elevator forward would also permit elimination of the forward upper-stage bomb elevator.

The Commander-in-Chief, Pacific Fleet, who operated in more benign waters, strongly disagreed, and the centerline elevator remained a dead issue. He had other suggestions. Sonar, for example, should be deleted. "While sonar might be considered desirable in an attack carrier, shortage of funds dictates against installation." SAMs, too, might be deleted in favor of reliance on other ships of the task force. But some gun battery, probably the conceptual lightweight 5-in/54s, was essential.

That is, CinCPACFLT considered Tartar at best a very limited blessing. "Improved intercept capability of N[T]DS-controlled interceptors and AAW surface forces should be relied upon. . . ." On the other hand, there was already a feeling that large ships operating near land would face a significant MTB threat, against which missiles would be useless. At a meeting of fleet representatives in March, "the only feature of the design [which brought agreement] was the armament. They all questioned the need for guided missiles and suggested gun batteries instead."

The SCB had somewhat different ideas; it decided to retain the sonar and preferred Tartar to guns, but agreed to place two lightweight 5-in/54s on the Tartar sponsons aft, leaving sufficient space and weight allowance for a later Tartar installation.

A 20 April SCB review gave rise to further changes.
—One 310-ft C 13 catapult replaced the no. 3 250-ft catapult.
—Sonar was finally eliminated as an economy.

The *John F. Kennedy* was completed without armament, although Sea Sparrow launchers soon occupied the sponsons shown. This 13 December 1968 photograph gives a good impression of the range of naval aircraft then operated by U.S. carriers. Forward of the island are the last of the heavy (strategic) attack bombers, two RA-5 Vigilantes, whose length necessitated the triangular cutouts in the *Kennedy's* elevators. Abaft the island are two Skywarriors, the direct predecessors of the Vigilante and, in effect, the reason for the entire class of heavy carriers. Inboard of the island are four F-4 Phantoms and a smaller delta-winged A-4 Skyhawk attack bomber. Darkened areas of the deck indicate the ends of the four catapults. A Phantom is in launch position on the forward port unit. Note, finally, the distinctive canted funnel and the SPS-48 three-dimensional radar, which replaced the SPS-30 as original equipment. SPS-48 is displacing SPS-30 in active carriers, and in 1982 was aboard the *Midway* and all or most of the *Forrestals* and later carriers. CVNs 68–71 all had it as originally completed.

—Two of the Tartar fire-control systems (Mk 74) were eliminated.

—In view of the reduced role of piston-driven aircraft, avgas was to be reduced to 25,000 gallons, JP 5 increased to 1,925,000.

—A shorter, wider island was to be studied as a means of improving resistance to nuclear blast.

The preliminary design for what was now designated SCB 127C was complete at the end of April 1962. Although the CVA 66 hull form had been duplicated, the new side protective system and consequent internal rearrangement required a completely new set of working plans. Their cost was, however, partly offset by the adoption of Tartar in place of the more expensive Terrier of previous carriers. Internal changes included increased magazine volume (with consequent lengthening of the after armored box and shortening of the forward one) and JP 5 stowage, and the new machinery arrangement; there was also improved ballistic protection. Some late changes included the movement of all pilot ready rooms to the gallery deck, the escalators of earlier carriers being eliminated.

As actually built, the new carrier had no guns and no heavy missile battery. Instead, space was reserved for the new short-range point defense missile system (Sea Sparrow, or PDMS), three box launchers being fitted (starboard side forward, and post and starboard quarters). She also had a bow sonar dome, although no sonar was fitted. In addition, her large port sponson was extended aft parallel to the centerline to improve air flow, and the 310-ft waist catapult required its forward extension. Finally, her radar suit was revised and simplified as planned. Her three half-sisters later had their obsolescent Terrier batteries removed in favor of Sea Sparrows.

As this is written, the *Kennedy* is the last U.S. oil-fired attack carrier to have been built. However, a repeat *Kennedy* was proposed in the late seventies as an alternative to the smaller CVV on the projected nuclear CVN 71. One reason for rejection of the project at that time was the sheer load of design required to take into account changes in such minor equipment as pumps and electronic motors over the decade and a half since the *Kennedy's* construction.

13

Carrier Modernization

World War II was a great watershed in most areas of naval warfare, seeing great shifts in missions and in weapons. The 1945 fleet carrier was an attempt to take some of the changes into account, although it was clear at the time that the carrier could never be built in quantity in peacetime, if indeed she could be built at all. As in the case of destroyers, there was too great an investment sunk in carriers of wartime and prewar design for Congress to authorize more. The only choice open to a navy determined to maintain its lead in naval aviation was an aggressive program of carrier modernization, which in the postwar decade transformed the carrier fleet nearly as thoroughly as did the advent of the new heavy carriers.

The carrier force received two great shocks in 1945–46. First there were jets. They accelerated far too slowly and had too little low-speed lift for conventional rolling takeoffs. They would have to be catapulted, and their catapults would have to be substantially more powerful, and therefore much longer and heavier, than the H 4s of the *Essex* and *Midway* classes. Landing speeds would also rise, requiring heavier and more powerful arresting gear. Although these improvements might involve some difficulties, they did not require major internal rearrangement of a carrier. However, the jets also had much greater appetites for fuel, which in 1945 was still avgas, the potentially explosive substance that had to be stowed under armor and inside an antitorpedo bulkhead system. Volume inside that armored box was already limited. Moreover, during the postwar years a new family of low-drag bombs well suited to jets was developed, requiring greater magazine volume

(within the armored box) for the same weight of bombs. Finally, when it appeared that the jet fuel problem could be solved through the advent of HEAF, an additional burden was placed on the limited internal armored volume of the carriers: the need for a protected blending room in which gasoline and HEAF could be combined to form jet fuel. Jet aircraft also required faster fueling, that is, larger fuel pumps inside the armored box.

The second shock was the new series of BuAer heavy attack bombers, which again required heavier catapults and arresting gear. They also required facilities for atomic weapon storage and assembly, as in CVB improvement program no. 1, and much heavier bomb elevators. These elevators were required for a new family of heavier air weapons as well, a 4,000-lb tactical bomb and a 14-in rocket, the latter not progressing far enough to enter service.

As early as 1945 wartime experience (particularly as it applied to the *Essex* class) had given rise to demands for protected ready rooms, a new arrangement of side armor, and more deck-edge elevators. Although these improvements could not be made in ships completed during and immediately after the war, they could certainly form part of any major carrier reconstruction program.

Beside these operational issues, the navy of 1945–46 was also developing a new family of guided weapons, ranging from antiaircraft missiles such as LARK to cruise missiles ("pilot-less aircraft," or P/A) such as Loon and the later Regulus, and even to ballistic weapons such as the captured German V-2 and its research successors. It was by no means clear what

---

The *Franklin D. Roosevelt* is shown off the Virginia Capes in July 1969, after her austere refit, with the centerline elevator replaced by a deck-edge unit and the bridge somewhat modified. Note the absence of a waist catapult, the retention of her original port deck-edge elevator position amidships, and the ECM antennas sponsored out just abaft it.

The *Essex*-class carrier *Oriskany*, suspended incomplete after World War II, was the prototype for carrier reconstruction. She is shown in the Atlantic, newly completed, on 6 December 1950. Note the heavy AA battery, including, at this time, fourteen twin 3-in/50s, and a few twin 20-mm guns. The 3-in gun arrangement followed approximately that adopted late in World War II for quadruple 40-mm weapons, but the newer weapons were heavier and their sponsons clearly more massive.

their role or their capabilities would be, but the naval leadership was anxious to explore the new technology they represented, since clearly it would have a major effect on the future of warfare. In 1946, then, there was considerable interest in modifying existing warships to test missiles, primarily for research but also for interim operational use. The first proposals for reconstructing Essex-class carriers were more for test than for combat purposes, and it was some time before the conversion program was reoriented.

As early as February 1945 BuAer was proposing a jet modification to existing *Essex*-class carriers to incorporate an increase in gasoline capacity of 100,000 gallons (although how such an increased amount of fuel could be accommodated was unclear). Further proposals included improved arresting gear, barriers specially adapted to jet-type tricycle undercarriages, electric outlets for starting jet engines on the flight deck, and perhaps most importantly, improved catapults. For example, the bureau was working on a 225-ft unit that could accelerate a 20,000-lb airplane to 125 mph, compared with the 18,000 lbs/90 mph of the *Essex*-class H 4B (96 feet) or the 28,000 lbs/90 mph of the *Midway*'s H 4-1. In fact, although it

proved impractical, the bureau did begin work on the H 8, the standard for *Essex*-class conversions (15,000 lbs/120 mph).

Meanwhile, plans to embody new developments aboard ships, particularly missiles, were devised. In 1946 the new SCB carried three separate conversions of existing warships for missile testing: SCB 26A, the large cruiser *Hawaii* (with a short flight deck forward), SCB 27, a carrier "capable of operating offensively with new heavy aircraft, jet aircraft, pilotless aircraft, or guided missiles, as selected," and SCB 28, a missile-launching submarine. To some extent SCB 27 would test features planned for the new heavy carrier (SCB 6A, the *United States*) then in the early design stage; it would also test missiles. Originally one of the *Midway*s was proposed as the SCB 27 carrier, but she was too valuable to remove from service for experimental purposes. Instead, the CNO approved a single *Essex*, the sole unit still under construction, the *Oriskany*, which would be completed to an SCB 27A design. She was ordered suspended 22 August 1946 to await completion to a new design under the FY 48 program.

At first her experimental function, with missiles

and then with the new aircraft, was emphasized. For example, space was to be reserved for stabilized platforms for two missile-control radars, probably SPG-49s, at either end of the island, as well as one forward and one on the island proper. The flight deck would have to be strengthened for 45,000-lb (later 60,000-lb) aircraft, and this and other top weight would have to be compensated by a blister. In addition, the flight deck would be strengthened forward and amidships to permit rocket launching (as from the flight deck of the *Midway* in Operation Sandy) and fitted with two new catapults, an H 8 and a slotted-tube type, as in the original *Forrestal* design. Fuel capacity would be increased to 300,000 gallons (that is, by almost 50 percent) and the gassing rate at the flight deck increased to 50 gallons per minute. In view of the BuAer heavy-attack-bomber program, provision was to be made for 12,000-lb bombs. The flight deck would be cleared of guns, the battery being reduced to ten twin 3-in/70s, one at each end and two at each quadrant.

Work began in June and by October BuShips had two studies in hand. An austere scheme A could handle the 45,000-lb Savage; it retained the conventional carrier island structure, and its after and deck-edge elevators would be enlarged to strike below a fully armed bomber. The catapult would be a single H 8, and conversion would cost about $25 million. For $33 million the bureau offered the flush-decker of scheme B, with the H 9 catapult then being developed for the *United States*, capable of handling a 60,000-lb bomber. Although plans showed only a single catapult, each scheme had space and weight reserved for later installation of a second (slotted-tube) unit. In each case structural limitations forward precluded any improvement of the forward centerline elevator. Large sponsons running three-quarters the length of the ship were needed to support the heavy 3-in/70 battery without interfering with the flight deck, which had to be shortened at the ends. The considerable additions of top weight required a 5-ft blister (for a total beam of 103 feet) running along most of the length of the ship. Full-load displacement was expected to rise from about 36,700 tons in a late *Essex* to about 39,700 tons, and conversion would require a year for scheme A or twenty months for the more ambitious scheme B.

By this time fiscal reality was much clearer; the FY 48 budget could not support even scheme A, and indeed there was no longer any great support for the experimental conversion of a valuable combatant ship. Op-05 wanted scheme B as the forerunner of its cherished flush-deck carrier, but had to admit that she could be built only at the cost of all other FY 48 programs. On 17 January 1947 the VCNO, Vice Admiral D. C. Ramsey, made changes to SCB 27A that were "the minimum alterations necessary to permit

The *Oriskany* shows her 3-in gun arrangement in this May 1951 publicity photo. Three more twin mounts were sponsoned out to starboard abreast below her island (as in the wartime carriers), and there was another at hangar-deck level aft, plus two at the stern. Most SCB-27A conversions omitted one or more of these mounts, particularly after top weight became critical in these ships with the adoption of heavier aircraft. Blistering the hull permitted, among many other things, sponsoning out the starboard 5-in guns so that they required no flight-deck cutouts. Note the Mark 56 director just abaft the forward port gun sponson, for 5-in and 3-in gun control, supplementing the two Mark 37s on the island.

Essex class carriers to operate present or prospective fighter type aircraft and the largest and heaviest attack type aircraft now considered feasible without requiring major structural changes. . . ."

Conversion now entailed clearing the flight deck by removing the gun mounts and also the stub supporting a quadruple Bofors abaft the island; the island was reduced in size, partly through the removal of its guns. The uptakes were rebuilt and angled aft, so that a massive pole radar mast could be built to support antennas without the sort of interference common in wartime arrangements.

The flight deck was strengthened to take 52,000-lb airplanes, the centerline elevators being strength-

The newly converted *Wasp* (*above* and *facing*) displays the major features of the SCB-27A conversion in these November 1951 photographs, taken in Gravesend Bay, off the Brooklyn Navy Yard. Her H 8 catapults are much longer (and more powerful) than those of the unconverted *Essex*es, as comparison with the photographs in chapter 7 will show. Note the concentration of all radar antennas into a single structure, which the reconstruction was intended to accomplish. In this case, the SX height finder and air search radar had its own platform atop the funnel structure, and the heavy pole mast carried two air search radars, an SPS-6A and an SR (on its after side). The starboard view shows the characteristic escalator housing, for moving pilots from protected ready rooms to the flight deck, as well as the hangar-deck 3-in mount well aft. The sponson projecting aft from the island was later occupied by an SPN-8 blind-landing radar, under development but not yet ready in 1951. The portside view shows clearly the heavy flight-deck structure required to accommodate the H 8 catapult.

ened to 40,000 pounds and enlarged to 58 by 44 feet. The deck-edge elevator was strengthened to 30,000-lb capacity. Heavy attack aircraft could then be armed and fueled in the hangar, raised to the flight deck by the centerline elevators, and struck below upon landing by the deck-edge unit. Both H 4B catapults were replaced by H 8s, and the former Mark 4 arresting gear replaced by a new Mark 5. Internally, avgas capacity was indeed increased by almost 50 percent to 300,000 gallons, despite the problems of limited protected volume.

As in CVB improvement program no. 1, the forward bomb elevator was enlarged to handle nuclear weapons, that is, "a package 15 feet long weighing 16,000 lbs." Elevator speed and capacity (forty-eight round trips per hour with 9,500 pounds or twenty-four with 16,000, allowing 10 seconds to load and unload) were based on the requirement that "a typical strike group of attack aircraft should, as an optimum, be rearmed and gassed within the period of time required to land the entire group." In 1949 the interim (1952) group was set at forty-two F9Fs and forty-two Skyraiders (AD-3s), the latter each with two 2,000-lb or one 4,000-lb bomb; the ultimate (1958) air group would be twenty-four 15,000-lb interceptors, twenty-four 30,000-lb escorts, and twenty-four 30,000-lb attack bombers, each with two 4,000-lb bombs. A typical strike would be half the air group, landing at 75-sec intervals.

Three ready rooms were relocated from the gallery deck to protected positions below the hangar deck. Since pilots would have to climb some considerable distance from them, a prominent escalator was installed outboard of the island structure. All of the alterations, including the new catapults, required additional electric power, and the original pair of 250-kw emergency diesel generators were replaced by 850-kw units. However, the four 1,250-kw turbogenerators were not replaced.

Defensive armament was a problem. There was no question of dispensing with it, but cost and structural change had to be minimized. Thus an Op-05 battery of six new twin 3-in/70 AA guns had to be rejected.

Instead, new sponsons were built for four open single 5-in/38s on the starboard side to supplement the four already mounted to port in standard *Essex*-class carriers, and they were supplemented by a battery of fourteen twin 3-in/50s, the guns originally developed in 1945 as an emergency replacement for the quadruple Bofors during kamikaze attacks. These weapons, already in production, presented relatively few installation problems. They were located in standard Bofors positions: two each at the ends, three outboard of the island structure, one right aft at hangardeck level to starboard, one each adjacent to the port forward and port and starboard after 5-in sponsons, and three at sponson level along the port side of the flight deck. The *Oriskany* also had sixteen twin 20-mm guns, weapons justified at General Board hearings in 1950 as useful for morale, since they would give the crew a sense of security even if it was unlikely that the guns would have much effect.

Protection was revised according to the 1945 concepts described in chapter 10. Blisters were required in any case to balance off the top weight of the many new flight-deck features, and they were designed to be flush with the ship's side, extending all the way up to the hangar deck. The side armor was removed entirely, and 60-lb STS was used for the blister plating. In addition, the hangar was subdivided by two fire and splinter bulkheads, a new fog/foam firefighting system, improved water curtains, and a new cupronickel fire main. BuShips argued that

> hangar damage resulting from fires has far exceeded the hangar damage resulting from the initial bomb or projectile detonation or suicide plane crash.... hangar deck fires primarily result from the presence of gasoline in planes in that space.... these fires readily detonate, by roasting, major ordnance material with ensuing great extension of damage. STS hangar bulkheads ... would be provided for the main purpose of preventing and limiting the damage resulting from gasoline fires on the hangar deck....

The *Oriskany* was completed to the revised SCB 27A design under the FY 48 program, a conversion approved by the CNO on 5 June 1947. She had been

Table 13-1. Carrier Modernization

	SCB 27A‡	SCB 27C**	SCB 27C††
Ships (CVA)	9, 10, 12, 15, 18, 20, 33, 34, 39	11, 14, 16††, 19, 31††, 38††	—
Light Ship Disp't (tons)	28,204	29,601	30,580
Full Load Disp't (tons)	40,600	41,944	43,060
LOA (ext)(ft-in)*	—	—	894-6
LOA (ft-in)	898-1.5	898-3.75	880-0
LWL (ft-in)	819-1.125	820-0	820-0
Beam (WL)(ft-in)	101-4.3125	103-3.75	103-0
Beam (ext)(ft-in)	151-10.75	166-9.5	166-10
Draft (full)(ft)	29-8.1875	29-7	30-4
Length of Angled Deck (ft-in)	—	—	520-0
FD (ft)	870×108	862×108	861×142
Aircraft (tons)†	382.3/662.5§	465.5/823.8‡‡	580
Av Ord (tons)	—	944.05	1,060
Av. Fuel (tons)	825.68	2,360§§	2,262
JP-5 (HEAF)(gals)	—	473,576	480,000
Avgas (gals)	302,194	360,000	360,000
Elevators			
Deck Edge (ft)	1 60×34	1 44×56, 1 34×60	2 56×44
Capacity (lbs)	46,000	57,000; 46,000	port: 46,000 stbd: 57,000
Centerline (ft)	2 58×44	1 44×58	1 70×44
Capacity (lbs)	46,000	46,000	46,000
Catapults			
Bow	2 H 8	2 C 11	2 C 11
Waist	—	—	—
SSTG (kw)	4 1,250	4 1,250	4 1,700
Diesel Generators (kw)	2 850‖	2 1,000	2 1,000
5-in/54 / 5-in/38	0/8	0/8	0/4
Twin 3-in/50	12#	12	—
Complement			
Ship (off/enl)	104/2,791	131/2,086	167/2,418
Aviation (off/enl)	—	—	171/769
Speed (full/sust)(kts)	31.7/30.0	32.0/?	30.7/29.1

*Over catapult booms where applicable.
†Empty weight unless otherwise indicated.
‡Data for USS *Oriskany*, 1955, unless otherwise noted.
§Air group: 23 AD, 13 F2H, 16 F9F-5, 22 F9F-6, 1 HUP; empty weight/takeoff weight.
‖1,000 kw in at least CVs 10, 20, 33, 39.
#Originally 14 mounts.
**Data for *Hancock*, 1955 (axial-deck version).
††Completed with angled deck.
‡‡Air group: 44 F9F-6, 12 F2H-3, 16 AD-6, 6 AD-4B, 10 AD-4NA, 1 HUP; empty weight/takeoff weight.
§§83 tons avgas, 1,530 of JP-5.
‖‖1,200 tons including equipment and stores.
##1,017 tons including JP-5.
***Including equipment and stores.
†††Fuel oil 8,990 tons compared with 10,030 in SCB 110; endurance reduced from 12,500 to 9,500 nm at 20 kts.
‡‡‡1978 figures.
§§§As in 1976.

SCB 110	SCB 110A	SCB 101.66	SCB 125	SCB 125A§§
41, 42	43	41	9, 10, 12, 15, 18, 20, 33	34
44,950	45,100	47,895	30,800	33,250
63,500	62,600	64,714	41,200	44,000
—	—	1,001-6	—	910-9.5
977.2-0	978-0	977-0	890-0	—
900-0	900-0	905-0	824-6	820-0
121-0	121-0	121-0	101-0	106-7
210-0	231-0	258-6	196-0	157-0
34-6	34-9	35-4	30-1	31-4
531-0	663-6	651-0	520-0	—
977.2 × 192	978 × 236	972.2 × 258.5	861 × 142	—
963‖‖	815***	767	—	—
1,376	—	1,210	—	—
956##	3,500†††	3,449	—	—
600,000	—	1,186,000	—	—
355,600	—	—	—	—
3 56 × 44	3 56 × 44	3 63 × 52	port: 60 × 40 stbd: 56 × 44	—
74,000	74,000	110,000	46,000	—
—	—	—	1 58 × 44	—
—	—	—	46,000	—
2 C 11	2 C 11	2 C 13	2 H 8	2 C 11-1
1 C 11	1 C 11	—	—	—
8 1,250	8 1,250	8 1,250	4 1,250	—
2 850	2 850	2 850	2 850	—
10/0	6/0	3/0	0/7	0/2
9	—	—	4	—
412/3,648	116/2,521‡‡‡	146/2,560	—	110/1,980
	201/1,537	214/1,766	—	135/1,050
30.6/29.5	—	31.6/29.7	32/30.3	32.0/30.3

The *Intrepid*, the second SCB-27C (steam catapult) conversion, nears completion at Newport News in this 14 May 1954 photograph. Note the starboard after deck-edge elevator, characteristic of these ships, and the heavy 3-in/50 battery, similar to that of an SCB-27A. The structures at the forward end of the flight deck protect portions of her two C 11 steam catapults not yet fully installed, and the length of the catapults is evident.

suspended 85 percent complete, and had to be torn back to a 60 percent state of completion before reconstruction could begin. The next two ships, the *Essex* and *Wasp* of FY 49, were drawn from reserve, but for the two under the FY 50 supplemental program it was hoped that some saving could be achieved by drawing ships from the active fleet, particularly since the active carrier force was scheduled to run down in FY 51. The *Kearsage* was decommissioned for reconstruction, but the *Leyte*, scheduled for withdrawal and modernization upon completion of the *Oriskany*, remained active instead because of the Korean emergency. Her place in the reconstruction program was taken by the *Lake Champlain*. The use of active carriers did save money, but it was opposed in view of the navy campaign to halt the decline of the active fleet, and in fact the *Kearsage* was the only *Essex* active in 1949 to be rebuilt. It was estimated that the *Leyte* and *Kearsage* would cost about $38 million each, compared with $111.7 million to complete the *Oriskany* and $55 million for the two FY 49 ships. Ships in reserve would cost about $50 million each,

the two FY 50 ships benefitting from interim modifications postwar and from reduced ordnance. By way of contrast, it was estimated in August 1950 that the *Franklin*, then described as one of the best of the reserve carriers, could be converted for about $43 million if some reduction in electronics were accepted.

Given the tightness of funds and the high cost of SCB 27A, interest in more austere conversions was also expressed. For example, as of May 1950 austere conversions, with blisters installed, flight-deck guns removed, new catapults, arresting gear, elevators, and barriers, would cost $21 million for the "long hull" ships and $26 million for the older ones; they would lack CCA (bad weather) equipment and the 3-in/50 guns, and their gasoline systems would remain unimproved. The most austere conversion, in which only the deck-edge elevator was replaced and no new deck-edge guns were fitted, would cost about $9 million and fifteen months in a yard, compared with nine months lead time and two years in the yard for the full SCB 27A.

The original program called for a mobilization base of ten carriers: seven SCB 27As and three *Midways*. By May 1950, before the outbreak of the Korean War, this requirement had been increased to twelve carriers; one proposal was to achieve this level with four partial conversions, with another four to bring the number of usable carriers to sixteen, since no further conversions within the first fifteen months of a war were anticipated. New carriers could be built to replace the unconverted older ones; a navy spokesman at this time estimated that one new carrier could be built for the price of three SCB 27As and forecast the completion of two new carriers by 1957–58.

In fact the Korean War opened the floodgates. Four full conversions were authorized in FY 51: one in the first supplemental, one in the second, and two more in the third. Four more were authorized in the FY 52 program, for a total of thirteen out of the twenty-four *Essex*-class carriers up to that time. In 1951 a tentative FY 53 program showed four more, two of which were approved. By that time the conversion (then SCB 27C) cost $63 million, and no more were approved.

SCB 27A did not quite exhaust the possibilities for *Exxex*-class conversion. In 1951 studies began of three additional improvements, a more powerful powder-fired slotted-tube catapult, new Mark 7 arresting gear and a new starboard deck-edge elevator to replace the revious after centerline one, which interfered with the flow of traffic along the deck. In an SCB 27 A, the elevator (with a capacity of 56,500 pounds, or 62,000 locked in) was expected to require 630 tons of weight compensation and the removal of four 5-in/38s. Instead, new 5-ft wide blisters were designed, which would reduce sustained speed from the original 32 knots to 30.6 (30.9 in SCB 27A). By this time the ship was marginal in stability. For example, the estimated list after two torpedo hits was 21°, compared with 19° in SCB 27A—and a standard requirement of 15°. Contemporary documents abound in statements like "stresses in the bottom plating are increased and approach the permissible limit."

The new SCB 27C was to be applied to the *Hancock* and later conversions. Where not all SCB-27As had been fitted with the improvement program (that is, with the capacity to stow nuclear weapons), all SCB 27Cs would be so fitted, which reflected increased acceptance of the navy nuclear role. One of the two H 8 catapults would be replaced by a C 10, a powder type arranged with its breech in the extreme bow, and all SCB 27Cs would also have the new fuel-blending system. The starboard after pair of 5-in/38s would have to be relocated aft to a position across from the port guns, and all fourteen twin 3-in/50s would be retained. Other new features were catapult blast deflectors, deck cooling, mechanical position-

ing of aircraft at the catapults, and the new nylon barricade specially adapted to jet aircraft. With fuel blending about 480,000 gallons of HEAF could be carried, at the expense of bunker oil. The optimum blending ratio was as yet not known, but at 2.6:1 the ship would be able to carry 739,000 gallons of jet fuel as well as 42,000 of gasoline for her piston-engine aircraft. The cost in steaming radius would be a reduction from 11,500 to 8,740 nautical miles at 20 knots. As in SCB 27As, the port deck-edge elevator and the forward centerline elevator were originally rated at 42,000 pounds, although characteristics of October 1951 show 46,000; the original *Essex* had been rated at 28,000.

The SCB 27C design emphasized the problem of the limited volume of the armored box of an *Essex*. Competition for protected volume in the SCB 27A conversion forced all 3-in/50 ammunition out into fourth-deck magazines. One problem was that the lion's share of the armored box, 64.2 percent, was filled with machinery spaces that could not be reduced; the next largest shares were ammunition, 14.8 percent, and gasoline, 14.5 percent, with only 3 percent devoted to control spaces and another 3.5 percent to "special shops" (nuclear weapons assembly). In SCB 27C the situation was aggravated by the addition of blending facilities, charges for the proposed powder catapult, and also the substitution of low-drag for conventional bombs. Blending alone required larger pump rooms, over and above those which had been required for the increased fueling rates envisaged in SCB 27A. Space was so scarce that the possibility of extending the armored box fore and aft was considered; however, the ends of the ship were too fine to accommodate extended torpedo protection. The 50 tons of catapult charges and part of the 5-in ammunition had to be moved out of the armored box, since gasoline was now squeezing out some of the magazines (avgas now consumed 15.3 instead of 14 percent of protected volume, while other proportions remained constant). Ammunition outside the armored box now amounted to 4.4 percent of the volume of the box. Even so, there were substantial sacrifices. For example, the original SCB 27C drawings showed 90 tons of catapult charges outside the armored box, carried well forward. After a review of explosive hazards, this was cut to 45 tons plus 5 tons of ready service charges, an amount considered barely acceptable in the outside location, and a plan to relocate it behind armor, with a two-stage dredger hoist to lift it to the catapult, was proposed.

Unfortunately there were delays in C 10 catapult development, so that in September 1951 BuAer recommended that the second and third conversions (the *Intrepid* and *Ticonderoga*) be completed to SCB 27A standard and the prototype 27C, the *Hancock*,

At sea on 10 August 1956, the *Intrepid* has no bow 3-in/50 guns, which were omitted to save weight in the SCB-27C design. She retains the other mounts of the SCB-27A. Only the first three SCB-27Cs were completed with this open-bow configuration; the others had the fully enclosed "hurricane bow," later fitted to the first three, together with an angled deck. The two fighters on the catapults are McDonnell F2H Banshees, standard tactical bombers and night fighters of this period. More are parked aft, together with two North American AJ Savages, the earliest fruits of the 1945 BuAer heavy-attack program. Radars on the island structure include an SPN-6 to the right, a zenith search set (SPS-4 or SG-6), an SPS-12 on the pole mast to the left, and a wartime-type SC-series antenna sponsored out from the stack structure. An SPS-8 height finder occupies the position forward of the pole mast. The ship astern, the command cruiser *Northampton*, was designed partly as a consequence of plans to make all future carriers flush-deckers; she would have to carry the long-range air search radar of a carrier task force, since the carrier would be unable to. In July 1982 the *Intrepid* became a museum ship in New York Harbor.

delayed. Alternatively they could be fitted with a lengthened H 8 designated H 8-1. In fact the steam catapult came to the rescue, the C 11 replacing both H 8s in an SCB 27C conversion. Three ships were completed to the original SCB 27C standard: the *Hancock*, *Intrepid*, and *Ticonderoga*. SCB 27C was modified to correspond to the new *Forrestal* design, the final three ships (the *Lexington*, *Bon Homme Richard*, and *Shangri-La*) all being completed with the successful angled flight deck and the new enclosed ("Hurricane") bow. They also had their forward centerline elevators enlarged. All of these ships had the new C 11 steam catapult, capable of launching 39,000 pounds at 136 knots or 70,000 at 107.5. By way of comparison, the larger C 7 of the *Forrestal* could launch 70,000 pounds at 116; the H 8 could launch 62,500 pounds at 61 knots. SCB 27Cs could not operate the 70,000-lb A3D because their flight decks were not sufficiently strong; they had a parking limit of 60,000 pounds. By way of weight compensation, the battery of the angled-deck SCB 27C was reduced to eight 5-in/38s and only five twin 3-in/50s.

The steam catapult was different enough from the earlier hydraulic type to prevent conversion of the SCB 27A ships to steam-catapult operation. Instead,

they were subject to an SCB 125 conversion in which they received the angled flight deck, enclosed bow, and an after starboard deck-edge elevator. The *Lake Champlain* alone was not converted. The *Oriskany* received an SCB 125A refit which brought her up to full SCB 27C standard, with Mark 7 (rather than improved Mark 5) arresting gear, C 11-1 steam catapults, and enlarged elevators of increased capacity.

All of the angled-deck carriers had the enclosed ("hurricane") bow introduced in the all-weather *Forrestal* design. It has been foreshadowed by the *Midways*' strengthened and partly enclosed bow, with its secondary conn, and was inspired by severe storm damage, when the edges of several *Essex* flight decks were smashed. On the hurricane bow, the flare of the hull was blended into the forward end of the flight deck. A secondary conn (with portholes in the forward part of the bow) occupied the space directly under the flight deck. Ships initially modernized with open bows showed a knuckle forward, whereas the final SCB 27Cs, completed with enclosed bows, had smoothly faired bows. Presumably that represented relocation of some catapult equipment to clear the emergency conn forward.

Given a fixed upper limit on the size of the active

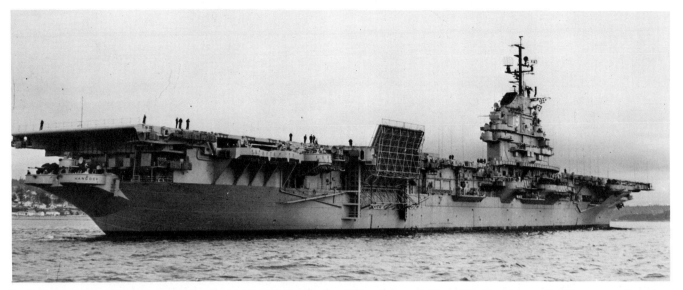

A starboard quarter view of the newly converted *Hancock*, off Puget Sound Navy Yard on 28 April 1954, shows her after deck-edge elevator folded up. She was the prototype SCB-27C. Note her 3-in and 5-in gun tubs, and the small radome of an SPN-8 blind-landing radar at the after end of her island structure. All *Essex* conversions involved blistering. However, since the blisters were carried up to the hangar deck and faired into the hull fore and aft, they are not readily apparent in these photographs.

attack-carrier force, the SCB 27A conversions displaced unconverted *Essex*-class ships, which were redesignated support carriers and assigned to ASW missions (see chapter 15). In their turn they were replaced by the *Forrestal*s and the SCB 27Cs. All of the converted *Essex*es were marginal in their stability as completed and required weight compensation for fixed improvements (such as heavier radars) and, it appeared, for the rising weight of aircraft. The only available compensation was the gun battery, which in any case was of increasingly less value for self-defense against enemy air attack. Few of these ships retained many of the original 3-in/50 guns by 1960, after which 5-in/38s were removed as well. For example, at the end of her career the *Oriskany* retained only two of the latter. The other surviving units all had four.

The other major carrier modernization program was applied to the *Midway*s. At first they were too valuable to withdraw from service, because their rather austere improvement program no. 1 made them the only carriers capable of launching Savage atomic bombers, and, indeed, of handling nuclear weapons. Their great advantage over the *Essex*es in this regard was their longer, more powerful, H 4-1 catapult, barely sufficient for an AJ. However, after the cancellation of the *United States*, conversion of the *Midway*s was the only way a platform for the new A3D strategic carrier bomber could be provided.

In May 1949, with the super-carrier barely dead, the CNO authorized a conversion study. BuAer expected to replace the existing H 4-1 with one of the new slotted-tube catapults; the flight deck would have to be strengthened to take a parking load of 80,000 pounds, and the deck-edge elevator enlarged to 60 by 40 feet (an 80,000-lb parking load). Fuel capacity would have to be increased and the crane strengthened to take a 60,000-lb weight. An air group of twelve A3Ds and seventy of the new F3D night fighters (which would prove unsuitable for carrier operation in the end) was contemplated. BuShips estimated that the new long catapult would require elimination of the forward flight-deck expansion joint, which in turn would require major changes in the structure supporting the flight deck. In effect a forecastle deck would have to be built up. The flight deck itself would have to be extended forward about 40 feet, the bow enclosed, and the two forward twin 3-in/50s eliminated. In addition, a deck-edge elevator would have to replace the forward centerline one. The need to allow for deck-landing reactions would require so great an alternation to the after elevator that the bureau proposed that it be replaced with a stern elevator, such as the one designed for the abortive *United States*. Alternatively, a deck-edge elevator might be installed on the starboard deck edge aft. The bureau believed that aviation-fuel capacity could be increased to 500,000 gallons by enlargement of the forward tanks at the expense of bunker oil; the after tanks could not be enlarged without major alterations to the shaft alleys. The net effect of such a conversion would be an increase of about 3,170 tons in displacement, for a full load of 64,495 tons. The cost would be about $45 million.

No conversion was planned at that time, as the FY 52 program was being drawn up. However, the Korean War made funds available, so that in August 1950 most of the FY 52 program had already been

In these Puget Sound photographs of 24 August (*above*) and 1 October 1956 (*facing*), the *Hornet*, with her angled deck and enclosed bow, illustrates the SCB 125 conversion of an already-modernized (SCB 27A) *Essex*-class carrier. The bow incorporates an emergency steering station indicated by a row of portholes. An after starboard deck-edge elevator was also fitted in place of the former centerline unit. Note the sharp reduction in gun battery: the ship mounted seven rather than eight 5-in/38s and apparently only three twin 3-in/50s, and one 5-in/38 gun was removed from the *starboard* after gun sponson, near the after deck-edge elevator. The flight-deck view is a blend of new and old, with a radical Vought Cutlass (F7U) parked just abaft a rather battered, wartime TBM Avenger, and a Skyraider and two Grumman Panthers parked forward.

incorporated in FY 50 and FY 51 supplementals. In April 1952 a *Midway* conversion was included in the prospective FY 54 program as SCB 110. Planning paralleled SCB 27C as it was then understood, except that the two long hydraulic catapults were to be replaced by the powerful C 7s and avgas stowage increased to 500,000 gallons. All three elevators would be enlarged to about 50 by 60 feet and strengthened to take the 70,000-lb A3D bomber. The C 7 was as yet a powder catapult, and space had to be found for 150 tons of charges. A 5-ft blister would keep the preconversion draft to maintain torpedo protection. The belt armor would be removed in favor of the 60-lb splinter plating of the *Essex* conversions and internal box protection for magazines and gasoline tanks. Later steam catapults (long-stroke versions of the C 11, rather than the much more powerful C 7) were specified, and the deck-edge elevators enlarged to the 63- by 52-ft type of the *Forrestal*s. The remaining centerline elevator could not be widened, but it was to be lengthened.

As in the *Essex* modernization, the next step was an angled deck. Indeed, the *Midway* herself had been used to test angled-deck concepts. SCB 110 differed from the *Essex* schemes in that provision to operate the new A3D was essential, with consequences for flight deck and elevator strength. Blistering was necessary to balance the top weight of the angled-deck sponson and maintain the limited freeboard of these rather wet ships. It was also argued that space needed for habitability might be gained along the

second and third decks, and that torpedo protection would be enhanced.

As in the *Essex*es, guns had to be removed for weight compensation and because gun positions had been covered by both the big angled-deck sponson and the new deck-edge elevator aft. Thus characteristics of September 1952 showed only eleven 5-in/54s and eight twin 3-in/50s, and the *Midway* actually emerged from reconstruction with even fewer guns. BuOrd had tried unsuccessfully to obtain a modernized battery of rapid-fire 5-in/54 guns. Similarly, after a long struggle for improved side protection, BuOrd was forced to settle for the 60-lb (1.5-in) STS of the SCB 27 series.

By this time HEAF and blending were available, so the enlargement of avgas tanks was abandoned in favor of stowage of 600,000 gallons of HEAF (replacing bunker oil); endurance fell to 11,200 nautical miles at 20 knots (plus 1,300 nautical miles if HEAF were burned in the boilers). By late 1952 the modernization was limited to $35 million exclusive of electronics (which would be paid for out of the material improvement program).

In view of the decision to provide the *Forrestal* with two waist catapults, the SCB began to reconsider a third C 11 for the *Midway* conversion and recommended its inclusion in SCB 110. BuShips undertook the study with the thought of adding a modified C 11 with a 150-ft stroke, which would be able to launch interceptors, at 30-sec intervals, when the ship was under way at not less than 15 knots. Space, weight,

The *Oriskany* was unique among SCB 27A carriers in being rebuilt, in an SCB 125A modernization, with steam catapults, an angled deck, and an enclosed bow. She is shown in September 1959, the galleries along her starboard side emphasizing her blister. Note, too, her new radar arrangement, with an SPS-37A long-wavelength air search set sponsored outboard and an SPS-8 height finder inboard. The air search set above them is an SPS-12, with an SPS-10, for surface search, above both. Note the lengthened centerline elevator forward. The aircraft are McDonnell F3H Demons, fleet-air-defense fighters that were the first operational carriers of the Sparrow long-range air-to-air missile.

and stability were all available because of the blistering; the installation would cost about $5 million. Alternatively, the full 211-ft C 11 might be installed; this would require relocation of a flight-deck expansion joint, and the new catapult would infringe on the arresting pendant area. Interceptors could, however, be launched while the ship was at anchor. A cost of $6.5 million would include the catapult itself.

The *Franklin D. Roosevelt* was reconstructed at Puget Sound under the FY 54 program at a cost of $48 million, with three catapults, a fully enclosed ("hurricane") bow, and a battery reduced to ten 5-in/50 guns and eleven twin 3-in/50s. She was completed 6 April 1956, followed into the yard by the *Midway*, authorized under the same program, and completed

1 October 1957. Finally, modernization of the *Coral Sea* was authorized under the FY 57 program (SCB 110A, with the forward centerline elevator replaced by a second starboard deck-edge unit). Her 5-in battery was, therefore, reduced to six guns and her 3-in battery entirely removed (she was recommissioned in January 1960). Both of her sisters had their 3-in guns removed at the same time, and all suffered further reductions in their 5-in batteries, so that in 1963 both SCB 110s had only four guns (and their sister only three).

The three *Midway*s occupied a position between the *Essex*es and *Forrestal*s. They had flight decks large enough to make operation of such modern types as the F-4 Phantom practical, and so were well worth

The axial-deck SCB 27C attack carriers were rebuilt to angled-deck configuration. The *Intrepid* is shown off Norfolk on 25 March 1960, with a Grumman Trader COD airplane on her starboard catapult and a Skywarrior and three Skyray fighters abaft her island. The port sponson 3-in/50 mount has been replaced by what appears to be oil tanks. Note the new radio antenna sponsoned out from the flight deck forward (to starboard) and the five arresting-gear pendants on her angled deck.

retaining in service longer than earlier ships. On the other hand, they were limited by their 17-ft 6-in hangar decks and C 11 catapults, the same type that had been installed in the reconstructed *Essex*es. In 1966, therefore, the *Midway* was again reconstructed at Puget Sound (SCB 101.66, FY 66 program). This project ultimately included replacement of the forward centerline elevator by a deck-edge unit, as in the *Coral Sea*, and of the three C 11 catapults by two C 13s located forward. Flight-deck area was increased considerably and new arresting gear was fitted. Aviation-fuel capacity rose from 873,000 gallons of JP-5 (plus 60,000 of avgas) to a new total of 1,200,000 gallons (the figure originally aimed at in SCB 110). This refit proved extraordinarily expensive. Budgeted at $84.3 million, it ultimately came to $200 million, a sobering figure. The *Midway* was recommissioned on 31 January 1970. Given her cost, a similar planned modernization of the other SCB 110, the *Franklin D. Roosevelt* (SCB 103.68 of the FY 68 program), was

cancelled in favor of an austere overhaul, which nonetheless included elmination of the forward centerline elevator in favor of a deck-edge unit. The waist C 11 was removed but the two bow units were not replaced by C 13s.

CVA 42 was stricken in 1977; reportedly she was the worst of the three in material condition. It was argued at the time that the 17-ft 6-in clear hangar-deck height of these ships was a fundamental limitation—it was better to retain *Essex*es in reserve, as the latter would be less expensive to operate if they were recommissioned. On her last cruise, for example, the *Franklin D. Roosevelt* had to operate E-1B rather than E-2 airborne radar aircraft. On the other hand, her sisters do operate modern combat aircraft. The *Coral Sea* (CV 43) remains in service as a limited attack carrier and is unlikely ever to receive a conversion equivalent to that accorded the *Midway*, the only one of her class really equivalent to later carriers.

As an ASW support carrier (CVS) in October 1969, the *Intrepid* shows even less armament (she appears to have only one 5-in/38 forward), but she does have a self-protective ECM (sponsored outboard of her island and flight deck). She was fitted with a bow anchor to clear a new SQS-23 sonar in her forefoot. Also evident is the greatly enlarged pri-fly structure at the rear of her island. The large dish antenna belonged to an SPS-30 height finder; the small dots visible abaft the island are spotlights for night operation.

Photographed on 10 November 1967, the *Ticonderoga* has the final appearance of *Essex*-class attack carriers, with greatly reduced gun batteries (only three or four 5-in/38s at the time of decommissioning) and the massive "mattress" of an SPS-43A. The enlarged and raised pri-fly clears the big radome of an SPN-35 blind-landing radar abaft the island, which is barely visible here. Note, too, the antenna mast aft, carrying monopoles for long-range radio communication, tilted outboard for flight operations. The aircraft on deck are A-4 Skyhawks and F-8 Crusaders forward; a Skywarrior has just landed on the angled deck. One obstacle to the proposed recommissioning of *Essex*-class CVAs is said to be a lack of suitability for current types of aircraft.

Off Rota on 10 June 1970, the *Wasp* illustrates the final appearance of the SCB 27A/125 ASW carriers. They could be distinguished from the steam-catapult ships by the absence of bridle arresters forward. Note the prominent fueling lines amidships, hung from a boom on the island: ASW carriers had to maintain their escorts' endurance. The big radome of an SPN-35 blind-landing radar is just visible abaft the island, and three Grumman Tracer AEW aircraft can be distinguished on deck among their cousins, the Grumman S-2 Trackers. Although by this time the 5-in battery had been reduced to four guns, the ship still retained both of her Mark 37 directors and two Mark 56 directors. Her bow anchor indicates the presence of a bow sonar; some consideration had also been given to providing these ships with variable depth sonars trailed from their fantails, which the Soviet *Kiev*-class carriers now employ.

These photographs are dated 23 May 1956, when the *Franklin D. Roosevelt* was on trials after her recommissioning on 6 April. She was the first *Midway* to be reconstructed under SCB Project 110. She retained a considerable gun battery. It proved impossible to replace the slow-firing single 5-in mounts with rapid-fire Mark 42s. The two radars on the new tower mast were an SPS-8 and, below it, an SPS-12. An SPN-8 blind-landing radar was mounted on the after end of the island. The waist catapult is clearly shown in the overhead view.

The *Midway*, rebuilt to a slightly different design, retained her original radar mast. She is shown off Puget Sound on 2 December 1957, having been recommissioned on 30 September. The success of the design effort for the two SCB 110 reconstructions inspired an attempt to design a new 45,000-ton attack carrier, CVA 10/53.

The *Coral Sea* had an elaborate reconstruction under SCB Project 110A, with her port deck-edge elevator moved aft to clear her waist catapult and her forward centerline elevator replaced by a deck-edge unit. All of her 3-in/50s were eliminated, and her gun battery was reduced to six single 5-in/54s, all of them on large sponsons (with none forward of the angled deck and its catapult). The mirror landing aid is visible on its sponson forward of the port deck-edge elevator. These photographs were taken off Puget Sound on 15 February 1960; the ship was recommissioned on 25 January, having entered the yard on 16 April 1957.

The *Midway* was reconstructed a second time, at San Francisco, under SCB Project 101.66; she is shown here emerging from the yard on 31 January 1970. Note her greatly enlarged flight deck, her new mast for an SPN-6 CCA radar, and her sharply curtailed AA battery. This refit was so expensive that a proposed SCB 101.68 (FY 68) refit of the *Franklin D. Roosevelt* was cancelled; she received an austere refit instead.

The *Coral Sea* is shown in the Pacific on 10 September 1977. Little altered since her SCB 110A refit, she had, by this time, only three 5-in/54 guns; within three years none were left. She can operate all current types of aircraft, except the F-14, but her limited hangar clear height makes some maintenance tasks difficult. The *Coral Sea* is now a limited attack carrier, scheduled to replace the *Lexington* as a training carrier at Pensacola in the mid 1980s.

The *Midway* is the oldest operational U.S. carrier and may well serve past her fortieth year as a first-line unit. She is shown in the Indian Ocean late in 1979, considerably modified since 1970. At the time of this photo she was armed with Sea Sparrow defensive missiles and was scheduled to be fitted with Phalanx close-in defensive guns; she retained none of her 5-in battery.

14

Nuclear Carriers

Carriers were the last class of warships to be considered for nuclear power. The advantages of utilizing such power were not nearly so obvious in a carrier as in, say, submarines or destroyers. The latter needed nuclear propulsion merely to operate with the high-endurance conventional carriers. For a carrier, the advantages of unlimited steaming endurance were far more difficult to quantify. For example, although the carrier could continue to steam for several years, her aircraft would need a fresh fill of fuel and ammunition after only a few strike days. On the other hand, a carrier on patrol in very distant waters flies relatively few sorties but burns a great deal of oil—as the U.S. Navy found to its disadvantage in the Indian Ocean in 1979–81. Nuclear power also obviates the use of uptakes and prevents stack-gas corrosion, both considerable problems in carrier operation. Aircraft riding the flight deck of a conventional carrier suffer corrosion damage from stack gases and sea water, a significant consideration in an era of very costly airplanes with long operational lives. In the late forties and early fifties, when the flush-deck carrier was the sine qua non for continued progress in naval aviation, the elimination of uptakes was considered to be a major advantage.

Several carrier commanders have said that the great advantage of nuclear power is the availability of vast reserves of electrical and steam power and the assurance that fuel will not be used up too rapidly. That is, even a carrier steaming at less than flank speed uses a lot of power to catapult aircraft. A modern carrier also uses huge quantities of electrical power, amounting to a significant fraction of her total power output. In a conventionally powered carrier, this drain on the boilers requires careful control. However, the reactors of a nuclear carrier have such large margins designed into them that the achievement of full electrical power is no problem. The nuclear carrier also has the freedom to steam at full speed, over 30 knots, for an extended period. That freedom became more and more important as the threat of Soviet submarines grew in the late fifties and early sixties. That is, the faster the carrier relative to the submarine, the less opportunity the submarine has to approach to within torpedo range. Missiles are admittedly a much more difficult problem, but even they have their limits. Moreover, the faster the carrier, the more difficult a target she is for pre-planned long-range air strikes, which since the late fifties have been the chief Soviet anticarrier tactic.

Because the value of nuclear power in large surface ships was so indistinct, it was probably not really appreciated until the very successful world cruise of the nuclear task force consisting of the *Enterprise*, the cruiser *Long Beach*, and the frigate *Bainbridge*. Again, because it was difficult to define the feasibility of the nuclear plant in quantitative terms, and because nuclear power was so very expensive, the advocates of nuclear carriers had a hard time convincing Secretary of Defense McNamara of their value in the controversy over CVA/CVAN 67.

Nuclear propulsion was first considered for aircraft carriers in 1946, as part of the super-carrier project resulting in the design of the *United States*. At

The newly completed nuclear carrier *Enterprise* shows only three Grumman S2F ASW planes on her vast flight deck. Her island shows the large flat panels of the SPS-32 and -33 electronically scanned radars, with a carrier approach radar (SPN-6) visible alongside her unique conical ESM array. The prominent antennas at the bow, for carrier-to-air communication, were replaced within a few years by the current Phasor-90 cones. Note also the portholes of the usual secondary conn in the bow.

that time one of its major advantages was the absence of uptakes; flush-deck carrier designers were plagued with the problem of smoke disposal. Moreover, it could be argued that, unlike a submarine or a destroyer, a carrier had sufficient reserves of space and weight to accommodate even a very large plant. Most versions of the SCB-6A project included provision for nuclear power in one or more of the four ships planned.

Reactor development was not quite fast enough to provide such a plant for the SCB-6A planned for FY 52, but from then on the expectation that it would soon produce an acceptable carrier power plant colored even the development of non-nuclear carriers. For example, proposals to develop a wholly new carrier design to succeed the *Forrestals* were abandoned because it was clear that very few such ships could be built before the shift to nuclear power for all future carriers. In fact the high initial cost of a nuclear power plant prompted a search for a less expensive nuclear carrier after the design of the *Enterprise*, and the next two carriers received conventional plants. The *Nimitz* design was economical in part because it incorporated new reactor technology, providing sufficient power in only two reactors.

Nuclear-carrier design entailed some unique problems. First the development of any given reactor was difficult and expensive enough to require ships to be designed around particular power plants. To some extent that was also true of non-nuclear carriers, because the design of a wholly new steam power plant was a complicated process. However, non-nuclear plants were infinitely more elastic in their design than nuclear ones were. That is, it was far easier to design a new non-nuclear plant say, 30 percent more powerful than an existing one, than to develop a wholly new reactor. The nuclear designers, for example, could not easily tolerate the sort of power plant growth experienced in the *Midway* design (see chapter 9). This consideration held for all nuclear ships, from submarines up. What was unique in a carrier was the role of oil fuel, which was antitorpedo protection as well as propellant. Thus even nuclear carriers had to incorporate extensive liquid loads, even though those loads were irrelevant to propulsion. Torpedo protection spaces, then, could carry enough fuel to propel escorts; their size also made for greater air-group fuel endurance, since jet fuel as well as bunker oil could fill them. However, the sheer weight of that fuel required large ships. That is, one might imagine that a nuclear carrier would be about the size of the corresponding conventional ship if only her reactor, boilers, and turbines weighed no more than the fuel, boilers, and turbines of an oil burner. However, she was unable to dispense with that fuel oil, unless she also dispensed with its protective value. This problem of excess fuel was a major incentive to develop a new and more compact torpedo protective system—which, ironically, first appeared in the non-nuclear carrier *John F. Kennedy*.

In the *Enterprise* design the apparent disadvantage of a heavy oil-fuel load was turned on its head; the ship accommodated enough aircraft to make full use of her very large aviation-fuel capacity and was provided with enough magazine space and quick-reloading equipment to make the larger air group fully effective.

One of the earliest indications of navy interest in a nuclear carrier was a 1 August 1950 request by the CNO, Admiral Forrest Sherman, for a BuShips study of the feasibility of such a ship. Captain H. G. Rickover proposed completion in 1953 of a land-based prototype, the large ship reactor (LSR), and in 1955 of a shipboard plant. So large a plant would have competed directly with the nuclear weapons program, which used the same highly enriched uranium, so a design study was ordered but no prototype built. However, the Joint Chiefs of Staff did establish a formal requirement for a carrier reactor in November 1951. At this time the only other naval reactor design in progress was the submarine type that ultimately powered the *Nautilus*. A carrier required a very different design, which was assigned in such a way as to preclude merely scaling up the submarine reactor for it. By 1952 the estimated cost of the land-based prototype was about $150 million, that is, almost as much as a conventional carrier itself. Given such a high cost, the Joint Chiefs sought to combine in a single plant a prototype land-based power reactor, a plutonium-making reactor, and the naval prototype.

The new Eisenhower administration was determined to cut military costs, just as authorization for the LSR was due. Question was raised within the navy as to the value of a carrier plant. Nuclear power was far easier to justify for a submarine or even for a short-range destroyer; carriers were so large that they could transport a sufficient amount of fuel with them. Moreover, there was some question as to whether the navy could obtain enough nuclear fuel for both a large fleet of submarines and surface ships, a fear particularly legitimate at a time of rapid nuclear-weapon production, with its great drain on national nuclear resources. Too, there was fear within OPNAV that support for a future nuclear carrier would undermine the existing (and urgent) program of conventional-carrier construction. Admiral Sherman appears to have been the only major naval exponent of the carrier project, and he died in July 1951. Therefore in the summer of 1953 the Atomic Energy Commission (AEC) cancelled the carrier-reactor project in favor of one for a land-based power station.

However, the carrier-reactor project did not die. In

The huge *Enterprise*, seen shortly after completion on 29 October 1961, introduced several new features: fixed (phased-array) radars for air search and height finding, a new flight-deck layout (retroactively applied to the two *Kitty Hawk*s), and provision for a missile battery for self-defense (also retroactively applied to the *Kitty Hawk*s). The missiles themselves were not mounted, for economy's sake; note the empty sponson on the ship's starboard quarter. When this photograph was taken, the only conventional radars on board were the SPN-6 and the SPN-10 of the CCA system. The cone above the massive flat search radars housed ECM antennas. The *Enterprise* emerged from a 1979–82 refit with conventional radars (an SPS-48 and an SPS-49) replacing her somewhat temperamental fixed arrays, and she is now armed with the Sea Sparrow and the Phalanx close-in defensive gun.

The *Enterprise* displays one of her Sea Sparrow launchers in this 21 June 1976 photograph. The SPS-12 conventional air search radar on her island was added partly because the big flat arrays were not entirely reliable, and partly because they had no IFF facilities. The small white radome above her bridge housed a British-type SCOT/satellite-communication antenna, allowing the ship to use British-oriented facilities in areas such as the Indian Ocean.

May 1954 Rickover proposed a program of five reactor prototypes, ranging from an attack-submarine power plant up through destroyer, cruiser, and carrier prototypes. The administration approved, and research and development of the carrier-reactor land-based prototype was approved by the AEC in August 1954. By the end of 1955 a land-based prototype, the A1W, consisting of two reactors driving a simulated single propeller shaft of a carrier, was planned. A frigate reactor, the F1W, was to use the same core in a somewhat larger reactor, and there was also to be a cruiser plant, the C1W, using four A1W reactors rather than the eight of the carrier plant. In these designations the first letter indicated the type of ship, the second the manufacturer (W for Westinghouse and G for General Electric). A two-reactor variant of the C1W powered the nuclear cruiser *Long Beach*. In fact, the *Long Beach* plant was used as a seagoing test version of that planned for the *Enterprise*. No F1W entered service; instead there were the D1G and D2G destroyer (frigate) reactors. As for carriers, the operational version of the A1W was the A2W; eight reactors of this type powered the first U.S. nuclear carrier, the *Enterprise*.

Both the A2W and C1W produced similar levels of power. The 280,000 SHP for the *Enterprise* equates to 35,000 SHP per reactor; the reported 80,000 SHP of the *Long Beach* equates to about 40,000 SHP per reactor. The destroyer reactors were somewhat smaller, the *Bainbridge* showing 60,000 SHP with two D2Gs, or 30,000 SHP each. By the late fifties individual reactor power was rising, since it appeared that the fewer reactors per ship, the lower the cost per ship would be. An abortive A3W was designed for the four-reactor attack carrier proposed under the FY 61 and FY 63 programs. Since these ships were slower than the *Enterprise*, one can conclude that the A3W came well short of a quarter of the 280,000-SHP plant, probably about 45,000 to 50,000 SHP. However, the pressure for more powerful reactors continued strong. In the early sixties there were attempts to design a single reactor that might replace the 60,000-SHP D2G plant. Although it was not built, experience in its design led directly to the huge A4W, the *Nimitz* plant, which reportedly produces 260,000 SHP (130,000 SHP per reactor). At each level of power some upgrading was possible, but not very much, given the delicacy of reactor design. Thus, for example, any attempt to design a range of nuclear aircraft carriers was very strictly constrained by the range of available reactors. The original A1W/A2W was sized on the basis of contemporary conventional-carrier power plants, the four-reactor C1W originally being intended to produce a level of power comparable with that of a *Des Moines*-class heavy cruiser capable of 120,000 SHP. Ultimately it did rather better on two

reactors, which gives some indication of the range of reactor-design flexibility, before details had been fixed.

Once the LSR project had been approved, a nuclear carrier (CVAN) design could begin. In fact a small nuclear carrier (CVAN 4/53) was studied in 1953, but the *Enterprise* (CVAN 65, SCB 160 design), the first American nuclear carrier, began with tentative characteristics set forth in a 16 February 1954 BuShips memorandum.

—Aviation features primary
—To be built and serviced in existing U.S. facilities (maximum dimensions 1080 LWL x 130 x 36 feet)
—Protection at least equal to that of *Forrestal*
—Strength deck at the top of the gallery deck (for the proposed new catapult arrangement)
—Canted flight deck
—Capable of operating 100,000 lb aircraft
—At least eight 5-in/54
—2000 tons of aviation ordnance
—Best speed
—4 elevators and 4 steam catapults, two of the latter to launch 100,000 lb aircraft
—3 million gallons of aviation fuel

There seems to have been a general feeling that with nuclear power and the steam catapult a radically new type of flight-deck configuration would be both possible and appropriate. The alternatives considered ranged widely and included dual-runway layouts with the island on the centerline, ramps replacing the elevators required to service the 100,000-lb aircraft, even a two-level arrangement reminiscent of some of the designs of the thirties. All called for rather large ships; in some cases two- or three-shaft plants were tried in *Forrestal*-size hulls, at the cost of speed. The net effect of all of the sketch designs was to force up the size of any future CVAN by showing how poor a bargain a small one would be. It was no great surprise that the radical flight-deck layouts were rejected. As for machinery, speed requirements ruled out anything short of the full four-shaft power plant ultimately adopted.

Given the need for considerable liquid weight in any conventional protective system, the designers of the *Enterprise* tried to limit the excess size of their ship by carrying no liquids outside the side protective system except for those requiring special handling: H202, lubricating oil, cleaning fluid.

The redesigned flight deck (island moved aft and thus interchanged with no. 2 starboard elevator, port elevator moved from the fore to the after end of the port sponson to feed the waist catapults) was derived from the abortive SCB 153 design. In contrast with previous carriers, there were only two hangar bays, each served by two elevators. The elevators themselves were redesigned: wedge-shaped additions to their outboard sides facilitated nose-wheel handling of aircraft taken on and off them.

HEAF fuel stowage was comparable with that of previous carriers, but could be increased by 850,000 gallons if the bunker oil normally carried for escorts were not required. On the other hand, compared with earlier ships, avgas stowage was reduced from 300,000 to 100,000 gallons, presumably on the theory that an all-nuclear strike carrier deserved only the most modern aircraft. H202 (300,000 gallons) was specified for the first time; it easily supplanted gasoline as the chief liquid hazard aboard ship.

The combination of nuclear endurance and voluminous tankage made it worthwhile to design the carrier for a much longer unreplenished strike mission than was possible previously, with a corresponding increase in aviation ordnance stowage. Another radical requirement, very fast re-arming of one-third of the fighter-attack group, was met by stowing ready-service aircraft ammunition on handling skids within the armored box. It was also important to be able to recover aircraft rapidly and easily: SCB 160 introduced the mirror-landing system. In consequence the number of arresting wires could be reduced from six to five.

Given the great cost of the nuclear carrier and the novelty of her power plant, people appear to have been tempted to incorporate other advanced naval technology in her. Thus the *Enterprise* had the very long-range electronically scanned fixed antennas of the Hughes SCANFAR system, as well as the first defensive guided-missile system (Terrier) in a U.S. carrier. Her designers believed that her nuclear power plant would be unsuitable for steam catapults, perhaps because nuclear reactors did not produce superheated steam. She was therefore to have had a new internal combustion catapult, the C 14.

There were, to be sure, problems. For example, aircraft weight was limited to 80,000 pounds, and aircraft-fuel capacity did not quite reach the 3,000,000 gallons specified. On the other hand, the boilers did prove well suited to steam-catapult operation; the *Enterprise* received four C-7s. As for the futuristic radar, it had its own problems, and for much of her career the *Enterprise* has carried a conventional SPS-12 as back-up. The complex radars were removed altogether during her 1979–82 refit at Puget Sound. Although space and weight were provided in the design for four (later two) twin Terriers, they were not ultimately fitted, the intention being to contain the explosive cost growth of the ship. She operated almost entirely unarmed (with four single 20 mm guns) for several years, but received the prototype Sea Sparrow (BPDMS) installation in 1968.

The SCB 160 preliminary design was completed in September 1956 for funding under the FY 58 program, with long lead items in FY 57. The *Enterprise* was so large that strong pressure was brought to reduce her size. In February 1957, for example, the preliminary designers sketched a similar design in

The *Enterprise* is shown on sea trials in February 1982 after a long Puget Sound refit begun in 1979. The most noticeable change is the removal of the futuristic electronic-scan radars from her island; she was fitted with an SPS-48 three-dimensional radar (forward) and an SPS-49 long-range air search set (aft), as well as an SPN-41 for CCA aft on the starboard side of her flight deck. At this time, too, the basic point defense system (Sea Sparrow) installed in 1967 was replaced by a NATO Sea Sparrow system, one of the three launchers for which is visible on the after port sponson. Two directors for the Mark 91 mod 1 fire-control system are visible in the vertical niche cut into her block-shaped island structure, at its after port corner. The ship was also fitted with three Phalanx close-in defensive guns, one of them on the port forward sponson and another at the after port edge of her quarterdeck. The cylindrical objects along the edge of the flight deck are encapsulated life rafts. The *Enterprise* has a unique (and complex) eight-reactor power plant, all of her machinery reportedly being concentrated to save piping and shielding weight.

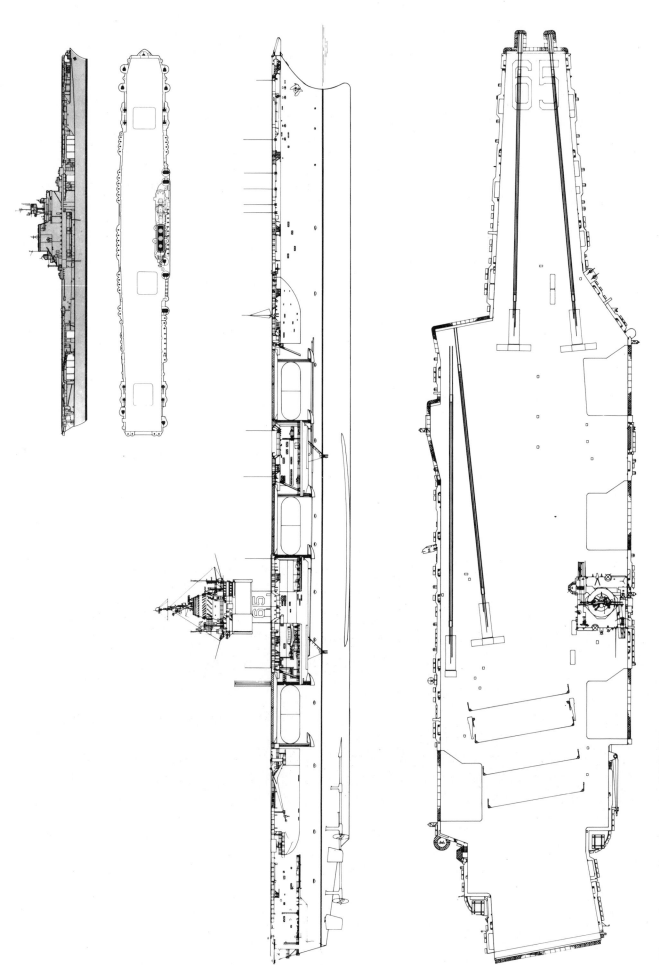

The nuclear carrier *Enterprise* (CVN 65).

Although several nuclear carriers were designed during the late fifties and early sixties, none was built; the *Nimitz*, completed in 1975, was the first to follow the *Enterprise*. Here the *Nimitz* is shown off the Virginia Capes on 1 March 1975. Her arrangement generally follows that of her non-nuclear forebears, with a "smooth" (non-spray-forming) hull forward and a lattice radar mast abaft her island. A Sea Sparrow defensive missile launcher occupies the sponson forward.

which all side protection was omitted, with only one side bulkhead (to carry essential liquids) retained. The result was a carrier whose hull dimensions were 1,015 by 132 by 35.75 feet, and displacement fell to 63,400 tons light and 80,500 fully loaded. It was estimated that $5 million could be saved on an *Enterprise* cost then estimated at $314 million. One reason for the 25-ft reduction in length was increased internal volume. On the other hand, it seemed that the loss of underwater protection was not balanced by any great gain in cost; in effect this study justified the very large size of the nuclear carrier, so long as the full eight-reactor power plant was employed. Any reduction in size would have to come from some more radical change, such as the use of a smaller number of individually more powerful reactors, the A3Ws.

The CNO, Arleigh Burke, laid out his strategy for the FY 59 and subsequent programs in a 3 August 1957 memo to the chairman of the shipbuilding committee (Op-03B). He already knew that future shipbuilding funds would not cover the types of ships he needed, that the navy's programs for advanced technology were encountering severe overruns.

Funds can usually be obtained more easily for ships and weapons of greatly improved performance than is possible for . . . weapons of lesser capability. In other words, funds for nuclear power, guided missiles, and atomic delivery systems can be obtained more easily than less funds for conventional power plants, guns, and other conventional weapons. Furthermore, initial installations of new equipment usually result in greatly increased performance of this equipment as experience is gained. . . .

There will be great pressure by the other services to eliminate any carrier from future programs. There was a warning by the House Appropriations Committee on future CVANs. Whether or not this warning was intended to apply only to nuclear power for car-

riers or whether it was intended to apply to any future carrier is not definitely known. The Navy should have at least three more attack carriers, which would give a total of 12 modern attack carriers. It may be that we will require one or two more than this but the decision does not have to be made now.

Certainly we must take the steps which will permit us to get new attack carriers. If we were assured of getting an attack carrier in 60 we could afford to take a holiday in 59 although it would be better if we could get one each year until we arrive at an adequate total.

The advantages of a CVAN over a CVA are not fully known. There are considerable advantages but the additional cost of $100 million may be a very high price to pay. . . . Actually the advantages of whether to include in the 59 shipbuilding program a CVA, a CVAN, or long-lead time components for a CVAN is determinable only by which program has the best chance of being approved by DOD [Department of Defense], BuBud [Bureau of the Budget], and Congress.

In view of the Committee's statement it is unlikely that a CVAN next year could be approved.

If a holiday for attack carriers in the 59 shipbuilding program is adopted, we must have assurance that such a carrier will be approved in the 60 program. If Congress were to appropriate considerable funds for long-lead items and if they made a statement of intent in the 59 hearings that they intended to support a carrier for 1960, such assurances would probably be the maximum we could obtain. The mortgage on the 60 carrier would have to be of such significance that it could not be cancelled with impunity. Therefore, the long-lead components should be in the order of $50 to $100 million, which money would actually be spent in 1959 so that cancellation would not be easily accomplished.

In fact no carrier was included in the FY 60 program, a navy request for such a ship having been turned down. However, a lot of work was done on a new and less expensive CVAN for FY 60, designed around a much more austere propulsion plant. No new design was possible for FY 59, given time constraints, so early navy versions of the FY 59 program showed a repeat *Enterprise.*

A series of studies of less expensive nuclear attack carriers (CVAN 7/57) was begun in the summer of 1957. It called for
—A 22.5- instead of a 25-ft hangar
—A sustained speed below 30 knots
—Six (rather than eight) reactors at most
—50,000-lb aircraft, with a total of 750 tons
—A length of about 950 feet
—About 60,000 tons
—Fewer catapults and elevators

Both two- and three-shaft designs were investigated, using the reactors already developed for the nuclear cruiser *Long Beach*, the frigate *Bainbridge*, and a quarter of the full *Enterprise* plant. It appeared, for example, that two *Long Beach* plants could be accommodated on 60,000 tons and a length of 900 feet, with two elevators, 90 percent of the complement and 75 percent of the aviation fuel and ordnance accommodated by the *Enterprise*. In effect, then, the ship might be able to sustain operations for a comparable time but could not hope to provide the intensity of operations possible with the *Enterprise*. Nor would she have the speed previously considered essential.

A parallel series of studies of much smaller carriers was also done to explore the effects of various types of limits (see table 14-1). Scheme G was sized to carry out a single air strike, with 600 tons of aircraft and

Table 14-1. 1957 Studies for the Small Attack Carrier

	G†	H	J	K
Light Ship (tons)	25,500	15,860	17,350	21,600
Full Load (tons)	34,700	20,000	24,300	25,000
LWL (ft)	725	660	710	710
Beam (ft)	105	88	88	94
Draft (ft)	30	24	26	—
Depth (ft)	80	74.5	76	81
SHP	140,000	90,000	105,000	80,000
Speed (sust) (kts)	30.3	29	30	28
Aircraft*	600	300	300	—
Av Ord (tons)	415	225	325	—
JP-5 (tons)	1,530	800	1,225	—
Catapults	—	—	2 C 11-1	2 C 14
Elevators (ft)	—	—	2 40×60	2 40×60
(lbs)			50,000	50,000
Complement (tons)	2,500	2,000	2,000	2,070
NSFO (tons)	4,500	1,515	3,915	—
Endurance (20 kts) (nm)	10,000	4,000	10,000	—

*Including spares, equipment.
†"One shot."

515,000 gallons of JP-5 (and no torpedo protection at all) on 34,700 tons fully loaded, the displacement of a wartime fleet carrier. However, it was much shorter and beamier than such a ship, and would require a 140,000-SHP non-nuclear plant to drive a 725-ft hull at a sustained speed of only 30.3 knots. In effect it was a scheme for the bare minimum, an expendable jet carrier. Scheme H explored the impact of size limits on capability. Non-nuclear, it displaced only 20,000 tons fully loaded, which put it in the large CVL category. As a consequence, it could accommodate only 300 tons of aircraft and only 264,000 gallons of fuel. A 90,000-SHP plant would drive its 660-ft hull at only 29 knots, below the usual 30-kt limit. In effect it demonstrated the futility of small carriers, and its endurance was extremely limited. Scheme J tested the effect of a 30-kt speed limit and a requirement for useful endurance. Displacement rose to 24,300 tons, with an incidental increase in length to 710 feet and in fuel tankage to 405,000 gallons of JP-5. Finally, in scheme K a *Long Beach* power plant was applied to the scheme J hull as a test of minimum CVAN standards. Displacement rose to 25,000 tons, and there was a loss in speed: scheme J had had a 105,000-SHP plant, well above what was available to the *Long Beach*. There were to have been two internal combustion C 14 catapults in place of the C 11-1s of the earlier design, and two 40- by 60-ft (50,000-lb) elevators, with a pair of twin Tartar missile launchers for self-defense. Hull volume freed of fuel stowage would have provided enough aircraft fuel and ammunition for a seven-day mission, albeit with a rather small air group.

The entire 7/57 project was suspended after October 1957 only to be revived the next January. By that time an upgraded cruiser reactor, presumably the abortive A3W, was in prospect, so that three- and four-reactor designs were attractive. A new series of design studies showed hangars reduced from 25 to 22 feet in clear height as well as reductions in side protection. All schemes were restricted to three catapults and three elevators and the landing run was held to 690 feet, as in CVA 64 (compared with 720 feet in the *Enterprise*). There was considerable skepticism; the standing committee on shipbuilding and conversion objected to cost cutting by eliminating self-defense and in February 1958 wrote that "if any reduction in the features is to result in a ship more appealing from the cost reduction standpoint, the reduction in cost over that of the CVAN 65 must be substantial. A few million dollars will not sell the ship."

The carrier of the first sketch design, 58A, was actually smaller than a *Forrestal*, at 65,000 tons fully loaded and 950 feet on the waterline (a 1,000- by 220-ft flight deck, 1.9 million gallons of jet fuel, and two Terrier or Advanced Tartar launchers for self-defense). Cost was estimated at $291 million, compared with $314 million for the *Enterprise*'s Terrier. Scheme 58B, similar except for a *Forrestal*-length (990-ft) hull, was expected to cost $8 million more. Neither ship could achieve a sustained speed of 30 knots, which was a major requirement. A three-reactor, three-shaft scheme 58C was even slower, but could be built for $242 million, the lowest of the series. Alternatively, the missiles could be foregone, but the standing committee found that unattractive.

Scheme 58A was the best of the lot, even though it had the unusual feature of a centerline elevator right aft to conserve space. It was chosen as the basis for a new CVAN design, with the understanding that the centerline elevator be eliminated. Ultimately all three elevators were set on the starboard side, two of them forward of the island. The landing run was extended to 740 feet by reducing the deck angle to 7°, that is, by reducing the overhang associated with that run and so saving off-center top weight.

Clearly the new carrier, designated SCB 203, was not nearly as attractive as the *Enterprise* or even the recent conventional carriers, since its air group was smaller (1,125 tons, against 1,280 for CVA 60 and 1,350 for CVAN 65). On the other hand, it could support that group for the longer mission contemplated in the design of CVAN 65. For example, it would have only nine heavy attack aircraft compared with the eighteen of both CVA and CVAN, and twelve rather than twenty-four medium attack aircraft; fighter and miscellaneous complements matched those of the other carriers, for a total air group of seventy-eight (ninety-nine in the *Enterprise*, eighty-seven in CVA 63).

By mid-1958, SCB 203 was no longer a totally austere carrier; it incorporated the big SPS-32/33 fixed radars as well as self-defense missiles. It died when Vice Admiral R. B. Pirie (Op-05) objected to its low speed, and smaller deck angle (hence reduced flight-deck area) and air group. No carrier was authorized for FY 60, a navy request for a CVA being turned down. Thus a new CVAN study began in 1959, to achieve aviation facilities at least equal to those of CVA 64 but once again at a cost below that of CVAN 65. It became SCB 211, 1,020 feet long (950 for SCB 203, 1,040 for the *Enterprise*), with the 25-ft hangar restored and a light displacement of 61,800 tons (compared with 54,000 for SCB 203 or 67,600 for the *Enterprise*).

By this time there were more improvements in reactor design, but speed still fell below operator requirements for the four-reactor design. Preliminary Design hoped for further progress and at the same time tried to improve speed performance by fining the ends of the ship. This in turn constricted

internal volume and so reduced the space available for torpedo protection, which brought about the development of the new system that later appeared aboard the non-nuclear carrier *John F. Kennedy*.

In light of the limitations of SCB 211, the FY 61 carrier (CVA 66) was given conventional propulsion; it was an improved CVA 64 rather than a new small CVAN. However, intense interest in further nuclear-carrier construction still existed. It now focussed on the FY 63 carrier, which was planned as a nuclear ship, a modified version of SCB 211. A parallel conventional design was carried as an alternative, given the uncertainty of Secretary of Defense McNamara's willingness to buy a nuclear carrier. Ultimately, in fact, he chose the conventional *John F. Kennedy* (CVA 67). However, the details of the CVA(N) design are of interest because they are the link between the austere carrier studies and the current *Nimitz*.

The principal forces driving the SCB 211A design were the desire for more accommodation and more jet fuel within the envelope developed for SCB 211. Typhon, the new weapon system being developed for fleet air defense, was also considered. Its big electronically scanned radar, SPG-59, could, at least in theory, replace air-search and height-finding sets and so greatly simplify carrier-island arrangements, particularly if it were mounted without any interference with uptakes.

Major changes in characteristics (as of September 1961) were

—C 13 steam catapults in place of the C 14 internal-combustion type originally specified for the nuclear carriers.
—2 million gallons of JP-5 instead of the 1.5 million of SCB 211.
—5,160 rather than 4,655 personnel, and seven rather than six ready rooms, although the ship would operate only six squadrons. It appears that the change in the number of ready rooms was due to an increase in the number of air crew: future fighters (F-4) and medium attack bombers (A-6) would carry two men rather than one.

BuShips suggested some simplification, as all of this would be impossible within the SCB 211 envelope. Full load would probably rise about 2,000 tons and, given the existing power plant, speed would probably fall by half a knot. The increased displacement, moreover, would buy only 150,000 more gallons of JP-5; the full 2 million would have to be bought by reducing fuel oil carried for non-nuclear escorts. As for Typhon, the ship could only afford the "small-ship" (3,400 element) version. Accommodation now exceeded the design figure for the *Enterprise*. Drastic measures, including a reduction in hangar length and fuller use of the space under the carrier's island, could not solve the volume problem.

At this point Secretary McNamara rejected the FY 63 nuclear carrier, but as the battle was clearly not yet over, BuShips continued work. Thus on 16 January 1962 it reported three alternatives to the SCB.

—Without any reduction in escort fuel the SCB 211 hull could accommodate 1.7 million gallons of JP-5, a small Typhon radar, two long-range Typhon launchers, and a complement of 480 officers and 4,450 enlisted men.

—At the cost of considerable growth (and a loss of speed) the full characteristics could be met: 2.05 million gallons of JP-5, a 20 percent increase in aviation ordnance, full Typhon (large radar), and 480 officers and 4,680 enlisted men.

—The bureau preferred a compromise in which 1.8 million gallons of JP-5 was bought at the expense of a reduction in escort fuel, Typhon had a medium radar and two Tartar-size launchers, and the complement was cut to 480 officers and 4,450 enlisted men.

Further development of the design was based on the BuShips preferred solution, except that Typhon was being abandoned in favor of the much simpler and less expensive Tartar. An increase in accommodation (relative to SCB 211) from 413 to 487 officers and from 4,171 to 4,845 enlisted men would be achieved in part by a reduction in habitability standards to those approved for ships between 300 and 600 feet in length. The SCB limited the cost of such a ship to $410 million, compared with $310 for its rival, the modified CVA 66 actually built. Studies showed that the sacrifice in habitability would actually buy only 480 officers and 4,650 enlisted men, but without it the ship would accommodate only 4,450 enlisted men. The full level desired would have required a larger ship, breaching the price limit.

Accommodations were not the only pressure on the design. In mid-January the SCB was being pressed by the Bureau of Naval Weapons (BuWeps), formerly BuAer, to provide at least one long-stroke (310- versus 250-ft) catapult (C 12). Without it, some of the aircraft planned for 1967 (presumably the F-111B) would be only marginally operable. Similarly, elevator loads would be increased from 80,000 to 90,000 pounds, and the aircraft load from 1,000 to 1,100 tons. On the other hand, the bureau was willing to downgrade air defense to four Sea Maulers, a point defense system later cancelled in favor of Sea Sparrow. Moreover, without Typhon radar costs could be considerably reduced.

The net effect of all of these demands was substantial growth in the ship: the new design, SCB 250, used an *Enterprise* hull but retained the four-reactor plant of its predecessor, by this time powerful enough to breach the 30-kt requirement. The 20-ft increase in waterline length solved the internal volume problem,

providing 2.6 million gallons of JP-5, 2,960 tons of aviation ordnance, and escort fuel. There would be two long and two short catapults, and fully loaded she would displace 90,530 tons; cost would rise to $425 million. SCB 250 was fully satisfactory as a carrier design, failing only because of Secretary McNamara's unwillingness to agree to pay for her nuclear power plant.

A four-year gap separated CVA 67 and the next carrier, the *Nimitz* (FY 67). As in the case of the Korean War, it wasn't until the experience of carrier air strikes in Vietnam that faith was restored in the carrier concept. Thus in February 1966 Secretary McNamara announced that his previous policy of maintaining a force of only thirteen attack carriers in the early seventies would be modified to a total of fifteen carriers with twelve air wings, with time out of service for overhaul and refit accounted for. The force would consist of four nuclear carriers (the *Enterprise* plus three new ships), the eight *Forrestal*s, and the three rebuilt *Midway*s; McNamara finally accepted the arguments put forward by nuclear advocates in the CVA/CVAN 67 debate. The new ships would be built at two-year intervals under a single integrated procurement plan: CVAN 68 would be completed in 1971, CVAN 69 in 1973, CVAN 70 in 1975, with funding under the FY 67, 69, and 71 programs. In fact CVAN 69 was funded in FY 70, and debates over CVAN 70 delayed it until the FY 74 program. Construction, too, was very slow: CVAN 68 was not completed until 1975, CVAN 69 not until 1977.

The principal advance reflected in the new design was a reactor so powerful that two sufficed to power the carrier; in effect the new carrier was conceived as an SCB 250 enjoying the economy of two rather than four reactors. At the same time the squeeze on internal carrier volume grew more severe, and this issue was reflected in a variety of unusual design measures. In addition, CVAN hull dimensions were constrained by available building ways, and so her hull form was somewhat fuller than that which would have given optimal speed. Pressure to improve aviation capabilities led to the use of four long (C 13-1) catapults.

Aviation requirements, particularly fuel and ordnance stowage, mandated the use of a large hull despite complaints that carrier growth had to be checked. In June 1964 Preliminary Design priced the two-reactor ship at $422 million, compared with $425 million for four reactors. The SCB working level asked for three alternatives: an *Enterprise* hull with four long catapults, a ship 10 feet shorter with the same catapults, and an *Enterprise* hull with a CVA 67 flight deck and two C 13-1 catapults. Costs were estimated at, respectively, $431.2 million, $430.4 million, and $430 million; in each case total payload would considerably exceed that of either the *Enter-*

The *Nimitz* is shown on sea trials, 4 March and 18 April 1975. Her lattice radar mast carries an SPS-43A for long-range air search, with an SPN-41 in the boxlike structure below it. There are two SPN-42 dishes bracketed out on the after port side of the island, and the small dish of the SPN-44 is just visible at the top (aft) of the island. The cones paired vertically are Phasor-90s for ship-to-air communication. Note the Sea Sparrow launchers on each quarter, and the SPS-48 height finder and SPN-43 CCA marshall radar on the island structure. The odd cutout of the flight deck aft was reportedly meant to reduce her overall length; the area eliminated was of no particular consequence, given the location of the landing runway.

prise or *Kennedy*, and a further increase of 2,500 tons (over 10,400 in the first case, 10,895 in the last, compared with 10,000 for the *Enterprise* and 8,400 for the *Kennedy*) could be bought for half a knot. This the SCB found well worthwhile.

The CNO, Admiral McDonald, was unwilling to accept the full *Enterprise*-sized hull now that a smaller power plant was available. Some saving might come from reduced habitability standards, but BuWeps insisted on four C 13-1 catapults. However, a proposal to use a phased-array radar, as in the *Enterprise*, was killed in November 1964. By that time

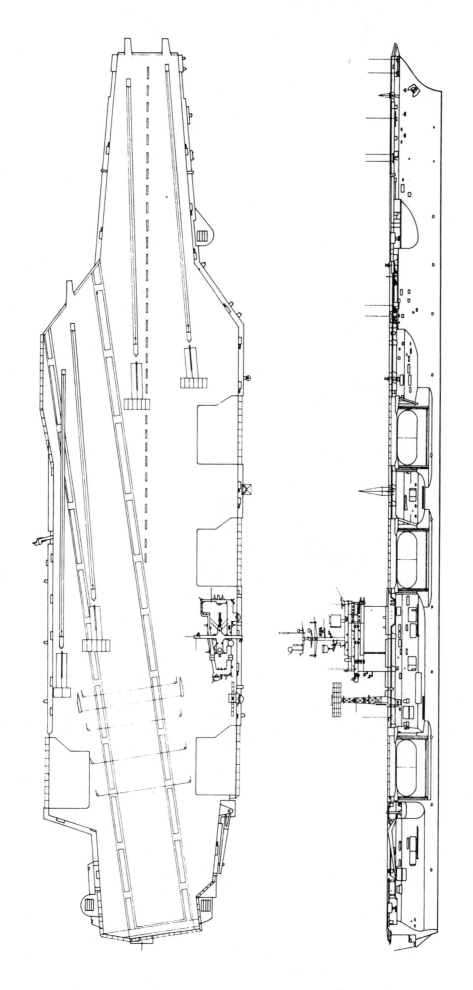

The nuclear carrier *Nimitz* (CVN 68).

there were two design alternatives under consideration: a ship with a shorter flight deck (1,047 feet) and only two long (and two short) catapults and a ship 1,040 feet long with a 1,100-ft flight deck, four long catapults, and slightly more beam (135 versus 134 feet as previously). The 1,030-ft ship, as sketched late in November, would have a 1,090-ft flight deck and a beam of 135 feet (draft 37 feet fully loaded); it would accommodate 3,150 tons of aviation ordnance and would be armed with a pair of Tartars, as in the original CVA 67 design; indeed, electronics would duplicate the CVA 67 suit, except for the addition of a satellite link. There would be four long catapults.

The short hull was rejected in the course of preliminary design because the designers could not afford the loss of hull volume. On the other hand, beam was set at 134 feet because of the limits of building docks. Some speed reduction was accepted in the interest of a fuller form, and indeed the designers later suggested that any increase in nuclear power be applied to a fuller form for more interval volume rather than for more speed.

Compared with those in previous carriers, the principal changes were in the flight-deck layout and the arrangement of magazines, the latter due to the adoption of two reactors. The flight deck changes resulted from continued interest in improving the air flow abaft the carrier; research showed that the principal, and perhaps the only, means to this end was a decrease in the angle of the angled deck. This angle in turn was determined by the requirement that the after end of the landing runway pass between no. 3 and 4 elevators, and that the forward end clear an airplane at the after end of no. 2 (portside) catapult. Thus one possible change was a relocation of no. 4 elevator, for example to a centerline position between the forward catapults. This would actually gain considerable internal floor space, but it was rejected by the operating forces and the carrier type desk. That left only the forward catapults. The forward end of the flight deck was held parallel to the centerline, so that the after ends of the two forward catapults could be swung to starboard.

With two widely separated machinery spaces, the conventional magazine arrangement would have been one amidships (between machinery spaces) and two at the ship's ends. However, this would have considerably increased vulnerability, since the three magazines would occupy more length than the two end magazines of earlier ships. The after magazine, then, was merged with the midships one. It was no longer possible to divide the hangar into two bays with a single midships fire bulkhead. The new design reverted to earlier (non-nuclear) practice, with three separate hangar bays, which provided both additional protection and some additional support (given

the extra doors) for the flight deck. At this stage it also appeared that, compared with earlier ships, these would have to surrender 40 more feet of hangar to aircraft maintenance shops.

The original CVAN 68 design incorporated a pair of Tartars, which were omitted in favor of twin 3-in/50 guns controlled by three Mark 56 directors interfacing with NTDS. For a time two quadruple 40-mm guns were to have replaced the three twin 3-in/50s, presumably in view of the weight criticality of the ships. These weapons were no more than space and weight reservations for BPDMS (Sea Sparrow); the ships were completed with three such systems, tied to a simple target-designation system.

As this is written the *Nimitz* design, about fifteen years old, is still the basis for U.S. carrier construction, having survived a number of attempts to find viable alternatives. Like the *Forrestal*, the *Nimitz* is no longer an example of warship growth, but rather a compromise between unrestrained growth and the costs of smaller size. Probably the attempt to develop a smaller carrier, the abortive CVV, was the best proof of capabilities lost at any carrier size substantially smaller than that of the *Nimitz*. The *Nimitz* itself reflects U.S. carrier operating experience in Vietnam, particularly in her large magazine and aviation-fuel volumes. It can be argued that Vietnam was an unusually benign environment for carrier operation, emphasizing the aircraft capabilities of carriers but not their survivability. That is, large magazine volumes such as the *Nimitz*'s may also be large liabilities in a ship subject to attack by numerous antiship missiles whose hits are distributed along her length. There is less of a chance that smaller magazines, although they are an operational liability, wil' be hit, and consequences may be less severe if the ship with smaller magazines is hit.

Like the *Hornet* of 1939, CVN 71 of FY 79, the fourth *Nimitz*, was in a sense a victim of time. Although the Naval Ship Engineering Center (NAVSEC) had worked out a design for a small carrier, it was in no position to design a new or even a greatly altered full-size attack carrier in less than several years. However, given the long interval since the last carrier authorization (FY 74), and given the urgent need to replace the aging *Midway*s, any such new design would probably not be practicable. Similarly, if the Reagan administration is able to obtain the two carriers it wants, most likely they will not differ substantially from the *Nimitz*. One might also speculate that the carrier program of the last few years has been far too unstable to encourage the investment involved in a wholly new design. Today's reasoning is not too far from that of the mid-fifties, when SCB 153 was rejected primarily because it would apply to too few ships.

15

Return to the Small Carrier: CVV, 1972–78

Although the series of small attack-carrier studies of the fifties was not continued into the sixties, the hope that somehow the size of the attack carrier could be pared down never completely died out. By the early seventies the issue of a new carrier design was becoming critical, as the *Midway*s would soon be thirty years old and therefore due for replacement. Moreover, by the early eighties even the *Forrestal*s would be nearing replacement age. Anticipation arose over the advent of VSTOL aircraft, which might permit a considerable reduction in carrier size. This hope was not based on analysis of the consequences of VSTOL operation aboard carriers so much as on the feeling that eliminating catapults and arresting gear would have to save size and cost. In fact, it turned out that VSTOL aircraft could indeed be accommodated aboard a much smaller carrier, but accepting a smaller ship would amount to endorsing reduced levels of carrier air power at sea. The British, for example, were indeed able to build a viable carrier, HMS *Invincible*, on less than 20,000 tons, but the price they paid in carrier function was probably unacceptable. If a VSTOL carrier attacked shore targets, it would be able to project only a small fraction of the weight of ordnance a conventional air group could move. To achieve a like level of destruction, several small carriers, costing perhaps several times as much as a single large-deck unit, might be required.

Another important issue was carrier vulnerability. Clearly a larger ship would be less vulnerable to many types of attack, simply because the effect of any given weapon would occupy a smaller fraction of its length. On the other hand, some weapons were so destructive that no ship could be expected to survive their effects. It might be argued as well that the magazine spaces of a small carrier would not accommodate enough explosives to destroy the carrier, were she to suffer a magazine hit. The large magazines of a modern nuclear carrier can be likened to a dormant volcano.

Through the seventies several attempts were made to trade off large carriers for small ones, VSTOLs for all-conventional air groups, and even medium VSTOL carriers for large ones. The belief that somehow the aviation community and the carrier designers are conspiring to hide the real advantages of smaller and less expensive carriers persists to this day. In addition, since the large carriers were generally nuclear, Admiral Rickover's powerful nuclear organization was believed to be adding to the confusion and the pro-big-carrier propaganda. Late in the seventies the Carter administration supported the smaller attack carrier in an attempt to reduce carrier

By the mid-seventies the *Franklin D. Roosevelt* badly needed replacement, and the Carter administration proposed a ship of similar size, the CVV, rather than another *Nimitz*-class CVN. Among the operational restrictions on the *Franklin D. Roosevelt* was her inability to operate the E-2C early warning aircraft; note the E-1Bs in this 1973 photograph.

unit cost. The ultimate victory of the big carrier was due to a combination of congressional pressure and American experience with carrier-operating requirements in the Indian Ocean. Current congressional interest in a 40,000-ton VSTOL carrier is an unrelated development which, however, illustrates the tenacity of the small-carrier concept. Perhaps this agitation partly explains the fact that no carrier-design effort has been announced; the new CVN 71 and her successors will essentially be duplicates of the fifteen-year-old *Nimitz* design.

Agitation in favor of the medium carrier began with Admiral Elmo Zumwalt, a CNO strongly in favor of reducing the unit cost of ships in order to increase their numbers and recover from the disastrous slide of the seventies. His initiatives included a limited-cost AAW escort (DG/Aegis), a limited-cost general-purpose escort (the *Perry*-class FFG), and the sea control ship (SCS), an austere helicopter carrier for ASW (see chapter 16). As for large-deck carriers, there was interest within Admiral Zumwalt's group in a 40,000-ton carrier for sea control. However, ultimately he proposed a new 50,000- to 60,000-ton design, which became the tentative conceptual base line (T-CBL) and the direct forebear of the later CVV of the Carter administration.

Secretary of Defense Melvin Laird issued a program decision memorandum on 21 September 1972 calling for the design of a smaller carrier limited in cost to $550 million (FY 73 dollars). At this time the SCS was conceived as a $100 million ship, and the FFG as a $45 million unit. Studies began in December 1972, work continuing through early 1974. Although a third *Nimitz*, the *Carl Vinson* (CVN 70), was authorized instead for the FY 74 program, the T-CBL idea did not die. Enough had been done to convince many observers that a medium carrier, displacing perhaps 60,000 tons fully loaded, was a practical possibility. Indeed, several reports compared the T-CBL design with the British CVA 01, the 54,000-ton ship cancelled by the Labour government in 1966. The existence of this design seemed to prove that a useful carrier could be built on a displacement considerably less than that of a *Forrestal* or a *Nimitz*, although the designers of CVA 01 had accepted some design practices that the U.S. Navy could not.

In July 1975 Secretary of Defense James Schlesinger, who succeeded Laird, directed the navy to begin a new round of studies, this time of a nonnuclear carrier. The navy appealed, citing the advantages of nuclear power, and the study was redefined as a 50,000-ton nuclear ship, CVNX, the cost of the lead ship not to exceed that of the *Nimitz* (FY 70 figures). In theory, it was to incorporate innovative approaches to catapult, elevator, defensive weapons,

and command and control problems. However, after reviewing three alternative CVNX designs, a characteristics study group concluded in January 1976 that on the basis of a three-ship buy a fourth *Nimitz* was the best means of maintaining the thirteen-carrier force beyond 1985.

As a result, President Ford requested long lead-time items for such a ship (CVN 71) in his FY 77 budget request of May 1976. However, he did not back it firmly, and in response to criticism of the defense budget he cancelled CVN 71 in favor of two smaller, oil-fired carriers to be built in FY 79 and FY 81. Although they were to be capable of operating all current aircraft, in fact it was hoped that they would be optimized for a new generation of VSTOLs then under development. A new carrier designation, CVV, was conceived with this prospect in mind. It was actually, however, a modified form of T-CBL, that being the only existing conceptual design in the appropriate size range.

The Carter administration found the CVV idea attractive, partly because it represented a reversal of the trend toward more and more capable carriers. Some of the costing involved seems odd in retrospect. For example, because the carrier air group had to be counted in the total cost of the carrier, a small carrier of a new design might be less expensive than a somewhat larger repeat unit, perhaps with the same limited air group. To some extent, too, Carter administration spokesmen justified the construction of a carrier of limited capability on the theory that it was replacing another limited carrier, a *Midway*. Congress was unmoved by this argument, authorizing a fourth *Nimitz* in the FY 79 budget. President Carter then vetoed the defense authorization bill, agreeing to sign only a version from which the carrier had been deleted. He hoped to include a CVV in the FY 80 budget, but in the end had to accept a *Nimitz*, at least partly because operations in the Indian Ocean had shown the great value of both the nuclear power plant and the large air group. Under the Reagan administration the navy seeks to achieve a total of fifteen deployable carriers (for a total carrier strength of sixteen, including one under SLEP) over the coming decade. The FY 83 budget includes two modified *Nimitz*-class carriers, CVN 72 and CVN 73. Thus the T-CBL/CVV exercise is primarily a demonstration of the cost, in carrier capability and even survivability, of reductions in carrier size.

Like the other Zumwalt projects, T-CBL was primarily constrained by cost and therefore limited in size and electronic sophistication. No particular air wing could be specified. Rather, ship size was determined by the other factors and a tentative air wing was molded to suit it, with little tactical rationale. In this sense T-CBL was reminiscent of the minimum-carrier studies of the fifties. Unlike the earlier carriers, however, it was intended primarily for tactical strike missions. Evidence of this change was that capacity was measured in A-7 (light attack) aircraft spots rather than in terms of larger aircraft, such as the A-3 (A3D) of the mid-fifties studies. As in the case of almost all carriers, the actual size of a T-CBL air group was indeterminate, navy figures for public consumption of about fifty-five contrasting with some more optimistic OSD figures of sixty-two to sixty-five aircraft. The T-CBL design report envisaged alternatives of fifty-two aircraft for the mixed CV mission, fifty-four for pure attack, and fifty-nine for ASW.

T-CBL was intended to achieve simplicity of design by using the modular aviation support of CVA 66 and the contemporary SCS; services not common to all alternative air groups would be mounted in vans so as to facilitate changes in air group. There were other sacrifices as well: a reduction to two catapults and two elevators. The elevators would have to supplement ammunition elevators during strike operations. Reduction of the usual four-shaft engineering plant to two shafts (in fact, to half a *Kennedy* plant) would also save money, weight, and internal volume, but at the cost of a great reduction in speed. It had to be reduced on full power (134,000 SHP); T-CBL would make 27.8 knots (sustained, 80 percent power would give 26.2). With all four boilers lit, firing off one airplane per minute would reduce speed to 27.2 knots with a clean bottom; but five years out of dock, with a 5 percent power-degradation factor, she would make only 23.8 knots, and with three boilers on line, 20.7 knots. It could be argued, then, that T-CBL was too slow for standard task force operations and far too slow to combine tactically with other attack carriers. Range would match that of other conventional carriers; the ship would displace 44,566 tons light (including margins) and 58,897 full load.

The *Kennedy*'s high-pressure steam plant was a type that the Secretary of the Navy had ordered dropped from destroyer design studies in 1967 because of maintenance problems with its 1,200-psi boiler. However, there was no space for the larger plant required at lower steam conditions. Indeed, the machinery spaces were so compact that a 1975 report on the T-CBL design observed that "should the CV-TCBL side protective system be defeated the ship is vulnerable to loss of power from side hits due to the short length of the aft Auxiliary Machinery Room." As in other modern carriers, machinery was arranged on the unit system, with two boilers and one turbine per compartment; machinery compartments were separated by one auxiliary machinery room—another was forward.

One element of the design not to be compromised was electronics, since the T-CBL might have to operate as the single carrier of a task force. The only major economy was omission of the carrier-controlled approach search radar (SPN-43), one of the two main air search sets (SPS-49, SPS-48C) having air control as a secondary role. Command and control facilities would include NTDS, an austere version of the TSC planned for all carriers, and the integrated operational intelligence center (IOIC). Electronic countermeasures would be standard types for a ship of her importance. For self-defense T-CBL would mount three Phalanx CIWS (as in other carriers) but none of the point defense missiles employed aboard other carriers.

The CVNX study of January 1976 approached carrier problems from the opposite direction, beginning with a mission and threat analysis. The study group found that the number of catapults and arresting gear were no longer driving forces behind a design. Given a fixed air group, the important issues were required internal volumes (for aviation ordnance, aviation fuel, and maintenance of the air group), seakeeping, and propulsion characteristics.

The *Nimitz* (model C) was taken as the baseline of the CVNX series. Model A was a minimum carrier, with reduced magazine volumes, a minimum-length angled deck, two shafts, two elevators, two catapults, and three arresting-gear wires (vice the four of the *Nimitz*): in effect it was a nuclear version of T-CBL. Its machinery was based not on that of a full-sized carrier but on that of a nuclear cruiser. It employed a four-reactor D2G (D2W) plant delivering about half the power of a *Nimitz*. The air group would consist of about forty-eight to fifty-three aircraft.

Model B was a minimum carrier designed to support about two-thirds of a *Nimitz* air wing, using an up-rated model A plant. Light displacement rose from the 51,900 tons of model A to 59,700 tons (full load, from 64,600 to 74,800 tons). Model B had three elevators and three catapults; in contrast with model A, it could carry 82 rather than 74 percent of the JP-5 of *Nimitz*. In both cases aviation fuel per aircraft would considerably exceed that of a *Nimitz*, presumably because of the demands of side protection systems. The volume of the latter would be proportioned according to the hull length and therefore take up an increasing fraction of displacement on a smaller ship—unless protective standards were relaxed.

One reason models A and B were not too different was that flight-deck dimensions were based not on the size of the air wing but on the types of aircraft to be supported: flight-deck length was determined by a requirement for simultaneous launch and recovery of aircraft. For example, the distance from the ramp to

The *Carl Vinson* (CVN 70), the latest U.S. carrier, is shown on sea trials, 26 January 1982. Although largely a repeat *Nimitz*, she shows several detail changes. The white radomes of Phalanx 20-mm close-in defensive cannon are visible on both sides forward and on her port quarter. It is not clear whether this reversion to forward sponsons will result in new spray-formation problems. Note, too, that she has only one bridle-catcher: fewer and fewer naval aircraft use wire bridles, and nearly all now have catapult hooks as part of their landing gear. The *Dwight D. Eisenhower* likewise has only one bridle-catcher. In the future this sort of boom will probably disappear altogether. Finally, the latticework boom projecting from the carrier's port sponson will ultimately carry ECM antennas; the boom's counterpart is mounted on the starboard side of the island. The dishes on the mast are for satellite communications, and the three radar directors control the carrier's Sea Sparrow point defense missiles.

the hook touchdown point was figured by the vertical hook-to-ramp clearance: a minimum figure of 11 feet (14 in *Nimitz*) and the standard 3.5° glide slope together gave a ramp-to-hook distance of 180 feet. The 11-ft point had to be within 3 feet of the second wire, which in turn had to be spaced 40 feet from the third, requiring a 350-ft runout with an additional allowance of 94 feet for barricade stretch and turnabout for the airplane being arrested. The end of the 672-ft distance would be the end of the port sponson; slamming (seakeeping) considerations dictated that the leading edge of this sponson be about 25 percent aft of the bow (in fact in model A some additional slamming was accepted and this distance was held to 21 percent). The resulting flight-deck length of 912 feet determined hull length (860 feet). The requirement of the 1954 and 1955 studies that the landing (angled deck) area not overlap with the catapults in the bow was dropped.

In model B the minimum length for a three-catapult, three-elevator flight deck was found to be about 900 feet. The most efficient hull depth was 94 feet, given a reduction in hangar-deck clear height to 20 feet (as compared with 25 in other modern carriers); special "high hat" areas would be arranged for maintenance requiring greater headroom. Other fixed factors in hull depth were machinery-box height, gallery-deck height, double-bottom tank depth, and the number of deck heights between hangar deck and armored box—a number closely related to questions of hangar-deck freeboard in carriers, such as this one, with deck-edge elevators. The hull depth in turn provided for optimum beam and length; in fact model B was somewhat longer in order to attain the best speed and seakeeping characteristics.

Models A and B were designed on the basis of a NAVSEC computer program. To check the program, model D was designed as a minimum carrier incorporating the *Nimitz* power plant and capable of supporting two-thirds of the *Nimitz* air group. Model D characteristics were strongly affected by the choice of power plant, but that in turn was required to achieve sufficient speed for the ship to be able to operate with other carriers. Other important design factors were the maximum allowable beam for building (135 feet) and magazine-arrangement considerations. The result was quite close to the *Nimitz*: for example, full load was 84,800 as opposed to 93,400 tons; light displacement was 68,200 as opposed to 72,700 tons. However, there were only three elevators and three catapults. Aviation fuel stowage was 92 percent of that in the *Nimitz*.

A variety of new arrangements was considered for the new moderate-size carriers. For launching aircraft, a stored-energy rotary drive (SERD) catapult,

broadly reminiscent of the old Norden flywheel of the *Lexington*, was evaluated. It had to be rejected because it would not be ready in time for CVNX installation. Reportedly the SERD catapult, which might have been installed in a future non-steam (gas turbine) carrier, was later abandoned, having failed to live up to its early promise.

Aircraft elevators were of the type installed in CV 67, the *Kennedy*. The conceptual designs required at least one elevator on each side of the ship. This would insure operation of the carrier under most sea conditions; it would also permit her to continue in action after hits were concentrated on one side of the ship. The hangar-bay access to the elevator on the starboard side was to serve as an underway replenishment station as well. Two such are generally required—model A, with only one starboard elevator, had another hangar-bay access cut in her starboard side.

Aircraft-maintenance features reflected a new Pallet-Van arrangement in which the contents of standardized shore vans would be mounted aboard ship on readily accessible shipboard locations; carrier reconfigurations reflecting alternative wings could be made within forty-eight to seventy-two hours. It appeared that adoption of this system would save $1.7 million in FY 76 construction dollars and $24.5 million in fifteen-year life-cycle costs, compared with the cost of a somewhat more primitive modular approach in which the vans themselves would be taken aboard.

At first the hangar deck was to accommodate only one-third of the air group specified for each carrier. However, this fraction had to be raised to the 40 percent of other postwar carriers; flight and hangar decks were too congested for a smooth flow of operations, and the forward end of the hangar was too far aft of the magazine for convenient access to the exit area of the weapons elevator. The elevator exit was located in the maintenance spaces forward of the hangar bay. Finally, it was necessary to extend the hangar bay aft to facilitate access to the portside (aft) elevator.

Manning reductions was a particularly important means of weight and cost savings. It was estimated that by the 1980s a variety of labor-saving innovations, including greater reliability in aircraft electronics, might cut personnel requirements by as much as 9 percent; the net effect of this cut on carrier size was estimated at 1,600 to 1,800 tons, or $50 to $80 million in life-cycle cost. The CVNX study also considered the effects of more austere habitability standards. A variant incorporating 1960 standards saved about 2,400 tons and $35 million; if it incorporated 1965 standards it would save 1,700 tons and $25 million.

This last result was very striking. The explosive cost growth of U.S. warships in recent years is often imagined to be directly related to habitability, to naval personnel who will not tolerate the spartan conditions of the past. However, naval architects have long known that among the least expensive components of a large warship is hull steel, which is the material used to improve habitability. For a very large ship, a few thousand tons make little difference in other ship features, so the additional cost is merely that of the excess steel; CVNX gave an example of how small the price would be. Reasoning further, one might determine that a larger carrier would be less expensive per ton because much of her cost would be in fixed items such as command-control communications (C³) and the reactor power plant. Indeed, for a fixed speed, she would require fewer horsepower per ton. Some costs, it was true, would rise with size, particularly those proportional to the size of her air group. However, in that case, if the analysis shifted to the problem of maintaining a fixed total of naval aircraft at sea, the cost per airplane would probably fall off for a smaller number of larger carriers.

The CVNX analysis did not cast favorable light on the austere two-shaft carrier. Even if the two shafts of that carrier were undamaged, her tactical mobility would still be inferior to that of the four-shaft carrier, a fact relating directly to the question of survivability. For example, a faster carrier would force Soviet missile-firing submarines to move faster and so would considerably increase their acoustic signatures. Wind-over-deck would be important in some circumstances. In the damaged condition, with only one shaft available, a two-shaft carrier would have insufficient speed for safe aircraft operations. As for catapults, the number of independent ones was extremely important in determining the tempo of air operations. The CVNX group found that three catapults would suffice. A reduction to two would result in a very significant reduction in the number of aircraft launched, or else in a requirement for prolonged steaming into the wind.

Studies were also conducted of seakeeping as it would affect aircraft handling and launch and of probable aircraft accident rates, using the *Essex* and *Midway* classes as comparisons for models A and B. Finally, there was the question of the adequacy of the CVNX air wing. A and B/D air wings were far less effective than the *Nimitz* air wing in offensive operations owing to the number of base or overhead aircraft any carrier would require for AEW, ASW, and CAP. In such circumstances, it would be difficult to provide an air strike with fighter escorts to make it effective. Moreover, in an extended campaign, the smaller carrier air wings might take longer to gain air superiority in a contested area and would suffer greater losses during that period. The study concluded that, in force projection, the A wing would be marginally capable in low-threat areas and ineffective in high-threat areas; the B or D wings would have sufficient flight-deck area and support facilities for a force-projection air wing, but not for the combined CV multipurpose air wings, and so would have to operate with other carriers for mutual support.

These arguments killed the CVNX, and CVN 71 was very nearly ordered as a fourth *Nimitz* in FY 78. Instead, the conventional T-CBL was revived, in slightly improved form, as CVV. After the completion of CVNX tradeoff studies in February 1977, Congress rescinded the authorization for long-lead items for CVN 71 and directed a smaller carrier to be designed for submission in the FY 79 budget. Therefore time was very short, and the T-CBL design had to be adapted in a design effort beginning in March 1977. Nine design alternatives were presented to the CNO on 1 April.

CVV 1 was an updated T-CBL with some deficiencies corrected, notably the imbalance between ship and air-wing manning (especially in the ship's supply department). Design alternatives included the SPY-1 AEGIS radar (which CVNX had indicated would lower manning but increase ship costs), an extra catapult and elevator, a flight-deck rearrangement, and the addition of two more boilers. The CNO approved the six-boiler plant as well as a rearranged flight deck. Some flight-deck features were spread out to improve survivability. Thus one of the two bow catapults was moved back into the waist, and one of the two original starboard elevators was moved to the port side aft.

He also wanted to reduce cost; the option adopted was to defer essential electronic purchases to keep within what was now a $1.3 billion (FY 79 dollars) limit. At the same time, the CNO approved rearrangement of the magazines and machinery spaces.

At this time contracts for detailed design and construction were to be awarded during FY 79; this assumed completion of contract design by 1 March 1979 and left only six weeks (where three months would normally be required) for the conceptual baseline design, if preliminary design were to begin on schedule on 1 June 1977. In fact, however, Congress relaxed this pressure by denying funds for the preliminary design in mid-May 1977. CVV work continued in view of the probability that the next carrier, whenever it was funded, would be a CVV—which certainly coincided with the administration's view.

Part of the effort was directed towards redressing imbalances in the original T-CBL design, which could be traced to lack of clarity in her air-group assignment. In particular, the original T-CBL design called for fuel for 1.35 strike days—but ordnance for

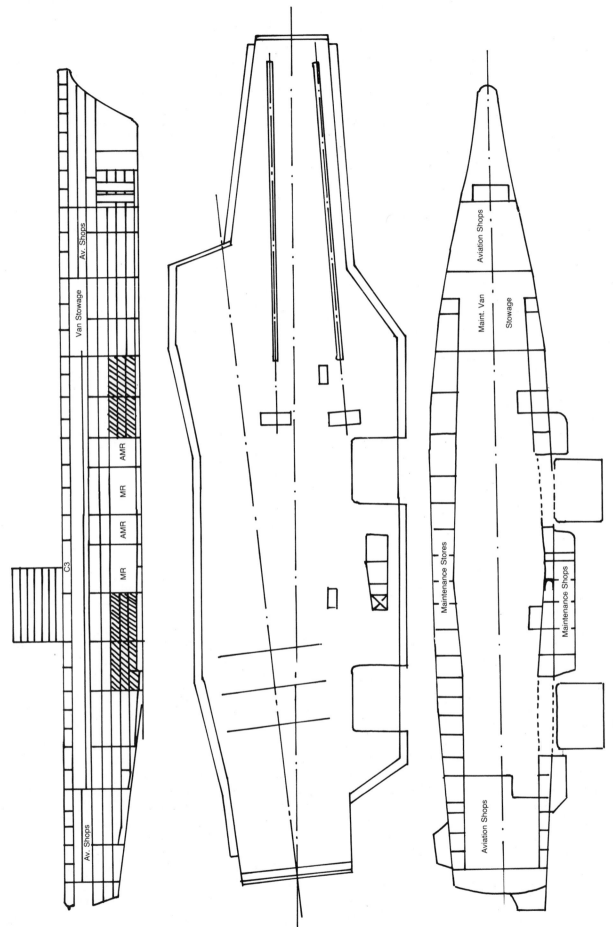

Van Stowage
Av. Shops
Av. Shops
C3
MR
AMR
MR
AMR

Aviation Shops
Maint. Van
Stowage
Maintenance Stores
Maintenance Shops
Aviation Shops

T-CBL carrier design, 1974, showing flight and hangar decks. Magazines are shaded.

4.5. When the notional T-CBL air wing was loaded with fighter aircraft, this latter figure rose to 5.0 strike days, but aviation fuel would be used even faster, giving further imbalance to the design. By January 1978 JP-5 stowage had been considerably expanded, partly to allow for uncertainties in future VSTOL fuel consumption.

In the absence of an agreed air group, flight-deck and hangar-deck design was also unbalanced. The flight deck was filled out to allow maximum area: it increased from the 95 deck spots (A-7) of T-CBL to an ultimate level of 112. However, this expansion was achieved without allowing for an increase in hull size and weight incident to an increase in the size of the supported air wing. Specific flight-deck changes included filling out the starboard side aft to allow maximum area to maneuver VSTOL aircraft prior to launch; the forward end of the landing area was shifted to port to allow a maximum safe parking area forward on the flight deck.

To some extent the dearth of internal space was alleviated by a 14 November 1977 CNO decision to increase the hangar-deck height from 19 feet 6 inches to 24 feet 6 inches, the beam from 122 to 126 feet, and to provide an 02 deck level forward, aft, and outboard of the hangar. These changes alone added 86,000 square feet of deck area. At the same time the CNO approved changes to provide additional damage-control voids and one more 2,500-kw ships service turbo-generator (five already in the design), and to increase the power of the two 1,500-kw emergency diesel generators to 2,000 kilowatts each. JP-5 stowage was increased from 2,700 to 4,000 tons, but nominal ship growth (in the design condition) was avoided by retaining the earlier figure for the full-load condition. That is, had full-load tonnage (design) risen 1,300 tons, engine power, for example, would have had to increase to maintain design speed in the new heavier condition. Finally, the CNO approved a 10 percent margin for crew size.

The fuel issue demonstrated how unrealistic the entire CVV exercise was. Surely sustained speed at a realistic full-load displacement was more important than speed under conditions that would never exist. Similarly, the cost target could be met only if the ship was delivered without a lot of her electronics (which would have to be supplied later).

—She would have an LN-66 navigational radar and an SPS-55 surface/low flier set, but no SPS-49 long-range air search radar. Instead, the SPS-48C pencil-beam three-dimensional radar, normally used for air control, would suffice. However, there would be the usual CCA radar systems: SPN-35A, -41, -44.

—Countermeasures would be limited to the passive WLR-8; installation of the SLQ-32 ECM system and the antitorpedo NIXIE (SLQ-25) would be deferred. So would the three CIWS close-in AA guns.

—The advanced C³ system, an austere tactical support center (TSC), the TFCC, and the integrated intelligence center (CV-IC) would be deferred.

—One of the two 2,500-kw ships service turbo-generators and the liquid oxygen plant would be deferred, as well as all boats other than two 26-ft motor whale boats in davits.

Hull depth was set by the requirement that elevators and hangar deck not be subject to sea damage. Because hangar-deck height was originally set at 19 feet 10 inches, this freeboard required unusually great deck heights (11 feet) for the two decks below. Another deck would have increased hull depth and weight. Hangar length was set by the length from the forward magazine bulkhead and lower-stage weapons elevator to a point aft of the portside elevator. Beam was set by the width of the machinery box (80 feet) and the side protective system; the unique internal arrangement of the ship had the machinery box placed farther aft than usual, so that the aftermost machinery bulkhead became a constraint.

Some of the CVV's protective arrangements were very un-austere. That is, although it had the defect of only two shafts, two elevators, and two catapults, the CVV's design did incorporate a new internal protection scheme and, apparently, improved side (antitorpedo) protection. The principal threat envisaged appears to have been the antiship cruise missile, and at a 1979 congressional hearing it was suggested that the only real danger to such a ship would be the detonation of her magazines. It could be argued, too, that although the number of elevators and catapults was half that of other carriers, the earlier designs showed such a concentration of them lengthwise that one hit alone would knock out one or two elevators and two out of four catapults. Thus appropriate lengthwise separation of the two elevators and the two catapults would confer considerable operational survivability.

Unlike a bomb or an aircraft rocket, a large cruise missile has a shaped-charge warhead capable of blowing through a considerable thickness of steel. The missile generally strikes the side rather than the upper deck of the carrier, and at a shallow angle it can be expected to penetrate to the magazine areas, even those at or below the waterline. The pressure for additional magazine volume in itself made for larger magazines of considerable length and height, so that there was a greater probability that cruise-missile hits randomly distributed around amidships along the length of the hull would strike a magazine and detonate it. In addition, the deeper double bottom pressed for would decrease internal deck height between the inner bottom and the waterline, forcing

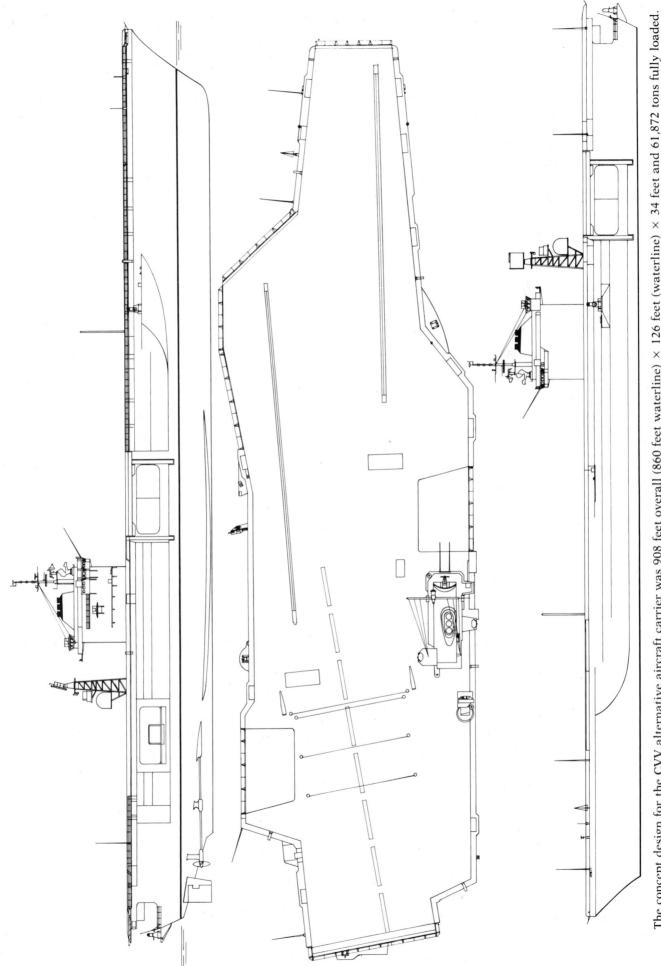

The concept design for the CVV alternative aircraft carrier was 908 feet overall (860 feet waterline) × 126 feet (waterline) × 34 feet and 61,872 tons fully loaded. Armament was limited to three 20-mm Phalanx antimissile guns, and there were to have been eight super-RBOC chaff rocket launchers. Radars were the SPS-48(V), SPS-49, SPS-55, LN-66 (navigational), SPN-35, two SPN-41, and SPN-44. Other major electronic equipment was the TACAN (URN-25), ESM (SLQ-32[V]3), SRN-9 (satellite navigation), and SRN-17 (Omega navigation).

magazines up into the area of the ship vulnerable to cruise-missile attack.

The CVV was the first U.S. carrier design to incorporate a new type of magazine protection intended specifically to defeat the cruise missile with its shaped-charge warhead. The censored transcript of a House Armed Services Committee hearing of February 1979 includes an account of a system of baffles or vanes intended specifically to break up or deflect the jet of hot metal produced by a shaped-charge warhead. It was claimed that "a cruise missile will make a mess, but it will not incapacitate the ship at all" and, moreover, it would not be able to sink the carrier because it would be unable to cause a mass detonation of a magazine. Evidently the new protection carried a high cost in ship volume. For example, a modified *Kennedy* proposed as an alternative to the CVV was to have had similar magazine protection, with aviation ordnance capacity reduced to 1,250 tons, compared with about 2,000 tons for the *Kennedy* herself. The CVV design, intended from the first to incorporate the new type of protection, was rated at 1,191 tons of aviation ordnance.

Probably the decision to employ a single magazine rather than the two of earlier non-nuclear carriers reflected confidence in the new form of protection. In addition, it could be argued that the single magazine would take up less of the ship's length, which would reduce the probability of a cruise missile striking the magazine. This probability could be further reduced by moving the magazine within the hull. If an incoming cruise missile homed on the centroid of the radar return of the carrier, for example, it would be less likely to strike substantially fore or aft of amidships. If that centroid were generated primarily by the corner reflectors represented by the carrier structure, then the location of the magazine relative to the sharp edges of the flight-deck sponsons might be significant. Again, the record of the hearing suggests that these issues were carefully considered in the CVV design.

In addition, the CVV incorporated a structurally improved and considerably deeper bottom for better protection. The level of improvement claimed was 66 percent, which was significant since most modern torpedoes and mines explode under a ship for shock and whipping effect rather than strike the side for flooding effect. The bottom changed the overall design enough so that the improved *Kennedy* could not incorporate it without total redesign.

The result is somewhat reminiscent of the prewar *Wasp*, whose design was far more a function of external constraints than of any tactical or strategic ideas. In the case of the CVV, it was sometimes argued that careful calculation would show that the cost per embarked airplane was quite comparable with that in a larger ship. However, that begged two major points, each of them fatal to the idea of the medium (60,000-ton) carrier. First, Congress and OSD tend to approve numbers of ships, not total carrier tonnage or total A-7 deck spots at sea. Therefore, requesting a CVV implied a political investment equivalent to that required for a *Nimitz*. It could not be attractive except on the basis of a credible pledge to buy more CVVs than the number of CVAs they were replacing— i.e., on a two-for-one or three-for-two basis. Given the explicit distaste of the Carter administration for carrier-based force projection, no such pledge was offered. Second, from an operational point of view, carrier capability is limited by the number of specialized ("overhead") aircraft in the air group: AEW, tanker, reconnaissance. (British and French experience with the use of relatively small carriers bears this point out.) The decision to adopt flexible (CV rather than CVA) air wings in U.S. carriers made sheer aircraft capacity particularly valuable. Finally, the ambitious VSTOL program with which the CVV was to have been compatible never approached its early promise. That left CVV as a small, slow, second-rate carrier with few supporters in the navy. Her demise was not surprising.

The CVV was envisaged partly as a means of bridging the gap between conventional carriers and their VSTOL successors. In his last days in office, Donald Rumsfeld, President Ford's last Secretary of Defense, envisaged the new carrier with catapults but no arresting gear, so that she could launch VSTOL aircraft with heavy fuel and weapon loads and then recover them in a vertical-landing mode. He directed that the CVV displace 40,000 to 50,000 tons (fully loaded). The new Carter administration allowed the navy to review this concept, which was then considered too risky. Thus the Carter administration's CVV had full arresting-gear capability for conventional operations and grew to over 62,000 tons fully loaded.

16

Postwar ASW Carriers

For the U.S. escort carrier, as for all other U.S. antisubmarine ships, the advent of the German Type 21 submarine was a major blow. No longer would submarines spend most of their transit time on the surface. At most they would expose only small snorkels. To restore useful radar-detection ranges much larger airborne radars would have to be used, hence much larger ASW aircraft, and even then the radars would achieve much shorter ranges than the simpler airborne radars of World War II had attained against surfaced submarines. Perhaps worst of all, after the war the Allied ASW forces would surely lose their greatest asset: the ability to anticipate enemy submarine dispositions through code breaking. That made hunter-killer tactics far less effective—they required some very-long-range means of finding the submarine in the first place.

All that was left to detect a submarine at a considerable range was radio direction finding. Even that seemed doomed by the German short-burst radio transmitter (*Kurier*) intended specifically to frustrate direction finders. For example, sonobuoys were developed in World War II primarily as a means of regaining contact with a submarine that dived as an airplane approached. After the war the sonobuoy became a prime search sensor, laid in fields or in barriers an airplane could monitor. The speed of the airplane could be exploited to lay a barrier relatively far from a screened force, with aircraft pouncing on submarines detected as they tried to penetrate. In typical convoy screen tactics, for example, aircraft would lay lines of sonobuoys to protect the flanks of a force, while helicopters with active dipping sonars protected the van. Additional fields of sonobuoys could be laid ahead of the screened formation to detect submarines trying to close to attack.

It seemed inevitable that the Soviets, who had captured examples of all the German submarine technology, would duplicate it. Indeed, the interest in direct attacks upon Soviet submarine bases at the outbreak of any major war, which was a major justification for the design and construction of the large carrier *United States* (see chapter 11), was largely a consequence of this expected decline in the value of wartime ASW technology and tactics.

With the failure of very-long-range means of submarine detection, entirely new tactics and weapons had to be developed. Wartime experience suggested that submarines would have to communicate by radio in order to achieve a useful degree of tactical coordination. The issue then was the extent to which such communication (and other submarine electronic emissions) could be intercepted. Code breaking exploited the other end of this communication net. Carriers were tried in both a direct support (screening) role and in hunter-killer experiments, the latter predicated on the continued viability of long-range direction finders and also on prompt notification of sinkings ("flaming datum" reports).

Hunter-killer tactics became much more profitable with the development of the very-long-range bottom-mounted hydrophones of the SOSUS system, which restored a significant capability for submarine detection at great ranges. ASW aircraft then took on a new importance, because only they could arrive at the SOSUS or flaming datum fast enough to find a

It took an *Essex* hull to accommodate postwar ASW aircraft comfortably, such as the Grumman Guardians (AF-2S and -2W) shown aboard the unconverted *Valley Forge*.

submarine in the vicinity. Moreover, until the appearance of the P-3 Orion, there were many areas in both the Atlantic and Pacific that could not be covered effectively by land-based aircraft and therefore required the attention of ASW carrier forces on station for extended periods. Indeed, initially the AOR-type underway replenishment ships of the sixties were designed specifically to support ASW hunter-killer groups on station in both oceans, although by the time they were in service most of the ASW carriers had been retired.

Postwar ASW strategy embraced two other techniques as well: the barrier and attack on Soviet bases. The former tactic would be carried out largely by U.S. submarines off Soviet bases, and it became economical only with the advent of very-long-range submarine sonars. The latter would employ the *United States*, and was limited by American willingness to attack the Soviet Union directly, and with nuclear weapons, early in a war. In the beginning of the fifties plans to use nuclear firepower early in a war were not frowned upon, but later doctrines of graduated escalation and limited warfare made the prospect of premature use of nuclear weapons unacceptable. The success or failure of attrition tactics (direct kill, barrier, and base attack) in turn determined the extent to which screening was necessary. Alternatively, one might say that the evolution of U.S. weapons, from numbers toward limited quantities of high effectiveness, favored attrition tactics enormously. The ASW carriers were part of this evolution, and in the end were eliminated because of it.

There was one other important consideration in post-1945 ASW operations, one the navy understood quite well but failed to explain to many in the Defense Department: deterrence. In order to deter the Soviets from depending upon a submarine offensive early in any war with the United States, the navy tried to demonstrate its ability to counter the Soviet submarine threat, usually by detecting and then tracking (and holding down) individual Soviet submarines. In the case of diesel-electric submarines, the submarine might actually be forced to the surface as her batteries became exhausted. Such "cold-war trailing" was also an effective deterrent to Soviet plans to use ballistic-missile submarines against the United States. The tactic could not be carried out by either submarines or "pouncer" aircraft, since in each case the target submarine might well be unaware of her vulnerability. Instead, the cold-war mission generally required the continuous attention of aircraft and surface ships. Some special devices were developed, such as a magnetic clicker (SCAT) that could be dropped onto the submarine, as both a noise source and a way of letting her crew know that she had been detected and cornered. The cold-war mission was first enunciated in the late fifties.

By 1960 the primary roles of the ASW carriers (CVS) were ocean-area surveillance against Soviet missile submarines, cover for fast-carrier strike groups, and protection of shipping. The role of fast-carrier protection was being emphasized in view of the availability of the P-3. The carrier group might make a high-speed run to a launch point or, as in Korea, might carry out lengthy operations in a relatively restricted (say, 100,000 square mile) area that the CVS would have to sterilize and maintain. The threat to fast carriers became particularly acute with the appearance of Soviet nuclear submarines that could overcome the speed advantage previously enjoyed by the carriers. Moreover, from the early sixties onward, it was assumed that the Soviets would develop a submarine-launched anticarrier missile equivalent to the U.S. Subroc, which in turn would require attacks on submarines as much as 100 nautical miles from the carriers. This particular threat only materialized, in the form of the Soviet *Charlie*-class submarine, in the late sixties, but it had an important impact on ASW tactics and weapons throughout the decade.

The CVS role in SOSUS contact prosecution declined as the long-range P-3 Orion came into service, leaving the CVS with the roles of intensive area search and carrier task-group escort. In the Mediterranean sonar conditions were relatively poor and CVS operations relatively successful. In particular, a CVS air group could search far more intensively than could a land-based patrol unit designed for pouncing on established contacts. There was also an increased demand for CVS deployment in the Western Pacific to cover the two operating areas off Vietnam. Even so, the CVS force was allowed to vanish in the early seventies as maintenance costs of the elderly carriers mounted and their effectiveness declined.

From 1962 onward the CVS air groups included four A-4B light attack aircraft operating as low-performance fighters. Their function was to counter a new and very significant Soviet threat to the sea-lanes: the over-the-horizon antiship missile, carried by Soviet surface ships and submarines. Firing the missile required target data, which was generally supplied by a Bear D reconnaissance bomber. Although the meager CVS fighter group could not deal with the missiles themselves, it could deal with the Bear D and thus frustrate an attack. A similar philosophy applied to the provision of Harrier (AV-8A) VSTOL fighters in the proposed SCS and VSTOL support ship (VSS) of the seventies. In each case, the area of relatively low air threat might shrink as the Soviets deployed longer-range missile-carrying bombers (Backfires rather than Badgers), which would themselves attack in large numbers and could not be defeated by a small number of low-performance fighters. As for the CVSs, despite repeated attempts to obtain a new fighter specially suited to them, their best was the Skyhawk, which was severely limited since it had no intercept radar.

In 1945 the potential force of ASW carriers comprised nineteen new *Commencement Bay*-class escort carriers as well as nine fast light carriers (CVLs), whose performance as attack carriers could be considered marginal at best. The escort carriers could be used for both ASW and amphibious support, and indeed the latter mission was a former alternative task for U.S. ASW carriers throughout the fifties. The earlier escort carriers were all laid up—some were even discarded. They were incapable of operating modern ASW aircraft such as the new Grumman AF-2S/2W. Thirty-six *Casablancas* were, however, retained for their possible future value as ASW helicopter carriers. Four of them were reactivated during the Korean War as aircraft transports. They were not economical in this service, however, and were later replaced by four of the earlier C-3 escort carriers. Some documents of this period suggest that another escort-carrier mission was contemplated: fighter support of convoys in areas such as the Mediterranean where the chief enemy threat would be air atttack.

The threat of fast-submarine attacks prompted the navy to seek faster surface ASW forces after the war. One example was the conversion of surplus *Fletcher*-class destroyers into "destroyer escorts" under SCB 7. Similarly, SCB 8 called for a new fast escort carrier, roughly comparable to the wartime CVL in size. Instead, the wartime CVL was selected for conversion. Thus in 1948 two experimental ASW task groups were planned, one (sufficient to counter a Type 21 submarine) built around a modernized *Commencement Bay*-class escort carrier, and one (designed to counter the faster Walter U-Boat, Type 26) built around an *Independence*-class CVL. Ultimately ten CVEs and two CVLs (the *Bataan* and *Cabot*, under SCB 54, FY 49, and FY 51) were modernized. The newer light carrier *Saipan*, used largely for training, received a more limited modification.

Improvements included stronger elevators and flight decks, torpedo-detection sonar (both passive and active), and provision for the new ASW munitions, both sonobuoys and homing torpedoes. In the CVLs, a new portside catapult (H 4B) replaced the former H 2-1, and the after elevator was strengthened to take 22,000-lb aircraft. Blisters provided weight and stability compensation, and the carrier could accommodate 500 sonobuoys as well as 36 homing torpedoes (Mark 24 "mines" of wartime design, or Mark 34 or Mark 41 torpedoes). Antiship torpedoes were an alternative load, if they could be accommodated at all. Both CVL and CVE were to be fitted with a new enlarged island structure that added command and communications spaces and, in a CVL, could

support the wartime SP or the new SPS-8 height-finding radar. A new 07 level was incorporated for the air-defense officer and his sector control stations, and the port island bulkhead was moved one foot inboard. In the CVLs, combining the first and second and the third and fourth funnels compensated for the new island and provision for Blimp refueling. These modified ships were to be provided with the homing-torpedo countermeasures, noise beacons fired from rocket launchers, found in some contemporary U.S. ASW destroyers and frigates.

The primary CVE improvements proposed at this time were the new island, new Mark 5 arresting gear, and decked-over (oil) cargo tanks, the latter to provide more internal space and improve damaged stability by reducing the free surface of the oil. Generally there was money and time enough only for two of the three improvements. For example, in April 1952 the Atlantic Fleet considered the new island its highest priority for a refit program to begin with the *Siboney*. The Pacific Fleet wanted the cargo-tank modification deferred because it would take valuable ships out of service for too long a time (about nine months).

Of the nineteen *Commencement Bay*-class escort carriers completed, seven were decommissioned immediately after World War II and saw no further service, although one of them, CVE 111, was scheduled for conversion to a communications relay ship in the early sixties. Two others, CVEs 114 and 118, were recommissioned to support marine fighter-bombers (Corsairs) in Korea. The other ten operated as ASW carriers. They had significant limitations, particularly after the introduction of the Grumman AF ASW attack bomber, one of the largest single-engine aircraft every built. Under peacetime conditions it was limited to 22 knots wind-over-deck for day and 26 knots for night operation; the CVE 105 class was designed only for 19 knots wind-over-deck, so that successful operation required additional wind. Writing in April 1953 the Commander, Carrier Division 18, Atlantic Fleet reported a large percentage of "no fly" periods in a recent exercise, Springboard. Moreover, recovery of so large an airplane aboard an escort carrier "places an extraordinarily high premium on pilot technique and upon the LSO's judgment. In addition, it is my opinion that with present planes and CVEs, continuous and adequate ASW operations would be limited to a period of about 48 hours or less because of the relatively small number of AFs embarked. Such a limitation indicates that Hunter-Killer groups, as presently constituted, do not compose the effective force . . . required. . . ."

There were three solutions: a new-construction CVE, which was then being designed, the use of surplus *Essex*-class carriers, which was actually the solution adopted in the end, or reconstruction of the CVEs. The problem was numbers: not enough

Newly recommissioned, the light carrier *Bataan* arrives at San Diego on 28 July 1950 to load aircraft for the Korean war zone. In this photograph she has some new radars (an SPS-6B and an SG-6 on her foremast) and new ship-to-air communications antennas (replacing the former main air search antenna between her funnels). But improvements were limited, and did not include the radio and radar direction-finders which, in 1950, were considered essential adjuncts to carrier ASW operations. The FJ-1 Fury aft was already obsolete at this time.

Fully modified for ASW, the *Bataan* (*above* and *facing*) shows the standard two-level bridge, and two rather than her previous four uptakes. These photographs are undated, but it appears that the *Bataan* underwent an ASW refit late in 1951. Her operational career, however, was spent in conventional air strikes during the Korean War, and she was decommissioned at its end. The aircraft on deck appear to be Grumman AF Guardians, and the mainmast carries an HF/DF antenna, barely visible among the surface-to-air dipole pairs.

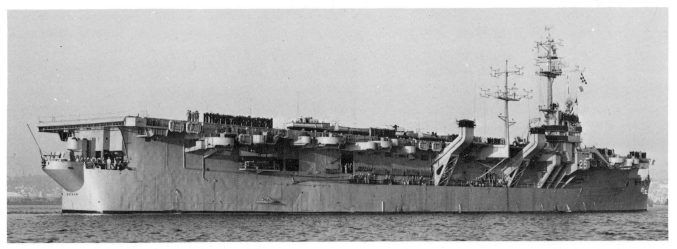

*Essex*es were available, and it seemed unlikely that a sufficient number of new CVEs would ever be funded. Indeed, despite the urgency of developing ASW tactics during the postwar period, entirely new ASW carriers, either CVEs or CVSs, never were built. Instead, ASW forces ran through the capital built up during World War II. As for the CVE, it appeared that she would require much higher speed, at least 26 knots. The only hope for less speed lay in the angled flight deck, already being demonstrated aboard the *Antietam* and, according to reports, easy to land on. The Commander, Air Force, Atlantic Fleet seconded the recommendation for CVE reconstruction, which alone could meet the need for numbers. Even the large air group possible in an *Essex* would not make up for the small number of that class, probably no more than nine, available. By way of contrast, there were twenty-three CVE 105 hulls, including four that had been completed but never commissioned.

BuShips considered two alternative levels of improvement. In one, the CVE was to be fitted with an angled deck strengthened to take 23,000-lb aircraft; the existing H 4C catapult moved onto the canted overhang; the existing H 2-1 bow catapult replaced by an H 4B at the forward end of the flight deck; and the centerline elevators relocated to the starboard deck edge. The cargo tanks would be decked over, cargo oil capacity being reduced from 9,360 tons to about 6,070, and about 200 tons of fixed ballast added. Weight compensation would include a reduction in the planned battery from eleven to six twin 3-in/50 mounts. Alternatively, in order to increase sea speed to about 24 knots, a new bow about 30 feet longer than the original one might be added, the hull blistered, and *Sumner*-class boilers and *Cleveland*-class turbines with new reduction gears installed; shore-based spares would suffice to equip two ships. Increased aeronautical features alone would cost

Much thought was given to the use of blimps, a major feature of postwar ASW, in conjunction with escort forces. Here one is secured aboard the escort carrier *Sicily* on 12 April 1949; the unusual flight-deck markings are probably intended to aid the blimp pilot. The ship is essentially in her wartime configuration, except that a tall topmast carries an HF/DF antenna.

about $13 million and twelve months in a shipyard; the increased speed could be had for another $9 million and six months, with lead times of, respectively, six and eighteen months.

BuShips considered these costs high enough to justify its favored solution, a new CVE, SCB 43, on which it was then working. The new carrier would be able to accommodate thirty S2F aircraft (compared with eighteen in a CVE 105 conversion), would be about a knot faster, and would have more oil for escorts, 2 rather than 1.68 million gallons. It would, however, cost $60 million.

The projected new CVE appeared in early versions of the FY 52 and FY 53 programs, succeeding the SCB 8 project proposed for FY 48, but replaced at that time by "essential features incorporated in the *Wright* and *Saipan*." As of July 1950 it was estimated that a prototype SCB 43 would cost $53 million, compared with $150 million for a large-deck carrier (which became the *Forrestal*). Work began in March 1950 as an "industrial preparedness" (that is, mobilization) measure. SCB 43 was envisaged as an austere type capable of operating thirty "single-package" (a hunter-killer, the Grumman S2F) ASW aircraft, steaming at up to 25 knots with an endurance of 8,200 (later 8,400) nautical miles at 17 knots, and carrying 2 million gallons of fuel for escorts, 230,000 gallons of gasoline for aircraft. There were to have been two catapults. As in the contemporary fleet carrier, a flush-deck design was desirable, but the General Board recognized that it might not be acceptable in view of its complexity and cost, so an alternative island design was requested. A size approximating that of the CVL was assumed, with a standard displacement of 14,000 tons and 25,000 fully loaded, and a 600- by 85-ft flight deck. Hangar height was to be the 17 feet 6 inches of wartime carriers.

The initial characteristics showed only ASW

ammunition, but as the design developed the role of furnishing close air support to the marines came to determine magazine volume, particularly as a new generation of low-drag bombs appeared. Ultimately that meant 414.9 tons of close-support ammunition for forty sorties per day for ten days, using early versions of the Skyraider bomber and the Banshee and Panther jet fighters. In 1953 it was assumed that from FY 55 onward higher-performance jets such as the Cutlass and Demon would operate at a higher tempo, fifty sorties per day for five days. On the other hand, the ASW weapon load, for a relatively long cruise, came in the end to only 386.6 tons. The only weapon common to both missions was the 5-in rocket.

The CVE mission differed considerably from that of a conventional attack carrier. In October 1950 BuShips (Code 512) analyzed desirable characteristics.

Any concept of an ASW carrier, either modification of an existing hull or new construction, should consider all components . . . in the light of all-weather, 24-hour-a-day operation. Although all carriers in a war zone are presumed to be operating 24 hours a day, the relentless, continuous operation of antisubmarine warfare over long periods of time warrants special consideration. . . .

Present concept of operations is that of three search teams of two aircraft each, operating an around-the-clock schedule. Search team flights would be of approximately three hours duration, teams being relieved on station. When the "one-package" aircraft comes into service use each search team will consist of one aircraft. One or more search teams may be airborne at one time with two aircraft on the catapults in condition eleven. Approximately 12 single package aircraft will be the complement of an ASW vessel of the CVE 105 class (sufficient aircraft

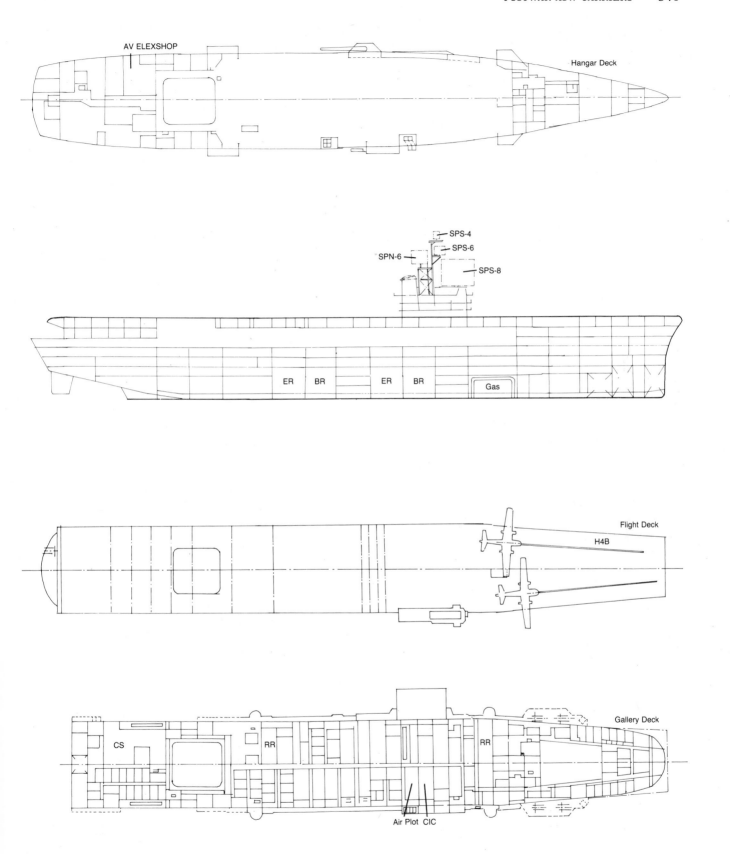

Scheme 10B for an ASW carrier (CVE), 25 June 1952, showing flight, gallery, and hangar decks.

should be assigned to permit hold down, continued search, and a reserve complement).

Since the carrier would be the core of a hunter-killer group, she would have to carry enough fuel for her accompanying destroyers, and all-weather operation would require a sophisticated CCA radar system. ASW operation would require both an active sonar and a "sonaramic" passive torpedo-detection unit. Effective command and control would require the carrier to maintain continuous plot on at least two of her aircraft flying at 1,000 feet 65 nautical miles or more from the ship. Since electronics would be a major contributor to ship cost, these features could not be entirely consistent with austere design. Round-the-clock operation would require three complete deck, gas, and ordnance crews, an enlarged operations department, and ready rooms designed for continuous operation with adjoining messes, heads, showers, and air-conditioned bunk rooms.

In a departure from BuShips practice, the contract for preliminary design was awarded to Newport News in 1950 for the FY 53 program. Since Newport News would also be the lead yard for the *Forrestal* and thus responsible for the detail design of that ship, speed was essential, and the yard had to proceed on the basis of the first preliminary characteristics of October 1951. As work continued, it became apparent that the original estimates of size had been somewhat optimistic. Displacement was reported in February 1952 as 15,000 tons (standard); twin-screw geared turbines would drive her at a trial speed of 26.5 knots or a sustained speed of 25. The battery was six twin and six single 3-in/50 rapid-fire guns. There were to be two elevators, one deck-edge forward and one centerline aft, and two H 4B catapults in the bow.

As the SCB 43 design continued to grow (to a full-load displacement, by July 1952, of 25,800 tons and a waterline length of 612 feet rather than the original 600 feet), alternatives were sought. In December 1952 OPNAV asked BuShips to investigate the conversion of a Maritime Administration hull, possibly with an angled deck. The new Mariner cargo ship would be suitable, provided two additional 600-kw ship's service turbo-generators were installed. Although at 20.5 knots it would be considerably slower than the new CVE, that would not prohibit S2F operation, since the Mariner could be fitted with a C 11 steam catapult. The chief drawback would be much-reduced escort fuel, 910,000 gallons, compared with 2,000,000 for SCB 43 and 2,410,000 for the existing CVE 105. Conversion would cost about $33 million. Since these characteristics were considered minimal, BuShips also investigated conversion of an AO 143-(*Neosho*-) class fleet oiler. She would have a slower (19.5 knot) speed but much larger displacement (17,825 tons light, compared with 14,027 for the Mariner and 15,000 for SCB 43; 35,900 tons fully

loaded, compared, respectively, with 21,000 and 22,000). As a tanker, she would carry far more oil: 4,060,000 gallons for escorts. Cost of conversion would rise to $38 million, but that was still far short of the $60 million estimate for SCB 43. BuShips remarked that "there is more ship available than can be efficiently utilized," although an extra catapult might be worked in.

Now BuShips tried another approach, CVE 2/53, a somewhat smaller escort carrier with reduced air group. Scheme 2, for example, carried twenty rather than thirty S2Fs, at a cost of $68.1 million rather than $69.5 million (SCB 43). If H 4B catapults were accepted, waterline length would be reduced from 612 to 550 feet, and the reduction in air group would save 30 officers and 40 enlisted men out of original totals of 200 officers and 1,150 men. Other 2/53 variants, with steam catapults, were credited with jet fighter (F4D) capability, possible air groups including sixteen S2Fs and four F4Ds and, on a larger hull, twenty-four S2Fs and six F4Ds. There was also an angled-deck version of SCB 43, limited operationally because it had only the two H 4B (*Essex*-type) catapults.

The new carrier was withdrawn from the FY 53 budget (with other projects) to fund the new attack-carrier *Saratoga*. In April 1954 DCNO (Air), Rear Admiral R. A. Ofstie, proposed cancellation of the project because SCB 43 would be unable to operate jet aircraft and so could not function in close support; he maintained that existing CVEs would suffice as a mobilization base, despite the extensive complaints of inadequacy in the recent past. The admiral went on to recommend a new design study, but his memo effectively ended the postwar CVE story.

That left the big unconverted *Essex*es, which became available for subsidiary tasks as the SCB 27A and 27C program progressed. In May 1952 Rear Admiral H. E. Regan, Commander, Carrier Division 17, proposed that these ships be used for ASW, a proposal approved by his commander, Admiral A. W. Radford. The *Valley Forge* was tested in a hunter-killer exercise off the California coast late in 1952 and proved extremely successful. She had sufficient deck space for two S2F squadrons and could easily operate the big AF, flying it off even in a dead calm. The ASW proposal was under OPNAV consideration by March 1953, and five carriers were ordered designated CVS (for support or for ASW) on 8 August 1953, two more following on 1 January 1954. Gradually the *Commencement Bay*s were retired as they took over the hunter-killer mission.

All seven operational unmodernized *Essex*-class carriers became CVSs. They were followed by the SCB 27As, beginning with the *Wasp* on 1 November 1956. In 1959 two of the original CVSs, the *Boxer* and *Princeton*, followed by the *Valley Forge* in 1961, became marine-helicopter assault carriers (see chap-

The *Siboney* displays the standard new ASW island in this 3 February 1956 photograph. The big air search radar was an SPS-6B, and she carried an HF/DF at her masthead, with a UHF/DF in the radome just below it. By this time the escort carriers had lost a considerable portion of their gun batteries: note the empty bow position and the empty beam gun tub.

Near the end of her combatant career, on 23 June 1955, the *Point Cruz* demonstrated that she could operate the twin-engine Grumman S2F (later S-2) Tracker "single-package" ASW aircraft. Although the S2F was designed with the *Commencement Bay* class in mind, it was almost invariably operated from converted *Essex*-class carriers, and later versions could not operate from the smaller ships. A ship-to-air antenna is visible at the after end of the flight deck, as is a hose for fueling escort ships—the *Commencement Bay*s were valuable partly for their immense cargo-fuel capacity, a consequence of their tanker heritage. The *Point Cruz* herself was reactivated in August–September 1965 as a civilian-manned aircraft transport of the Military Sea Transportation Service.

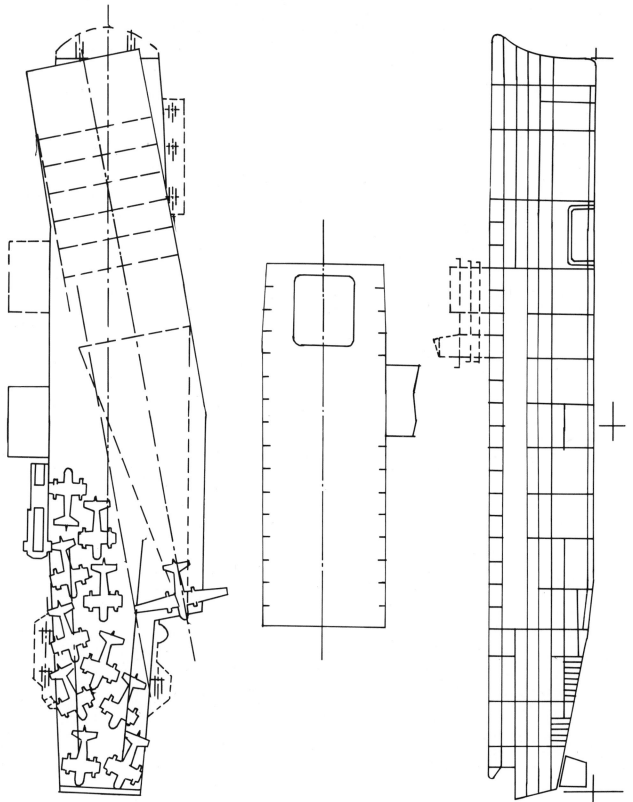

Scheme 3a for CVE 2/53, March 1953, with angled deck, showing S2F ASW aircraft on deck. The guns are twin 3in/50s.

ter 17); the other four were the first *Essex*es to be decommissioned after Korea, in 1959–60 (except for the training carrier *Antietam* in 1961).

By 1960 typical CVS tactics required four S2Fs continuously on station for sonobuoy searches, one AEW airplane on station for radar and ESM search (requiring a total of six for continuous coverage), and four helicopters on station (requiring a total of twenty for continuous coverage). Typically, too, a carrier would be accompanied by eight destroyers, four for a close screen against penetrating submarines and four for distant contact prosecution. An unconverted *Essex* would have enough fuel oil for the carrier and her destroyers to operate for twelve days and enough gasoline for eight days of S2F and AEW operation. She would have JP-5 for the HSS-2 helicopters. The *Essex* conversion traded off ship fuel oil for increased aviation fuel, so that a ship like the *Randolph* could steam for ten days with her destroyers, could operate her piston-engine aircraft for twelve, and her helicopters for twenty-one. In a typical pattern of operations, one S2F was assigned to each distant destroyer, the ship acting to prosecute air contacts. However, improvements in sonobuoy technology (such as Jezebel) promised greatly increased ranges and thus made expanded S2F complements potentially very useful; the commander of the experimental task group Alfa proposed that eight be maintained airborne, requiring in turn a complement of thirty-two such aircraft. For the future, it appeared that a VTOL ASW airplane could replace both the S2F and the helicopter. It would be faster than a helicopter, and faster movement to and from the ship (and between dips of its sonar) would permit one VSTOL to replace two helicopters. At this time a typical future VSTOL complement was estimated as forty aircraft, and potential designs included a Bell D2022, McDonnell 113P, and a Vertol 116.

The new sonobuoy technology required a new level of data processing, entirely beyond the capacity of the Grumman S2F. The Pacific Fleet proposed that the requisite scarce personnel and equipment be concentrated aboard the carrier in an antisubmarine contact analysis center (ASCAC). It was tested aboard the carriers *Yorktown* and *Bennington* in 1961. The first were ad hoc productions, but in November 1964 the CNO approved four system-engineered ASCACs, two per fleet (one in a CVS, one ashore). The *Randolph*, in the Atlantic, had the first, replacing an earlier version. A related development was an ASW ship command and control system (ASWSCCS), related to NTDS, developed at San Diego and installed aboard the carrier *Wasp* and the frigates *Voge* and *Koelsch*. It was, in effect, an application of NTDS concepts to ASW warfare; presumably its further expansion was stopped by the war in Vietnam.

The other major CVS modification was the addition of a large SQS-23 bow sonar, primarily for carrier self-defense. That is, a carrier proceeding at moderate speed could expect to detect a submarine at sufficient range to evade a quiet (slow) torpedo or to detect a fast (noisy) torpedo at sufficient range to evade it directly. The prototype was the *Randolph*. In June 1962 the commanders of ASW forces in both fleets proposed the installation of a variable depth sonar on an SQS-23-equipped CVS under the FY 64 program. In 1964 the CO of the *Wasp* argued that all carriers should be fitted with sonar and also with an ASW standoff weapon; he considered a VDS preferable to a bow-mounted sonar. In particular, compared with a fast attack carrier, a CVS was vulnerable to submarine attack by the nature of her operations.

The *Wasp* found her bow sonar quite valuable. It could generally surpass the performance of similar sonars in destroyers because of its greater depth and the inherent steadiness of the carrier. Many exercises showed that nuclear submarines could penetrate screening destroyers and that the carrier would have to detect and evade them herself. For example, during the exercise MASTER STROKE in 1964, the *Wasp* detected submarines that had penetrated the screen; she was able to hold contact at over 7,000 yards while evading and vectoring in aircraft and destroyers. In several cases the submarine penetrated by using the carrier's wake as a screen, and a VDS-equipped destroyer had to cover that sector. Hence the desirability of a VDS aboard the carrier. The other problem was with the nuclear submarine, which might close so suddenly that there would be no time to react with aircraft or with surface escort forces. Thus snapshot weapons such as Asroc were highly valued. Although both the VDS and Asroc were rejected, the Royal Navy at this time designed its new carrier (ultimately cancelled) to mount the Ikara ASW standoff weapon: it was standard British practice to place large sonars aboard carriers.

By the late fifties the war-built *Essex*-class carriers, in common with most of the destroyer force, were wearing out. In 1958 a special committee on fleet readiness proposed an extensive reconstruction program, which became FRAM (Fleet Rehabilitation and Modernization program). Simultaneously new construction was planned, since FRAM would only add a few years to the life of a ship. However, in the case of both the CVS and destroyer, the new construction program fell a victim to the Vietnam War, and numbers could be kept up only through maintaining FRAM ships past their nominal life times.

ASW carriers were subject to the more austere of the alternative FRAM programs, FRAM II; the *Randolph* was the first, under the FY 61 program (October

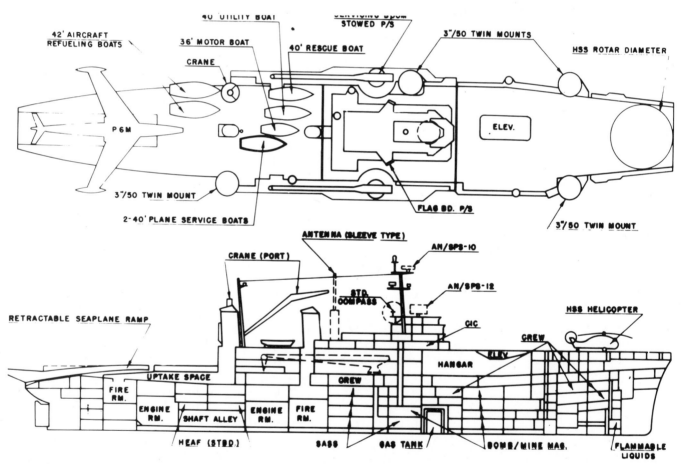

The ships of the *Commencement Bay* class were withdrawn from service in the mid-fifties with a considerable amount of potential life left in their hulls and machinery. This was one of the more unusual conversions proposed: a seaplane tender for the new P6M jet seaplane bomber, for the FY 58 program (SCB Project 176). It was to have followed two seaplane-tender conversions, the *Albemarle* in FY 56 and the *Currituck* in FY 57. The CVE 105 conversion would have two seaplane-servicing booms (rather than one, as in the ex-tenders), as well as a recovery ramp aft; the P6M was far too heavy to be hoisted aboard. It would also accommodate far more JP-5 (1,100,000 versus 307,000 gallons for the *Currituck*), conventional ammunition (900 versus 400 tons), and "special" (nuclear) weapons (80 versus 70 tons); only avgas stowage (45,000 versus 283,000 gallons) would be less. In addition the CVE, unlike the tenders, would handle six HSS helicopters. Conversion cost was estimated at $29 million, compared with $14 million for the *Albemarle* and $70 million for a new tender with only marginally better characteristics. There would be room for 570 air-group personnel, compared with 470 in the *Albemarle* conversion. The entire program died when the P6M was cancelled to offset the cost of the new Polaris missile program.

1960 through March 1961). She was fitted with the bow-mounted SQS-23, an Iconorama tactical display in her CIC, a new ECM, and a data link permitting her to operate the new WF-1B AEW airplane with its APS-82 radar. Ultimately seven more were modernized: CVSs 9 and 33 under FY 62; CVS 20 under FY 63; CVSs 11, 12, and 18 under FY 65; and CVS 10, the *Yorktown*, under FY 66. CVS 11, the *Intrepid*, was the only SCB 27C to be modernized in this fashion.

Thus the new attack-carrier program provided CVS tonnage through the retirement of modernized fleet carriers during the fifties and sixties. However, it was clear that a new CVS would ultimately have to be built. The design studies of the early sixties were the only ones for medium-size carriers made before the abortive CVV of the mid-seventies, and as such are of some interest.

As in the case of the CVV, the primary determinant of carrier size was the flight deck, and that depended in turn on the aircraft the carrier would operate. High-performance types such as the new Phantom fighter required long (C 13) catapults, whereas all other aircraft, including the new E-2 AEW type, could make do with the much shorter C 11. In 1960 it appeared that fleet air defense would soon be taken over by a 50,000-lb Missileer (F6D) fighter, in which aircraft performance was traded off against the performance of six very large long-range air-to-air missiles. The F6D was, in an avionics sense, a distant ancestor of the modern F-14. From a carrier point of view, its success would have been a prerequisite for the design of limited-size ASW carriers. Its failure mandated the use of the Phantom, which in turn required a larger flight deck (for landing runway) and larger, more powerful catapults. Alternatively, a positive choice might have been made for a CVS unable even in the support role to operate the highest-performance fleet air defense fighters. When the new CVS design studies were being made, the navy shifted back and forth between these two positions, the Missileer project having been cancelled late in 1960.

Internal volume requirements had a lesser impact on total carrier size. As in the CVE studies, an ASW carrier needed far less ordnance than an attack carrier, so that magazine capacity could be greatly reduced. An ASW carrier did need a lot of aviation fuel, and as long as the air group included the piston-engine S2F, that meant protected stowage of gas. By the mid-sixties a new ASW airplane, the VSX or S-3A, was in prospect, finally ending the need for such stowage and permitting a shift to a single-fuel (JP-5) carrier. In addition, the S-3A was designed (at least at first) to be self-sufficient, so that the ASCAC might no longer be needed.

As in many other ship types, carrier cost was largely determined by the sophistication of carrier electronics. At the high end of the spectrum, most of the design studies included a large hull sonar, the naval tactical data system, and CCA radars for all-weather operation. Most also had self-defense missiles, either the large Terrier of the big fleet carriers or the much more compact Tartar.

Work began in June 1959 on the basis of an air group of eight fighters (either Missileer or Phantom), twenty S2F-3s, sixteen HSS-2 helicopters, four AEW aircraft (W2F-1s, now designated E-2As), and two rescue helicopters (HU2K-1s). The new carrier was to have the standard endurance of 12,000 nautical miles at 20 knots and a sustained speed of 30 knots, slightly below that of most fleet carriers but still sufficient to keep up with strike groups. Radars were, at first, to have included the big fixed arrays of SPS-32 and SPS-33 (as on the *Enterprise*), and a big SQS-26 bow sonar was specified to replace the SQS-23 on converted *Essex*es. The defensive missile was to have been the large Terrier. A CVS designed on this basis was very expensive, with an estimated cost of $222 million. Omission of the advanced radar would save $18 million, and without Terrier the cost would fall again to $179 million. Ultimately a shorter endurance (8,000 nautical miles at 20 knots) and the omission of Phantom capability (C 11 rather than C 13 catapults) had to be accepted (see table 16-1).

This study was attractive enough to encourage inclusion of a new CVS in tentative long-range plans; on 31 December 1960 the CNO requested feasibility studies of a CVS as an alternative to a new-construction attack carrier. By this time Missileer had been cancelled, and the impact of the Phantom on the overall design accepted. Indeed, the eight Missileers of the FY 60 study were replaced by twenty-four Phantoms. It might be argued that, whereas each Missileer could account for up to six targets per sortie, each Phantom could account for no more than two, so that the vast increase in fighter numbers corresponded to an attempt to maintain air-defense capability. Terrier was also reinstated, presumably again to balance a loss of fighter capability.

The result was, in effect, a minimum Phantom carrier, the impact of the fighter showing in the heavier catapult (one in the bows, one in the port sponson) and heavier elevators (the Phantom took off at 59,000 pounds and, with a tractor, the elevator load was 65,000 pounds). An unusual requirement called for eight Polaris missiles: at this time the Polaris special-project office was offering sketch designs of installations in virtually every class of surface warship, down to missile frigates (DLGs). The missile installation had to be combined with a suitable elevator arrangement, the port elevator being set abaft four missile tubes and the port catapult. Another new feature was the more compact side pro-

Table 16-1. Selected CVS Studies

	FY 60 Apr 1960	Scheme 62 B Jan 1962	Scheme 62 P Jan 1962	FY 66 Aug 1963	SCB 100.68 Sep 1963	SCB 100.71 Apr 1964	New CVS March 1967	New CVS March 1967
Light Ship Disp't (tons)	35,250	39,550	47,300	41,953	—	39,360	42,502	43,030
Full Load Disp't (tons)	46,500	54,520	58,600	52,700	43,400	50,000	56,869	57,497
LOA (ft)	900	900	950	850	860	815	—	—
LWL (ft)	850	850	900	800	830	770	820	820
Beam (ft)	112	116	122	120	101	122	124	124
Draft (ft)	30.5	32	32	33.8	29.6	32	34	34
Depth (ft)	—	85	—	—	—	92.2	—	—
Aircraft	50	20 S-2, 4 E1B	16 SH-3	50	20 S-2, 16 SH-3, 2 UH-2, 1 C-2, 4 E-2, 4 A-44	47	42–52	42–52
Catapults	2 C 11-1	2 C 13	2 C 13	2 C 13	2 C 13	2 C 11	2 C 13	2 C 13
Elevators	3	3	3	3	3	3	3	3
Capacity (lbs)	60,000	89,000	74,000	60,000	—	80,000	80,000	80,000
FD (ft)	900×170	900×200	—	850×170	860×190	—	—	—
Hangar Height (ft)	17.5	17.7	19	—	22	—	22	22
Runway (ft)	520	660	660	530	—	—	—	—
Av Ord (tons)	535	1,200	1,200	500	500	600	600	600
JP-5 (tons)	1,600*	1,600	54,000	2,425 (800,000 gal)	— (400,000 gal)†	1,100‡	3,031 (1,000,000 gal)	—
Complement (off/enl)	329/2,703	350/3,000	350/3,000	300/3,000	300/3,000	350/2,986	340/2,896	—
SHP	180,000	212,000	—	140,000	135,000	140,000	150,000	190,000
Speed (sust)(kts)	30.3	31.2	—	28	28	28	28	30
SSTG (kw)	6 1,500	6 2,500	—	—	—	—	—	—
DG (kw)	2 1,000	3 1,000	—	—	—	—	—	—
Armament	none	2 Terrier 8 Polaris	2 Terrier 8 Polaris	2 Mauler	2 Tartar	2 Tartar	2 Tartar	—

*Plus 750 tons of avgas.

†Plus 200,000 gallons of avgas.

‡Plus 500 tons of avgas.

tective system introduced in CVA 67 at about the same time. In this case it saved more than space: the full attack-carrier system could be fitted, whereas the CVS of 1960 had had to make do with a reduced conventional liquid-loaded type. The sonar was the standard SQS-23 rather than the -26 proposed in 1960.

All of this was to be achieved on 45,000 to 50,000 tons, which was at best a tight fit. Both conventional and nuclear versions were developed, the latter based on the small nuclear carrier (SCB 203) of 1957. The requirements were difficult to meet. For example, a first cut, scheme 62A, could not meet the sustained 80-percent-power requirement using *Essex*-size machinery, and in an alternative scheme 62B, power had to be increased to *Midway* level (212,000 SHP) to achieve 31.2 knots. Endurance was to be based on bunker oil alone, whereas in the FY 60 study both 4,550 tons of bunker oil (NSFO) and 2,350 of aviation fuel had been counted.

There were two nuclear studies, both of them unable to meet the 30-kt requirement: schemes 62N, with three reactors and three shafts, and 62 P, with four of each. The three-reactor ship was cheaper, smaller (42,600 tons light versus 47,300 tons), sim-

pler, and considered less vulnerable to attack in view of the slightly smaller fraction of length occupied by machinery. However, it was almost two knots slower. Moreover, merely by virtue of her greater length, scheme 62P could accommodate 90,000 more gallons of JP-5 in her side protective system.

Fully loaded, all four sketch designs exceeded the 50,000-ton limit; scheme 62A was the smallest at 53,170 tons, and 62P the largest at 58,600. Aviation ordnance was much less than in an attack carrier, 1,200 tons, but was still well above the levels later accepted. As for aviation fuel, the two conventional ships had minimum capacities of 1,600 tons of JP-5 and 800 tons of gasoline. In the nuclear ships the JP-5 capacity was set by the dimensions of the side protection, at 5,100 tons in scheme 62N and 5,400 in 62P.

As in the case of the 1960 studies, these results were too encouraging to abandon, but money was too tight for immediate construction, so design work continued. No further nuclear studies were done, but a lower sustained speed of 28 knots was accepted and half a *Forrestal* plant proposed. Thus a design of 8 April 1963 showed a 52,700-ton ship (41,953 tons light) with two C 13 catapults and a proposed air group of fifty. Aviation-fuel capacity was about the

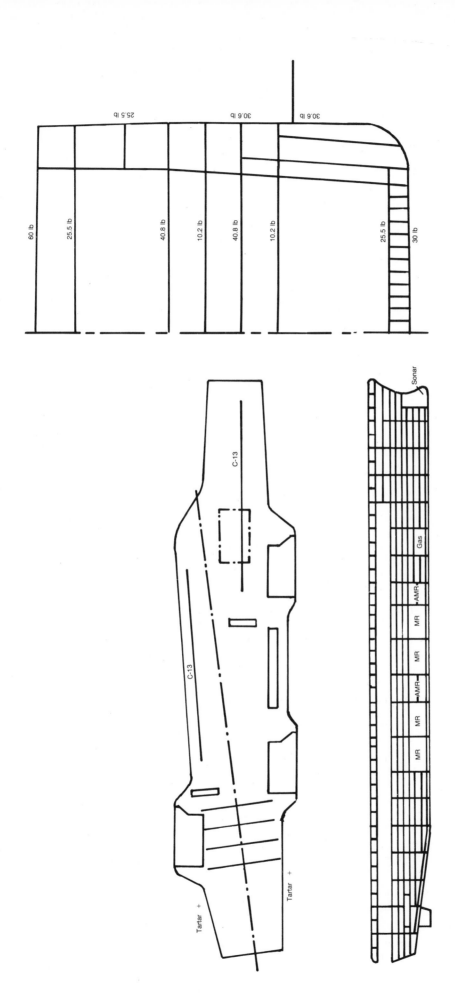

SCB 100.68, FY 68 ASW carrier (CVS) sketch design.

same previously required, 2,377 tons (800,000 gallons), but the ordnance load fell to 500 tons. As a result, an unusual internal arrangement could be adopted, with a single armored box 60 feet long separating two machinery spaces, each comprising a 52-ft engine and boiler room and a 30-ft auxiliary space. This study was used as the basis for cost and feasibility studies of new CVS construction for the prospective FY 66 to FY 69 programs.

A modified version was prepared in the fall of 1963 as SCB 100.68, a CVS for FY 68 construction. As in the new attack carriers, care was taken to minimize the angle of the angled deck to "decrease the effects of island induced turbulence during no-wind conditions as well as to permit [the design of] a ship with better length-to-beam ratio." The boilers were to be JP-5-burning pressure-fired types, to permit a freer trade-off between ship and air-group fuel when the carrier was operating two light attack squadrons in the close-support role. Endurance rose again to 12,000 nautical miles at 20 knots, with aviation ordnance and fuel for a month of wartime ASW, plus stowage for close-support munitions; self-defense was provided by two Tartars. In addition, the design was to be compatible with the VSTOL aircraft then expected to be operational in 1970–75. Aviation-fuel stowage was sharply reduced to 360,000 gallons of JP-5 and 190,000 of gas (for helicopters and S2Fs), readily convertible to JP-5. As in earlier studies, the high-performance aircraft drove the design, so that displacement rose to 53,622 tons fully loaded. The primary hope for a smaller (and less expensive) CVS, then, was to abandon the requirement to operate Phantoms and accept instead the lower-performance aircraft, which in turn would be able to operate with the smaller C 11 catapult and with a shorter landing area.

The fundamental issue was the rationale for a $235 million CVS for which there was no concrete mission, or rather, for which Secretary of Defense Robert McNamara was unable to recognize a valid mission. Also VSTOL technology was becoming a major rival, in that it appeared to promise a far less expensive ship. For example, at a SCB working-level conference on 1 October 1963 the Op-07 representative mentioned a proposed $70 million VSTOL carrier. Design work continued, and indeed the CVS still had very strong support within the navy, but more and more efforts turned to means of cutting ship size and cost. Thus, in the scheme K that BuShips developed in detail in 1964, the catapults were C 11s and ship endurance was cut back yet again to 8,000 nautical miles. Of three elevators, one would be on the centerline forward, serving the two catapults in the bows. That location in turn decreased the requirement for port sponson structure and duplicated the arrange-

ment of an SCB 27C modernized *Essex*. As in many earlier ASW carrier designs, this one was to have carried reloads (torpedoes and Asroc missiles) for her escorts.

The result was truly a minimum carrier, displacing only 39,360 tons light, with a waterline length of 770 feet (compared with 850 feet for scheme 62A and 820 feet for an *Essex*). Loads included 600 tons of aviation ordnance, 1,100 tons of JP-5, and 500 tons of avgas (compared with a total of 2,425 tons in the earlier study or 2,354 in a modernized *Essex*). In addition, the ship could divide a liquid load of 2,500 tons between bunker oil and JP-5. Even so, the direction of events was evident in its designation: SCB 100.71, for a projected FY 71 program, rather than SCB 100.68—and this was only April 1964.

The last gasp of the new-CVS studies followed in 1967, after the failure of a proposal to rebuild the existing *Essexes* for a second time. It was essentially a revival of the FY 68 project, but both 28- and 30-kt alternatives were considered. Once again there was a shift back toward high-performance aircraft, the new design showing a pair of 250-ft C 13 catapults. A clear hangar height of 22 feet was predicated on the requirements of the E-2A, and aviation-fuel needs rose to 1,000,000 gallons of jet fuel (3,031 tons) and 7,000 gallons of bunker oil, with an air-group weight of 700 tons. Aviation ordnance was held at the 600-ton level of the earlier studies. Ship size again rose, this time to 57,497 tons (43,030 light) in the 30-kt version, and waterline length returned to *Essex* dimensions (820 feet), although the new ship would have been far beamier. Endurance was set at the usual carrier figure of 12,000 nautical miles at 20 knots.

These were all ships, but they differed significantly from the later CVV in that they had far less stowage for ammunition and hence could not have functioned effectively as attack carriers. Indeed, their aviation-ordnance requirement was somewhat below the level specified for the SCB 27A *Essex* conversion and was about half of what the CVV carried later with her greater magazine protection.

Although the CVS studies were diligently pursued for almost eight years and Secretary McNamara did include CVS construction in his out-year projections, in fact the estate of the ASW carriers declined sharply through the late sixties. For example, in FY 66 the navy proposed the modernization of the last straight-deck CVS, the *Lake Champlain*. Secretary of Defense McNamara and Deputy Secretary Cyrus Vance refused the move, partly on the basis of internal Defense Department studies questioning the effectiveness of the CVS, particularly in view of the inadequacy of her S-2 aircraft. They ordered CVS force levels reduced to seven ships (three rather than five in the Atlantic) for the balance of the Vietnam

War, and then to five (with four air groups) thereafter. Four CVSs were retained in the Pacific to support operations in Vietnam during the war, and in 1967 the Secretary did approve development of the new S-3A CVS airplane, the standard CVS air group being set at twenty-four VSXs, eight SH-3 helicopters, and four fighters. However, Defense Department projections were based on an expectation that the war would end in 1970 and five SCB-27Cs with steam catapults would become available for CVS duty to replace the seven operational SCB-125s.

With the failure of projects for new CVS construction, attention turned to *Essex*-class reconstruction. For example, in May 1965 BuShips reported a study of the installation of two C 11 catapults and the strengthening of elevators in an SCB-125 to take a 56,500-lb load, at a cost of half a knot. About a year later cost estimates showed that $65 million and forty months would be required to bring a CVS 10- (SCB-125-) class carrier up to full CVA 19 standards, with lower costs for some of the steam catapult ships (such as $28 million and thirty months for the *Intrepid*, $30 million and thirty months for the *Lexington*). Almost the same conversion had been rejected in the early fifties at the outset of the SCB-27C program, as the SCB-27As had been dropped from the attack-carrier force.

By December 1966 there was a special OPNAV/NAVMAT study group seeking means of keeping the elderly carriers in service through the 1980s. The existing cycle (five-month overhauls every thirty-five months) would keep them operating almost indefinitely, but it allowed no time for modernization, which was becoming increasingly urgent. For example, the ASW command and control system tested in the *Wasp* would soon be essential, and when the S-3A entered service it would require a ship inertial navigation system, new maintenance facilities, and more JP-5 stowage, avgas being eliminated. Habitability was well below current standards.

Structural strength was a major problem. For example, whipping in storms had caused structural failure in the main (hangar) deck of *Essex*-class carriers. One possible answer to the problem was to rebuild the ships from the second deck up, making the flight deck the strength deck, but that was ruled out by top weight. The best that could be done was to strengthen the longitudinals under the main deck. There was also some fear that a modernized ship would exceed her limiting displacement for longitudinal strength. In addition, the wooden flight deck had to be removed, as it had become an increasingly severe maintenance problem. The modernization program called for replacement of remaining areas of wooden deck with aluminum-clad hickory.

Other features of the proposed reconstruction were an automatic carrier landing system for all-weather operation and satellite communications (which would require both a new mast and an antenna tower abaft the island); greatly improved habitability (including six 200-ton air-conditioning units); new facilities for aircraft maintenance; and the elimination of avgas stowage in favor of a total of 760,000 gallons of JP-5. The ship would need more electrical generating capacity; the four existing 1,500-kw turbo-generators would be replaced by 2,500-kw units; the two 1,000-kw emergency diesel generators and increased displacement would reduce sustained speed to 28.8 knots. In effect, all ship systems, even the ship girder itself, would be affected, but the result would still be somewhat less than satisfactory. That it was considered feasible at all indicates some of the reasoning behind more recent proposals to modernize the surviving *Essex*es as limited attack carriers for the eighties.

In fact the war lasted longer than expected, and money was far too tight to allow for maintenance (let alone modernization) of the CVS force. The last ship converted was the *Ticonderoga*, redesignated in October 1969 and converted at Long Beach, operating in the Western Pacific for the last time in the summer of 1972. After she was decommissioned, three CVSs remained in the Atlantic, although one of them, the *Shangri-La*, was actually a light attack carrier, replacing the *Intrepid*. The latter then reverted to her original CVS mission. Despite the success of CVS deployments in the Mediterranean in 1967–68, by late 1970 the Sixth Fleet had concluded that it could no longer maintain an active CVS at all times. The *Intrepid* was the last Atlantic ASW carrier, with two Mediterranean deployments in 1971–72. She deployed again in November 1972 as a "mini CV" with a mixed tactical and ASW air wing, replacing the *Saratoga*, which was in Vietnam. She was the last active CVS.

Admiral Zumwalt, who was now CNO, determined to overcome the decline of U.S. naval forces. Admiral Holloway, himself a CNO later, proposed that the large attack carriers be modified to carry enough ASW aircraft for force defense, that is, for the task force protection mission of the CVS. In addition, Admiral Zumwalt sought the construction of a new class of small ASW support ships (SCS) that might take over much of the CVS mid-ocean ASW task. In 1969 and 1970 two Atlantic attack carriers (the *Forrestal* and *Saratoga*) added half-squadrons (eight SH-3Ds) of ASW helicopters to their air groups without loss of tactical aircraft, inspiring the decision to try a more radical conversion. Admiral Zumwalt ordered implementation of Project 60 Decision 9 for this flexible-carrier concept on 27 August 1970. The *Saratoga* was the prototype, operating S-2s and SH-3s on her

Mediterranean deployment in June 1971 and being redesignated a CV rather than a CVA on 31 June 1972.

Some modifications were required. The existing S-2 needed avgas as well as an ASCAC for real-time classification. The newer S-3A would need neither, but it would require a ship inertial navigation system as well as the special maintenance facility (VAST) of the new F-14 fighter. It would also need a TSC to maintain the programs of its computer; ultimately the TSC would also perform real-time processing of S-3A acoustic data. Modifications in the *Saratoga* and the next two CVs included installation of an ASCAC adjacent to the flag war room, refurbished avgas stowage, stowage for ASW torpedoes and sonobuoys, and an ASW ready room, at a total cost of $7 million and three months, work being completed in March 1971. Late in 1972 it was estimated that conversion would cost $5 million for equipment and another $2.4 million for conversion proper. Half of an ASW air wing (twenty S-2Es, eight SH-3Ds) could be operated at the cost of four fighters, four attack bombers (A-7s), and four heavy reconnaissance aircraft. The beauty of the CV concept was that the ship could shift from a CVA air wing to a mixed (CV) air wing to an air wing with a full CVS load of ASW aircraft with full flexibility.

It was soon decided to convert all active large-deck carriers by FY 77, the *John F. Kennedy* being the first with an all-jet air group (S-3As). These CV conversions solved only half the CVS replacement problem, since clearly the big carriers would be far too valuable to waste on areas of low air threat in wartime. There had never been enough CVSs for sea-lane protection, and now there were no low-value carriers at all. The proposed solution was the helicopter.

From the early fifties onward, ASW helicopters had been recognized as a viable means of detecting and, perhaps more importantly, of keeping contact with a submarine. In particular, they could operate active (dipped) sonars where a destroyer could not, since a submarine could not torpedo a sonar-dipping helicopter. In 1959, for example, the Long Range Objectives (LRO) group proposed a new escort, the PE or patrol escort, which would support six helicopters specifically for the "cold-war trail" task. The PE was rejected because more conventional destroyer escorts seemed far better suited to wartime operations, but the idea of a marriage between a surface ASW ship and a strong force of ASW helicopters with active sonars persisted.

Within a decade advances in Soviet submarine quieting threatened to defeat the passive SOSUS system. Convoy tactics would have to be reintroduced by a U.S. Navy badly lacking in escorts. Small helicopter carriers were proposed as an equalizer by LRO-81 (that group's last study) in 1969. There were two

alternatives: escort carriers (CVHEs, modified *Commencement Bay*s) and a new class of 12,000- to 14,000-ton DHKs (30 knots, with twelve advanced ASW helicopters deploying sonobuoys or towed-sled sensors not amenble to aircraft use). The LRO envisaged a total of fourteen DHKs and fifteen CVHEs, the latter supporting amphibious assaults and covering underway replenishment groups, and lacking the destroyer armament of the DHKs.

In theory the new helicopter carriers would replace the last six CVSs, whose S-3 aircraft would transfer to shore bases to replace early-model P-3s. A single helicopter carrier could also replace two or three destroyers, based on her ability to maintain two ASW helicopters continuously on station. The substitution would not be a simple one, since destroyers would still be required as a secondary forward convoy screen, as pouncers to prosecute contacts, and for covering the rear sectors of a formation, using passive towed-array sonars against submarines attempting to overtake at high speed. In this way the high technology for the DHK/CVHEs might begin to balance the number of more conventional escorts which a return to convoy tactics would require—and which the LRO-81 planners could not hope to achieve.

Admiral Zumwalt was not part of the group that prepared LRO-81, but as head of Navy Systems Analysis he would have been well aware of its conclusions. When he became CNO in 1970 he sought a combination of new navy initiatives that would reverse the decline of U.S. forces. One idea was an air-capable ship that could provide maintenance and depot facilities for destroyer-borne LAMPS ASW helicopters, to keep them continuously airborne over a convoy. It was conceived by the deputy chief of Naval Materiel for Development (and chief of Naval Development), Rear Admiral Tom D. Davies, as a destroyer-size ship totally dependent on her aircraft for offensive and defensive capability. In 1971 Vice Admiral E. P. Aurand, Commander, ASW Forces, Pacific, proposed that ASW helicopters be concentrated aboard a platform able to keep one (or, better, two) airborne continuously. That in turn implied six and then twelve helicopters on a 15,000-ton platform. Ultimately the air group was set at twelve to fourteen helicopters and three or four VSTOL fighters, the latter for conventional air defense (the anti-Bear mission) in low-air-threat areas such as the North Atlantic.

Admiral Zumwalt envisaged up to twenty convoys at sea requiring air support in mid-ocean before reaching carrier-operating areas. He set a cost ceiling of $100 million (about one-eighth the cost of a full-size carrier) for an SCS, which required a hangar large enough to accommodate most of her aircraft, as in an LPH (amphibious helicopter carrier). A series of design studies (temporarily designated DH) was ordered in September 1970, and fifteen alternative schemes were developed. They ranged from 8,400 tons (ten SH3D helicopters and a single-screw 15,000-SHP steam turbine) to 21,850 tons (twenty CH53s, four LAMPS, five AV-8 Harriers, two Harpoon launchers, two Sea Sparrow launchers, and nuclear steam turbines on a length of 720 feet). Four were presented in November: the 8,400-tonner, an 11,230-tonner (six SH-3s, six Harriers, one 3-in gun, and twin-screw 70,000-SHP steam turbines), a 15,160-tonner (fifteen SH-3s, six Harriers, one Harpoon and two Sea Sparrow launchers, and twin-screw 69,000-SHP steam turbines), and a 21,480-tonner (twenty CH-53s, four LAMPS, five Harriers, two Harpoon and two Sea Sparrow launchers, and twin-screw 46,000-SHP steam turbines). None of the original sketch designs called for gas-turbine propulsion. Although virtually no defensive or offensive weapons were specified, standard policy was to provide two Harpoon launchers on any ship over 20,000 tons and two Sea Sparrows on the larger ships. In each case a 20-ft clear hangar height was provided. The 11,230-ton design, which formed the basis for subsequent development, had an elevator right aft and another abeam the island, the enclosed hangar stopping just forward of the island structure. It was unprotected but incorporated alternating engine and fire rooms

for protection against underwater attack. Blast deflectors for the Harriers were worked into the flight deck abaft the island, giving these aircraft about a 320-ft run to take off.

The designation SCS was adopted in May 1971. The preliminary design was complete by January 1972 (see table 16-2). It showed a capability for intermediate-level maintenance; the power plant was set at two LM-2,500 gas turbines, of a type being standardized in the fleet, and a single screw. No guns other than the Phalanx close-in weapon system were to be mounted. At this time the lead ship was expected to cost $175 million in FY 75 dollars, with follow ships at $117 million each; one was to be included in the FY 75 program for completion in FY 78, three more in FY 76, and two each in FY 77 and FY 78, for a total of eight, equivalent to one big-deck carrier. Design money was appropriated in FY 72 and FY 73, and the navy requested $29.4 million for advanced funding for FY 74.

One SCS was to have operated with each convoy, supporting *Perry*- (FFG-7-) class ocean escorts. The helicopters of the SCS were to have localized and attacked submarines detected by the towed arrays streamed by the frigates, which were credited with convergence zone range. In addition, VSTOL fighters aboard the SCS would provide air defense up to 100 nautical miles from the convoy, backed up by the

Table 16-2. VSTOL Ships

	SCS	VSS I	VSS II	VSS III
Light Disp't (tons)	9,773	15,210	17,380	20,116
Full Load (tons)	13,736	22,490	26,334	29,130
LOA (ft-in)	610	—	717-0	717-0
LWL (ft-in)	585	69-0	690-0	690-0
Beam (WL/EXT)	80	98.45/133.5	105.7/166.5	109.2/178.0
Draft (full load)(ft-in)	21.62-0	23.23-0	24-5	25.3-0
Depth (ft-in)	67.5-0	73.50-0	77-1	77-1
SHP	45,000	90,000	90,000	90,000
Speed (kts)	26 (24.5 sust)	28 sust	—	—
CIWS	2	2	2	2
Harpoon Canisters	—	2	2	2
Aircraft	3 AV-8A	4 AV-8A	4 AV-8B	—
	2 LAMPS	6 LAMPS	6 LAMPS III	
	14 SH-3	16 SH-53	16 SH-53	
	545×105	655×133.5		
Hangar Height (ft)	19.0	19.0	20.1	20.1
Elevators (ft)	1 60×30	1 60×30	2 45×45	2 45×45
	1 35×50	1 35×49.3		
Capacity (lbs)	60,000	60,000	85,000	85,000
JP-5 (tons)	950	1,140	2,791	—
Av Ord (tons)	180	—	292	—
LM 2500 GT	2	4	4	4
SSG (GT)	3 2500	5 2500	5 2500	5 2500
Complement				
Ship	76/624	30/446	44/636	49/910
Aviation	—	79/492	79/492	87/541

standard missiles of the frigates. They would be particularly valuable against the Bear Ds used by the Soviets to provide over-the-horizon target information for submarines and surface ships firing long-range antiship cruise missiles. The SCS air group was set at eleven ASW and three AEW helicopters and three Harriers; the carriers would maintain two ASW and one AEW helicopter continuously on station in the air, with a ready VSTOL fighter on deck to intercept incoming aircraft, and two ready helicopters to pounce on submarine contacts. In experiments, the VSTOLs were used to lay sonobuoy barriers on the flanks of the convoy, the helicopters providing the screen in the van.

Admiral Zumwalt blames Admiral Rickover for the disaster that followed; Rickover found the concept of austere warships such as SCS entirely unacceptable and had ready allies in the naval aviation community, which considered VSTOL a dangerous threat to the large-deck carrier. Despite Admiral Zumwalt's protest that the SCS was by no means conceived as an alternative carrier, the fight within Congress killed the small carrier. During the FY 75 budget review, Congress denied the $143 million required to build the prototype, citing Defense Department studies questioning the ability of the SCS to survive submarine torpedo attack or to counter the submarine-launched cruise missile. Congress allocated the $29.4 million of FY 74 money for studies of a low-cost conventional carrier, which became the CVV. The SCS plans were sold to Spain, which laid down one such ship, the *Principe de Asturias*, at Bazan on 8 October 1979.

Meanwhile, the SCS operational concept was being tested at sea. Alternative platforms were evaluated during 1971, the best being a *Commencement Bay*-class escort carrier—which it would cost $73 million merely to make seaworthy. The next best choice was a helicopter carrier, the *Guam* being selected and modified from October 1971 through January 1972. Major modifications included an ASW sensor analysis TSC, additional aircraft control and direction facilities, and improved aircraft maintenance facilities. The experimental air group consisted of SH-3G Sea King helicopters and AV-8A Harriers.

Tests continued through April 1974 and were generally considered successful despite material problems with the SH-3 helicopter. However, the Operational Test and Evaluation Force questioned whether the ship could meet a fifteen-day mission requirement of maintaining two sonobuoys, and the General Accounting Office wondered whether she was worth building when the advanced ASW helicopter and the advanced VSTOL (both of which she would operate) were so far away. Admiral Zumwalt

had to retreat, omitting the ship from his last (FY 75) budget.

Admiral Zumwalt's successor, James L. Holloway III, asked for a larger and more powerful ship; he planned a transition to an all-VSTOL navy by the early twenty-first century. The VSS, much more capable than the SCS of handling large VSTOL aircraft, was one element of this plan. Although in theory she was not a conventional-carrier replacement, the VSS was required to achieve speeds much closer to those of fleet carriers. The complementary NavAir program called for three generic VSTOL air frames which would fill all sea-based aviation requirements, and which, it was hoped, would enter service in the late 1980s or early 1990s: VSTOL A (utility, e.g., ASW and AEW), B (supersonic fighter/attack), and C (LAMPS III replacement). But navy requests for VSTOL design funds received no congressional support, perhaps in part because of the opposition of carrier aviators. The VSS itself, however, was developed through concept design, and in 1982 it remains one option for future carrier construction. Moreover, the sea-based VSTOL is hardly dead, since the AV-8B Harrier can approach VSTOL B in function and performance.

The Naval Ship Engineering Center then developed about fifty alternative VSTOL support ships (VSS) between November 1974 and December 1975; they included alternatives capable of operating only VSTOL and helicopters as well as more conventional carriers with catapults and arresting gear. The VSS was conceived as an enlarged SCS, not as an alternative to the large-deck carriers. General requirements had been established by January 1976 and a conceptual design was developed between January and June 1976. It could accommodate sixteen SH-53s, six LAMPS, and four Harriers, and was thus somewhat larger than the SCS. In addition, the VSS was provided with two Harpoon launchers and with NTDS for air control. In contrast to the SCS, the machinery was twin screw, with four LM-2500 gas turbines for a speed of 29 knots. Aircraft maintenance was to be based on the use of vans for avionics shops and spares in order to achieve flexibility of air wing. There was a considerable cost in clear deck area to accommodate alternative van arrangements. Structurally, the VSS differed from other U.S. aviation ships in having a "notched" hull, the flight deck terminating forward of the stern, with a semi-enclosed elevator at its after end. Several advantages were claimed for this unusual configuration: the elevator would have the immunity to sea damage of an inboard installation and the flexibility of a deck-edge elevator and, aircraft could extend beyond its periphery. By ending the flight deck short of the stern, the designers could limit enclosed volume and, they claimed, the tendency to

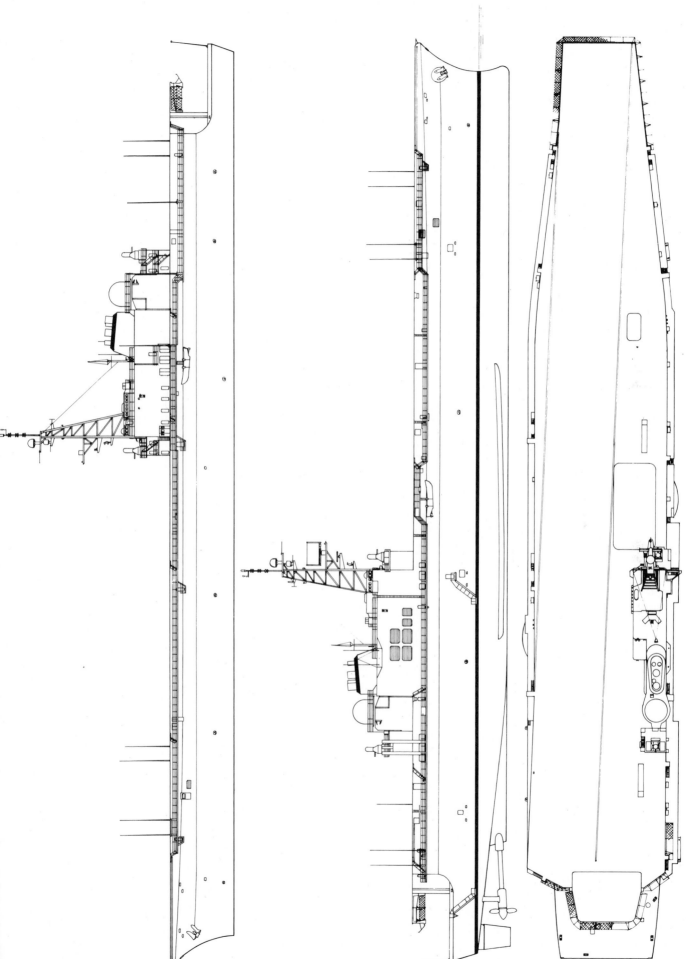

Sketch design for the sea control ship, 1974.

add loads aft for increased displacement. The hull length of 690 feet was chosen to provide sufficient hangar-deck area for shops and to achieve the required speed at minimum power. Finally, the VSS design provided for a second (30- by 60-ft) inboard elevator forward.

Funds were not provided to develop a contract design in 1976, but a congressional Defense Authorization Conference Report of 20 June 1977 directed a VSS to be evaluated in comparison with other sea-based air platforms. The VSS design was revised to reflect a new air group: twelve Type As (ASW), four Type As (AEW), six LAMPS III, and the original quartet of Harrier (AV-8A) fighters. In addition, on 3 August OPNAV added a requirement that the VSS be capable of supporting a marine-assault air wing; twelve Type As (marine Assault), four CH-53 D/F helicopters, six AH-IT gunship helicopters, and two UH-1Ns. Two more alternative air wings were added in September: an ASW/AEW group (sixteen Type As for ASW, four Type As for AEW, and four Type B fighters) and a revised marine-assault air wing (twelve Type As for marine assault, six Type As for fire support and command and control, and four CH-53 D/Fs—later CH-53Es were also to be operated). The major shift from the 1976 VSS was a decision, made early in October, that a sufficient number of personnel would be carried to replace the deferred maintenance of the original VSS with a more conventional form of maintenance. Finally, the revised VSS would incorporate a deck-edge elevator forward rather than the earlier centerline type.

These changes required considerable reworking of the original VSS design, the result being designated VSS II. It was completed in February 1978 and continues, four years later, to figure in navy studies of future sea-based air forces. As in large carriers, air-group considerations dominated the design at all levels. One problem throughout was that neither Type A nor Type B VSTOL was well defined in 1977; indeed, neither type exists in 1982. The Naval Air Systems Command had to develop generic characteristics of alternative lift/cruise fan, tilt rotor, and compound helicopter configurations of Type A; Type B was better defined and required only one set of characteristics. The situation was reminiscent of that in the design for the super-carrier *United States*, whose large strategic bomber was never fully defined.

Each of the alternative air wings had a different effect on the design. The VSS could not park all of its aircraft on the hangar deck; the designers remarked that in a smaller ship it would be necessary to provide a maximum density "storm spot" for all in the protection of the hangar, whereas in the VSS a safe parking area on the flight deck could be used. For ASW, the old SCS requirement of two ready helicopters and

one ready VSTOL translated to a flight deck on which two SH-53s could be "spread" while still leaving a takeoff lane for an AV-8A. Requirements for combined flight- and hangar-deck area were driven by the VSTOL ASW/AEW air wing. In the absence of existing VSTOLs, a notional list/cruise fan airplane was used for purposes of estimation, since it had the largest spotting factor. Clear hangar height, 20 feet 1 inch (rather than the 19 feet of VSS I), was determined by the CH-53E helicopter (SH-53 in VSS I). Helicopter dimensions (45 by 45 feet) were determined by the expected size of the Type B VSTOL. Magazine capacity, which could be increased slightly in VSS II owing to greater beam, was set by the VSTOL ASW air wing. Similarly, this air wing was responsible for an increase in aviation-fuel capacity from 1,140 to 2,791 tons.

A deck-edge elevator was justified on strength grounds; as in larger U.S. carriers, the flight deck was the strength deck, and any centerline elevator amidships made for a concentration of stresses. In addition, a deck-edge elevator saves hangar space. However, it cannot be used in heavy seas, which would affect a VSS far more than a large carrier; in that case the VSS would be limited to its after elevator.

Neither VSS I nor VSS II included any special protection, although magazines were kept below the waterline. Late in November 1977 Under Secretary of the Navy James Woolsey asked for alternative designs of a protected VSS, and late the following January the Secretary of the Navy requested a "class D" cost estimate for a VSS armored to the level of "scheme D," submitted in reply to Woolsey's inquiry. It included a torpedo decoy system, Nixie, and was designated VSS III. The added weight could be accommodated either by a sacrifice of freeboard or of speed, which latter NAVSEA considered marginal. VSS III, then, incorporated a new hull form of reduced freeboard (but gaining 0.8 knots in speed). Her concept design was completed in July 1978; she incorporates the British-type ski-jump as well as protection. This design study was considered in several navy studies of future platforms for sea-based air, in some of which it was an alternative to full-deck carriers. The central issue remains the success of advanced VSTOL aircraft, which for more than two decades has been just over the horizon. In most of these studies a VSS force capable of providing an air effort equivalent to that of a CV force is much more numerous and also more expensive, since each VSS requires much of the electronic suit of the larger ship. However, particularly when life-cycle costs are included, the air wing dominates carrier cost. The issue then is the cost of each notional VSTOL compared with that of current fixed-wing aircraft. The other

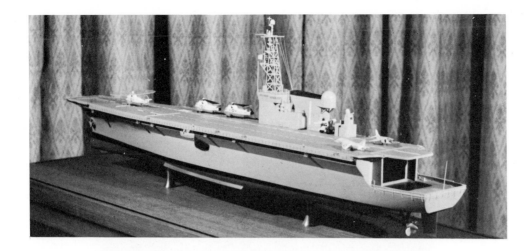

The design of a sea control ship was an attempt to develop an inexpensive ASW carrier, but proponents were never able to convince Congress that the ship would have a worthwhile role. The VSS design that followed was similar in outline but longer, with Harpoon cannisters on the fantail, twin propellers, and a deck-edge elevator. A modified SCS with a British "ski-jump" ramp incorporated in the bow was launched in May 1982 in Spain.

central issue is vulnerability. No small ship is likely to be survivable as a large one. However, in the face of nuclear weapons, any one of which can destroy even a large carrier, it can be argued that the VSS force can preserve a larger fraction of its air power against a given level of attack. It is also often argued that, given their independence from catapults and arresting gear, VSTOL aircraft aboard a large carrier can greatly reduce that ship's vulnerability to disabling damage from conventional hits.

Proposals were repeatedly made for VSS construction. For example, the Congress almost funded conversion of a helicopter carrier to an SCS in FY 79. The Senate Armed Services Committee added $40 million for such a conversion and $25 million for the design of a new type of VSTOL carrier, as well as $70 million for long-lead items for a sixth LHA (see chapter 17) to more than replace the LPH withdrawn for SCS duty. All of these items were deleted from the FY 79 bill finally passed after President Carter vetoed the orig-

inal version (which had included a large-deck nuclear carrier). However, interest in limited carriers persists, some proponents of large-deck ships wanting medium-capability carriers of about 40,000 tons in addition. For example, in the fall of 1978 Rear Admiral George Jessen of the Naval Air Systems Command pointed out that modern jet fighters had such high thrust-to-weight ratios that they, like the VSTOLs, would benefit from ski-jump takeoff—thus catapults might be dispensed with (or at least considerably reduced in size and power) aboard a sufficiently fast (for wind-over-deck), long carrier. Tests of this concept began in 1982 at Patuxent River with T-2J and F-14 aircraft.

In FY 82 testimony, navy representatives reported that a VSS III (a hardened VSS) was well-enough advanced for translation to contract design, but that the more exotic light (40,000 tons) ski-jump carrier would not be at the same stage until about 1985.

17

The Amphibious-Assault Carriers

Outside the mainstream of attack and ASW carriers lies the amphibious-assault or helicopter carrier, represented in the current fleet by the LPH and LHA. It was the direct result of a marine corps study, ordered in August 1946, of the effects of nuclear weapons on future amphibious operations. Lieutenant General Roy S. Geiger, Commander, Fleet Marine Force, Pacific, witnessed the Bikini tests and concluded that a few atomic bombs could easily destroy the concentrated shipping and also the beachhead of any classical amphibious assault. Clearly ships would have to be dispersed, but that would risk defeat on the beach, since the troops would not be able to concentrate as they contacted enemy forces. A special board considered a variety of alternatives, including transport aircraft, gliders, and parachute assault, but each was defective. Transport submarines were an interesting possibility, ultimately discarded because of their very limited troop-carrying capacity, not to mention their great cost. That left the helicopter and a transport seaplane. The General Board recommended that parallel programs be developed in a December 1946 report endorsed by General Alexander A. Vandegrift, the commandant of the marine corps.

The course that followed was marked by considerable optimism: the rate at which effective troop-carrying helicopters might materialize looked promising. From a carrier point of view, the larger the individual helicopter, the smaller the number required for a single assault lift. In theory, too, the use

of helicopters able to shuttle back and forth quickly would reduce the total number of helicopters needed. The 1946 board envisaged alternative types lifting 3,500 and 5,000 pounds, the former sufficient for a rifle squad, the latter for a rifle squad plus a skeletonized machine-gun squad or a mortar squad. Moreover, 5,000 pounds would lift light artillery. The larger helicopter was so much more attractive that by 1949 the development of the smaller one had been abandoned. Even larger helicopters were proposed, but the marines were reluctant to adopt one that could lift many more than twenty men in view of the high vulnerability of individual craft.

The reality was rather less impressive. The first marine troop carriers were observation helicopters, Sikorsky HO3S-1s, which could carry only six men each. They were replaced on an interim basis by Piasecki HRP-1s, each of which could carry only a fifth of the desired payload, or eight troops, a minimum for landing troops on combat formation. By 1949 the marines recognized that helicopter development would not be as rapid as expected, and a new marine board wrote out a requirement for a helicopter that could fit existing escort-carrier elevators, lift thirteen to fifteen troops (a 3,000- to 3,500-lb payload), and fly 3,500 nautical miles. It ultimately became the first large troop carrier, the Sikorsky HR2S, which in developed form could carry twenty to twenty-five troops. While it was under development, the marines received the smaller Sikorsky HRS, orig-

LHD 1, shown in a Litton artist's sketch, is the latest incarnation of the amphibious assault, or helicopter, carrier. It is to be developed from the existing Litton LHA design, the principle change being redesign of the internal well deck to support the new air cushion landing craft, or LCAC. Because the LCAC would be launched about 50 miles from the beach, the LHD is to abandon the shore-bombardment gun armament of its predecessors. In addition, special provision will be made for support of AV-8B VSTOL fighters, both for ground attack and for a secondary sea control carrier mission. The first LHD is planned for the FY 84 program.

inally developed for ASW, which could carry a full squad of ten marines. The HR2S was the basis for helicopter-carrier conversion and design in the fifties, although it never quite reached the weight envisaged. That is, its typical takeoff weight was about 31,000 pounds, but the planners of the mid-fifties expected it to reach 50,000 or even 60,000 pounds, and designed flight decks and elevators accordingly. By way of comparison, the current heavy helicopter, the CH-53D, lifts thirty-eight troops but takes off at up to 41,435 pounds, and the current medium marine helicopter, the CH-46F, lifts twenty-six troops and takes off at 23,000 pounds.

Tactically, the marines considered a flight of ten helicopters best for effective control, so that helicopter carriers were generally designed to accommodate multiples of that unit. The marines concentrated on the requirements of a divisional assault, which were considerable. For example, a January 1951 study envisaged lifting 10,000 men and 3,000 to 4,000 short tons of material. Total lift, then, would be 520 HRSs or 208 HR2Ss, which in turn would require, in the former case, 20 escort carriers with 20 helicopters each, accommodating 150 to 200 tons of cargo, 500 to 600 assault marines, and a 200-man helicopter squadron. At this time it did not appear that the CVE would be able to support the larger helicopter; the study envisaged construction of eight new carriers or conversion of eight existing ones, each to carry 20 HR2Ss, 1,200 to 1,500 assault marines, the 200-man helicopter unit, and 450 to 550 tons of cargo. Although the detailed requirements varied over time, this level of effort was typical—and daunting, given the size of the shipbuilding budget and the demands for other warship types, such as new attack carriers and new missile-armed escorts for them.

The marines commissioned their first helicopter squadron, HMX-1, on 1 December 1947. It was able to test the new vertical-assault concept the following year in an amphibious exercise, Packard II: 5 HO3S-1 light observation helicopters flew from the escort carrier *Palau*. In Packard III, May 1948, 8 helicopters from the *Palau* stimulated a full helicopter attack of 184 aircraft flying from six CVEs, to lift a complete regimental combat team, which would seize a strategic crossroads inland of the beach. Simultaneously, landing craft were to assault the nearby shore. High winds and rough seas prevented a successful landing but did not stop the helicopter operation; each HRP carried six passengers about ten miles from the carrier under heavy-fighter cover. In all, 230 men and 14,000 pounds of cargo were lifted.

On 1 January 1951 the marine Tactics and Techniques Board set 1 November 1951 as the target date for the first CVE conversion, with four ships to be in service by 1 September 1952. *Commencement Bay*-class carriers were initially envisaged for use, but all those in service were urgently needed for ASW or for marine support in Korea. Instead, the marines would have to make do with the *Casablanca*s (CVE-55 class), which had been retained in reserve precisely because of their potential as helicopter carriers. The marines sought a new-construction helicopter carrier or a conversion in the FY 52 program, but no such ship appeared in that or in the FY 53 budget. However, the CNO did direct the Atlantic Fleet to test the vertical-assault concept, with two exercises conducted early in 1952 from the *Siboney*. The CVE-55 class would be suited to operation of the HRSs, although alterations would be required if the HR2Ss were to be operated. Again, it was estimated that twenty ships would be required to lift a marine division using the smaller helicopter, or thirteen CVEs with the larger. Since there were hardly enough helicopters available, only four CVEs were requested, each to carry twenty HRSs, 850 troops, and 75 tons of cargo.

The CNO asked BuShips for a feasibility study on 8 September 1952; it was completed in November, too late for inclusion of a conversion in the FY 54 program. The marine commandant now renewed his request to obtain four ships in FY 55. Within a short time he had reverted to the much larger target, again to lift an entire division: four CVE-105s and twelve CVE-55s. This was well in advance of what the shipbuilding budget could support, given the costs of other types of technology. Of two carrier conversions in the FY 55 budget, one was deferred. The other, the CVE *Thetis Bay*, emerged on 20 July 1956 as CVHA-1, carrying twenty HRS helicopters. The *Thetis Bay* was considered an experimental ship rather than an operational prototype, and her conversion was extremely austere. In order to provide sufficient elevator capacity for the HR2Ss, her after elevator was enlarged, the after end of the flight deck being cut away. Troop berthing and sanitary facilities were installed at the forward end of the hangar deck, and all 5-in and 20-mm mounts removed, leaving only eight twin 40-mm guns as armament. Troop capacity was 38 officers and 900 enlisted men.

The second ship, the larger CVE *Block Island*, appears to have been intended as the prototype for further SCB 159 conversions, and was the first ship designated as a helicopter-assault ship or LPH. Work began in January 1958 but was never completed, and the program for CVE conversions was cancelled in favor of a combination of new construction and the conversion of larger fleet carriers. The big CVEs had become available as the unconverted *Essex*es dropped out of the attack-carrier force and became CVSs; in turn, as the SCB-27As dropped out, the unconverted *Essex*es became available for further service as LPHs, and the CVE-105 conversions became less and less attractive.

An assault-forces study group, designated by the

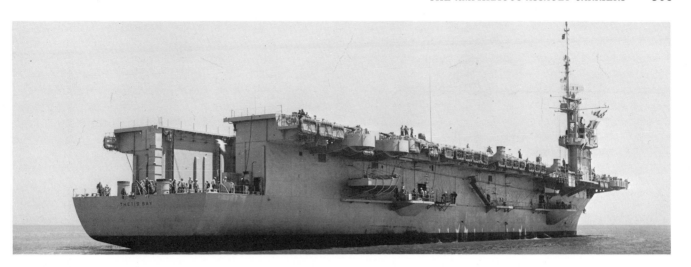

The former escort carrier *Thetis Bay* was the first U.S. carrier dedicated to transporting marines and their helicopters. Note that, although she could carry twenty-two HR2S troop helicopters, her flight deck was marked out for only five spots. The flight deck was cut away aft to increase the clearance of the elevator there. The *Thetis Bay* was never intended as a prototype for mass conversion, although many *Casablanca*-class carriers of her type were retained through the fifties solely as a mobilization reserve for conversion to helicopter ships (they could not operate modern fixed-wing aircraft, even with modernization).

Ad Hoc Committee (predecessor of the LRO) in September 1954, reported the next April that over the next ten to fifteen years most existing attack cargo and transport (AKA and APA) ships would be replaced by helicopter carriers. "This will be occasioned by the VTOL aircraft becoming the principal means of placing personnel ashore under assault conditions. Supporting personnel and heavy equipment will still be landed by water-borne means but the majority of assault troops will be air-landed." The lift per marine division and air wing (one per coast) was estimated as one command ship (possibly a converted Mariner), twelve CVHAs (twenty HR2Ss each), four APAs (converted Mariners), three AKAs (converted Mariners), twelve LSTs, nine LSDs, one assault submarine, and one APD (an improved type with a sustained sea speed of 25 knots). That set a requirement for twenty-four CVHAs. The type chosen would have to be as economical as possible to build or convert; any conversion candidate would have to be a hull of some numbers not badly needed for any other purpose. Moreover, it would have to have a considerable amount of hull life left. Desired characteristics included twenty helicopters, 20 knots sustained speed, 1,800 troops, and 2,000 measurement tons of troop cargo. This was a measure of volume, not weight. Its weight equivalent, estimated at 1,000 tons at the time, depended on the details of marine equipment.

In November OPNAV members of the SCB strongly proposed installation of two Tartars, and despite many foreseeable problems it was approved. However, this decision was later reversed, in view of the increase in ship size and cost involved and the problems of procurement for FY 57 ships. BuAer objected on grounds of missile blast on the flight deck.

Many alternatives were considered: cruisers (the *Cleveland* and *Baltimore* classes), the *North Carolina*-class battleship, the *Independence*-class light carrier, CVE-55- and CVE-105-class escort carriers, a Mariner-class merchant ship, and a special design. Of the conversions only the CVEs were available in sufficient numbers, but they could not meet the desired characteristics. On the other hand, a newly designed ship would be relatively expensive.

Early studies were based on an existing 20-kt seaplane tender design, the LPH benefitting from the elimination of boat and vehicle stowage. By April 1955 it appeared that the new ship (then designated a CVHA) would displace about 11,160 tons light (18,000 fully loaded) and would be 625 feet long on the waterline. It would cost $47 million for the lead ship and $40 million for a follow-on, that is, about a fifth the cost of an attack carrier. OPNAV asked for an alternative with about half the capacity, and BuShips reported that it could develop such a ship

on 7,500 tons (12,500 fully loaded) at a unit cost of $31 million for the lead ship and $24 for follow-ons, which was even less attractive, given the much greater numbers required for the full program. By way of comparison, it was estimated that the CVE-55 could carry fifteen helicopters, the CVE-105, eighteen, and the battleship, the largest hull in the study, twenty-eight; the latter would have to retain one of her turrets for trim.

Work now began on a twenty-helicopter LPH. By August waterline length had been reduced to 550 feet and two basic configurations were under consideration: a conventional small carrier, based on SCB 43, and a single-deck type in which hangar and flight deck would be on the same level. The latter was rejected because considerable turbulence would be generated on the flight deck and the hangar would be obstructed by stanchions. Moreover, without elevators, it would have had only restricted cargo-handling facilities. Hangar clear height in the conventional design under development was set at 20 feet, and there were to be two deck-edge elevators. The marines wanted 300,000 gallons of avgas, a minimum speed of 20 knots (to match that of the amphibious force), and an endurance of 10,000 nautical miles at 20 knots. Marine flexibility demanded that the new ship be able to pass through the Panama Canal.

In May 1956 the marine commandant agreed to a parallel program of LPH new construction and conversion, with two ships in each of the FY 58–62 programs. Thus the new LPH, SCB 157, and a CVE-105 conversion, SCB 159, were developed in parallel. Work began in June 1955 as the proposed FY 57 program then showed two new-construction LPHs. By December, when the new carrier had been dropped from the FY 57 program, the design was much in its final form, 550 feet long, with a displacement of 10,000 tons (light; 17,000 fully loaded) and an expected trial speed of 21.5 knots. Roll stabilization was proposed to permit operation of her helicopters in heavy weather and embarkation of her troops in other ships' boats. Work continued into 1956 since an LPH was still scheduled for the FY 58 program.

The CVE-105 conversion needed about 2,500 more tons to do the same job but enjoyed far more endurance. The new-construction LPH had several advantages. Since it was the minimum hull that would meet the characteristics, it required significantly less maintenance. It would also suffer less from a seaway; a study showed that the same sea that would reduce it to 13 knots would reduce the CVE to 8 knots. Finally, the LPH, sized for the helicopter expected to appear in the sixties, enjoyed a significant advantage in hangar capacity. Since the CVE flight deck was not to be altered, vehicle parking (on the hangar deck) was reduced from an original requirement of 6,000 square

Still in much her CVS configuration, the *Boxer* rides at anchor at Vieques, Puerto Rico, 5 December 1966, with H-34 assault helicopters on her flight deck. In contrast with the other two ex-*Essex* LPHs, she retained all of her flight deck and none of her sponson guns. Ventilating ducts on the side of her hull can be made out just abaft the accommodation ladder. The principal element of new electronics was the big conical-monopole antenna, common to all the converted carriers, on the island just forward of the no. 3 5-in gun mount.

feet to 4,500 on two levels; in the new ship, all vehicles would be one level, hangar-deck length being reduced in the CVE conversion from 306 feet (304 in the new design) to 214. The new LPH would have the great advantages of a gallery deck, adding over 11,000 square feet of usable area, improvements in control and accommodations, 20 percent more avgas, and 20 percent higher flight-deck loads. The original carrier design of the CVE also had important limitations. For example, since the CVE hangar deck was the strength deck, it could not be altered significantly. Sheer at the hangar deck cost, in effect, a full deck level fore and aft. There were also arrangement problems. Where the new LPH could accommodate all her troops on one level, the former CVE had to distribute hers among spaces built atop wing tanks and voids; in some cases troops were two levels from their sanitary facilities.

The CVE was far less expensive, but she would not have had the twenty- to twenty-five-year life of a new ship, even though she would have had relatively little time on her machinery. At an SCB meeting on 20 May 1957 the vote was six to four in favor of the new ship. Cost savings were suggested. For example, elimination of the roll stabilization would save $1 million, as would replacement of the proposed twin-screw plant by a single-screw Mariner (merchant) type. A proposal to reduce hangar height from 20 to 17.5 feet was rejected. The other cuts were accepted, as was a reduction in accommodation, a $1.5 million cut in air-conditioning, and a reduction in flight-deck strength from 60,000 to 50,000 pounds.

There was some controversy over propulsion. For example, BuAer argued that by 1961, when the ship would be ready, helicopters would all be burning JP-5, so that the ship might well operate as a single-fuel type, perhaps with pressure-fired boilers. The marines asked for a study of the cost of an increase in speed to 25 knots. The original design had called for two 600-lb boilers; the higher speed would require four of the more complex 1,200-lb type, and the design was not pursued very far.

By July 1957 the LPH hull was being carried at a waterline length of 570 feet (11,000 tons light, 18,000

As an LPH, the *Valley Forge* had the standard arrangement of two twin and two single 5-in mounts, as in this 30 May 1964 photograph. She retained her entire CVS radar suit, including the height-finding SPS-8 sponsored outboard of the funnel.

The big *Essex*-class flight deck was useful for aircraft transport as well as for helicopter operation. Photographed in February 1966, the *Valley Forge* transports a deck load of cocooned Crusader fighters, Skyhawk light bombers, and a solitary Skyraider. The helicopters forward of the planes have their air intakes covered by protective material. Her own H-34s line the forward part of the flight deck and fly overhead.

The converted LPHs saw combat service in the Dominican Republic and Vietnam. Here the *Princeton* prepares to launch an assault in January 1967. Note her tower mast and modified funnel arrangement, as well as the new SPS-30 height-finder radar. By this time she had already been modernized under the FRAM II program (FY 62, between December 1960 and June 1961); the *Boxer* was modernized under FY 63 and the *Valley Forge* under FY 64. The *Princeton* and the *Valley Forge* were stricken in January 1971, the *Boxer* in December 1969, being replaced by ships built from the keel up as helicopter carriers.

fully loaded) and a cost of $46.2 million for the prototype, $38.2 million for follow-ons. She would carry 300,000 gallons of JP-5 or avgas. Although a single-screw plant was ultimately adopted, the final design showed excess fuel stowage, since tankage could not be reduced very late in the design; a change would have thrown off the stability of the ship and thus required fixed ballast. As for arrangement, the marines wanted four takeoff areas, but in the end only three could be provided (two forward and one aft when twenty helicopters were aboard, since only nine could be accommodated on the hangar deck). Beam was increased from an initial estimate of 80 feet to 84 for stability; no increase was tolerable at the flight deck because the ship had to be able to pass through the Panama Canal.

Throughout, the characteristics required that the ship be convertible for ASW helicopter operation, not surprising given the importance of ASW and the enthusiasm for helicopters with dipping sonars.

The *Iwo Jima*-class LPH had several advantages over the principal alternative, a converted *Essex*-class CVS. At a time of shortage of sailors, she needed 400 rather than 1,200 men for base manning, that is, she could be operated by the sort of complement an attack transport required. That was partly thanks to the simple propulsion plant adopted. In addition, she concentrated the marines on board to an extent impossible in a converted carrier: for example, the *Princeton* (*Essex* class) had twenty-seven separate berthing compartments, with capacities ranging from 4 to 157 men. Finally, there were specialized

control facilities, an HDC (helicopter directing center) and an FSCC (fire support coordinating center). Given straitened financial resources, the construction program took far longer than had originally been expected, seven ships being built under the FY 58, 59, 60, 62, 63, 65, and 66 plans.

Essex-class ASW carriers were converted as an interim substitute. The SCB first considered a complete conversion in March 1957, with four boilers and two turbines removed to increase internal space. In that case 300 officers and 2,700 enlisted troops would be carried (compared with about 200 officers and 1,800 troops in the new LPH), and cargo would be stowed in no. 1 and 2 boiler rooms. No. 1 and 4 main turbines would be removed, the flight deck strengthened, and the forward centerline elevator removed to provide troop spaces. Accommodation could be increased 50 percent by building two more decks into the hangar deck at its forward end. There would be 9,000 square feet for vehicles (compared with the earlier 6,000) and 1,300 to 1,500 tons of cargo (compared with the earlier 900), as well as 10,000 rather than 5,000 gallons of gasoline for vehicles. But the ships were old and tired, and the SCB did not find so radical a conversion (which would have cost about $25 million for the lead ship) worthwhile compared with the new ship, SCB 157.

The plan actually adopted was much simpler, the SCB concentrating on cutting maintenance and operating costs. It decided that all guns except four 5-in ones on the flight deck and two single 5-in ones on the sponsons be removed, the radar suit be greatly re-

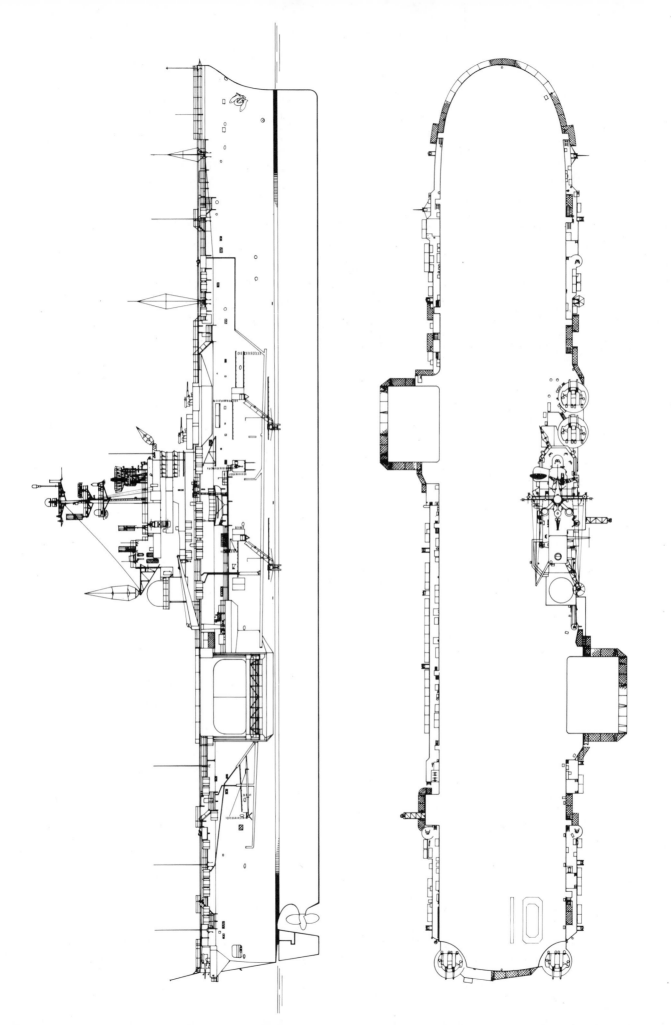

The helicopter carrier *Tripoli* (LPH 10), 1972.

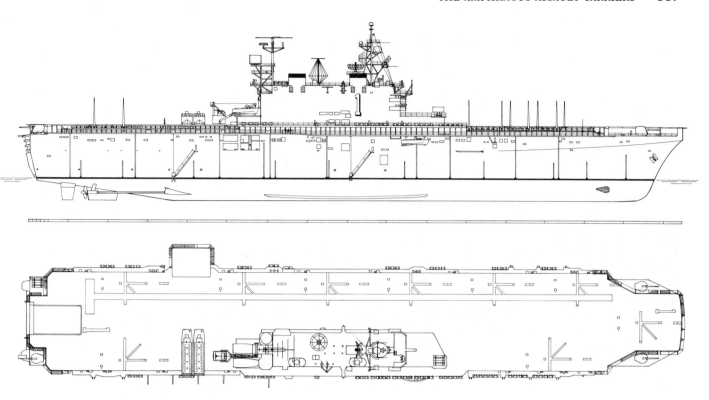

The prototype helicopter assault ship *Tarawa* (LHA 1), July 1976. She was armed with three lightweight 5-in/54s (Mark 45), two Sea Sparrow launchers (Mark 25), and six single 20-mm guns (Mark 67). Radars were the SPS-10F, SPS-40B, SPS-52B, SPN-35, SPQ-9A, SPG-60, and Mark 115 (for Sea Sparrow). TACAN was URN-20.

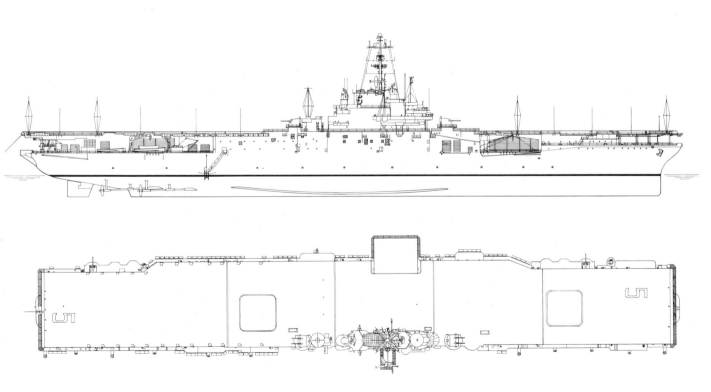

The *Essex*-class carrier *Princeton* (CV 37) as a helicopter carrier, LPH 5, in 1965. She retained six 5-in/38s as well as two Mark 37 and two Mark 56 directors, the latter on her port side. Radars were the SPS-10, SPS-12, SPS-30, Mark 25, and Mark 35. ECM was ULQ-6 (lattice outriggers). TACAN was URN-20. Note her twin funnel caps.

The *Iwo Jima* was the prototype keel-up helicopter carrier, considerably less expensive to operate than an *Essex* and better adapted to comfortable troop carrying. In peacetime amphibious ships may deploy for several months at a time with full marine complements aboard, so that troop habitability becomes extremely important. The newly completed ship is shown off Puget Sound on 2 November 1961.

Modifications to the original LPH in service have included the addition of SPN-35 blind-landing radar (in the large radome) and the replacement of half of the original quartet of twin 3-in/50 mounts by Sea Sparrow BPDMS point defense missiles (before the island and on the port quarter). A self-protective ECM antenna, cantilevered out from the ship's port side at flight-deck level just abaft the island, is distinguishable by its shadow. This is the *Tripoli*, in Subic Bay after Operation End Sweep, on 20 July 1973. The helicopters of the mine clearance force operated from LPHs, which also have a secondary ASW role. However, none of the large CH-53 minesweeping helicopters appear on the *Tripoli*'s flight deck.

duced, and four of the eight boilers be removed from service (speed would then fall to 25 knots). The resulting ship could stow ten HR2Ss on her hangar deck, with another twenty on the flight deck (four in flight positions and sixteen folded).

Three ships, the *Boxer*, *Princeton*, and *Valley Forge*, were converted; a fourth, the *Lake Champlain*, was dropped in view of manning difficulties. All were later refitted under the FRAM II program. The *Essex* concept (and the concept of concentrated LPH operations) was tested in LANTPHIBEX 1-58 early in 1958, when the carriers *Tarawa*, *Valley Forge*, and *Forrestal* delivered an entire regimental landing team to the beach. The converted carriers later saw combat in the Dominican Republic and Vietnam.

The amphibious force commanders criticized the *Iwo Jima* design for its "complete lack of landing craft, so that it is of doubtful utility under non-flying conditions and must depend on other types with landing craft to give it an over-the-beach capacity. This is probably the result of the . . . so-called LPD/LPH concept," in which landing ships with well decks (LPDs) were also provided with helicopter landing facilities. In 1965, then, the LRO group proposed a new LPH with integral over-the-beach capability, carrying twelve LCVPs or air-cushion vehicles, but with a flight deck as in the original LPH. In April 1965 the CNO asked whether what was then expected to be the last of the *Iwo Jima* class, the *New Orleans* (LPH 11), could be lengthened and provided with her own landing craft. The SCB asked for twelve LCVPs and two LCPLs, as well as ninety-seven more personnel. The cost would be a 52-ft section added amidships and 1,800 tons more displacement. It was rejected because the building yard, Philadelphia, was already badly behind schedule on a new amphibious command ship and a new LST; in addition, without considerable redesign damaged stability would become marginal and there might be an unacceptable trim by the stern. All that could be done, then, was to provide the FY 66 ship, the *Inchon* (Ingalls), with davits for two landing craft (LCVPs).

The ultimate solution was a new type of helicopter carrier, the LHA, incorporating an LSD-type well deck for landing craft and considerable cargo capacity. It also had improved command and control facilities, and so could function as an amphibious flagship, replacing (to some extent) the specialized AGC (LCC). In common with the contemporary *Spruance*-class destroyer and the abortive forward-deployment logistics ship, it was designed entirely by a private builder, Secretary of Defense McNamara favoring a "single package" procurement policy. The Litton design team won all three competitions, and on 28 May 1968 the Secretary announced an award for nine 39,000-ton ships. But massive cost overruns caused

the cancellation of four ships on 20 January 1971. The LHA is about the size of an *Essex*, although it is substantially slower, and from time to time it is proposed as the basis for an inexpensive aircraft carrier. For example, an LHA derivative was among the options offered to the Royal Australian Navy in 1980. Litton also offered a revised LPH, which for a time was the favored candidate. It lost out to the British *Invincible* class, which was attractive because it was being offered at an extremely low cost. However, after the Falklands Crisis it became politically impossible for Britain to sell the *Invincible*.

Both LPH and LHA were part of a massive buildup of modern amphibious lift during the sixties; the marines finally achieved the 20-kt amphibious force they had sought since 1946. All of these ships will require replacement beginning at the end of the eighties, and in 1982 there is already some interest in the form that replacement will take. The VSS described in chapter 16, intended to operate at times as an amphibious ship, was sometimes designated LH-X/VSS.

In March 1981 Vice Admiral W. H. Rowden, DCNO (Surface Warfare), testified before a Senate committee that the navy remained short of helicopter lift and hoped to obtain a sixth LHA in FY 83. In the FY 85 program the navy hoped to begin construction of a new class of amphibious ships, tentatively designated LHDX, between an LHA and an LPH in size. The Reagan administration's Five-Year Program (FY 83–87) of February 1982 showed no new LHAs, but instead two new LHDs (FY 84 and FY 87), which would replace the existing LPH force in the 1990s. A table of "notional ship characteristics" released in 1981 showed a 34,570-ton ship, 764 by 106 feet, carrying 1,800 troops, as well as boats and helicopters. "Spots" would be provided for medium helicopters (CH-46s). A well-deck capacity for two air-cushion vehicles or ten LCM-6s was claimed. A year later the LPD was described as an LHA (39,500 tons, 817 by 106 feet) modified to carry three air-cushion landing craft (or twelve LCM-6s) as well as maintenance facilities for eight to ten AV-8B Harrier VSTOL aircraft. The LHD was described as convertible for a secondary power projection/sea-control role, embarking specialized vans to expand her air group to a minimum of twenty AV-8Bs and six SH-60B LAMPS III ASW helicopters. Troop capacity increased to 1,903. This design replaced an October 1981 Lockheed Shipbuilding proposal based on the existing LSD-41 steam plant and limited to about two-thirds the size of the LHA.

The other proposed new design was an LPDX, a replacement for the existing LPD, with six helicopter spots and space for 858 troops on a displacement of about 17,300 tons. By way of comparison, an LHA has

Perhaps the greatest single criticism of the LPH concept was that the ships would be entirely useless in bad weather, since they could unload their troops only by helicopter. The LHA was a solution, but before it was implemented the last ship of the class, the *Inchon*, shown here emerging from Ingalls Naval Yard on 11 May 1970, was redesigned to carry a pair of landing craft in davits aft.

thirty-eight CH-46 "spots," an LPH twenty-seven. However, the LHA can accommodate only one air-cushion vehicle. Ship size was dictated by the structure of the minimum marine amphibious unit (MAU), which had to be transported by one LHDX, one LPDX, and one LSD-41. Indeed, a Lockheed LPDX proposal of October 1981 was derived directly from the LSD-41 design by the insertion of a hull plug amidships. In theory, the three ships together can transport eight air-cushion vehicles, 1,700 marines riding the LHDX, 850 the LPDX, and 440 the LSD, and the two air-capable ships can support the thirty-four CH-46s the MAU requires.

As this is written in 1982, the future of some sort of sea-based air platform seems assured. The Reagan administration believes that the large-deck carrier remains both sensible and uniquely capable, and that continuing congressional interest in smaller types (such as the VSS) is unlikely to bear fruit for some time, if at all. Describing the LHD as a secondary power-projection ship is, for the moment, a sop to the critics. As long as there is no viable VSTOL AEW aircraft, the VSTOL carrier is unlikely to displace her big sister, as the Falklands Crisis appears to show.

One exotic possibility is a space-based early-warning radar, which might conceivably take over enough of the AEW role to justify a non-AEW carrier. Given such early warning, and given very powerful air- and ship-launched defensive missiles, the carrier might no longer need high-performance aircraft except for the strike mission. In that case the large-deck carrier might become an even more powerful means

of force projection. Alternatively, a small VSTOL carrier might become at least viable, if still unimpressive in the strike role. A less exotic means of achieving early warning without AEW would be the proposed long-endurance manned or unmanned radar airship—which, however, might be much more vulnerable to adverse weather (not to mention enemy action) than a conventional AEW airplane. Certainly projects such as the autonomous HARP balloon have not prospered.

VSTOL continues, as this is written, to be the main alternative to the big carrier. There is one other, the large surface combatant with a very large number of cruise missiles, supported by sophisticated surface-based AAW and ASW systems. The chief justification for such ships is the prospective manning crisis of the latter part of this century: there may not be enough draft-age men to operate labor-intensive carriers. On the other hand, the variety of surface-based systems that would be needed even to approach carrier capability is a demonstration of the power that can be concentrated in the carrier. Moreover, the surface force could not approach the carrier's versatility—in a carrier, changing the air group changes the capability of the ship. In a surface ship, it is not only the missiles, but also the controlling systems, that must be changed, a very expensive (and at least now, time-consuming) option.

Given the Reagan administration's choice to emphasize force growth over new system development, the chance that any radical alternative to the large-deck carrier will appear within the next two

In 1982 the *Tarawa*-class LHA is the largest of the helicopter carriers. She is so close in overall size to an *Essex* that some advocates of the small attack carrier have proposed fixed-wing carriers based on her hull; Litton went so far, at one point, as to offer the Australian government such a ship to replace the aging *Melbourne*. However, the result was far too expensive and a modified LPH had to be offered instead. The name ship of the class clearly shows the stern gate that permits her to discharge large landing craft as well as helicopters. The forest of antennas on her island proclaims her a command ship as well as an assault carrier. Also visible are Sea Sparrow launchers for self-defense and three 5-in guns for shore bombardment. The future LHD will be similar in concept, but her well deck will accommodate the new air cushion landing vehicles, which will permit the unloading of heavy equipment and troops from a position well beyond the horizon, out of range of most enemy counterattack.

decades is slim. Too much still has to be done before VSTOL, for example, can take over the vital AEW role. The main prospective replacement for the carrier-based interceptor, a ship-launched but air-targeted missile, is at least as far away. Nor does it seem likely that big surface-effect craft (SES) will replace conventional carriers. Although they might dispense with catapults, they would still have to support viable—which means large—air groups, and that would entail the sort of weight and volume to be found in big carriers, which are beyond current SES capabilities.

The reason for the big carrier, the unsettled state of the world and the need to project U.S. power into it, is hardly likely to vanish in the foreseeable future. The story of this book, then, will surely continue into the next century.

A

Out of the Mainstream

A few exotic carrier projects warrant mention in this volume, even though none of them had any great effect on the development of the U.S. carrier. One of these carrier types was actually built, in order to fill the requirement for flight decks to train the vast number of naval aviators in 1942, when the navy was busily expanding its air arm. Two large side-wheeler steamers, the *Seeandbee* and the *Greater Buffalo*, were acquired for use on the Great Lakes and renamed the *Wolverine* and the *Sable*. They are remembered as the only paddle-wheel carriers. The *Sable* had the first steel flight deck in U.S. service. They had no hangars and no catapults, their flight decks being intended primarily for practice landings. As the CVE program gained momentum, escort carriers were assigned in numbers for carrier pilot training, and the two paddle-wheelers no longer provided the sole practice flight decks.

After the war, the obsolescent carrier was generally assigned to Pensacola for training, the *Saipan* being a case in point. In 1955 the early versions of the FY 57 program proposed that she be rebuilt with an angled deck, so that she could continue to function as a training carrier and even as a limited attack carrier in wartime.* However, no design studies appear to have been done, and the *Saipan* was laid up in October 1957.

In December 1954 Admiral Daniel V. Gallery, then chief of Naval Air Reserve Training at Glenview, Illinois, proposed a new training-carrier conversion based on a freighter hull for service on the Great Lakes. The following January BuShips sketched a 650 (oa) × 75 × 20-ft flush-decker, displacing 9,900 tons light, 13,600 tons fully loaded, and capable of 20 knots on 14,000 SHP. She would have a cargo-ship hull; her main deck would be the flight deck. Aircraft facilities included six Mk 7 arresting-gear pendants, a C 11-2 catapult forward, and an elevator (70 × 44 feet) forward. The entire flight deck was canted at 5° to simulate that of a fleet carrier. An estimated cost of $27 million, based on that of the CVE 105 class, was well above Admiral Gallery's expectations, and the proposal died. The cost indicates what the limit was for effective aircraft operation.

The ad hoc committees of 1955 produced a variety of exotic carrier designs, primarily based on the great hopes then entertained for VSTOL aircraft. For example, a progress report of 28 March 1955 on "studies originated as a result of Norfolk Meeting of Special Committee for Advanced Ship Design" lists a "self-escorting CVN" of *Forrestal* size and speed. She would carry twelve attack aircraft, twenty-four VTOL planes, sixteen helicopters, Terrier batteries for each quadrant, and two Talos launchers. It was also suggested that the *Saipan* be converted to a missile ship with escort capabilities, probably the CVHG of the 1955 ad hoc report, with a reduction of the flight deck to mount Terriers fore and aft and six helicopter spots remaining on deck.

In fact, navy interest in VSTOL was of long standing, and VTOL fighters (Pogos) were carried in navy development plans of the early fifties as "convoy fighters," a concept probably inspired by the British CAM-ship concept of World War II. For example, the new *Mariner*-class merchant ships of the early fifties were designed to accommodate a pad for a helicopter or a VTOL fighter. The precise origins of the navy program are not clear, but both air force and navy issued study contracts in 1947, and the navy program for operation from helipads began the following year.

*At this time, too, there was an SCB 144 project to reconstruct *Essex*-class CVSs with angled decks, enclosed bows, relocated pri-fly, HEAF stowage, and improved arresting gear. As of 1955, three carriers were planned for FY 57: the *Essex*, *Princeton*, and *Tarawa*. SCB 144 was, however, a victim of the general shortage of shipbuilding and conversion funds.

There was no pure jet of sufficient thrust to lift itself, so the VTOL was designed around a big turboprop. Both Lockheed and Convair designs were chosen for evaluation in March 1951. Both were intended as interceptors, armed with two or four 20-mm cannon or forty-eight FFAR rockets. Not much was written about their mission, but in May 1955 the Naval Air Development Center (Johnsville, Pennsylvania) did propose the use of Pogos aboard a converted light-cruiser hull as an inexpensive nuclear strike system. The poor weight-carrying capability of the VTOL would be balanced by the effectiveness of a single hit. Somewhat similar arguments can be made for more modern VTOLS.

The two tail-sitting turboprops flew in the summer of 1954, by which time they were probably already relegated to the ranks of experimental aircraft. By this time the navy was also interested in jet tail-sitters, one of which, made by Ryan, led to a cockpit mockup about 1951 and then to an X-13 prototype which flew in December 1955. In turn, the success of the X-13 project contributed heavily to interest in specialized VTOL carriers, such as the self-escorting CVN.

The other radical project of the postwar period was a seaplane fighter, the Seadart. It began with a 1945 proposal by the Edo Corporation, an experienced builder of floats for floatplanes. New float (and hull) technology promised radical improvements in fineness ratio and hence in the aerodynamic behavior of sea-based aircraft. This progress led both to fighter proposals and to the P6M Seamaster Bomber. In the case of the fighter, Convair proposed a rather efficient aerodynamic form based on a hull blended into the wings. In 1946, moreover, NACA (the predecessor of NASA) devised a water-ski undercarriage that could act as a shock absorber yet in flight could lie flat against a streamlined fuselage. In 1948 Convair proposed a hydro-ski/blended body fighter, which became the delta-wing Seadart (F2Y); it would match the performance of existing land-based fighters, yet operate out of coastal waters without any need for long concrete runways.

Although the Seadart proved too advanced to achieve operational status, it was much more than a test of new technology. After letting a contract for two prototypes in January 1951, the navy ordered twelve production articles on 28 August 1952. Later it ordered five more. Experience with the prototypes, however, suggested that the airplane was nowhere near production status, and ten were cancelled in December 1953. Even then serious interest remained, and the program limped on until 1956. Indeed, the plane was given a new designation (F-7A) under the 1962 DOD redesignation of naval aircraft, which suggests continuing interest. As with the Pogos, the Seadart was a pure interceptor, with four 20-mm cannon or forty-four 2.75-in rockets (FFAR); since its wings rode the water, it could not carry underwing stores of any type, and it had no enclosed weapons bay.

BuAer developed a Seadart support ship, a converted escort carrier with a powerful flight-deck catapult. The forward elevator was eliminated, and the deck abaft the after elevator cut away so that a Seadart could land on a flexible mat aft, then taxi up the ramp to the elevator for recovery. In sheltered waters, the carrier could use cranes to recover Seadarts, taxiing onto rafts nearby. Given calm enough waters, the CVE with her new catapult and her stern ramp would provide the kind of fighter cover for a landing that otherwise only a fleet carrier could furnish. The use of the carrier would also limit exposure of the fighters to corrosive salt water. In an alternative basing study, the marines considered operating Seadarts or similar fighters from an unimproved beach, using an LSD that had already unloaded her cargo to hose them down in her well deck. Finally, there was hope around 1953 that the Seadart would be able to operate from a flexible flight deck.

In December 1952 DCNO (Air) took the idea seriously enough to recommend a CVE 55–class conversion as his sixth priority for the FY 55 program; his higher priorities were *Midway* modernization (SCB 110), one CVE (ASW), two CVE 55 helicopter conversions, an aviation stores ship (AVS, SCB 115), and a new-construction light seaplane tender (AVP).

What is interesting in retrospect is the similarity in operational concept between the Seadart and the current Harrier: each is independent of prepared airfields ashore. Such autonomy was particularly attractive to the marines as conventional aircraft performance pushed up the length (and therefore the cost in time and in material) of air fields ashore. At the same time the marines faced the loss of carrier air support with the demise of the escort carriers, which had often served as close-air-support ships in Korea; it was by no means clear that ASW support carriers (CVS) would be available for such duty in wartime, when the submarine threat would be most intense.

Finally, there were several attempts to find new uses for the *Essex*-class hulls as they left the active fleet. Three did become helicopter carriers (see chapter 17). Other proposals included a specialized satellite launching ship to boost payloads into polar orbits inaccessible from U.S. territory, a fast replenishment ship or aviation stores ship, and a 30-knot amphibious ship, a more complete conversion than the LPH. It was also proposed in the sixties that a CVS be loaded with forty C-2 logistics aircraft as marine troop transports for very rapid intervention capability. In one version, the marines would parachute in to seize particularly critical objectives. Alternatively, they might be landed while a key airport remained in friendly hands.

During World War II the rapid expansion of the carrier force demanded a similar expansion of the pilot corps, and carriers were required for deck training. Many escort carriers served in this vital role, but for training on the Great Lakes two former pleasure steamers were converted. The only paddle-wheel carriers ever built, they were also the first U.S. carriers with steel flight decks. The design was extremely austere, the conversions quick. Here the USS *Wolverine* has just been completed in Buffalo early in August 1942; at left the side-wheeler *Greater Buffalo* is beginning her conversion to the similar *Sable*. The *Wolverine* could accommodate 12,000-lb aircraft on her 550- x 85-ft flight deck. She had arresting gear but no catapult and no hangar; she carried 6,000 gallons of avgas. Maximum speed was reported as 18 knots.

The *Sable* steams through the Great Lakes near the end of her career, in June 1945. She had only two funnels; her near sister had four. However, she was the larger of the two ships, with a 587.5- x 85-ft flight deck. She probably did not carry gasoline. Her only electronic equipment appears to have been a pair of aircraft homing beacons, a YE and the mattress-like YG.

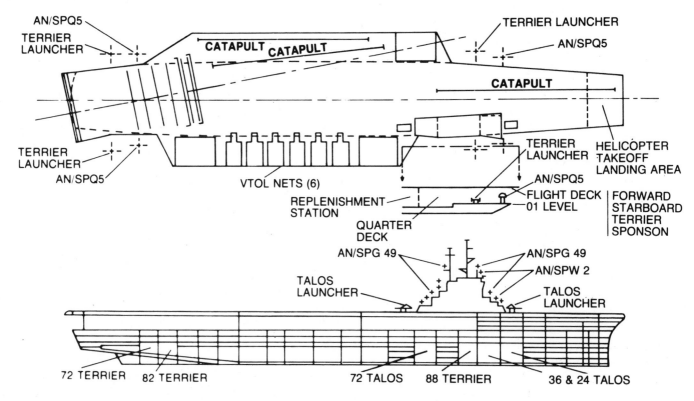

This "self-protecting CVAN" was sketched in 1955 as part of a BuShips attempt to forecast warship possibilities. It suggests the promise of VTOL technology (presumably based on the Bell X-13, which was partly funded by the navy, and which could have landed in the "VTOL nets" abaft the island) and of the new surface-to-air missiles. The power plant would have duplicated that of the new *Enterprise*. Its dimensions were 990 feet (wl), 1,030 feet (oa), by 132 feet (wl) by 36 feet, for a light-ship displacement of 64,875 tons (81,150 fully loaded). Self-defense would have been achieved with two Talos launchers (fore and aft of the island) and four Terriers (in quadrants). With three C 7 catapults, the CVAN would have operated conventional aircraft as well as VTOLs; her air group was listed as eight heavy bombers (A3D size), twenty-four VTOL interceptors, four night fighters (F3H-1N), and sixteen ASW helicopters (HRZS). Note that the carrier had no sonar and no ASW missile battery, although she would operate without escorting ships. Costs were estimated as $375 million for the lead ship and $340 million for follow ships. In fact the much simpler *Enterprise* cost about $451 million, without defensive missiles.

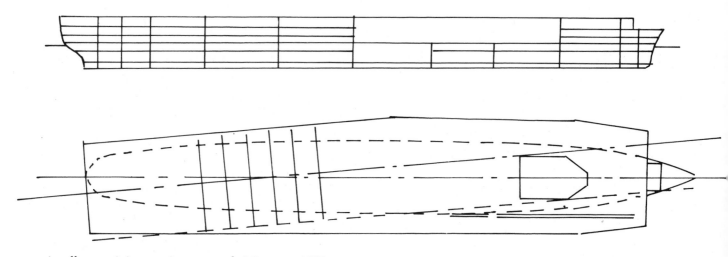

A gallery training carrier proposal, 3 January 1955.

B

Catapults

Although catapults were either planned for or installed aboard every U.S. carrier, they did not achieve any great operational importance before World War II, partly because conventional rolling takeoffs were both simpler and faster. However, they were essential to the success of the escort carriers (CVEs), which would have been limited to observation aircraft (OS2Us) and light fighters (F4Fs) without them. For example, with an empty flight deck, a CVE steaming at 18 knots could barely launch a Grumman TBF torpedo bomber that had only two-thirds gasoline and no torpedo. With a catapult, the same airplane could be launched fully armed and fueled, and the entire CVE air group could be spotted on deck for takeoff. The catapult takeoff interval was estimated at thirty seconds, compared with twenty for a conventional rolling takeoff.

Aboard the large fleet carriers, rolling takeoffs presented no problem initially. However, as aircraft loads increased in wartime, the length of deck required for takeoff increased. Moreover, with air groups increasing in size, less of the deck was actually available when a deck-load strike was spotted for takeoff.

Typically, the entire strike would be spotted on deck, leaving just enough room forward for catapult takeoffs. As soon as enough aircraft had been launched, the ship would revert to rolling takeoffs. Since they did not cause aircraft to swerve as did conventional rolling takeoffs, catapults could be used without lights at night. Moreover, catapults permitted takeoffs in a cross-wind, so that carriers did not have to turn into the wind to launch. It was claimed that at Samar catapults saved the escort carriers, which otherwise would have had to turn towards the Japanese fleet to launch their aircraft. In the Gilberts (*Tarawa*) operation, it was estimated that catapults aboard fleet carriers saved two days of fuel because search planes had been catapulted during the run from Hawaii. Finally, it was argued that catapults

were an important element of operational survivability, since a carrier with a damaged flight deck might still be able to launch with them; otherwise she would probably have to back down to launch her aircraft over her stern.

By the end of World War II, some fleet carriers were making 40 percent of their launches by catapult. An *Essex* , for example, could spot forty-seven Avenger torpedo bombers, allowing a 450-ft takeoff run (with a wind-over-deck of 30 knots). A loss of 5 knots in wind-over-deck would so increase the takeoff run that fifteen of those aircraft would have to be struck below to gain 150 feet of clear deck. However, the same carrier could catapult Avengers at only 3 knots. Aboard CVEs catapults made possible the launch of high-performance fighter aircraft to resupply the fast carriers and also to supply army forces ashore. In North Africa, for example, the quick appearance of large numbers of P-40 fighters after paratroopers had secured the airfield was an important factor in the success of the invasion. In the Gilberts there were no docks left undamaged, but P-39s could still be delivered by catapult. By the end of World War II, all Mustang and Thunderbolt fighters destined for the Pacific were being fitted for catapulting on the assembly line. Even two-engine fighters, Lightnings and Black Widows (P-61s), were modified. Work on adapting land-based fighters to catapult operation continued for several years postwar; Shooting Stars and Thunderjets were the last types so fitted.

Catapults have been increasingly important since 1945, because they have substituted for long concrete runways and thus permitted carriers to operate the highest-performance aircraft, both jet fighters and large attack bombers. As a result, catapults were required to launch most postwar aircraft and their characteristics because the primary limitation on new naval aircraft during the fifties. Thus the improvement due to the development of the steam catapult was crucial to the post-Korea success of U.S. carrier aviation.

U.S. interest in shipboard catapults predated interest in carriers as such, and the development of the former was very rapid after World War I. Both compressed-air (A series) and powder (P series) catapults were developed, primarily for battleships and cruisers. In addition, Carl Norden (of bombsight and gyro gunsight fame) developed a flywheel catapult for the *Lexington* and the *Saratoga*. One of the great defects of using it was a lengthy interval between launches, presumably required to spin up the flywheel. Most carrier catapults were either hydraulic (H series) or slotted-cylinder (C series)—the latter is still in service today.

Hydraulic catapults employed a ram that drove a shuttle through a cable and sheave arrangement, which in turn multiplied the speed and stroke of the ram mechanically. Growth was limited by the weight and inertia of the mechanism, and by the strength of the wires through which force was transmitted. Although a very powerful hydraulic catapult, the H 9, was designed for the carrier *United States*, it was at the limit of technical feasibility and therefore not pursued. Instead, attention was focussed on the alternative direct-acting slotted cylinder. The latter was more attractive mechanically, since the piston in the cylinder drove the catapulted aircraft directly. Activating the piston was not simple, though; the earliest designs called for powder (explosive) drive, and indeed several U.S. carrier designs included special magazine space for catapult charges. But the development of the powder catapult did not prove successful. Fortunately, the British designed a steam-powered slotted cylinder, solving the major problem of sealing the catapult cylinder against excessive steam escape. The slotted cylinder became the standard for U.S. carriers. The sole major exception was the design of an internal-combustion catapult for the *Enterprise*, presumably to avoid steam being vented from her propulsion plant. As completed, however, she was fitted with a conventional steam catapult and development of the internal-combustion unit was abandoned.

Recent interest in gas-turbine light carriers has raised the question of a successor to the steam catapult. In the ski-jump carrier high-performance aircraft can presumably take off under their own power, but it is still necessary to launch slower ones such as the Grumman E-2. One proposal (recently dropped) was to revive the flywheel type of the twenties.

CATAPULT LIST

Catapults were originally designated in a single Mark series. The A-type, P-type, etc., designations were introduced in December 1923.

Type A

A Mk I. Design began in March 1919 and manufacture that July, with pier tests in May 1920. The catapult car was attached to the step of the float rather than to the landing gear or fuselage, as it was previously. The first installations were aboard the battleships *Maryland*, *Nevada*, and *Oklahoma*. The *Maryland* fired the first aircraft in 1922. Of twenty more units completed, fourteen went aboard *Omaha*-class cruisers. The other six were installed aboard the battleships *California*, *Mississippi*, *Idaho*, *Tennessee*, *Pennsylvania*, and *Arizona*. Later two were installed aboard the *New Mexico* and *Colorado*. A Mk I was superseded by a Mk III, the last pair being removed from the cruiser *Raleigh* late in 1929. Capacity was 3,500 pounds at 50 mph in 60 feet.

A Mk II. This was first delivered in January 1923, and had a capacity of 6,000 pounds at 60 mph. It was superseded by Mk III, with a similar capacity.

A Mk III. This was a modified A Mk IB (which reverted to attachment to landing gear). It passed its pier test in the summer of 1927, with the first installation aboard the light cruiser *Memphis*. Most A Mk IIIs were produced by modifying Mk Is. Initial installations were aboard ten light cruisers, three battleships, and three shore stations.

A Mk IV. A very successful catapult, this was designed originally for installation aboard the surviving armored cruisers and had hydro-electric training. One version was intended for destroyer installation. The first two went aboard the light cruiser *Richmond* in May 1931, and the whole *Omaha* class was to have been fitted by November 1932. Capacity was 6,300 pounds at 61 mph in 60 feet. This about reached the limit of the turntable air catapults, and attention soon turned to powder types.

A Mk V. This flush-deck-carrier catapult was tested in 1935 for bow installation. About six years earlier a Mk IV, mounted on the catapult pier, had a simulated deck built around it to show that land planes could be launched.

Note: No designation was applied to the track-type catapult originally installed in the *Langley*, although in December 1923 BuAer proposed an A Mk III, the A Mk IV being a battleship-superstructure type then under consideration. The A Mk III was similar to those formerly aboard the armored cruisers. Capacity was 6,000 lbs at 55 mph in 95 feet.

Type P

P Mk I. The first model of this turret-top catapult was completed in October 1922. It was superseded by the Mk III production model.

P Mk II. This was an abortive battleship-super-structure catapult for the *New Mexico* class, with an athwartships track.

P Mk III. Tests for this catapult were completed early in 1924, and the first was installed aboard the battleship *Mississippi* that fall. It was superseded by the Mk IV, which had a larger capacity. There were also two Mk IIs, one for the *West Virginia*, one for the *Idaho*. Typical capacity was 6,350 pounds at 64 mph.

P Mk IV. This was the ultimate U.S. turret-top catapult, in service through 1941. All first-line battleships were fitted, and first deliveries were made late in 1925. Its performance matched that of Mk III.

P Mk V. This powder turntable catapult was to replace battleship air catapults and to be fitted in cruisers. However, the only ship fitted with it was the battleship *Colorado*.

P Mk VI. Originally the Mk V Mod 1, lighter than the Mark V, this catapult was installed aboard U.S. battleships and cruisers, the latter beginning with the *Salt Lake City* class. Tests began early in 1929. Its typical performance was 6,500 pounds at 65 mph.

P Mk VII. This athwartships double-ended powder catapult, similar to the P Mk IV in performance, was intended for installation aboard the *Maryland* and other battleships. One was tested at Washington Navy Yard in the fall of 1930, but installation was cancelled.

P Mk VIII. This athwartships powder catapult, designed for the carrier *Ranger* in 1930, was abandoned to cut costs during construction. Mk IX was another land-plane catapult, but it never went beyond the early design stage. A fixed-track type for hangar decks, it would have used Mk VII material.

Type F

F Mk I. This was a test catapult at Dahlgren.

F Mk II. This Norden catapult, used aboard the *Lexington* and the *Saratoga*, had a 6-ton flywheel, which revolved at high speed and then was friction clutched. One problem with this catapult was burned-out clutches. An F Mk II was installed aboard the *Langley*, but was not usable. Capacity was 10,000 pounds at 35 mph.

Type H

H Mk I. This was the prototype for carrier installations in 1935, with a capacity of 5,500 pounds at 45 mph in 34 feet.

H Mk II. This was the *Yorktown*- and *Wasp*-class deck catapult, with a capacity of 5,500 pounds at 65 mph in 55 feet (later 7,000 pounds at 70 mph). H 2-1 was designed for escort carriers and later installed in the *Enterprise* and the *Saratoga* when they were refitted in wartime. Capacity was 11,000 pounds at 70 mph in 73 feet. The first tests of Mark II aboard the *Enterprise* were delayed by an explosion in December 1938. This catapult was suitable for flight- or hangar-deck operation.

H Mk III. Experimental seaplane-launching catapult, 1937–40. Capacity was 60,000 pounds at 120 mph. It was intended for launching Mariner (PBM-2) seaplanes from the catapult lighter AVC-1. It led to the development of the H 6.

H Mk IV. This was the *Essex*-class catapult. Work began on 3 November 1939 with a request for design studies of a new flight-deck catapult to launch aircraft up to 16,000 pounds at 90 mph, accelerating them at up to 2.8 G over a 95-ft run, with a one-minute recharge interval. A range of weights of 3,500 to 16,000 pounds was envisaged, and in April 1940 the new catapult was required to launch seaplanes as well. The latter requirement led to a modified version, the H 5. In August 1940, a requirement for a hangar-deck catapult with a 73.5-ft run was added; it became the H 4A, the flight-deck type the H 4B. A modified H 4A for CVE use was designated the H 4C; it differed from H 4A in having one rather than two shuttles, and it was generally mounted on the port side of the carrier. The H 4-1 was a modified, lengthened type for large carriers of the *Midway* class. The first deadweight launch by an H 4 made in November 1942, the first airplane launch in January 1943; the first installation was aboard the carrier *Lexington* at Boston, tests being completed 13 March 1943. The first H 4A was tested at sea aboard the *Yorktown* on 1 May 1943. The characteristics of each catapult are as follows: H 4A, 16,000 pounds at 85 mph in 72 feet 6 inches, acceleration 3.13 G, recharge in 60 seconds with two pumps; H 4B, 18,000 pounds at 90 mph in 96 feet 8 inches (2.8 G), recharge in 42.8 seconds with four pumps; H 4-1, 28,000 pounds at 90 mph in 150 feet (1.8 G), recharge in 60 seconds with four pumps. Hangar-deck catapults were ordered removed from *Essex*-class carriers in May 1943, and all units were converted to conventional H 4s.

H 5. This catapult was for launching marine seaplane scout bombers from seaplane tenders upon arrival at a base. It was derived from the H Mk IV, and installations were approved for the *Currituck* and *Tangier*; the first was installed aboard the *Currituck* at Philadelphia, but tests were unsuccessful and there was insufficient time for correction. All H 5s removed from seaplane tenders were converted to H 4s. Performance was 16,000 pounds (SB2C-2 seaplane) at 90 mph in 96 feet 8 inches (2.8 G), with recharge (two pumps) in 86 seconds.

H 6. This seaplane catapult was developed from XH Mk III. Capacity was 60,000 pounds at 120 mph.

H 7. This catapult for very large seaplanes was to have been housed in a special self-propelled barge. It was cancelled in view of changes in the patrol-plane program in 1942. Capacity would have been 120,000 pounds at 130 mph.

H 8. This postwar high-capacity hydraulic catapult, replacing the wartime H 4B aboard modernized carriers, had a capacity of 15,000 pounds at 120 mph, or 62,500 pounds at 70 mph (61 knots). It represented the practical upper limit of hydro-pneumatic catapult design.

H 9. This hydraulic catapult was designed for the abortive super-carrier *United States*; it was to launch 100,000-lb aircraft at 90 mph (78 knots) or 45,000 pounds at 120 mph (105 knots). Its stroke was 210 feet, compared with 190 feet in the *Midway* (260 feet including holdback).

Type C

C Mk 1. The experimental slotted-cylinder type for carriers was begun in 1945. Installation was completed at the end of January 1951, and that April it accelerated 30,000 pounds at 60 kts (69 mph) with twenty-two 100-lb charges. Later parts of it were used to test C 10 components.

C Mk 7. This high-capacity slotted-cylinder catapult, originally intended for powder operation, was redesigned as a steam catapult. Its capacity was 40,000 pounds at 171 mph (148.5 knots) or 70,000 pounds at 133 mph (116 knots). The original version used 500 psi steam, owing to the limits of the *Forrestal* plant, but a 1,200-psi version was later developed. Stroke was 250 to 275 feet.

C 8. This was a target catapult with a capacity of 350 pounds at 110 mph (96 knots). Two were built.

C 9. This was a target catapult with a capacity of 2,000 pounds at 192 mph (167 knots). Four were built, two for the air force.

C Mk 10. This powder (later gasoline/LOX) catapult was intended as a lower-power unit for *Forrestals* and as a primary unit in SCB 27C conversions. Capacity was 40,000 pounds at 144 mph or 125 knots. Mod 3 was steam-powered (indirect) and was proposed in 1953 for CVE use.

C 11. This was the first U.S. steam catapult, based on the British BXS-1 but using higher steam conditions. The BXS-1 was 203 feet long, using a pair of 18-in power cylinders at 3/5 psi and 450°. Test shots aboard HMS *Perseus* began at Philadelphia Navy Yard on 9 December 1953, although a decision in favor of steam catapults had been made in April 1952, after British tests. The destroyer *Greene* supplied high-pressure steam. The C 11 launched a 23,670-lb deadweight at 138 knots, and 55,300 pounds at 109.5 knots, all well beyond U.S. requirements. The C 11 was rated at 39,000 pounds at 156 mph (136 knots) and 70,000 pounds at 124 mph (107.5 knots). The first was installed on the *Hancock* in May 1954.

C 13. This heavy-duty catapult, successor to the C 7, is aboard newer attack carriers, operating at 1,000 rather than 550 psi. It exists in both 250-ft and 310-ft (Mod 1) versions. Capacity of the 250-ft version is 78,000 pounds at 160 mph, once per minute.

C 14. This internal-combustion catapult for the *Enterprise* was never built. Capacity was to have been 50,000 pounds at 200 mph (175 knots) or 100,000 pounds at 144 mph (125 knots), or 70 million ft-lbs, compared with 54 million ft-lbs for C 13 and 42 million ft-lbs for C 7.

C 15. This abortive catapult had a capacity of 60,000 pounds at 230 mph (200 knots) and a 260-ft stroke. As proposed in 1957, the first was to have been dockside in January 1963, but the program never got that far.

Type J (Jet Propelled)

J Mk 1. This merchant-ship catapult was to have been similar to British developments of 1942–43; it was diverted to development of water buffers. Performance was 7,500 pounds at 83 mph in 85 feet.

J Mk 2. This LST catapult was successfully tested in 1944. Capacity was 1,100 pounds at 45 mph to launch observation planes.

Type M (Missile Launching)

M 1. This was the 1944 CVE catapult for launching Loon missiles (V-1 copies). Capacity was 5,000 pounds at 250 mph in 1944.

M 2. This was a 1945 shipboard turntable launcher. Capacity was 1,650 pounds at 150 mph in 50 feet in 1945.

C

Arresting Gear

Arresting gear sets as much of a limit on aircraft performance as flight-deck size and catapult capacity do. In the case of axial-deck carriers, U.S. flight-deck practice also required a barrier to protect the parking area forward from aircraft missing the arresting gear wires. Originally this was a simple wire that could tip over an airplane or at least foul its propeller. However, wire could not be used with jets, since there was the danger of it riding up over the airplane's nose and decapitating its pilot. Instead, a nylon barrier was adopted from the Royal Navy for jets.

As for the arresting gear proper, early U.S. practice followed the British in fitting both longitudinal and transverse wires. The former were intended to keep an airplane from tipping over as it braked (the British had suffered several casualties late in World War I as aircraft were blown overboard by gusts of wind). This danger receded as aircraft became heavier, and the U.S. Navy abandoned longitudinal wires in 1929. The Royal Navy abandoned all arresting gear for a time, a practice unacceptable to the U.S. Navy, since something had to stop an airplane from plowing into the deck park forward of the landing zone.

The primary issue was how to absorb the energy of landing within a reasonable space. Early tests on a turntable at Hampton Road led to the use of heavy weights at either end of the wire "pendant" stretched across the deck for the arresting hook to engage. In 1924 Carl Norden and T. H. Barth designed the Mark I and Mark 2 brakes; these generally operated by tightening a brake band against the surface of a drum. The Mark 2 was installed in the *Lexington* and the *Saratoga*. The first truly hydraulic type was the Mark 3, the development of which was begun by the Experimental Division of the Naval Air Station at Hampton Roads in 1928. The Mark 3 had a designed capacity of 8,000 pounds at 60 mph. It replaced the Mark 2 in the *Lexington*s and was installed in the *Ranger*.

The Mark 4, with an even higher capacity (10,000 pounds at 70 mph), was installed in the *Yorktown*s. Mod 2 engines (8,500 pounds at 60 mph) allowed for a longer runout for the after section of the landing area, while Mod 1, with a shorter runout, was mounted closer to the barrier. The latter, originally a broach type developed in connection with Mark 3, was soon replaced by a barrier directly connected to Mark 4 Mod 2 arresting-gear engines, for more efficient energy absorption. Aircraft weight and performance continued to rise, and Mod 3A (on the *Hornet*) was rated at 16,000 pounds and 85 mph. The capacity of existing Mod 2s as increased by the substitution of heavier hydraulic cylinders and plungers, with sheaves being regrooved for larger-diameter cables. The *Enterprise* was modified during May 1941, but the *Yorktown* could not be refitted owing to damaged cylinders and plungers shipped to Pearl Harbor for that purpose.

Later Mods of Mark 4 were the standard for World War II carriers, with Mods 5 and 6 rated at 19,800 pounds at 64 mph (55 knots). By the end of the war, seven *Essex*-class carriers (beginning with the *Bennington*) had the improved Mark 5 (30,000 pounds at 90 mph, or 78 knots). Mark 5 was fitted postwar to the remaining *Essex*s, to the two *Saipan*s, and to carriers refitted for ASW (CVs 8–105). However, *Independence*-class light carriers so refitted received an eighth Mark 4 arresting gear engine. This was only marginally sufficient for jet operation, and the *Forrestal*s and later carriers were fitted with an improved Mark 7 system (50,000 pounds at 121 mph, 105 knots, or 60,000 pounds at this speed in an emergency). Mark 6 was the abortive (and much more powerful) unit designed for the super-carrier *United States*, which was to have operated 100,000-lb aircraft (100,000 pounds at 104 mph, 90 knots or 70,000 pounds at 120 mph, 105 knots).

The new generation of very high-performance jet aircraft envisaged in the mid-fifties would need much more. One possibility was to use the mobile arresting gear (MOREST) engine then being developed for the marines, with double-sheaving to add its capacity to that of the existing Mark 7. Alternatively, new types of arresting gear could be developed. A Mark 8, with a capacity of 50 million foot-pounds (compared with 8 million for Mark 5) was abandoned in 1958, as was the smaller Mark 9. Instead, BuAer concentrated on a new Mark 10, for 28,000- to 60,000-lb aircraft at up to 230 mph (200 knots, or 62 million foot-pounds). However, as in the case of the proposed C 14 catapult, this increased capacity was not needed, and the Mark 7 remains the standard U.S. arresting gear in 1982.

D

Magazine Loads

Magazine capacity is generally listed in the accompanying carrier data tables in terms of total tonnage, but this figure can be deceptive, since the weight of weapons in a carrier magazine depends to a great degree on the mix of weapons in a given magazine volume or even in a given magazine stowage area. For example, a given volume of streamlined (low-drag) bombs weighs much less than a similar volume of World War II–type bombs of similar unit weight, since the latter are much stubbier. Similarly, missiles generally have lower densities than do unguided bombs, and the shift toward missiles has reduced munitions weights aboard modern carriers.

The accompanying tables indicate some of the important shifts over the past six decades. First, there was the abandonment of the very light bomb (30 pounds) and the attempt to reduce to a minimum the number of different bomb types in service, as reflected in table D-1. Before World War II all navy fighters were equipped to drop 100-lb bombs, and dive-bombers were designed to drop either the 500- or the 1000-lb weapon (the latter was carried, for a time, only by special heavy bombers and by horizontal [torpedo] bombers). The number of weapons in each category was determined by a formula analogous to that used to estimate the appropriate number

of shells per gun. However, the figure of two torpedoes per torpedo bomber appears to have been more arbitrary.

With the approach of war, new types of munitions were introduced: first semi-armor-piercing (SAP) and armor-piercing (AP) bombs, then aircraft depth bombs (DB) for antisubmarine patrol from carriers, and then a variety of rockets, from the solid 3.5-in ASW type up to the 11.75-in "Tiny Tim," the warhead of which was a 500-lb bomb. Rocket accuracy often exceeded that of conventional bombing or even dive-bombing, and in 1945 Tiny Tims were being added at the expense of 500-lb bombs, as in the *Midway* magazine load-out.

An important magazine load factor *not* evident in these tables is aircraft gun ammunition, which could represent a considerable weight and volume, particularly after the shift from 0.50-cal to 20-mm amunition. As aircraft speeds increased after the war, guns gradually gave way, first to unguided aircraft rockets (the 2.75-in "Mighty Mouse" folding-fin aircraft rocket or FFAR, and to a much lesser extent, the 5-in FFAR or Zuni) and then to missiles (the Sidewinder and Sparrow in 1956, then the Phoenix). The latter is not represented on the accompanying tables, but its predecessor, the Eagle, is.

There was also a great postwar increase in the variety of weapons, as evidenced particularly in table D-6. The ships shown did not carry exotic standoff missiles, but they did carry a great variety of specialized bomb dispensers, such as the Rockeye. The Corvus, shown in one case, was a proposed standoff missile that was cancelled in 1959. The Walleye was in service by 1968, but it is not shown in the partial list of *Enterprise* ordnance. One standoff weapon that is shown is Shrike, the antiradar missile. The relatively small number of Shrikes carried is quite striking, given reports of the limited lethality of the missile.

Table D-1. Prewar Fleet Carriers

	Langley 1920	Lexington 1936	Ranger 1934	Ranger 1941	CV 9* Sep 1939	CV 9* Jan 1940
30 lb	500	—	30	—	—	—
100 lb	200**	804	749	600	288	522
500 lb	—	391	174	515	246	450
1,000 lb	—	240	130	177	108	148
325 lb DB	—	—	—	200	—	—
Torpedoes	24	36	—	—	36	36

*100 percent mobilization reserve.
**165-lb and 220-lb type.

Table D-2. Wartime Fleet Carriers

	Essex 1942	Enterprise Oct 1943	Bennington 1944	Bunker Hill 1945
100-lb GP	504	504	508	300
250	—	—	—	50
500 GP	296	288	292	400
SAP	—	288	292	60
1,000 GP	146	378	147	75
SAP	129	378	128	—
AP	110	378	110	—
1,600 AP	19	18	18	—
2,000 GP	19	18	18	15
325 DB	296	288	292	48
100 INC	296	288	292	240
100 F	—	—	—	—
220 F	—	—	—	300
Torpedoes	36	36	50	—
3.5 AR	—	—	366	300
5.0 HVAR	—	—	4,006	1,700
11.72 AR	—	—	—	108

Table D-4. Light Carriers

	CVL 1942	Cowpens 1947	Saipan Design 1943	Wright 1953*
100-lb GP	162	240	228	707
250	—	—	—	340
500 GP	72	72	144	280
SAP	—	—	—	—
1,000-lb GP	36	18	60	34
SAP	36	27	60	—
AP	36	18	48	—
1,600-lb AP	—	9	12	—
2,000-lb GP	—	9	12	—
325-lb DB	36	72	144	45
100-lb INC	180	72	144	—
100-lb F	—	—	—	—
220-lb F	—	—	—	94
Torpedoes	24	36	36	8 (ASW)
3.5 AR	—	—	—	250
5 HVAR	—	1,500	—	1,400
11.75 AR	—	—	—	—

*As ASW carrier, with an air group of 18 AF-2 aircraft.

Table D-3. Large Carriers

	Midway Design Mar 1942	Midway 1945	United States 1949
100 GP	552	828	832
250	—	—	1,296
500 GP	480	470	1,296
SAP	—	—	216
1,000 GP	216	324	360
SAP	204	306	144
AP	—	—	64
1,600 AP	120	180	—
2,000 GP	—	—	—
325 DB	480	720	—
100 INC	480	720	672
F	—	—	608
220 F	—	—	864
Torpedoes	168	96	—
3.5 AR	—	486	—
5.0 HVAR	—	5,324	3,670
11.75 AR	—	250	250
2.75 FFAR	—	—	5,520

Under intensive operating conditions, carriers would not conduct strikes for more than a few days at a time, so that any stock of one munition might not exceed a three days' expenditure. At the end of World War II, the standard cycle was five days of operation and then one day of retirement for replenishment; the cycle was dictated by the requirement to service the Okinawa battle with sufficient firepower, not by carrier-magazine capacity. Some accounts suggest that the critical factor was crew fatigue. In Korean waters, the operating cycle was rather shorter, keyed to the need to replenish aviation fuel rather than munitions. For example, unconverted Essex-class carriers generally spent two days operating and one off, and the SCB 27 conversions could increase operating time to three or four days. A similar tempo was main-tained off Vietnam. However, recent published official accounts of carrier design suggest that magazine capacities are equivalent to eight to eleven days of steady operation on the basis of 1.55 sorties per airplane per day at a range of about 300 nautical miles.

Nuclear weapons have been an important issue in carrier-magazine design since 1949. Originally only non-nuclear components were carried, and the bombs had to be assembled on board, a process that might, in the early 1950s, require twenty-four hours. Thus the nuclear provisions of CVB improvement project no. 1 had to include special nuclear workshops. The weight and volume of nuclear weapons has never been very great. For example, at one time the Forrestals were credited officially with 1,650 tons of conventional ordnance and 150 of special (nuclear) weapons. Even the United States, designed specifically for nuclear attack, would have carried only 100 weapons (100 sorties), and at about 7,600 pounds per bomb that would have been only 339 tons, compared with a total magazine capacity of about 2,000.

Only very recently has magazine volume per se had much of a direct effect on carrier design. The Nimitz was designed specifically with an increased capacity for greater effectiveness in conventional warfare. Statements at the congressional hearings concerning the proposed light carrier (CVV) suggest that it would have required some weapon stowage above the waterline, and that efficient defense against cruise missiles striking nearly horizontally would have required the evacuation of some magazine spaces.

Finally, some magazine capacity may have to be devoted to the requirements of the ships accompany-

Table D-5. Escort Carriers

	Sangamon Aug 1942	Sangamon Jul 1945	Commencement Bay Nov 1944	Block Island Jan 1953	Kula Gulf May 1954	SCB 43 (ASW) 1952	SCB 43 (Close Support) 1952
100 GP	150	240	180	360	360	—	—
250	—	—	—	24	24	—	725‡
500 GP	85	72	120	228	228	—	135‡
SAP	—	—	—	24	24	—	—
1,000 GP	40	18	30	48	48	—	90‡
SAP	40	27	45	12	24	—	—
AP	—	18	30	—	—	—	—
1,600 AP	24	9	15	—	—	—	—
2,000 GP	—	9	15	24	24	—	45‡
325 DB	110	72	120	193	216	400	—
100 INC	175	72	121	—	—	—	—
100 F	—	—	—	—	—	—	—
220 F	—	—	—	—	—	—	—
Torpedoes	46	36	9	25 (Mk 24)	22	100 (Mk 41)	—
3.5 AR	—	132	132	1,500	1,000	5,140†	5,140†
5.0 HVAR	—	1,452	1,188	1,000	1,000	2,000	2,000
11.75 AR	—	—	—	—	—	—	—
7.2-in Charge*	—	—	—	—	212	2,000	—
Depth Charges*	—	—	—	—	—	264	—

*For escorts.

†2.75 FFAR.

‡LD bombs.

Table D-6. Carrier Reconstruction

	SCB 27C Dec 1951	Hancock (27C) Feb 1955	Intrepid (27A) 1954	SCB 110 Sep 1953	SCB 144 Mar 1955
250 LD	1,000	700	750	1,239	300
500 LD	400	160	380*	413	300
1,000 LD	430	200	183†	372	150
2,000 LD	225	60	23‡	182	12
350 DB	—	48	100	—	450
100 INC	—	300	—	700	—
100 F	—	—	—	—	180
250 F	—	750	165	—	500
Sparrow	300	—	—	575	—
5.0 HVAR	850	1,000	1,000	1,350	2,000
2.75 FFAR	5,000	—	352§	14,000	5,600
Torpedoes (ASW)	8	8	18‖	8	32#
100 GP	—	750	200	—	600

*Old type: 350 GP, 30 SAP.

†Old type: 100 GP, 18 SAP, 65 AP.

‡Old type.

§3.5-in AR.

‖Of which 8 were ASW (MK 34).

#MK 34; or 96 MK 43 lightweight.

ing the carrier. The only example in these tables is the need for Hedgehog and depth-charge stowage in the postwar escort carriers to replenish surface ships of the hunter-killer group. However, some fleet carriers do have facilities for surface-to-air missile stowage. For example, plans of the *Oriskany* (1974) show a Terrier assembly area. Such stowage is essential, given the very limited magazine space aboard most surface escorts.

Although it is difficult to discern the logic of bomb allocations made after about 1942, the rationale of prewar load-outs is well established. It followed gun practice: the navy procured an amount of ammunition equal to the accuracy life of the gun tube, stowing half on board and half (the "mobilization supply") at a shore depot, at least in peacetime. For example, the first characteristics for the *Essex*-class listed a peacetime load-out and required sufficient magazine volume to accommodate the "mobilization supply," that is, a 100-percent increase.

The prewar problem was to establish both the effective life of each airplane aboard a carrier (including the 50-percent spare-aircraft allowance) and to allocate the alternative bomb loads among the missions each airplane was likely to fly. Aircraft lifetime gradually increased during the prewar period, as did the carrying capacity of each plane. In 1929, for example, the General Board set the average fighting lifetime of an airplane at 100 hours (fifty flights). Fighters would carry bombs perhaps a quarter of the time.

Given the number of missions, some estimate had to be made of the loads aircraft would carry. The board proposed to allow 80 percent of all bombing raids by fighters to 30-lb bombs, and 20 percent to 100-lb bombs. Both bombs were suited only to attacks on light structures and exposed personnel; the 50-lb and 1,000-lb weapons were the only ones considered capable of inflicting serious structural damage. Observation aircraft could dive only with the lighter bombs, and they were allocated 40 percent of the flights with 30-lb bombs, 30 percent with 100-lb bombs, and 30 percent with 500-lb bombs. The heavy torpedo bombers would divide their time between medium and heavy (1,000-lb) bombs.

Table D-6A. Reconstructed Carriers

	Intrepid* Feb 1966†	Hornet* Mar 1967	Shangri-La# Jul 1963	Hancock Feb 1967	Coral Sea†† May 1967
250 LD	1,015/39‡	—	720/260†	1,236	72/32‡
500 LD	133‡	—	60†	798	500/90‡
1,000 LD	18‡	—	—	123	35/12‡
2,000 LD	—	—	—	4	3/4‡
Napalm	—	—	—	—	350
Sparrow	—	—	—	330	—
Sidewinder	—	—	—	—	—
Bullpup	—	—	—	100	—
Shrike	—	—	—	36	—	—
2.75 FFAR	—	3,800	—	3,800	7,524
5.0 FFAR	676	600/50‖	—	600	420
CBU	10§	—	—	20**	—
Depth Bombs	—	100	—	—	10
Torpedoes (ASW)	—	120	—	—	—
FRAG	18	—	200	—	—

*ASW carriers.
†As limited attack carrier: bombs aboard. In other cases only allowance is listed.
‡High-drag.
§Cluster chaff bombs.
‖5-in HVAR.
#Also had 82 100-lb high-drag aboard, but not part of allowance.
**Aboard, but not part of allowance.
††Also had 48 100-lb high-drag aboard.

BuAer preferred to calculate in terms of missions, and wanted enough bombs for a major surface action and for the campaign immediately preceding and following it. Replacement aircraft would arrive with their own bombs, so that a carrier need only accommodate sufficient weapons for the life of her air group. The bureau also pointed out that, since existing arresting gear could not allow the landing of heavily loaded aircraft, all bombs would generally be jettisoned before landing, so that bombs would have to be provided for both effective and ineffective missions. As for wastage, BuAer followed the standard Army figure of 25 percent per month, which was why it provided 50 percent spare aircraft aboard each carrier.

Carriers would be limited to no more than two or three flights per bomber per day. This projection compares well to postwar accounts of six deck-load strikes per day (half of the air group each time) in intense air operations in 1944–45. Further, BuAer assumed that operations prior to the major surface action would require no more than two or three bombing flights per airplane, for a total of perhaps ten aircraft loads per bomber, and probably fewer for specialized types such as dive-bombers. Moreover, World War I experience indicated that, except for strafing, smaller aircraft probably carried out a smaller percentage of bombing runs than large ones, so that they would often fly without bombs. Nor would they have to jettison their light bombs before landing.

Some distribution of bomb loads among the ten flights per plane also had to be assumed. For example, in 1932 it was estimated that the torpedo bombers would fly three times with 500-lb bombs, five times with 1,000-lb bombs, and two times with torpedoes. Heavy dive-bombers, on the other hand, were expected to attack four times with 500-lb bombs and six times with 1,000-bombs. Expected attrition somewhat reduced total ship loads—8 percent per raid (based on 1918 experience) was often used as an estimated rate. The General Board considered BuAer's attrition rates far too low, suggesting instead 50 percent for torpedo attacks on surface ships, 50 percent for strafing attacks by fighters, 40 percent for dive-bomber attacks on surface ships, 40 percent for fighters in combat, and 33⅓ percent for spotting and scouting. Shore targets were not considered in these estimates, although a few years later they would be a major factor.

By the early 1930s the General Board was trying to rationalize bomb loads for different types of aircraft. For example, since dive-bombers had to pass through antiaircraft fire each time they attacked, the board saw no excuse for dividing their bomb load into sizes smaller than 1,000 pounds. Similar, a single 1,000-lb bomb was the simplest load a torpedo bomber could carry, representing minimum complication and minimum extra weight; there was no point in arranging for smaller loads. As for carrier fighters, the board wanted provision for a 500-lb bomb but knew that such an arrangement would impair performance; it settled for two 100-lb bombs per airplane, retaining the 500-pounder aboard special scouts. Ultimately

Table D-7. Modern Carriers

	*Ranger** Nov 1967	SCB 127A Feb 1956	SCB 127A Apr 1959	SCB 127B Feb 1960	*Kitty Hawk* Jul 1962	*America* Feb 1965	*Constel- lation* Jun 1967	SCB 127C 1963	*Enterprise* Feb 1968
250 LD	1,300	1,200	1,379	1,040	1,730	1,898	1,522	1,250	2,352
500 LD	2,600	1,040	761	520	1,593	683	1,285‖	1,040	5,133
1,000 LD	170†	180	596	540	499	46	41	180	442#
2,000 LD	20	95	301	270	101	36	25	95	38
Napalm	150	—	—	240	600	102	—	—	150
Corvus	—	—	—	24	—	—	—	—	—
Eagle‡	—	—	—	200	—	—	—	200	—
Sparrow	—	500	600	400	300	260	—	400	250
Sidewinder	—	700	900	600	450	350	—	600	150
Bullpup	—	500	500	200	220	100	—	240	40
Shrike	—	—	—	—	14,046/651§	72	—	72	30**
2.75 FFAR	3,800	10,000	10,000	6,000	—	4,750	11,400	4,408	9,747
5.0 FFAR	600	1,500	1,500	1,200	1,735	1,220	960	1,200	1,600
Incend	—	—	—	—	—	—	—	—	—
CBU	—	—	—	—	—	140	—	198	
Sadeye	—	—	—	—	—	—	—	100	—
Rockeye	—	—	—	—	—	—	—	100	—
Gladeye	—	—	—	—	—	—	—	100	—
Weteye	—	—	—	—	—	—	—	100	—
MK 12 POD	—	—	—	—	—	—	—	30	—

*Missiles were not listed, but were undoubtedly aboard.

†Plus 165 750-lb bombs.

‡Predecessor to Phoenix, not actually fielded. Recent reports give the standard Phoenix load-out as 96 missiles per carrier.

§5-in HVAR.

‖Plus (not in allowance, but on board) 448 750-lb bombs and 340 napalm bombs.

#Plus 544 750-lb bombs.

**Plus 51 Walleyes, 44 Standard ARMs.

scout and dive-bomber categories merged in aircraft like the Douglas Dauntless, which could dive with a 1,000-pounder.

By 1933 landing-on with heavy bombs was no longer considered hazardous, and bomb capacities were being computed on the basis of aircraft lifetime and expected expenditure. For example, fighters were credited with a combat life of 60 hours (thirty flights), half with bombs, of which 20 percent would involve drops. Two-seat bombers would fly 80 percent of their missions with bombs, dropping them 30 percent of the time, but two-seat scouts would always fly with bombs (two 100-lb bombs), which they would drop 20 percent of the time. Torpedo bombers, attacking half the time, were credited with fifteen 3-hour flights, twelve of them with bombs. Allowances were based on two months of operations. Thus a fighter capable of carrying two 100-lb bombs might be provided with three flights' worth of bombs; a two-seat bomber with seven flights' worth; a two-seat scout with six flights' worth; and a torpedo bomber with six flights' worth.

These allowances were increased somewhat in 1939 (for example, the fighter allowance rose from six to ten light bombs), and in 1942 the General Board set new standards which remained in force through the Pacific War: ten 300-lb bombs per fighter; four 100-lb,

four 500-lb GP, three 1,000-lb GP, two 1,000-lb SAP, and two 1,000-lb AP bombs per scout (dive-) bomber; and eight 500-lb GP, two 1,000-lb GP, three 1,000-lb SAP, two 1,000-lb AP, and one 1,600-lb AP bomb per heavy (torpedo) bomber. In addition, the scout bomber was allowed four and the torpedo bomber eight 325- or 350-lb depth bombs. This allocation was later sharply criticized because it did not take account of variations in mission requirements—it was too balanced. For example, in the Pacific Island campaigns, the AP bombs were not nearly as valuable as light demolition types, and sometimes depth bombs had to be used against Japanese buildings. Some of the shifts are evident in the load-outs of the *Bennington* and the *Bunker Hill*. In addition, in 1944 fleet fighters began to operate as fighter-bombers, carrying 500-lb rather than 100-lb bombs. The disappearance of most of the Japanese fleet largely ended the value of torpedo bombing, although early in the war allowances were sharply increased (as in the case of the *Midway* design).

After the war, antiship requirements were sharply reduced. The *United States*, for example, carried no torpedoes, and those torpedoes carried aboard other ships were usually for ASW only. That is only beginning to change as this is written, with Harpoon missiles assigned to some carrier aircraft.

E

Carrier Characteristics

NOTES TO TABLES

The following data tables give complete information for ships of wartime or prewar construction or for ships stricken before 1980; less comprehensive information for the conventionally powered ships of the current fleet; and an even more incomplete account of the nuclear fleet.* The tables of modern types incorporate the recently adopted system of weight breakdowns (which emphasizes the new roles of C^3 and of electrical systems) introduced in the mid-1950s. *Forrestal* data has been given in both forms for comparison. Note that the endurance figures in the tables of modern ships refer to the characteristics according to which they were designed and thus bear little resemblance to operational figures.

Data are *representative* of each class as built and, where possible, as subject to standard modification. Displacement and loading data are taken from inclining experiment (IX) reports, and the names and date refer to those reports.

Dimensions are given in feet and inches; for example 161–10 is 161 feet 10 inches. Fractions of feet are used only when the original source material was given in that form.

Where two trial figures are given, they refer to separate runs at light and heavy displacements, as noted. Trial endurance is a prewar figure; the wartime figure takes into account practices such as split-plant operation, which considerably reduced effective endurance. The design figure is that stated in the characteristics.

Generator capacity is given in kilowatts (kw), and is AC unless otherwise noted. Steam conditions are given in boiler pressure/temperature (psi/F). In armament figures, numbers in parentheses indicate numbers of multiple mounts, for example, (5 × 4) means five quadruple mounts. Avord includes bombs, torpedoes, and gun ammunition (at times the latter outweighed the former).

Weight data in parentheses are designed as opposed to returned (actual) weights. In many cases the returned weights of the ship in light condition do not match the light-ship displacement deduced from the inclining experiment, and the figure *below* the light-ship weight is that found upon inclining. The same convention applies when the light-ship-weight breakdown refers to a sister ship of the one inclined; such instances are noted.

Among the weights, the margin is a designer's figure. Applied to returned weights, it is the very small weight still remaining to be placed aboard at the time of the final weight report. Machinery liquids include lubricating oil and fuel oil "in the system," that is, not in storage tanks. Note that prewar standard displacements were computed on the basis of a "normal," or design, condition, with 2/3 stores and other loads (except ammunition) aboard. Generally, standard displacement did not include gasoline or aviation lubricating (lube) oil, although it did include the aircraft. Late in the prewar period, the potable-water allowance for standard displacement was cut to 5 gallons per man to reduce the displacement. Among the weight groups, *aeronautics* generally included both aircraft *and* equipment under BuAer cognizance, except as noted. After World War II, however, aircraft were treated as a load item and excluded from the light-ship displacement. *Protec-*

*The ships of the nuclear fleet are subject to the most severe security restrictions.

tion includes only vertical *armor* and not splinter plating (STS) or deck armor, a point particularly evident in the *Midway*-class table.

For modern ships, no breakdown of loads is given owing to security classification.

All weights are given in long tons of 2,240 pounds. Stability data refer to the loading noted. GM is the metacentric height, GZ the maximum righting arm (with the corresponding angle in parentheses), and the range is the range of stability.

Name *Langley* (CV 1)
Date May 1922
LOA 542–2½
LWL 520–0
Beam (wl) 65–2 13/16
Beam (ext)
Hull Depth 39–9⅝
Depth to FD
CB 0.70
C⊗ 0.97
SHP (trial) 7,152*
Speed (trial) 15
AT (displacement)

Endurance (service)
Tactical Diameter (yds/kts)
Hangar Clear Height None
Flight Deck 523 × 65
Elevators 1—45–6 × 36
Capacity 10,000
Catapults 2
Fighters 12†
Spotters 12
Torpedo Bombers 4
Other 6 Seaplanes
Design Displacement 12,700
Design Standard Displacement 11,500

Design Full Load
Boilers (conditions) 3 D.E. (190 psi)
SSTG 2–350, 1–200, 2–35
Diesel Generators None
SHP (design) 6500
Speed (design) 15.5
Fuel Capacity (design) 2,002.6
Endurance (design)
Battery 4 5 in/51
Aviation Ordnance
Aviation Gasoline (gals) 251,000
Complement: Ship ⎫
⎬ 53/415
Aircraft ⎭

WEIGHTS

	Normal	Full Load
Hull		
Hull Fittings		
Protection		
Machinery (dry)		
Armament		
Equipment and Outfit		
Aeronautics		
Ballast: Concrete	2,000	
Water	314	
Margin		
Light Ship	10,669	
Aircraft‡		
Ammunition		
Machinery Liq		
Complement		
Stores and PW§	307	
Lube Oil: Ship		
Aviation	106	
Std Displacement		
RFW	410	
Fuel Oil		
Diesel Oil	1,834	
Avgas ⎫ Seawater Pro. ⎭	672	
Displacement	13,990	15,150
GM	3.28	4.58
GZ	4.30 (51)	5.35 (54)
Range	g.t. 90	g.t. 90
Draft	20–7	22–1

*As a collier.
†As reported about 1924.
‡Loads are 1919 design estimates.
§Including 90 tons of lube oil and 15 tons of galley coal.

Name *Lexington* (CV 2)
Date June 1936 (as refitted)
LOA 888–0
LWL 850–0
Beam (wl) 105–5¼
Beam (ext) 106–0
Hull Depth 74–3
Depth to FD Same
CB 0.564
C⊗ 0.980
SHP (trial) 212,702*
Speed (trial) 34.99
AT (displacement) 37,600
Endurance (service) 10,950/11,9,490/15
Tactical Diameter (yds/kts) 1,950/33
                    (model)
Hangar Clear Height 20–0

Flight Deck 866–2 × 105–11¼
Hangar Deck 393 × 68
Elevators 29–2¾ × 34–10¾†
Capacity 6,000
Catapults F Mk 1 (removed)
Arresting Gear Mk 4
Fighters 18 (6/3) F2F–1‡
Bombers 18 F4B–4
Scouts 20 (2/8) SBU–1
Torpedo Bombers 18 (2/7) BG–1
Other 2 (1/0) JF–1, 3 (0/1) 02U–3
Design Displacement 38,746
Design Standard Displacement 36,000
Design Full Load
Boilers (conditions) 16 W.F. (300 psi, 522 F)
SSTG 6–750
Diesel Generators None

SHP (design) 180,000
Speed (design) 33.25
Fuel Capacity (design) 2,637
Endurance (design) 10,000/10
Battery 8 8 in/55, 12 5 in/25
Fire Control System
Protection: Flight Deck/Gallery Deck None
Hangar Deck None
Protective Deck(s) 2 in (50 lbs or 30 lbs)
Belt 7 in–5 in
Bulkheads
Conning Tower 80-lb side, top, tube
Steering Gear 150-lb plus 30-lb (incl deck)
Aviation Ordnance
Aviation Gasoline (gals) 137,450
Complement: Ship   } 100/1,840 (1942)
            Aircraft } 141/710 (1942)

WEIGHTS§

	Normal	Full Load	Emergency
Hull	21,186.9	(21,471)	
Hull Fittings	2,820.0	(2,705)	
Protection	1,436.7	(1,460)	
Machinery (dry)	6,893.9	(6,267 wet)	
Armament	833.7	(751)	
Equipment and Outfit	629.1	(1,270)	
Aeronautics	267.1	(273)	
Ballast			
Margin			
Light Ship	34,067.4		
	(34,597.9)		
Ammunition	856.2		
Machinery Liq	617.1		
Complement	227.8		
Stores and PW	812.6	1,248.4	
Lube Oil: Ship	22.2	22.2	33.3
Aviation	32.0	48.0	
Std Displacement			
RFW	500.0	750.0	1,977.3
Fuel Oil	2,400.0	3,600.0	7,227.7
Diesel Oil	47.5	47.5	
Avgas }Seawater Pro.	461.0		
Displacement	41,187.7	43,054.6	47,879.4
GM	6.78	7.31	8.77
GZ	6.70 (46.5)	7.14 (48)	7.48 (51)
Range	g.t. 90	g.t. 90	g.t. 90
Draft	29–2¾	30–4¾	33–3½

Saratoga, Dec 1928.
†And FWD: 29–4¾ × 59–4¾ (16,000 lbs)
‡Number in parentheses: aircraft triced up/stowed.
§Light ship weights for *Saratoga*; AVORD weight for *Saratoga* as built; aeronautics include aircraft.

Name *Ranger* (CV 4)
Date Apr 1934
LOA 769–0⅜
LWL 730–0
Beam (wl) 80–0
Beam (ext)
Hull Depth 51–0
Depth to FD
CB 0.457
C⊗ 0.813
SHP (trial) 54,201
Speed (trial) 29.89
AT (displacement) 16,140
Endurance (service) 11,490/15*
Tactical Diameter (yds/kts)
Hangar Clear Height 18–11
Flight Deck 709 × 86

Hangar Deck 510 × 56
Elevators 2–51–10¾ × 41–0¾†
Capacity 15,000
Catapults None
Arresting Gear Mk 4
Fighters 18/9 (18 F4F–3)‡
Bombers 18/9 (37 SB2U–1/2)
Scouts 18/9
Seat Fighters 2, 18/9
Other 2/1 VJ, 2/1 VO (4 SOC–1, 2 J2F–1
Design Displacement 15,799
Design Standard Displacement 13,800
Boilers (conditions) 6 B & W
SSTG 4 500 DC
Diesel Generators None
SHP (design) 53,500
Speed (design) 29.25

Fuel Capacity (design) 1,567
Endurance (design) 10,000/15
Battery 8 5-in/25, 40 0.50-cal MG
Fire Control System 2 Mk 33
Protection: Flight Deck/Gallery Deck None
Hangar Deck None
Protective Deck(s) None
Belt None
Bulkheads None
Conning Tower None
Steering Gear 2-in sides, bhds; 1-in top
Aviation Ordnance 266.3 tons
Aviation Gasoline (gals) 135,840
Complement: Ship } 81/1,288 (1941)
Aircraft } 120/659 (1941)

WEIGHTS

	Normal	Full Load	Normal	Battle Condition
Hull		(8,485)		
Hull Fittings		(1,789)		
Protection		(48)		
Machinery (dry)		(1,604 wet)		
Armament		(162)		
Equipment and Outfit		(391)	As refitted Sep 1941, with 6 quad	
Aeronautics		(191)	1.1-in and 12 0.50-cal MG	
Ballast				
Margin		(152)		
Light Ship	(13,398.3)	(12,822)	(14,227)	
Aircraft				
Ammunition	512.5		839	
Machinery Liq	159.7		99	
Complement	96.0		214	
Stores and PW	384.6	571.7	572	860
Lube Oil: Ship	24.9	64.4	16	13
Aviation			25	37
Std Displacement	14,576		16,092	
RFW	66.7	100.0	67	100
Fuel Oil	1,566.7	2,350.0	1,567	2,350
Diesel Oil			26§	38§
Avgas }	368.8	325.0	200	300
Seawater Pro. }			250	211
Displacement	16,578	17,577	18,202	19,907
GM	3.26	4.10	2.91	3.85
GZ	4.70 (50)	5.45 (50)	4.27 (45.4)	5.47 (46.1)
Range	78.75	82.75	76.1	83.3
Draft	21–6¼	22–4⅞	22–11½	23–11

*Wartime steaming, based on 2,350 tons oil.
†Plus aft elevator: 39–9¾ × 34–9¾ (9,000 lbs).
‡Operational/triced-up (1941 complement in parentheses).
§Including one ton of kerosene.

Name *Enterprise* (CV 6)
Date Mar 1938
LOA 809–6 (824–9 over flight deck in CV 8)
LWL 770–0
Beam (wl) 83–2½
Beam (ext) 109–6¼
Hull Depth 79–8
Depth to FD
CB 0.527
C⊗ 0.959
SHP (trial) 120,517
Speed (trial) 33.65
AT (displacement) 22,959
Endurance (service)
Tactical Diameter (yds/kts) 790/30
Hangar Clear Height 17–3
Flight Deck 802 × 86 (814 × 86 in CV 8)

Hangar Deck 546 × 63
Elevators 3 48 × 44
Capacity 17,000
Catapults 3 H 2
Arresting Gear Mk 4
Fighters 18 (36 F6F–3)*
Bombers 18
Scouts 37 (SBD–5)
Torpedo Bombers 18 (TBF–1)
Other 5 VJ, 1 VM
Design Displacement 23,661
Design Standard Displacement 20,000
Boilers (conditions) 9 B & W
 (400 psi, 648F)
SSTG 4 1,000
Diesel Generators 2 200 (250 in CV 8)
SHP (design) 120,000

Speed (design) 32.5
Fuel Capacity (design) 4,280
Endurance (design) 12,000/15
Battery 8 5-in/38, 16 1.1-in, 24 0.50-cal MG
Fire Control System 2 Mk 33†
Protection: Flight Deck/Gallery Deck None
Hangar Deck None
Protective Deck(s) 60 lbs
Belt 4-in–2.5-in on 30 lbs
Bulkheads 4-in
Conning Tower 4-in side, 2-in top, 60-lb tube
 (30-16 splinter pro in CV 8)
Steering Gear 4-in side, 60-16 deck
Aviation Ordnance 387.2‡
Aviation Gasoline (gals) 177,950
Complement: Ship   86/1,280 (1941)
         Aircraft   141/710 (1941)

WEIGHTS§

	Normal	Full Load	Optimum Battle	Full Load
Hull	12,467.2	(12,111)	As refitted	
Hull Fittings	1,984.2	(1,906)	Nov 1943	
Protection‖	922.4	(914)		
Machinery (dry)	2,770.0	(2,645 wet)		
Armament	193.9	(188)		
Equipment and Outfit	460.7	(466)		
Aeronautics#	238.4	(213)		
Ballast				
Margin		(200)		
Light Ship	19,036.8	(18,643)	(21,622.2)	
	(18,267.2)			
Aircraft				
Ammunition	670.0		1,237.1	
Machinery Liq	123.0		178.5	
Complement	243.8		315.0	
Stores and PW	495.8	743.6	679.0	1,018.5
Lube Oil: Ship / Aviation	75.2	94.3	52.6	78.9
Std Displacement**	19,576		24,128	
RFW	310.3	482.5	321.6	482.4
Fuel Oil	2,682.5	4,270.9	4,814.0	6,511.1
Diesel Oil	71.5	89.5		
Avgas	544.2	464.6	618.4	550.7
Seawater Pro.	23.8	35.0		
Displacement	23,507	25,484	29,882.3	32,060.2
GM	5.41	6.38	9.28	9.64
GZ	6.38 (47)	7.12 (47)	7.07 (41)	7.61 (41)
Range	85.5	g.t. 90	81	84
Draft	24–4¾	25–11½	26–10½	28–4½

*1943 air group in parentheses.
†Mk 37 in *Hornet* (CV 8).
‡*Hornet* (CV 8) data.
§Light-ship weights for *Yorktown* (CV 5).
‖Total of 3,860 tons of STS in CV 8.
#Including aircraft (218.3 tons empty in *Hornet*).
**Based on 75 tons mach liq, 544 of ammunition, 198 complement, 492 stores & PW, no lube oil.

Name *Wasp* (CV 7)
Date Estimates; no IX
LOA 720–0¼ (741–4⁷⁄₁₆ over flight deck)
LWL 690–0
Beam (wl) 80–7
Beam (ext) 90–8¹⁵⁄₁₆ (hangar deck:
    111–10½ over flight deck)
Hull Depth 55–0
Depth to FD 79–10⅞
CB 0.583
C⊗ 0.872
SHP (trial) 71,302/73,906
Speed (trial) 28.2/30.73
AT (displacement) 19,187/17,260
Endurance (service)
Tactical Diameter (yds/kts)
Hangar Clear Height 17–2

Flight Deck 727 × 93
Hangar Deck 522 × 63
Elevators 2 48 × 44*
Capacity 17,000
Catapults 4 H 2
Arresting Gear Mk 4
Fighters 18 F4F–3
Bombers 38 XSB2C–1
Scouts 18 SBD–1
Design Displacement 17,200
Design Standard Displacement 14,700
Design Full Load
Boilers (conditions) 6 3 drum (565 psi, 700 F)
SSTG 2 1,000, 2 850 (DG)
Diesel Generators 1 25 (emergency)
SHP (design) 70,000
Speed (design) 29.5

Fuel Capacity (design) 3,345.95
Endurance (design) 12,000/15
Battery 8 5-in/38, 16 1.1-in, 24 0.50-cal
Fire Control System 2 Mk 33
Protection: Flight Deck/Gallery Deck None
Hangar Deck None
Protective Deck(s) 50 lbs
Belt 25- to 30-lb backing only
Bulkheads None
Conning Tower 60-lb STS
Steering Gear 3.5-in side, 50-lb deck
Aviation Ordnance
Aviation Gasoline (gals) 162,000
Complement: Ship   86/1,302
              Aircraft   120/659

WEIGHTS

	Normal	Full Load	Normal	Full Load
Hull	9,066.5	(8,609)		
Hull Fittings	2,295.6	(1,755)		
Protection	222.1	(205)		
Machinery (dry)	2,049.6	(2,020 wet)		
Armament	196.1	(192)		
Equipment and Outfit	463.5	(430)		
Aeronautics	253.1	(253)		
Ballast				
Margin		(100)		
Light Ship	14,546.5	(13,564)		
Aircraft				
Ammunition	546	546		
Machinery Liq	47	47		
Complement	198			
Stores and PW	395	593		
Lube Oil: Ship } Aviation }				
Std Displacement	15,752			
RFW	164	246		
Fuel Oil	1,602	2,403		
Diesel Oil				
Avgas } Seawater Pro. }	734†	734		
Displacement	18,252	19,116		
GM		6.42‡		
GZ				
Range				
Draft	22–2**			

*Plus one spar-elevator at deck-edge.
†Including lube oil.
‡At 18,450 tons.
**At a trial displacement of 17,200 tons.

Name *Essex* (CV 9)
Date Dec 1942
LOA 872–0*
LWL 820–0
Beam (wl) 93–0
Beam (ext) 147–6
Hull Depth 54–8¼
Depth to FD 81.7
CB 0.573
C⊗ 0.980
SHP (trial) 154,054
Speed (trial) 32.93
AT (displacement) 34,346
Endurance (service) 15,440/15
Tactical Diameter (yds/kts) 765/30
Hangar Clear Height 17–6
Flight Deck 862 × 108

Hangar Deck 654 × 70
Elevators 2 48–3 × 44–3
Capacity 28,000
Catapults 1 H 4A, 1 H 4 B‡
Arresting Gear Mk 4
Fighters 36§ F6F–3‖
Bombers 37 SB2C§
Torpedo Bombers 18 TBF§
Design Displacement 33,400
Design Standard Displacement 27,500
Design Full Load 36,380
Boilers (conditions) 8 B & W (565 psi, 850F)
SSTG 4 1,250
Diesel Generators 2 250
SHP (design) 150,000
Speed (design) 33
Fuel Capacity (design) 6,330

Endurance (design) 20,000/15
Battery 12 5-in/38, 32 (8 × 4) 40 mm, 46 20 mm
Fire Control System 2 Mk 37, 8 Mk 51
Protection: Flight Deck/Gallery Deck None
Hangar Deck 1.5 in
Protective Deck(s) 1.5 in
Belt 4 in–2½ in (508 × 10 ft)
Bulkheads 4 in
Conning Tower 1.5-in STS top, 1-in STS side
  of pilot house
Steering Gear 2.5-in deck
Aviation Ordnance 625.5
Aviation Gasoline (gals) 231,650
Complement: Ship } 268/2,363
  Aircraft

WEIGHTS

	Optimum Battle	Full Load	SCB 27C**	CVS‡‡
Hull	16,021.5	(16,500)	21,425	
Hull Fittings	2,500.2	(2,478)	3,240	
Protection	996.7	(969)	295	
Machinery (dry)	3,123.2	(3,401 wet)	3,474 (wet)	
Armament	438.1	(421)	135	
Equipment and Outfit	519.1	(739)	669	
Aeronautics#	474.9	(766)	125	
Ballast				
Margin		(248)	211	
Light Ship	24,073.7	(25,522)	29,547	
	(23,785)			
Aircraft	418.1		900††	365
Ammunition	1,195.6		1,286	1,247
Machinery Liq	241.5			
Complement	284.2		365	369
Stores and PW	1,066.7	1,601.6	1,739	1,553
Lube Oil: Ship	13.0	16.9	} 80	18
Aviation	82.7	82.7		63
				16§§
Std Displacement	26,668.8		33,793	32,652
RFW	335.2	502.7	503	503
Fuel Oil	4,758.3	6,330.0	4,555	5,944
Diesel Oil	108.2	162.2	165	160
Avgas	} 678.5		} 2,354	853
Seawater Pro.				1,430 (JP–5)
Displacement	32,549	34,881	41,370	41,542
GM	8.95	9.59	9.5	9.64
GZ	7.46 (42.7)	7.94 (42.5)		
Range	81.5	84.8		
Draft	25–11¾	27–5¾	28–6	30–3⅝

*In "long hull" ships 888–0; as completed, 855–10 before addition of sponsons.
‡Two H 4B in later ships.
§Plus 60 0 × 34–0 deck-edge (18,000 lbs).
‖Spare aircraft in parentheses.
#Including aircraft.
**Axial-deck version.
††Including spares and eq't.
‡‡*Lake Champlain.*
§§Aviation liquids.

Name *Midway* (CVB 41)
Date Aug 1945
LOA 968–0
LWL 900–0
Beam (wl) 113–0
Beam (ext) 136–0
Hull Depth 57–6
Depth to FD 84–0
CP 0.605
C⊗ 0.976
SHP (trial) 215,520*
Speed (trial) 33.03
AT (displacement) 58,600
Endurance (service) 15,000/15 (split plant)
Tactical Diameter (yds/kts) 990/30
Hangar Clear Height 17–6
Flight Deck 924 × 113

Hangar Deck 692 × 95
Elevators 2 54–1 × 46–1†
Capacity 26,000
Catapults 2 H 4–1
Arresting Gear Mk 5–0
Fighters 64 F4U–4
Bombers 64 SB2C–5
Other 4 F6F–5N, 4 F6F–5P
Design Displacement 55,450
Design Standard Displacement 45,000
Design Full Load 60,100
Boilers (conditions) 12 B & W
  (565 psi, 850F)
SSTG 8 1,250
Diesel Generators 2 850
SHP (design) 212,000
Speed (design) 33

Fuel Capacity (design) 10,000
Endurance (design) 20,000/15
Battery 18 5-in/54, 84 (21 × 4) 40 mm
Fire Control System
Protection: Flight Deck/Gallery Deck 3.5 in‡
Hangar Deck 80 lb
Protective Deck(s) 70 lb (80 lb outboard) STS
Belt 7.6 in on 30-lb STS (7-in starboard)§
Bulkheads 6.3 in; 40 lb above armor box‖
Conning Tower 6.5-in side, 3.5-in top, 4-in tube
Steering Gear 7.6-in sides, 5-in above, 6.3-in
  bhds, 100-lb deck
Aviation Ordnance 2,167#
Aviation Gasoline (gals) 332,000
Complement: Ship 106/2,006 (1943)
  Aircraft 210/1,121
  Flag 14/126

WEIGHTS

	Optimum Battle	Full Load	SCB 110	(Std Loads)
Hull**	27,340	(26,834)	29,848	
Hull Fittings	3,340	(3,336)	3,901	
Protection	3,425	(3,423)	604	
Machinery (dry)	5,165	(5,166)	5,547 (wet)	
Armament	1,170	(1,167)	810	
Equipment and Outfit	815	(816)	821	
Aeronautics	1,060	(1,059)‡‡	440	
Ballast				
Margin		(500)	1,179	
Light Ship	(42,215)		43,150	
Aircraft	869††		815	
Ammunition	2,653	2,712	1,889	2,118
Machinery Liq	466			176
Complement	384		439	384
Stores and PW	1,280	1,910	2,681	667
Lube Oil: Ship	77	116	}101	
Aviation	144			
Std Displacement			50,075	45,660
RFW	413	628	628	
Fuel Oil	6,003	10,032	8,728	
Diesel Oil	168	252	252	
Avgas / Seawater Pro. }	1,042	1,042	2,931	
Displacement	55,103	59,901	62,614	
GM	9.61	11.62	13.9	
GZ				
Range				
Draft	32–2	34–5¾	34–6	

*Trial Data for *Coral Sea.*
†Plus one deck-edge: 56–0 × 34–0.
‡30 lb fore and aft of armor box.
§Two in to HD above protective deck; belt is 512 ft long.
‖And two double 25-lb doors (40-lb doors) dividing hangar.
#Of which 805 were bombs, 476 rockets, 92 torpedoes. Based on total ammunition load of 3,369 tons on trial, 2,519 std.
**Including (approx) 3,650 tons FD armor, 240 tons HD, 1,850 tons Protective Deck, 130 tons over steering gear (beyond structural weight).
††Armed and fuelled (168 tons).
‡‡Including aircraft, empty (701 tons).

Name 1945 Fleet Carrier (Study C–2)
Date Nov 1946
LOA 960–0
LWL 890–0
Beam (wl) 106–6
Beam (ext) 160–0 (134–0 over sponsons)
Hull Depth 57–0
Depth to FD
CB
CⓍ
Tactical Diameter (yds/kts) 1200/25
Hangar Clear Height 17–6
Flight Deck 870 × 111
Elevators 4
Capacity 45,000 lbs

Catapults 3 H–8
Arresting Gear
Fighters 35 F7F
Bombers 18 BT3D
Design Displacement 51,000
Design Standard Displacement 40,400
Design Full Load 54,500
Boilers (conditions)
SSTG
Diesel Generators
SHP (design) 220,000
Speed (design) 33.1
Fuel Capacity (design)
Endurance (design) 11,700/20
Battery 26 (13 × 2) 3-in 170, 16 (4 × 4) 40 mm,
    40 (20 × 2) 20 mm

Fire Control System
Protection: Flight Deck/Gallery Deck 3-in/—
Hangar Deck 1.5 in
Protective Deck(s) 1.5 in
Belt 1.5 in
Bulkheads 4 in
Conning Tower 30-lb STS over ship controls
Steering Gear 4-in side/1.5-in top
Aviation Ordnance 1,430
Aviation Gasoline (gals) 500,000
Complement: Ship 142/1,598
    Aircraft 114/912

WEIGHTS

	Normal	Full Load
Hull	25,180	
Hull Fittings	2,950	
Protection	990	
Machinery (dry)	4,655	
Armament	890	
Equipment and Outfit	800	
Aeronautics*	634	
Ballast		
Margin	400	
Light Ship	36,499	
Aircraft	406	
Ammunition	2,000	
Machinery Liq		
Complement		
Stores and PW		
Lube Oil: Ship		
Aviation		
Std Displacement†	43,200	
RFW / Fuel Oil / Diesel Oil	7,000	10,500
Avgas / Seawater Pro.	742	
Displacement	51,000	54,500
GM		
GZ		
Range		
Draft		

*Excluding aircraft.
†This estimate does not take into account reduced stores and potable water in the standard condition.

Name *United States* (CVA 58)
Date Contract Design Mar 1949
LOA 1088–0
LWL 1030–0
Beam (wl) 125–0
Beam (ext) 190–0
Hull Depth 101–0
CP 0.976
CⓍ 0.582
Hangar Clear Height 28–1
Flight Deck 1,034 × 190
Hangar Deck 856 × 113
Elevators 3 52 × 63, 1 60 × 60

Capacity 100,000
Catapults 4 H 9
Arresting Gear Mk 6
Fighters 80 F2H–1
Bombers 18 ADR–62 (100,000 lb)
Design Displacement 79,000
Boilers (conditions) 8 (1,200 psi, 950F)
SSTG 8 2,000
Diesel Generators 4 1,000
SHP (design) 280,000
Speed (design) 33.0
Fuel Capacity (design)
Endurance (design) 12,000/20

Battery 8 5-in/54 RF, 16 (8 × 2) 3-in/70, 20 20mm
Fire Control System 4 Mk 67, 5 Mk 56, 7 Gunar
Protection: Flight Deck/Gallery Deck 2-in/1-in
Hangar Deck 1.5 in
Protective Deck(s) 1.5 in*
Belt 60-lb hull side, 30-lb and 25-lb hangar sides
Bulkheads 30 lb
Conning Tower
Steering Gear 5-in deck, 4-in sides, 4-in bulkheads
Aviation Ordnance 2,000
Aviation Gasoline (gals) 500,000
Complement: Ship / Aircraft 349/3,778

WEIGHTS

	Trial§	Full Load	Normal
Hull	41,832		
Hull Fittings	8,237		
Protection	1,214		
Machinery†	6,450		6,215
Armament	1,049		
Equipment and Outfit	1,137‖		
Ballast			
Margin	1,650		
Light Ship		61,569	
Aircraft		1,339	1,339
Ammunition		2,735	2,656
Complement		436	425
Stores and PW		2,769	680
Lube Oil: Ship			
Aviation		87	0
Std Displacement			66,434
RFW	372	565	
Fuel Oil ⎱	8,126	11,545	
Diesel Oil ⎰		678	
Avgas‡ ⎱	1,513	⎱ 1,526	
Seawater Pro. ⎰		⎰	
Displacement	78,946	83,249	
GM	9.69	10.45	
GZ		7.0	
Range		63	
Draft	34–6		

*Three-in over magazines and gasoline.
†Machinery liquids: 45 tons full load, 180 std.
‡Plus 87 tons of aviation liquids.
§Full stores and PW, two-thirds RFW and ship fuels.
‖Includes aeronautical equipment.

Name *Forrestal* (CVA 59)	Hangar Clear Height 25–0	Boilers (conditions) 8 B & W (615 psi, 850F)
Date	Flight Deck 1,018 × 237	SSTG 8 1,500†
LOA 1039–0	Hangar Deck 740 × 101	Diesel Generators 3 1,000
LWL 990–0	Elevators 4 63 × 52	SHP (design) 260,000
Beam (wl) 129–4	Capacity 79,000	Speed (design) 32**
Beam (ext) 249–11	Catapults 2 C 7, 2 C 11*	Endurance (design) 12,000/20
Hull Depth 97–4	Arresting Gear Mk 7–1	Battery 8 5-in/54
CP 0.601	Fighters 12 F3H	Fire Control System 3 Mk 56, GUNAR
C⊗ 0.978	Bombers 32 A3D	Aviation Ordnance 1,650
SHP (trial) 251,460	Design Displacement 72,250 (flush deck)	Aviation Gasoline (gals) 750,000‡
Speed (trial) 32.88	Design Standard Displacement 59,900	Complement: Ship 123/2,641§
AT (displacement) 76,400	Design Full Load 75,870 (flush deck)	Aircraft 237/1,675

WEIGHTS

	Normal	Full Load	1974 Figures
Hull		(39,201)	
Hull Fittings		(7,634)	
Protection		(85)	
Machinery		(6,251)	
Armament		(767)	
Equipment and Outfit		(1,249)	
Aeronautics		(282)	
Ballast			
Margin		(400)	
Light Ship		(55,587)	59,076

Aircraft	1,000	902
Ammunition	2,368	1,718#
Complement	929	
Stores and PW	1,279	2,479
Lube Oil: Ship	} 165	
Aviation		
Std Displacement	(61,163)	

RFW	590	
Fuel Oil‖	8,570	
Diesel Oil	160	
Avgas }	4,766	4,326
Seawater Pro. }		

Displacement	76,614	78,509
Draft	33–9	

*Four C–7 in CVA 61–62.

†Plus 2 600 (400 cycle) later.

‡And 789,000 of JP–5.

§Total of 446/3,360 in 1974.

‖Fuel load from *Ships Data* 1952; recent unofficial figure is 7,800 tons, perhaps reflecting JP–5 in NSFO tanks (a recent endurance figure, again unofficial, is 8,000/20).

#Aviation ordnance only.

Name *Constellation* (CVA 64)	Heavy Attack 8 A–3†	Designed Displacement (light) 56,300
Date 1967	Special Types 9	Designed Displacement (full) 76,870
LOA 1,047–6	Hull‡ 38,384 (37,482)	Boilers (conditions) 8 F.W. (1,200 psi, 950F)
LWL 990–0	Propulsion 3,971 (3,381)	SSTG 8 1,500§
Beam (wl) 129–4	Electrical 909 (1,132)	Diesel Generators 3 1,000
Beam (extreme) 251–8	C³ 358 (342)	SHP (design) 280,000
Hangar Clear Height 25–0	Auxiliaries 8,257 (8,601)	Speed (design) 33.6
Flight Deck 1,047 × 238	Outfit 3,071 (3,352)	Endurance (characteristics) 12,000/20
Hangar Deck 740 × 101	Armament 984 (1,237)	Battery 2 Terrier
Elevators 4 70/85 × 52	Margin	Aviation Ordnance 1,800
Capacity 89,000	Light Ship 60,005 (55,528)	Aviation Fuel: JP–5 1,837,512
Catapults 4 C 13	Loads 20,940 (20,967)	Aviation Fuel: Avgas 93,384
Arresting Gear 5 Mk 7–2	Full Load 80,945 (76,495)	Aircraft Total Weight (design) 1,000
Fighters 28 F–4, 16 F–8*	Draft 35.5	
Light Attack 36 A–4		

*As envisaged in Feb 1956.

†Or 16 A–5 in place of A–4 and A–3 aircraft.

‡Weights for *Kitty Hawk* (CVA 63), 1958; weights in parentheses refer to *Forrestal*. Displacements are 1967 data; CVA 63 weights sum to 55,934 tons (light ship).

§Plus 2 750 (400-cycle) later installed.

Name *Enterprise* (CVAN 65)	Catapults 4 C 13	SHP 280,000
Date Feb 1968	Arresting Gear 6 Mk 7–3	SSTG 16 2,500
LOA 1,123–2⅜*	Fighters 24	Diesel Generators 4 1,000
LWL 1,040–0	Light Attack 24	Battery None
Beam (wl) 133–0	Medium Attack 24	Aviation Ordnance 1,800†
Beam (extreme) 255–0	Heavy Attack 18	Aviation Fuel: JP–5 2,478,358
CB 0.603	Special Types 9	Aviation Fuel: Avgas 95,976
C⊗ 0.991	Actual Light Load 71,277	Aircraft Total Weight 1,347
Hull Depth 99–6	Actual Loads 17,807	Complement: Ship 136/3,189
Hangar Clear Height 25–0	Actual Full Load Displacement 89,084	Flag 20/75
Flight Deck 1079 × 235.3	Draft 37.1	Air 244/1,647
Hangar Deck 732 × 96	Designed Displacement (light) 68,443	Marines 2/69
Elevators 4 85 × 52	Designed Displacement (full) 85,480	
Capacity 89,000	Reactors 8 A2W	

*Over booms; 1,093–0 on centerline. LOA reported as 1,101–2 in 1974.

†Aviation loads, 1974: 2,524 tons of avord, 8,240 of fuel (including sea water to protect avgas); and 892 of aircraft.

Name *America* (CVA 66)
Date Feb 1965
LOA 1069–9
LWL 990–0
Beam (wl) 129–4
Beam (extreme) 252–0
CP 0.600
C⊗ 0.987
Depth 97–4
Hangar Clear Height 25–0
Hangar Deck 740 × 107
Flight Deck 1,025 × 238.6
Elevators 4 85 × 52
Capacity 80,000
Catapults 3 C 13, 1 C 13–1
Arresting Gear 5 Mk 7–3
Fighters 14 F–4, 14 F–8*
Light Attack 24 A–4

Medium Attack 12 A–6
Heavy Attack 12 A–3
Special Types 6 E–1B, 4 RF–8,
  2 SH–2, 1 C–1
Hull 38,443
Propulsion 3,952
Electrical 1,117
C³ 535
Auxiliaries 8,265
Outfit 3,622
Armament 1,067
Margin 677
Light Ship 56,200
Loads 22,500
Full Load 78,700
Draft 34–11⅞ fwd, 36–11⅞ aft

Designed Displacement (light) 57,750
Designed Displacement (full) 78,250
Boilers (conditions)
SSTG 6 2,500, 4 300 (400 cycle)
Diesel Generators 3 1,000
SHP (design) 280,000
Speed (design) 33
Battery 2 Terrier
Aviation Ordnance 1,800
Aviation Fuel: JP–5 1,172,768 gals
Aviation Fuel: Avgas 50,658 gals
Aircraft Total Weight (design) 1,000
Complement: Ship 168/3,138
            Flag 2/56
            Air 299/1,080
            Marines 2/62

*FY 63 air group.

Name *John F. Kennedy* (CVA 67)
Date Design data
LOA 1,051–3*
LWL 990–0
Beam (wl) 129–4
Beam (extreme) 251–6
CP 0.628
C⊗ 0.978
Hull Depth 97–4
Hangar Clear Height 25–0
Flight Deck 1,028 × 238.8
Hangar Deck 688 × 106
Elevators 4 85 × 52
Capacity 80,000
Catapults 3 C–13, 1 C 13–1
Arresting Gear 5 Mk 7–3
Fighters 14 F–4, 14 TFX†

Light Attack 24 A–4
Medium Attack 12 A–6
Heavy Attack 9 A–3/A–5
Special Types 6 E–2, 3 RF–8
Hull‡ 37,139
Propulsion 4,106
Electrical 1,083
C³ 527
Auxiliaries 8,581
Outfit 3,466
Armament 626
Margin 1,100
Light Ship 56,628
Loads 21,517
Full Load 78,145

Draft 35–4
Designed Displacement (light) 61,000
Designed Displacement (full) 83,000
Boilers (conditions) 8 (1,200 psi)
SSTG 6 2,500
Diesel Generators 2 1,500
SHP (design) 280,000
Speed (design) 33.5
Battery 3 Sea Sparrows
Aviation Ordnance 1,800
Aviation Fuel: JP–5 } 5,919§
Aviation Fuel: Avgas }
Aircraft Total Weight (design) 1,000
Complement 470/4,495

*1,072–1 over catapult booms.
†1967 air group as planned in 1962.
‡Weights refer to original design with 2 Tartar launchers.
§1974 figure, when she carried 2,149 tons of avord and 1,000 of aircraft. JP–5 can be traded off against ship fuel.

Name SCB 203
Date Preliminary design (Jul 1958)
LOA 1,000–0
LWL 950–0
Beam (wl) 125–0
Beam (extreme) 230–0
Hangar Clear Height 25–0
Flight Deck 1,000 × 230
Hangar Deck 664 × 93
Elevators 3
Capacity

Catapults 3 C 14
Arresting Gear Mk 7
Landing Length 740
Fighters 24
Light Attack 24
Medium Attack 12
Heavy Attack 9
Special Types 9
Light Load 54,000
Loads 12,000
Full Load Displacement 66,000

Draft 34–0
Reactors 4 A3W*
SHP 180,000 (est)
Battery 2 Terrier
Aviation Ordnance 1,350
Aviation Fuel: JP–5 1,800,000 gals
Aviation Fuel: Avgas 80,000 gals
Aircraft Total Weight
H202 210,000 gals
Complement 4,195

*This was a "paper" reactor, no prototype was built. Performance was, therefore, only an estimate, presented here as an indication of the sacrifices inherent in the design.

Name SCB 211
Date Preliminary design (Nov 1959)
LOA 1,068–0
LWL 1,020–0
Beam (wl) 131–0
Beam (extreme) 238–0
CP 0.584
C⊗ 0.990
Hangar Clear Height 25
Flight Deck 1,070 × 238
Hangar Deck 710 × 95

Elevators 4 70/85 × 52
Capacity
Catapults 4 C 13
Arresting Gear Mk 7–3
Landing Length 750
Fighters 24
Light Attack 24
Medium Attack 12
Heavy Attack 18
Special Types 9
Light Load 61,800

Loads 14,800
Full Load Displacement 76,600
Draft (full) 34–6
Reactors 4 A3W
SHP 200,000 (est)
Battery 2 Terrier
Aviation Ordnance 1,650
Aviation Fuel: JP–5 1,500,000 (4,500 T)
Aviation Fuel: Avgas 100,000 (265 T)
Aircraft Total Weight 1,000
Complement 413/4,587

Name CVAN 67
Date Contract design (1963)
LOA
LWL 1,040–0
Beam (wl) 133–0
Beam (extreme)
CB
C⊗
Depth 99–6
Hangar Clear Height 25–0
Catapults 2 C 13, 2 C 13–1

Arresting Gear
Fighters 12 TFX*
Light Attack 51 VAX (A–7)
Medium Attack 9 A–6A
Heavy Attack 6 SH–3A
Special Types 3 EA–6A, 6 RA–5,
  6 E–2A, 1 C–1A
Light Load 70,097
Loads 17,303
Full Load Displacement 87,400
Capacity Displacement 90,530

Draft (full) 36–7, (37–7 capacity)
Reactors 4 A3W
Battery 2 Tartar
Aviation Ordnance 2,329/2,960†
Aviation Fuel: JP–5 6,305/7,930 tons‡
Aviation Fuel: Avgas 82§
Aircraft Total Weight 1,300
Complement: Flag 21/48
  Ship 133/2,672
  Aviation 236/1,758

*Notional 1970–75 air group, as understood in 1963.
†Weights are for full load/capacity displacement.
‡2,080,000/2,610,000 gals.
§25,000 gals.

Name *Nimitz* (CVN 68)
Date Design data
LOA 1,088–0
LWL 1,040–0
Beam (wl) 134–0
Beam (extreme) 257–6
CP 0.613
C⊗ 0.991
Hull Depth 100–6
Hangar Clear Height 26–6
Flight Deck 1,092 × 250.8
Hangar Deck 684 × 108

Elevators 4 70/85 × 52*
Capacity 105,000
Catapults 4 C 13–1
Arresting Gear Mk 7–3
Actual Light Load 73,973
Actual Loads 17,467
Actual Full Load Displacement 91,440
Draft (full) 36–8
Draft (combat) 37–8
Designed Displacement (light) 72,805
Designed Displacement (full) 88,896

Designed Displacement (combat) 91,878
Reactors 2 A4W
SHP 260,000†
SSTG 8 8,000
Diesel Generators 4 2,000
Battery‡ 3 Sea Sparrow
Aviation Ordnance 2,470/2,970
Aviation Fuel: JP–5 2/2.7 million gals§
Aviation Fuel: Avgas None
Aircraft Total Weight
Complement 439/5,182

*Inboard/outboard.
†Unofficial figure; trial speed reported as 31.5 kts. Endurance reported as 1.5 million miles at 20 kts.
‡As designed, 2 Tartar P&S aft, 2 twin 3-in/50 P&S fwd.
§Full load/combat load; also reported as 11,064 tons in congressional testimony.

Name CVA 3/53
Date June 1953
LOA 922–0
LWL 850–0
Beam (wl) 119–0
Beam (ext)
Hull Depth 91–0
CP 0.590
C⊗ 0.986
Hangar Clear Height 23–0

Flight Deck 900
Elevators 3 44 × 56
Capacity 70,000
Catapults 3 C 11
Boilers (conditions) 8 (1,200 psi, 950 F)
SHP (design) 200,000
Speed (design) 31.6 (30 sust.)
Fuel Capacity (design)
Endurance (design) 12,200/20
Battery 8 5-in/54 RF

Fire Control System 4 Mk 67
Protection: Flight Deck/Gallery Deck 55/20 lb
Hangar Deck 35 lb
Protective Deck(s) 35 lb*
Belt 45-lb hull side, 20- & 25-lb hangar
Aviation Ordnance 1,565
Aviation Gasoline (gals) 494,000†
Complement: Ship ⎫
Aircraft ⎭ 3,826

WEIGHTS

	Normal	Full Load
Hull	26,100	
Hull Fittings	5,996	
Protection	200	
Machinery	5,140	
Armament	637	
Equipment and Outfit	1,101§	
Ballast		
Margin	1,600	
Light Ship	40,554	
Aircraft	900	
Ammunition	2,310	
Complement	420	
Stores and PW	836	2,452
Lube Oil: Ship		⎫ 125
Aviation		⎭
Cleaning Fluid		11
Std Displacement	45,020	
RFW		575
Fuel Oil‡		9,500
Diesel Oil		325
Avgas ⎫		2,000
Seawater Pro. ⎭		
Displacement		59,392
GM		10.35
GZ		
Range		
Draft		35–0

*65-lbs over magazines, gasoline.
†And 3,500 tons of HEAF.
‡Including HEAF (3,500 tons).
§Including aeronautical equipment.

Name Study 62B
Date Jan 1962
LOA 900
LWL 850
Beam (wl) 116
Beam (extreme)
CB
C⊗
Hull Depth 85
Hangar Clear Height 17.5
Flight Deck 900 × 200
Elevators 3 44 × 56
Capacity 89,000
Catapults 2 C 13

Runway 660
Fighters 20 F–4
ASW 20 S–2, 16 SH–34
Special Types 4 E–1B
Hull 24,280
Propulsion 3,530
Electrical 970
C³ 590
Auxiliaries 5,800
Outfit 2,420
Armament 850
Margin
Light Ship 39,550
Loads

Full Load 54,520
Draft 32.0
Boilers (conditions)
SSTG 6 2,500
Diesel Generators 3 1,000
SHP (design) 212,000
Speed (design) 31.2
Endurance (characteristics) 8,000/20
Battery 2 twin Terrier, 8 Polaris
Aviation Ordnance 1,200*
Aviation Fuel: JP–5 1,600 tons
Aviation Fuel: Avgas 800
Aircraft Total Weight (design) 618.2†
Complement 350/3,000

*Total ordnance: 1,462 tons.
†Empty; 1,031.3 tons ready for takeoff.

Name CV–TCBL
Date Preliminary design (Feb 1975)
LOA 902–0
LWL 850–0
Beam (wl) 120–6
Beam (extreme) 245–6
Hull Depth 87–6
Hangar Clear Height
Flight Deck 902 × 221
Elevators 2 70 × 52
Capacity 110,000
Catapults 2 C 13–1
Arresting Gear 3 wires
Fighters 12 F–14A
Light Attack 20 A–7E

AEW 4 E–2C
ASW 7 SH–3H
Special Types 4 KA–6D, 4 EA–6D
Hull 28,154
Propulsion 1,986
Electrical 1,110
C³ 494
Auxiliaries 5,837
Outfit 2,525
Armament 631
Margin 3,827
Light Ship 44,566
Loads 14,331
Full Load 58,897

Draft 34–0
Boilers (conditions) 4 (1,200 psi)
SSTG 6 2,500
Diesel Generators 2 1,500
SHP (design) 134,000 (2 shafts)
Speed (design) 27.8 (26.2 sust)
Endurance (characteristics) 8,000/20
Battery 3 CIWS
Aviation Ordnance 1,075
Aviation Fuel: JP–5 2,700 T
Aviation Fuel: Avgas None
Aircraft Total Weight (design) 607
Complement: Aviation 218/1,287
                          Ship 119/1,907

Name CVV
Date Design study (Aug 1977)
LOA 912–0 (923–0 over booms)
LWL 860–0
Beam (wl) 126–0
Beam (extreme) 256–6*
Hull Depth 87–6
Hangar Clear Height 24–6
Flight Deck 912 × 256–6
Elevators 2 70 × 52
Capacity 110,000
Catapults 2 C 13–1
Fighters 10 F–14A
Light Attack 12 A–6D/E
AEW 4 E–2C

ASW 10 SH–3A, 8 LAMPS III
Special Types 2 KA–6D, 4 EA–6B
Hull† 29,740
Propulsion 2,171
Electrical 1,335
C³ 565
Auxiliaries 6,239
Outfit 3,155
Armament 673
Margin 3,177
Light Ship 47,055
Loads 15,372
Full Load 62,427
Draft 34–7

Designed Displacement (light) 45,192
Designed Displacement (full) 59,794
Boilers (conditions) 6 (CV 66 type)
SSTG 6 2,500
Diesel Generators 2 2,000
SHP (design) 140,000‡
Speed (design) 27.8 (26.3 sust)
Endurance (characteristics) 8,000/20
Battery 3 CIWS
Aviation Ordnance 1,191
Aviation Fuel: JP–5 2,700§
Aviation Fuel: Avgas None
Aircraft Total Weight (design) 607
Accommodation: 4,024

---

*Including removable extension (14.6 ft).
†Weight data as of spring 1979.
‡Two shafts: four boilers on line at any one time.
§Also reported as 4,400 tons, presumably representing a trade-off against ship fuel.

Name *Independence* (CVL 22)
Date Jan 1943
LOA 622–6
LWL 600–0
Beam (wl) 71–6
Beam (ext) 109–2
Hull Depth 41–11⅝
Depth to FD
CB
C⊗
SHP (trial) 106,001*
Speed (trial) 31.46
AT (displacement) 14,200
Endurance (service) 8,325/15
Tactical Diameter (yds/kts)
Hangar Clear Height 17–4
Flight Deck 552 × 73

Hangar Deck 258 × 55
Elevators 2 42 × 44
Capacity 28,000
Catapults 1 H 2–1†
Arresting Gear
Fighters 12
Bombers 9
Torpedo Bombers 9
Other 1 utility
Design Displacement 14,220
Design Standard Displacement 11,000
Design Full Load 15,100
Boilers (conditions) 4 B & W (565 psi, 850F)
SSTG 4 600
Diesel Generators 2 250
SHP (design) 100,000
Speed (design) 31.6

Fuel Capacity (design)
Endurance (design) 12,500/15
Battery 24 (2 × 4, 8 × 2) 40mm, 16 20mm
Fire Control System 10 Mk 51
Protection: Flight Deck/Gallery Deck
Hangar Deck
Protective Deck(s) 2 in
Belt None‡
Bulkheads 5 in and 3.75 in
Conning Tower None; 15-lb STS on bridge
Steering Gear 5-in bhds, 2.25-in above, 0.75-in below
Aviation Ordnance 331.4
Aviation Gasoline (gals) 122,243
Complement: Ship } 140/1,321
Aircraft }

WEIGHTS

		Normal
Hull	6,393.9	*Cabot*, CVL 28,
Hull Fittings	1,066.8	as an ASW carrier,
Protection	254.2	Jan 1955
Machinery (dry)	1,812.0	(IX Jul 1951)
Armament	86.5	
Equipment and Outfit	254.8	
Aeronautics§	143.4	
Ballast	82.1	
Margin		
Light Ship	9,133.5 (9,849.5)	11,118.6
Aircraft (empty)	114.0	
Ammunition	604.6	
Machinery Liq	124.2	
Complement	157.1	
Stores and PW	686.1	
Lube Oil: Ship } Aviation }	73.9	
Std Displacement‖	11,495.8	
RFW	179.7	179.7
Fuel Oil	2,632.6	2,686.4
Diesel Oil	84.3	84.3
Avgas‡ } Seawater Pro. }	358.6	
Displacement	14,751	16,185
GM	5.76	3.73
GZ	3.35 (40–18)	
Range	80–36	
Draft	24–2¾	26–1½

*Data refer to *Cabot* (CVL 28).
†Second H 2–1 added 1944–45; 1 H 4B in ASW conversions.
‡5-in–3¼-in belt in CVLs 24–30; 2-in forward belt in all ships over forward magazine.
§Including aircraft (empty).
‖Based on full rather than two-thirds loads.

Name *Saipan* (CVL 48)
Date
LOA 683–6⁹⁄₁₆
LWL 664–0
Beam (wl) 76–8½
Beam (ext) 108–0
Hull Depth 43–4*
Depth to FD 71–6
CB
C⊗
SHP (trial) 119,247/117, 568
Speed (trial) 32.26/32.02
AT (displacement) 17,490/18,160
Endurance (service) 11,700/14
Tactical Diameter (yds/kts)
Hangar Clear Height 17–8
Flight Deck 611–0 × 80–0

Hangar Deck 284–0 × 68–0
Elevators 2 48 × 44
Capacity 30,000
Catapults 2 H 2–1†
Arresting Gear Mk 5–0
Fighters 18 F6F–3‡
Bombers 12 SB2C–2
Torpedo Bombers 12 TBF–1C
Design Displacement 17,800
Design Standard Displacement 14,500
Design Full Load 18,750
Boilers (conditions) 4 B & W (600 psi, 850 F)
SSTG 4 750
Diesel Generators 2 500, 2 60
SHP (design) 120,000
Speed (design) 33 (clean)
Fuel Capacity (design) 2,550

Endurance (design) 11,000/15
Battery 42 (5 × 4, 11 × 2) 40 mm, 32 (16 × 2) 20 mm
Fire Control System Mk 51
Protection: Flight Deck/Gallery Deck
Hangar Deck
Protective Deck(s) 2.5 in
Belt 4 in–2.5 in§
Bulkheads 4 in–1.5 in
Conning Tower
Steering Gear 4-in side, 2.5-in top, 0.75-in bottom
Aviation Ordnance 370
Aviation Gasoline (gals) 143,500
Complement: Ship 78/1,339
            Aircraft 48/212 (for 18 AF–2, 1955)

WEIGHTS

	Full Load	
Hull‖	7,998.6	(8,100.3)
Hull Fittings	663.8	(1,079.6)
Protection	705.1	(697.0)
Machinery (dry)	1,500.4	(2,240.0)
Armament	215.5	(215.5)
Equipment and Outfit	171.7	(383.8)
Aeronautics	173.7	(381.0)
Ballast		
Margin		(151)
Light Ship#	13,753	(13,248)
Aircraft**	289.3	
Ammunition	713	801
Machinery Liq	85	177
Complement	201	200
Stores and PW	310	1,042
Lube Oil	56	10
Std Displacement	15,118	
RFW	224	
Fuel Oil	2,830	
Diesel Oil	180	
Avgas	413	
Seawater Pro.	69	
Displacement††	19,086	
GM	7.90	
GZ		
Range		
Draft	25–9¾	

*To main deck: 48–7¼ to hangar deck.
†One replaced by H 4B postwar.
‡Air group contemplated Jan 1944.
§Plus 2-in lower belt forward.
‖Based on returned weights, Dec 1945, may not include same GFE.
#LS weight from contractor's estimate.
**183.4 tons empty.
††CVL 49 IX, 1951.

Name *Long Island* (CVE 1)
Date Jan 1944 (aircraft ferry)
LOA 492–0
LWL 465–0
Beam (wl) 69–6
Beam (ext)
Hull Depth
Depth to FD
CB
C⊗
SHP (trial) 7,965
Speed (trial) 17.8
AT (displacement) 16,620

Endurance (service)
Tactical Diameter (yds/kts) 800
Hangar Clear Height 17–6
Flight Deck 418 × 70–10*
Hangar Deck 98 × 54
Elevators 1 34 × 38 (aft)†
Capacity 7,400
Catapults 1 H 2
Arresting Gear Mk 3
Scouts 6 SBC‡
Observation 10 SOC
Design Displacement
Design Standard Displacement

Design Full Load
Boilers (conditions) Diesel (Busch-Sulzer)
SSTG 2 300 DC, 3 275 DC
SHP (design) 8,500
Speed (design) 16.5
Fuel Capacity (design) 1,360
Endurance (design)
Battery 1 5-in/38, 2 3-in/50
Aviation Ordnance
Aviation Gasoline (gals) 105,165
Complement: Ship ⎫
            Aircraft ⎬ 408

WEIGHTS

		As converted, 1941
Hull		(BAVG 1)
Hull Fittings		
Protection		
Machinery (dry)		
Armament		
Equipment and Outfit		
Aeronautics		
Ballast: Concrete	2,638.7	1,616
Water	1,119.1§	1,415
Margin		
Light Ship		10,675
Aircraft	350.0	28
Ammunition	292.4	271
Machinery Liq	86.7	72
Complement	124.6	65
Stores and PW	729.3‖	372#
Lube Oil: Ship	19.6	20
Aviation	140.0	21
Std Displacement	13,324	
RFW	62.0	260
Fuel Oil		
Diesel Oil	1,316.8	1,434
Avgas ⎫	234.9	309
Seawater Pro. ⎭		
Displacement	14,937.9	
GM	3.38	
GZ		
Range		
Draft	24–9¾	

*Originally 360 × 70.
†In 1943, as a training carrier.
‡1941 air group.
§Including 138.6 tons for torpedo protection.
‖Including 462.5 tons of potable water.
#Including 62 tons of potable water.

Name *Card* (CVE 11)
Date Feb 1943
LOA 495–8
LWL 465–0
Beam (wl) 69–6
Beam (ext)
Hull Depth 42–6
Depth to FD
CB
C⊗
SHP (trial)
Speed (trial) 17.6
AT (displacement) 16,620
Endurance (service) 26,340/15

Tactical Diameter (yds/kts) 750/15
Hangar Clear Height 17–6
Flight Deck 436–8 × 80–0
Hangar Deck 261 × 62
Elevators 41–3 × 33–3*
Capacity 14,000
Catapults 1 H 2
Arresting Gear Mk 4–5A
Fighters 12 F4F
Torpedo Bombers 12 TBF
Design Displacement 16,620
Design Standard Displacement
Design Full Load 15,700
Boilers (conditions) 2 F.W. "D" (285 psi, 577 F)

SSTG 3 250 DC
Diesel Generators 2 300 DC (ship service)
SHP (design) 8,500
Speed (design) 16.5
Fuel Capacity (design) 3,290
Endurance (design)
Battery 2 5-in/38, 20 (10 × 2) 40 mm
Fire Control System Mk 51
Aviation Ordnance 195†
Aviation Gasoline (gals) 186,286
Complement: Ship ⎫
Aircraft ⎭ 100/808

WEIGHTS

	Full Load	Glacier (CVE 33): HMS Atheling, Jul 1943
Hull		
Hull Fittings		
Protection		
Machinery (dry)		
Armament		
Equipment and Outfit		
Aeronautics		
Ballast: Concrete	289.2	1,579.7
Water		
Margin		
Light Ship		(9,432.2)
Aircraft		
Ammunition	400	393.3
Machinery Liq	47	50.4
Complement	99	91.4
Stores and PW	416	559.4
Lube Oil: Ship	} 74	6.3
Aviation		64.8
Cargo Oil	1,672	1,672.3
Std Displacement		
RFW‡	529	263.6
Fuel Oil	1,615	1,745.3
Diesel Oil	131	
Avgas	509	509.0
Seawater Pro.	37	39.2
Displacement	14,914	14,863.4
GM	3.62	4.24
GZ	4.29 (46.8)	4.71 (48)
Range	89.3	90
Draft	24–8¾	24–8

*Fwd; 33–3 × 41–3 aft.
†Includes seawater ballast.
‡Of which 100.8 were bombs and torpedoes.

Name *Sangamon* (CVE 26)
Date Aug 1942
LOA 553–0
LWL 525–0
Beam (wl) 75–0
Beam (ext) 105–2
Hull Depth
Depth to FD
CB
C⊗
SHP (trial) 16,905*
Speed (trial) 19.28
AT (displacement) 23,235
Endurance (service) 23,920/15†

Tactical Diameter (yds/kts) 865
Hangar Clear Height 17–6
Flight Deck 502 × 85–0
Hangar Deck 198 × 69
Elevators 2 34–1 × 42–1
Capacity 14,000
Catapults 1 H 2
Arresting Gear Mk 4–5A
Fighters 12 (26 F6F–5)‡
Scouts 9
Tortedo Bombers 4 (6 TBM–3)
Design Displacement 23,235
Design Standard Displacement
Design Full Load 24,275

Boilers (conditions) 4 B & W (450 psi, 750 F)
SSTG 2 400
Diesel Generators 3 150
SHP (design) 13,500
Speed (design) 18.0
Fuel Capacity (design) 5,880
Endurance (design)
Battery 2 5-in/51, 8 (4 × 2) 40mm, 12 20mm
Fire Control System Mk 51
Aviation Ordnance 305§
Aviation Gasoline (gals) 148,285 (1945)
Complement: Ship ⎫
                        ⎬ 830
                Aircraft ⎭

WEIGHTS

	Normal	Full Load	Normal
			Jul 1945
Hull			
Hull Fittings			
Protection			
Machinery (dry)			
Armament			
Equipment and Outfit			
Aeronautics			
Ballast			
Margin			
Light Ship‖		9,336.7	10,576.3
Aircraft			
Ammunition		344.8	500.9
Machinery Liq		17.8	58.8
Complement		93.5	114.6
Stores and PW	227.3	676.5	1,636.4**
Lube Oil: Ship		⎫ 24.3	12.1
Aviation		⎭	23.0
Std Displacement	10,044.6		
RFW	26.4	39.6	58.9
Fuel Oil#	10,935.9	12,876.3	10,446.3
Diesel Oil	120.6	180.9	357.0
Avgas		265.3	⎫ 435.7
Seawater Pro.		19.5	⎭
Displacement	21,412.3	23,875.2	24,220.0
GM		5.11	3.49
GZ		2.05 (27.5)	1.27 (23)
Range		64.8	48.5
Draft		30–7½	31–0

*Data for *Cimarron*.
†Based on 4,780 tons of oil fuel.
‡1945 air group in parentheses.
§Of which 160.5 tons was bombs and torpedoes.
‖Including aircraft.
#Including fuel oil carried as cargo.
**Including 1,367.2 tons of potable water.

Name *Liscombe Bay* (CVE 56)
Date Jul 1943
LOA 498–10
LWL 490–0
Beam (wl) 65–0
Beam (ext)108–1
Hull Depth
Depth to FD
CB
C⊗
SHP (trial)
Speed (trial) 20.75*
AT (displacement) 9,650
Endurance (service) 10,240/15

Tactical Diameter (yds/kts) 450/15
Hangar Clear Height 17–6
Flight Deck 474 × 80–0
Hangar Deck 256 × 56
Elevators 41 10¾ × 33 9½†
Capacity 14,000
Catapults 1 H 2–1
Arresting Gear Mk 4–5
Fighters 9
Bombers 9
Torpedo Bombers 9
Design Displacement 9,570
Design Standard Displacement
Design Full Load 10,200

Boilers (conditions) 4 B & W (285 psi, 577 F)
SSTG 3 300
Diesel Generators None
SHP (design) 9,000
Speed (design) 20
Fuel Capacity (design) 1,890
Endurance (design)
Battery 1 5-in/38, 8 (4 × 2) 40mm, 12 20mm
Fire Control System
Aviation Ordnance 276
Aviation Gasoline (gals) 129,713
Complement: Ship } 764
Aircraft }

WEIGHTS

	Normal	Full Load
Hull		(3,801.1)
Hull Fittings		(682.2)
Protection		
Machinery		(1,082.6)
Armament		(46.0)
Equipment and Outfit		(193.6)
Aeronautics‡		(76.0)
Ballast		
Margin		(84.8)
Light Ship	(6,854)	(5,966.3)
Aircraft		197.0
Ammunition		492.0
Complement		88.0
Stores and PW	165.4	506.0
Lube Oil: Ship }		36.0
Aviation }		
Std Displacement§	7,847.6	
RFW		102.8
Fuel Oil		2,228.0
Diesel Oil		10.0
Avgas		} 373.0
Seawater Pro.		
Displacement	10,122.5	10,902
GM	(trial)	3.88
GZ		
Range		
Draft		20–9¼

*Trial data for *Casablanca* (CVE 55).
†Fwd; aft 37 10¾ × 41 9½.
‡Equipment only.
§Standard figure estimated on the basis of half stores, 5 gals of potable water per man.

Name *Commencement Bay* (CVE 105)
Date Nov 1944
LOA 557–1
LWL 525–0
Beam (wl) 75–0
Beam (ext)105–2
Hull Depth 51–0 (39–0 to main deck)
Depth to FD 72–0
CB 0.672
C⊗ 0.983
SHP (trial) 17,800
Speed (trial) 20.2
AT (displacement) 23,000

Endurance (service) 8,320/15
Tactical Diameter (yds/kts)
Hangar Clear Height 17–6
Flight Deck 501 × 80
Hangar Deck 216 × 69
Elevators 2 44 × 42
Capacity 17,000*
Catapults 1 H 2–1, 1 H 4C
Arresting Gear Mk 4–5
Fighters 18 F6F–3
Torpedo Bombers 15 TBF–1
Design Displacement 23,100
Design Full Load 24,275

Boilers (conditions) 4 "D" (450 psi, 750 F)
SSTG 4 500
Diesel Generators None
SHP (design) 16,000
Speed (design) 19.0
Fuel Capacity (design) 3,380
Endurance (design)
Battery 2 5-in/38, 36 (3 × 4, 12 × 2) 40mm, 20 20mm
Fire Control System Mk 51
Aviation Ordnance 515
Aviation Gasoline (gals) 150,806
Complement: Ship ⎫ 134/920
                        Aircraft ⎭

WEIGHTS

	Normal	Full Load
Hull		(6,561.6)
Hull Fittings		(851.4)
Protection		
Machinery (dry)		
Armament†		(153.1)
Equipment and Outfit		(265.5)
Aeronautics		(212.2)
Ballast		
Margin		
Light Ship	9,499.3	
Aircraft		
Ammunition		801.0
Machinery Liq		4.0
Complement		70.6
Stores and PW	251.7	801.4
Lube Oil: Ship		⎫ 30.1
Aviation		⎭
Cargo Oil		7,358.7
Std Displacement‡	10,975.9	
RFW		247.3
Fuel Oil		1,788.5
Diesel Oil		23.8
Avgas		⎫ 453.1
Seawater Pro.		⎭
Displacement		21,397
GM		4.04
GZ		5.12 (51)
Range		g.t. 90
Draft		27–10½

*23,000 lbs on ships modified for ASW postwar.
†Estimated from weapon weights.
‡Estimated on the basis of half stores, no cargo oil, and 5 gals potable water per man.

Name CVE–ASW (SCB 43)
Date Jun 1952
LOA 644–3
LWL 612–0
Beam (wl) 92–0
Beam (ext)112–0
Hull Depth 76–6
CP 0.588
C⊗ 0.98
Hangar Clear Height 17–6

Flight Deck 600 × 85
Elevators 1 50 × 44, 1 50 × 30
Capacity 34,000
Catapults 2 H 4B
Arresting Gear Mk 5
Bombers 30 S2F (S–2)
Design Standard Displacement 14,500
Design Full Load 25,890
SSTG Total 4,500 kw
SHP (design) 70,000

Speed (design) 26.5
Fuel Capacity (design) 2,456
Endurance (design) 8,400/17
Battery 18 (6 × 2, 6 × 1) 3-in/50
Fire Control System 4 Mk 56, 1 Mk 63
Aviation Ordnance 415
Aviation Gasoline (gals) 230,000
Complement: Ship }
                 Aircraft } 200/1,150

WEIGHTS

	Normal*	Full Load
Hull	7,820	
Hull Fittings	1,930	
Protection		
Machinery	2,093	
Armament	202	
Equipment and Outfit	531	
Aeronautics	97	
Ballast		
Margin	500	
Light Ship	13,173	
Aircraft	402	402
Ammunition	541	551
Complement	151	151
Stores and PW	225	723
Lube Oil: Ship		} 38
Aviation		
Cargo Oil		7,400
Std Displacement	14,492	
RFW	69	104
Fuel Oil	1,637	2,456
Diesel Oil	45	68
Avgas	672	} 672
Seawater Pro.		
Displacement	24,861	25,738
GM	10.07	10.12
GZ		
Range		
Draft	26.85	27.60

*Trial condition includes cargo oil, lube oil, full stores and potable water.

Name Sea control ship (SCS)
Date Contract design (1973)
LOA 610–0
LWL 585–0
Beam (wl) 80–0
Beam (extreme) 105–0
CP 0.600
C⊗ 0.793
Hangar Clear Height 19–0
Flight Deck 545 × 105
Elevators 1 60 × 30, 1 35 × 50
Capacity 60,000 lbs
Catapults None
Arresting Gear None

Fighters 3 AV–8A
ASW 14 SH–3, 2 LAMPS
Hull 5,288
Propulsion 369
Electrical 605
C³ 85
Auxiliaries 1,401
Outfit 954
Armament 137
Margin 934
Light Ship 9,773
Loads 3,963
Full Load 13,736

Draft 29–9
Boilers (conditions) 2 LM 2,500 gas turbines
SSTG 3 2,500 (gas turbines)
Diesel Generators None
SHP (design) 45,000
Speed (design) 26 (24.5 sust)
Endurance (characteristics) 8,400/17, 7,500/20
Battery 2 CIWS
Aviation Ordnance 180
Aviation Fuel: JP–5 545 tons
Aviation Fuel: Avgas None
Aircraft Total Weight (design)
Complement 76/624

Name VSTOL support ship (VSS III)
Date 1979
LOA 717–0
LWL 690–0
Beam (wl) 109–2
Beam (extreme) 178–0
Hull Depth 77–1
Hangar Clear Height 20–1
Flight Deck
Elevators 2 45 × 45
Capacity 85,000
Catapults None

Arresting Gear None
Fighters 4 AV–8B
ASW 6 LAMPS III, 16 SH–53
Hull 12,114
Propulsion 822
Electrical 754
C^3 197
Auxiliaries 2,264
Outfit 1,835
Armament 266
Margin 1,864
Light Ship 20,116

Loads 9,014
Full Load 29,130
Draft 25–3
Boilers (conditions) 4 LM 2500 (gas turbines)
SSTG 5 2,500
Diesel Generators None
SHP (design) 90,000
Battery 2 Harpoon cannisters, 2 CIWS
Aircraft Total Weight (design) 353*
Complement: Ship 49/910
            Aviation 87/541

*VSS II, 292 tons of avord, 2,848 of JP–5.

Name *Guam* (LPH 9)
Date Mar 1969
LOA 592–0
LWL 556–0
Beam (wl) 84–2¾
Beam (extreme) 161 (108)*
CB 0.517
C⊗ 0.909
Hull Depth 73–6
Speed (trial) 23.5
Hangar Clear Height 20–0
Flight Deck 602–3½ × 108
Elevators 2 50 × 34
Capacity 44,000†

Catapults None
Arresting Gear None
Helicopters: 20 HR 2S‡
Hull 6,782.5§
Propulsion 600.8
Electrical 254.0
C^3 173.1
Auxiliaries 1,641.8
Outfit 1,148.7
Armament 115.7
Margin
Light Ship 11,280
Loads 7,194

Full Load 18,474
Draft 23–9 fwd, 28–9 aft
Designed Displacement (light)
Designed Displacement (full)
Boilers (conditions) 4 B & W (600 psi, 850 F)
SSTG 2 2,500
Diesel Generators 2 750
SHP (design) 22,000
Speed (design) 22
Battery 8 (4 × 2) 3-in/50‖
Aviation Fuel: JP–5 209,442#
Complement 90/577
            Troops 193/1,864

*Elevators folded.
†50,000 lbs in LPH 2–3, 11–12.
‡LPH 9 is unique in having an ASCAC for ASW operation. Typical air group: 20–24 CH–46, 4 CH–53, 4 UH–1 or AH–1.
§Weights for *Iowa Jima* (LPH 2).
‖Later 2 Sea Sparrows, 4 3-in/50, 2 CIWS.
#A typical recent (1982) figure is 405,000 gals, presumably reflecting use of NSFO tanks for JP–5. These ships also carry 6,000 gallons of vehicle gasoline.

Name *Tarawa* (LHA 1)
Date Aug 1976
LOA 820–0
LWL 778–0
Beam (wl) 106–8
Beam (extreme) 126–0
CB
C⊗
Hull Depth 90–6
SHP (trial)
Speed (trial)
AT (displacement)
Hangar Clear Height 20–0
Flight Deck 820 × 106.5
Elevators 1 59¾ × 34¾*

Capacity 80,000
Catapults None
Arresting Gear None
Helicopters: 19 CH–53 or 30 CH–46
Hull 16,154
Propulsion 1,352
Electrical 759
C^3 411
Auxiliaries 3,587
Outfit 2,348
Armament 226
Margin
Light Ship 25,588
Loads 13,173
Full Load 38,761

Draft 25.74
Designed Displacement (full) 39,300
Boilers (conditions) 2 (600 psi, 850 F)
SSTG 4 2,500, 4 150 (400 cycle)
Diesel Generators 2 2,000
SHP (design) 70,000
Speed (design) 24
Endurance (characteristics) 10,000/20
Battery 2 Sea Sparrows, 3 5-in/54, 6 20mm
  Mk 67
Aviation Fuel: JP–5 400,000
Vehicle Fuel: 10,000
Complement 90/812
            Troops 172/1,731

*And one deck-edge elevator: 34 × 50 (40,000 lbs).

F
Vital Statistics
of Carrier Types

BUILDING YARDS

ASB	American Shipbuilding Corp.
BETHQ	Bethlehem, Quincy (Fore River)
BETHSI	Bethlehem, Staten Island
CIW	Commercial Iron Works, Portland
DET	Detroit
FED	Federal (Kearny)
ING	Ingalls Shipbuilding, Pascagoula
K	Kaiser, Vancouver
LITT	Litton, (formerly Ingalls)
MINY	Mare Island Navy Yard
NN	Newport News
NORNY	Norfolk Navy Yard
NYNY	New York Naval Shipyard, Brooklyn Navy Yard
NYSB	New York Shipbuilding Corp., Camden
PHNY	Philadelphia Navy Yard
PSNY	Puget Sound Navy Yard
SEATAC	Seattle-Tacoma Shipbuilding
SUN	Sun Shipbuilding
TODD	Todd Pacific, Tacoma
WILL	Williamette
WP	Western Pipe & Steel, San Francisco

FATES

Acq	acquired
BU	broken up
Ret	returned
Str	stricken
WL	war loss

FLEET CARRIERS

		LD/Launch	Comm	Decomm	Fate
CV 1	*Langley*	18 Oct 11	7 Apr 13	25 Oct 36	Conv to seaplane tender (AV 3)
	MINY	24 Aug 12	20 Mar 22		21 Apr 37; WL 27 Feb 42
CV 2	*Lexington*	8 Jan 21	14 Dec 27		WL 5 Aug 42
	BETHQ	3 Oct 25			
CV 3	*Saratoga*	25 Sep 20	16 Nov 27		Expended at Bikini test, 25 Jul
	NYSB	7 Apr 25			46
CV 4	*Ranger*	26 Sep 31	4 Jun 34	18 Oct 46	Str 29 Oct 46; BU 47
	NN	24 Feb 33			
CV 5	*Yorktown*	21 May 34	30 Sep 37		WL 7 Jun 42
	NN	4 Apr 36			
CV 6	*Enterprise*	16 Jul 34	12 May 38	17 Feb 47	Str 2 Oct 56; BU 58 after drive to
	NN	3 Oct 36			preserve her failed
CV 7	*Wasp*	1 Apr 36	25 Apr 40		WL 15 Sep 42
	BETHQ	4 Apr 39			
CV 8	*Hornet*	25 Sep 39	20 Oct 41		WL 27 Oct 42
	NN	14 Dec 40			
CV 9	*Essex*	28 Apr 41	31 Dec 42	9 Jan 47	CVS 8 Mar 60; FRAM FY 62; str
	NN	31 Jul 42	1 Feb 51	30 Jun 69	15 Jun 75; BU
CV 10	*Yorktown*	1 Dec 41	15 Apr 43	9 Jan 47	CVS 9 Jan 57; FRAM FY 66; str 1
	NN	21 Jan 43	2 Jan 53	27 Jun 70	Jun 73; museum ship (South
					Carolina)
CV 11	*Intrepid*	1 Dec 41	16 Aug 43	22 Mar 47	SCB–27C; CVS 31 Mar 62;
	NN	26 Apr 43	18 Jun 54	30 Mar 74	FRAM FY 65; museum ship
					(New York), 1982
CV 12	*Hornet*	3 Aug 42	29 Nov 43	15 Jan 47	CVS 27 Jun 58; FRAM FY 65
	NN	30 Aug 43	1 Oct 53	26 Jun 70	
CV 13	*Franklin*	7 Dec 42	31 Jan 44	17 Feb 47	Str 1 Oct 64; BU
	NN	14 Oct 43			

		LD/Launch	Comm	Decomm	Fate
CV 14	Ticonderoga NN	1 Feb 43 7 Feb 44	8 May 44 1 Oct 54	9 Jan 47 1 Sep 73	CVS 21 Oct 69; SCB–27C; str 16 Nov 73; BU
CV 15	Randolph NN	10 May 43 29 Jun 44	9 Oct 44 1 Jul 53	25 Feb 48 13 Feb 69	CVS 31 Mar 59; FRAM FY 61; str 15 Jun 73; BU
CV 16	Lexington BETHQ	15 Jul 41 26 Sep 42	17 Mar 43 1 Sep 55	23 Apr 47	SCB–27C; CVS 1 Oct 62; CVT in 1982 (still active)
CV 17	Bunker Hill BETHQ	15 Sep 41 7 Dec 42	24 May 43	Jan 47	Str 1 Nov 66; BU; had been used as an electronics test ship
CV 18	Wasp BETHQ	18 Mar 42 17 Aug 42	24 Nov 43 28 Sep 51	17 Feb 47 1 Jul 72	CVS 1 Nov 56; FRAM FY 64; str 1 Jul 72; BU
CV 19	Hancock BETHQ	26 Jan 43 24 Jan 44	15 Apr 44 1 Mar 54	9 May 47 30 Jan 76	SCB–27C; str 31 Jan 76; BU
CV 20	Bennington NYNY	15 Dec 42 26 Feb 44	6 Aug 44 30 Nov 51	8 Nov 46 15 Jan 70	CVS 30 Jun 69; FRAM FY 63
CV 21	Boxer NN	13 Sep 43 14 Dec 44	16 Apr 45	1 Dec 69	CVS 15 Nov 55; LPH Jan 59; FRAM FY 62; str 1 Dec 69; BU
CV 22	Independence NYSB	1 May 41 22 Aug 42	14 Jan 43	Jul 46	Bikini test; sunk as target 29 Jan 51
CV 23	Princeton NYSB	2 Jun 41 18 Oct 42	25 Feb 43		WL 24 Oct 44
CV 24	Belleau Wood NYSB	11 Aug 41 6 Dec 42	31 Mar 43	13 Jan 47	French Bois Belleau Sep 53–Sep 60; str 1 Oct 60; BU
CVL 25	Cowpens NYSB	17 Nov 41 17 Jan 43	28 May 43	13 Jan 47	Str 1 Nov 59; BU
CVL 26	Monterey NYSB	29 Dec 41 28 Feb 43	17 Jun 43 15 Sep 50	11 Feb 47 16 Jan 56	Str 1 Jun 70; BU
CVL 27	Langley NYSB	11 Apr 42 22 May 43	31 Aug 43	11 Feb 47	French Lafayette Jan 51–Mar 63; str 63; BU
CVL 28	Cabot NYSB	16 Mar 42 4 Apr 43	24 Jul 43 27 Oct 48	11 Feb 47 21 Jan 55	Str 1 Nov 59; Spanish Dedalo 30 Aug 67
CVL 29	Bataan NYSB	31 Aug 42 1 Aug 43	17 Nov 43 13 May 50	11 Feb 47 9 Apr 54	Str 1 Sep 59; BU
CVL 30	San Jacinto NYSB	26 Oct 42 26 Sep 43	15 Dec 43	1 Mar 47	Str 1 Jun 79; BU
CV 31	Bon Homme Richard NYNY	1 Feb 43 29 Apr 44	26 Nov 44 1 Nov 55	9 Jan 47 2 Jul 71	SCB–27C
CV 32	Leyte NN	21 Feb 44 23 Aug 45	11 Apr 46	15 May 59	CVS Aug 53; str 1 Jan 69; BU
CV 33	Kearsage NYNY	1 Mar 44 5 May 45	2 Mar 46 1 Mar 52	16 Jun 50 13 Feb 70	CVS 1 Oct 58; str 1 May 73; BU
CV 34	Oriskany NYNY	1 May 44 13 Oct 45	25 Sep 50	15 May 76	SCB–27A prototype; steam catapults fitted in SCB–125 conversion completed 29 May 59
CV 35	Reprisal NYNY	1 Jul 44 46			Cancelled 12 Aug 45 (40% complete); hulk used for explosive tests beginning 1 Apr 48 in Chesapeake Bay; sold Aug 49; BU
CV 36	Antietam PHNY	14 Mar 43 20 Aug 44	28 Jun 45	8 May 63	Angled deck prototype; CVS 8 Aug 53; str 1 May 73; BU
CV 37	Princeton PHNY	14 Sep 43 8 Jul 45	18 Nov 45 28 Aug 50	21 Jun 49 30 Jan 70	CVS 12 Nov 53; LPD 2 Mar 59; FRAM FY 61; str 30 Jan 70; BU
CV 38	Shangri-La NORNY	15 Jan 43 24 Feb 44	15 Sep 44 1 Feb 55	7 Nov 47 30 Jul 71	SCB–27C; CVS 30 Jun 59
CV 39	Lake Champlain NORNY	15 Mar 43 2 Nov 44	3 Jun 45 19 Sep 52	17 Feb 47 2 May 66	CVS 1 Aug 57; str 1 Dec 69; BU
CV 40	Tarawa NORNY	5 Jan 44 12 May 45	8 Dec 45 3 Feb 51	30 Jun 49 13 May 60	CVS Jan 55; str 1 Jan 67; BU
CVB 41	Midway NN	27 Oct 43 20 Mar 45	10 Sep 45		
CVB 42	Franklin D. Roosevelt NYNY	1 Dec 43 29 Apr 45	27 Oct 45	1 Oct 77	Original name: Coral Sea; str 1 Oct 77; BU
CVS 43	Coral Sea NY	10 Jul 44 2 Apr 46	1 Oct 47		
CVS 44					Construction cancelled 11 Jan 43
CV 45	Valley Forge PHNY	7 Sep 44 18 Nov 45	3 Nov 46	15 Jan 70	CVS 12 Nov 53; LPH 1 Jul 61; FRAM FY 62; str 15 Jan 70; BU
CV 46	Iwo Jima NN	29 Jan 45			Cancelled 11 Aug 45; BU on slip
CV 47	Philippine Sea BETHQ	19 Aug 44 5 Sep 45	11 May 46	28 Dec 58	CVS 15 Nov 55; str 1 Dec 69; BU
CVL 48	Saipan NYSB	10 Jul 44 8 Jul 45	14 Jul 46 27 Aug 66	3 Oct 57 14 Jan 70	Communications ship Arlington (AGMR–2) 1966–70; str 15 Aug 75; BU

		LD/Launch	Comm	Decomm	Fate
CVL 49	*Wright*	21 Aug 44	9 Feb 47	15 Mar 56	Command ship (CC–2) 1963–
	NYSB	1 Sep 45	11 May 63	22 May 70	70; str 1 Dec 77; BU 80
CV 50–55, CVB 56–57					All cancelled Mar 45
CVA 58	*United States*	18 Apr 49			Cancelled 23 Apr 49
	NN				
CVA 59	*Forrestal*	14 Jul 52	1 Oct 55		
	NN	11 Dec 54			
CVA 60	*Saratoga*	16 Dec 52	14 Apr 56		
	NYNY	8 Oct 55			
CVA 61	*Ranger*	2 Aug 54	10 Aug 57		
	NN	29 Sep 56			
CVA 62	*Independence*	1 Jul 55	10 Jan 59		
	NYNY	6 Jun 58			
CVA 63	*Kitty Hawk*	27 Dec 56	29 Apr 61		
	NYSB	21 May 60			
CVA 64	*Constellation*	14 Sep 59	27 Oct 61		
	NYNY	8 Oct 60			
CVAN 65	*Enterprise*	4 Feb 58	25 Nov 61		
	NN	24 Sep 60			
CVA 66	*America*	9 Jan 61	23 Jan 65		
	NN	1 Feb 64			
CVA 67	*John F. Kennedy*	22 Oct 64	7 Sep 68		
	NN	27 May 67			
CVAN 68	*Nimitz*	22 Jun 68	3 May 75		
	NN	13 May 72			
CVN 69	*Dwight D. Eisenhower*	14 Aug 70	18 Oct 77		
	NN	11 Oct 75			
CVN 70	*Carl Vinson*	11 Oct 75			
	NN	15 Mar 80			
CVN 71	*Theodore Roosevelt*	31 Oct 81			
	NN				

ESCORT CARRIERS

		LD/Launch	Comm	Decomm	Fate
AVG 1	*Long Island*	7 Jul 39	2 Jun 41	26 Mar 46	Acq 6 Mar 41; str 12 Apr 46; merchant ship *Nelly* (1949)
	SUN/NN	11 Jan 40			
AVG 2					Reserved for planned conversion of transport *Wakefield* (ex-*Manhattan*)
AVG 3					Reserved for planned conversion of transport *Mt. Vernon* (ex-*Washington*)
AVG 4					Reserved for planned conversion of transport *West Point* (ex-*America*)
AVG 5					Reserved for planned conversion of liner *Kungsholm*
ACV 6	*Altamaha*		15 Nov 42		Acq 31 Oct 42; HMS *Battler*, 31 Oct 42; ret 12 Feb 46
	ING	4 Apr 42			
ACV 7	*Barnes*		10 Oct 42		Acq 30 Sep 42; HMS attacker 30 Sep 42; ret 5 Jan 46; merchant ship *Castel Forte* (1948)
	WP	27 Sep 42			
ACV 8	*Block Island*		11 Jan 43		Acq 9 Jan 43; HMS *Hunter* 9 Jan 43; ret 29 Dec 45; merchant ship *Almdijk* (1948)
	ING	22 May 42			
ACV 9	*Bogue*	1 Oct 41	26 Sep 42	30 Nov 46	Acq 1 May 42; str 1 Mar 59; BU 60
	SEATAC	15 Jan 42			
ACV 10	*Breton*		9 Apr 43		Acq 9 Apr 43; HMS Chaser 9 Apr 43; ret 12 May 46; merchant ship *Aagtekerk* (1948)
	ING	19 Feb 42			
ACV 11	*Card*	27 Oct 41	8 Nov 42	13 May 46	Acq 1 May 42; str 15 Sep 70; BU 71; aircraft transport 1958–70
	SEATAC	21 Feb 42	1 Jul 58	10 Mar 70	
AVG 12	*Copahee*	18 Jun 41	15 Jun 42	5 Jul 46	Acq 8 Feb 42; str 1 Mar 59; BU 61
	SEATAC	21 Oct 41			
ACV 13	*Core*	2 Jan 42	10 Dec 42	4 Oct 46	Acq 1 May 42; str 15 Sep 70; BU 71; aircraft transports 1958–69.
	SEATAC	15 May 42	1 Jul 58	25 Nov 69	
ACV 14	*Croatan*		20 Feb 42		Acq 27 Feb 43; HMS *Fencer* 27 Feb 43; ret 11 dec 46; merchant ship *Sydney* (1948)
	WP	4 Apr 42			
ACV 15	*Hamlin*		30 Dec 42		Acq 21 Dec 42, HMS *Stalker* 21 Dec 42; ret 29 Dec 45; merchant ship *Riouw* (1948)
	WP	5 Mar 42			

	LD/Launch	Comm	Decomm	Fate
ACV 16 *Nassau* SEATAC	27 Nov 41 4 Apr 42	20 Aug 42	28 Oct 46	Acq 1 May 42; str 1 Mar 59; BU 61
ACV 17 *St. George* ING	18 Jul 42	14 Jun 43		Acq 14 Jun 43; HMS *Pursuer* 11 Jun 43; ret 12 Feb 46; BU
ACV 18 *Altamaha* SEATAC	19 Dec 41 22 May 42	15 Sep 42	27 Sep 46	Acq 1 May 42; str 1 Mar 59; BU 61
ACV 19 *Prince William* WP	7 May 42	29 Apr 43		Acq 28 Apr 43; HMS *Striker* 28 Apr 43; ret 12 Feb 46; BU
ACV 20 *Barnes* SEATAC	19 Jan 42 22 May 42	20 Feb 43	29 Aug 46	Acq 1 May 42; str 1 Mar 59; BU 59
ACV 21 *Block Island* SEATAC	19 Jan 42 6 Jun 42	8 Mar 43		Acq 1 May 42; WL 29 May 44
ACV 22 *Searcher* SEATAC/CIW	20 Jun 42	8 Apr 43		Acq 27 Jul 42; RN 7 Apr 43; ret 29 Nov 45; merchant ship *Capt. Theo* (1947)
ACV 23 *Breton* SEATAC	25 Feb 42 27 Jun 42	12 Apr 43 1 Jul 58	30 Aug 46	Acq 1 May 42; str 6 Aug 71; BU 72; aircraft transport 1958–71
ACV 24 *Ravager* SEATAC/WILL	16 Jul 42	26 Apr 43		Acq 1 May 42; RN 25 Apr 43; ret 26 Feb 46; merchant ship *Robin Trent* (1948)
ACV 25 *Croatan* SEATAC	15 Apr 42 1 Aug 42	28 Apr 43 16 Jun 58	20 May 46 23 Oct 69	Acq 1 May 42; str 15 Sep 70; BU 71; aircraft transport 1958–69
ACV 26 *Sangamon* FED/NN	13 Mar 39 4 Nov 39	25 Aug 42	24 Oct 45	Acq 22 Oct 40 as oiler; str 24 Oct 45; BU 48
ACV 27 *Suwannee* FED/BETHSI	3 Jun 38 4 Mar 39	24 Sep 42	28 Oct 46	Acq 26 Jun 41 as oiler; str 1 Mar 59; BU 62
ACV 28 *Chenango* SUN/NORNY	10 Jul 38 4 Jan 39	19 Sep 42	14 Aug 46	Acq 31 May 41 as oiler; str 1 Mar 59; BU 62
ACV 29 *Santee* SUN/PSNY	31 May 38 4 Mar 39	24 Aug 42	21 Oct 46	Acq 30 Oct 40 as oiler; str 1 Mar 59; BU 60
AVG 30 *Charger* SUN	19 Jan 40 1 Mar 41	3 Mar 42	15 Mar 46	Acq 4 Oct 41; str 28 Mar 46; merchant ship *Fairsea* (1949)
ACV 31 *Prince William* SEATAC/PSNY	18 May 42 23 Aug 42	9 Apr 43	29 Aug 46	Str 1 Mar 59; BU 61
CVE 32 *Chatham* SEATAC/WILL	25 May 42 19 Sep 42	11 Aug 43		HMS *Slinger* 11 Aug 43; ret 27 Feb 46; merchant ship *Robin Mowbray* (1948)
CVE 33 *Glacier* PSNY	9 Jun 42 7 Sep 42	3 Jul 43		HMS *Atheling* 31 Jul 43; ret 13 Dec 46; merchant ship *Roma* (1950)
CVE 34 *Pybus* SEATAC	23 Jun 42 7 Oct 42	31 May 43		HMS *Emperor* 6 Aug 43; ret 12 Feb 46; BU
CVE 35 *Baffins* SEATAC	18 Jul 42 18 Oct 42	28 Jun 43		HMS *Ameer* 19 Jul 43; ret 17 Jan 46; merchant ship *Robin Kirk* (1948)
CVE 36 *Bolinas* SEATAC	3 Aug 42 11 Nov 42	22 Jul 43		HMS *Begum* 2 Aug 43; ret 4 Jan 46; merchant ship *Raki* (1948)
CVE 37 *Trumpeter* CIW	25 Aug 42 15 Dec 42	4 Aug 43		RN 4 Aug; ret 6 Apr 46; merchant ship *Alblasserdijk* (1948)
CVE 38 *Carnegie* SEATAC	9 Sep 42 30 Dec 42	9 Aug 43		HMS *Empress* 8 Jun 43; ret 4 Feb 46; BU
CVE 39 *Cordova* SEATAC	22 Sep 42 30 Jan 43	6 Aug 43		HMS *Khedive* 25 Aug 43; ret 26 Jan 46; merchant ship *Rempang* (1948)
CVE 40 *Delgada* SEATAC/CIW	9 Oct 42 20 Feb 43	20 Nov 43		HMS *Speaker* 20 Nov 43; ret 17 Jul 46; merchant ship *Lancero* (1948)
CVE 41 *Edisto* SEATAC	20 Oct 42 9 Mar 43	7 Sep 43		HMS *Nabob* 7 Sep 43; RCN; WD 1944; ret 16 Mar 45; merchant ship *Nabob* (1948)
CVE 42 *Estero* SEATAC	31 Oct 42 22 Mar 43	3 Nov 43		HMS *Premier* 3 Nov 43; ret 12 Apr 46; merchant ship *Rhodesia Star* (1948)
CVE 43 *Jamaica* SEATAC	13 Nov 42 21 Apr 43	27 Sep 43		HMS *Shah* 27 Sep 43; ret 6 Dec 45; merchant ship *Salta* (1948)
CVE 44 *Keweenaw* SEATAC	27 Nov 42 6 May 43	25 Oct 43		HMS *Patroller* 22 Oct 43; ret 13 Dec 46; merchant ship *Almkerk* (1948)
CVE 45 *Prince* SEATAC/WILL	17 Dec 42 18 May 43	17 Jan 44		HMS *Rajah* 17 Jan 44; ret 13 Dec 46; merchant ship *Drente* (1948)
CVE 46 *Niantic* SEATAC	5 Jan 43 2 Jun 43	8 Nov 43		HMS *Ranee* 8 Nov 43; ret 21 Nov 46; merchant ship *Friesland* (1948)

		LD/Launch	Comm	Decomm	Fate
CVE 47	Perdido	1 Jan 43	31 Jan 44		HMS *Trouncer* 31 Jan 44; ret 3 Mar 46; merchant ship *Greystoke Castle* (1949).
	CIW	16 Jun 43			
CVE 48	Sunset	23 Feb 43	19 Nov 43		HMS *Thane*; torpedoed 15 Jan 45; ret 15 Dec 45; BU
	SEATAC	15 Jul 43			
CVE 49	St Andrews	12 Mar 43	7 Dec 43		HMS *Queen* 7 Dec 43; ret 31 Oct 46; merchant ship *Roebiah* (1948)
	SEATAC	2 Aug 43			
CVE 50	St Joseph	25 Mar 43	22 Dec 43		HMS *Ruler* 22 Dec 43; ret 29 Jan 46; BU
	SEATAC	21 Aug 43			
CVE 51	St Simon	26 Apr 43	31 Dec 43		HMS *Arbiter* 31 Dec 43; ret 3 Mar 46; merchant ship *Coracero* (1948)
	SEATAC	9 Sep 43			
CVE 52	Vermillion	10 May 43	20 Jan 44		HMS *Smiter* 20 Jan 44; ret 6 Apr 46; merchant ship *Artillero* (1948)
	SEATAC	27 Sep 43			
CVE 53	Willapa	21 May 43	5 Feb 44		HMS *Puncher* 2 May 44; RCN; ret 16 Jan 46; merchant ship *Muncaster Castle* (1949)
	SEATAC	8 Nov 43			
CVE 54	Winjah	5 Jun 43	21 Feb 44		HMS *Reaper* 18 Feb 44; ret 20 May 46; merchant ship *South Africa Star* (1948)
	SEATAC	22 Nov 43			
CVE 55	Casablanca	3 Nov 42	8 Jul 43	10 Jun 46	Ex-*Alazon Bay*; str 3 Jul 46; BU 47.
	K	5 Apr 43			
CVE 56	Liscombe Bay	9 Dec 42	7 Aug 43		WL 24 Nov 43
	K	19 Apr 43			
CVE 57	Anzio	12 Dec 42	27 Aug 43	5 Aug 46	Ex-*Coral Sea*, ex-*Alikula Bay*; str 1 Mar 59; BU 60
	K	1 May 43			
CVE 58	Corregidor	17 Dec 42	31 Aug 43	30 Jul 46	Ex-*Anguilla Bay*; str 1 Oct 58; BU 60; aircraft transport 1951–8
	K	12 May 43	19 May 51	4 Sep 58	
CVE 59	Mission Bay	28 Dec 42	13 Sep 43	21 Feb 47	Str 1 Sep 58; BU 60
	K	26 May 43			
CVE 60	Guadalcanal	5 Jan 43	25 Sep 43	15 Jul 46	Ex-*Astrolabe*; str 27 May 58; BU 60
	K	5 Jun 43			
CVE 61	Manila Bay	15 Jan 43	5 Oct 43	31 Jul 46	Ex-*Bucareli Bay*; str 27 May 58; BU 60
	K	10 Jul 43			
CVE 62	Natoma Bay	17 Jan 43	14 Oct 43	20 May 46	Str 1 Sep 58; BU 60
	K	20 Jul 43			
CVE 63	St Lo	23 Jan 43	23 Oct 43		Ex-*Midway*, ex-*Chapin Bay*; WL 25 Oct 44.
	K	17 Aug 43			
CVE 64	Tripoli	1 Feb 43	31 Oct 43	22 May 46	Ex-*Didrickson Bay*; str 1 Feb 59; BU 60; aircraft transport 1952–8
	K	2 Sep 43	5 Jan 52	25 Nov 58	
CVE 65	Wake Island	6 Feb 43	7 Nov 43	5 Apr 46	Ex-*Dolomi Bay*; str 17 Apr 46; BU Baltimore 47
	K	15 Sep 43			
CVE 66	White Plains	11 Feb 43	15 Nov 43	10 Jul 46	Ex-*Elbour Bay*; str 27 Jun 58; BU 59
	K	27 Sep 43			
CVE 67	Solomons	19 Mar 43	21 Nov 43	15 May 46	Ex-*Nassuk Bay*; str 5 Jun 46; BU 47
	K	6 Oct 43			
CVE 68	Kalinin Bay	26 Apr 43	27 Nov 43	15 May 46	Str 5 Jun 46; BU 47
	K	15 Oct 43			
CVE 69	Kasaan Bay	11 May 43	4 Dec 43	6 Jul 46	Str 1 Mar 59; BU 60
	K	24 Oct 43			
CVE 70	Fanshaw Bay	18 May 43	9 Dec 43	14 Aug 46	Str 1 Mar 59; BU 59
	K	1 Nov 43			
CVE 71	Kitkun Bay	31 May 43	15 Dec 43	19 Apr 46	Str 8 May 46; BU 47
	K	8 Nov 43			
CVE 72	Tulagi	7 Jun 43	21 Dec 43	30 Apr 46	Ex-*Fortezela Bay*; str 8 May 46; BU 47
	K	15 Nov 43			
CVE 73	Gambier Bay	10 Jul 43	28 Dec 43		WL 25 Oct 44
	K	22 Nov 43			
CVE 74	Nehenta Bay	20 Jul 43	3 Jan 44	15 May 46	Str 1 Aug 59; BU 60
	K	28 Nov 43			
CVE 75	Hoggatt Bay	17 Aug 43	11 Jan 44	20 Jul 46	Str 1 Sep 59; BU 60
	K	4 Dec 43			
CVE 76	Kadashan Bay	2 Sep 43	18 Jan 44	14 Jun 46	Str 1 Aug 59; BU 60
	K	11 Dec 43			
CVE 77	Marcus Island	15 Sep 43	26 Jan 44	12 Dec 46	Ex-*Kanalku Bay*; str 1 Sep 59; BU 60
	K	16 Dec 43			
CVE 78	Savo Island	27 Sep 43	3 Feb 44	12 Dec 46	Ex-*Kaita Bay*; str 1 Sep 59; BU 60
	K	22 Dec 43			
CVE 79	Ommaney Bay	6 Oct 43	11 Feb 44		WL 4 Jan 45
	K	29 Dec 43			

		LD/Launch	Comm	Decomm	Fate
CVE 80	*Petrof Bay*	15 Oct 43	18 Feb 44	31 Jul 46	Str 27 Jun 58; BU 59
	K	5 Jan 44			
CVE 81	*Rudyerd Bay*	24 Oct 43	25 Feb 44	11 Jun 46	Str 1 Aug 59; BU 60
	K	12 Jan 44			
CVE 82	*Saginaw Bay*	1 Nov 43	2 Mar 44	19 Jun 46	Str 1 Aug 59; BU 60
	K	19 Jan 44			
CVE 83	*Sargent Bay*	8 Nov 43	9 Mar 44	23 Jul 46	Str 27 Jun 58; BU 59
	K	31 Jan 44			
CVE 84	*Shamrock Bay*	15 Nov 43	15 Mar 44	6 Jul 46	Str 27 Jun 58; BU 59
	K	4 Feb 44			
CVE 85	*Shipley Bay*	22 Nov 43	21 Mar 44	28 Jun 46	Str 1 Mar 59; BU 61
	K	12 Feb 44			
CVE 86	*Sitkoh Bay*	23 Nov 43	28 Mar 44	30 Nov 46	Str 1 Apr 60; BU 61; aircraft transport 1950–54
	K	19 Feb 44	29 July 50	27 Jul 54	
CVE 87	*Steamer Bay*	4 Dec 43	4 Apr 44	1 Jul 46	Str 1 Mar 59; BU 59
	K	26 Feb 44			
CVE 88	*Cape Esperance*	11 Dec 43	9 Apr 44	22 Aug 46	Ex-*Tananek Bay*; str 1 Mar 59; BU 61; aircraft transport 1950–59
	K	3 Mar 44	5 Aug 50	15 Jan 59	
CVE 89	*Takanis Bay*	16 Dec 43	15 Apr 44	1 May 46	Str 1 Aug 59; BU 60
	K	10 Mar 44			
CVE 90	*Thetis Bay*	22 Dec 43	21 Apr 44	7 Aug 46	CVHA–1, 1 Jul 55; LPH–6, 28 May 59; str 1 Mar 64; BU 66
	K	16 Mar 44	20 Jul 56	1 Mar 64	
CVE 91	*Makassar Strait*	29 Dec 43	27 Apr 44	9 Aug 46	Ex-*Ulitaka Bay*; str 1 Sep 58; target ship (Pacific Missile Range); grounded on San Nicholas Island (Apr 61) and broke her back
	K	22 Mar 44			
CVE 92	*Windham Bay*	5 Jan 44	3 May 44	Jan 47	Str 1 Feb 59; BU 61; aircraft transport 1951–59
	K	29 Mar 44	31 Oct 51	1959	
CVE 93	*Makin Island*	12 Jan 44	9 May 44	19 Apr 46	Ex-*Woodcliffe Bay*; str 1 Jul 47; BU 47
	K	5 Apr 44			
CVE 94	*Lunga Point*	19 Jan 44	14 May 44	24 Oct 46	Ex-*Alazon Bay*; str 1 Apr 60; BU 66
	K	11 Apr 44			
CVE 95	*Bismarck Sea*	31 Jan 44	20 May 44		WL 21 Feb 45
	K	17 Apr 44			
CVE 96	*Salamaua*	4 Feb 44	26 May 44	9 May 46	Ex-*Anguilla Bay*; str 1 Sep 46; BU 47
	K	22 Apr 44			
CVE 97	*Hollandia*	12 Feb 44	1 Jun 44	17 Jan 47	Ex-*Astrolabe Bay*; str 1 Apr 60; BU 60
	K	28 Apr 44			
CVE 98	*Kwajalein*	19 Feb 44	7 Jun 44	16 Aug 46	Ex-*Bucareli Bay*; str 1 Apr 60; BU 61
	K	4 May 44			
CVE 99	*Admiralty Islands*	26 Feb 44	13 Jun 44	26 Apr 46	Ex-*Chapin Bay*; str 8 May 46; BU 47
	K	10 May 44			
CVE 100	*Bougainville*	3 Mar 44	18 Jun 44	3 Nov 46	Ex-*Didrickson Bay*; str 1 Jun 60; BU 60
	K	16 May 44			
CVE 101	*Mantanikau*	10 Mar 44	24 Jun 44	11 Oct	Ex-*Dolomi Bay*; str 1 Apr 60; BU 60
	K	22 May 44			
CVE 102	*Attu*	16 Mar 44	30 Jun 44	8 Jun 46	Ex-*Elbour Bay*; str 3 Jul 46; BU 49
	K	27 May 44			
CVE 103	*Roi*	22 Mar 44	6 Jul 44	9 May 46	Ex-*Alava Bay*; str 21 May 46; BU 47
	K	2 Jun 44			
CVE 104	*Munda*	29 Mar 44	8 Jul 44	13 Sep 46	Ex-*Tonowek Bay*; str 1 Sep 58; BU 60
	K	8 Jun 44			
CVE 105	*Commencement Bay*	23 Sep 43	27 Nov 44	30 Nov 46	Ex-*St Joseph Bay*; str 1 Apr 71
	TODD	4 May 44			
CVE 106	*Block Island*	25 Oct 43	30 Dec 44	28 May 46	Ex-*Sunset Bay*; str 1 Jul 59; BU 60
	TODD	10 Jun 44	28 Apr 51	27 Aug 54	
CVE 107	*Gilbert Islands*	29 Nov 43	5 Feb 45	21 May 46	Ex-*St Andrews Bay*; str 1 Jun 61; in service as AGMR–1, 7 Mar 64–20 Dec 69; str 15 Oct 76
	TODD	20 Jul 44	7 Sep 51	15 Jan 55	
CVE 108	*Kula Gulf*	29 Nov 43	12 May 45	3 Jul 46	Ex-*Vermillion Bay*; str 15 Sep 70; MSTS service 1965–69 (aircraft transport)
			15 Feb 51	15 Dec 55	
	TODD/WILL	20 Jul 44	30 Jun 65	6 Oct 69	
CVE 109	*Cape Gloucester*	10 Jan 44	5 Mar 45	5 Nov 46	Ex-*Willapa Bay*; str 1 Apr 71
	TODD	12 Sep 44			
CVE 110	*Salerno Bay*	7 Feb 44	19 May 45	4 Oct 47	Ex-*Winjah Bay*; str 1 Jun 61; BU 62
	TODD/CIW	29 Sep 44	20 Jun 51	16 Feb 54	
CVE 111	*Vella Gulf*	7 Mar 44	9 Apr 45	9 Aug 46	Ex-*Totem Bay*; str 1 Dec 70; BU 71
	TODD	19 Oct 44			
CVE 112	*Siboney*	1 Apr 44	14 May 45	Nov 47	Ex-*Frosty Bay*; str 1 Jun 70; BU 71
	TODD	9 Nov 44	22 Jan 50	3 Jul 56	

		LD/Launch	Comm	Decomm	Fate
CVE 113	*Puget Sound*	12 May 44	18 Jun 45	18 Oct 46	Ex-*Hobart Bay*; str 1 Jun 60; BU 62
	TODD	30 Nov 44			
CVE 114	*Rendova*	15 Jun 44	22 Oct 45	27 Jan 50	Ex-*Mosser Bay*; str 1 Apr 71; BU 71
	TODD/WILL	28 Dec 44	3 Jan 51	30 Jun 55	
CVE 115	*Bairoko*	25 Jul 44	16 Jul 45	14 Apr 50	Ex-*Portage Bay*; str 1 Apr 60
	TODD	25 Jan 45	12 Sep 50	18 Feb 55	
CVE 116	*Badoeng Strait*	18 Aug 44	14 Nov 45	20 Apr 46	Ex-*San Alberto Bay*; str 1 Dec 70; Bu 72
	TODD/CIW	15 Feb 45	6 Jan 47	17 May 57	
CVE 117	*Saidor*	30 Sep 44	4 Sep 45	12 Sep 47	Ex-*Saltery Bay*; str 1 Dec 70; BU 71
	TODD	17 Mar 45			
CVE 118	*Sicily*	23 Oct 44	27 Feb 46	5 Jul 54	Ex-*Sandy Bay*; str 1 Jul 60; BU 61
	TODD/WILL	14 Apr 45			
CVE 119	*Point Cruz*	4 Dec 44	16 Oct 45	30 Jun 47	Ex-*Trocadero Bay*; aircraft transport 1965–69; str 15 Sep 70; BU 71
	TODD	18 May 45	26 Jul 51	31 Aug 56	
			23 Aug 65	16 Oct 69	
CVE 120	*Mindoro*	2 Jan 45	4 Dec 45	4 Aug 55	Str 1 Dec 59; BU 60
	TODD	27 Jun 45			
CVE 121	*Rabaul*	2 Jan 45	30 Aug 46	30 Aug 46	Completed, not commissioned; str 1 Sep 71; BU 72
	TODD/CIW	14 Jul 45			
CVE 122	*Palau*	19 Feb 45	15 Jan 46	15 Jun 54	Str 1 Apr 60; BU 60
	TODD	6 Aug 45			
CVE 123	*Tinian*	20 Mar 45	30 Jul 46	30 Jul 46	Completed, not commissioned; str 1 Jun 70; BU 71
	TODD	5 Sep 45			
CVE 124	*Bastogne*	2 Apr 45			Suspended 12 Aug 45; BU on slip
	TODD				
CVE 125	*Eniwetok*	20 Apr 45			Suspended 12 Aug 45; BU on slip
	TODD				
CVE 126	*Lingayen*	1 May 45			Suspended 12 Aug 45; BU on slip
	TODD				
CVE 127	*Okinawa*	22 May 45			Suspended 12 Aug 45; BU on slip
	TODD				
CVE 128–139					Cancelled 11 Aug 45

AMPHIBIOUS CARRIERS

LPH 2	*Iwo Jima*	2 Apr 59	26 Aug 61	
	PSNY	17 Sep 60		
LPH 3	*Okinawa*	1 Apr 60	14 Apr 62	
	PHNY	14 Aug 61		
LPH 7	*Guadalcanal*	1 Sep 61	20 Jul 63	
	PHNY	16 Mar 63		
LPH 9	*Guam*	15 Nov 62	16 Jan 65	
	PHNY	22 Aug 64		
LPH 10	*Tripoli*	15 Jun 64	6 Aug 66	
	ING	31 Jul 65		
LPH 11	*New Orleans*	1 Mar 66	16 Nov 68	
	PHNY	3 Feb 68		
LPH 12	*Inchon*	8 Apr 68	20 Jun 70	
	ING	24 May 69		
LHA 1	*Tarawa*	15 Nov 71	29 May 76	
	LITT	1 Dec 73		
LHA 2	*Saipan*	21 Jul 72	15 Oct 77	
	LITT	18 Jul 74		
LHA 3	*Belleau Wood*	5 Mar 73	23 Sep 78	
	LITT	11 Apr 77		
LHA 4	*Nassau*	13 Aug 73	28 Jul 79	
	LITT	28 Jan 78		
LHA 5	*Peleliu*	12 Nov 76	3 May 80	
	LITT	6 Jan 79		

Note: LPH–1 was the *Black Island* (ex-CVE, conversion cancelled); LPH–4 was the *Boxer* (ex-CV 21); LPH–5 was the *Princeton* (ex-CV 37); LPH–6 was the *Thetis Bay* (ex-CVE 90); LPH–8 was the *Valley Forge* (ex-CV 45).

TRAINING CARRIERS

IX 64	*Wolverine*		12 Aug 42	7 Nov 45	Former *Seeandbee*, paddle steamer; acq 12 Mar 42; str 28 Nov 45; BU 47
	DET	1912			
IX 81	*Sable*		8 Mar 43	7 Nov 43	Former *Greater Buffalo*, paddle steamer; acq 7 Aug 42; str 28 Nov 45; BU 48
	ASB	1923			

Note: Dates of completion are date of commissioning as converted by the navy; conversions were at Erie Plant, American Shipbuilding Corp., Buffalo.

Notes on Sources

This book is based on navy internal papers held by the National Archives, the Federal Record Center (FRC) at Suitland, Maryland, the Naval Historical Center (NHC) at the Washington Navy Yard, the NavAir historical office at Jefferson Plaza (in Washington), and the DCNO (Air) or Op-05 historical office at the Washington Navy Yard. Important postwar historical records are also held by the Center for Naval Analyses (CNA) (which does not consider itself an archive). CNA is, in effect, the repository of OpNav and Operations Evaluation Group (OEG) concepts, and holds probably the most complete existing collection of LRO papers.

The primary sources were the records of C & R and BuShips; of the Secretary of the Navy (SecNav); of the General Board; of OPNAV; of BuAer and its successor, the Naval Air Systems Command (NavAir); and of the Naval Ship Engineering Center (NavSEC). The wartime OPNAV (CominCh/CNO) files include the VCNO files, which reflect most wartime ship production and modification decisions. Also extremely valuable, particularly for carrier policy and tactics, were the prewar reports of CinC U.S. Fleet, the files of the prewar fleet problems, and the wartime combat analyses carried out under the aegis of the CominCh/CNO staff. The combat analysis reports of the Pacific Fleet during the Korean War provided a similar operational view of the lessons of that conflict. Unfortunately there is, as yet, no comparable coverage of the lessons of the Vietnam War, although they are clearly reflected in the *Nimitz* design. A more explicit account of the lessons of World War II is to be found in the reports of four special boards convened by CinCPAC: ship and aircraft characteristics, ordnance, radar, and radio (including sonar). The first of these is, in effect, an evaluation of the designs of ships used during the war and is quoted in this book. The radar report includes comments on CIC location and organization.

The prewar SecNav, OPNAV, and bureau files are all held by the Navy and Old Army Branch (NNMO) of the National Archives. Wartime BuShips files are held by FRC. Recently the wartime SecNav and CNO/CominCh records were transferred from NHC to NNMO. NHC still holds the General Board records and a variety of miscellaneous files, such as those of the prewar OPNAV War Plans division. FRC holds the SCB files as well as many wartime and postwar BuShips files, such as those of the Preliminary and Contract (Code 440) Design divisions. SCB memoranda for the period 1945–50, including notes on annual programs and tentative ship characteristics, are duplicated in the General Board files at NHC.

Naval aviation files are held by two separate organizations: NavAir history and the DCNO (Air) historical unit, representing, respectively, the technical and operational histories of U.S. naval aviation. The OPNAV unit, important in the fight over the super-carrier, holds much of the navy material generated at the time. It also holds an important series of administrative reports written under DCNO (Air) auspices in 1945–46 and a full collection of the BuAer confidential *Bulletin*. The latter carried accounts both of new aircraft and of new carrier concepts, including operational concepts for the use of the new Seadart fighter. The NavAir historical collection includes very extensive chronological summary reports of the various technical divisions, such as those which developed catapults and arresting gear. There are also detailed historical files on various naval aircraft, which include material on their policy origins and fates, and the "Ten-Year History of BuAer Technology, 1935–45," prepared late in 1945 by Dr. Lee Pearson and including full accounts of catapult and arresting gear development during the period.

From a policy point of view, the primary papers on carrier design for the period up through 1950 are those of the General Board: series 420 (construction program), 420-2 (building programs on an annual basis), 420-7 (carriers), and 430 (naval ordnance, such as AA weapons and aviation ordnance); during World War II, however, the ship modification role of the General Board was largely taken over by the VCNO.

Ship design files in the C & R/BuShips correspondence series are CV/S1-1 (design) and CV/L9-3 (modifications); in addition the individual ship files sometimes include comments on trials experience. There were also Preliminary and Contract Design files (design books and flat files, respectively), collections of relevant correspondence and, sometimes, notes of actual design decisions. NNMO holds design books for the battle cruiser conversions of 1922 (*Lexington* class) and flat files for all carriers actually built from the *Langley* conversion through the *Wasp*. The C & R correspondence files at NNMO include early notes on the *Essex* class.

FRC (RG 19) holds design books on all carriers designed after 1922. Major files included 6487 for carrier designs up through the *Wasp* class; 9844 for wartime types including the CVEs, CVLs, *Essex*, and *Midway*; 11221 for the *United*

States and the *Forrestal*; 10537 for the postwar ASW escort carrier; and 63A3172 for the 1946 fleet carrier and for the considerable material on the *United States*, including the 1949 symposium on her design. This latter material included formal design reports on the SCS, the VSTOL support ship, the T-CBL medium carrier, and the CVNX study of 1976. Unfortunately, although 6487 was available when I began research in 1974, it was destroyed by FRC the following year, before I could copy the material on CV 4, CV 5, or CV 7; thus the design material on these classes is somewhat less complete than had been hoped. The accounts of their early design are based on C & R papers and talks found in other files rather than on raw design notes, as in the case of the later carriers. However, the material on the studies of 1923 is taken from this file.

Two special BuShips files deserve mention. In 1945 the Preliminary Design group compiled a series of special design histories, which are held in FRC entry 344-74-564. They include studies of the *Essex*, *Midway*, *Saipan*, *Independence*, and CVE types, as well as a draft of a general history of U.S. carrier design. In each case details of design rather than overall considerations are emphasized. These files also generally include a collection of the references used to prepare the history, and some of these papers have not survived in the original correspondence files. The other special file is RG 19 entry 1036 in FRC, which contains the inclining experiments of most U.S. warships from about 1914 through 1945; it is the source for most of the breakdowns of loads in appendix D. Preliminary Design also compiled extensive notes on war damage, from which some of the details in chapter 11 have been taken.

From an operational point of view, the most valuable sources of the interwar period are probably the records of the hearings of the General Board and the accounts of the major fleet exercises, or fleet problems (microfilmed by the National Archives). The latter include critiques that illustrate fleet doctrine of the day in considerable detail. They are supplemented by fleet tactical publications, such as those for carrier aircraft doctrine, which are held by the Naval Historical Center. For the wartime period there are also tactical publications, but they are not as revealing. For this period the standard histories have been supplemented by the "lessons learned" reports prepared by the CominCh staff and culminating in a 1946 report of the final wartime operations.

For the immediate postwar period, operational concepts can be derived from the Op-05 and other OPNAV files built up first during the development of the 1946 fleet carrier, and then during the design development of CVB-X and the *United States*. Dr. David Rosenberg's papers on the navy policy of this period, prepared as part of the Office of the Secretary of Defense study of the strategic arms competition from 1945 onward, are probably the best source on this period. Some of his work also appears in the published record of the Air Force Historical Symposium of 1978.

There is also a most unusual source: the notes compiled by the group led by Samuel E. Morison during the writing of the *History of United States Naval Operations in World War II*. They include considerable data on the origins and use of the escort carriers. They are held by the Operational Archives.

These files generally consist of masses of correspondence often duplicated in other files, so that a citation from one source does not indicate the absence of a document from others. Policy papers were generally found in SecNav and General Board files. The SCB correspondence reflects policy choices, but on a much more limited basis. Similarly, the post-1950 records of BuShips sometimes include policy documents prepared by OPNAV. There are also, for the late fifties and early sixties, the reports of the LRO group, which was sometimes quite influential. In general, BuAer policy can be inferred from BuShips documents on design requirements. For carriers, the relevant General Board files are 420 (construction program) and 420-7 (carriers). Since the General Board did not make aircraft design policy, a search of its aircraft (449) files was not useful. However, the board hearings of the interwar and early war periods do reflect navy attitudes toward carrier operations.

For detailed technical data on prewar carriers, I have relied on the general information books (ship information books) held by NNMO. They include hull and, in most cases, armament and armor data. They do not include details of machinery or aeronautical equipment. However, the trials booklets held as part of the SecNav records include such information. There were also the volumes of *Ships Data, U.S. Naval Vessels*, which were regularly published through 1952 and which include accurate dimensions as well as details of electrical generators and weapons of 40-mm and larger caliber. This printed source was supplemented by a compilation of prewar ship data prepared by Preliminary Design, which included hull characteristics and protection as well as designed steaming endurance. Other endurance data were taken from the compilation of ship endurance prepared in 1945 as a fleet tactical publication (FTP 218). Plans came from the records of BuShips, including microfilms of the older C & R plans formerly held by NavSea at the Washington Navy Yard.

Besides manuscript files including such things as correspondence, there are official handbooks. Especially important is BuOrd's *Armament Summaries*, updated on a biweekly basis during World War II and issued annually since; fleet tactical publications, both prewar and postwar (held by the NHC); and for carrier aircraft facilities, such as flight- and hangar-deck dimensions, the annual NavAir reports. This category also includes official classified magazines, such as the wartime and early postwar *CIC*, the postwar *Combat Readiness*, and the postwar BuAer confidential *Bulletin*, which until about 1955 was a major source of information on the bureau's aspirations.

In general, published accounts were used to organize the material taken from the primary sources. In a number of cases the major value of the published handbooks turned out to be the photographs they contained, which drew attention to the significance of items in official correspondence.

Chapter 1

The major secondary source for U.S. naval aviation policy in the prewar period was Turnbull and Lord, *History of United States Naval Aviation* (New Haven: Yale University Press, 1949). Major primary sources included the fleet problem microfilms, the General Board hearings, and the War

Plans division publications, which described the ORANGE war strategy. Carrier air group assignments are taken from the annual reports of CinC U.S. Fleet, held by NNMO, and from NHC records. For the postwar period I have relied heavily on the Rosenberg papers already mentioned. More recent policy papers have included the navy material presented in 1970 at the congressional hearings on the proposed CVAN-70 and in the published version of the CVNX study of 1976. The text of NSC-68, as well as the background documents, was published in the U.S. Department of State's *Foreign Relations of the U.S., 1950* (volume 1). The texts of LRO reports are held by CNA, and some of them (used here) have been declassified.

Chapter 2

The account of the initial U.S. attempts to design carriers is taken largely from the NNMO Preliminary Design files, with supplementary material from General Board files; also used was the account in a very abbreviated "design history" of the *Lexington* conversion held by DCNO (Air) history. The latter includes reduced-scale copies of sketch designs for flush-deck carriers and is the source for the photo captions of the two preliminary design models shown in this chapter. No formal Preliminary Design books appear to have survived for these designs, although the books predating 1924 were almost all deposited in NNMO collections. Very complete documentation exists on the *Lexington* design, in Preliminary and Contract (flat file) Design files held by NNMO. Material on the AA experiments of the thirties was taken from General Board file 430 on ordnance. Wartime improvements to the *Saratoga* are described in the CominCh/CNO files and, indirectly, in the inclining experiment files; the prewar proposals are taken from C & R files. The situation is far worse for the *Langley*: there is only a very brief and incomplete file on the conversion, and the inclining experiment has not survived. It appears that no preliminary design was done as such.

Chapter 3

Most of the *Ranger* design history is taken from General Board hearings and from the 420-7 file, which reflects proposals for alternative configurations, including the island itself. The death of the torpedo plane is described in the annual reports of CinC U.S. Fleet. Some of the 1922 designs are described in some detail in a design summary in FRC entry 6487. Material on wartime modifications is taken from the CominCh/CNO files.

Chapter 4

The *Yorktown*-class preliminary design history is taken largely from General Board 420-7 files, supplemented by the files of the SecNav, which include some of the design alternatives considered. In addition, the flat files were consulted; they include the issue of torpedo protection. Catapult notes are from NavAir history files. War refit notes are taken from the CominCh/CNO files, the wartime BuShips files, and the inclining experiment files.

Chapter 5

This chapter is based primarily on General Board files, supplemented by the flat file in NNMO records. No full

inclining experiment was found, although the flat file refers to the considerable overload found when a realistic air group was included; this file also includes the proposal for higher power, as do the General Board 420-7 files. The concepts of 1938 and 1940 are taken from those files, which contain the sketch plans for these ships.

Chapter 6

Material on the ORANGE war plan came from War Plans division publications from 1929 onward, including the list of "ships not on the (existing) Navy list" (WPL-10). There were also references to the converted liners in General Board hearings on the basic naval policy of the United States. Correspondence in the SecNav file described the attempt in 1935 to procure elevators as long-lead items for mobilization conversion, and the miscellaneous envelope files (entry 152) of RG 19 included blueprints for liner conversions drawn at that time. Several Maritime Commission spokesmen described the P4-P design in 1940 in connection with the commission's long-term planning, and the sketch published here was made from a photograph of a model of the P4-P published in the *Pacific Marine Reporter* in connection with bidding on this ship. Attempts to find a plan or a photograph showing the unique arrangement of the funnels have, as of publication, proven fruitless. Data on the 980-ft liner (but not on its armament) is taken from Williams and De Kerbreck, *Damned by Destiny* (Brighton: Tredo Books, Ltd., 1982). This book also has additional material on the P-4P design.

Chapter 7

Primary material on the *Essex*-class characteristics was taken from General Board 420-7 and from the Preliminary Design files. The design history was used for Contract Design; post-1940 modifications were taken largely from BuShips files. To some extent, too, armament modifications were obtained from the wartime BuOrd *Armament Summaries*. Late-war alterations (such as emergency improvements in close-range AA capabilities) were taken from the SCB weekly accounts of decisions in NHC(CominCh/CNO) files. Finally, the critique of the internal ventilation of these ships is taken from a 1945 Pacific Fleet report, in NHC, on materiel lessons learned in ship characteristics.

Chapter 8

Sources for this chapter included a BuAer administrative history of the small carrier, held by the Op-05 historical unit; the design histories of the CVE and CVL classes (which were concerned primarily with contract design); the raw historical files in FRC; the Morison notes in NHC; and General Board 420-7, which included the early BuShips proposals for light cruiser conversion. The design history material in FRC 9844 included the original Gibbs & Cox proposals for convoy escort carriers, with BuShips notations that they were not the ones ultimately adopted; apparently that was very much a sore point with the bureau. British files at the National Maritime Museum, Greenwich, were also used, since the Royal Navy did much of the early work on trade protection conversions of existing merchant ships. Note that ship design files in the museum include British comments on U.S. carrier design and operations during World War II as observed by British officers in Washington and in the Pacific; such observation corresponds to the U.S. reporting of British work from the fall of 1940 onward.

Chapter 9

Midway-class material was taken from General Board files as well as the raw Preliminary Design files and the compiled Contract Design history of 1945.

Chapter 10

This material is taken primarily from BuShips files at FRC and from material in General Board and in CominCh/CNO files of 1945–46 at NHC; it includes the papers of the special board formed to develop characteristics for a new carrier and the testimony of officers such as Captain Raisseur. Some parts of the story can also be found in the Op-05 historical files. The story of the new heavy attack bomber is largely taken from NavAir historical files. The details of wartime carrier damage come from BuShips war damage reports.

Chapter 11

For the political background of the super-carrier, I have relied on a combination of the Rosenberg paper and the Op-05 historical files; these are, of course, implicitly partisan. General Board files included much of the design background of the ship as well as details of its rationale; these files also yielded reports on the 1949 symposium on the design of the *United States*. BuShips files at FRC provided design details as well as reports of the preliminary design and parts of the design history; these files also included the ammunition load-out data cited in the text. The CVB-X sketch came from General Board postwar files, and the model photographs came from postwar CNO files held by NHC. Data on the design characteristics of the ship came from General Board files, since in 1948–49 the General Board was still deeply involved in the characteristics process.

Chapter 12

The *Forrestal* was the last carrier for which the General Board had any responsibility, and the files of that organization include the earliest discussions of characteristics. However, the notes on the politics of the ship, and particularly on the 60,000-ton limit, come from NavSEC files, as do the early design notes. SCB materials yielded the sketches of flush-deck flight-deck arrangements and an (unreproducible) photograph of a model of the flush-deck version of the ship. Unfortunately, this model appears no longer to exist. The detailed port and starboard views are Contract Design drawings, representing the ship as she was actually laid down. As in the case of later carriers, BuShips files and current NavSEC files filled out this information; they included the formal report of Preliminary Design, notes on the angled-deck version of the ship, and miscellaneous papers such as those on the choice of machinery. These last two sources were also used for the accounts of other modern carriers in the balance of the chapter. Some unclassified

but official data on these ships was obtained from the now-declassified 1952 edition of Ships Data and also from the NavAir annual reports. In addition, considerable data on current U.S. carriers was published in the course of congressional hearings on the choice of design for CV 71 (CVV, repeat *Nimitz*, or repeat CV 67).

Chapter 13

Material on early carrier modernization projects was taken from postwar CNO files (NHC), from SCB papers, and from internal classified accounts in the monthly BuAer confidential *Bulletin*. No design file for SCB-27 was located, but the post-1950 BuShips correspondence files (FRC) were quite useful in this regard. Details of the 1949–51 projects were taken from SCB project files. The latter were also used for the later *Essex*-class conversion. SCB-110 (at least in its early stages) was described by a design file and also by an SCB file. Details of the most recent *Midway*-class refits were taken from SCB papers.

Chapter 14

All material on nuclear carrier design was taken from BuShips preliminary design files (at FRC) and NavSEC files; NavSEC also held a contract design history of the *Nimitz* class.

Chapter 15

CVV material is based partly on the formal NavSEC design report on the T-CBL, which was the design predecessor of the CVV, and partly on material released as part of the congressional hearings on the CVV design in 1979. There was also a formal OpNav CVNX study released in 1976, comparing various carrier options and describing major carrier desiderata.

Chapter 16

Material on the overall development of U.S. airborne ASW was taken from a variety of sources, including declassified issues of *Combat Readiness* and declassified sections of later documents. CVE and CVL modifications were described in detail by BuShips correspondence files, as were the ASW modifications to *Essex*-class carriers. The 1959 CVS studies were described in FRC 63A3172; later CVS studies were taken from NavSEC files. There was a formal NavSEC design history of alternative DHK configurations, including the one selected by Admiral Zumwalt for the SCS. NavSEC also produced design histories of the SCS and the VSTOL support ship, the latter in several variants. The SCS operational test was described in detail in congressional hearings in 1974.

Chapter 17

BuShips files at FRC include a design history of the various LPH projects, and OPNAV files give the rationale for the LHA; since the latter was a private design, the navy files include no formal design history. Much of this chapter is based on marine corps experience and doctrine as recounted in the two-volume official history, *Marines and Helicopters, 1946–62 and 1962–73* (GPO, 1976 and 1978).

Index

Numbers in italics refer to illustrations.